MW01248747

John McKeen

HISTORY

OF

BRUNSWICK,

TOPSHAM, AND HARPSWELL,

MAINE,

INCLUDING THE ANCIENT TERRITORY KNOWN AS

Pejepscot.

BY

GEORGE AUGUSTUS WHEELER, M. D.,

AND

HENRY WARREN WHEELER.

"*Histories make men wise.*" — BACON.

BOSTON:
ALFRED MUDGE & SON, PRINTERS.
1878.

Facsimile Reprint

Published 1989 By
HERITAGE BOOKS, INC.
1540E Pointer Ridge Place, Bowie, Maryland 20716
(301)-390-7709

ISBN 1-55613-232-8

1988
Surname index
Compiled By Shirley Simington Schilly
and
Furnished By Pejepscot Historical Society

TO

The Memory of

THE ESTEEMED CITIZEN,

AND

FAITHFUL AND EARNEST HISTORICAL STUDENT,

THE LATE

JOHN MCKEEN, ESQUIRE,

WHOSE RESEARCHES IN THE EARLY HISTORY OF THE

PEJEPSCOT REGION

JUSTLY ENTITLE HIM TO OUR GRATEFUL

REMEMBRANCE,

This Volume is Dedicated.

- Notice -

The foxing, or discoloration with age, characteristic of old books, sometimes shows through to some extent in reprints such as this, especially when the foxing is very severe in the original book. We feel that the contents of this book warrant its reissue despite these blemishes, and hope you will agree and read it with pleasure.

PREFACE.

THE labor of compiling a local history, though not necessarily requiring a very high order of talent, does require a careful and conscientious examination of a large amount of miscellaneous material. The difficulties attending a compilation of this kind are numerous and, many of them, not easily to be anticipated In the words of Sterne, "When a man sits down to write a history, though it be but the history of Jack Hickathrift or Tom Thumb, he knows no more than his heels what lets and confounded hindrances he is to meet with in his way."

So much is said by way of apology for the unavoidable errors that may, perchance, be discovered in this volume. The undertaking itself needs no apology, as the value of such compilations, not only to the writers of general history, but also to the public more immediately interested, is now everywhere admitted.

The aim of the compilers has been to furnish a work which should be valuable rather than merely entertaining They have endeavored to give a faithful and complete *history* of the three towns, and although they have tried to make the volume more interesting by the introduction, when proper, of narratives and traditions, yet this they have considered of secondary importance.

The methodical arrangement of a work of this kind, so as to embrace all that is desired and at the same time to avoid frequent repetition, is involved with difficulties, and is, after all, somewhat a matter of taste. In this work the arrangement by the topics into which the subject is most naturally divided has been adopted as, on the whole, the best. Each division of the subject has, however, been arranged in chronological order, and for further convenience of reference full indexes have been appended.

It is proper, in this place, to acknowledge the assistance which the compilers have received, in various ways, in the prosecution of their work. Their very great indebtedness to the labors of the late John McKeen, Esquire, has already been shown, and is still further shown by the frequent reference to him throughout the book; but they desire also to acknowledge the kindness of Miss Frances A. McKeen in furnishing them with the private papers of her father.

The name of the late Moses E. Woodman, Esquire, is also entitled to be held in grateful remembrance for the work he did in collecting and tracing the genealogy of Topsham families.

Much interesting information has also been obtained from notes made by the late James McKeen, M. D.

It is proper also to acknowledge to the public the great obligations of the compilers to the late Doctor John D Lincoln, both for the material assistance rendered by him, and for his steadfast encouragement in their undertaking, from its very inception up to his last hours.

The thanks of the compilers are also especially due to Mr. A. G. Tenney, for his personal help and advice, as well as for the great assistance afforded by his file of the *Brunswick Telegraph*, and for the many courtesies extended by him; to Professor A. S. Packard, for valued advice and assistance, and for his kindness in affording unusual facilities for examining the books and papers in the historical and college libraries; to General Joshua L. Chamberlain, Honorable Charles J. Gilman, Professor Stephen J. Young, and Professor George L. Vose, for valuable advice and assistance; to Reverend Elijah Kellogg, for his manuscript lecture on the history of Harpswell; to Messrs. Charles J. Noyes, Stephen Purinton, Edwin Emery, Professor Henry Carmichael, Reverend George T. Packard, and Doctor Asher Ellis, for assistance in the collection and preparation of material for the work; and to the many others who have, in one way or another, assisted them, the compilers return their sincere thanks.

The various illustrations given in the book will, it is hoped, be satisfactory to the public. The *portraits* were furnished by and inserted at the expense of the friends of the persons whom they represent.

The Pejepscot plan of the Brunswick and Topsham lots was made from two of the original plans, and was reduced and engraved by the photo-lithographic process, by J. H. Bufford's Sons, Boston. The map of Brunswick and Topsham villages in 1802 was compiled from a written description of Brunswick by the late John McKeen, Esquire, and from verbal descriptions of Topsham by Mr. James Wilson and the late Mrs. Nathaniel Green.

All of the maps and most of the illustrations are from drawings made by Mr. Charles G. Wheeler, Bowdoin, Class of 1876.

Whatever praise or censure may be due the authors for the manner in which they have executed their work should be equally divided between them, as it has been a joint production, in which they are themselves unable to specify their respective claims of authorship.

In conclusion: To the citizens of the three towns, and more especially to those of Brunswick and Harpswell, whose interest in the work has been so fully shown by their liberal appropriations in aid of its publication, this volume is offered with gratitude and respect, and its favorable reception will be deemed an ample remuneration for their labors by

THE AUTHORS.

CONTENTS.

PART I.

PART II.

PART III.

APPENDICES.

ILLUSTRATIONS.

MAPS AND PLANS.

PART I.

"THIS is the place,—stand still, my steed,
Let me review the scene,
And summon from the shadowy past,
The forms that once have been!"

LONGFELLOW, *A Gleam of Sunshine.*

HISTORY

OF

Brunswick, Topsham, and Harpswell.

CHAPTER I.

ABORIGINAL INHABITANTS.

THE Indian race, formerly occupying the territory now embraced by the State of Maine, was divided, as most authors state, into two considerable nations, called the Etechemins and the Abenákis. The former nation occupied the region east, and the latter that west, of the Penobscot River.[1]

The Abenaki nation was composed of four principal tribes, viz.: —

1. The Sokokis, who had their principal encampments upon the Saco River.

2. The Anasagunticooks, who occupied the entire valley of the Androscoggin River.

3. The Canibas, who dwelt upon the Kennebec, from its tide waters to its source.

4. The Wawenocks, who reside between the Sagadahock and the river St. George, and upon the latter.[2]

The Anasagunticooks were, at the first advent of Europeans, a very numerous, powerful, and warlike tribe. The Pejepscot Indians were, in all probability, a sub-tribe of the Anasagunticooks. They had customary places of resort, if not permanent places of residence, at the Brunswick Falls, at Maquoit, and at Mair Point. It is now considered probable, from the remains and relics found there, that the latter was the place of one of their villages in the sixteenth century.[3]

Like most of the native tribes, the Anasagunticooks were, at first,

---

[1] *Willis, Maine Historical Collection*, 4, p. 96. *Vetromile, The Abenakis*, p 17.

[2] *Kidder, Maine Historical Collection*, 6, p. 235 *Williamson and others.*

[3] *John McKeen, Manuscript Lecture.*

probably friendly to the whites. At least, our settlers are represented as living with them upon the most friendly terms up to about the time of King Philip's War.[1]

They soon, however, became extremely and inveterately hostile to the settlers upon their domain, and until their extermination by disease and by the aggressions of the whites, they continued to exhibit their animosity by frequent attacks upon isolated settlements and habitations and by lying in ambush for individuals or small parties.

The plague which broke out among them about the year 1615 or 1616 so reduced them that, in the latter year, they numbered only 1,500 warriors.[2]

They were still further reduced in number by warfare and other causes, so that there were, according to one authority,[3] on November 24, 1726, only five Indians in the tribe over sixteen years of age. John Hegon was their sachem at this time.

Twenty-five years later there were one hundred and sixty warriors in the tribe.[4] This is a large increase in number, but yet it shows how weak the tribe had become.

The most celebrated sagamores of this tribe were Darumkin, Worumbo, and Hodgkins, — called sometimes Hawkins. Of the former but little is known, except that he was the father of Terramugus, and on several occasions served as orator for the tribe.

Worumbo is better known on account of his deed to Richard Wharton, July 7, 1684, confirming to him the lands formerly conveyed to and possessed by Thomas Purchase.

Hodgkins (or Hawkins), whose Indian name was Kankamagus, was, in reality, a sachem of the Pennacooks, but he joined the Androscoggins about 1684, and lived with Worumbo.

Mugg is thought to have been another of their sachems,[5] although by some authors he is supposed to have belonged to the Penobscot tribe.[6] He was very conspicuous in the Indian war of 1676–77. On October 12, of the former year, he assaulted Black Point, now Scarborough, with one hundred men, and captured it. In 1677 he again besieged that garrison for three days, and killed three men and took one captive. He was himself killed, May 16 of that year. Prior to this war he had lived for some time with the English, and had been very friendly to them.[7]

---

[1] *McKeen, MSS. Lecture. Woodman, Manuscript History of Pejepscot.*

[2] *Williamson*, 1, *p.* 483.

[3] *Gyles's Statement, Maine Historical Collection*, 3, *p* 357.

[4] *Williamson*, 1, *p.* 483.

[5] *Drake. Book of Indians*, 3, *p.* 110.

[6] *History of Pemaquid, p* 122.

[7] *Drake, Book of Indians*, 3, *p.* 110.

This chief must not be confounded with Mogg, — generally known as Mogg Megone, — who was killed at the time of Rasle's death (1724), and who belonged to the Saco Indians.

Another of their sagamores was Philip Will, originally a Cape Cod Indian; he was captured by the French, at the siege of Louisburg, when only fourteen years of age. Remaining with the Abenaki Indians, he became, eventually, a chief of this tribe. Will was brought up in the family of a Mr. Crocker, in which he was taught "to read, write, and cipher." He prevented, for many years, the final extinction of his tribe. He was six feet three inches in height, and possessed a good development.[1]

The fact that the lands occupied by the whites were duly purchased of and conveyed to them by the Indians themselves, and that the earlier settlers in this region endeavored to conciliate and make friends of them, seems to have had but little effect in restraining the savage disposition of the natives. After the first outbreak, they rarely lived on really peaceable terms with the settlers, and when there were no actual hostilities going on, they were continually strolling about and annoying the inhabitants,[2] and even isolated acts of friendship on the part of individuals amongst them were comparatively rare.

The settlement of the region occupied by this tribe, subsequent to the time of King Philip's War, presents continual scenes of carnage and destruction, midnight massacres and conflagrations, until the tribe itself became extinct.

The language of the Abenaki nation has been carefully studied by many competent students, but the difficulties in the way of thoroughly understanding the different dialects are so great that much uncertainty still exists, both as to the correct pronunciation and derivation, and also as to the meaning, of very many of the names formerly applied to localities. The Indian names, and their signification in English, of some of the more important places, will, nevertheless, prove interesting, and are therefore given in this connection.

ABAGADUSSET River and Point. — The original name of the point was Nagusset.[3] At a later day it was called Point Agreeable. Abagadusset, or *Bagadusset*, one of its forms, means "to shine," the reflection of the light from the waters of the bay probably giving the name.[4] This river and point is not included within the present territory of either of the three towns, but was within the limits of the Pejepscot tract as originally claimed, and reference to it is often made.

---

1 *Williamson*, 1, *p.* 481. 2 *McKeen. MSS. Lecture.* 3 *Pejepscot Papers.*
4 *Dr. Ballard in the United States Coast Survey Report*, 1868, *p.* 246.

AH-ME-LAH-COG-NETUR-COOK, which means a place of much game, of fish, fowl, and beasts, was the Indian name for Brunswick near the Falls.[1]

ANDROSCOGGIN. — The river now known as the Androscoggin, and from which the tribe inhabiting its shores received its name, was variously called the *Anasagunticook*, the *Anconganunticook*, *Amasaquanteg*, and *Amascongan*. The latter is the original of Androscoggin, as appears by the deposition of the Indian Perepole.[2] The name has been written in some sixty different forms, as its sound was received by the ancient hunters, owners, and settlers. There seems to have been a disposition to make it conform to known words in the English usage. The name "Coggin" is a family appellation in New England; and it was easy to place before it, according to each man's preference, other familiar names, and to call the stream "Ambrose Coggin," "Amos Coggin," "Andrews Coggin," "Andros Coggin," and "Andrus Coggin."[3] Vetromile[4] says that Coggin means "coming"; that *Ammascoggin* means "fish coming in the spring," and that Androscoggin means "Andros coming," referring to the visit of a former governor of the province. But the visit of Governor Andros was not made until 1688, while the river is called Androscoggin in an indenture, made in 1639, between Thomas Purchase and Governor Winthrop.[5]

Another authority[6] says the word means "the Great Skunk River." By another,[7] it is said to be derived from *naamas* (fish), *kees* (high), and *auke* (place), and to mean "the high fish place." According to Reverend Dr. Ballard,[8] its derivation is from the word *namās* (fish), abbreviated, as is the frequent practice, by dropping the first letter, and *Skaughigan* (Skowhegan), a fish-spear. The name may therefore be translated the Fish Spear, or Fish *Spearing*. The name, as furnished by Perepole, with his description, marked the part of the river above the *Amitigonpontook* — that is, the "Clay-land Falls" at Lewiston, — upward to "*Arockamecook*," that is, the "Hoe-land," at Canton Point. The rips and shallows in this portion were favorable for *spearing fish* beyond any part below.

BUNGANUNGANOCK, commonly shortened to Bunganock, is the name

---

[1] *Pejepscot Papers.*

[2] *Maine Historical Collection*, 3, *p.* 333, *taken from the Pejepscot Papers.*

[3] *Dr. Ballard in United States Coast Survey*, 1868, *p.* 247.

[4] *History of the Abenakis*, *p.* 24. [5] *See next chapter.*

[6] *Willis, Maine Historical Collection*, 4, *p.* 115.

[7] *Potter, Maine Historical Collection*, 4, *p.* 189.

[8] *Report of the United States Coast Survey*, 1868, *p* 247.

of a small stream flowing into Maquoit Bay. It runs at the bottom of a deep ravine, suggesting the name of Bunganunganock, which means the "High-bank Brook."[1]

CATHANCE River, pronounced by the Indians *Kat-hah-nis*, is said by them to mean *bent*, or *crooked*.[2]

MAQUOIT means the "bear-place" or "bear-bay."

MERRICONEAG. — This name was originally applied only to the Indian "carrying-place" at the upper end of Harpswell Neck, but finally denoted the whole peninsula. The word in full would be *Merrucoonegan*, from *merru* (swift, quick), and *oonegan* (portage), meaning the "quick carrying-place."[3]

PEJEPSCOT. — That portion of the Androscoggin River extending from Brunswick Falls to Merrymeeting Bay, and the adjacent land upon the south, was called Pejepscot. The word was originally applied to the water, and meant "crooked, like a diving snake."[4]

QUABACOOK, meaning "the duck water place,"[5] was the Indian designation of Merrymeeting Bay. The English name of this bay, according to one, and the most probable, tradition, had its origin from the meeting of the waters of five rivers. According to another account, the name was due to the meeting of two surveying parties, and their enjoyment of the occasion upon its shores.[6]

SAWACOOK, as the land upon the north side of the river where Topsham is situated was called, signifies, according to one authority,[7] "the burnt place"; according to other authorities it means either "a tree forking in many branches," or else it means "the place to find many cranberries."[8]

SEBASCODEGAN is the Indian name of the Great Island in Harpswell. This name is supposed to be derived from *k'tche* (great) and *t'bascodegan* (measure), and this solution of the name shows that the natives had taken some means of *measuring* the island and had found it *great*.[9]

There are other Indian names of localities in the vicinity of Brunswick, Topsham, and Harpswell which have been preserved by tradi-

---

[1] *Dr. Ballard in United States Coast Survey Report for* 1868, *p.* 248. [2] *Ibid.*

[3] *Dr. Ballard in United States Coast Survey Report for* 1868, *pp.* 248, 258.

[4] *Willis, in Maine Historical Collection*, 4, *p.* 108.

[5] *Pejepscot Papers, Perepole's Deposition. Also, Dr. True, in Brunswick Telegraph*, 1864.

[6] *Dr. Ballard in United States Coast Survey Report for* 1868, *p.* 253.

[7] *Dr. N. T. True, of Bethel.*

[8] *Potter, Maine Historical Collection*, 4, *p.* 191.

[9] *Dr. Ballard in United States Coast Survey Report for* 1868, *p.* 258.

tion, but those that have been mentioned are the best known. The others hardly require particular mention in this connection.

The Indians, in their travels from place to place, went by water whenever possible. The places where they were obliged to leave the water, either to go around falls and rapids or to cross from the salt water to the fresh, or from stream to stream, were called carrying-places, because at these places they were obliged to leave the water and carry their canoes. The paths they made from one carrying-place to another were called trails. The principal carrying-places were in Harpswell, at CONDY'S POINT, Sebascodegan, the trail leading across the point, and at Indian Point Landing, on the northeast corner of Sebascodegan. There was also one across the upper end of MERRICONEAG NECK. In Brunswick, the chief carrying-places were: THE UPPER CARRYING-PLACE. This was at the bend of the river above the falls, and was the place where the Indians left the river on their way to Maquoit. The name was given to distinguish it from the lower or STEVENS'S CARRYING-PLACE. The latter was at the narrow neck of land between the New Meadows River and Merrymeeting Bay. The land was owned in 1673 by Thomas Stevens, hence its name. WIGWAM POINT, a small point of land extending into the New Meadows River, a short distance above the dike or bridge at the foot of Ham's Hill, though not strictly a carrying-place, was a landing-place of the Indians, who probably had a wigwam there. It was once called *Indian Town.*

In Topsham, the chief carrying-place was at the Androscoggin River, above Merrill's, and the trail led to Cathance Pond. It is probable there was another carrying-place at the head of Muddy River, with trails leading to the Androscoggin and Cathance Rivers.

After Lovewell's war, the Indians dwelling on the Androscoggin, finding they were too weak to protect themselves either from the settlers or from other tribes, moved to Canada and joined the Saint Francis tribe. Even the bones of their ancestors are no longer to be found, and naught but a few names remains to remind us of the exist ence of this once powerful tribe.

CHAPTER II.

THE PEJEPSCOT PURCHASE, AND PRIOR SETTLEMENTS, 1605-1714.

THE earliest voyage of discovery made to the immediate vicinity of the Androscoggin River was possibly that of Captain George Weymouth, in the spring of 1605. He is supposed to have come up to the falls.[1] That it was the Sagadahoc River, and not the St. George's or the Penobscot, which Weymouth visited, has not, however, been fully settled.

[1607.] He was followed in the year 1607 by Captain George Popham, who arrived near Monhegan, July 31, in two vessels, the "Gift of God" and the "Mary and John," carrying one hundred and twenty planters. From Monhegan they went to Cape Small Point, and built a fort on Atkins Bay. This fortification was named Fort Saint George. Though the place was abandoned the next summer, it was intended to be a permanent settlement, and was occupied sufficiently long to establish its claim to be called the first English settlement on the New England coast.

[1620.] In the year 1620 a charter was granted by King James I to forty "noblemen, knights, and gentlemen," constituting them a body corporate, called the Council of Plymouth. Their territorial limits extended from the fortieth to the forty-eighth parallel of latitude, and from sea to sea.

The Council of Plymouth, in addition to the grant to the Plymouth Company of New England, granted patents in the Province of Maine to the Kennebec (or New Plymouth) Company, the Muscongus (or Waldo) Company, and to the Pemaquid Company.

[1632.] They also, June 16, 1632,[2] granted a patent to Thomas Purchase and George Way. By some this patent is thought to have emanated directly from King James.[3] The patent itself was lost,[4] and no record of it has been found. It is known to have existed from the frequent references to it in old deeds and other documents.[5]

---

1 *McKeen, Maine Historical Collections*, 5, *p.* 335.

2 *Willis, History of Portland, p.* 64.   3 *Pejepscot Records, Statement of Title.*

4 *Very likely when Purchase's house was burned.*

5 "*A Pattent for a Plantation att Pechipscot," is recorded in the " Cattalogue of such*

The Thomas Purchase above named was undoubtedly the first individual to settle in this region of the Androscoggin. He came about the year 1628, before the issue of the patent, therefore, and located himself somewhere within the limits of the present town of Brunswick. Whereabouts he established his house is a matter of doubt. The question is discussed at some length in the Pejepscot Records.[1] Abram Whitney, who lived at Little River in 1796, Samuel Wilson, Symonds Baker, a Mr. Tebbetts, and Andrew Dunning all testified, about 1796, that according to common report, prevalent during their childhood, Thomas Purchase lived at the Ten-Mile Falls (Little River), and that they had seen there an old chimney and a cellar, which the aged people called Purchase's cellar. John Moulton, Gideon Hinkley, and Richard Knowles testified in 1794, Thomas Thompson and James Hunter, of Topsham, in 1795, to the effect that they had been told by their parents and other aged people that Purchase formerly lived at New Meadows River, at a place afterwards known as "Stevens's Carrying-Place." A great many others testify, on one side or the other, and a certain number of them to the effect that his residence was at the Pejepscot Falls.[2]

The opinion has been expressed by some that Purchase, on first settling down as a trader with the Indians, dwelt at what was subsequently known as Stevens's Carrying-Place, and that when the English settled in somewhat near proximity to him, he, in order to monopolize, as much as possible, the trade with the natives, moved up to the Pejepscot Falls, and subsequently to the Ten-Mile Falls. Since it is known, however, that he very early went into the fishing business, it would seem quite as probable that he first settled at the falls, and afterwards, when too old to carry on the fishing business, took a farm at New Meadows. There is, probably, no reasonable basis for the supposition, entertained by some, that there were three individuals of the same name, situated near each other.[3]

Nothing has been found to show that George Way was ever settled in this vicinity. At the time the patent was issued Way lived in Dorchester, England; and though his widow and sons afterwards resided in Hartford, Conn., it is not known, with certainty, that he himself ever came over to this country.

Pattentes as I know granted for making Plantacons in New England," No. 16, *Vol* 2, *Colonial Records, in the Public Record Office, London.* (*See Maine Historical Collections, Memorial Volume*, p. 124)

[1] *Statement of Title.*

[2] *There are said to be nearly one hundred depositions in the Pejepscot Records, in reference to the residence of Thomas Purchase.*

[3] *See Sketch of Purchase in Part III.*

The grant to Purchase and Way was not very extensive. It is defined as "certain lands in New England called the river Bishopscotte, and all that bounds and limits the main land adjoining the river to the extent of two miles" only.[1] The river called Bishopscotte is undoubtedly that portion of the Androscoggin known as the Pejepscot. The old patents were apt to be indefinite, and oftentimes conflicted with one another, but this grant seems unusually definite as to its width, and tallies well with the following indenture, between Thomas Purchase and Governor Winthrop: —

"This indenture, made the 22th day of the 5th M^{o}, @ 1639, betweene Thomas Purchas, of Pagiscott, gentleman, of the one parte, and John Winthrope, Esq: Governo^{r} of the Massachusets, on the behalfe of himselfe, the Governo^{r} & Company of the Massachusets, on the other parte, witnesseth, that the said Thomas, for divers good causes & considerations him therevnto moveing, hath given & granted, & by these p^{r}sents doth give & grant, vnto the said John Winthrope & his successors, the Governo^{r} & Company of the Massachusets, forever, all that tract of land at Pagiscott aforesaid, vpon both sides of the ryver Androscoggin, being four miles square towards the sea, wth all liberties & priviledges therevnto belonging, so as they may plant the same wth an Inglish colony when they shall see fit, and shall have as full power to exercise iurisdiction there as they have in the Massachusets; provided, that the interest & possession of such lands as the said Thomas now vseth, or shall make vse of, for his owne stock, & improvement wth in seaven yeares next ensuing the date hereof, shall bee & remaine to the said Thomas & his heires & assignees forever vnder the iurisdiction aforesaid; and as well the said Thomas himselfe, & his family, & his heires & assignes, as all other the inhabitants vpon said lands, are forever to bee vnder the due ptection of the said Governo^{r} & Company, by order of the Generall Court, as other inhabitants of the same iurisdiction are: This grant by approbation of the said Generall Court to bee recorded and exemplified vnder the comon seale, or otherwise to be voyde — In witnes whereof the parties above said have herevnto interchangably set their hands & seales the day & yeare first above written.

THOMAS PURCHES.

Signed, sealed & deliv'ed in the p^{r}esence of
STEPHEN WINTHROPE
THOM: LECHFORD
AMOS RICHARDSON.[2]

---

[1] *Maine Historical Collections*, 1, p. 152.

[2] *Records of the Colony of the Massachusetts Bay in New England*, 1, pp. 272, 273.

It is generally considered that this deed gives the right of jurisdiction only, and not the right to the soil. The "four miles square towards the sea" can only refer to the direction towards Casco Bay, which is only about four miles distant. Up to this time Purchase was, probably, the only settler within the limits of what constitutes the present towns of Brunswick, Topsham, and Harpswell.

[1657.] There was about this time considerable uncertainty as to what government had jurisdiction over this region. It was determined, in the year 1657, by an action brought for the purpose, by the widow Elizabeth Way against Purchase.[1] The matter was referred to the General Court of Massachusetts. In the legislature there was a difference of opinion on the subject, and that body appointed Mountjoy to run the easterly line of Massachusetts. He did so, and it was found that it extended to the mouth of the Sagadahock.[2]

[1669 to 1676.] About the year 1669 Thomas Gyles settled at Pleasant Point, on Merrymeeting Bay, in what is now Topsham. He purchased a tract of land two miles long and one mile broad, on the left bank of the Pejepscot, of Thomas Watkins, one of the residents on the Kennebec, and also of the Indian sachem, Darumkin.[3] His brother James settled near him,[4] as did also James Thomas and Samuel York, who, July 20, 1670, bought of Robinhood and Daniels all the tract of land between Gyles's lot and Terramugus[5] Cove.[6]

In 1675 Thomas Purchase added to the land granted by the Council of Plymouth, a large tract on the river, which he had bought of the Indians.[7] July 3d of this year, Thomas Stevens, who had previously owned land in North Yarmouth, settled at New Meadows, and bought a tract of land on the New Meadows River, of three Indian sagamores, Robinhood, Eramket Daniels, and Manessumet.[8] He had previously bought land of Thomas Purchase.[9]

The land purchased of the above-mentioned sagamores was "a certain piece or parcel of land adjoining to Pejepscot River, butted and bounded as follows: To the land of Thomas Stephens, now in possession, east, and to Alister Coombs, his land, south, and from the head of Alister Coombs, his marsh, westerly, to a certain path,

---

[1] *Massachusetts Bay Colony's Records, Vol.* 4, *Part* 1, *p.* 334.

[2] *McKeen, MSS. Lecture.*

[3] *York County Records*, 10, *p.* 82.

[4] *Gyles Memorial, p.* 103, *et seq.*

[5] *This cove, named for an Indian chief, is between the flour mill of Purinton, Beaumont, & Co., on the "Granny Hole" stream, and the Topsham end of the railroad bridge.*

[6] *Maine Historical Collection*, 3, *p.* 315, *et seq.*

[7] *Williamson. Hubbard.*

[8] *York County Records*, 9, *p.* 254.

[9] *Maine Historical Collection*, 3, *p.* 315.

called the carrying path, or carrying place, and from said path upon a strait line to a certain island, commonly called the Stave Island, standing at the lower end of Pejepscot Narrows, and to Pejepscot River north, and to the aforesaid land of Thomas Stephens easterly, to hold in fee with general warranty."[1]

June 30, 1676, Stevens sold the above-described piece of land to Lancellot Pierce, who resided there for "some time." What became of him is not known, but as William Pierce, of Milton, in 1715, claimed this land as heir of Lancellot Pierce,[2] it is probable that the latter moved to Milton or that vicinity, and died there. Stevens probably lived on the land which he bought of Purchase.

In 1672 Nicholas Cole and John Purrington bought of Sagettawon and Robin Hood, Indian sagamores, "all the Land Lying & Being between the Two Carrying Places Upon Merriconeag Neck Beginning at the head of the Westermost Branch of Wiggen Cove so directly over to Wester Bay to the Bight, and so up along the neck from side to Side untill they come to the Uppermost Carrying place at the head of the Wester Bay at the Meadow which George Phipping has formerly mowed, so over to the head of the crick that Comes in from the Easter Bay"; also "That whole Tract of Meadow which they have formerly possessed Upon the Great Island lying and being at the head of the Cove against the Little Cove on Great Jebege Island" The deed was witnessed by Thomas Stevens and his wife, Margaret.[3] It is probable that Purrington himself did not occupy this land. If he did, he afterwards moved to Arundel.[4]

Nicholas Shapleigh, of Kittery, had, about the year 1659, though the exact date is unknown, purchased and caused to be settled Merriconeag (Harpswell) Neck and the island of Sebascodegan. The purchase was made of the Indians, and the price paid for the deed was "a considerable sum of wampumpeag, several guns, and a parcel of tobacco."[5] There is no special reason for supposing, however, that Shapleigh actually settled there himself.

[1683.] This land of Purchase and Way, and of Nicholas Shapleigh, all came into the hands of Richard Wharton, a Boston merchant. July 4, 1683, John Shapleigh, the heir of Nicholas, sold to Richard Wharton "all that tract or neck of land called Merryconeg in Casco Bay, Province of Maine, and is bounded at head or upper end, with the plains of Pejepscot or lands late belonging to or claimed by Mr.

---

[1] *Pejepscot Papers*; *Statement of Title.* [2] *Pejepscot Papers.*
[3] *Pejepscot Papers.* [4] *Ibid.* [5] *Pejepscot Records.*

Purchase, and on all other sides or parts is incompassed and bounded with and by the salt water; and also all that the aforesaid island called Sebasco, alias Sequasco-diggin."[1]

October 10, 1683, Eleazer Way, of Hartford, son and heir of George Way, the partner of Thomas Purchase, sold to Richard Wharton, for £100, "one moiety or half part, or whatever share or proportion, be the same more or less, he the s^{d} Eliazer Way, now hath, may, might, should, or in anywise ought to have or claim, of, in or to a certain tract or parcel of land commonly called and known by name of Pejepscot, situate, lying, and being within the Province of Maine in New England aforesaid," together with one half of all lands, uplands, meadows, etc., belonging to the same, "which said tract of land and premises for the space of forty years, or thereabouts, before the late war with the Indians, was in the actual possession and improvement of Mr. Thomas Purchase, and was actually given by patent from the Council of Plymouth within said Kingdom of England, to the said George Way, and Thomas Purchase, deceased."[2]

October 25, 1683, John Blaney, of Lynn, and Elizabeth, his wife, the former widow of Thomas Purchase, of Pejepscot, deceased, and the administratrix of his estate, testified "that said Eliazer Way had sold his [Purchase's] moity to s^{d} Wharton in s^{d} Patent by the consent of the children of s^{d} Purchase for their support and settlement for £150," reserving seven lots which were secured to the children by articles in the deed. The portion sold was, "All that moiety, half deal and remaining share, whatsoever the same is or may be, of the said lands late belonging to the s^{d} Thomas Purchase by virtue of the said patent or any other right in partnership with the said George or Eliazer Way, and all the right and title, propriety and interest which the said Thomas Purchase died seized of, or that he might, should, or ought to have had in the said Province of Maine." The children of Purchase signified their consent to the sale on the deed itself.[3]

It will be seen, from the above extracts, that at this time Wharton owned the whole of what is now the town of Harpswell, — except a few islands, — the greater portion of Brunswick, and a tract on the river in what is now the town of Topsham.

[1684.] On July 7, 1684, Worumbo and five other Indian sagamores signed and delivered to Wharton the following deed: —

"To ALL People to whom these presents shall come, Know Yee that whereas near three score years since Mr Thomas Purchase deceas'd

---

[1] *Pejepscot Papers, Statement of Title.* [2] *Ibid.* [3] *Ibid.*

came into this Countrey as wee have been informed and did as well by Power or Patent derived from the King of England as by consent contract & agreement with Sagamores & Proprietors of all the Lands lying on the Easterly Side of Casco Bay & on the both sides of Androscoggen River & Kennebeck River, enter upon & take possession of all the Lands lying four Miles Westward from the uppermost Falls in S^d^ Androscoggan River to Maquoit in Casco Bay & in the Lands on the other side Androscoggan River from above s^d^ Falls down to Pejepscot and Merrymeeting Bay to be bounded by a South West & North East Line to run from the upper part of s^d^ Falls to Kennebeck River & all the Lands from Maquoit to Pejepscot & to hold the same Breadth where the Land will bear it down to a place called Atkins his Bay near to Sagadahock or the Westerly side of Kennebeck River & all the Islands in the S^d^ Kennebeck River & Land between the said Atkins his Bay & Small Point Harbour the Lands & Rivers & Pond interjacent containing in breadth about three English Miles more or less, And whereas we are well assured that Maj^r^ Nicholas Shapleigh in his lifetime was both by purchase from the Indian Sagamores our Ancestors and consent of M^r^. Gorges Commissioner possessed & dyed Seized of the remainder of all the Lands lying & adjoining upon the Maine & all the Islands between the said Small Point Harbour & Maquoit afores'd & particularly of a Neck of Land Merryconege & an Island called Sebasco Diggin. And whereas the Relicts & Heirs of said Mr Purchase and Maj^r^ Nicholas Shapleigh have reserved accommodations for their several Families sold all the remainder of the aforesaid Lands & Islands to Richard Wharton of Boston Merch^t^, And for asmuch as the said Mr Purchase did personally possess improve & inhabit at Pejepscot afores^d^ near the Centre or Middle of all the Lands afores^d^ for near fifty years before the Late unhappy War, And Whereas the s^d^ Richard Wharton hath desired an enlargement upon and between the s^d^ Androscoggen & Kennebec Rivers & to encourage the Said Richard Wharton to settle an English Town & promote the Salmon and Sturgeon Fishing by which we promise our Selves great Supplyes & Relief. Therefore & for other good causes & consideration, & especially for & in consideration of a Valuable Sum received from the S^d^ Wharton in Merchandize. Wee Warumbee, Darumkine, Wihikermet, Wedon-Domhegon, Neonongasset, & Nimbanewet Chief Sagamores of all the aforesaid and other Rivers & Land Adjacent have in conformation of the said Richard Whartons Title & Propriety fully freely and absolutely given granted ratifyed & confirmed to him the said Richard Wharton all the afores^d^ Lands from the uppermost part of

ANDROSCOGGAN FALLS FOUR MILES Westward & so down to MAQUOIT & by Said River of Pejepscot & from the other side of Androscoggan Falls all the Land from the Falls to Pejepscot & Merrymeeting Bay to Kenebeck & towards the Wilderness to be bounded by a SOUTH WEST & NORTH EAST LINE to extend from the upper part of the said Androscoggan UPPERMOST FALLS to the said River of KENEBECK & all the Land from Maquoit to Pejepscot & to run & hold the same Breadth Where the Land will bear it unto ATKINS his BAY in Kenebeck River & SMALL POINT HARBOUR in Casco Bay and all ISLANDS in Kenebeck & Pejepscot Rivers & Merrymeeting Bay & within the afores[d] Bounds. Especially the aforesaid Neck of Land called MERRYCONEGE & Island called SEBASCO DEGGIN Together with all Rivers Rivulets Brooks Ponds Pools Waters Watercourses. All wood Trees of Timber or other Trees & all Mines Mineralls & Quarries and especially the Sole & absolute use & benefit of Salmon and Sturgeon Fishing in all the Rivers Rivulets or Bays afores[d] & in all Rivers Brooks Creeks or Ponds within any of the Bounds aforesaid. And also Wee the Said Sagamores have upon the considerations aforesaid given granted bargained & sold enfeoffed & confirmed & do by these presents give grant bargain sell aliene enfeoffe & confirm to him the said Richard Wharton all the Land lying FIVE MILES ABOVE the uppermost of the said Androscoggan Falls in Breadth & Length holding the same Breadth from Androscoggan Falls to Kenebeck River & to be bounded by the afores[d] South West and North East Line & a parcell of Land at Five Miles Distance to run from Androscoggan to Kennebeck River as afores[d] Together with all the Profits Priviledges Commodities Benefits & Advantages & particularly the Sole Propriety Benefit & Advantage of the Salmon & Sturgeon Fishing within the Bounds & Limits aforesaid To have & to hold to him the said Richard Wharton his heirs & assignes for ever all the aforenamed Lands Priveledges & Premises with all benefits rights appurtenances or advantages that now do or hereafter shall or may belong unto any part or parcell of the Premises fully freely & absolutely acquitted & discharged from all former & other gifts grants bargains sales mortgages & Incumbrances whatsoever, And Wee the said Warumbee Derumkine Wihikermet Wedon-Domhegon, Neonongasset & Numbenewet do covenant & grant to & with the said Richard Wharton that we have in our selves good right & full power thus to confirm & convey the premises & that we our heirs and successors shall & will warrant & defend the said Richard Wharton his heirs & assignes for ever in the peaceable enjoyment of the Premises & every part thereof against all and every person or persons that may legally claim any right Title Interest or Propriety in the Premises by from or under us the abovenamed Sagamores or any of our Ancestors or Predecessors, Provided nevertheless that nothing in this Deed be construed to deprive us the Sd Sagamores our Successors or People from improving our antient planting grounds nor from hunting in any of the said Land being not inclosed nor from fishing for our own provision so long as no Damage shall be to the English Fishery, Provided also that nothing herein contained shall prejudice any of the English Inhabitants or Planters being at present actually possessed of any of the Premises & legally deriving right from Sd Mr. Purchase &c or Ancestors. In witness hereof we the aforenamed Sagamores well understanding the Purport hereof do set to our hands & Seales at Pejepscot the seventh Day of July in the thirty fifth year of the Reign of our Sovereign Lord King Charles the Second One Thousand Six hundred eighty four.

THE MARK OF WARUMBEE [His seal]

THE MARK OF DARUMKINE [Seal]

THE MARK OF WIHIKERMET [Seal]

THE MARK OF WEDON DOMHEGON [Seal]

THE MARK OF NEHONONGASSET [Seal]

THE MARK OF NUMBENEWET [Seal]"

Sealed and Delivered In presence of

JOHN BLANEY
JAMES ANDREWS
HENRY WALTERS
JOHN PARKER
GEO. FELT

Upon this deed was the following indorsement: —

"Upon the day of date of the within written deed the several Sagamores whose names are subscribed thereto & inserted therein did at the Fort at Pejepscot deliver quiet and peaceable possession of the premises with livery and seizen to Mr. John Blaney and wife in their own right as she is administratrix of the estate of Thomas Purchase dec'd and in the right of his children. Also the Sd Mr. Blaney Attorney to Mr. Eleasar Way did the same day deliver quiet & peaceable possession, with Livery & Seizen of the Premises to Mr. Richard Wharton, the Quantity of Seven hundred Acres of Land being excepted according to a Former Agreement." This was signed by Henry Waters and John Parker, and sworn to July 19, 1684, before

Edward Tyng, justice of the peace. On July 21 following, Warumbee, for himself and the other sagamores who sealed and delivered the foregoing deed, acknowledged it to be his and their free and voluntary act, before the same justice. James Andrews, on July 21, 1684, and John Parker, July 9, 1684, two of the subscribing witnesses, made oath before the same justice, that they saw this deed signed, sealed, and delivered

John Parker furthermore swore, at the same time, and before the same justice, that he saw possession given, together with livery and seizin of the premises, in presence of the several witnesses before named, and further stated that upon the eleventh day of July, he with Henry Waters was present and saw Worumbo deliver possession and livery and seizin "by a turf and twig and a little water taken by himself off the land and out of the main river above Androscoggin Falls, to Richard Wharton in full compliance with the conveyance of the premises within granted and confirmed."

This deed, with the several proofs thereof and possession given thereon, were recorded in the Province (York) records, July 26, 1684.[1]

Wharton found his deed encumbered by prior deeds, one of which was an Indian deed, dated 1659, to John Parker, the consideration for which was "one Beaver skin received and the yearly rent of one bushel of corn and a quart of liquor, to be paid on or before the 25th of December."[2] It is probable that this was the same tract of land (Sebascodegan) which Wharton, in behalf of his son William, sold to John Parker on July 20, 1684.[3]

The fort referred to in this Worumbo deed was not, as will be noticed by the date, the one built by Governor Andross in 1689, nor Fort George, which was built still later.

In this connection, it is proper to speak of the claim of the Eaton family to the territory now comprising the town of Brunswick. According to tradition, Jacob Eaton came here from Salisbury, Massachusetts, about 1680, or earlier, with one Michael Malcom, as a trader and trapper with the Indians. They are said to have bought this tract of land of the Indians, and the family believe, and it has been thought by members of the legal profession, that there was a valid claim. There are no deeds in possession of the family, and none were found in the York County records to substantiate this claim. It is very probable, however, that there was such a purchase from the Indians, and that this was one of the "prior claims" referred to as com-

---

[1] *Pejepscot Records.* [2] *Ibid.* [3] *York County Records,* 4, *p.* 19.

plicating Wharton's deed. Unfortunately for the family, however, a deed from the Indians would not be valid if there was at any time a grant from the throne of England covering the same territory. Such a grant Purchase and Way undoubtedly had, and as this land came legally into the possession of Wharton, and as, at a later day, the claim of the Pejepscot proprietors was acknowledged to be valid by the Commonwealth of Massachusetts, there can be no question that, whatever claim the Eatons may have once had, it is now irrecoverably lost. The case would be no better if the Eaton claim should be proved to have been derived from the Kennebec or Plymouth Company.

[1691.] About the year 1691, one Nicholas Cole, who had previously settled on Harpswell Neck under a title derived from the Indians, set up his claim to possession under an old title of Harvard College. It seems that on February 7, 1682, the General Court of Massachusetts granted "Merriconeag Neck with 1,000 acres of land adjacent," to the President and Fellows of Harvard College.[1] The same year the same Court also granted to Richard Wharton 1,000 acres of land "in the Province of Mayne, either upon any free Island or place upon the Mayne."[2] The college afterwards became anxious to secure the grant which had been made in 1682, and applied to the legislature for its confirmation; the decision was, however, in favor of the Pejepscot proprietors, into whose possession the property had come. The college obtained permission to review the case, but were again defeated.[3]

Notwithstanding these decisions, the General Court, on May 7, 1684, granted "to the Honoured Deputy, Governour Thomas Danforth, Esq., President of the Province of Maine, and to Sumner Nowell, Esq., for their great Pains and good Service, done by order of this Court, in the expedition in several Journeys to Casco, for which no Recompense hath been made them, an Island called Shebiscodego, in Casco Bay, in the Province of Maine, Provided they take the said Island in full satisfaction for all service done, referring to the Settlement of the Province of Maine to this day."[4]

OTHER EARLY SETTLERS.

[1653.] In 1653 the General Court of New Plymouth appointed Thomas Prince a commissioner to institute a civil government in this portion of the Province of Maine. A meeting of the inhabitants was notified by Prince, to be held at the house of Thomas Ash-

---

1 *Attested Copy of Court Record in Pejepscot Papers.* 2 *Ibid.*

3 *McKean, MSS. Lecture.*

4 *Attested copy of Court Record in Pejepscot Papers.*

ley at Merrymeeting Bay, in what is now called Dresden,[1] on May 25, 1654.

At this meeting "Thomas Purchase of Pejepscot" was chosen "Assistant to the Government," and John Ashley, constable. Prince, also, at this meeting, administered the oath of allegiance to sixteen men.[2] The residence of these men was, for the most part, on the east bank of the Kennebec and on the Sagadahoc. Alexander Thwait, one of the number, was settled, according to McKeen, on the part of Merrymeeting Bay opposite Fulton's Point,[3] and if this was the case, he and Richard Collicutt, who lived near him soon after, must have been Mr. Purchase's nearest neighbors. Sewall,[4] however, locates Thwait at Winnegance.

[1658.] Thomas Haynes is thought to have settled this year at Maquoit,[5] where he retained land as late as 1678. His wife's name was Joyce.[6]

[1672.] Richard Potts was settled as early as 1672,[7] and probably a year or two earlier,[8] on what was known as New Damariscove Island. In 1673 he owned and lived upon the point which still bears his name, at the extremity of Harpswell Neck.[9]

The following individuals are known to have been settled about this time, certainly prior to 1700, within the limits of what was afterwards called the Pejepscot purchase: at Middle Bay, John Cleaves; on White's Island, Nicholas White; at Mair Point, James Carter, Thomas Haynes, Andrew and George Phippeny; at Maquoit Bay, John Swaine, Thomas Kimball, of Charleston, who settled on Hoeg Island in 1658,[10] John Sears, Thomas Wharton, Samuel Libby,[11] who subsequently resided in Scarborough, Henry Webb, Edward Creet (or Creek),[12] and Robert Jordan; on Smoking Fish Point,[13] Christopher Lawson, an Antinomian; at or near New Meadows, in 1675, was Alister Coombs.[14]

The island of Sebascodegan was settled as early as 1639 by Francis Small and his wife Elizabeth, whose child was the first born on the island, of English parents. He was from Kittery,[15] and was a

---

[1] *McKeen, MSS. Lecture.*
[2] *Maine Historical Collections*, 5, *p.* 194.
[3] *McKeen, MSS. Lecture.*
[4] *Ancient Dominions of Maine, p.* 131.
[5] *Willis, History of Portland, p.* 98.
[6] *York County Registry of Deeds*, 4, *p.* 20.
[7] *Pejepscot Papers.*
[8] *York County Records*, 2, *p.* 366.
[9] *York County Records*, 10, *p.* 89.
[10] *York County Records*, 2, *p.* 90.
[11] *York County Records, various references.*
[12] *York Records*, 4. *p.* 20. *Land adjoined Thomas Haines's.*
[13] *What is called Ireland, McKeen.*
[14] *Pejepscot Papers, Statement of Title.*
[15] *McKeen, Harpswell Banner, Oct.*, 1832.

tenant under Colonel Shapleigh. The latter also owned Merriconeag Neck. The neck at this time had a number of settlers upon it who were all driven off by the Indians at the commencement of King Philip's War in 1675.[1] In 1683 Shapleigh, finding his property almost worthless on account of the Indian troubles, sold the neck and island to Richard Wharton, of Boston.

After Wharton's purchase of Sebascodegan, the Indians continued possession of the island, for the purpose of catching fish, seal, and porpoise. This prevented any further settlements there for some years.[2]

[1689.] In the year 1689 that portion of the Pejepscot tract adjacent to Brunswick, known as the "Gore," which formerly belonged to the town of Yarmouth, but is now a part of Freeport, began to be settled. Eight or ten families who had been driven from Eleutheria, one of the West India Islands, by the Spaniards, and who were dependent on Boston for support, came thither for a home.[3] The Gore was a triangular strip of land left between the southwestern boundary of Brunswick and the northeastern line of Yarmouth.

[1702.] In 1702 Benjamin Marston received possession by deed, of Thomas Potts, of Dover, New Hampshire, son of Richard Potts, of the estate at Potts's Point and the island near by, which was previously owned by Potts.[4] He is thought to have made a settlement there.

Among the Pejepscot Papers is the following memorandum, which, though in part a repetition of what has already been given, is inserted on account of the more particular information it conveys about certain matters. No date or authorship is given to the paper, but there is no doubt that it was made about the year 1714, by one of the Pejepscot proprietors.

"AN ACC'T OF THE EASTERN PARTS AND OF THE SEVERAL SETTLEMENTS THAT HAVE EVER BEEN MADE ON THE LANDS FORMERLY PURCHASED BY MR. WHARTON AND NOW[5] BOUGHT BY EIGHT OF US.

"The narrow carrying place that parts Casco Bay from Merrymeeting Bay, settled by Stevens, who has a son now at New Haven married to Parkers' daughter.

"Settlements on the Eastern side of Small Point Neck.

"Next to above s^{d} Stevens, at the upper Whigby, or Wiskege, by Lawson owned by Ephraim Savage.

---

[1] *McKeen, Harpswell Banner, Oct.*, 1832. [2] *McKeen, Ibid.*

[3] *McKeen, "Gleanings" in Brunswick Telegraph*, 1859.

[4] *York County Records*, 10, *p.* 88.

[5] *The Pejepscot Company was formed in* 1714.

"William Rogers about 2 leagues lower.

"Thomas Watkins about a mile lower.

"Mr. Gooch, the minister, about a mile lower down the river.

"John Filman about a mile lower.

"Capt. Reynolds about a mile lower.

"John Layton at the neck just above Winegance.

"Mary Webber about 2 mile lower — her son goes now with Captain Bracket.

"William Baker about a mile lower.

"Sylvanus Davis, now suppose Nelson.

"John Parker.

"Thomas Humphreys.

"Ichabod Wiswall.

"John Verin.

"Samuel Newcomb.

"William Cock and John Cock within half a mile.

"Robert Edmunds, said to be claimed now by Sr Charles Hobby.

"James Mudge within a quarter of a mile.

"Thomas Atkins, said to have bo't the whole neck down to Small Point of Indians and to have sold their interest to the other inhabitants. Some of his heirs supposed to be now living at Roxbury or Dorchester.

"Ambrose Hunniwell the lowest settlement on that side, about 4 mile short of Small Point. Hunniwell that works for Captain Belcher, one of that family.

"On the western side of that neck only Drake who settled at Small Point harbour — lived there but a little while.

"On Merriconege Neck only 2 settlements.

"Richard Potts who lived at the lower end.

"John Damarell about 3 miles above him.

"But one settlement at Mair Point by John Phippany.

"But one settlement at Maquoit by Robert[1] Haines.

"Settlements between Pejepscot & Swan Island on the north side of Merrymeeting Bay.

"Samuel York about 4 or 5 mile down from the Falls on the Eastern side. Living now at Squam, Cape Ann, he supposed the likeliest man to inform how far Merriconege Neck or Shapleys Island have been possessed or improved.

"James Thomas ½ a mile below. He and his heirs supposed to be wholly extinct.

---

[1] *Possibly Thomas is meant.*

"Williams ½ a mile farther — only a man & his wife — had no children — supposed to be extinct.

"James Giles about 4 miles up Muddy River.

"Thomas Giles at Point on south side of Muddy River mouth. Of these families Gyles of Winnissemet Ferry and Giles the Interpreter now live at Salisbury.

"Thomas Watkins at Shildrake Point, between Muddy River and Cathance.

"Alexander Browne east side of mouth of Cathance River.

"Dependence Collicut at point of Abegedasset River claims that point — no settlement between s[d] Collicut & Swan Island.

"One settlement at Swan Island by Collicut, Alexander Brown and Humphrey Davis, by turns — "

Samuel White, in 1714, produced the testimony of George Phippen and wife that his grandfather, Nicholas White, was settled at the upper end of Mair Point about forty-four years previously, and that Phippen and his wife were for several years the nearest neighbors. Two other testimonies, of persons living "on Pulpit Island or New Damariscove," were given to the same effect. The names of these two witnesses are not recorded.[1]

ORIGIN OF THE PEJEPSCOT COMPANY.

[1693.] Richard Wharton, who had become possessed of the greater portion of the lands already mentioned, having died in England, administration *de bonis non* on his estate was granted Dec. 30, 1693, to Ephraim Savage, of Boston.

[1697.] On Oct. 26, 1697, the Superior Court at Boston authorized and empowered Savage to sell Wharton's estate in order to liquidate his debts.[2]

[1714.] On Nov. 5, 1714, Savage, acting in accordance with the authority above mentioned, sold the whole of the above tract of land to Thomas Hutchinson, Adam Winthrop, John Watts, David Jeffries, Stephen Minot, Oliver Noyes, and John Ruck, of Boston, Massachusetts, and John Wentworth, of Portsmouth, New Hampshire, for the sum of £140, to hold in fee as tenants in common. The conveyance was acknowledged the next day and was recorded in the York records on the nineteenth of the following November.[3]

These "tenants in common" constituted the original company of the Pejepscot proprietors. On Oct. 20, 1714, the General Court of

---

[1] *Pejepscot Papers.* [2] *Pejepscot Records.* [3] *Pejepscot Papers, Statement of Title.*

Massachusetts passed a resolution that it was for the public interest that some townships be laid out and settled in the eastern country, and John Wheelwright and others were appointed a committee to receive the claims of all persons claiming lands there.

[1715.] On the 18th of February, 1715, the Pejepscot proprietors made certain proposals to the above-mentioned committee: —

1. That the General Court should give confirmation to their purchase, in order that they might "be better able to encourage substantial farmers to remove with their stock from England."

2. For the encouragement of a fishing town at Small Point.

3. That whenever twelve or more persons offered themselves for any new settlement, they should be "covered"[1] with such a force and for such a time as the General Court should deem necessary.

4. That those settling in the limits of the Pejepscot tract should, for the first seven years, have some assistance from the public towards the maintenance of a ministry, and should be exempted from the payment of any Province tax.

The proprietors agreed that, if the General Court would consent to the foregoing proposals, they would, on their part, agree to enter into the following arrangements: —

1. To lay out three or, if the land would admit, four plats or towns, and have them surveyed and platted that same summer, at their own cost.

2. "In seven years, if peace continues with the Indians," they would settle "each of said towns with fifty families or more, in a defensive manner, having already offers of very considerable numbers, both in this country and from England." And in order thereto they were willing to grant them such house-lots, in fee, and such accommodations in regard to their lands, as might induce them to settle there.

3. That they would lay out a convenient portion of land in each town, for "the subsistence of the first minister, the ministry, and a school."

4. "Being desirous that the people might not live like heathen, without the worship of God, as had been too frequent in new settlements," they engaged, for the more speedy procuring of a minister, and to make it easier for the inhabitants at their first settling down, that as soon as there should be twenty householders in each of the towns, who would provide a frame for, and raise a meeting-house

---

[1] *i. e., protected.*

they would, at their own expense, furnish glass, lead, nails, iron work, and other materials, and finish the meeting-house for them, and pay towards the maintenance of an "orthodox gospel minister" in each town, the sum of £40 per annum, for five years. These proposals to the committee received the signature of all the proprietors.[1]

On the twenty-seventh of the following May, the committee reported favorably on these proposals, and the General Court, on the tenth of June, passed resolutions in accordance therewith. Thus this company became undoubted legal owners of the territory they had purchased.

STATEMENT OF THE TITLE.

The Pejepscot tract, in consequence of the varied mode of its acquisition and the uncertainty of its true bounds, became the subject of a lengthy and severe controversy between the proprietors and several other claimants, — more particularly the Kennebec Company, — which lasted until about 1814. In order to understand this controversy, as well as the decision arrived at, it becomes necessary to state the several questions involved, and to make some explanatory remarks.

It is not, however, necessary to reproduce the exact points urged by the opponents of the Pejepscot Company. The questions to be considered are evidently as follows: —

1. In regard to the validity of the original titles to the land.
2. In regard to the extent of these titles.
3. In regard to the validity of the subsequent sales and conveyances.
4. In regard to the jurisdiction.

In regard to the first, it is proper to state that the original claims to all lands in this section could only originate in one of three ways: *first*, by grant from the King of England, direct or indirect; *secondly*, by purchase from the Indians; *thirdly*, by right of occupation of unclaimed land, in other words, by the right of "squatter sovereignty."

The validity of the claims to land obtained in these three ways may be considered as strong in the order given. The right in virtue of a grant emanating from the government holding possession of the country has ever been considered indubitable, unless conflicting with some prior grant from the same source. The right in virtue of a grant from the Indians is more than doubtful, though it may, we presume, sometimes have been deemed valid in those cases where no other grant

---

[1] *Pejepscot Records.*

existed,[1] and where there had been no prior sale by parties representing the same tribe, and the right either of those selling, or of the tribe they claimed to represent, was not contested. The right by virtue of occupation simply, is valid after the lapse of a certain number of years, determined by legal enactments.

In applying these principles to the different grants of the Pejepscot lands, it will be seen at once that the grant by the council of Plymouth to Purchase and Way was perfectly valid, unless it conflicted with a previous grant, by the same council, to the Kennebec Company. The evidence that a grant was issued to Purchase and Way was virtually proved. The deed of land bought by Purchase of the Indians, if any such there was, would only serve to strengthen his other claim.

The title to the lands, purchased of the Indians by Thomas, York, Gyles, and Stevens, should be considered valid, except as to any portion which might overlap the territory belonging either to Purchase and Way or to the Kennebec Company. The purchase of lands from the Indians by Nicholas Shapleigh was valid, there being no prior grant. That of Wharton from Worumbo, etc., was equally valid for the same reason, except where it conflicted with the other grants. The ground assumed by the Kennebec Company was that they owned, by virtue of their charter, all the land up and down the Kennebec River for fifteen miles upon each side, and that consequently some of the before-specified titles, being later, were null and void. They also claimed that the Pejepscot Company had not located their lands in accordance with the Worumbo deed.

The question, in regard to the boundaries of the lands granted, is the most important. The descriptions used in the old conveyances were often very indefinite. The bounds, said to have been given in the patent to Purchase and Way, are, however, sufficiently explicit as to one direction, and Purchase's deed to Massachusetts gives the bounds in the other direction. The territory granted in the sale to Nicholas Shapleigh is also clearly defined, being bounded by Purchase's possessions and by the sea. The point of the long dispute lay in the description given in the Worumbo deed. This deed included all the lands before granted. Did it include more? It could not include more on the south and east, but it undoubtedly did on the west and north.

The description reads: —

" All the aforesaid lands from the uppermost part of Androscoggin

---

[1] *Maine Historical Collections*, 2, p. 273. *Kent's Commentaries*, 3, p. 385. *Wheaton's International Law* (*Dana*), p. 40, *note.*

falls four miles westward and so down to Maquoit," and on the other side of the river from the same falls to the Kennebec, on a line running southwest and northeast

The principal question to be decided is as to what falls were meant. Were such terms to be used in a deed at the present day, there would be but little doubt that a point above all the falls in the river was intended. At the time of the deed, however, the river was not so well known as now, and serious doubts might justly be entertained as to whether the falls at Lewiston, Lisbon, or Brunswick were intended. If the Lewiston Falls were meant, the territory would consist of about 500,000 acres,[1] whereas if the falls at Brunswick were meant, the extent of territory embraced by the deed would not be one quarter so large. The opponents of the Pejepscot Company claimed that the Brunswick Falls were the ones intended. The proprietors, however, took the ground, doubtless correct, that the river below Brunswick was called the Pejepscot by both Indians and settlers, and that the lower falls were uniformly described, at that date, as the Pejepscot Falls, and consequently, that the falls referred to were those at Lewiston. The proprietors, however, came to a settlement with the Plymouth (or Kennebec) Company, on February 20, 1758, and released to them all the lands to the northward of a line drawn through the mouth of the Cathance River, and running west-northwest to the west-side line of the Plymouth claim.[2]

This settlement, however, proved unsatisfactory, and, June 17, 1766, the southern line of Bowdoinham and the Kennebec River were fixed upon and agreed to by the contending parties,[3] and on the 8th of March, 1787, the legislature of Massachusetts passed a resolution to the effect that the Twenty Mile or Lewiston Falls should be considered the uppermost falls referred to in the Worumbo deed.[4]

The difficulties do not seem to have terminated even then ; for in the year 1800, the Supreme Court of Massachusetts, acting on the report of referees, made substantially the same decision that had been made by the legislature,[5] adding, however, certain stipulations in regard to the assignment of lots to settlers. The proprietors for a long time refused to abide by the terms of the decision, and the controversy was not finally settled until 1814.[6]

The claims of individual settlers under other titles were disposed of by confirmatory grants from the Pejepscot Company, unless their titles

---

[1] *Vide Douglass Summary*, 1748.
[2] *Lincoln County Registry of Deeds*, 1, *p.* 21.
[3] *Pejepscot Records.*
[4] *Pejepscot Papers, Statement of Title.*
[5] *Pejepscot Records.*
[6] *Williamson, History of Maine.* 2, *p.* 585.

were proved to be illegal and void, or to have lapsed. The territorial limits of the company, at the time of the final decision of the contro versy with the Plymouth Company, embraced the present towns of Danville, Lewiston, Greene, a part of Lisbon, a part of Leeds, a part of Poland and Minot, Durham, Bowdoin, Topsham, Brunswick, and Harpswell. The territory, as previously claimed by the company, would have included Bowdoinham and Richmond in addition.

In regard to the validity of the conveyance by Wharton's administrator to the proprietors, there can, of course, be no doubt. There is also no doubt as to the jurisdiction of Massachusetts after Independence was declared. As to prior governments, it is only necessary to say, that although the jurisdiction over this part of the present State of Maine was claimed at different periods by different rulers, and went under the several names of the Province of Laconia[1] (1622), the Province of Lygonia (1630), the Province of Maine (Gorges–1639), and the Massachusetts Colony (1651–1677), yet the transfer of jurisdiction by Purchase to the latter gave her the strongest claim to the *Pejepscot tract*, though the fairness of her title to the Province of Maine is still a mooted question.

At this early date, however, the jurisdiction was merely nominal, there being but little actual enforcement of the laws in this portion of the Province.

---

[1] *The grant of the Province of Laconia was rather indefinite, but as it included the lands "betwixt ye lines of West and North West conceived to pass or lead upwards from ye rivers of Sagadehock & Merrimack in ye country of New England afores'd," it must have included all of Maine west of the Kennebec, and consequently included the Pejepscot tract.*

CHAPTER III.

DOINGS OF THE PEJEPSCOT PROPRIETORS, AND SETTLEMENTS UNDER THEM.

UP to the time of the formation of the Pejepscot Company, in 1714, comparatively few persons had made settlements in this region, and there had been no organized efforts to induce settlers to come hither. From this time new settlers appear oftener than before, though not very rapidly at first.

[1715.] Among other projects of the proprietors to encourage immigration to their lands, they voted, at a meeting held Sept. 14, 1715, "That the present projection for laying out the Town of Brunswick in one Line of Houses be accepted and the Town laid out accordingly.

"That each Proprietor will take up a Lot and build upon it as soon as may be. That we consent to Mr. Noyes taking his Lot next Maquoit (he promising to build a Defensible House thereon next Spring). That the Meeting House shall be in the midway between the Fort & Maquoit. That the Lots for the Ministry, the First Minister & the School be the Centre Lots, and as for the other Lots, Those persons, whether Proprietors or others, that first take up the Lots & build upon them, shall take their choice. And that the Outbounds & the plan of Topsham be likewise laid out now, three Sides of a Square, the Houses Twenty Rods distant according to the plan offered to the Generall Court." [1]

[1716.] The Pejepscot proprietors, some time in 1716, or perhaps 1717, bought a large tract of land extending from Abbacadasset Point up the west side of the Kennebec River, as far as the north end of Swan Island, and thence into the country for four miles. The title came from Kennebis, and Clark and Lake, but mediately through Richard Collicut and Samuel and Hannah Holman, of whom the proprietors bought.

---

[1] *Pejepscot Records.*

The proprietors at this time had to send everything necessary for the carrying on of their operations from Boston, and we accordingly find that at their first meeting, held Feb. 21, 1716, they voted to have twenty hundred weight of screwed hay, for the use of their cattle there, sent to Brunswick by the first sloop that went; and that the other things that had been requested should be sent to their servant, James Irish.[1]

At a meeting of the proprietors, held Sept. 5, of this year, it was voted: (Agreeably to their previous vote of the twenty-seventh of April, granting liberty to Adam Winthrop, one of their partners, to make choice of some island, neck, or tract of land within their territory) That Swan Island should be appropriated to Winthrop as his share of their first division, and that it should be reckoned at 1,000 acres, whether it proved to be more or less; "That Mair-Point be divided into Two Lots, The Lower half part to be Lot No. 2 — The upper half to be Lot No. 3"; that the portion of land lying between Cathance River and the eastern part of Abagadasset Point, and a line running northerly from the latter, should be divided into five lots, equal in front, and that the lot nearest Cathance River should be called No. 4, and that they should be numbered from that lot, successively, Nos. 5, 6, 7, and 8; that each lot should run back from Merrymeeting Bay, until it embraced 1,000 acres; that if either half part of Mair Point should fall short of 1,000 acres, the deficiency should be made up in some part of the township of Brunswick.

After the passage of the preceding votes, the proprietors proceeded to draw lots for their respective choices, with the following results: —

Lot No. 2 fell to John Wentworth, Esq.
" 3 " Mr. Stephen Minot.
" 4 " Thomas Hutchinson, Esq.
" 5 " Oliver Noyes.
" 6 " Mr. John Ruck.
" 7 " David Jeffries, Esq.
" 8 " John Watts, Esq.

The above lots were called the First Division.

It was then voted that there should be eight lots laid out on Small Point Neck, etc., and that these lots should be called their Second Division.[2]

At a meeting of the proprietors, held on the 13th of November following, it was agreed that they should give Captain Nowell a deed of

---

[1] *Pejepscot Records.* [2] *Ibid.*

five hundred acres of land within the township of Topsham, on the condition that he would build a house there and dwell there for the next five years, and that he would not leave except by consent of the proprietors, and on condition that the land allotted him should be so laid out as not to interfere with the plan of the town. As no other reference is made to Captain Nowell in the Pejepscot Papers, it is not probable that the conditions were fulfilled.

[1717.] On the third of May, 1717, Brunswick was, by vote of the General Court of Massachusetts, constituted a *township*, and the Pejepscot proprietors, with a view to the settlement of the town, "*Voted:* That all persons that shall offer themselves and be Excepted Inhabitants of the said Town And have a Lott of Land Laid out to them in S^{d} Township of ninety five Acres as also five acres of meadow in some Convenient place They building an house on Each Lott so Taken up within one year next after their taking up the S^{d} Lotts & Dwelling upon & improvin their Lands for the Terme of Three Yeares, And having their Said Lands Discribed & recorded in this Town Book by a Clerk Leagually Chosen & sworne It shall be accounted a Sure Lawfull Title of an absolute State of Inheritance in fee To them their Heirs & assignes forever, Provided nevertheless If any of ye before recited Conditions are not Complyed with by the said Inhabitants according to ye True intent thereof That then ye S^{d} Lotts of Land Shall be wholly forfited to ye use of the S^{d} Proprietors as fully as Ever here to fore any thing in this Book Recorded notwithstanding." [1]

At a meeting of the proprietors, June 13, 1717, Lieutenant Heath was instructed to survey and make a plot of each of the proprietor's lots. It was also voted that the township of Topsham be likewise surveyed and plotted in an oblong square, if the land would allow it, fronting on Merrymeeting Bay, so as to leave about two hundred acres, and that this town plat be laid out into fifty lots, each lot to be twenty rods wide.

It was also decided at this meeting to have a general plan of the whole territory made as soon as might be. The proprietors also desired Mr. Hutchinson to write to a friend in England for a copy of the patent to Purchase and Way, and to send it to them, well attested, as soon as possible.[2] The document is not on file with the Pejepscot Papers, and it is probable that it was never obtained.

At a meeting of the proprietors, June 17, 1717, it was "*Voted*, That a mile and a half upwards from Potts's Neck, and the other prongs

---

[1] *Brunswick Records, in Pejepscot Collections.* [2] *Pejepscot Records.*

of Merryconeag Neck, be left on the lower end of said Merryconeag Neck, for a Town or Fishing Settlement, the rest of said Neck to be divided in eight parts equal in Front, to run across said Neck, in paralel lines, from the North West to the South East side, according to the bearing of the said land, the Lowest Lott to be No. 1.

"The Lotts being fairly drawn came out as follows, viz.: —

No. 1. David Jeffries.
2. John Watts.
3. John Ruck.
4. Adam Winthrop.
5. John Wentworth.
6. Oliver Noyes.
7. Stephen Minott.
8. Thomas Hutchinson."[1]

[1718.] At a meeting of the proprietors, held April 23, 1718, it was "*Resolved:* That whereas it will tend much to the advantage of the Settlements for each Partner to settle his Severall Lotts laid out to him, and that it may be a means of preventing Troublesome disputes, we agree, as soon as may be conveniently, to build upon our Severall Divisions and to put them under Improvement."

[1719.] The next reference to this subject that has been found is in the proceedings of a meeting of the inhabitants and a committee of the Pejepscot proprietors, held May 8, 1719.

At this meeting a vote was passed, "That all Persons who have or Shall Take up any Lott or Lotts in Brunswick & Shall for ye space of halfe a year neglect to put Forward Building on & improving the s^d Land Shall be Liable to be forever Deprived of their Lott or Lotts; By the vote of this s^d Town." The land for a town commonage was granted by the proprietors at this time, but the vote passed will be given in connection with that subject.

[1731.] In 1731 Phineas Jones was employed to survey the lands and make plans. He found Brunswick and the lands above, on both sides of the Androscoggin River, to be 480,543 acres, Merriconeag Neck to be 4,670 acres, and Sebascodegan Island to be 5,790 acres. He made his survey in the winter season with five or six assistants, protected from the Indians by a file of soldiers. They selected the winter because there were fewer Indians about, and also because, the ponds and brooks being frozen, they could travel over them. In deep snow they could use snow-shoes.[2]

---

[1] *Pejepscot Papers.* [2] *McKeen, MSS. Lecture.*

Joseph Heath, Esquire, had been up to this time the agent and clerk of the company, but June 30, of this year, Captain Benjamin Larrabee was appointed agent, and the record book, containing the doings of the settlers, was transferred to him.[1] The proprietor, also, on the twelfth of July, 1737, gave John Booker, of New Meadows, the power of attorney to keep all unauthorized persons from settling upon Sebascodegan Island, or from cutting wood or timber or hay there, and to seize upon and ship to Bôston any timber or wood cut there without permission, one half the proceeds to go to Booker for his services, and the other half to the proprietors.[2]

The proprietors at the same time gave the power of attorney to Colonel Johnson Harmon, of Merriconeag, for the purpose of keeping off intruders from the Neck.[3]

July 16, 1737, the proprietors gave Benjamin Larrabee full power of attorney to execute deeds to the settlers in Brunswick and Topsham.[4]

In a letter of instructions to Larrabee, dated two days later, the following information was given in regard to the prices of the lots, and as to his duties: —

"The first settlers were to pay but five pounds for each hundred acres — Since that, Giveen and those near him were to pay Sixteen pounds for each hundred acres — Some that have more lately taken Lotts at Brunswick Road Ten pounds for each hundred Acres, those at Topsham and New Meadows Twenty five pounds for each hundred acres —

"As fast as you can receive money for the deeds you execute we would have you apply it to discharge the debts of the propriety viz: Mr. Pearse the Carpenter and Mr. Wakefield the Glazier for Brunswick Meeting house.

"If the Lotts at Brunswick Road to Maquoit and Topsham are not all filled up or granted you may go on to grant them on as good Terms as you can for the Proprietors — not lower than Ten pounds in Brunswick and Twenty five pounds in Topsham." [5]

[1739.] In June, 1739, Mr. Larrabee sent a representation to the proprietors of the difficulties the settlers labored under, in regard to paying for their lots in money, and the proprietors agreed that they might send the pay for their lots in wood or timber, to Boston, without charge.[6]

[1741.] At a meeting of the proprietors held at the "Sun" tav-

[1] *Pejepscot Records.* [2] *Pejepscot Papers.* [3] *Ibid.* [4] *Pejepscot Records.*
[5] *Ibid.* [6] *Brunswick Recórds in Pejepscot Collection.*

ern, Boston, April 22, 1741, it was voted that the following instructions be given to their partner, Henry Gibbs, to act upon while he was at Brunswick: —

"[1.] Whereas the Lotts were laid out but 20 rods wide from Fort George to Maquoit, the inhabitants complain they are too long and narrow, therefore for Accommodation of the settlers it is now proposed that they be 30 rods wide & to be laid out on one Side of the Road and to be one hundred acres exclusive of the marsh & to be valued at Fourteen pounds p Lott.

"[2.] Att every 10th Lott a Road of four rods wide to be laid out the whole length of said Lott if it fall out convenient. The County Road if any be laid out to be laid down on the Town plan & to be reckoned as one of said Roads and in case the Lott next said Road be more than 30 Rods wide yet to run an equal length with the rest & it be left to be appropriated as shall be Judged Most for the Interest of the Propriety.

"[3.] The Lotts on the East side of the Road to Maquoit to be Forty Rods wide as the Land will allow because the Land is not so good & necessary roads to be on that side.

"[4.] We are willing that a Priviledge be granted to such as will undertake to build a Grist Mill at a little stream near the Fort."[1]

The stream referred to in the preceding paragraph had its source in the swamp which formerly existed where the depot is now. This swamp extended as far east as the mall, as far north as Pleasant street, and westerly beyond Union Street. The brook ran along between Union and Maine Streets, passing back of the factory store and entering the river about where the factory is now. After the swamp was filled and drained, of course the brook no longer existed.

[1750.] At a meeting of the Pejepscot proprietors, held July 9, 1750, it was voted that an advertisement should be posted upon the meeting-house at Brunswick, stating that it was the intention of the proprietors to defend the inhabitants of Brunswick and the neighboring towns in the propriety, in their possessions, and that any person who should be so imprudent as to take up land under any other title, would be prosecuted. At the same meeting it was also voted to dispose of the vacant land at New Meadows, viz., that extending from Charles Casida's lot to Wigwam Point, exclusive, for the most that it would bring, and out of the proceeds of the sale to pay the expense of finishing the meeting-house in Brunswick. The remainder was to be

---

[1] *Brunswick Records in Pejepscot Collection.*

kept subject to the order of the proprietors.[1] A note at the bottom of the above entry in the records says, "Not accepted by the Town."

[1751.] On March 19th of this year, 1751, a letter was sent to the selectmen of Brunswick, by the proprietors, recommending that no one should take a title of land from the Plymouth Company, and promising them that if any of the inhabitants of Brunswick or Topsham should be molested or disturbed by that company, the proprietors would stand by them and indemnify them against the Plymouth Company's claim.[2]

This letter, however, seems not to have fully satisfied all the settlers, as some few did take up land under titles derived from the Plymouth Company. Learning this fact, the proprietors, at a meeting held April 15, voted, "to unite in defence of their Title to the Lands comprehended in said Township, and that an advertisement be forthwith printed, Cautioning all persons against making any Encroachment, Strip, or Waste, on any Land belonging to this Propriety, as they will answer it to the utmost perill of the Law."[3] In addition to this vote the proprietors, at a meeting held May 15, in order to show to all interested the exact bounds of the several lots, voted that the several deeds, or sufficient extracts from them, should be at once printed at the company's expense.[4]

The people of Topsham not having, at this time, the advantage of a local government, were apparently inclined to do about as they pleased, without reference to the proprietors, and some lawless acts were undoubtedly committed by them. The following letter from Belcher Noyes, the proprietors' clerk, to Adam Hunter, of Topsham, will show what some of these acts were: —

"BOSTON, May 12, 1753.

"MR. ADAM HUNTER:

"I wrote you last fall by Ste Gatchell to which have never had any answer from you, the Proposal made us by Capt. Willson is quite mean & unworthy any notice, I am sorry to hear your People have so generally combined in the old Trade of destroying the Lumber on ye Proprietors Interest this is very Abusive Treatment & convinces us you have no Regard to the Laws of God and man, for such a small frontier Settlem^t to live in such an abandoned State in the open violation of all Law, will expose you to the vengeance due to such Behaviour & it will one day fall heavy on your Heads.

---

1 *Brunswick Records in Pejepscot Collection.*

2 *Ibid.* 3 *Ibid.* 4 *Ibid.*

"For shame then be persuaded to leave of such actions, Topsham is become the Reproach of everybody. The Donlaps & Willsons are famous in this Trade. I should be glad when you come to Boston you might come prepared w^{h} some scheme to render your settlm^{t} capable of a better Improvement & encourage the Increase of Inhabitants.

"I enclose you a plan Delineating ye Bounds of the Plymouth Claim & our answer to their Remarks on said Plan I pray you would peruse the same & give me your sentiments in so doing you will oblige,

"yours to serve

"B. NOYES."[1]

[1757.] At a meeting of the proprietors, held May 31, 1757, Belcher Noyes was chosen clerk, and in the following June, treasurer and collector of taxes. At the meeting in June, a committee was chosen to conclude an agreement with the proprietors of the Kennebec purchase. It was also voted that the proposals from the Plymouth Company, for the accommodation of the disputes between them, should be accepted.

At a meeting of the Pejepscot proprietors, held at the Exchange tavern in Boston, on Wednesday, June 8, the subject of an agreement with the Plymouth Company was debated and decided upon.

[1758.] The deeds of the Pejepscot proprietors to the Plymouth proprietors, and of the latter to the former, were made and executed, in accordance with the above-mentioned agreement, on February 20, 1758.[2]

[1760.] The people of Topsham, at this time, are still at opposition with the proprietors, as appears from a letter of Belcher Noyes, their clerk, to E. Freeman, dated July 30, in which he states that there are some in Topsham who deny the title of the Pejepscot Company, the ringleaders being Captain Adam Hunter and Captain Thomas Wilson. He further states that there are "pyrates" there, who have made their living out of the proprietors by destroying the lumber, and that "none so guilty as this said Hunter who has gott an estate out of those woods." He says also that Mr. Gibbs had sold his right to one John Merrill, of Arundell, who would go down in the fall.[3]

[1761.] At a meeting held Oct. 8, 1761, Enoch Freeman, Esq., was desired and empowered to have a regular plan made of the township of Topsham, and to have the lots for settling so delineated that it

---

[1] *Pejepscot Papers.* [2] *Pejepscot Papers. Records.* [3] *Pejepscot Papers.*

could be known what land remained undisposed of. He was to make the line between the Plymouth and Pejepscot Companies' lands the boundary of his survey, and was to have the lands plotted by a skilful surveyor, into lots of one hundred acres each, so far as the land would admit. At the same meeting, he and Belcher Noyes were empowered to dispose of the settling lots in Topsham that were not already taken up, and to apply the proceeds towards finishing the meeting-house, the frame of which was already raised. At this meeting authority was given to Belcher Noyes "to execute a Deed of the old Stone Fort, with the Buildings and Land adjacent, in the Town of Brunswick, in behalf of this Propriety, viz. The one half to Jeremiah Moulton Esq. The other half to Capt. David Dunning; they paying unto the said Belcher Noyes the sum of one hundred and thirty three pounds six shillings and eight pence, lawful money, — for which sum he is to account with the Proprietors. Also, the privilege of the stream at the Falls, and its appurtenances."[1]

[1762.] At a meeting of the proprietors, June 3, 1762, it was voted to sell to Stephen Staples one hundred acres of land above the Cathance Mill, in Topsham, for five shillings and four pence per acre, and to apply the money towards finishing the meeting-house. It was likewise voted to sell to William Patten sixty-six acres of land situated in a gore of land on Cathance River — it being the balance of the land belonging to Cathance Mill — for whatever price could be obtained.[2]

In a letter from Belcher Noyes, dated October, 1762, and written to some unknown person, reference is made to the encroachments of the Plymouth Company upon the settlers at Topsham. In this letter he says: —

"The Plymouth Company have at the last session of our General Court gott a Tract of Land without Inhabitants, incorporated into a Township by the Name of Bowdoinham, the Bounds of which are enclosed. This takes off a small part of Topsham and some few families on Cathance Point, and by this means they have crowded themselves on us, contrary to their agreement. This was perfected before I knew anything of it. The People of Topsham are uneasy that their township is not laid out."

[1763.] The trouble between the settlers at Topsham and the Pejepscot proprietors has not yet been quieted. Mr. Belcher Noyes writes to Mr. Freeman that "Capt. Wilson is at the head of this Rebellion — you will find him a very troublesome fellow."[3] In another

[1] *Brunswick Records in Pejepscot Collection.* [2] *Pejepscot Records,* 1, *p.* 216.
[3] *Pejepscot Papers.*

letter, dated June 22, 1763, and probably to the same person, he says, referring to a meeting of the committees of the Plymouth and Pejepscot Companies to settle the dividing line between their respective territories, that the former, " in order to induce us to a complyance with their construction of the matter, produced a delusive plan taken by their surveyor, whereby the points of land called Summerset Point and Pleasant Point were so laid down as to persuade us, if they could, that they made the mouth of Cathance river." He says, moreover, that the Plymouth Company " intend to make a point of it and to force us to a complyance and by the fixing the southerly line of Bowdoinham I take it we are foreclosed and must submit to their terms." He concludes by saying that this land " we have lost absolutely by our neglect in the survey of Topsham and getting the same incorporated which has been settled 30 years ago."[1]

There are numerous letters from the proprietors' clerk, all complaining of the delay in completing the plan of Topsham.[2]

This survey was made by Stephen Gatchell, whom Noyes describes as " a poor, miserable, shufling fellow and indebted to everyone." It was completed Oct. 28 of this year.[3] It took Gatchell forty-seven days to perform this work with the aid of three assistants. He charged for his work £25 1*s.* 4*d.*

The inhabitants of Topsham, having suffered long enough from the rival claims of the Plymouth and Pejepscot Companies, from taxation by the town of Brunswick, and from the want of power to control whatever turbulent element there might be amongst them, decided to apply for an Act of incorporation as a town, and accordingly a petition was this year sent to the General Court, praying for the passage of such an Act.

[1766.] On May 29, 1766, an agreement was made between the Kennebec and Pejepscot proprietors, whereby the southerly line of the township of Bowdoinham was made the line between the territory of the two companies, and as compensation for which the former proprietors granted to the latter five hundred acres of land " to be hereafter agreed upon." They also allowed one hundred and ninety acres of land in the possession of John Fulton, on Cathance Point. On June 11, it was mutually agreed that in lieu of the five hundred acres to be allowed to the Pejepscot proprietors, they should have " 400 acres as laid out on Cobbasecontee Pond, in Pond Town, so called." This agreement, as amended, was duly and legally confirmed by both parties, June 17, 1766.[4]

---

[1] *Pejepscot Papers.* [2] *Ibid.* [3] *Ibid.* [4] *Ibid.*

[1787.] At a meeting of the Pejepscot proprietors, held Aug. 13, 1787, Josiah Little was elected as their clerk, in place of Belcher Noyes, deceased.[1]

[1799.] On the 3d of May, of this year, Josiah Little, Esquire, was chosen by the Pejepscot proprietors as their agent, to take care of their undivided interest in the town of Brunswick; to prosecute any trespassers; or to dispose of any or all of the property as he should judge to be most for their interest.[2]

SETTLEMENTS UNDER THE PROPRIETORS.

The efforts made by the Pejepscot proprietors to settle their lands were, for the most part, quite successful, though the rapidity with which settlers came in varied very much at different times. Many of these earlier settlers, it is said, ran away from England, and upon their arrival in this country changed their names.

Between 1717 and 1722 forty-one persons are known to have settled in Brunswick, and there were doubtless others whose names have not been preserved. Many of these settlers, however, forfeited their lots in consequence of their non-fulfilment of the required conditions. In 1722 the fourth Indian, or Lovewell's, war commenced, and the situation of the settlers here became so disagreeable that they nearly all abandoned their homes, and it was not until about 1730 that the settlement was renewed.

Those who are known to have remained are John Minot, Andrew Dunning and his sons, William Woodside and Ebenezer Stanwood and their sons, William Simpson and David Giveen and sons, of Brunswick; and Lieutenant Eaton, John Vincent, Thomas Thorn, James Ross, John Malcom, James McFarland, William Stinson, James, Isaac, and John Hunter, of Topsham. The most of these had garrisons.[3]

David Giveen, mentioned above, had been living at Mair Point, but about 1727 he bought three hundred acres of land at Middle Bay of the proprietors, and moved to the latter place.[4]

On June 30, 1733, the proprietors granted to Benjamin Larrabee, gratis, a lot of land in Brunswick, — one hundred acres, — on certain specified conditions of improvement and tenancy.[5]

In September of the following year, Samuel Woodward paid Benjamin Larrabee, agent for the proprietors, £5 towards the purchase of a lot of one hundred acres, situated between Captain Woodside's land and Bungamunganeck, the conditions of the sale being that Woodward was to build a suitable dwelling-house on the lot, and clear

---

[1] *Pejepscot Records.* [2] *Ibid.*
[3] *McKeen, MSS. Lectures.* [4] *Ibid.* [5] *Pejepscot Records*, 1, *p.* 117.

and inhabit it by the last of the following May (1735), and to pay £13 additional, or forfeit the £5 already paid; and if there were not one hundred acres in the lot specified, it was to be made up elsewhere.[1]

In the year 1738 the township of Brunswick was incorporated as a body politic by the Commonwealth of Massachusetts, and a considerable increase at once took place in the number of new settlers. On June 27, 1739, there were thirty-nine individuals who had recently come into possession of lots at New Meadows.[2] Whether all these persons actually lived upon their lots is unknown, but doubtless the greater number did. There were also, at this time, in other parts of the town, twenty-nine [3] individuals who were either new settlers or the sons of early settlers who had now become of age.

In June, 1740, the proprietors voted to give Benjamin Larrabee a lease of the lands adjacent to Fort George, and also the privilege of the salmon fishery, on such terms as might be agreed upon by the committee, to whom all such matters were referred.[4] Larrabee was at this time the agent of the proprietors, and probably the terms agreed upon with the committee were quite liberal. The following list of the land deeds issued by him, while agent, will prove interesting in this connection: —

MEMº OF ALL DEEDS ON RECORD MADE BY BENJAMIN LARABEE ESQ AS ATTORNEY TO THE PROPrs OF BRUNSWICK AND TOPSHAM.[5]

	Names of the Persons to whom Benj. Larabee Esq atty &c. sold.	Quantity of acres sold.	The time when sold.	The consideration.
1	Nathan Adams	100 acres	March 9th 1737	£25 0 0
2	John Adams	100 "	March 9th 1737	25 0 0
3	William Malcome	200 "	March 6th 1737	10 0 0
4	Robert Spear	200 "	March 29th 1738	32 0 0
5	William Spear	203 "	April 11th 1738	26 0 0
6	John Malcome	100 "	Jany 16th 1737	5 0 0
7	John Malcome	100 "	Jany 16th 1737	5 0 0
8	John Gyles Esqr	100 "	Sept 6th 1738	5 0 0
9	Jacob Eaton	100 Topsham	March 24th 1739	5 0 0
10	Henry Gibbs	95 & 115 poles	May 20th 1740	25 0 0
11	Jonathan Sayward	200	June 19th 1740	Quit claim as an heir to Parker.
12	John Barrows	100	July 15th 1740	25 0 0
13	John Adams	135	July 28th 1741	25 0 0
14	John Barrows	100	Octo. 16th 1741	25 0 0
15	Saml Clarke	200	May 19th 1742	32 0 0
16	David Given	100	Nov 8 1742	16 0 0
17	William Dunning	200	May 21st 1742	10 0 0
18	Benjamin Thompson	100	Nov 3d 1742	25 0 0

[1] *Pejepscot Papers.* [2] *Ibid.* [3] *McKeen, MSS. Lecture.*

[4] *Brunswick Records in Pejepscot Collection.*

[5] *Extracted from York County Records of Deeds, etc., Jan. 9, 1749, by Daniel Moulton, Reg.*

	Names of the Persons to whom Benj. Larabee Esq atty &c. sold.	Quantity of acres sold.	The time when sold.	The consideration.
19	James Hervey	103	Octo 24th 1741	£16 0 0
20	James McFarland	200	May 28th 1739	10 0 0
21	James McFarland	206	June 23d 1742	10 0 0
22	James McFarland	206	June 23d 1742	10 0 0
23	John Adams	100	Nov 3d 1742	25 0 0
24	Charles Casedy	100	May 7th 1742	25 0 0
25	Thomas Skolfield	103	May 26th 1742	25 0 0
26	Benj Bunker	115	Jany 12th 1740	25 0 0
27	Eben Stanwood	206	May 19th 1742	30 0 0
28	Isaac Snow	100	Nov 3d 1742	25 0 0
29	Jacob Eaton	100	Nov 28th 1737	25 0 0
30	Jacob Eaton	74 & 40 rods more or less being Lot No 9 at N. Meadows.	Nov 3d 1742	25 0 0
31	Saml Clarke Jacobs' Admr.	400	April 14th 1742	56 0 0 Old tenor
32	Patrick Drummond	100	April 7th 1738	25 0 0
33	Benj Bunker	63 & 112 rods	Jany 10th 1740	25 0 0
34	Alex Tyler	200	Octo 20th 1740	50 0 0
35	Saml Hinkley	200	May 21 1742	50 0 0
36	Lemuel Gowen	100	Feby 25 1740	50 0 0
				£828 0 0

On July 25, 1743, William Woodside, who had lived for some time at Maquoit, received a deed from the First Church in Boston, conveyed by its deacons, of three hundred and fifty acres of land at the westernmost end of Maquoit, "beginning at mouth of Puggy-muggy River." The price paid was £50.[1] Although there was a considerable number of settlers in the town at this time, they must have been quite scattered; for in 1747, according to the statement of Joshua Filbrook, there were but two houses to be seen from Fort George.[2]

June 19, 1751, Benjamin Thompson, of Georgetown, bought of Rebecca Morely, of Dorchester, Mass., "daughter of Thomas Stephens, formerly of the eastward parts now called Stephens' Carrying place, or near a place called the Head of Stephens's River," etc., all her interest in her father's lands, "being one sixth part of his estate."[3]

In 1752 there were, according to a map of the Plymouth Company of that date, but twenty dwelling-houses in Brunswick. For the location of these houses the reader is referred to the accompanying map, which is reduced from the original: —

[1] *York County Records*, 26, *p.* 256.

[2] *Journal of James Curtis in Library of the Maine Historical Society.*

[3] *York County Records*, 29, *p.* 120.

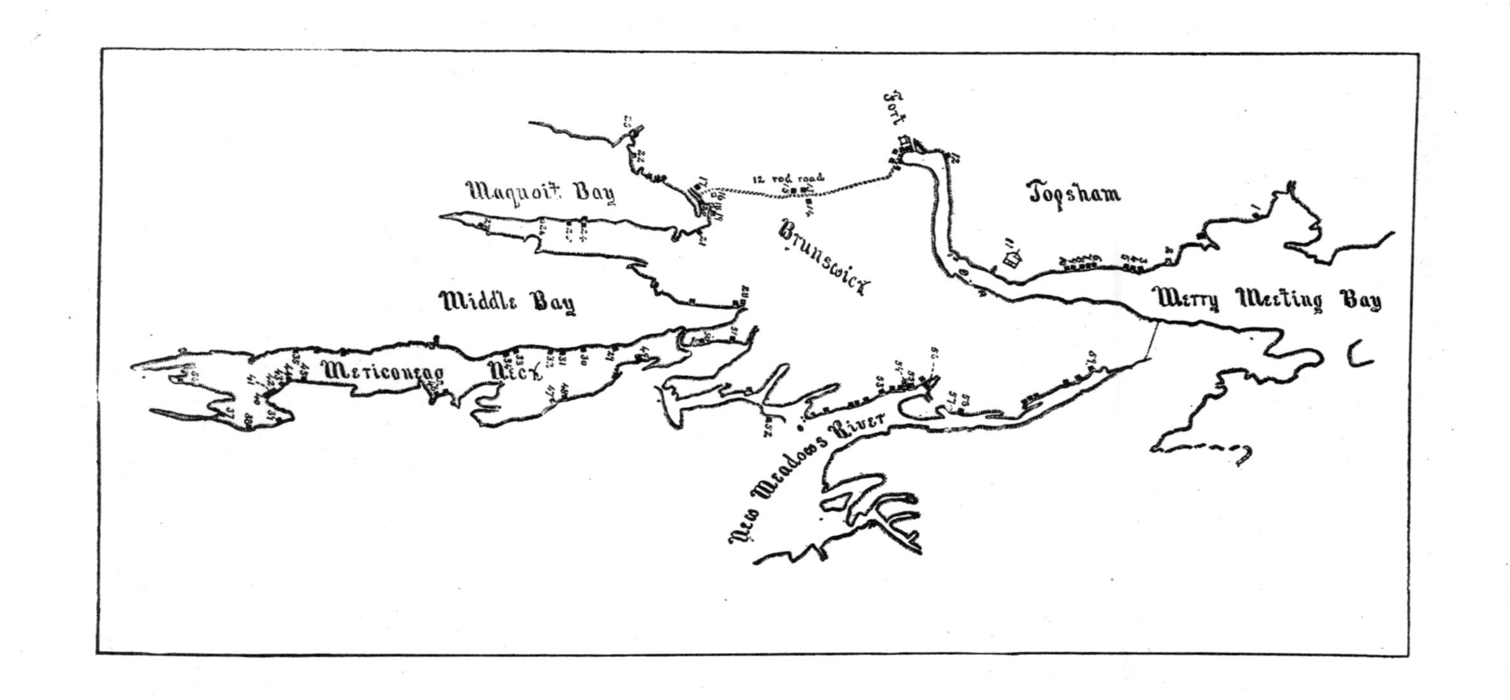
Fort
12 rod road
Topsham
Maquoit Bay
Brunswick
Middle Bay
Merry Meeting Bay
Mericoneag Neck
New Meadows River

REFERENCES TO THE FOREGOING MAP.

Topsham.

1. Gowan Fulton (1749).
2. Mr. Reed.
3. Samuel Beveridge.
4. Charles Robinson.
5. William Vincent.
6. William Thoms.
7. Jacob Eaton.
8. Robert Lithgow.
9. William Malcom.
10. William Thoms, Jr.
11. Lieut. Hunter.
12. Captain Willson.

Brunswick.

13. Speer.
14. Meeting-house.
15. Finney.
16. James Dunning.
17. Woodside.
18. Mill.
19. Stanwood.
20. Mill.
21. Smart.
22. V. Woodside.
23. Mill.
24. Captain Minot.
25. Beverage.
26. J. Orr (1742).
27. Camp.
28. Giveen.

Harpswell Neck.

29. Widow Adams.
30. McNess.
31. McGregory.
32. Willson.
33. Whelan.
34. Dyer.
35. Hays.
36. A negro.
37. Pinkham.
38. Do.
39. Widow McCraw.
40. Pinkham.
41. Webber.
42. Do.
43. Do.
44. Stover.
45. Toothaker.
46. Allen.
47. Warren.
48. Watts.
49. Mill.

Brunswick.

50. Starbord.
51. Skolfield.
52. Hall (on Sebascodegan Island).
53. Snow.
54. Mill.
55. Coombs.
56. Mills.
57. Deacon Hinkley.
58. Captain Thompson.
59. Smith.

In an estate bill for this year forty-five new names are to be found, but probably many of them are those of the children of parties who had previously settled in town, while some, undoubtedly, were of those who had purchased lots of previous settlers. Some whose names appear on this bill may have resided elsewhere.

The town continued to increase in population, however, and about 1760 a number of new citizens moved in, among whom were the families of Stone, Pennell, Melcher, Harding, Weston, Gross, Curtis, and perhaps others.[1]

[1] *McKeen, MSS. Lecture.*

In 1771 Robert Goddard moved into town, and Batcheldor Ring settled a little southwest of him, but also in Brunswick. The house of the latter was shortly afterwards burned, and he rebuilt a little farther west, and in the town of Durham. Owing to this fact, Brunswick lost a small portion of her territory when the line between that town and Durham was run.[1]

A year or two later several Quakers settled in town, near the western line. Some of them had previously been living in Harpswell. Among these new-comers were the families of Jones and Hacker.[2]

The first settlers on the Topsham side of the river all left their homes before the formation of the Pejepscot Company.

Between 1717 and 1722, however, thirty-three persons took up lots in Topsham, though many of them, doubtless, not fulfilling the conditions required by the proprietors, forfeited their claims. It appears from an entry made in 1717 by the proprietors' clerk, that the second island going out of Merrymeeting Bay into the Pejepscot River was deeded by Messrs. Minot and Watts to the Reverend Mr. Baxter of Medfield, Mass., and was thereafter to be known as Baxter's Island.[3] Three years later the proprietors granted to Mr. Baxter "the Island over against Topsham of about twentythree acres," upon condition that he would build two houses on it, and settle two families there who should be able to provide their own subsistence.

On July 30, 1720, the proprietors granted to Captain John Gyles the "First Lott of Land in the Township of Topsham, in consideration that he build a suitable dwelling house thereon and by himself or some meet person Inhabit the same for the space of three years," also "Five hundred and fifteen acres lying on Cathance Point opposite thereto." Gyles probably did not comply with the conditions, as we find that in 1741, the old title to land in Topsham derived through Thomas Gyles was brought forward, and the proprietors, therefore, on July 21, of this year, "In consideration of five shillings current money of New England, to us in hand paid by John Gyles, Esq., of a place called St. Georges, in the County of York aforesaid, and in consideration of a quit claim for lands at a place called Topsham, in the County of York aforesaid, signed by said John Gyles and his brethren, baring date the 15th of August, A. D. 1727," transferred to the Gyles's "a Point of Land containing 60 acres" in Topsham, "bounded southerly by Lott number one, easterly and Northerly by Merrymeeting

---

[1] *McKeen, MSS. Lecture.* [2] *Ibid.*

[3] *Brunswick Records in Pejepscot Collection.*

Bay, and westerly by the entrance or mouth of Muddy river"; also, another tract of land "lying Westerly from the former, bounded southerly by Lott Number one, westerly by Cathance River, Northerly by land belonging to us, and easterly by Merrymeeting Bay and the entrance of Muddy River . . . containing 515 acres."[1] This latter tract of land appears to be the same as that mentioned in the former deed.

On June 30, 1721, Samuel York, of Ipswich, relinquished all title to land in Topsham claimed by his father, Samuel York, deceased, by virtue of an Indian deed, etc., the proprietors granting him three hundred acres in lieu thereof.

About 1731 quite a number of new settlers moved to Topsham. Some forty-three persons took up lots this year or a short time previous. As many of the names of these persons do not appear in subsequent lists of settlers, however, it is probable that they either forfeited or sold their lots. Between this date and 1738, some fourteen families moved into town. The proprietors about this time especially encouraged settlements in Topsham, as that place was much behind Brunswick in the number of settlers. This was because Topsham was much more exposed to the incursions of the Indians, it having but few strong garrisons.[2]

[1746.] In 1746 it had only thirty-six settlers, and many of these were afterwards killed by the Indians. There are not more than ten or a dozen of these whose descendants have lived in Topsham during the present century. Some of these settlers removed and settled in the neighborhood of Boston.[3]

[1749.] The population of Topsham at this time was "about twenty-five inhabitants."[4]

Owing to the attacks of the Indians during what is known as the Spanish, or Fifth Indian war, the settlement at this place became much reduced, so that in 1750 there were but eighteen families remaining.[5]

In 1752 the number of polls in the Topsham precinct was twenty-eight. The number of dwellings at this time can be seen by reference to the map on page 40.

In 1757 the population of Topsham had nearly doubled, the number of polls being at this time forty-nine.[6] The whole number taxed in town in 1758 was forty-four.[7]

---

[1] *Pejepscot Records.* [2] *Pejepscot Papers.*
[3] *Ibid* [4] *Brunswick Records in Pejepscot Collection.*
[5] *Massachusetts Historical Collection*, 3, p. 142. [6] *Pejepscot Papers.* [7] *Ibid.*

On November 11, 1763, the following named settlers near Cathance proposed to buy of the proprietors the amount of meadow land affixed to their names, and agreed to pay six shillings per acre. The proprietors, however, limited the quantity to five acres each. This amount, it is to be presumed, they all purchased. The names and amounts desired were as follows: —

Hugh Wilson, six acres.
James Potter, Jr., eight acres.
James Mustard, five acres.
John Mallett, six acres.
Alexander Potter, six acres.
William Alexander, eight acres.
Samuel Wilson, ten acres.

On June 17, 1766, David Jeffries, of Boston, clerk to the Kennebec proprietors, and James Bowdoin, of Roxbury, Mass., a grantee of the same proprietors, deeded to John and William Potter and Gowen Fulton, all of Topsham, all of the land in Bowdoinham claimed by them under their previous deeds from the Pejepscot proprietors.[1]

[1768.] At a meeting of the Pejepscot proprietors, July 23, 1768, it was voted to allow John Merrill's claim to land bought of Henry Gibbs, in Topsham. The quantity of land which Merrill held was four hundred acres, which was forty acres more than the amount of his claim, and he was required to account for the overplus at a meeting held August 5; however, the proprietors gave him fifty acres in consideration of £39 due him from them.

A memorandum in the Pejepscot Records gives the dimensions of several log-houses built in Topsham, about 1738, as follows: "thirty feet long, eighteen feet wide and eight feet high."

The earliest transfer of land in Harpswell, after the formation of the Pejepscot Company, of which we have found any record, was in 1720. On May 20, of this year, Nicholas Cole and Samuel Littlefield, of Wells, deeded to Samuel Boone, of Kingston, Rhode Island, one half of Merriconeag Neck, one half of Great Chebeag Island, and one half of Great Island, being the land formerly owned by Nicholas Cole, Senior, and John Purrington.[2] Boone is not, however, known to have settled in Harpswell.

In the year 1727 several new families moved to Harpswell and settled upon the Neck. On the twenty-sixth of May of this year, Thomas Westbrook, one of the Pejepscot proprietors, deeded to

---

[1] *Original deed in our possession.*

[2] *Pejepscot Papers.*

Colonel Johnson Harmon, formerly of York, one twenty-fourth part of two thousand acres of land on Merriconeag Neck.[1]

In October of the same year, Colonel Harmon leased of the Pejepscot proprietors, for seven years, "that farm or tract of land called Merriconeage Neck in Casco Bay, and so running up to the upper carrying place including ye whole breadth of ye s^d^ neck." The proprietors, however, retained the right to settle one or more families on the Neck, without opposition from Harmon.[2]

The authorities of Harvard College, however, though defeated in their appeal to the legislature, as stated in the preceding chapter, had not given up their claim to the land, and in January, 1732, they instituted a suit of ejectment against Harmon, in the Court of Common Pleas of the County of York. In October, 1733, a verdict was rendered in favor of Harmon. The plaintiffs appealed the case to the Superior Court, which was held in 1737, and it was eventually decided again in favor of Harmon, or rather of the proprietors from whom he leased. Having been four times defeated, Harvard College made no further attempt to recover this property.[3]

In Dec. 21, 1741, Colonel Harmon deeded all the foregoing land (excepting fifty acres which he had previously sold to John Stover) to his son, Joseph Harmon, of York, together with his dwelling-house, barn, and all other buildings and appurtenances. The price paid was £70 in bills of credit.[4]

On May 17, 1731, Moses Gatchell leased of the Pejepscot proprietors, for two years, the land on Merriconeag Neck, between the Carrying-Place and the land then occupied by Colonel Harmon.[5]

At the same date Gideon Conner, then residing on the Neck, leased of the proprietors, for two years, a tract of land having the same bounds as Gatchell's,[6] and it is probable that the two men leased the land together, but each was held by a separate lease. It is possible, however, that Conner was the "Iresh Neighbour" referred to in the following letter: —

"MERECONEAG June 25, 1731.

Hon^d^: Colo^ll^ sr: I am still in your posession on y^e^: upor end of ye neck but I have there an Iresh Neighbour which pretends to hold pos^n^: for mr. Porenton by a Leas under his hand as I am sr in yours by Colo^ll^ Westbrook And I hope by your cosent: I am Redy and will^n^ to sarve your intrust: and desier your Counsel and asistance from time to time: and sr if you will plese to send me ½ Barrel of Molases

---

1 *Pejepscot Papers.* 2 *Ibid.* 3 *Ibid.* 4 *Ibid.* 5 *Ibid.* 6 *Ibid.*

and one Sythe you will greatly oblige me: and I will indever to pay you ye next faul who am yours to Cd

"MOSES GATCHEL."[1]

There had been but two houses at the upper part of Merriconeag Neck previous to 1741, as will be seen by the following testimony: —

"Hannah Smith Testifyeth & Saith y^t she with her late Husband James Smith lived at ye upper end of Mereconege Neck where her late Husband & her Father Moses Gatchel Built a House & lived there from June 1731 to 1735 at which Coll Westbrook told us y^t if we liked any place on said Neck better we might Remove to it upon which my late Husband [Smith] & Father [Gatchel] Removed about 1½ mile loer down on s^d neck & Built a House there where we lived till 1741, as Tennants to S^d Westbrook & $Comp^y$ & Built Houses in both Places & further that when her Father Gatchell Removed from the upper House on S^d neck he Lett it to $Nath^{ll}$ Barnes who lived there 2½ years from 1735 & paid my Father Rent for the Same for S^d Westbrook & $Comp^y$ the S^d Barnes Removing away to Topsham left s^d House in the Posession of W^m McNess for y^e S^d Westbrook & $Comp^y$ — and no persons whatsoever lived on the upper half of S^d Neck but my Father & My Husband & owre Familys while we lived there & there was no sign of any other habitation nor improvement but where we first lived."[2]

The proprietors, notwithstanding their devotion to the interests of the settlers, were men who knew how to look out for their own physical wants and how to enjoy good living. It appears that on the 8th of August, 1733, the proprietors leased to William Cady and his associates, for seven years, the "island called Sebasco Deggin," with liberty to use and occupy it; and they also agreed to deliver to Cady the frame of a house, then in the possession of Colonel Harmon, and to furnish Cady with four thousand feet of boards, and with nails sufficient for finishing the house, which Cady was to set up and finish. The proprietors reserved to themselves the right of "improving any mine or mineral," which might be discovered on the island, and also the right "to settle a fishery there," or to make other settlements there, which should not, however, interfere with the improvements of Cady and his associates.

Cady agreed to erect and finish, forthwith, at least one dwelling-house on the island, and occupy it before the next winter, and that before the next summer he would settle, at least, three other families

[1] *Pejepscot Papers.*

[2] *Ibid.*

besides his own on the island, and keep off all intruders from settling without leave, in writing, from the proprietors, and from cutting wood or grass there. He further agreed to clear the fresh meadows, and to clear and break up and bring to tillage and English grass as much of the land upon the island as he and his associates could (the proprietors finding grass-seed), and to endeavor to raise a nursery of fruit trees and an orchard; and as an annual rental he agreed to pay to Adam Winthrop, or his heirs in Boston, "for the use of him and the rest of the Lessors *twenty good fat geese*, or in failure thereof £5 per annum, in bills of credit on this Province."[1] Although his name is not mentioned in this deed, there is little doubt that William Condy was one of Cady's "associates," as a blank form of a deed in the Pejepscot papers mentions Condy's name in connection with that of Cady. The harbor known as "Cundy's" was undoubtedly named for William Condy.

It will be noticed that this lease reserves the right to the proprietors to allow other settlers on the island. And in 1737 or 1738 some twenty families were settled there.

An attempt was made to re-settle the island for the purpose of building a fishing-town. Mr. Nathaniel Donnel, of York, selected a spot which was to be divided into small lots of an acre each, for the convenience of dwelling-houses, with a convenient harbor adjacent. The project was abandoned on account of the increased hostility of the Indians. The harbor referred to was probably Condy's, as the land on the western shore of that harbor is well calculated for the site of a village.[2]

Dec. 23, 1742, Joseph and Clement Orr, of Pemaquid, turners by trade, bought of Henry Gibbs, of Boston, a tract of land at the northerly end of Merriconeag Neck, containing one hundred and twenty-two acres.[3] The next day they received from the same party another tract of sixty-nine acres near the former,[4] and the "southeast prong" of Merriconeag Neck, containing, by estimation, two hundred acres."[5]

In 1743 Richard Jaques, of North Yarmouth, bought one hundred acres of land, on Little Sebascodegin (Orr's) Island.[6]

He is believed, therefore, to have been the first purchaser of land on this island, though tradition has it that a man by the name of Fitzgerald was the first occupant of the island. What disposition he

---

[1] *Pejepscot Papers.* [2] *McKeen, in Harpswell Banner.*
[3] *York County Records*, 26, *p.* 201.
[4] *Ibid.*, 26 *p.*, 202. [5] *Ibid.*, 28, *p.* 99. [6] *Ibid.*, 25, *p.* 112.

made of this property is unknown, but the whole island afterwards came into the possession of Honorable William Tailer, of Dorchester, Mass., and of Honorable Elisha Cook, of Boston, whose heirs sold it in 1748 to Joseph Orr.[1] Joseph Orr had previously been living on Merriconeag Neck, but after he purchased the island he, with his brother Clement and sons, moved on to it and erected a garrison-house. The island has since gone by his name.

In his purchase of half of the island from the heirs of William Tailer, Orr did not secure the signature to his deed of one of the daughters, the wife of Reverend Matthew Byles, of Boston, who accordingly put in her claim to a share. In consequence of this claim, on July 22, 1760, Orr set off and released to her one tenth part of the island, and received a quitclaim of the remainder.[2] On October 16th of this year, Joseph Orr deeded the whole of his property on this island to his brother Clement as a life estate, and to his heirs after him. In case of the death of Clement's heirs it was to revert to the heirs of Joseph.[3]

In 1755 there were on Sebascodegan Island, sixteen persons, and on Merriconeag Neck, six persons, who, living north of the Yarmouth line, were taxed in Brunswick.

The number of settlers in these three towns, during the first half of the last century, is so large as to prevent a mention of their names in this connection, and a list of these settlers is therefore given in the Appendix. The doings of the proprietors, which are not given in this, will be found in their appropriate connection in other chapters.

---

[1] *York County Records*, 35, *pp.* 31, 32. [2] *Ibid.*, *p.* 232.
[3] *Original deed, in possession of S. Purinton.*

CHAPTER IV.

PERIOD OF THE INDIAN WARS, 1675-1760.

In the earliest years of the Pejepscot settlement the whites were few in number, and although they oftentimes, doubtless, excited the jealousy and even the personal animosity of the natives, still, on the whole, they conducted themselves with sufficient caution to prevent any outbreak. For a few years previous to 1675 the ill-feeling and jealousy on the part of the Indians had been increasing and was particularly directed against Thomas Purchase, who was thought by them to have charged unfair prices, and otherwise to have overreached them in trade. The custom of the English at this time was, as is said by an early writer, "first to make them [the Indians], or suffer them to make themselves, drunk with liquors, and then to trade with them, when they may easily be cheated both in what they bring to trade, and in the liquor itself, being one half or more nothing but spring water, which made one of the Androscoggin Indians once complain that he had given an hundred pound for water drawn out of Mr. P. his well." [1]

KING PHILIP'S WAR. 1675-1678.

The animosity of the natives culminated in an outbreak in 1675. The war commenced in the Plymouth Colony, June 24, 1675. By September the fourth or fifth, hostilities commenced at Pejepscot. On that day, a party of about twenty Indians went to Purchase's house and pretended to his wife that they wished to trade. Discovering, however, that her husband and son were both absent, they gave up all further disguise, and proceeded to rob the house. They took what weapons, powder, and liquor they could find, ripped up the featherbeds for the sake of the ticking, killed a calf and several sheep, and proceeded to make merry. Purchase's son returned home while this was going on, and being discovered by the party, was obliged to

---

[1] *Drake, Hubbard's Indian Wars, p.* 256.

flee for his life. He was followed for some distance by an Indian with a gun, but succeeded in making good his escape. The party offered no violence to any one in the house, but told them that "others would soon come and treat them worse." Some few days later, a party of twenty-five settlers, having collected for the purpose, went in a sloop and two boats to the New Meadows River, near to the house of Mr. Purchase, to gather and secure the growing crops, and also to reconnoitre. Here they found a number of Indians pillaging the neighboring houses. In attempting to get between the Indians and the woods, they came upon three of their spies. One of these, attempting to reach the river, they shot. The second was wounded, but escaped across a stream to a canoe. The third escaped and gave the alarm. The Indians, however, remained concealed until the corn was all gathered and the boats loaded, when they suddenly gave their war-whoop, rushed upon them, wounded several, and carried off the boat-loads of corn in triumph.[1] Some time the next year Purchase's house was burned and he was compelled to leave.[2]

The war now having fairly opened, the settlers were all obliged to flee, and the Indians, emboldened by their success, "sought trophies for the tomahawk and scalping-knife in every direction, at the door of every plantation" throughout the Province of Maine.

The Androscoggin Indians were the most active of all the tribes, and it was thought, in 1676, that if a treaty could be effected with them there would be a general peace with the Eastern tribes.[3] This could not be accomplished this year, however, and so the General Court, in 1677, ordered Majors Waldron and Frost, with one hundred and fifty men, sixty of whom were Natick Indians, to the Kennebec, with instructions "to subdue the Indians in those parts, and deliver the English captives detained in their hands."

The force landed at Mair Point, Feb. 18, 1677. They were immediately hailed by an Indian party, among whom were Squando and Simon, "the Yankee-killer." After some preliminary questions, Waldron inquired of Simon whether they desired peace. The latter answered, "Yes, and we sent Mugg to Boston for that purpose; he told us you'd be here." Upon being asked if they would release their English captives, Squando replied, "I will bring them in the afternoon." Nothing further was seen of them, however, until the

---

[1] *Williamson, History of Maine,* 1, *p.* 520 *et seq.*
[2] *Maine Historical Collection,* 3, *p.* 315.
[3] *Drake, Book of Indians,* 3, *p.* 104.

next day at noon, when fourteen canoes were seen up the bay, pulling for the shore, and soon a house was seen in flames, and the Indians appeared and challenged Waldron's soldiers to fight. Major Frost then attacked them and killed and wounded several. Another parley was then held. On being asked why they had not brought their captives, as they had agreed to do, and why they had fired the house and challenged the soldiers, the Indians replied, through their interpreter, that "the captives were a great way off, and that the snow and cold weather had prevented their coming, that the house took fire by accident, and that the soldiers fired at the Indians first." Major Waldron, finding himself unable to recover the captives or to fight the Indians with advantage, sailed for the Sagadahock.[1]

This was the last engagement of this war that occurred in this vicinity, though peace was not declared until April 12, 1678. Although in the first three months alone of this war, eighty persons were slain between the Piscataqua and the Kennebec, it is not known that any of the settlers in the Pejepscot tract were killed.

KING WILLIAM'S WAR. 1688-1699.

The peace concluded with the Indians in 1678 lasted just ten years, when, from various causes, they became excited and again took the war-path. Governor Andros was at first inclined to adopt pacificatory measures, but at last, finding war inevitable, he took the opposite course, and in November, 1688, he made an expedition into the Eastern country, as it was then called, and established garrisons. At the time of his visit to Pejepscot, "the weather was exceedingly cold, the snow deep, and the travelling exceedingly tedious." While here he caused a fort to be erected under the charge of Anthony Brockhold, one of his counsel,[2] and garrisoned it with a part of his army.[3] This fort stood on what is now Maine Street, a few rods south of Bow Street, and about where the store of J. T. Adams & Co. is now.

The first attack in this vicinity was in the spring of 1690, when the fort was taken by the savages. In September, Colonel Benjamin Church was sent from Massachusetts with between three hundred and four hundred men, to drive them off from Brunswick and other places in this region, and, if possible, recover their captives. He landed his force at Maquoit, Sept. 13, and marched them by night towards Fort Andros. They surrounded the fort, but at daybreak it was discovered that the enemy had left shortly before their arrival. The soldiers

---

[1] *Williamson, History of Maine,* 1, *pp.* 545, 546.

[2] *McKeen, MSS. Lecture.*

[3] *Williamson, History of Maine,* 1, *p.* 590.

found some plunder and a barn of corn. They left the same day for an Indian fort on the Androscoggin. After capturing the latter and releasing several prisoners, they returned to Maquoit, went aboard their vessels, and sailed for Winter Harbor.[1]

Church had no conflict with the Indians at Brunswick as stated by Cotton Mather, the contest referred to having occurred at Cape Elizabeth.[2]

In September, 1691, Captains King, Sherburne, March, and Walton landed, with their several companies of Massachusetts militia, at Maquoit and visited Fort Andros, expecting to find some Indians there. They found none, however, and accordingly returned immediately to Maquoit. While re-embarking, they were assaulted by a strong force of Indians who had been watching them. In this skirmish Captain Sherburne, of Portsmouth, New Hampshire, was killed.[3]

The war lasted some eight years longer, but there was no further skirmishing in this vicinity. Probably the settlers had all left. A conference between the commissioners from Massachusetts and the sagamores of the Penobscot, Kennebec, Androscoggin, and Saco tribes was held at Mair Point, and a previous treaty of peace, which had been made at Pemaquid, Aug. 11, 1693, was ratified between them on Jan. 7, 1699. This treaty quieted the fears of the settlers and encouraged those who were engaged in the resettlement of Maine.

QUEEN ANNE'S WAR. 1703–1713.

Peace with the Indians lasted only about four years. In 1703 the third Indian war commenced. Although during this war engagements and skirmishes were quite frequent in the vicinity and to the westward of Falmouth, there is no evidence that there was any contest in this vicinity. The statement made by the late John McKeen,[4] that there was an attempt to undermine the fort here, in 1702, by a Frenchman named Bobazier and five hundred Indians, is an error. The fort referred to was at Casco, the present city of Portland.[5]

In 1704 some companies from Massachusetts and New Hampshire went East, "Indian hunting," as it was termed, and one Peter Rogers, of Newbury, stated that he came to Pejepscot in a company of some twenty or thirty. That it was in the winter time, and that they trav-

---

[1] *Dexter, "Church's Expeditions against the Eastern Indians," pp.* 50 *to* 56.

[2] *McKeen, Manuscript Lecture.*

[3] *Williamson, History of Maine,* 1, *p.* 628.

[4] *Pejepscot Papers. McKeen, MSS. Lecture.*

[5] *Penhallow, p.* 20. *Willis's History of Portland, p.* 315.

elled with snow-shoes from there to Rocamoco,[1] or Jay Point, now Canton. No mention is made of his meeting with either settlers or savages.

LOVEWELL'S WAR. 1722–1725.

Although during Queen Anne's war there is not known to have been any conflict in this vicinity, yet the whole Province was in such a disturbed state on account of the Indian troubles that the Pejepscot proprietors, in 1715, felt it necessary to offer the following.

ENCOURAGEMENTS TO ENLIST.

"Wee the Subscribers Proprietors of the Lands in Brunswick & Topsham, do offer the following encouragements to such as shall Voluntarily enlist themselves as Souldiers to garrison the Fort at Brunswick.

"1 That immediately upon their enlistment, they shall enter into Pay & Subsistence.

"2. That the Military Service expected from them at present is like to be so small as to permit them, besides their wages, to earn money by Labour.

"3. That during the time of the Forts Repair, we will employ them all as Labourers, (except the Warders), & pay Two Shillings a day for every day they work.

"4. That afterwards we will endeavour to find employment for them, by splitting staves, shingles or clapboards or any other Service that may prove beneficiall to us & them.

"5. That when they have served six months as Souldiers if they desire to become Inhabitants, we will endeavour to obtain a General Order from His Ex^{c}y the Govern^{r} to release them, they finding another man in their room, & when so dismist they shall have One hundred Acres of Land granted to each of them equall with the other Inhabitants & on the same Terms & conditions with them.

"6. If they don't see cause to settle there, when they have served twelve months, we will use our endeavour to obtain His Ex^{cy} Favour to get them discharged, which we hope we shall be able to accomplish.

"*Approved by the Governour*
& Signed by several of the
Proprietors.

"BOSTON, Aug. 3d, 1715."

The proprietors, at a meeting held the thirtieth of the same month, voted to provide a free passage in a sloop to Brunswick and Topsham to the enlisted soldiers.

---

[1] *McKeen, Manuscript Lecture.*

The fourth Indian, called the Three Years' or Lovewell's War, commenced in this vicinity, June 13, 1722, by a party of sixty Indians in twenty canoes appearing at Merrymeeting Bay, on the north side, perhaps near Pleasant Point or Fulton's Point. They captured nine entire families, but released all except five men, — Hamilton, Hanson, Trescott, Love, and Edgar, — whom they detained as hostages for the safe return of the four Indians in the hands of the English at Boston.[1]

In June or July of this year, they made an attack upon the settlement at Brunswick, which they set fire to and entirely destroyed. Several citizens were also taken prisoners. Mr. David Dunning and another soldier were on the plains at the time, and when about where the First Parish Meeting-House now is, their attention was arrested by an unusual noise. They looked among the bushes and discovered a large number of Indians about the house of Thomas Tregoweth, and just moving away towards the fort. Mr. Dunning went to his home at Maquoit, but the soldier ran towards the fort, giving the alarm as he went. He was fired at, but escaped. Some of the citizens who were captured were cruelly murdered, and the houses were rifled and burned. In regard to the fate of Thomas Tregoweth nothing is definitely known.[2]

After their work of destruction was accomplished the Indians repaired to a dwelling on Fish-House Hill[3] for purposes of revelry. They were soon dislodged, however, put to flight, and the house partially destroyed by a chain-shot from the cannon in the fort. This fort was not Fort Andros, but a stone fort named Fort George, which was built in 1715 by the Pejepscot proprietors, and which stood quite near the site of the former. The Indians took their boats and went with their captives to Pleasant Point.

Captain Gyles sent Samuel Eaton, with a letter done up in his hair and covered with an eel-skin, to let Colonel John Harmon, who was stationed at Arrowsick, know of the attack, and that the Indians were on their way to Pleasant Point.[4] Harmon, discovering the village to be on fire, concluded that the Indians had made an attack upon it, and at once, before the message from the fort had reached him, manned two whale-boats, and, accompanied by Major Moody, proceeded with muffled oars up the river. It was night when he entered Merrymeeting Bay. Perceiving the fires of the Indians upon Pleasant Point, he carefully approached and noiselessly landed.

---

[1] *Williamson, History of Maine*, 2, *p.* 114. [2] *McKeen, MSS. Lecture.*
[3] *On Water Street, near the present residence of Miss Narcissa Stone.*
[4] *McKeen, Manuscript Lecture.*

Ascending the banks, he found a large number of Indians lying before their fires, all sleeping very soundly, being much fatigued by the labors of the day and their subsequent revelry. His men immediately arranged themselves, fired into them, and killed sixteen or eighteen, and took some prisoners, though some, doubtless, escaped. A few of the Indians, who were some little distance off, alarmed by the report of fire-arms, fired at them, but without doing any harm.

Harmon, on his return to his boats, found the body of Moses Eaton, of Salisbury, Mass., whom the Indians had first tortured by depriving him of his tongue and cutting off his arms and legs, and had then killed. As no one of the party was shot at the time of the attack, Eaton must have been taken captive while separated from his comrades. His body was buried near the spot.[1]

An account of this affair has been preserved in doggerel rhyme Harmon is represented on the bank of the river, watching the Indians sleeping before their fires. It is introduced here as a specimen of the literature of the times: —

> "Oh, the sweet and pleasant morning
> While we around them stood,
> But oh! the dreadful and grievous groaning,
> Englishmen lying in their blood.
> 'Come,' said valiant Colonel Harmon,
> 'This, their neglect, is our gain;
> Therefore let us fall upon them, —
> Our cause is good we will maintain.'
> Then on them we fired two volleys,
> And, with haste, we made away.
> For fear the Indians would surround us,
> And we should not get away.
> Some did say that we did kill thirty,
> Others say that we did kill more;
> The number to us is uncertain,
> I believe we hardly killed a score."[2]

This attack upon the settlement at Brunswick is supposed to have been specially in retaliation for that upon Norridgewock, the preceding year, by Colonel Westbrook.[3]

Early in August, 1724, "Captains Harmon, Moulton, Brown, and Bean were now preparing for Norridgewock, with two hundred men

---

[1] *Williamson, History of Maine*, 2, *p.* 116 *According to McKeen (Pejepscot Papers), Moses Eaton was son of Samuel Eaton, of Brunswick, who then lived about where the Bowdoin Hotel is now.*

[2] *Pejepscot Papers.*

[3] *Maine Historical Collections*, 3, *p.* 311.

in seventeen whale-boats. After they landed at Triconnick, they met with Bomazeen at Brunswick (who had slain an Englishman some days before), whom they shot in the river, as he attempted to make an escape. They afterwards killed his daughter, and took his wife captive; who gave an account of the state of the enemy, which encouraged them to march on[1] briskly."

No further fighting is known to have occurred in this vicinity until 1725. On April 13th of that year two Indians captured a man belonging to the garrison at Maquoit, named James Cochran, about eighteen years of age. He was on the marshes in pursuit of fowl when he was surprised by the two Indians. He was pinioned, taken to the carrying-place, put in a canoe, and carried up to the Ten-Mile Falls. There the Indians made their arrangements for the night. A fire was made and supper prepared. Cochran expected all this time that he would be killed when the savages met some of their companions, and determined, in consequence, to make his escape, if possible. The second night his bonds were removed, and he was placed between the two Indians to sleep. Each of the savages slept with his hatchet under his head and his gun by his side. Cochran feigned sleep, while in reality he watched every movement. As soon as he found his captors asleep he rose up. This movement awakened one of them, who, seeing their prisoner apparently suffering from cold and endeavoring to warm himself, went to sleep again. When all was again quiet, Cochran took the hatchet from under the head of the one who had waked, and killed him instantly. He killed the other as he was getting up. He then scalped them both, took their guns and hatchets, and went down the river in great haste, fearing lest he should meet their companions. In fording a river on the way, he lost a gun and one of the scalps. When he arrived opposite the fort, he shouted, and a boat was sent across for him. He narrated his adventure to Captain Gyles, and some men were sent up the river, who found the bodies of the dead Indians, and also their canoe which they brought back.[2] He was both rewarded for his bravery and promoted in his rank.

At this time, Captain John Gyles was in command of the fort, which was crowded with the inhabitants who had gone to it for safety. This war was closed by the ratification of a treaty between the Indians and commissioners on behalf of the government, August 6, 1726.

---

[1] *i. e., to Norridgewock. Penhallow's Indian Wars, p.* 102. *Query: Bomazeen Island is east of Gurnet Bridge. May not Bomazeen have been killed there and the name applied to the island in consequence?* — EDS.

[2] *McKeen, MSS. Lecture. Penhallow's Indian Wars, p.* 109.

SPANISH OR FIFTH INDIAN WAR. 1745-1749.

The fifth war with the Indians grew out of the war between Great Britain, France, and Spain, which commenced about 1739, although the formal declaration of it was not made until June, 1744. In anticipation of this war, and in expectation that the Indians would take part in it, the forts along the coast were put in order and garrisoned.

In 1740 the commanding officer of Fort George was furnished with a quantity of goods, of suitable kinds, sufficient to supply the Indians who commonly resorted there. This was done to attach them to the interests of the government.[1] So much reliance was placed upon this method of dealing with the Indians, that in 1742 the government refused to strengthen it at all,[2] and in 1743 only six men were sent to this fort. In 1744 block houses were built in Brunswick and Topsham, "all of massive timber," and a regiment, consisting of 1,290 men, was organized and placed under the command of Colonel Samuel Waldo, of Falmouth. The proportion of Brunswick and Topsham men in this regiment was fifty. Another regiment was also organized, from the towns west of Falmouth, under the command of Colonel William Pepperell, of Kittery. These soldiers were all, however, discharged December 2d, except one hundred men from the latter regiment, who were formed into eight guards and stationed between Berwick and St. George. Fourteen men scouted from New Marblehead to Brunswick, and ten from Topsham to Richmond fort. There was a block house with a company of soldiers at Maquoit, under command of Captain William Woodside. There were also storehouses and other buildings there.[3]

In 1745 a call was made for men to serve in the expedition to Louisburg. This expedition was very popular in this vicinity, and many persons enlisted, including some of the principal and most promising young men in each of the towns. From twenty-five to thirty men went from Brunswick, as many more from Harpswell, and a number from Topsham. It is said that in Brunswick a day of fasting and prayer was held before any soldiers enlisted, so unwilling were the people to allow their own capability of defence against the Indians to be weakened. The Harpswell forces were commanded by Richard Jaques, the same who shot Sebastian Rale at Norridgewock.

During the continuance of the Louisburg campaign, the settlers were continually alarmed for their own safety, and were calling upon the government to send a military force hither from the West. The

---

[1] *Massachusetts Records*, 1740, *p*. 481. [2] *Ibid.*, 1742, *p*. 416. [3] *McKeen.*

glad tidings that Louisburg was reduced was received with great joy, and the return of the volunteers, who nearly all came back, was hailed with the utmost enthusiasm.[1]

The first outbreak of the Indians in this war occurred at Saint George and Damariscotta, July 19, 1745.[2]

July 30 of this year, a man and a boy, at Topsham, were surprised by the Indians, who knocked them down and beat them with clubs. The man was killed and the boy was scalped and left for dead.[3] About this same time, a mounted man and his horse were shot at New Meadows.[4]

This was not, however, the first blood shed in this vicinity, as three years previously Alexander McFarland was killed by the Indians while crossing the Androscoggin River. This was, however, an isolated case and may have been due to personal animosity. About the time of the Topsham and New Meadows massacres, Captain Mochus was scouting[5] with his company between Brunswick and Falmouth, and Captain John Gatchell was scouting north of Brunswick. The following is a copy of the Journal of the latter: —

"1747/8 MARCH — JOURNAL OF A MARCH UP THE KENNEBECK RIVER BY CAPT. JOHN GATCHELL OF BRUNSWICK.

"7 Mett this day at Brunswick took allowance of Provision & ammunition but no Rum marcht 6 mile & lodged at Topsham.

"8 Marcht across Merrymeeting Bay 8 Mile & then up Kennebeck River 4 mile to Richmond Fort & bought some Rum to carry with us then lay down & slept.

"9 Took Mr Call to pilott us to a pond Marcht N. N. West ab^t 12 Mile & came to a pond about 4 mile long hardly a mile wide the Pond lays N. E. & S. W. a River came & went out both at one end of ye pond, went up the River that came into ye pond a mile & campt, sent out 2 men about a mile round then sett out our Sentrys & lay down & slept.

"10 Marcht up said River 3 mile abt N. W., went one mile N. E. then one mile N by E & came to a small pond about a mile & half long & half a mile wide — Went still by ye River 2 mile N W. then went N. 2 mile & came to a pair of Falls that had an Indian Ware made w^h stones to catch fish — went up the River 6 mile about N &

[1] *Pejepscot Papers. McKeen, MSS. Lecture.*

[2] *Williamson, History of Maine*, 2, *pp.* 215 *to* 236.

[3] *Drake, French and Indian Wars, p.* 80. *If this lad was Thomas Thorn, he afterwards recovered.* — EDS.

[4] *Smith's Journal, p.* 40.

[5] *Massachusetts Records*, 1745, *p.* 40.

came to a large Pond, went 2 mile on the Pond & campt on an Island Sent out 3 men 2 mile round, sett out our Sentrys & then lay down & slept.[1]

"11 Marcht across ye pond 3 mile N. by E. this pond is about 10 or 12 mile long & about 2 or 3 mile wide & has near 20 Islands in it — it lays N. E. & S. W. Went four mile N. by E. & came to a pond about 3 mile long & half a mile wide & trackt some Moose Went N 2 mile & came to a meadow, Went 4 mile N & came to a long meadow then marcht about 4 mile N by W & campt Sent out 2 men that went 2 mile round, sett out our Sentrys then lay Down & slept.

"12 Went up a high hill & sent a man up a tree that he see a pond about five mile off, it bore from us E. N. E. went 3 mile N & came to a pond & a Small River that run N. E. We went N E 2 mile on said River & came to a large pond, it appeared to be 4 mile to y^e South End of y^e pond, we went N. up y^e pond 6 mile & came to a narrow place & a small Island in y^e narrows N N E up to y^e head of the pond ab^t 5 mile then went into y^e woods N. a mile & $camp^t$, sent out 3 men about 2 mile round then lay down & slept — it snowed —

"13 Rise This Morning, it being Sabbath day & the Trees very full of Snow we Marcht none only sent some men out on Discovery, they went about 4 mile to a high mountain & went up & see a pond that appeared to be very large it lay east from our Camp, & they see another pond y^t lay North from y^t large pond. it appeared to be about 4 or 5 mile long they returned to ye Camp and at night we sett out our Sentry, then lay down & slept.

"14 Marcht this morning ab^t 2 mile & came to that large pond that we see a Sabbath day, this pond appeared to be about 15 mile long & about 4 mile wide & lay N^o & S^o, it has about 28 Islands in it went about 12 mile South down ye pond then went into the woods S. W. & came to a Small River that vented out of that long pond that we went up on Saturday, Went down ye small River about three mile South & came to a pair of Falls that had 3 Indian Wares made w^h stones went still down ye River it run to ye eastward 4 mile & campt, sett out our Sentrys lay down & slept.

"15 Went down y^e River 5 mile & crost y^e River on y^e Ice the River run Easterly went down the River 6 mile & came to another large pond[2] ab^t 10 mile long & 2 mile wide it lay N. E. & S W^t, we crost y^e pond at y^e S W^t end then $March^t$ S W 8 mile & came to Ken-

---

[1] *These ponds appear to be the Winthrop chain.*

[2] *Snow's Pond in Sidney.*

nebeck River, went down y^e^ River a mile & Campt sett out our Sentrys, and lay down & slept.[1]

"16 It snowed but we went down the River in y^e^ Storm 8 mile & came to where y^e^ Tide flows,[2] went still down ye River 20 mile & came to Richmond Fort lay Down & slept.

"17 Marcht down said River to Merrymeeting Bay & some of the Men gott home.

"18 this day the Remainder of our Men gott home.

signed

"JONATHAN PHILBROOK, *Clerk*."[3]

April 23, 1747, Smith writes in his journal, "A scout of men are now out from North Yarmouth, another going out from Purpooduc. We are in the most distressed circumstances, Swarms of Indians being about the Frontier, and no soldiers save Captain Jordan's company of fifty men, thirty of whom have been for some time at Topsham guarding the government timber."

May 5, of this year, the Indians shot Mr. Seth Hinkley, near the garrison of Joseph Smith and Tobias Ham, at New Meadows. They were tanners, and Hinkley had been there to get a strap for a cowbell.[4] The following letter, from Isaac Hinkley, gives a rather more detailed account: —[5]

"BRUNSWICK, May ye 6, 1747.

"LOVEING BROTHER AND SISTER.

"I hope that these few lines will find you in good health as we that are alive through the tender mercys of God.

"God has taken away by his providence our brother Seth by the Indians May ye 5 day. thay kiled him about 8 o'clock in the fournoon and scalped him and stript of all his cloes save only his briches and stockens. thay carid away his gon. thare was three men gest back behind a hill in a swamp near a gainst him when he was kiled and thay heard the gons when the Indians fiard at him and one of them said thay have shot sombody and presently after heard a Larm at Smiths and then thay ran out to Smiths and when thay came thare thay said that Seth was kiled and thay went whare thay heard the gons and found him Liing in the path thay shot about 33 fete at him. The night before the Indians ambush Mr. Ham. 11 of us went to see if we culd find them but we culd not find them. one our and ahalf after thay ware sen to go over merremeting bay into Cathance river.

---

[1] *Below Waterville.* [2] *Augusta.* [3] *Pejepscot Papers.* [4] *McKeen, MSS. Lecture.*
[5] *Copied from the original in possession of H. W. Bryant, Esq., Portland.*

"The Lord has maid a breach upon us and by taking away our brother from us the Lord has be reved father and mother of thare son and us of our brother. yeat thaey and we must say with Job the Lord gaive and the Lord hath taken away Blessed be the name of the Lord.

"Sister reliance is brought abaed and has lost hur child but she is like to do weal but she has bin near to the gates of death but through the tender mearcies of God she is like to do well.

"So I remain your loving brother

"ISAAC HINKLEY.

"TO MR. SAMUEL SCAMMON Saco."[1]

Four days subsequently the Indians fired upon a canoe, containing four persons, as it was coming up through the narrows below Cow Island. The boat contained Mr. and Mrs. Moffitt, William Potter, and William Thorn, a soldier in Topsham, under Captain William Burns. Moffitt and Potter were killed. Thorn had his arm shot off. Mrs. Moffitt succeeded, with some assistance from Thorn, in paddling the canoe to the Brunswick side of the river, and thus enabled them both to escape.[2] Thorn asked for aid from the General Court, and on May 31, 1748, twelve pounds were allowed him.

August 19th a man was wounded somewhere in Brunswick, and a boy taken prisoner. In the early part of September four men were killed and scalped in a corn-field, in Topsham, only about twenty rods from the garrison, by twelve Indians. Probably one of these was Richard Crain, said to have been killed August 27th. One, of the men had seven bullets shot through his body.[3] In the same magazine from which the above extracts were taken occurs the following account: —

"BOSTON, NOV. 16.

"We are informed by Capt Woodside, that on the fifth Instant towards Evening, a Lad about 16 Years old, going out of Brunswick Fort at the Eastward, saw eleven Men dressed with Coats and Hats coming towards him, which he took for Englishmen, till they came up to him, when he found them to be Indians, one of which seized him as his Prisoner, which the Lads Father observing from the Fort, discharged his Gun (loaded with Swan-Shot) at the Indian and wounded him, upon which he immediately quitted the Lad, who ran towards the Fort, but was unfortunately shot down by the other Indians. The

---

[1] *Scammon married Mehitable Hinkley.*

[2] *Williamson, Smith, McKeen, et als. Massachusetts Records, Vol.* 73, *pp.* 163, 164.

[3] *Historical Magazine, Vols.* 9 *and* 10. *Extracts from New York Gazette, dated Sept.* 14, 1747.

People of the Garrison got the Lad into the Fort alive, but he died of his Wounds soon after: He said the Indian that took him was mortally wounded by his Father's Shot, one of which struck him (the Boy) in the Ball of his Hand."

In 1748 the Indians made their appearance rather earlier than usual, — on the last of April. A company of soldiers kept open communication between Fort George and Maquoit. They were, however, frequently annoyed by the Indians, who lay in ambush. On their first appearance this spring, a number of them hid in the bushes on the west side of Mair Brook and fired upon Captain Burns as he was crossing the brook with a file of men. They killed him and a Mr. Bragg, and captured a Mr. Werburn, whom they took to Canada. A day or two afterwards a boy of Doctor Spear's was watering a horse at a well near the house, when he was fired at, and he and the horse were both killed.[1]

May 3d of this same year, Captain Burnell and one other were killed at Brunswick, and on another occasion Lieutenant Mackburn was killed at the place called "Spawell."[2]

Although during the winter of 1748 there were some prospects of a peace, and the Indians were comparatively quiet, yet troops were kept in service for the defence of the Eastern inhabitants, and twelve men were left to garrison Fort George. A treaty of peace was concluded October 16, 1749.

Although the war was now declared at an end, yet the Indians had been too much excited to remain perfectly quiet, and fresh outbreaks and massacres occasionally occurred.

Early in the year 1750 a woman on the old "Skipper Malcom" place in Topsham had died. She was to have been buried one afternoon in March, and a new grave was dug. At the time appointed the house was filled with neighbors. The burial services had closed, and the procession formed for the march to the grave, when a snow-squall came up and prevented the burial, which was deferred until the next day. The storm was the severest that had been known for many years, and lasted four days. No interment could take place until the fifth day. Some three years afterwards it was ascertained that a large party of Indians, who had been making an unsuccessful foray upon the settlements around Yarmouth, were making their way north, toward the Chaudiere River, when they learned, from a prisoner whom they had captured at Flying Point, that a funeral was to take place on

---

[1] *Smith's Journal*, p. 133. [2] *Spawell was near Mair Brook. Pejepscot Papers.*

the afternoon of the next day, at the graveyard near the upper part of Merrymeeting Bay. They resolved to ambush the procession and massacre the whole settlement at one blow. They waited for the funeral procession the whole afternoon and the first night. The storm saved the settlers, but nearly destroyed the Indians, who suffered severely.[1]

In July, 1751, the Indians came upon a party of seven settlers who were getting in their hay at New Meadows. These men were at work on the side of the hill north of the railroad at Harding's Station, on the farm now occupied by Mr. Chapin Weston. The Indians, discovering that the party were some way from their guns, ran and cut off their retreat. This party of farmers consisted of Edmund, Isaac, and Gideon Hinkley; Deacon Samuel Whitney and his son Samuel, who was only a boy; Hezekiah Purington and Samuel Lumbers. Isaac Hinkley was killed while attempting to escape. He fell in the gully at the lower part of the field, south of the railroad track, and his body was not found until the next spring. The rest were all taken prisoners and carried to Canada, where they suffered many hardships.

They were afterwards exchanged and returned home. The government provided for their families during their captivity.[2]

The following memorial to the General Court, of one of the captives, will be read with interest in this connection: —

"TO THE HONBLE SPENCER PHIPS, ESQ LT. GOVR & COMMANDER IN CHIEF FOR THE TIME BEING. THE HONBLE HIS MAJESTYS COUNCILL & HOUSE OF REPRESENTATIVES IN GENERAL COURT DECEMBER 4, 1751.

THE MEMORIAL OF SAMUEL WHITNEY OF BRUNSWICK
HUMBLY SHEWETH

"That your Memorialist & his Son Samuel, with five more of the Inhabitants, While at work together mowing their Hay, on Wednesday ye 24 day of July last about two o'clock in the afternoon were surrounded & surprised by nineteen Indians & one Frenchman, who were all armed, & in an hostile manner did seize upon & by Force of Arms, obliged them to submitt their Lives into their hands, and one of our said number, viz. Isaac Hinckley in attempting to make his escape was killed in a barbarous Manner & Scalped. After we were secured

---

[1] *The foregoing tradition is from the diary of the late James McKeen, M. D., of Tops ham.*

[2] *Pejepscot Papers.*

by said Indians, they destroyed and wounded between 20 & 30 head of Cattle belonging to ye Inhabitants, some of which were the property of your Memorialist. The said party of Indians were nine of them of Norridgewalk Tribe, one of whom was well known, the other were Canada Indians. That the Norridgewalk Indians appeared more forward for killing all the Captives but were prevented by the other Indians.

"Your memorialist was by them Carried to Canada & there sold for 126 Livres — And the said Indians when they came to Canada were new cloathed & had New Guns given them with plenty of Provisions as an encouragement for this exploit. That the Govr of the Penobscot Tribe was present when your memorialist was sent for to sing a Chorus, as is their custom of using their captives. & manifested equal Joy w^{h} the other Indians, that took them. And the Norridgewalk Tribe had removed from Norridgewalk & were now sett down on Canada River near Quebec, supposed to be drawn there by the Influence of the French. These things your memorialist cannott omitt observing to y^{r} Honours, and his Redemption was purchased by one Mr. Peter Littlefield formerly taken a captive & now resident among them, to whom your memorialist stands indebted for said 126 Livres being the price of his Liberty, which when he had so far obtained, he applied to ye Govern^{r} of Canada for a Pass, who readily granted it, that his Return to Boston was by way of Louisbourgh, when said Pass was taken from him by the lord Intendant, on some Pretence which he could not obtain of him again.

"Your memorialists son yet remaining in Captivity among the Indians with three more that were taken at ye same time, and he has a wife and 8 children under difficult circumstances by reason of this misfortune.

"Your memorialist having thus represented his unhappy sufferings to this Honble Court humbly recommends his Case to the Compassion of this Honble Court hoping they will in their great Goodness provide for ye Redemption of his Son & enable him to answer his obligation to said Mr. Littlefield, who was so kind to pay for his Ransom. Your memorialist being in no Capacity to answer that Charge as thereby he is reduced to great poverty otherwise grant him that Relief as in their Wisdom & Goodness shall seem best —

"Your memorialist as in duty bound shall ever pray &c

"SAMUEL WHITNEY."

On the back of this paper is the following indorsement: —

"1751. CAPTIVES TAKEN.

"Hez. Purington } returned.
Sam'll Whitney }
Edm[d] Hinkley
Gideon Hinkley
Samuel Lombard
Samuel Whitney Jun[r] returned.
Isaac Hinkley killed.

"July 24th 1751."[1]

There is a tradition that the friends of young Hinkley, supposing that he was carried off by the Indians, did not search for him. Early in the spring of the following year, it was noticed that a dog, which had belonged to Hinkley, went every day to the gully where he fell. The dog was followed and the remains were thus discovered, but they had been so long exposed to the weather and to the ravages of wild beasts that they were in such a condition as to be unrecognizable by dress or features, and it was only by a peculiar string found in one of the shoes that the remains were identified.

FRENCH, OR SIXTH INDIAN WAR. 1754–1760.

When the last of the series of Indian wars commenced, in 1754, the government of Massachusetts deemed it unnecessary to retain Fort George any longer, but voted the sum of £470 towards building a fort at the Ten-Mile Falls instead, and for other military purposes.[2] This action, so far as the fort was concerned, was premature.

Early this year, Adam Hunter, of Topsham, received a commission as captain, with authority to raise an independent company. The following is a copy of the commission:—

"*PROVINCE OF THE MASSACHUSETTS BAY.*

"WILLIAM SHIRLEY ESQ., CAPTAIN-GENERAL AND GOVERNOR-IN-CHIEF IN & OVER HIS MAJESTY'S PROVINCE OF Y[E] MASSACHUSETTS BAY IN NEW ENGLAND &C.
[L. S.]

"TO ADAM HUNTER, GENTLEMAN, *Greeting:*

"By virtue of y[e] power & authority, in & by his Majesty's Royal Commission to me granted to be Captain General, &c., over this his Majesty's Province of y[e] Massachusetts Bay aforesaid; I do (by these

[1] *Pejepscot Papers.*

[2] *Massachusetts Records*, 1754, *p.* 325.

presents) reposing especial trust and confidence in your loyalty, courage, and good conduct, constitute & appoint you to be a Captain of an Independent company of fifteen volunteers forthwith to be raised in ye town of Topsham & parts adjacent in ye County of York; for marching upon any sudden alarm to ye relief & protection of any neighbouring English Fort or settlement (mentioned in ye instructions herewith s[ent]) which shall be attacked or molested by Indians; & for cutting off their retreat.

"You are therefore carefully & diligently to discharge ye duty of a captain in leading, ordering & exercising said Company in Arms, both inferiour officers and soldiers, & to keep them in good order & discipline; hereby commanding them to obey you as their captain — & yourself to observe & follow such orders & instructions, as you shall from time to time receive from me, or ye commander in chief for ye time being, or other your superiour officers for his Majesty's service, according to military rules & discipline, pursuant to ye trust reposed in you.

"Given under my hand & seal at arms at Boston, the fourth day of March, in ye twenty seventh year of ye Reign of his Majesty King George ye Second, Annoq: Domini, 1754."

[Signed] W. SHIRLEY.

By His Excellency's
Command.
[Signed] J. WILLARD *Secr'y.*[1]

Hostilities commenced in this vicinity, May 9, 1756. On that day a party of Indians assembled on the high lands of Topsham, concerted their plans, and agreed to meet there on their return. They divided into two parties. One party was to go to Flying Point, and the other to Maquoit, Middle Bay, and New Meadows. The second party skulked about Maquoit for a while and then went to Middle Bay, where they looked into the house of John Giveen, who, with his wife, had gone to meeting at Harpswell. In the afternoon, while the Indians lay concealed in the bushes at Smith's Brook, three men — Abijah Young, and John and Richard Starbird, who were on their return from meeting at New Meadows — passed by. These men belonged, probably, to Captain Samuel Goodwin's company, which scouted between Fort George and Maquoit.[2] They were well armed. The Indians darted from their concealment and fired at them. In

---

[1] *Copied from the original, Sept.* 23, 1833, *by Lithgow Hunter, of Topsham.*
[2] *Pejepscot Papers.*

their surprise and fright, the men dropped their guns and ran. Young was wounded and carried off a prisoner.

The other party of Indians appeared Sunday, at daylight, at the house of Thomas Means, at Flying Point, in what is now Freeport. This was a fortified house and the doors were securely fastened. The Indians, however, battered it open by means of a log and thus effected an entrance. Thomas Martin, the father of Captain Matthew, was asleep in his chamber, and being so suddenly aroused was unable to find his gun, and consequently remained in concealment. One of the children concealed herself in the ash-hole. This daughter, Alice, afterwards married Mr. Clement Skolfield, eldest son of Thomas, and was the mother of Captain George Skolfield. Mr. Means, his wife, child, and wife's sister, Miss Molly Finney, were taken out of the house. Mr. Means was held by the arms between two stalwart Indians, while a third one shot him through the breast and scalped him. While this was being done, Mrs. Means, with a child in her arms, ran into the house, closed the door, and placed a chest against it. The Indians, on their return to the house, finding the door refastened, pointed a gun through a hole and fired at her. The ball passed through her breast, killing the infant in her arms. They succeeded in getting into the house again, and while they were in the entry, Martin, who had found his gun, fired down through his chamber-floor and wounded one of them. This frightened them off and they left the place, taking with them the wounded Indian and Miss Finney, who was heard crying loudly for rescue. She was carried off in her night-clothes. When they got to the hill in Topsham they were met by the second party, who had Young a prisoner. The latter advised Miss Finney to seize the first blanket she could. She succeeded in getting and retaining one. The subsequent adventures of this lady, though interesting, are not so exciting as what has been related.

The Indians took their prisoners through the wilderness to Quebec. Here Miss Finney was sold to a farmer and put to work in the field. The farmer, not satisfied with her work there, afterwards put her in his kitchen. While here, she attracted the attentions of a Frenchman. Her master, in consequence, being displeased, used to lock her in her chamber when she was not at work. Not many months after this, Captain McClellan, of Falmouth, was at Quebec with a cartel of exchange. Having been formerly acquainted with Miss Finney, he sought after and finally found her. A time and mode of escape were agreed upon. At the time fixed he went to her window and threw her a rope. She let herself down, escaped to his vessel, and after a fair voyage arrived at Portland. She afterwards married the man who had been so instrumental to her release.[1] Young obtained his liberty in about a year, but died in Halifax of the small-pox.[2]

In 1756 a garrison was built in Topsham and the defence of it was given to Captain Lithgow.[3] On May 18, 1757, a party of seventeen Indians waylaid Captain Lithgow and a party of eight men, at Topsham, and had a short but sharp engagement with them. Two of Lithgow's party were wounded and two of the Indians were killed.[4] Disheartened at the result, the savages withdrew, taking with them the dead bodies of their companions. They afterwards, however, as they went up the river, took their revenge by killing two white men.[5]

Shortly after this event John Malcom and Daniel Eaton were going to Maquoit for salt hay, or were returning with some, when they were waylaid by some Indians. Malcom escaped, but Eaton received a bullet in his wrist, was captured, and was carried to Canada, where he remained about a year. He was the son of Moses Eaton who was killed at Pleasant Point in 1722.[6] According to another account, he was the son of Samuel Eaton, of Salisbury, Mass.[7] Eaton was captured by the famous Indian chief, Sabattis, who sold him for four dollars. The only food they had to eat, on their way to Canada, was a partridge which Sabattis shot, and of which he gave Eaton all the better part, reserving for himself only the *head* and *entrails*, which he ate with apparent relish. Years after (about 1800), Sabattis passed through Brunswick, and while there entered the store of John Perry, which was on the site of the store now occupied by Barton Jordan. Quite a crowd of villagers collected to see the old chief, and Dean Swift, then a lad of eight years, was sent to inform Daniel Eaton, who was then an old man, that Sabattis was in the store. Eaton, who was at work piling shingles for Colonel William Stanwood in what is now the yard of the estate of the late A. C. Robbins, Esquire, came to the store, and was at once recognized by Sabattis, who seemed to be really glad to see him. At the request of some of those in the store, Eaton drew up his sleeve to show the buckshot in his arm, which were fired by Sabattis at the time of Eaton's capture. Sabattis looked at the arm with reluctance, saying, "That long time ago; war time too."

---

[1] *McKeen, MSS. Lecture. Massachusetts Historical Collections, 4 Ser. Vol. 5, p.* 415.

[2] *Williamson, History of Maine, 2, p.* 320.

[3] *Sewall, Ancient Dominions of Maine, p* 306.

[4] *Williamson, History of Maine, 2, p.* 325.

[5] *Sewall, Ancient Dominions of Maine, p.* 308.

[6] *Pejepscot Papers.*

[7] *McKeen, MSS. Lecture.*

After a short but friendly chat with Eaton, Sabattis shook hands and left the store and went on his way.[1]

Although a treaty of peace was not made until the spring of 1760, yet the war had virtually ceased at this time, and accordingly the fort was dismantled, and on Dec. 19, 1758, was leased by the proprietors, to whom it had reverted.

These Indian wars occupied a period of nearly eighty-five years, and during nearly all this time the settlers were accustomed, at every alarm, to congregate in the fort at Brunswick or the block house at Maquoit, though towards the close many were in garrisons in other parts of the town and in Topsham. At times these defences were so crowded that temporary booths and camps were made outside of, but near to them. There were but few garrisons in Harpswell, as from its local situation it was not subject to assaults by the Indians.[2]

There were a few other cases of massacres and violence on the part of the Indians, besides those which have been related, but accounts of them are, for the most part, entirely traditional and indefinite, both as to dates and localities, and often as to the individuals concerned in them.

An account of the manners and customs of life at this period belongs to another chapter, but one tradition is here given to show the expedients to which those in the fort, during the raids of the Indians, were often obliged to resort. It is said that at one time, when the inhabitants were obliged to seek refuge in Fort George, they had no neighbors nearer than at Bath, then called "The Reach." This place was distant fifteen miles by water, which was the only safe way of communicating between the two posts. In Fort George was a dog which had been taught to carry letters and which would take one to Bath in about two hours' time. On arriving there he would howl until he gained admission to the fort at that place, and would receive an answer, which he would as speedily fetch back to Brunswick. At last he was killed by an Indian. The garrisons were now deprived of this means of communication. An active and zealous youth undertook, however, to take the place of the four-footed messenger. "I," said he, "will carry your messages by water." For two successive summers this brave youth went between the two posts, swimming a great part of the way. He went chiefly in the night-time, resting by day in the rushes that grew around the shores of Merrymeeting Bay. At

---

[1] *Reminiscences of Dean Swift.*

[2] *Memoranda of Rev. Samuel Eaton, in Pejepscot Papers.*

length he was captured by the Indians and carried to Canada. From the latter country he soon, however, made his escape, and returned to Fort George, where he soon "resumed his swimming mail route." He was afterwards captured a second time by the famous Indian chief, Sabattis. What further became of him is unknown.[1]

---

[1] *Putnam, Description of Brunswick, Me., by a gentleman from South Carolina,* p. 32.

PART II.

TOPOGRAPHICAL AND DESCRIPTIVE.

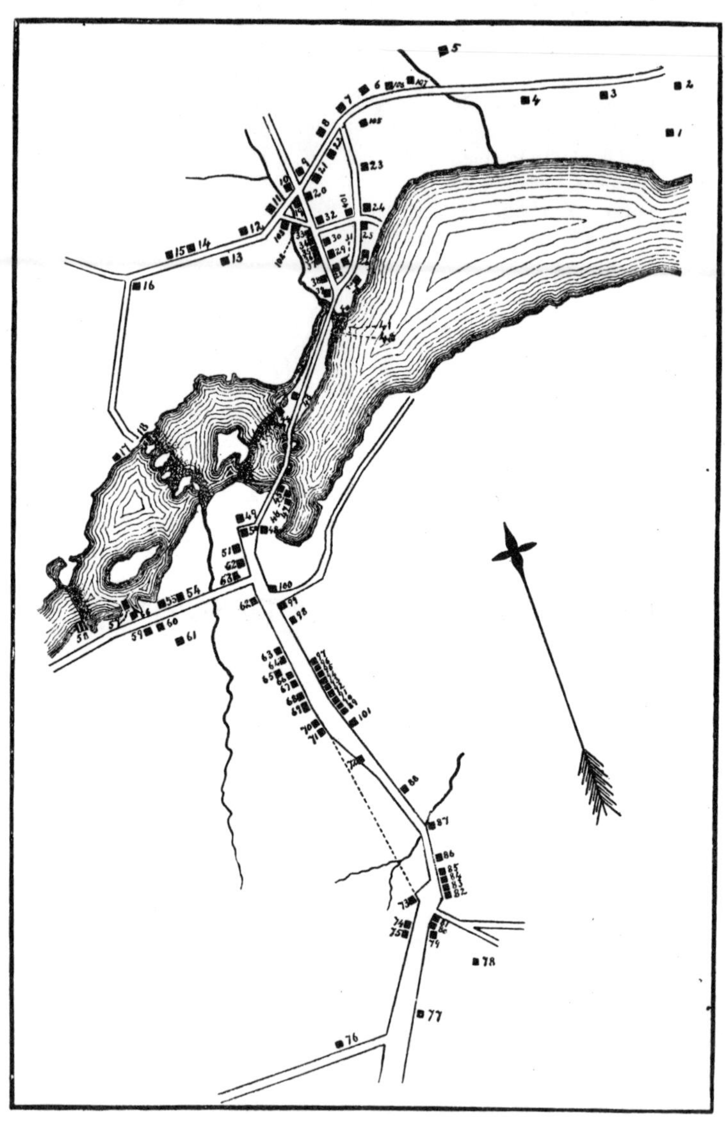

Map of Brunswick and Topsham Villages in 1802.

REFERENCES TO THE FOREGOING MAP.

1. Mrs Hinkley.
2. James Purinton.
3. Humphrey Thompson.
4. Capt. Nathl. Melcher.
5. Dr. Benj. J. Porter. (Residence.)
6. Luther Kimball. (Cabinet-maker's shop)
7. School-house.
8. Blacksmith's shop.
9. James Stone.
10. James Stone. (Store.)
11. Dr. Porter.
12. Hugh Wilson.
13. John Hern.
14. Eben Ferrin.
15. John Haley.
16. Joseph Haley.
17. Lawrence Humphreys.
18. Saw mill.
19. Shoemaker's shop.
20. Gideon Walker.
21. Joseph Swett.
22. Stephen Bradford.
23. Jairus Fuller.
24. Obed Burnham. (Pump and block-maker's shop.)
25. James Blanchard. (Store.)
26. Ezra Smith.
27. Larrabee & Emery. (Dwelling.)
28. Humphrey Purinton.
29. Store.
30. Store.
31. Isaac Johnson.
32. Larrabee & Emery. (Hatters.)
33. Porter & King. (Store.)
34. Henry Wilson. (Store.)
35. James Cushman. (Store.)
36. Francis Tucker. (Inn.)
37. Blacksmith's shop.
38. David Flagg.
39. Shoemaker's shop.
40. Hodge mill.
41. Granny Hole mill.
42. Grist mill and fulling mill.
43. James Thompson.
44. Saw mill.
45. Grist mill.
46. Saw mill.
47. Saw mill.
48. Waldron.
49. Ruins of Fort George.
50. Jere Moulton.
51. Cutting Noyes.
52. Store.
53. Daniel & Jotham Stone. (Store.)
54. Amos Lunt.
55 John Brown.
56. Bisbee's shop.
57. Grist mill.
58. 2 saw mills and grist mill.
59. Mr. Bisbee.
60. Thos Pool.
61. John Dunlap's mansion.
62. Trueworthy Kilgore.
63. Store.
64. Capt. Richard Tappan.
65. Store-house.
66. Major Swift.
67. William Owen.
68. Law office.
69. P. O. Alden.
70. John Dunning.
71. John Swartkin & Caleb Cushing's store.
72 School-house.
73. Robert D. Dunning.
74. Charles Ryan.
75. Store.
76. Samuel Stanwood.
77 President's House (being built).
78. Massachusetts Hall.
79. Inn.
80. Col. Estabrook's bakery.
81. Timothy Weymouth.
82. Barn.
83. Cabinet shop.
84. Shimuel Owen
85 Col. Thomas Estabrook.
86. Rev. Ebenezer Coffin.

87. Mr Heath.
88. Mr. Brooks.
89. Aaron Melcher.
90. Dr. Charles Coffin.
91. Ebenezer Nichols.
92. John Perry's store.
93. Samuel Emerson.
94. Store and office.
95. John Perry.
96. Store.
97. Col. Stanwood.
98. Store.
99 Daniel Coombs.
100. James Carey.
101. Caleb Cushing.
102. Eli Cox. (Pottery.)
103. Eli Cox.
104. Noah Tobey.
105. James Wilson.
106 Mr. Carr (Tailor.)
107. Court House.

CHAPTER I.

BOUNDARIES AND NOTABLE FEATURES.

THE territory now covered by the towns of Topsham, Brunswick, and Harpswell, forming an extensive portion of the old Pejepscot purchase, is situated between Casco and Merrymeeting Bays, and on both sides of the Androscoggin River. The railroad station at Brunswick is distant from Portland twenty-nine miles, from Bath, nine miles, from Augusta, thirty-three miles, and from Lewiston, eighteen miles. Its latitude is 43° 54′ 37″ N., and its longitude 69° 57′ 26″ W. from Greenwich.

TOPSHAM, the most northerly of the three towns, is bounded on the north by Bowdoin and Bowdoinham; on the east by Merrymeeting Bay; on the south by Brunswick; on the west by Brunswick and Durham; and on the northwest by Lisbon. Its area is about 22,600 acres.

BRUNSWICK is bounded on the north by Topsham, from which it is separated by the Androscoggin River; on the east by the New Meadows River, which divides it from Bath and West Bath; on the south by Casco Bay and the town of Harpswell; on the southwest by Freeport; and on the northwest by Durham. It has an area of about 28,200 acres.

HARPSWELL is bounded on the north by Brunswick; on the east by the New Meadows River; and on the south and west by Casco Bay. It consists of a peninsula called Harpswell, or Merriconeag, Neck, which extends southwest from Brunswick into Casco Bay, and of the following islands: Sebascodegan, or Great Island, Orr's, Bailey's, and Haskell's Islands, with Whaleboat Island, Birch Island, and several smaller ones. The area of the Neck is 4,570 acres, and that of Great Island 5,790 acres, according to the measurement made in 1731, by Phinehas Jones, a surveyor.[1] The whole town probably contains above 12,000 acres.

Through the Pejepscot region, and separating Brunswick from Tops-

---

[1] *McKeen, in Harpswell Banner, October*, 1832.

ham. runs the ANDROSCOGGIN RIVER, noted for its numerous falls and abundant power. The other rivers are the Cathance and Muddy, in Topsham, and the New Meadows, which separates Brunswick and Harpswell from Bath, West Bath, and Phippsburg.

The CATHANCE rises in the lower part of the town of Litchfield, flows in a southeasterly direction through the town of Bowdoin, and continues on this course until it reaches about the centre of Topsham, where it takes an easterly course for a short distance, then runs nearly north by northeast until it reaches the village of Bowdoinham, when it takes a bend and flows to the southeast until it reaches Merrymeeting Bay. A few miles south of Bowdoinham, this river has an arm which extends northwesterly for about a mile, where it drains two small branches. Its whole length is about twenty-seven miles.

MUDDY RIVER rises in the southeastern part of Topsham, about midway between the old Bowdoinham road and the Foreside road, and flows in a northeasterly direction until it reaches Merrymeeting Bay. Its length is not far from four and a half miles.

NEW MEADOWS RIVER rises in the town of Bath, about half a mile from Merrymeeting Bay, and flows south into Casco Bay. It was anciently called Stevens's River.

The only pond of considerable size in this whole region is Cathance Pond, sometimes called Bradley's Pond, in Topsham. It is little more than an expansion of Cathance River, and is a few acres only in extent.

MERRYMEETING BAY is formed by the confluence of the waters of the Androscoggin, Muddy, Cathance, Abagadusset, and Kennebec Rivers. It is about six miles in length and three in breadth, at its widest part. In a deed from Sir Ferdinando Gorges to Sir Richard Edgecomb in 1637, this sheet of water was called the "Lake of New Somersett."[1] In other ancient deeds it was called "Swan Pond."[2]

It is doubtful if there is in New England a tract of land of the same extent, possessing a more diversified scenery than does the territory just described. Each differing phase of the landscape may be surpassed in many other places, but the *tout ensemble* is rarely equalled. There is but one place where this extended view can be obtained, and comparatively few have ever enjoyed it. On the north of the village of Topsham, and about a mile distant from the bridge, is an abrupt elevation of land called Mount Ararat. In the innocence of childhood we long supposed this to be the veritable mount whereon the ark

---

[1] *Pejepscot Papers.* [2] *Ibid.*

rested. Upon the summit of this hill once stood a very respectable observatory, rising higher than the surrounding trees. From the top of this observatory, or from the summit of one of the tallest trees, could be seen in one direction the Cathance River, winding like a silver thread through the evergreen foliage; in another direction, the bright waters of Merrymeeting Bay; farther still gleamed the broad line of the New Meadows River and the wide expanse of Casco Bay, the latter dotted with islands and swept by the white sails of vessels of every size. At the west, about sixty miles distant, the White Hills of New Hampshire are distinctly visible on clear days, while a glass reveals the observatory and church spires at Portland.

The scenery of the three towns is widely different. Topsham, on the north or left bank of the Androscoggin, is for the most part hilly; while Brunswick, on the opposite bank of the river, consists (with the exception of the western and extreme eastern portions) of low, sandy plains. Harpswell is made up of islands, and the long, high peninsula of Merriconeag.

In the western part of the town of Brunswick a rocky elevation is to be observed, extending quite from the Androscoggin to Casco Bay. Many citizens are familiar with the picturesque scenery at Rocky Hill, some four miles up the river road, where this ridge begins. At the deep cut, some three miles west of the village, the railroad passes through a depression of this ridge, but at Oak Hill it again rises to full height.

A few miles farther, another depression is succeeded by Brimstone Hill, in Freeport, which completes the line quite to Harraseekit Landing, on Casco Bay. From Oak Hill and the higher points of the parallel ridge west of it, the sea is usually visible. From all elevated points, for miles around, appear also the spires of the villages of Brunswick and Topsham, the highest among them being the twin towers of King's Chapel. On the approach from up river, Powder-House Hill (at an earlier date known as Sunset Hill) hides much of the villages from view. A bend of the river, with a broad expansion at this point, gives all the effect of a lake, with the accessories of high, rocky banks, green hills, low, grassy shores, and sandy beaches.

At the upper railroad bridge, where the banks of the river approach each other and the compressed waters go rolling on between the firm bounds of rock, the scene begins to change. Here is the beginning of the notable BRUNSWICK FALLS, the finest water-power on the Atlantic coast. This magnificent fall of water, though lacking in the grandeur which attaches to the more famous falls of some other rivers, has yet a beauty of its own, which should by no means be overlooked. Its numerous cascades afford not only varied and picturesque views, but furnish a motive-power probably unsurpassed in New England within so small a space. The natural bed of the fall consists of coarse graphic granite and gneiss. The rock upon the middle fall projects above the water at several points, serving as natural abutments to the several sections of the dam. Shad Island, the former site of mills, divides the lower fall about midway. There are three pitches: the first has a vertical descent of about eleven feet, the middle of fourteen feet, and the lower of about fifteen feet. The total height of the fall is about forty-one feet above high tide, which flows to the foot of the fall, causing a variation in the height of the water of about three feet. The whole horizontal distance of the descent is 1,980 feet.

LOCALITIES.

In the Androscoggin River, from Lisbon to Merrymeeting Bay, there are twelve islands, besides numerous rocks at the Brunswick Falls, which have acquired distinctive names.

BEECH ISLAND — probably so called on account of the growth of beech-trees found upon it — is the first island above the upper railroad bridge.

MERRILL'S ISLAND is a short distance above the former. It was named after John Merrill, Esquire, who purchased it in 1768.

GOOSE ROCK is the rock upon which the middle pier of the upper railroad bridge rests. It is not a bowlder, as is generally supposed, but is part of a ledge extending to the shore.[1] Why the rock bears its present name is not known; but it is quite probable that it was so called from a supposed similarity to a swimming goose. It has, however, been suggested that it may have been a resort for fowlers, when after wild geese.

GOAT ISLAND is a short distance above the Factory, or second dam. The origin of its name is unknown; but it is conjectured that one of the early settlers pastured his goats upon it.

DEVIL'S ROCK is the name given to a large rocky island about midway of the second, or Factory dam. The traditional origin of the name is as follows: In the early settlement of the place, a man and his wife occupied a lone house a little way back from the river, on the Topsham side. This man was very superstitious, and probably addicted to the habit of taking both frequent and deep potations. One

---

[1] *Survey by C. J. Noyes, Esq.*

day during an ice freshet, as he was sitting at his window watching the ice go by, he imagined he saw Satan, *in propria persona*, floating down the stream on a log, and that he could hear the clanking of his chains as he climbed the rock. He informed his wife of this imaginary occurrence, and after the waters had sufficiently subsided, the pair visited the rock and found the footprints left there by his supposed Satanic Majesty. These holes in the rock — one of which does bear quite a resemblance to a huge footprint — are still to be seen.

Fishing Rock Island, Salmon Island, Shad Island. — All these names have been, at different periods, applied to the island at the lower falls, between the long dam and the gulf dam. Tradition gives the origin of the latter name as follows: The law formerly prohibited the catching of shad between sunset on Saturday and sunrise on Monday. Fish-wardens were annually chosen by some towns to see that this law was enforced. One Sunday some men went out and caught several of these fish, and hid them on this island, not daring to be seen carrying them home. Mr. Johnson Wilson and some friends started out after them in boats, pretending to be the fish-wardens, and went ashore on the island, found the fish, and, for sport, carried them away. The joke was discovered, and some complaint made against Mr. Wilson for breaking the Sabbath. Afterwards, when he built a mill, — the first one on the island, — those who had blamed him for taking the fish called his mill the "Shad Mill," and from that the island subsequently became known as Shad Island.

Freshet Rock is the name by which the rock between Shad Island and the Topsham shore is known. It is thus called from its being an index to the height of water in the river. It is never entirely covered by water except in freshets.

Granny Hole Mill, Stream, and Bridge. — The channel which carries the water from the river above the lower falls, around the island in Topsham, was originally only a ravine; but about 1760 it was excavated so as to afford a continuous flow of water. Tradition gives the following account of the origin of its name: On one occasion, in midwinter, Mr. Thomas Wilson, grandfather of Mr. James Wilson, of Topsham, went over the ice to a fulling-mill near the fort in Brunswick, to obtain a web of cloth. He stayed until after dark; and while coming home he heard a woman's voice in the direction of a mill which stood just south of where the flour mill in Topsham now stands. Going in the direction from which the sound came, he found a woman named Betty Watts, who had broken through the ice, and was clinging to the edge of it, screaming for help. Having his web of cloth with him, he held on to one end and threw the roll to the woman, who caught hold of it and was drawn out. In memory of this incident, the mill was called the "Granny-Hole Mill," and the name was afterwards applied to the whole ravine. The "Granny-Hole Bridge" is mentioned a number of times in the town records of Topsham.

THE GOLDEN PIPE. — This was a natural drain or outlet for what is now a stagnant pond in front of Flagg's brick-yard, in Topsham. It crossed Summer Street just west of Mr. Cyrus Flagg's residence, and so kept on till it entered the Granny-Hole Stream. In times of freshet, the water from the river flowed across the sand-bed through the Golden Pipe into the Granny-Hole Stream, which afforded an opportunity for lumbermen to run logs that way and save them from being carried down river and out to sea. The benefit thus derived from this channel doubtless gave rise to its name. When Summer Street was laid out, a portion of the drain was filled up and the street raised high enough to prevent the water from crossing it except in unusually high freshets. This drain is referred to in the town records under the name given above.

GREAT ISLAND is the name given in the Topsham town records to the island formed by the Granny-Hole Stream and the main river. It has also been called Thompson's Island, because it was at one time owned by Brigadier Thompson. It is usually called simply "The Island."

MIDDLE ROCK is the name of the rock upon which one of the piers of the Androscoggin Bridge (formerly the toll-bridge) rests.

MASON'S ROCK. — There are two traditions accounting for the name of the large rock below the falls, known as Mason's Rock. One is, that a Mr. Mason was once saved from drowning by getting upon this rock. The other is that, while upon the rock, he was killed by the Indians. There are no means of determining which of the two traditions is most reliable. "Samuel Mason" occupied lot number ten (within the present limits of Brunswick village) in 1717. He occupied it less than three years, and what became of him is now unknown.

FERRY POINT is the point of land at the Topsham end of the iron railroad bridge. It is so called from the fact that, previous to the erection of the toll-bridge, a ferry was maintained between this point and the "Landing" in Brunswick.

TERRAMUGUS COVE is the name applied in honor of an Indian chief, Terramugus, to the cove between Ferry Point and the Granny-Hole Mill. It is probable, however, that the river formerly covered the low land where the town landing used to be, back of the residence of Mr. Samuel Jameson, and that the name was applied to that particular part of the cove.

OLD SUNDAY. — About midway between Mason's Rock and Ferry Point, but nearer the Topsham shore, is a large stone, now seldom exposed to view, which was placed there by Brigadier Thompson to form the anchorage for a boom. Tradition accounts for its name from its being placed there by the Brigadier on Sunday.

COW ISLAND is the name applied to the island just below the present iron railroad bridge. The name was given early in the last century, and was doubtless suggested by the fact of its affording good and safe pasturage for cows. It was owned, prior to 1797, by John Sandford.[1]

THE NARROWS, where the river is compressed into narrow limits by two high rocky points, are about two miles below the Falls. The point on the Brunswick side was formerly occupied by Humphrey's steam-mill and ship-yard.

BAXTER'S ISLAND, FREYER'S OR FRIAR'S ISLAND, MUSTARD'S ISLAND. —These are different names for the island near the Topsham end of the Bay Bridge. The island was deeded in 1717 to the Reverend Joseph Baxter of Medfield, Mass., who came here as a missionary to the Indians. The name "Freyer's Island" is laid down on some of the maps of a recent date, but the origin of the name is unknown. It is called "Mustard's Island" from its present owner, Mr. John Mustard, of Topsham.

HUNTER'S ISLAND is the large island at the foot of the Narrows. In Stevens's deed from the Indians, in 1675, it is called "Stave Island." It may have borne other names, but we have not been able to ascertain them.

PLEASANT POINT lies between the Androscoggin and Muddy Rivers, extending into Merrymeeting Bay. Although this name is appropriate, and has the prestige of antiquity, yet it would appear still more appropriate to perpetuate the name of its original owner, the first settler in Topsham, by calling it *Gyles's Point*.

CATHANCE POINT is the point of land in Bowdoinham formed by the bend of the Cathance River near its outlet into Merrymeeting Bay.

FULTON'S POINT and PATTEN'S POINT are names which have been successively applied to a point on the eastern side of Cathance Point, by former residents of the vicinity, — James Fulton having been one

---

[1] *Deed to Brigadier Thompson.*

of its earliest occupants, and John Patten, its owner at a later period.

CENTER POINT, formerly called Moffitt's, and still earlier Somerset Point, is the point of land between the Abagadusset and Cathance Rivers. In a deed from Sir Ferdinando Gorges to Sir Richard Edgecomb, dated 1637, this point was called "Somerset Point."[1] The name has often been spelled "Samoset," and the explanation has been given that it was named in honor of the Indian chief of that name; but it is evident that the latter name is a corruption of the former. In the last century, the point was occupied by a family named "Moffitt," for whom it was named; and in like manner its present name was given because of its occupation for many years by a family named Center. It is in the town of Bowdoinham.

ABAGADUSSET POINT is the striking name which attaches to the last projection which engages our attention on the north side of the bay. It lies between the Kennebec and Abagadusset Rivers, and is a part of the town of Bowdoinham. The meaning and derivation of the name have already been given in Chapter I of Part First.

OAK HILL is about four miles north of Topsham village. The origin of the name is obvious.

In Brunswick the following localities are more or less familiar: —

FISH-HOUSE HILL, upon which stands the residence of Miss Narcissa Stone, received its name from the fact that there was once a fish-house upon it, where salmon and sturgeon were cured and packed for shipment.

EATON BROOK — the first brook west of the village — bears this name from Daniel Eaton, who lived near it in the last century.

HARWOOD'S BROOK was named for George Harwood, one of the early settlers, who built a house and attempted to clear a farm on what was afterward the "Captain Adams Place," which included the very noticeable hill, with the large house at the top, on the west bank of the Androscoggin, about a mile above the village.

SANDY GULLY — as its name indicates — is a sandy ravine on the River road, where it crosses Harwood's Brook.

ROCKY HILL is about four miles from the village on the road leading up the river. It is the beginning of the broad, rocky ridge to which reference has been made. The scenery of the locality is the boldest of any in the three towns.

THE PINNACLE is the name of a hill, probably the highest in the three towns, situated on the north side of the Durham road, at the

---

[1] *Pejepscot Papers.*

extreme western border of Brunswick. It is well covered with trees, except a space on the east and south, the latter side being marked by a precipitous ledge of light-colored granite.

BALD ROCK is a massive projection of ledge on a western slope of the ridge of which Oak Hill is a spur on the eastern side, nearly opposite.

OAK HILL is a spur of the granitic ridge which extends from the Androscoggin River to Casco Bay. It is on the Portland road, about four miles west of the village.

GROWSTOWN, a neighborhood about two miles west of the colleges, derives its name from the numerous families named Grows who formerly resided in the vicinity.

BUNGANUCK LANDING is the western side of Maquoit Bay, near Freeport. The origin of the name is given elsewhere in the volume.

WHARTON'S POINT, at Maquoit, was named for Thomas Wharton, who owned the lot in 1717. It was afterwards sold to William Woodside.

MAIR POINT, MARE POINT, MERE POINT. — These are the varied spellings of the name applied from a very early date to the peninsula which extends into Casco Bay and Maquoit Bay. The derivation, and consequently the spelling, of the name has been the subject of some discussion, and there still exists a difference of opinion concerning it. In the earliest deeds and other documents which we have seen, the name is spelled Mair; and for this reason we have so spelled the name whenever reference is made to it. We incline to the opinion that some time previous to the Pejepscot purchase, a man named Marr (or Mare) lived on the point, and that "Mair" is a corruption. Williamson[1] states that John Mare was an early settler on Mare Point. Some are of the opinion that at a very early period the point was occupied by French settlers, who gave it the name of *Mer* Point, which in English would be Sea Point. There is no proof, however, that the locality was ever occupied by the French.

NEW WHARF is the name of a wharf at Middle Bay, built in 1837. It was then spoken of as "The New Wharf," and never having received any other name, it is still called New Wharf, though now old and dilapidated.

PENNELLVILLE is a neighborhood near Middle Bay, which includes a number of families of the name of Pennell. Much ship-building has been done in this vicinity.

MAIR BROOK rises a short distance west of the Twelve-Rod road,

---

[1] *History of Maine*, 1, *p.* 564, *note.*

and crossing that road about half a mile below the colleges, thence runs in an easterly direction and empties into Harpswell Harbor, between Prince's Point and Harpswell Neck. The origin of the name is unknown, but it is doubtless the same as that of Mair Point.

THOMPSON'S BROOK, in the eastern part of the town, was named after Cornelius Thompson, an early settler, through whose lot the brook ran.

COOK'S CORNER, two miles east of Brunswick village, on the road to Bath, was named for Stephen Cook, who resided there in 1764 and probably earlier.

PRINCE'S POINT extends into Harpswell Harbor, between the Neck and Great Island. It received this appellation after a family named Prince, who have lived on the point many years.

HAM'S HILL, near New Meadows River, on the upper road to Bath, was named for Tobias Ham, who settled upon it previous to 1742.

BULL ROCK is a rock in New Meadows River, upon which rests one of the piers of the bridge below the railroad.

The following are localities in Harpswell: —

HARPSWELL NECK is what was formerly and is now, often, called MERRICONEAG.

The "GREAT ISLAND" is the English and SEBASCODEGAN the Indian name for the largest of the islands included in the township of Harpswell. Richard Wharton, in 1683, speaks of it as "Sebacoa, *alias* Chebascoa diggin." [1]

ORR'S ISLAND is the name now applied to what, in 1758, was known as LITTLE SEBASCODEGAN.[2] It received its later name from one of its first English occupants, Joseph Orr, who owned nearly the whole island. Orr's Island and Bailey's Island were, also, prior to 1683, called "The Twins." [3]

BAILEY'S ISLAND, situated south of the Neck, is the present name of what was called WILL'S ISLAND in the Act of Incorporation of Harpswell. Captain James Sinnett, now upwards of eighty years of age, who has resided upon the island all his life, gives the following account of the origin of these names. The first settler upon the island was a man named Black, who, with his wife and a boy, moved there from Kittery. They were of mixed breed, having in their veins the blood of the Anglo-Saxon, Indian, and African races. Black and his wife died and were the first persons ever buried upon the island. Their son, Will Black, lived to old age and became generally known

---

[1] *Pejepscot Papers.* [2] *See Act of Incorporation of Harpswell.* [3] *Ibid.*

by the name of Uncle Will. The island consequently took its first name from him. Afterwards, Deacon Timothy Bailey, of Hanover, Mass., purchased the island and moved there with his family. The Blacks were squatters, and, having no legal claim to the land, they moved to Orr's Island, and settled on the lot now owned by Mr. Ralph Johnson. Thereafter Will's Island was called Bailey's Island.

NORTH YARMOUTH ISLAND is situated south of, and in close proximity to Sebascodegan, or Great Island. The explanation of its bearing the name of a distant town is probably as follows: —

The town of North Yarmouth formerly embraced the peninsula of Mair Point and Harpswell Neck, with Sebascodegan and the lesser islands within the limits indicated by these points. When the town of Harpswell was formed, all the larger islands intended to be set off from Yarmouth for the new town of Harpswell were named in the Act of Incorporation, with the exception of the one now under consideration. The omission was probably unintentional; yet this island — nearly the most remote of all — still remained the legal territory of North Yarmouth. This anomaly among the islands led to its acquirement of the name of the town to which it belonged. At a later period it was annexed to Harpswell.

DAMARISCOVE ISLAND, now called "Haskell's Island," lies opposite Potts's Point. In the Act of Incorporation of Harpswell it was called Damariscove Island, but assumed its present name after its purchase by a Mr. Haskell.

FLAG ISLAND is said to derive its name from the fact that large quantities of flags grew upon it.

WHALE-BOAT ISLAND is, perhaps, so called from its fancied resemblance in shape to a whale-boat. It lies west of the lower part of the Neck.

GOOSE ISLANDS — two of them — lie west of the middle of the Neck. At the southeast of the lower one are a pair of small islands called "The Goslings."

SHELTER ISLAND, in Middle Bay, probably received its name from its affording a place of refuge for the settlers on Mair Point and vicinity in times of Indian hostility. Tradition says that this island was for many years the resort of smugglers, who obtained their goods in the British provinces, and stored them on this island if so fortunate as to escape the customs officers along the coast. The name was probably given by the smugglers.

BIRCH ISLAND, between Mair Point and the Neck, was doubtless so named for its abundant growth of birch-trees.

WHITE'S ISLAND, near Mair Point, was named for Nicholas White, who occupied it as early as the year 1675.

POTTS'S POINT, at the lower extremity of the Neck, was named for Richard Potts, its first occupant, who settled there previous to 1672.

THE PRONGS are the three points at the lower end of the Neck, which bears a resemblance to the form of a fork.

LOOKOUT POINT, on the western shore of the Neck, is so called because it affords an extended view of the bay. The scenery at this locality is very picturesque.

CONDY'S POINT is the southeastern extremity of Great Island, and, with the adjacent harbor, takes its name from William Condy, who settled there in 1733.

BOYLE'S POINT is the northeastern extremity of Orr's Island. It was probably named for the Reverend Matthew Byles, who had one hundred acres of this island set off to him by Joseph Orr, in lieu of his previous claim as heir to Honorable William Tailer.

The following are the names of the smaller islands of Harpswell, which are mostly uninhabited. There are a few others, without established name by which they might be recognized, and of which we therefore have made no special record.

ROGUE ISLAND is southeast of Condy's Point.

JENNY'S ISLAND is south of North Yarmouth Island.

LONG LEDGE is south of Jenny's Island.

POLE ISLAND, SMALL ISLAND, and SNOW ISLAND are situated in the eastern part of Quahaug Bay.

ELM ISLAND is east of the lower part of Orr's Island.

RAW ISLAND is east of the north part of Bailey's Island.

CEDAR LEDGES, five in a row, — seven or more in all, — are east of Raw Island.

POND ISLAND is east of the middle of Bailey's Island.

RAGGED ISLAND is east of the lower part of Bailey's Island. Its municipal connection has been disputed.

JAQUES'S ISLAND, south of Bailey's Island, receives its name from Lieutenant Jaques, who resided on the Neck opposite, and who was one of the officers in the final expedition against the Indians at Norridgewock.

TURNIP ISLAND is west of Jaques's Island.

GREAT MARK ISLAND is south of Haskell's Island.

LITTLE MARK ISLAND is south of Great Mark Island.

EAGLE ISLAND is west of Haskell's Island.

LITTLE BIRCH ISLAND is southwest of west prong of Harpswell Neck.

HORSE ISLAND is east of Little Birch Island.

BARNE'S ISLAND is between the west prong of the Neck and Great Whale-Boat Island.

LITTLE WHALE-BOAT ISLAND is northwest and near Great Whale-Boat Island.

IRONY ISLAND is east of the Goslings.

BRAINING'S LEDGE is between the Goose Islands.

LOOKOUT ISLAND is adjacent to Point Lookout.

LITTLE BIRCH ISLAND is northeast of Birch Island.

SCRAGG ISLAND is east of White's Island.

LITTLE IRONY ISLAND is south by southwest of Scragg Island.

CROW ISLAND is southwest of New Wharf, at head of Middle Bay.

CLARKE'S ISLAND is east of New Wharf.

BOMAZEEN ISLAND is between Brunswick and Great Island.

Other localities in Harpswell are: —

HIGH HEAD, on the east side of the northern part of the Neck, and JAQUES'S HARBOR, at the southern extremity of Bailey's Island.

HARPSWELL HARBOR is on the east of the Neck, between it and Great Island and Orr's Island.

CONDY'S HARBOR is on the east side of the point of the same name, south of Great Island.

QUAHAUG BAY extends into Great Island from the south and nearly divides the island.

ASH COVE is west of Potts's Point, between the eastern and middle prongs of the Neck.

MILL-POND BASIN is between the western and middle prongs of the Neck. It furnishes a tide power of great value, from its accessibility by sea, the depth of water admitting the passage of vessels of several hundred tons, quite to the dam. Upon it there is now a large grain mill.

LONG REACH is an extensive cove in the western side of Great Island, opening northward.

LONG COVE nearly divides the northern half of Orr's Island.

LOWELL'S COVE is on the southeast side of Orr's Island.

MACKEREL COVE is on the southern part of Bailey's Island.

WILL GUT is the passage between Orr's and Bailey's Islands.

THE GURNET is the name of the point in Brunswick opposite to Great Island, Harpswell. Between the point and island is the Gurnet Bridge. In the English Channel there are several headlands bearing the name, having taken it, probably, because of the number of gurnet fish found in the neighborhood, and it is probable that the name was given to the point in Brunswick from a fancied resemblance to one of the English headlands referred to.

FAUNA.

From the varied character of the region about Brunswick Falls, comprising sea-shore and forest, sandy plains, granite hills, and rich intervales, this narrow territory, prior to its occupation by the English, must have drawn a numerous representation of almost the entire fauna of the State. Among the MAMMALIA formerly found here were bears, wild-cats, loup-cerviers, wolves, moose, beaver, and otter. Cathance Pond is said to have been once a great resort for the latter, while traces of beaver-dams are found on almost every stream. Of the carnivora, wolves were the most common. The town many times voted bounties for the destruction of these animals, which prowled about the premises of the settlers in search of food, and sometimes even followed the settlers themselves.

About the year 1786, Mrs. Thomas, wife of Lewis Thomas, walked from Harpswell to Brunswick, bearing her baby in her arms, and in addition carrying half a quintal of fish. While coming through the woods near Middle Bay, she was followed by wolves. With remarkable presence of mind, she threw down a single fish, which the pursuing pack stopped to devour, while she pressed forward as rapidly as possible. The animals soon resumed the pursuit, and she threw down another fish, and again they stopped to make a quarrelsome meal. This operation was repeated at intervals until she reached her home. Ephraim Thomas was the name of the man who, when a babe, made this dangerous journey. He died in Greene, Maine, in 1849, at sixty-three years of age.

In 1792 Samuel Stanwood, who then lived on the site of the present residence of Mrs. Joseph McKeen, had a saw mill at Maquoit at which he worked during the day, carrying his dinner with him. One day, desiring to accomplish all he could and not feeling very hungry, he did not stop to eat the dinner which he had brought with him, but took it back with him when he started for home at night. When he reached Mair Brook, a wolf came out of the thicket, looked at him a moment, then went back and uttered his hideous yells, which soon brought four or five others of his species to the scene. Stanwood, finding he was pursued, threw out a handful of meat, and while the wolves were fighting over it he hastened forward, soon, however, to be overtaken by the animals, to whom he again threw fragments of food. This operation was repeated until, when nearly to his home, the last fragment of food was gone and the wolves were in hot pursuit of him. He screamed to his wife to open the door. Fortunately she heard him and flung open the door, just in time to secure his escape from the wild beasts at his heels.

Mr. Dean Swift says that when he was a boy and living with his parents in the house which is now the residence of Mrs. Rodney Forsaith, on Maine Street, he has many a night heard the wolves howling a short distance east of the house, in the woods which then extended to Federal Street.

Reverend Samuel Veazie, in 1767, purchased the farm adjoining the old Harpswell Island Meeting-House, and cleared a place for the erection of his dwelling. Back of his house there was a dense growth of wood, and in this the wolves sometimes collected in large numbers during the winter season, making the night hideous with their howls. The wolves would remain on the island until just previous to the breaking up of the ice, when they would leave it for the mainland. It is stated that they never failed to make the removal before the breaking up of the ice, seeming in this matter to show an intelligence akin to reason.[1]

Bears, never so troublesome as the wolves, have hardly been heard of within the limits of our three towns for many years. Some time in the last century Johnson Stover pastured hogs at Goose Island, and one day, hearing an unusual squealing, he found a bear holding one of the pigs in his paws, and occasionally nipping it with his teeth.

Alcot Stover once, while lying on his bed, saw one looking in at the window, but before he could get his gun his wife accidentally frightened it away.

About 1775 a woman, known as Granny Young, went to Bomazeen Island after berries. After filling her dishes, she started for home, having only a stave for a paddle. Hearing a noise in the water behind her she turned, and saw that a large bear was swimming after the boat. She plied her awkward paddle as vigorously as possible, but the bear overtook the boat and attempted to upset it. She fought him with the stave, striking him upon the head and nose until he was stunned; then she held his head under water until he was dead, when she towed him ashore.

The latest appearance of bears in Harpswell, of which we have the date fixed, was in 1800, when three were killed on the farm now owned by W. S. Purinton.

---

[1] *Mrs. Price, ninety-two years old; formerly a resident of the island.*

The common red deer must have been quite numerous in this region at the time of settlement. Even now they are occasionally met with. As late as 1858 two were seen in Brunswick, — one, a full-grown animal, at New Meadows; the other, a fawn, on the old Freeport road. On Oct. 20, 1859, three were shot on Topsham Plains. Some sixteen years ago caribou were seen at the western border of Brunswick by several persons, and in two instances some pursuit was made.

Raccoons are still caught every year in one quarter or another of the town. A live one was found in the Factory yard in Brunswick in 1844.

The wild-cat, though heard of occasionally in neighboring towns, has not been reported within our limits for many years. The "lucifee" (*loup cervier*), or Canada lynx, is believed still to haunt, occasionally, the extensive woods at the west of the town.

Foxes are alternately numerous, then rare, and seem to be somewhat migratory, according as mice, grouse, and hare are plenty.

The rabbit exists in favorable situations through the towns, but is not common enough to do much damage to the crops. A few young trees are each spring found with the bark gnawed from the trunk near the ground, but this has usually been laid to the mice.

Both the common and the star-nosed moles are occasionally met with, but are not sufficiently numerous to be regarded in any degree a pest, as in some localities southward. Gray, red, and striped squirrels are frequent, but not troublesome. The flying squirrel is not often seen, but still haunts the old woods. The weazel is infrequent; and its cousin, the mink, puts in an appearance in the vicinity of brooks with just sufficient frequency to incite the boys to unprofitable attempts at trapping. The muskrat seems equally, but sparingly diffused The skunk still taints the air with his mephitic odor each season, in many localities. Woodchucks are rare, but here and there a farmer complains of their ravages among his early bean-plants.

BIRDS.

Probably a list of the birds occurring in this vicinity, a century or two ago, would not differ from one of to-day, except in a few instances. It is certain, however, that certain species were vastly more numerous. The golden eagle is said to have been found upon our coast in the earlier days of its settlement; but the bird is not now known here, even as a visitant. On the other hand, there is not, that we are aware, any evidence that the eider duck was found upon our shores a century since, while it is now quite regularly a winter sojourner. Yet the seasons have not been growing colder, neither can we think them to have grown greatly warmer, though another bird associated with a higher temperature has become a *habitué* of this vicinity, as well as of other localities in the State. It has been said that the Baltimore oriole was an unknown bird until within a few years, yet it may be that the change of the country by human occupancy, rather than any change of climate, is the cause of its immigration. The scarlet tanager, also regarded as an inhabitant of mild climates, is occasionally seen here as early as May.

Among *winter* visitants are the grosbeaks, — the pine and the rose-breasted, — the pine finch, the Arctic or snowy owl, the Canada jay, and perhaps one or two others. The common birds are, no doubt, the same here as in most other portions of the State. The cuckoo is said to have been unknown in Aroostook until within three or four years, but here it has been observed for a generation, at least. It is, however, reported to have become more numerous in this vicinity of late. This, if a fact, may be owing to an increase of its insect food, for it is believed by some to feed largely on the caterpillar. Another bird, one of the woodpeckers, known as the sapsucker, has become rather rare of late years, from the relentless war waged upon it by the guardians of young fruit orchards. The crow, the pest of cornfields, in scornful disregard of public opinion, persists in making itself very much at home among the farms. Hawks in the usual variety, though reduced in numbers, are found in all the more rural quarters of the towns.

The several sorts of owls common in the State are met with here, their number in any locality seeming to depend more on the frequency of hollow trees, which afford them congenial shelter, than on any other condition. The blue jay, eminent for its disagreeable voice, its striking appearance, and remarkable foresight, is a frequent inhabitant. Ruffed grouse (here commonly called partridges) are frequent, but not numerous. Woodcocks, from their retired habits, are an almost unknown bird to our people, yet are really much more plentiful than grouse. The plovers, sandpipers, snipes, and quails are not usually numerous. Wild pigeons are frequent, but not to the hundredth part of their former numbers.

Of the birds that seek the neighborhood of human habitations we have the usual variety, the common dove, three or more kinds of swallows, and the martin. The last has diminished in number, the others appear to have increased. The robin is, perhaps, more numerous than any other single variety. Others of this family are the wood-thrush, whose vocal expression is the long, pensive, but musical whistle and trill heard in almost every wood in early summer; and Wilson's thrush, which is less common. Another songster, the brown thrush, or the brown mocker, is found, it is said, in only one locality of our towns, and this is in the western part of Brunswick.

The song sparrow, that frequents cool ravines, and sings all through the season, and the white-throated sparrow, are familiar to the ears of our inhabitants, if not well known to the eye. The chickadee, or black-cap titmouse, and the kingbird, are also quite common. Something like the last in appearance and voice is the kingfisher, present on most of our larger streams during the summer.

About the marshes on these streams the great blue heron is sometimes seen, but it is more frequent about the salt marshes and sea-shore. Around the sea-shore the coot is more numerous than any other of the large birds. Our water-fowl generally are not different from those found in other sections of the State. On our fresh-water ponds, as well as on the salt-water, are found in spring and autumn the wild goose, the black duck, teal, sheldrake, and merganser, while the wood-duck and the pintail or whistler, make their habitat all over our territory; yet they are not abundant. There is a tradition that at the period of settlement, wild fowl sometimes congregated in certain localities in our vicinity in such numbers, and made so much noise in the night, that the settlers were unable to sleep until they had driven the intruders away. It is said that to accomplish this they sometimes found it necessary to fling firebrands among them. Merrymeeting Bay was formerly a great resort for wild geese. The middle portion of the bay was, at low water, a sand-bed covered with a species of reed, on the roots of which the geese were supposed to subsist from about the first of September until the extreme cold weather sent them southward. The loon is met with at the proper season; the gulls and fish-hawks are quite common, and the white-headed eagle is frequently seen.

Of INSECTS, the chief food of our feathered friends, but often the bane of our orchards and growing crops, we probably have the same variety that is to be found in the rest of the State. Our list of REPTILES and AMPHIBIANS is not extensive. Turtles are not often met with, except the variety found in muddy ponds. Our serpents are the striped snake, the little brown snake, the green snake, the black snake, the milk snake, and the water snake. The water snakes are believed to have poison fangs; in regard to the brown and milk snakes we have no knowledge; the others mentioned are not deemed venomous.

The bull-frog, pickerel-frog, and green frog inhabit all our fresh waters, and the leopard-frog is to be found in the meadows, and the delicate, pale brown wood-frog is of frequent occurrence in our forests. The common toad is found in all cultivated lands, and tree-toads in all our localities. There are few persons who have not listened to the multitudinous cry of the latter during hot summer nights.

We have no lizards; the creature sometimes called so is the salamander. There are several species, varying much in size and color. They are found only in moist places, while some are amphibious.

Of CRUSTACEANS, our principal species are the king crab (or horse-shoe), the common crab, and the common salt-water lobster, the last abundant and of well-known value.

Our chief MOLLUSKS are the fresh-water clam (unio) and the various snails; the common clam, abundant in our salt-water flats, and familiar as an article of diet; the hen, or sea clam, found only at unusually low tides; and the quahaug, infrequent, except in Quahaug Bay, in Great Island.

Of the MARINE MAMMALS, the seal is quite frequent in our bays, and sometimes ascends the rivers for short distances. In 1868, one was seen near the Toll Bridge, and being pursued in boats, was captured near Cow Island. It weighed two hundred pounds. The porpoise is quite common, frequently disturbing the schools of various fish upon which the fisherman counts for his gain. Whales are rarely seen, but not unknown. The blackfish, or round-headed dolphin, is common off shore in its season. It was probably this species about which the *Androscoggin Free Press* gave the following account: —

"On Monday, Oct. 6, 1828, a shoal of dolphins, called by the sailors 'blackfish,' seventy or eighty in number, made their appearance near Orr's Island. The inhabitants, to the number of twenty-one men, in nine boats, armed with muskets and axes, went out to attack, and, if possible, catch them. After four or five hours of hard fighting they had been able to despatch but six or seven, but they had learned that the dolphins could be driven with as much facility as a flock of sheep. It was finally decided to attempt to drive them into a narrow cove which penetrated to the distance of a mile into the interior of Orr's Island, and which there terminated in a circular basin. In this design they were successful. All of the boats pressed closely upon their retreat and cut off all possibility of escape.

"Captain John Curtis, being in advance of the little fleet, caused his boat to be rowed alongside one of the largest dolphins, himself standing with one foot braced on the bows of the boat and the other on the back of his antagonist. He had taken this position to make the attempt of splitting open the head of the fish; but, the boat veering in its course, he must either fall into the water or jump upon the back of his intended victim. He did the latter, and in the next moment the company saw their gallant captain riding off astride upon the back of the dolphin. A full quarter of a mile was the hero thus borne over the water by this novel mode of navigation, when he safely alighted upon a vehicle of a more artificial construction.

"Captain Curtis did not, however, like Arion, entertain his dolphin with harmonious strains of godlike music. So far from this, in fact, he was constantly inflicting blows with his axe deeply into the monster's blubber.

"As the tide ebbed away, the dolphins began to drag themselves heavily through the mud, and it became advisable to find some more expeditious way of destroying them. Before sunset the whole number were despatched. About one hundred and thirty barrels of oil were obtained from the fish, realizing about $2,000.

"This singular fish is not the common dolphin, but the round-headed dolphin, being much larger. Those captured at Harpswell varied much in size. The largest was twenty-three feet long and eighteen feet in circumference. There were some that measured not more than six or seven feet in length. These were probably pups, as some of the females yielded large quantities of milk, resembling very much cow's milk."

The FISHES, inhabiting the salt water of our bays and off our shores, are the cod, haddock, hake, pollock, cusk, mackerel, blue-fish, herring, menhaden or porgy, sun-fish, sword-fish, rock-cod, sculpin, ling, flounder, cunner, frost-fish, and tom-cod. Our fresh waters contain brook-trout, pickerel, perch, chub, sucker, bream or kiver, bull-head, and others of lesser note. Among the fish that frequent both the fresh and salt water are the smelt, alewife, salmon, and sturgeon. In early times the last two were very abundant in the Androscoggin, but their number has greatly diminished. Since the construction of fishways in the dams a few years ago, there has, however been a manifest increase in the number of salmon, and it is to be hoped that by careful diversion from the waters of all matters deleterious to fishes, the river may again become abundantly stocked.

GEOLOGICAL FEATURES.[1]

The universal underlying rock of this region, extending to unknown depths, is gneiss. This is easily distinguished from granite, which consists of the same minerals, — mica, quartz, and feldspar, — by its appearance of stratification.

The layers or strata of gneiss are curiously bent and twisted, as if, while in a soft and plastic condition, at some early period of the earth's history, they had been crumpled like pieces of cloth by some gigantic force. This folding of the strata is well exhibited in a railroad cut on the Topsham shore, near the Lewiston bridge. In general, however, they dip to the southeast.

Intersecting these layers, in immense veins or dikes, is found the granite. The granite dikes have clearly been formed by the filling of vast chasms in the earth's crust, probably at a high temperature.

Withstanding better the wear of time than the gneiss, these dikes now form prominent features of our landscape at Powder-House Hill and the hills of Topsham, and have been the cause of the rapids which furnish our villages with their magnificent water-power.

The granite dikes are here an extensive source of building material, and, farther north, of the feldspar ground for the glazing of pottery and the quartz crushed for sand-paper. In these dikes, too, are found the crystals that have rendered the vicinity so famous for its mineral wealth.

On Powder-House Hill and other places, and probably throughout the village of Brunswick, were it accessible, the surface of these hard and almost imperishable rocks is found deeply scored and furrowed in lines parallel with one another, and having the direction of northwest and southeast. These it is well known, and has been abundantly proved, have been formed by the action of an immense glacier which once extended over the whole northern part of the United States.

Over four thousand feet in thickness, covering all but our highest mountains, as Washington and Katahdin, this stream of solid ice moved slowly southward with crushing force, grooving the surface, grinding down the hills, and transporting the huge bowlders that were, later, stranded in our fields. By this same agency were formed the deep fjords or inlets of our coasts and the islands that stud Casco Bay.

Following the period of ice came a period of thaw. At the same

[1] *This description is by Professor Carmichael of Bowdoin College, and though written with especial reference to Brunswick and Topsham, is undoubtedly equally applicable to Harpswell.*

time the coast of Maine, which once had been higher than now above the ocean level, sank below its surface, and an arm of the sea flowed over the highest building sites of Brunswick. Then were deposited the beds of brick clay which immediately cover the solid rock and crop out at the brow of the "Hill."

In sinking wells in different parts of the village, not unfrequently mussel-beds (*Mytelus edulis*) are met with in this day. Their perfection and disposition prove that here they have lived and died.

Other shells, as *Leda truncata*, which is not found to-day south of Spitzbergen, attest to the coldness of the salt waters which then covered the lowlands.

Two bison teeth, a fragment of a walrus tusk, a large and curious tooth resembling that of the walrus, found in a clay bed of the same period at Gardiner by the late Mrs. Allen, and deposited in the Museum of Bowdoin College by Mrs. M. Allen Elton, prove at this early day, long before Adam walked the earth, strange beasts occupied the morasses and briny waters of the Kennebec and Androscoggin valleys.

At a later period, immense streams of water from the still melting ice flowed southward through the Androscoggin, forming the high terraces of which six, one above the other, may be seen on the Brunswick, and two upon the Topsham shore.

Then was deposited the expanse of sand forming the arid plain surrounding the village of Brunswick. Happy the agriculturist on whose land the Leda clay breaks through the barren terrace sand!

Ice, then, is the sculptor to whom we owe all the physical features of our vicinity. It carved out our hills, valleys, and river-beds; brought bowlders and gravel from afar, and supplied the water which formed the terraces upon which the town of Brunswick has been built.

MINERALS.

This region is remarkably rich in the number of its minerals. The attention of the Pejepscot proprietors was early attracted to this fact, and with prudent forethought they passed the following vote, Jan. 15, 1718: —

"Voted, that if it shall so happen that there be any Mine or Mineral found out within any Proprietor's or Inhabitant's Lott; that the Said Mine or Minerall shall be held in common to the Proprietors: The Person in whose Lott it shall fall to have the same Quantity of good land elsewhere." [1]

---

[1] *Pejepscot Records.*

The following list of the minerals of this region, and the localities where they are chiefly to be found, is furnished mainly by Professor Carmichael: —

FELDSPAR is found in large and handsome crystals in Cobb's quarry. In Topsham, crystals a foot in diameter have been found in Sprague's quarry. Fine crystals of Amazonian spar from an old feldspar quarry are found on the banks of the Cathance River.

MICA, BIOLITE, PHLOZOPITE, in crystals, are found at the railroad cut near the upper bridge, and at the Tarbox quarry, Topsham. Near the Old Feldspar quarry slabs have been found a foot wide. Green mica is found at New Meadows. The green mica extensively exchanged by the late Professor Cleaveland was found in a bowlder near the river.

LEPIDOLITE is found at Topsham.

QUARTZ. — At Sprague's quarry large crystals, and at the Old Feldspar quarry crystals a foot in diameter are found. Decahedral quartz and smoky quartz are found in various quarries.

BERYL. — At Cobb's quarry, small but perfect crystals, with interesting pyramidal faces, are found in the railroad cut near the upper bridge. At Fisher's quarry, Topsham, crystals of a hundred pounds' weight have been found.

The EMERALD is said to have been found in a cut near the upper fishway, in Topsham.

GARNET. — Small but fine crystals are found in Cobb's quarry. A fine, perfect specimen, nearly as large as a man's fist, in the Museum of Bowdoin College, was found in Sprague's quarry. At Fisher's quarry are fine, large specimens. Large quantities of crystals, of medium color and large size, have been taken from a quarry near the road, beyond the Old Feldspar quarry. The most ordinary form is the ikositetrahedron modified by the octahedron and dodecahedron.

MAGNETITE is found in many localities. Crystals over two inches in diameter have been taken from Sprague's quarry.

TOURMALINE. — Large masses are found at Rocky Hill. Fine, large, perfect hemimorphic crystals are found at Tarbox's quarry, Topsham. Brown tourmaline is found at New Meadows, near the railroad bridge.

COLUMBITE. — Large and perfect crystals have been found at Fisher's quarry. One specimen weighed upwards of two pounds. It is found also at the railroad cut near the upper bridge.

GALENITE and IRON PYRITES are found (good specimens) near Cathance River.

APATITE is found near Cathance River, and crystals are also found at New Meadows, near the railroad bridge.

TITANITE is found at Cobb's quarry, and small but fine crystals are found near Miss Narcissa Stone's house.

CHLORITE is found at Cobb's quarry.

BISMUTHENITE is found at Fisher's quarry and at Tarbox's quarry, associated with columbite.

AMPHIBITE is found at Sprague's quarry.

SPHALENITE is found at Cathance River.

MOLYBDENITE is found in the bed of the river near the Topsham paper mill, at New Meadows, and at the Old Feldspar quarry.

GOHNITE is found in a quarry near the road, beyond the Old Feldspar quarry.

The following minerals have also all been found in some one or more of the three towns, though the exact locality we are unable to designate: COPPER PYRITES, MALACHITE, CALCITE, HEMATITE, CUPRITE, EPIDITE, and MOLYBDITE.

TUNGSTITE is supposed to have been found, but it is not known with certainty.

SOIL AND CROPS.

The soil of Topsham is, for the most part, a light, sandy loam, with some clay at the northwestern and northeastern parts. In the main, it is tolerably productive. The best farms are on what is called the Foreside, and on Cathance stream.

The soil of Brunswick varies from the sandy loam of the plains to a gravelly loam at the westward. Rich loams and heavy clays are found in a few localities. Peat has been found in the low ground east of Miss Narcissa Stone's house and has been used by her. The best farms were formerly[1] (and probably are now) at Middle Bay and Maquoit. The land is said, however, to have been much more fertile in former times than at present.[2]

Harpswell can hardly be considered an agricultural town, though portions of it are very productive. Some excellent farms are to be found upon the Neck and upon some of the larger islands. The soil of the Neck is largely granitic rather than a gravelly loam, with small tracts of clay loam. On Great Island the soil varies from a hard, tenacious clay to a sandy loam, while in some localities are found a fine sand, and in others slaty and granitic soils. Most of the farms are equal to those on the Neck, being excellent hay and grazing land, while the higher parts are suitable for corn and wheat. Orchards do not flourish well.

---

[1] *McKeen, MSS. Lecture.* [2] *Maine Historical Society Collection*, 3, *p.* 318.

Potatoes, barley, wheat, oats, and beans are the crops chiefly cultivated hereabouts. The mode of cultivation has improved very much of late years from what it was in Revolutionary times, when people "banked up their corn very high, and placed their potatoes very deep in the ground, and raised but little of either."

FLORA.

The flora of this region is, in general, like that of other similar localities in the central and coast region of Maine. The description here given is confined solely to the trees found here. At the time of the first settlement the wood growth was very different from what it is now. At that time there is said to have been an oak grove where the depot now stands in Brunswick, and the plains were covered with a growth of beech, instead of pine as at present. Then the prevailing growths were of hard wood. Among the forest trees now commonly met with are the alder, beech, birch, cedar, fir, juniper (or hackmatack), hemlock, four varieties of maple, two of oak, four of pine, and poplar, spruce, and willow. Those which are less commonly found are the ash, cherry, elm, horse-chestnut, larch, and arbor-vitæ.

CLIMATIC AND METEOROLOGICAL.

The climate of this region is somewhat different near the sea-coast from that a few miles farther inland. In Harpswell, and around the bays of Brunswick, the temperature is as uniform as it usually is on the coast of Maine. Topsham, from its greater elevation, is cooler than Brunswick in the summer and, probably owing to its southern slope, is slightly warmer in the winter. The following meteorological statement is from the Annual Report for 1867, of the Smithsonian Institution: —

"Between the years 1807 and 1859 inclusive, meteorological records were made with great regularity by the late Professor Parker Cleaveland, of Bowdoin College, at Brunswick, Maine, and after his death were consigned to this institution for reduction and publication. The observations, though not intended by their author to be of a strictly scientific character, were yet found sufficiently valuable to warrant the expenditure of considerable labor in preparing them for the press.

"The observations were made at 7 A. M., 1 P. M., and 6 P. M., and relate to indications of the thermometer and barometer, direction of the wind, state of the weather, amount of rain and snow, character of clouds, occurrence of thunder-storms, fogs, frost and hail, earthquakes, auroras, etc. The observations present, during a period of 52 years, a mean temperature of 44° 4′ Fahrenheit, which reduced to the level of the sea becomes 44° 6′.

"The lowest mean temperature for any year occurred in 1859 and was 40° 31′, and the highest was in 1840, 51° 60′, giving a range of 11° 29′, which is considerably larger than at places farther south in the United States.

"According to the average of 52 years, the warmest day falls on the 22d of July, or 31 days after the summer solstice, and has a mean temperature of 67° 7′.

"The coldest day, on an average, is the 18th of January, or 28 days after the winter solstice, having a temperature of 19° 9′ Fahrenheit.

"On an average, the 20th of April and the 24th of October have the same temperature as the mean of the entire year. The lowest record for the whole time is 30° below *zero*, and the highest 102° above.

"The northwest wind on an average reduces the temperature 4° 6′. The north lowers it 3° 1′, and the northeast 3° 8′. The southwest wind, on the contrary, elevates the temperature above its normal value, 2° 6′. In summer the effect of rain and fog is to lower the temperature 6° 5′. In winter, snow, sleet, or rain increases the temperature 4° 3′. From 54,097 observations, the following is the proportional number of winds in 1,000: —

SOUTH.	NORTH.	WEST.	EAST.	S. W.	N. E.	N. W.	S. E.
29	40	51	29	311	143	320	77

"From this it results that the most frequent are the northwest and southwest, the former in winter and the latter in summer.

"The least number of days in which rain fell was in February, the greatest in May. The greatest number of days in which snow fell was in January. The earliest snow occurred on the 26th of September, 1808, and the latest on the 8th of June, 1816. On an average, snow falls in Brunswick on some day in May once in five years, and in October once every other year. The average number of rainy days is 64, the average number of snowy days is 30.

"The average amount of rain and snow is 44.68 inches. The greatest amount of rain during any one day was 8¼ inches, November 4, 1845. The greatest fall of snow was on the 10th of March, 1819, and measured 30 inches.

"The greatest number of rainfalls occur while the wind is from the northeast, and the least number while it is from the west. The northeast wind in winter is almost constantly accompanied by rain or snow, while in summer the southeast surpasses it as a vehicle of rain, — a result evidently due to the position of the place of observation with respect to the ocean. The number of storms of thunder and lightning recorded during 51 years is 472, or about 9 a year. The greatest number occurred in July and August, the least in January and February. The total number of fogs is 1,135, or 22 in a year, the most dense of which occur in summer, the least dense in winter.

"July is the only month in which no frost is recorded. The earliest frost observed was August 3d and the latest June 19th. On an average, the spring frost ceases after the first week in June, and the autumn frost commences after the first week in September.

"There were 34 hail-storms, — the greatest number in January, the least in August. The records notice the occurrence of 7 earthquakes and 86 auroras, the greatest number of the latter in September and October.

"The aurora also exhibits a maximum and a minimum. The maximum occurred in 1808, 1818, 1830, 1838, 1848, 1857, giving differences of 10, 12, 8, 10, and 9 years. This indicates an average period of about 10 years.

"Unfortunately, the temperature of the barometer is not given, and therefore a reduction on account of the expansion of the mercury is not possible, and consequently the only use which has been made of the record has been to exhibit the monthly extreme values, together with their annual variations. The barometric maxima reach their greatest value in December, and their least value in June. The minima occur in August. The monthly range is the greatest at the period of greatest cold, in January, and the least range at the period of greatest heat, in July."

The coldest season ever experienced here was probably in the winter of 1780–81. It was, however, nearly, if not quite, as cold in 1751. As early as January 14 of that year (1751), Parson Smith gives an account of an excursion he took with his wife and others from Falmouth to Brunswick *on the ice*, "passing over Harrasicket Bay a-going, and venturing on their return to come directly from Brunswick across the Bay without Maquoit Island to New Casco,[1] and over thence to the Beach home."[2] In 1780 Casco Bay was frozen over as far into the

[1] *Near where the United States Marine Hospital now stands at Falmouth Foreside.*
[2] *Smith's Journal.*

sea as the island called the White Bull, and was travelled upon from *Harpswell* to *Portland.*

The mildest winter was that of 1838. On January 8, of this winter, David Johnson ploughed all day on Goat Island, Harpswell.

Destructive gales and thunder-storms have not been of exceptional frequency in this vicinity. The earliest one of any severity, of which mention has been found, occurred June 29, 1809, when there was a violent thunder-storm. The Gun House was struck by lightning, which struck also in twelve other places in that vicinity. On June 7, 1814, about 8 A. M., there was heard a report in the air resembling that of a gun, and gradually dying away. There was no storm at the time; it was doubtless the bursting of a meteor. April 1, 1815, various sized balls of snow were found in the woods. They were from less than one inch to fifteen inches in diameter, of an oval or globular shape, loose and uniform in texture, and very irregularly distributed. The tracks could be seen where they had been rolled over the surface of the snow by the wind. On May 7 and 21, 1816, there were severe thunder-storms. On the latter date the storm was accompanied with hail, the form of which was very remarkable. The hail-stones were in hexangular pyramids, sometimes half an inch in length. In some the base was almost transparent. On August 6, 1834, there was a severe thunder-shower, during which the vanes on Professor Cleaveland's and Captain Given's barns were struck by lightning. August 20, 1835, there was a severe hail-storm, and hail-stones which measured three inches in diameter were picked up at Mustard's tavern. September 3, 1845, there was a violent thunder-shower, during which Common's Hall was struck by lightning. May 6, 1850, there was also a violent storm. The lightning struck Captain Minot's buildings at Mair Point, and in several other places. February 18, 1853, probably the severest storm of all occurred. The lightning struck in over twenty different localities; among others, Deacon Perkins's house on the island in Topsham. October 30, 1866, the steeple of the First Parish Meeting-House in Brunswick was blown off.

In 1869, on September 7, a terrible gale began at seven o'clock P. M., and lasted for several hours. In the Lemont woods fourteen trees were blown down in one spot, and over two hundred trees were blown down in David Marriner's woods. A large number were also prostrated in Topsham. The depot woodshed in Brunswick, and two chimneys on the Medical College, were also blown over. A great deal of damage was done, of which the above constituted but a small portion. August 16, 1867, there was another severe storm, during which seven and one half inches of rain fell. Seventy-five feet of an embankment on the Androscoggin railroad in Topsham was washed out. It was twenty-five feet deep. July 15, 1868, a severe thunder-storm occurred, during which two houses and a barn in Brunswick, and an old wooden warehouse in Topsham, were struck by lightning. June 23, 1874, the Jordan House in Brunswick was struck by lightning.

Accounts have been preserved of some ten shocks of earthquake which have occurred here since the first settlement of Brunswick. The first and severest was the one which was felt throughout New England, and is called the "Great Earthquake." It happened on Tuesday, Nov. 18, 1755, at about a quarter past four o'clock A. M. The undulation of the earth's surface in this vicinity was so violent as to rock houses, and throw down chimneys, log fences, and crockery from the shelves. The chimney of Reverend Mr. Dunlap's house fell in, and some of his children narrowly escaped injury. The inhabitants generally were greatly alarmed, and viewed the occurrence as an omen of evil. Reverend Mr. Dunlap preached a sermon with especial reference to this event.[1] The other earthquakes were much less severe, though some of them were sufficient to cause a degree of trepidation amongst the timid. They occurred Nov. 22, 1755; June 12, 1805, at 7.30 A. M.; June 26, 1808, at 2.51 P. M.; Nov. 28, 1814, at 7 P. M.; the oscillations moved from north to south, lasted fifty seconds, and were followed by an explosion; May 23, 1817, at 3 P. M., — lasted one minute; March 7, 1823, at 10 A. M.; July 25, 1828, at 6 A. M.; Aug. 26, 1829, at 9 P. M. and at 9.15 P. M.; and Oct. 17, 1860.

---

[1] *Pejepscot Papers.*

CHAPTER II.

MUNICIPAL HISTORY OF BRUNSWICK.

THE town of Brunswick first received its name legally, in the year 1717, when it was incorporated as a township. This name was probably given to the town in honor of the house of Brunswick, to which family the then king of Great Britain belonged. The reason for this presumption is, that this town, being earlier settled and incorporated than any of the other nine or ten towns of the same name in the United States, could not have been named after either of them, and as there were, so far as known, no Germans among the earlier settlers here, it was hardly likely to have been named for the German city.

UNDER COMMONWEALTH OF MASSACHUSETTS.

[1717.] The vote of the General Court, constituting Brunswick a township, was passed on the third of May, 1717, and provided "That ye Land Plotted for a Town from Pejepscot Falls to Maquoit in Casco Bay be Constituted A Township to be laid out the Quantity of Six miles Square as the Land will allow & to be Called by the name of Brunswick to be forth-with Settled in a Defensible Manner." [1]

This action of the General Court gave the settlers municipal rights similar to those of plantations of the present day. Thus, for instance, they held public meetings, raised money for their common welfare, and chose their own town officers. Records were kept by an officer styled the town clerk, who was the first time appointed by the proprietors, and afterwards elected by the people.

On the second of May, of this year, Lieutenant Joseph Heath was chosen by the proprietors "To be their Clark for the Town of Brunswick until the town is Qualified to make their own election and Sworn to the faithful Discharge of that Trust." [2]

The first meeting of the inhabitants was held November 3, 1717. The first election of town officers was in March, 1719, when Captain John Gyles, Thomas Wharton, James Starrat, John Cochran, and

---

[1] *Massachusetts Records*, 1717.

[2] *Brunswick Records in Pejepscot Collection.*

Joseph Heath were chosen selectmen for the ensuing year. Joseph Heath was also chosen clerk and town treasurer, and Peter Haines, constable.

At a regular meeting of the inhabitants, held May 8, it was voted to purchase a *bos taurus* for the common benefit. It was also at this meeting voted, "That whereas Some of the Inhabitants of this Town have already Brought on Cattle & others expect to have some come before Winter, Therefore our first rate to our Minister shall be raised on Lotts & poles onley."[1]

Other meetings were held at different periods, at which action was taken relating chiefly to the support of a minister. The doings of those meetings will be found in the chapter upon Ecclesiastical History.

[1735.] In the year 1735 the inhabitants of Brunswick had become so numerous and felt so great need of a more perfect system in the management of their common concerns, that they made application to the government of Massachusetts for an Act of Incorporation as a town. The petition was as follows: —

"To His Excellency Jonathan Belcher Esq. Captain General and Governour in Chief. The Honourable His Majesties Councill, and the Honourable House of Representatives of his Majesties Province of the Massachusetts-Bay In New England In General Court assembled May 1735.

"The Petition of us the Subscribers Inhabitants of the Town of Brunswick in the County of York Humbly Sheweth — That your Petitioners being arrived to a competent number to transact Town affairs & in Expectation of having others very soon added to us, having now a commodious Meeting-House chiefly erected at the charge of the Proprietors, and having also obtained a pious & othodox Minister to settle with us, we now find it necessary to be vested with Power to lay a Tax or assesment in order to raise money for his maintenance — Therefore your petitioners Humbly pray your Excelency and Honours that you will pleas to Erect us into a Township & vest us with the Power & authorities belonging to other Towns excepting only the Power of Granting & Disposing of Land, which we acknowledge to be in the Proprietors who placed us here — and your Petitioners as in Duty bound Shall ever pray &c."[2]

This petition was signed by John Rutherford, Anthony Vincent, James Dunning, David Dunning, Richard Flaherty, — an Irish school-teacher, — James McFarland, James Carter, William Gibson, Andrew

---

[1] *Brunswick Records, in Pejepscot Collection.* [2] *Pejepscot Papers.*

Dunning, Ebenezer Stanwood, Samuel Stanwood, David Giveen, James Henry, William Spear, John Giveen, Robert Giveen, Thomas Neal, Thomas Washburn, Samuel Lindsey, Reverend Robert Rutherford, Benjamin Larrabee, Samuel Clarke, Nehemiah Giffen, — a stranger, — Robert Spear, Sr., Robert Spear, Jr., Robert Dunlap, William Woodside, Jonathan Dunlap, John Linsay.

The legislature, June 20th of this same year, granted the request of the petitioners and enacted a bill in accordance therewith. This bill for some reason, however, failed to receive the signature of the governor, and did not therefore take effect.[1]

[1737.] On the 25th of May, 1737, another petition for incorporation was presented to the General Court, by Benjamin Larrabee, in behalf of the inhabitants of Brunswick, which set forth the reasons urged in the former petition and stated the fact of a bill having been enacted, which had failed to be valid on account of its wanting the governor's signature. The prayer of this petition was granted in the House of Representatives on the 24th of June, and concurred in by the Senate three days later. A bill was accordingly prepared, and at the next session of the General Court, January 26, 1738–9, the following Act was passed, and received the sanction of the governor: —

"ACT OF INCORPORATION OF BRUNSWICK.

ANNO REGNI REGIS GEORGIJ SECUNDI DUODECIMO.

AN ACT

For Erecting a Township in the County of York by the Name of Brunswick.

"*Whereas* there is a Competent Number of Inhabitants already settled upon a Tract of Land lying within the County of York hitherto called and known by the name of Brunswick containing the Quantity of about six miles square and lying convenient for a Township; and *whereas* said Inhabitants have humbly petitioned this Court, that in order to provide a Suitable Maintenance for the Minister Settled among them, they may be Erected into a Township, and vested with the Powers and Authorities belonging to other Towns. THEREFORE for encouragement of the said settlement

"*Be it Enacted* by his Excellency the Governor, Councill and Representatives in General Court assembled, and by the authority of the Same. That the said Tract of Land described in a Plat now returned to this Court as follows: —

"Beginning at the mouth of a brook or Rivulet called Bungamunga-

---

[1] *Pejepscot Papers.*

nock, running into Maquoit Bay where it touches upon North Yarmouth line, and from the mouth of said Brook to run upon a course north northwest, half westerly five miles into the wilderness leaving a wedge or strip of Land between said line and North Yarmouth,[1] and from thence upon a course northeast four miles to the Second Falls of Amascoggin alias Androscoggen River from thence down said River by Fort George, and down Merry Meeting Bay so far as Stevens carrying Place including several small Islets lying in said River above Said Carrying Place, and over said Carrying Place to the head of the Creek or River that runs up to the other side of the said Carrying Place, thence down said creek or River to the mouth thereof, including an Island therein, and from the mouth of said River to run by the Waterside southwesterly to the Southwest point of a place called the New Meadows, thence to strike across the cove upon course north northwest, till it meets and intersects the upper end of Merryconeag Neck four rods above the Narrows of said Neck, commonly called the carrying place, thence to run along the Shore to a Neck of Land called Mair point, about a mile and a quarter down said Neck, thence to cross over said Mair point and Maquoit Bay, upon a course northwest till it comes to the place first above mentioned, be and henceforth shall be a Township to be called Brunswick and the Inhabitants thereof shall have and enjoy all such immunities, privileges and powers as Generally other Towns in this Province have and do by Law enjoy: —

"This Bill having been read three Several times in the House of Representatives Pass'd to be Enacted.

"[Signed] J. QUINCY, *Speaker.*

"This Bill, having been read three several times in Council, Pass'd to be Enacted.

"[Signed] SIMON FROST, *Dep'ty Sec'ry.*

"By his Excellency the Governour.

I consent to the Enacting this Bill.

"[Signed] J. BELCHER.

"Jany. 26, 1738, Copy Exam^{d}.

"[Signed] SIMON FROST, *Dep'ty Sec'ry.*"

Brunswick thus became the eleventh corporate town in Maine. At the same time that the foregoing was passed, the General Court also

---

[1] *Known as the "Gore."*

passed an Act authorizing and empowering Benjamin Larrabee, Esquire, "to warn the Inhabitants of said Town, qualifyed by Law to vote in Town affairs, to assemble and meet together in some Sutable Place on the first Monday of March next, to choose a Moderator, Town Clerk, and other Town Officers for the year then next ensuing." The date of the incorporation of the town, it will be noticed, is given as Jan. 26, 1738. This is according to the old method of reckoning time. The date, according to the new style, would be Feb. 4, 1739.[1]

[1739.] There were six town meetings in 1739. The first meeting of this year, and the first under the Act of Incorporation, was held March 28th. At this meeting the following officers were chosen: —

Samuel Hinkley, Moderator and Town Clerk; Captain Benjamin Larrabee, Samuel Hinkley, John Getchell, James Dunning, and David Dunning, Selectmen; John Malkeon, John Barrows, Constables; Thomas Washburn, William Vincent, Samuel Whitney, and James Howe, Tything-Men; Captain William Woodside, Wimond Bradbury, John Whitney, and Joseph Berry, Surveyors of Highways; Robert Spear and Cornelius Thompson, Fence-Viewers; James Thompson, Town Treasurer; John MacGregor and John McFarlin, Hog Constables; Israel Mitchell and William Spear, Field-Drivers.

One hundred and fifty-three pounds and fifteen shillings were voted for town expenses for the year. At this meeting John Getchell, Robert Spear, Samuel Clark, James Thompson, Benjamin Parker, and Thomas Skolfield were chosen a committee to lay out highways for the convenience of the town.

Some proposition looking to the extermination of, or protection from wolves was doubtless made, as the town this year voted, "That the wolves should be left till further consideration."

In July it was voted, "That the Minister Shuld Preach att ye Southeast end of S^d^ Town (att a place cal^d^ Newmedows) according to what Rates and taxes they shall Pay towards the Support of the Ministry it being agreed upon by the whole Town."

Against this action of the town, however, a protest was entered by Benjamin Whitney, Jean Brown, and William Woodside.

A meeting held December 25th elected Captain Benjamin Larrabee a representative "to go to answer the presentment commenced against this town at the general Sessions of the Peace." It does not, however,

---

[1] *Town Records, Vol.* 1; *also Pejepscot Papers.*

appear from the records what was the nature of the action against the town or by whom it was brought. Possibly it may have been in consequence of their being no provision made that year for a school, as the law was then obligatory upon all towns to make such provision.

On May 30, of this year, the inhabitants of Mair Point petitioned the General Court, since one half of that point was within the bounds of the township of North Yarmouth and was twenty-five miles distant from the meeting-house in that town, by land, and ten miles distant by sea, with two dangerous bays to be crossed, and since the northerly portion of the point was but two miles distant from Brunswick, that they might be set off from North Yarmouth and annexed to the town of Brunswick. An Act was passed, granting this privilege, which took effect, October 2d following.

[1740.] The total appropriation for defraying the expenses of the town in 1740 was £248 16*s*. 0*d*. Of this amount £150 was for the salary of Reverend Mr. Rutherford, and £80 for support of a schoolmaster, leaving but £18 for contingent expenses. It was also voted this year to raise £200 as a settlement for Mr. Rutherford, "if he lives and dies minister of Brunswick," and a little more than one fourth of this amount was to be raised that year. The town voted not to send any representative this year to the General Court, and also voted to allow *hogs* to run at large, provided they were properly yoked and ringed.

Harpswell Neck was this year set off from North Yarmouth and annexed to Brunswick as an "adjacent,"[1] but was soon after set back again.

[1742.] There were five meetings of the town this year. At the annual meeting in March, £246 was raised for current expenses, £150 of which was for the support and £66 for the settlement of the minister.

At a meeting held May 15th, Mr. Henry Gibbs, a freeholder and resident in town, was admitted as "an inhabitant thereof," and he was, at the same meeting, elected to represent the town at the General Court. This action was evidently not the will of a majority of the voters of the town, as another meeting for the choice of a representative was held on the 29th of June, and "it being put to vote whether to send one or not it was passed in the negative."

Several matters pertaining to the vacant lands came up for discussion this year, and at a subsequent meeting it was voted, "That all

---

[1] *Massachusetts Records*, 1740, *p.* 351; *also* 303.

the vacant Land one the east side of the Maine Rode that buts one Brunswick falls Runing from s^d falls a Loung the Shore till it coms to the south corner of the Cove near s^d falls thence running a south Corse to the Rode that Leades to the Landing place; to lay common for convenency of Landing botes and cornews [boats and canoes] and for the Uce of the Inhabetence of the Town of Brunswick forever."

It was also, at the same meeting, voted "that all that corner of vacant land from the southwest corner of Fort George, thence running a west course till it comes to the river, thence down said river till it comes to the main road, thence along said road to the place of beginning," be left in common for the privilege of a grist mill and "for the Uce of the Inhabatence of the Town of Brunswick forever."

The selectmen this year petitioned the General Court for an abatement of the tax assessed upon the town. The reasons for this request are best given in the petition itself, which is as follows: —

"TO HIS EXCELLENCY JOHNATHAN BELCHER ESQ^R. CAP^T. GENERALL AND GOVERNOUR IN CHIEF, THE HONOURABLE HIS MAJESTIES COUNCILL AND THE HONOURABLE HOUSE OF REPRESENTATIVES OF HIS MAJESTIES PROVINCE OF THE MASSACHUSETTS BAY IN NEW ENGLAND IN GENERALL COURT ASSEMBLED MAY, 1741.

"THE PETITION OF US THE SUBSCRIBERS SELECTMEN OF THE TOWN OF BRUNSWICK IN THE COUNTY OF YORK.

HUMBLY SHEWETH.

"That the Great and Generall Court were pleased to lay a tax of Thirty pounds (New tenner) upon the town of Brunswick which they are very unable to pay, and the Constables of S^d Town has Collected but a very small part by reason of their great poverty, for the Greater part of the Settlers have not been able, (as yet) to pay for their lots of land of one Hundred Acres Each which they have taken of the Proprietors tho at a Reasonable price, for the best lots do not exceed five shillings per acre, & other lots not above half so much, & tho some have lived upon S^d lots, more than ten years, & some near twenty, yet by Reason of our Great Poverty & being often allarmed with the Rumour of Warr, & being often disturbed by the Insulting Indians, and many times are oblidged to Garrison our houses, which is very expensive, and always obliged to be well provided with arms & aminition, or Retire to other places of Safety with our familys & Cattle, & so oblidged to neglect our Husbandry whereby our familys have greatly sufered & have been Impoverished, and many families not being able to raize their own Provisions, are beholden to other parts of the Province for them, & in these times of rumour of Warr do the duty of Souldiers, in Defending ourselves & neighbours, we being a frontier town, & so of service to the Province, the fort being Remote from the greatest part of the Inhabitants which Cant be avoided, for the benefit of Husbandry, which Fort is a Great terror to the Indians and keeps them in some aw, yet they oftentimes Insults us in our private houses & when they are in any want of victuals, they kill our Cattle, which keeps us under fears & Discouragements. therefore your Petitioners Humbly pray that this Honourable Court would take the premisses into your wise Consideration and abate the tax laid upon the town of Brunswick for the year 1740, and Excuse S^{d} Town from paying Province taxes, for some time to come which will greatly incourage the Inhabitants to settle the remote parts of the Province where they can at present, (but with Great Difficulty) get a living, & Defend themselves & neighbours in these Exposed parts, tho the Greater part of the Inhabitants are not able to pay for the lots of land they are settled upon, The Honourable Courts compassion will greatly Incourage the Eastern Settlements, & by the smiles of Heaven, in a few years, may become a usefull part of the Province and by their Industry enabled cheerfully to pay such rates & taxes as shall be laid upon them for the future, and as in Duty bound your Petitioners shall ever pray.[1]

"SAM^{LL} HINCKLEY.
ROBERT SPEER. } *Selectmen.*"
DAVID DUNING.

[1742.] The town in 1742, for the first time, sent a representative to "the Great and General Court," and David Dunning was elected to fill the office.

[1743.] Two boards of selectmen were chosen in 1743. At the annual meeting held in March, Isaac Snow, Samuel Hinkley, and Wymond Bradbury were chosen selectmen. There was some informality, however, about this meeting, A protest was made against it as illegal, by Captain William Woodside, James Dunning, Robert Finney, Robert Spear, David Dunning, David Giveen, and Samuel Clark, and the General Court ordered another meeting to be held on the 30th of August. This latter meeting "being purged of all illegal voters," an election of town officers was had, and Captain John Minot, Eben Stanwood, and James Dunning were chosen selectmen and David Dunning, representative. At this meeting Wymond Bradbury was authorized to provide a pair of stocks for the town.

---

1 *Pejepscot Papers, original document.*

The decision of the General Court in regard to the illegality of the *first* meeting was based on the fact that the meeting was not legally warned, and that the assessors were not under oath when they took the valuation of the town.[1]

[1744.] The Court of General Sessions for the County of York, having decided that the special meeting of the town, held by order of the General Court in August, 1743, was likewise illegal, a new election was ordered and had, January 17, 1744, at which a new board of town officers was chosen to serve out the unexpired portion of the fiscal year. Thomas Skolfield, Ebenezer Stanwood, and James Dunning were elected selectmen.

At the annual meeting in March, a new board of selectmen was chosen for the ensuing year. No representative to the General Court was chosen. A committee was chosen at this meeting, to examine all the accounts of the town since its incorporation, and to settle all its affairs, and it was voted to raise no money for town purposes until the committee had reported. The committee were Deacon Samuel Hinkley, Captain William Woodside, James Thompson, and Robert Finney, and they were authorized to call in to their assistance, if necessary, Mr. Samuel Dinne (Denny?), of Georgetown. This committee, in December, brought in a full and detailed report of all moneys which had been received by the town treasurer, and of what had been disbursed by him, together with a statement of what was due the town from all sources; with recommendations for the payment of various sums claimed from the town for services rendered, etc. Among these items was one of six pounds due Deacon Samuel Hinkley "for ten days going after a minister to supply the town," and another of £3 10*s*. for a "constable's staff." The report of the committee was accepted.

At a special meeting of the town in May, a committee was chosen to secure "a schoolmaster upon as reasonable terms as possible." At this meeting Deacon Samuel Hinkley was chosen "a commissioner to appear at the Great and General Court held at Boston, to prefer a petition or petitions in behalf of the town." He was to receive his instructions from a committee consisting of the selectmen, and David Dunning, Ebenezer Stanwood, and Robert Finney. His compensation was to be 12*s*. per day and £5 for expenses. For what object a petition was to be presented does not appear from the records. It was, however, in all probability, in reference to an unfortunate differ-

---

[1] *Massachusetts Records*, 1743, *p*. 99.

ence that had arisen between the town and the proprietors. The latter were exempt from taxation, and refused to assist in making the county roads which passed through their lands.[1] The result was that the passions of the people were excited in relation to the matter, and the town, believing that unoccupied land might be taken and sold for public purposes, very injudiciously granted one hundred acres of land each to Deacon Samuel Hinkley, Timothy Tibbets, Cypron Cornish, and Aaron Hinkley, it being stipulated in each grant, "Provided, that he make improvement on said land in defiance of the proprietors, Henry Gibbs & Company, and begin said settlement in three years from date hereof by building, fencing and improving, except he or they (his heirs) be put off by an enemy." This trouble between the town and the proprietors was after some years amicably adjusted.

The taxation bore so heavily upon the people at this time that the town voted not to exempt even the "listed soldiers of the inhabetence" from payment.

[1745.] The town this year voted to pay an annual salary of fifteen shillings to the town treasurer, as a compensation for his services.

The committee appointed in 1744 to receive the town money from the constables, and to settle all the accounts of the town, having made no report of their doings subsequent to the report of December of that year, the selectmen were directed to call them to an account, and to ascertain what money had been received and disbursed by them and what remained due to the town, and to report at the next town meeting.

[1746.] The selectmen were unable to make any settlement of the financial affairs of the town with the committee who had been appointed as receivers, and accordingly in February, 1746, "Robert Finney was elected a Commissioner to the next Court of General Sessions in order to get the Report of the Committee chosen to end all debates and adjust all accounts appertaining to the town since it has been erected into a town." Finney was to be allowed twelve shillings per day for his services. The purpose for which he was appointed, as stated in the vote of election given above, may have been to obtain a writ of mandamus against the town committee to compel them to do their duty, or it may have been to have a decision upon the merits of the question made by the Court.

At this same meeting, David Dunning was elected a commissioner to appear at the General Court in Boston, to prefer a petition in

[1] *Pejepscot Papers.*

behalf of the town. He was to receive his instructions from a committee consisting of Robert Spear, David Giveen, and Robert Finney, and was to receive £5 for his services and to be allowed £4 for his expenses. In the absence of any evidence in the matter, it is to be presumed that the object of the petition was the same as of the one presented the next year, and that, for some reason, this petition was never presented, or if presented was not acted upon.

The town also voted at this meeting to raise no money for current expenses, until that already assessed had been paid in by the constables to the receivers appointed by the town.

[1747.] At the annual meeting in March, 1747, the town voted "to apply to the General Court for protection" against the Indians, and David Dunning was chosen to prepare a petition in behalf of the town, under instructions from Ebenezer Stanwood, John Getchel, and Thomas Skolfield. He was to receive £9 for his services. This petition was, in all probability, favorably considered by the General Court, as the whole region from Wells to Topsham was at this time infested with savages.[1] At all events, it was either considered and acted upon, or else previous action on the matter had already been taken, for in May following, Captain Jordan was stationed at Topsham with thirty men.[2]

[1748.] The town, at its annual meeting in March, 1748, voted to send a petition, signed by the selectmen in behalf of the town, to the General Court, requesting to have Western men sent there for soldiers, instead of calling upon the inhabitants of Brunswick and its vicinity.

The financial affairs of the town were still in an unsettled condition, and consequently a committee was chosen at a special town meeting held in May, "to shew[3] the Receiver and Treasurer that refuse to pay in the town's money according to vote of the town, and said committee is instructed to make up accounts with all or any person who have any legal demands on the town."

The town, moreover, at this meeting chose Deacon Samuel Hinkley, Lieutenant Ebenezer Stanwood, and Robert Finney a committee to appear in behalf of the town at the quarter sessions for the county of York, to be held in October following, "to recover the town's legal debts and prosecute any person in whose hands the town's money may be found not paid out in the town's legal debts."

In October of this year the selectmen assessed £50 on the citizens as a town fund, and to pay a premium for wolves' heads.

---

[1] *Williamson, History of Maine*, 2, *p.* 252. [2] *Smith's Journal, p.* 129.

[3] *i. e., to instruct.*

[1749.] The town, at a special meeting in January, 1749, appointed Ensign William Vincent to inspect the fishery at Brunswick and to regulate the same according to instructions from the selectmen.

A proposition was also made at this time to petition the General Court for the annexation to Brunswick of the precinct of Topsham. The question was laid on the table for consideration at a future meeting.

[1750.] At the annual meeting in March, 1750, the town voted a present of £40, old tenor, to Reverend Mr. Dunlap, and voted to take up a contribution four times a year for the support of the Widow Mitchell. In May the town voted to raise £40, *lawful money*, for Reverend Mr. Dunlap. £26 13*s*. 4*d*. of this amount was to pay his salary and the balance to be a gratuity. It was also voted to raise £21 6*s*. 0*d*., lawful money, of which £13 6*s*. 8*d*. was for Mr. Dunlap's settlement, £5 6*s*. 8*d*. to make good the town stock of ammunition, and £2 13*s*. 4*d*. for other town expenses. The town declined this year to raise any money for a schoolmaster.

[1751.] At a town meeting in February, 1751, a committee was appointed to have the care and control of the common lands of the town, with authority to assess damages upon trespassers and to prosecute all such claims should recourse to law become necessary. It was also voted to add £13 6*s*. 8*d*. lawful money, to the salary of Reverend Mr. Dunlap, "providing he will take his pay in such specie as the town can pay him in at the market price, otherwise Mr. Dunlap must adhere to his first agreement with the town."

A bounty of £1 was offered by the town for each wolf killed by traps or pits within the limits of the town. It was also voted to raise £40, lawful money, in such specie as the town can produce in *lumber*, at the market price, and also to raise £8 in cash, to pay the minister's salary, £3 6*s*. 8*d*. for "Granny Mitchell," and £4 13*s*. 4*d*. for town expenses.

[1752.] At the annual town meeting £4 was voted to Robert Smart "for building a pair of stocks and whipping-post at our meeting house."

This year the town records begin to be double dated, in consequence of an Act of Parliament adopting the new style of reckoning time. As the difference between the old and new methods of reckoning time is now so generally understood, it is unnecessary here to enter into any explanation of the matter. The records appear to be double dated from the first, but this is probably due to the interpolation of the second dates by some later town clerk. The previous dates in this book have all been old style, but what follow will all be according to the new style.

[1753.] At the annual town meeting in March, 1753, a vote was passed to petition the General Court for power to tax the lands in town belonging to non-resident proprietors, unless they should speedily grant some satisfactory assistance to the inhabitants to enable them "to finish the Meeting house, settle the Minister and defray other publick charges." This vote was reconsidered at the October meeting, and it was then voted to delay action upon it until the following spring. At this October meeting Captain David Dunning was appointed a commissioner, in behalf of the town, to join the other towns in the county in signing a petition to have the county divided.

The town also voted to raise £10, in lawful money, for a supply of ammunition and £20, old tenor, for the relief of Widow Mitchell.

The ratable polls in Brunswick at this time were about eighty.[1]

[1754.] The town, in 1754, voted to raise £55 for current expenses, "to be paid in lumber landed in Boston on or before September 1st."

At the annual meeting in March, the question of taxing the lands of non-resident proprietors again came up, but the town then voted not to petition the General Court, at that time, for power to assess these lands, on account of the anticipation of a war. In September, however, the town voted that their representative should prefer such a petition to the General Court, and suitable instructions were accordingly given, October 1st, to John Minot, Esquire, by a committee consisting of Samuel Hinkley, David Dunning, James Thompson, and Samuel Stanwood, who were appointed for that purpose.

Those instructions were, in brief, that he should, with the assistance of an able lawyer, draw up a petition to the General Court, in which it should be stated that the town had undergone much difficulty and its settlement been retarded by reason "of the wars and incursions of the enemy"; that the town had not equal privileges with other towns, which could sell or grant vacant lands for public uses, whereas those who were settled upon lands derived from proprietors could not do so. For this reason, the petition was to state further that the town prayed "for power to rate the non-resident Proprietors' land for the sum of £200 for the following uses."

1. For finishing the meeting-house.
2. For the settlement of their minister.
3. For establishing a school in the town.

---

[1] *Memorandum on cover of Brunswick Records, in Pejepscot Collection.*

4. To help clear and keep good the county road through the proprietors' lands; which, "if it should be insisted upon to make it a complete road would take the bigger part of said money."

The representative was also instructed that in case the proprietors would give security for the payment of £100 for the above-mentioned uses, he was authorized to withdraw his petition.[1]

[1755.] In 1755 the town passed the following votes: —

To pay John Orr £1, lawful money, "for collecting the Province rate at Topsham for 1752," and to pay William Spear an annual salary of 6*s*. "for sweeping the meeting-house, locking doors, and taking care of the key."

The town decided not to petition the General Court for the annexation of Topsham this year.

The vote of the town in 1744, in regard to taxing soldiers, seems not to have been fully enforced, as instructions were this year given to the *former* constables of the town to proceed according to law to collect the taxes which had been assessed upon the officers and soldiers belonging to Fort George. Against this action of the town John Orr, John Smart, James Ellet, Samuel Clark, and Thomas Skolfield entered their dissent and protest.

The selectmen this year sent the following petition to the General Court, applying for military relief: —

"*PROVINCE OF THE MASSACHUSETTS BAY.*

"TO HIS EXCELLENCY WILLIAM SHIRLEY ESQ. CAPTAIN GENERAL AND COMMANDER IN CHIEF OF SAID PROVINCE, THE HON^{BLE} HIS MAJESTYS COUNCILL, AND HOUSE OF REPRESENTATIVES IN GENERAL COURT ASSEMBLED AUGUST 11TH 1756.

THE MEMORIAL OF THE SELECTMEN OF THE TOWN OF BRUNSWICK

HUMBLY SHEWETH,

"That in Consequence of a Memorial presented to this Court at their Sessions in May last representing the exposed circumstances of said Town by reason of the Enemy, this Hon^{d} Court was pleased to order 14 men out of Capt. Samuel Goodwin's Company to scout on the back of the Inhabitants from Fort George to Maquoit untill the further Order of this Court; the Benefitt of which they enjoyed but a very short time, not more than two weeks, when the aforesaid Order was superceeded on the Petition of Thomas Hancock Esq and others and

---

[1] *Pejepscot Papers.*

on the 7th July it was ordered by this Court that said 14 men be returned to said Company again by which means the Inhabitants at this Critical Season of their Husbandry are greatly exposed to the Incursions of the Indian enemy. As the former Memorial was in behalf of a Garrison situate near the meeting house on the main road from Maquoit necessary for the entertainment of Expresses, or any other Travellers in time of Warr kept by Mr Robert Speer who is greatly advanced in age, and very decrepid, the support of which Garrison would be a kind of Barrier to the Inhabitants, and a great Security to the House of Publick Worship, these & many other reasons that might be urged in favour of said Garrison, induced your Memorialists then to apply to this Hond Court for such Relief as should in their Wisdom seem meet.

"And we now again humbly apply ourselves to this Hond Court in behalf of said Town, and the aforesd Garrison that they would be pleased to give such further Direction for their Relief as that they may be enabled to pursue their Husbandry without that Danger to which they might otherwise be exposed.

"And your Memorialists as in Duty bound Shall ever pray &c.[1]

"THOMAS SKOLFIELD, } *Selectmen of*
SAM'L STANWOOD, } *Brunswick.*"

[1757.] In February, 1757, John Getchell and Captain David Dunning were appointed commissioners "to represent to the Colonel of this Regiment the difficult circumstances of this town, and to try for an abatement of the men he has sent for." This regiment was Colonel Ezekiel Cushing's at Falmouth.[2]

The first set of weights and measures for sealing purposes was purchased this year.

The number of polls in Brunswick at this time was ninety-two, and in the adjacent region it was eighty-one, of which number thirty-two were in that portion of Harpswell included within the boundary lines of North Yarmouth and Brunswick, and forty-nine were in Topsham.[3]

[1758.] This year the selectmen were instructed by the town "to acquaint the Honorable Board for levelling the province tax, concerning the adjacents that are taken of us." Harpswell was this year incorporated as a distinct town.

[1760.] In compliance with an order of the General Court, a committee was chosen by the town, in 1760, to communicate to the session

---

[1] *Pejepscot Papers.* [2] *Massachusetts Records, Vol.* 21. [3] *Pejepscot Papers.*

of the legislature to be held in Boston, on the first Tuesday of May, 1761, their desire that Brunswick might be comprehended in the new county of which it was desired that Falmouth might be the shire town. The various petitions sent in had the desired effect, and on June 19th, of this year, the county of York was divided into three counties, the most western one retaining the name of York, and the other two being named Cumberland and Lincoln, of which the latter was the most eastern. The dividing line between these two last commenced at the mouth of the New Meadows River, extended up that river to Stevens's Carrying-Place at its head, thence to and upon Merry-meeting Bay, and up the Androscoggin thirty miles. Owing to this division, Topsham came into Lincoln County.

It was voted this year that hereafter the eastern and western portions of the town "repair their own roads, and that the eastern end of the great pitch pine plains be the partition between each end of the town." Three shillings per day was allowed for men, and two shillings for each yoke of oxen employed upon the roads. £26 13*s*. 4*d*. was raised this year for the schoolmaster, and £45 for a town stock of ammunition.

[1761.] John Minot was requested by the town this year to urge upon the General Court the propriety of taxing the lands of non-residents, but he was unable to accomplish anything, because, as he says in a letter to "Gentlemen and neighbors," dated May 22, "upon the Carpet there was nothing but the Bloody Sword drawn forth by our bitter enemys & no man living then could give any judgment where or how things would end."[1]

The petition of the selectmen in 1760, desiring the General Court to include Brunswick in the new county to be established, was considered in council, June 16, and dismissed, it appearing that the whole town was already in the county of Cumberland.[2]

[1762.] A petition from a number of the residents at New Meadows, for separation from the western part of Brunswick, was this year presented to the General Court, and the following letter was sent to the proprietors: —

"BOSTON, May ye 14th, 1762

"GENTLEMEN

"I with a number of the Inhabitance of Brunswick Have Pettitioned the Court to have that Part of said town Called New Meadows, made

[1] *Pejepscot Papers.* [2] *Ibid.*

into a seperate Distrect — for we find by Longe expereance that it is Imposable for us to Injoy the preaching of the Gosple while togather — We likewise want to be Joyned to the Lower County as we can then attend Court with Greater ease and less Charge — as we have had our Lands from you, gentlemen, and as I Have endevored to serve the Intrest of your Company so far as it was in my power; and am ready still to do so — and tho' it was but Lettel I Could or Can do to serve you — yet Gentlemen I have some reason to Hope that you will look on my Honest Intentions to serve you to be equal to the thing, shall therefore request of you Gentlemen who have a Seat in the general Court to use your Intrest in favor of said Pettition, and you Gentlemen that Have no Seat in that Honourable House, I must also beg of you not to say anything to its predigue. In the mean while Gentlemen I remain

"Your most obedient Humble Servant

"AARON HINKLEY.[1]

"TO BELCHER NOYES ESQ.
Clerk of the Pejepscot Company
to be communicated"

[1763.] The town in 1763 again voted to petition the General Court to have the lands of non-resident proprietors taxed, and also that this petition should be signed by the selectmen and town clerk, and that some gentleman in Boston should be employed to present it and to speak in behalf of the town. It was also voted to set off and sell thirteen pews on the floor, and sixteen pews in the gallery, of the west meeting-house, "the oldest inhabitants that have no pews to have the preference in buying said pews," and the proceeds of the sale to go towards defraying the expenses of repairing and finishing the meeting-house.

[1766.] January 13, 1766, John Miller, his wife Jane, and his daughter Margret, and their families, were warned to leave town, in accordance with law, to prevent the possibility of their coming upon the town for assistance. Since this was, doubtless, the Reverend Mr. Miller who was settled three or four years before over the First Parish, it shows that the town paid no respect to persons in this matter, but served all alike who had no visible pecuniary means of support. This law was enforced here as late as 1792.

[1767.] The town this year voted to pay Mr. Hunt three dollars for building a new pair of stocks. This is the first mention made of *dollars* in the town records.

---

[1] *Pejepscot Papers.*

The town also voted sixteen shillings per year for a sexton for the west meeting-house, and two dollars per year for one for the east meeting-house.

[1768.] At a meeting held September 22d, Aaron Hinkley was elected a delegate from Brunswick "to join the committee at Boston in order to consult and advise such measures as should be thought best for the peace and safety of his Majesty's subjects in this Province," and Thomas Skolfield, Isaac Snow, Captain Dunning, Samuel Thompson, and William Woodside, Jr., were appointed a committee to furnish him with instructions. By the term "committee" in the above extract from the records must be meant the Provincial Convention of delegates, which commenced its session that very day at Boston, in place of the General Court, which the governor had refused to convene without the consent of his Majesty, the king. The invitation to send a delegate from Brunswick was not received until two days before the convention met.[1]

[1771.] In 1771 Aaron Hinkley, Isaac Snow, and Thomas Skolfield were chosen a committee "to answer the petition that the selectmen of Topsham put into the General Court in May last." This petition was to have the boundary line between the two towns so defined as to give the islands in the river to Topsham.

[1774.] The selectmen were instructed, in 1774, to lay out the 1,000 acres of Commons, and have a plan made of the same, in order that a deed of it could be obtained from the proprietors.

It was voted, at the annual meeting, to again petition the General Court for power to tax land belonging to non-residents.

At a meeting held August 3d, "the town took under consideration the difficulties of the Province, and unanimously agreed to the non-importing of English goods, until the matter in dispute between Great Britain and her colonies be reconciled."

The selectmen were directed to ascertain the quantity of ammunition the town had in stock, and to purchase, if necessary, a new supply. The port of Boston having been closed by Act of Parliament on account of the seizure of the tea, it was thought best to assist that town by subscription.

At a meeting held on the seventeenth of September, Captain Moulton, Samuel Stanwood, and Samuel Thompson were chosen a committee "to meet the Falmouth committee that are to meet at Falmouth, on Wednesday, the twenty-first day of September, instant, to consider

---

[1] *McKeen, Manuscript Lecture.*

what measures will be best to adopt for the good of the country and town."

At a meeting of the town held on the seventeenth of November, the proceedings of the Continental Congress and of the Provincial Congress were read. The Provincial Congress had passed a resolution which was, in substance, that the inhabitants of the Province should immediately provide themselves with arms and ammunition, and should use their utmost diligence to perfect themselves in military skill; and if any town was not provided with a full stock of ammunition, according to law, that the selectmen of such town should take effectual care without delay to provide the same.[1] The Provincial Congress also appointed Henry Gardner, Esquire, of Stow, receiver-general of all moneys for the use of the Province.[2]

The town, accordingly, adopted a resolution, "that it be our opinion that it is very proper to choose Militia officers in this town forthwith and act agreeably to the directions in the Provincial Congress." An election of militia officers then took place; Samuel Thompson being chosen captain, Robert Dunning, lieutenant, Thomas Thompson, ensign, and Stephen Getchell, clerk. A resolution was also adopted, "That the money voted in May last by our representatives be paid in to Henry Gardner, Esq., of Stow, and that, if any other or former collectors have any Province money in their hands that they pay the same to the said Henry Gardner, Esq."

Brunswick was represented in the Provincial Congress by Samuel Thompson.

The Continental Congress at Philadelphia, on the twentieth of October, entered into an association or agreement, providing for the non-importation of goods, wares, or merchandise from Great Britain, Ireland, or other of the British possessions; also, providing for the non-consumption of such articles, and for the non-exportation of home products. There were also articles abolishing the slave-trade; providing for improvement in the breed of sheep, and to prevent their being killed, unnecessarily, for food; encouraging frugality, economy, and industry, and looking to the promotion of agriculture, the arts, and manufactures in this country, and discountenancing every species of extravagance; guarding against extortion on the part of traders on account of the scarcity of goods, etc. The eleventh article, to which allusion is made below, was, in substance, that a committee should be chosen in every town to observe the conduct of all persons, and when

---

[1] *American Archives, Fourth Series, Vol.* 1, *p.* 852. [2] *Ibid*, *p.* 851.

the committee were satisfied that any person had violated the provisions of the agreement, the truth should be published in the *Gazette*, " to the end that all such foes to the rights of British Americans may be publicly known & universally contemned, as the enemies of American Liberty: and thenceforth we will break off all dealings with him or her." [1] These proceedings having been read in full to the meeting, the town resolved, " that the proceedings of the Grand Congress be adopted and much applauded by this town, quite unanimous," and Tobias Ham, Nathaniel Larrabee, James Curtis, Samuel Stanwood, Ebenezer Stanwood, and Thomas Thompson were elected " a committee to see to the due observance of the eleventh article in the proceedings of the Grand Congress."

There is on file a warrant of this year, in his Majesty's name, calling the voters to choose a representative to the legislature at Salem, but no meeting was held, as the citizens no longer recognized the royal authority.[2]

[1775.] At a meeting of the town held January 10, 1775, the proceedings of the Provincial Congress, at Concord, in December, were unanimously approved, with the exception of the article relating to " storing the goods after the tenth of October next," in regard to which article the vote was seventy-nine yeas and twelve nays.

A vote was also passed " that if a Number out of the several companies of militia should list as minute men," then each town ought " to make them such reasonable satisfaction as shall be thought proper by the town where they belong " Samuel Thompson, who was now a colonel, was elected as delegate to the Provincial Congress.

At a meeting held March 9, Benjamin Stone, Nathaniel Larrabee, James Curtis, Deacon Stanwood, and Aaron Hinkley, Esquire, were elected " a Committee of safety to consult what they shall think best at this crisis and make report at the adjournment of this meeting."

At a meeting held six days later, in the west meeting-house, the town voted " to pay Henry Gardner Esq. all the Province Money in the hands of the collectors of the town, agreeable to the advice of our Congress."

At a meeting held April 27, Aaron Hinkley, Deacon Samuel Stanwood, Benjamin Stone, Captain Curtis, and Captain William Stanwood, Jr., were chosen a Committee of Correspondence and also a Committee of Supplies, to provide ammunition and whatever else was thought necessary for the safety of the town.

---

[1] *American Archives, Fourth Series, Vol.* 1, *p.* 915. [2] *Pejepscot Papers.*

At a subsequent meeting, Reverend John Miller, Benjamin Rideout, Gideon Owens, Joseph Melcher, Joseph Allen, Colonel Samuel Thomson, David Brown, George Hayden, Benjamin Hinkley, and Benjamin Larrabee were added to "the Committee of Inspection," as the Committee of Safety was also designated. Samuel Thompson was elected delegate to the Provincial Congress, from Brunswick and Harpswell, and he was to serve for one year after the last Wednesday in the following May. The selectmen were instructed to inform the Committee on Supplies why the town did not comply with their request in regard to coats, etc., for the army.

At a meeting held on the fourth Tuesday in May, it was voted that the powder and flints provided by the town should be equally divided to each man in town, and the town was to pay the cost of procuring the powder; and "if the men who enlist under Captain Curtis should be called away, for them to carry their ammunition with them." A patrol was established this year, under the direction of the officers of the militia.

In consequence of the public distress and the grievousness of the taxes, Reverend Mr. Miller and Mr. John Farren, the schoolmaster, voluntarily gave up a portion of their salaries, and Thomas Skolfield and Nathaniel Larrabee, two of the selectmen, served the town in that capacity gratuitously.

[1776.] At the annual meeting in March, 1776, James Curtis, Samuel Stanwood, Thomas Thompson, Andrew Dunning, and Nathaniel Larrabee were chosen a Committee "of Correspondence, Inspection and Safety."

At a subsequent meeting, held May 27, it was voted "to send a petition to the Great and General Court," and the selectmen, together with the Committee of Correspondence and Samuel Thompson, now a brigadier-general, Thomas Skolfield, and Thomas Cotton, were elected a committee to draft the petition. What the object of this petition was has not been ascertained. Deacon Samuel Stanwood was chosen a commissioner to present this petition at the General Court.

A meeting was held May 31st at which "It was unanimously voted that if the Honourable Congress should, for the safety of the United Colonies, Declare themselves Independent of the King of Great Britain, that they will solemnly engage with their lives and fortunes to support the Congress in that measure." The selectmen were instructed to deliver the powder that was brought by Brigadier Thompson to the captains of the militia, for them to deliver to the men, when necessary. Brigadier Thompson received fifty, and Deacon Samuel

Stanwood thirty-nine votes for representative to the General Court, and the town then voted to send them both, — they agreeing to serve for half-fees.

At a meeting held December 24th, "after due consideration on a Resolve of the Great and General Court of this State, dated September 17, 1776," it was voted, "That the present House of Representatives of this State, with the Council, should consult and agree on some form of Government that shall most conduce to the safety, peace, and happiness of this State in all after generations."

Brigadier Samuel Thompson was chosen to represent the wishes of the town at the General Court, agreeably to the above-mentioned resolve.

[1777.] At a special town meeting, held in February, 1777, Deacon Snow and Captain Robert Dunning were elected to fill the places of Deacon Stanwood and Captain Curtis, and at the annual meeting, March 4, Major Nathaniel Larrabee, Doctor Samuel Dunken, Captain Robert Dunning, Robert Spear, and Andrew Dunning were chosen a Committee of Correspondence, etc.

At a meeting held May 22, Thomas Skolfield was elected a recognizee, *i. e.*, an officer empowered to take recognizances. The selectmen were instructed to execute the law "concerning monopoly and oppression." Notwithstanding the exciting and trying circumstances connected with the war of Revolution then going on, the citizens were not unmindful of the interests of education, for the town voted to have a school this year and to pay a schoolmaster £30. A committee was at this time appointed to procure a teacher.

At a meeting held on the twenty-seventh day of November, in pursuance of an Act of the General Court, entitled "An Act for supplying the Families of the Soldiers in the Continental Service," the town voted to supply the families of the men thus engaged, agreeably to the aforesaid resolve. For this purpose, £20 were voted and Benjamin Stone, Samuel Stanwood, James Curtis, Nathaniel Larrabee, and Robert Dunning were elected a committee to attend to its disbursement.

[1778.] At the annual meeting of the town in March, 1778, it was voted to allow Mr. Josiah Simpson eight pounds and four shillings for his service in carrying the baggage of twenty-two men from Brunswick to Boston the previous year. It was also voted "to supply the wives of those men that went for this town into the Continental army, by way of subscription, — they to be allowed the market price for s^{d} articles that they shall find for s^{d} use." Lieutenant Thomas Berry, Nicholas Rideout, Captain Robert Dunning, John Dunning, and

William Woodside were elected as Committee of Correspondence, etc.

The proprietors made an agreement with Aaron Hinkley for him to survey the town Commons. This he had done, but the survey differed so much from the plan made by James Scales, "and the inhabitants made so much uneasiness about it," that it was laid one side, and the Scales plan was accepted. The proprietors complain, however, of the neglect of the selectmen in the matter.[1] This explains why, at a subsequent meeting, held May 12, the town voted to have the Commons surveyed, but laid upon the table till the next meeting the clause in the warrant relative to applying to the proprietors for a deed. At this meeting, Aaron Hinkley, William Stanwood, and Andrew Dunning were chosen to consult as to the best method for supporting the families of soldiers.

"Then the votes were brought in for the proposed form of government, and there appeared to be for said form three, and against said form seventy five." This vote was in regard to a proposed new constitution for the Commonwealth of Massachusetts, which was not ratified by the towns in consequence of several serious defects contained in it.

At a meeting held June 2, Aaron Hinkley, William Stanwood, Jr., and Captain Curtis were chosen "to give our Representative Instructions." What these instructions were has not been ascertained. A vote was also passed at this meeting that the one hundred and fifty-eight dollars given, as an additional bounty, to the five men who went into the service, agreeably to a resolve of the General Court, of April 20, 1778, should be paid by a tax on the polls and estates of the west end of the town. The only explanation of this vote which we can suggest is, that the east end of the town may have furnished the five men called for, and should therefore be exempt from paying any bounty.

At a meeting held on the tenth of June, the town voted "to lay out the Commons agreeable to the minutes that were read, viz., S^d Commons to be bounded on the head of Middle Bay lots and to extend northerly between and adjoining upon the lots that front upon the twelve rod road and the lots that front upon Mericonege marshes, and upon the lots that front upon New Meadows river, until 1,000 acres be completed." Captain James Thompson protested against this vote, probably for fear lest the Commons might encroach upon his lot. A committee was chosen, however, to lay out the land in conformity with this vote, and Stephen Getchell was chosen surveyor.

---

[1] *Brunswick Records, in Pejepscot Collection.*

At a meeting held on the 10th of September, it was voted "that such shirts as are fit to be sent to our brethren in the army be 48/ each; that good shoes for said service be 54/, each pair; that good stockings for said service be 30/, each pair."

At a meeting held December 25, the town voted to accept of the survey of the Commons as laid out by the committee chosen the previous May, but not to accept a deed of them from Noyes, if made according to Hinkley's survey. A committee was chosen to consult with the proprietors' agent in regard to the matter.

[1779.] Brigadier Thompson, William Stanwood, and Doctor Dunken were chosen a committee to supply the families of those men who went from this town into the Continental service with such necessaries as they might need. The town also voted an appropriation of £200 for that purpose. James Elliot, Jr., Samuel Dunlap, Samuel Stanwood, Jr., Thomas Godfrey, and Stephen Pennell were chosen a Committee of Correspondence, Inspection, and Safety.

The selectmen were, at this meeting, instructed to procure a deed of the Commons, and the committee chosen to lay out the Commons were directed to complete their work as speedily as possibly. The selectmen were also instructed to take effectual means to secure, for the benefit of the town, the growth of lumber on the Commons.

Thomas Pennell was allowed £4 8*s*., "it being for so much *Counterfeit Money* he took in part of his tax in the year 1776."

Four prisoners — probably British soldiers — were taken care of in Brunswick this year, and the town consequently voted the following sums as compensation to those having charge of them: —

	£	s.	d.
To Captain Dunlap	£6	8*s*.	0*d*.
" " Thompson	4	4	0
" Lieutenant Berry	1	4	0
" Mr. John Dunning	2	14	0

The sum of three pounds was also voted to Jacob Anderson for services in carrying shirts, shoes, and stockings to Portland.

At a special meeting in August, the town voted its approval of the transactions of the convention held at Concord on the fourteenth of July preceding. The object of that convention was to establish a State price-current, and to adopt other measures to prevent monopoly, extortion, and unfair dealing, and spirited resolutions were passed, fixing the prices of several articles of merchandise.[1]

---

[1] *History of Concord, Mass.*, p. 122.

Aaron Hinkley, William Stanwood, Thomas Skolfield, Joseph Curtis, and Deacon Stanwood were chosen a committee "to set the prices on the articles in the town and carry the resolution into effect." They were also directed to inform the committee of the town of Boston concerning the action taken in this matter by Brunswick.

At a meeting on the ninth of November, an account of the proceedings of the convention held at Concord in the previous month was read, and it was thereupon unanimously voted, "to stand by the proceedings of said convention," and Aaron Hinkley, Deacon Stanwood, Thomas Skolfield, Captain Curtis, and Captain William Stanwood were elected a committee "to see said resolutions put into execution." The convention referred to was held at Concord on the sixth of October, at which a revision of the price-current adopted at the July convention was made, and resolutions were passed relating to trade, currency, etc. County and town meetings were recommended to carry these resolutions into effect.[1]

[1780.] At the annual meeting in March, 1780, the following appropriations were voted: The sum of $4,050 for highways, and to pay out of this thirty dollars per day for the labor of each man, twenty-five dollars for each pair of oxen, and five dollars for each cart, £12 to William Spear for his services for two years as sexton of the west meeting-house, and twenty-five dollars per day as compensation to the selectmen, "they to find themselves and paper."

The town at this time elected Brigadier Thompson as its agent to the General Court, in conformity with a resolve of that body, passed December 4, 1779.

At a meeting held May 15th, the town postponed voting in regard to a change of the State Constitution until the next meeting. Probably the next meeting of the town occurred too late for the vote of Brunswick to have any effect, since no vote of the kind was recorded at any subsequent meeting this year.

About this time a circular letter was received from Jere Powell, President of the General Assembly of Massachusetts Bay, desiring, in urgent terms, the town to furnish its proportion of blankets needed for the army at once,[2] as called for, amongst other things, by a resolve of that body passed the previous year.

The town accordingly voted to furnish the blankets and other articles and "to allow for each pair of good shoes, such as the agent will receive so much of the present currency as will purchase seven

---

[1] *History of Concord, Mass*, *p.* 122. [2] *Pejepscot Papers.*

pecks of Indian corn, and for stockings of the like quality, the value of five pecks of corn, and for shirts the same price as of shoes, and for blankets — them that are good — the value of four bushels in said currency."

At a meeting held September 4th, the town cast its first vote for governor of the Commonwealth of Massachusetts, lieutenant-governor, and senator. Whom the town voted for as governor is not mentioned, but undoubtedly it was John Hancock. Honorable Samuel Adams received a majority of eleven votes as lieutenant-governor, and John Lewis, Esquire, fourteen votes as senator. Honorable James Bowdoin received three votes as lieutenant-governor.

At a meeting in October, Brigadier Thompson, Doctor Dunken, and John Given were chosen as a committee to procure the beef which had been demanded by the General Court for the supply of the army. They were instructed that, if they were unable to procure the whole amount, they should, with the selectmen, make known to the General Court the reasons why they were unable to furnish all, and were authorized to make up the deficiency in the amount, in money. The selectmen were instructed to assess sufficient to cover the amount paid out by this committee.

[1781.] At the annual meeting in March, 1781, the selectmen were directed to inform the General Court that the resolve of December 4, 1780, concerning beef, was not received in season for the town to comply with its requirements.

At a meeting held on the nineteenth of July, the town voted to comply with the last requisition of the General Court, in regard to furnishing beef for the army, and to raise £204, cash, to procure the beef. A committee was also chosen to obtain the beef.

At a meeting held on the twenty-fifth of December, Samuel Stanwood, Captain William Stanwood, Jr., William Woodside, Aaron Hinkley, Doctor Samuel Dunken, and Captain James Curtis were chosen a committee to prepare a petition to the General Court, "concerning our present circumstances and our inability of paying our taxes in specie, and to lay the petition before our March meeting, for approbation or amendment."

[1782.] The above-mentioned petition was presented to the town at its annual meeting in March, 1782, and adopted. At this meeting Samuel Woodward, Jacob Anderson, and Samuel Stanwood, Jr., were chosen a Committee of Correspondence, Inspection, and Safety. This was the last time such a committee was raised by the town.

At a meeting in June, it was voted that "the several classes in this town procure the three men called for by the General Court without delay." To promote the enlistment of soldiers, the town was divided into districts, which are designated above as "classes."

Wolves must have become very troublesome at this time, for the town, at this meeting, offered a bounty of 20*s*. for each and every grown wolf killed within its limits, and 40*s*. to every person who would make pits or traps for their destruction.

On January 2, 1783, the following petition to have the town excused from paying a fine, for not furnishing the three men called for in 1782, was presented to the legislature by a committee of the town: —

"TO THE HONOURABLE THE SENATE & HONOURABLE HOUSE OF REPRESENTATIVES OF THE COMMONWEALTH OF MASSACUSETTS IN GENERAL COURT TO BE ASSEMBLED ON THE LAST WEDNESDAY OF JANUARY 1783.

"THE PETITION OF US SUBSCRIBERS (BEING A COMMITTEE CHOSEN BY THE FREE HOLDERS AND OTHER INHABITANTS OF THIS TOWN OF BRUNSWICK IN THE COUNTY OF CUMBERLAND REGULARLY ASSEMBLED),

HUMBLY SHEWETH.

"That whereas the Inhabitants of this Town have exerted themselves to the utmost of their power, in answering all requisitions that has been required of them During the present warr, but could not procure the last three men which was required for want of money; and whereas we understand that we have been overated in our taxations for some years past, both for men, money, & Beef, we Humbly pray y^r^ Hon^rs^ to Excuse us from the fine that is laid on us for said three men — Your Hon^rs^ cannot be Ignorant of our Circumstances in these parts — How our Coast is (almost continually) Invested with the Enemy Depriving us of our Vessels & Substance, So as we cannot gett to markett such commodities as we could spare. We are well assured that the farr Greater part of the Inhabitants here would be willing to suffer, and has suffered, in order to help on the present occation but for want of a Markett Cash is exceeding scarce among us — and many has & are moving back into the wilderness, because they cannot pay their taxes, therefore we Humbly pray that we may be eased of the above mentioned fine but as for the average part we mean to endeavour to pay as soon as possible but If executions should be issued out against us suddently, it would (we fear) Discourage the poor Inhabitants very much, therefore Relying on your Hon^rs^ great wisdom, to consider our Circumstances, not Doubting but that you will Endeavour to promote our Wellfare & Happiness in these parts as well as in the other parts of this commonwealth, And your Humble Petitioners as in Duty bound shall ever pray.[1]

"THOS. SKOLFIELD
JAMES CURTIS
SAM'LL STANDWOOD
NATH'L LARRABEE } *Committee.*

"BRUNSWICK, Jany 2d 1783."

In answer to this petition the legislature passed a resolve, which was approved by the governor, excusing the town from payment of any fine, provided they would pay into the treasury of the Commonwealth the sum of £185 4*s* 1½*d*., which was the average price paid for the enlistment of three men.[2]

The town this year voted to pay Brigadier Thompson £30 16*s*. 3*d*. for his services as delegate to the Provincial Congress in the years 1774 and 1775. Reverend Mr. Miller, Nathaniel Larrabee, Thomas Skolfield, Deacon Dunning, and Captain Gross were chosen a committee to answer a letter which had been received from the Committee of Correspondence of Boston. Their answer was as follows: —

"At a legal Town meeting held in Brunswick, on Thursday, the 26th of June, 1783, in answer to your letter respecting the return of the Refugees and Conspirators who endeavored to deprive us of our rights and privileges by joining with the King of Great Britain, it is the unanimous opinion of this town that they ought never to be suffered to return but to be excluded from having lot or portion in any of the United States of America."

November 20th, of this year, the Pejepscot proprietors gave to the town a deed of the town Commons. (See chapter on Public Lands, Roads, etc.)

[1784.] At the annual meeting in March, 1784, the town voted to take no action upon the article in the warrant concerning paying Brigadier Thompson's demands for expenses incurred in hiring men to serve in the army in the year 1781. He had probably acted in the matter on his own responsibility, and the town did not consider itself legally bound to repay him. The selectmen were, at this time, instructed to take proper care of the town Commons, and to dispose of the lumber on them as they might think to be for the best advantage of the town.

[1785.] In 1785 William Owen was elected representative to the General Court, and it was voted that in case that body refused to receive him in that capacity, he was to act as the town's agent to

[1] *Pejepscot Papers.* [2] *Massachusetts Records, Vol.* 44, 413

answer the Topsham petition. This petition was the renewal of a former one, to have the islands in the Androscoggin River annexed to Topsham.

[1786.] At a special meeting in January, 1786, a committee was chosen to petition the General Court for some abatement of the town's assessment in the next State tax. The town voted to hold every alternate town meeting at the east meeting-house. A resolution was adopted that it was the unanimous desire of the town that a canal be cut through from New Meadows River to Merrymeeting Bay. It was also voted to be the unanimous wish of the town that the counties of York, Cumberland, and Lincoln be made a separate State, and Aaron Hinkley was elected a delegate to a convention to be held at Portland (Falmouth) for the consideration of this subject.

[1787.] The town this year again voted in favor of making York, Cumberland, and Lincoln Counties a separate State.

At a meeting held on the eighteenth of December, the town voted — twenty-three to seven — "to accept of the proposed form of Government for the United States as it now stands," and Captain John Dunlap was elected a delegate to an assembly which was to meet at the State House in Boston, on the second Wednesday in January, 1788, for its adoption or rejection on the part of Massachusetts. This was the vote of Brunswick on the question of the acceptance, by the States, of the Constitution of the United States.

[1788.] At the annual town meeting in 1788, Captain John Peterson, Deacon Dunning, and Nathaniel Larrabee were chosen a committee to petition the General Court for a modification of the "Fish Act."

The town very injudiciously voted to lease one hundred acres of the Commons to William Marriner, and the selectmen were authorized to lease as much more to other parties as might be desired. A vote was passed this year, that all future town meetings should be held at the west meeting-house.

On the eighteenth of December, the town, for the first time, voted for Presidential electors, and Honorable Dummer Sewall and Samuel Freeman received a majority of the votes cast.

[1789.] The town this year decided to hold one annual meeting out of three at the east end of the town, and to hold all its other meetings alternately at the east and west ends.

[1790.] This year Benjamin Chase, his family and estate, were set off from the town of Freeport and annexed to the town of Brunswick.[1]

---

[1] *Massachusetts Special Laws*, 1, *p.* 277.

[1791] The vote for representative to Congress in November, 1790, seems to have been in some way illegal, as a special meeting was called January 25, 1791, for the purpose of another election, at which General Lithgow received a majority of eighteen votes.

At the annual meeting this year, a committee was chosen to locate a canal from Maquoit Bay to the Androscoggin River, but the town afterwards reconsidered the vote.

An address from the senators and representatives in the district of Maine was read, and the town then voted — seventy-one to twenty-five — in favor of a separate State.

[1792.] The town, in 1792, voted against the separation of the District of Maine from Massachusetts, by a vote of sixty-one to sixteen.

[1793.] In 1793 the town voted that the selectmen should be instructed to take an account of the *paper-money* in Captain Stanwood's hands, and direct him to dispose of it in the best manner he could, and deposit the proceeds in the town treasury.

The town also voted to dismiss the article in the warrant, concerning building a new meeting-house.

[1794.] In 1794, the question of making the District of Maine into a State was again voted on. The vote stood four in favor and thirty-five against so doing.

The town also voted "to allow Nathaniel Larrabee five pounds in full for his past service as town clerk, which is twenty-eight years."

The town this year voted, unanimously, "in favor of revising the Constitution." Whether it was the State or national Constitution is not specified. It was, perhaps, the latter, as the eleventh article of the Constitution of the United States was offered in Congress in 1794, and probably was not presented to the State, for ratification or rejection, much earlier than this.

[1795.] The town again, in 1795, voted — sixty-three to twenty-three — against the formation of a new State.

[1796.] "At a very full and respectable meeting of the town of Brunswick, legally assembled the fourteenth day of May, 1796, for the sole purpose of taking into consideration the state of our public affairs with respect to the treaty between Great Britain and America, voted unanimously to support the Constitution of the United States."

[1797.] The town, in 1797, again voted against the formation of a new State.

[1798.] In 1798 it was voted by the town that the selectmen should give a deed of the two hundred acres of land which the town had previously voted for the benefit of Bowdoin College, and they were instructed, if necessary, to petition the General Court for the requisite authority.

A committee was also chosen "to settle some accounts disputable between the Baptist and Congregational societies in this town."

At a meeting held in October to consider in regard to the formation of a new county from several of the towns in Cumberland and Lincoln Counties, the town voted to send Nathaniel Larrabee as a delegate to a convention to be held in Hallowell, with instructions to vote against the project of a new county, unless Brunswick could be made the shire town.

[1799.] In 1799 the town, although there was no war, raised one fifth as large an amount of money for gunpowder as it did for schools; thirty pounds being appropriated for the former and one hundred and fifty pounds for the latter.

[1802.] Appropriations by the town in 1802 were $1,000 for schools, and three hundred and fifty dollars for contingent expenses. This year men were allowed for labor on the highway one dollar per day, and sixty-six cents per day for each pair of oxen.

[1806.] The town, in 1806, appointed a committee to consult with the towns of Durham and Freeport, to see if they would join with Brunswick in building a workhouse or a poorhouse, and upon what terms they would do so.

[1807.] The records do not state what the decision of these towns was, but it may be inferred from the vote of Brunswick, in 1807, to build a house for the town poor, which should be thirty-six feet long, twenty feet wide, and two stories high. The town voted to have it located in the vicinity of Samuel Beals's,[1] and appropriated two hundred and seventy-five dollars to finish the outside.

[1808.] In 1808 the town voted that at the annual meetings in March, April, and May, every legal voter should take his seat in the meeting-house, and there remain until the moderator of the meeting should by name call upon him to come forward and put in his vote. This rather dilatory method of voting was, undoubtedly, tried as a remedy for the disorderly conduct so often prevalent at municipal meetings.

A committee was chosen this year to apply to the Pejepscot proprietors for permission to sell and dispose of the town Commons, ministry and school lots, "and marsh," the interest of such sales to be appro-

---

[1] *It stood on the lot in the rear of Mrs. Frances Owen's residence, on Federal Street.*

priated for the use of schools, or in such other way as the town should think proper. As no answer to any request of this kind can be found in the town records, or in the Pejepscot Papers or Records, it is sufficiently evident that no such permission was ever granted.

The effect of the Embargo Law, passed in Congress on the previous December, was severely felt throughout New England, and Brunswick formed no exception. The town therefore voted to present a respectful petition to the President of the United States praying him to suspend the law laying an embargo, either wholly or in part.

The selectmen were also requested to transmit to the selectmen of the town of Boston a copy of the proceedings of the town of Brunswick, and to assure them of their cordial co-operation with the inhabitants of that metropolis in any constitutional measures necessary to obtain a removal or alleviation of the grievances they suffered from a suspension of commerce.

[1809.] On January 23, 1809, the town adopted the following resolutions: —

"1st. *Resolved*, That the inhabitants of this town do consider the Act of Congress laying a permanent embargo as directly repugnant to the spirit of the Constitution of the United States and the several supplementary acts, but especially the act passed on the sixth of January inst., as alarming violations of the express provisions of that Constitution; that they tend directly to the annihilation of the revenue, while they greatly increase the expenses of the United States; to produce and daily aggravate distress among the great body of the people, and if long continued to excite domestic convulsions.

"2d. *Resolved*, That the last act of Congress designed to enforce the embargo, when its utter inutility either as a measure of precaution or as a measure of coercion, upon those belligerents whose decrees and orders effect our commerce, is acknowleged by all, forces upon us the apprehension that the embargo originated in the will of that Emperor who has declared that he will compel the United States to take part in the war either as friends or allies.

"3d. *Resolved*, That we believe it is the intention of the administration to unite with France in a war against Great Britain, a war which we deprecate as neither just, necessary or wise; since we are persuaded that all matters of dispute between the United States and that government might by sincere and honorable negotiation be amicably settled and a friendly commercial intercourse re-established on principles mutually advantageous.

"4th. *Resolved*, That the organization of a large military force in a time of peace, for purposes concealed from the people, excites in our minds the most alarming apprehensions, while the unlimited powers vested in the President and in officers of his appointment for enforcing the Embargo Laws present to our astonished view the monstrous image of a military despotism, erected by the rulers of a free republic and the property, the liberty, and even the lives of citizens placed under the control of numerous petty tyrants in defiance of the express provisions of the Constitution of the United States and in contempt of the Constitution and laws of this Commonwealth.

"5th. *Resolved*, That deeply afflicted by the evils incident to the embargo, but infinitely more distressed by these violations of our dearest rights, we will by every constitutional and peaceable measure seek the redress of our wrongs, declaring at the same time our determination to refrain from all violent opposition to the laws under which we suffer, and to discountenance such opposition in others.

"6th. *Resolved*, That we despair of obtaining relief from our distress and our fears by any further application to the President or the Congress; and that we will therefore present a respectful petition to the legislature of this Commonwealth praying that they would specially pursue such measures as they in their wisdom may judge most conducive to the redress of individual wrongs and best adapted to the portentous crisis of our public affairs.

"7th. *Resolved*, That we are ready to make any sacrifice of property and life for the preservation of the honor, the peace, and the liberty of our country.

"8th. *Resolved*, That whereas several merchants in this town have loaded their vessels by permission of the President of the United States, we do highly approve of their determination to refuse compliance with the law requiring them to unload their vessels or give heavy and unreasonable bonds."

The following *Memorial* was at the same time sent to the General Court of Massachusetts: —

"TO THE HONORABLE SENATE AND HOUSE OF REPRESENTATIVES OF THE COMMONWEALTH OF MASSACHUSETTS.

"THE MEMORIAL OF INHABITANTS OF THE TOWN OF BRUNSWICK IN THE COUNTY OF CUMBERLAND,

HUMBLY SHEWS:

"That, possessing the right to express their sentiments on the measures of government, and the state of public affairs, they are impelled by a strong sense of duty to themselves and to their posterity to exercise that privilege of freemen in the present distressed and alarming situation of the United States; considering silence at such a crisis as has now arrived as approbation of those measures which have produced it and an indication of stupid insensibility to the aggravated evils resulting from their operation.

"Your memorialists presume not to point out to your enlightened and honorable body the grievous sufferings inflicted, or the essential rights violated by the Acts of Congress laying a permanent embargo, and especially by the Act for enforcing the several embargo laws; but deeply impressed with an awful sense of the dangers in which their liberties are involved, they address you as their deputed guardians praying protection from that ruin in which those Acts, if not speedily revoked, must overwhelm them.

"Your memorialists see in those Acts no equivocal proofs of a subservient attachment to one of the belligerents and an inveterate enmity to the other, alike inconsistent with the dignity and injurious to the interests of an independent nation. That the embargo was the result of a necessity imposed by the decrees of France or by the orders in council of Great Britain we can never admit; since it was laid thirteen months after the decree of Berlin and a considerable time before the knowledge of orders in council reached the administration, and it has been acknowledged by Mr. Pinckney, Minister of the United States at London, that these orders made no part of the motives to that measure.

"Your memorialists are persuaded that had the administration been animated by that spirit and guided by that wisdom which pervaded the councils of the nation in 1794 and 1798 in respect to our foreign relations, the same happy result would have followed; but unhappily the reverse has been realized and our government have discovered a fixed determination to reject every proposal of accommodation with one of the belligerents and disposition to submit with astonishing [alacrity?] to gross and wanton violations of a solemn treaty and [to] unceasing insults from the other [belligerent.]

"Your memorialists disdain to be the apologists for the aggressions or insults of any nation, but justice compels them to declare what they fully believe that Great Britain has manifested a disposition to adjust in an amicable manner our differences with that nation, while France has not only disregarded the obligations of a treaty, but has declared her determination to compel the United States to take part in the war either as friends or allies.

"Your memorialists see with extreme [solicitude?] the organization of an extraordinary military force in a time of peace, the object of which is concealed from the people; and we declare our utter detestation of the Act of the sixth instant, designed to enforce an embargo, which even its advocates on the floor of Congress acknowledged to have produced no effect as a measure of coercion against the belligerents, while the evils affecting the people of the United States have been incalculably severe and are still increasing; and we do consider the provisions of that Act as unconstitutional, tyrannical, and oppressive in the highest degree, and are bound by the strongest obligations to resist them in every legal and constitutional way.

"We pray your Honorable Body to adopt such measures as you shall deem wise and expedient in this singularly awful crisis of public affairs."

It was also *voted* that the foregoing memorial should be signed by the moderator and town clerk, be presented to the legislature of the Commonwealth by the representative of the town, and that he be instructed to use his best endeavors to promote the object contained in said memorial.

A proposition was made this year to purchase the old meeting-house for a town-house, but it was defeated.

A committee was chosen to ascertain the *limits* of the 1,000 acres of town Commons, in order that the overplus, if any, which was given to the First Parish, might be determined.

[1811.] In 1811, the town elected Isaac Gates, Esquire, and Peter O. Alden, Esquire, as special agents to petition the legislature, in behalf of the town, for permission and authority to divide, set off, and convey to the President and Trustees of Bowdoin College the two hundred acres of land which was granted to them by a vote of the town passed May 2, 1791, and afterwards approved or confirmed by a vote of the Pejepscot proprietors.

[1812.] At a meeting held on the seventeenth of August, 1812, Jacob Abbot, Henry Putnam, Isaac Gates, Robert D. Dunning, and Jacob Anderson were chosen a committee to draft, and submit to the town, resolutions concerning "the present alarming state of national affairs." The committee reported the following, which were adopted, and the moderator and clerk instructed to sign and forward a copy of them to the President of the United States, and also one to the Portland *Gazette* for publication: —

"The people at all times, under an elective government, have the right of peaceably assembling to consult for the public good. When doomed to experience the most awful calamities that can afflict a nation, the right is not only unquestionable, but *essential* to the existence of liberty and expressly sanctioned by the Constitution. The freedom of speech and the liberty of the press and the undisturbed privileges of an individual, or united expression of sentiment, are the *vital* principles of a pure republic. The electors of rulers have a right to examine their conduct, and when measures are adopted bringing poverty and ruin in their train, and death and wretchedness in their consequences, under a pretext that the people demand them, it is the duty of every citizen to raise his voice to convince the deceived of their error and arrest the progress of destruction.

"Therefore, *Resolved*, That we view the union of the States as an *inestimable blessing* while the government is administered agreeably to the original compact, but we fear that a cruel and oppressive course of measures, and admission of new States into the Union whose inhabitants in habits and education are adverse to republican principles, will tend to *disaffect* the people and eventually dissolve the compact which has heretofore been a source of so much wealth and happiness to these States.

"*Resolved*, That we consider the declaration of war as *premature*, *unjustifiable*, and *groundless*. That it was produced by an undue attachment for the greatest tyrant and most sanguinary monster that ever disgraced the civilized world. That we consider it as directed by the finger of the same hand which has not ceased for years past to impose restrictive measures upon the commerce of the United States; in short, that we consider the declaration of war as merely the promulgation and approbation of an edict of the Court of St. Cloud.

"*Resolved*, That a treasury without money, an exposed commerce without naval protection, an army without soldiers, and a war without adequate and just cause, show the *weakness* or *wickedness* of our rulers, and tend to a direct sacrifice of everything dear to free men.

"*Resolved*, That William Widgery, member of Congress from this district, in voting for war contrary to the *known* wishes of his constituents and to the destruction of great maritime interests of New England, has added *shame* and disgrace to the good people of this district, without injury to his *own* moral or political reputation.

"*Resolved*, That we fully approve of the *minority* in Congress upon the question of war, and we pride ourselves upon having one representative from Maine who preferred the interests of his constituents to the *mandates* of the executive.

"*Resolved*, That we view with abhorrence and detestation the late *daring* and sanguinary attack upon the liberty of the press at Baltimore by a lawless and cannibal mob, and the assassination of the veterans of the Revolution and the voluntary defenders of liberty.

"*Resolved*, That we cordially approve of the sentiments expressed by our brethren in Boston, at their late town meeting, upon the same subject, and of the measures by them adopted, for the purpose of aiding the civil authority in the *prevention* and *suppression* of similar outrages.

"*Resolved*, That the liberty of speech and of the press is the bulwark of freedom, and the most glorious prerogative of free men, and that we will never relinquish this liberty but with our lives.

"*Resolved*, That we cordially approve of the moderate, firm, and dignified conduct of our excellent governor, whose measures have always tended to promote the interests of the State and individual happiness, and we rejoice in again having a chief magistrate who will not sell himself to a party, who holds the scale of equal justice and is above the reach of venalty.

"*Resolved*, That the districting of the Commonwealth for the choice of State senators and representatives to Congress under the administration of Elbridge Gerry, so that twenty-nine senators are chosen by a less number of votes than were necessary to choose the other eleven, is a most tyrannical and wicked exertion of power, a violation of the spirit of the Constitution, and a prostitution of the rights of the people, and must have originated in a desire to deprive them of their constitutional privileges.

"*Resolved*, That the senators so chosen, by refusing the various equitable modes for the choice of electors proposed by the House of Representatives, have evinced their approbation of this iniquitous system and have rendered themselves totally unworthy of the confidence of a free people.

"*Resolved*, That we will hold ourselves in readiness to obey the orders of our commander-in-chief in repelling any invasion of our shores or to aid the civil authority in executing the laws.

"*Resolved*, That we will exert ourselves by every constitutional and honorable measure to effect a change of our national rulers, that peace, commerce, and free trade may be enjoyed with all liberal and civilized nations, and all possible means be used to secure and preserve the union of the States.

"*Resolved*, That from the foregoing considerations, and from a belief that only when life or liberty are jeopardized the rulers of a nation are completely justified in declaring war, and as the great ostensible causes of the present one are removed by Britain herself, and as amicable adjustment of the only remaining difficulty is now offered, it is the imperious duty of our government to suspend hostilities without delay, and restore the blessings of peace to a brave but abused and suffering people.

"PETER O. ALDEN, *Moderator.*
DAN'L GIVEN, *Town Clerk.*"

The following address was also adopted: —

"To the Hon. Eleazer W. Ripley, Jonathan Page and Ebenezer Poor, senators of the district of Cumberland and Oxford.

"After having seen the various modes offered by the committee of conference from the House of Representatives to the Senate through their committee for the choice of electors of President and Vice-President of the United States, we are alarmed at the pertinacious adherence of the Senate to a partial and unequal mode of choosing electors, whereby a majority of the people are liable to be overruled by the minority, contrary to the spirit and letter of the Constitution and the principles of republican liberty.

"That this Commonwealth may have a voice in the next election of President and Vice-President a manly and just concurrence of the Senate with the House of Representatives is wanting, and this town hereby calls upon you to co-operate with them by your best exertions and procure a concurrence of the Senate with the House in some one of their propositions.

"In this day of peril and difficulty for the public good your best services are required. To stifle the voice of the people and deprive them of their elective rights would be a stride at usurpation too alarming for us to behold in silence and too flagrant to be borne.

"We consider the proposition made by the House fair, honorable, and constitutional, and we are sorry to assert that the Resolves of the Senate do not appear to us to be of that character.

"If our liberties, so dearly purchased by the blood and treasure of our fathers, must be lost, we most sincerely hope and fervently pray that they may never be destroyed under the forms of judicial nor legislative proceedings."

The town voted that four attested copies of the above address be made out by the town clerk, and that one be forwarded to each of the above-named senators, and one to the president of the Senate, to be laid before that body.

[1814.] Nothing especially worthy of record occurred in 1813, but at a meeting held in February, 1814, the town appointed a committee to write an address, setting forth "the present most unjust and iniquitous restrictions upon our trade." It was also voted to have this address published in the Portland *Gazette*. No copy of it appears on the records of the town, and the number of the *Gazette* supposed to contain it has not been found by the compilers of this work.

An article in the warrant, "to see if the town will accept of the Engine belonging to individuals of this town," was dismissed.

Some of the town officers elected at the annual meeting, not presenting themselves to take the oath of office, a warrant was issued to John Owen, constable, to notify them to appear at a specified time and take the oath, as required by law. Owen, on his return, certified that he had notified all "except Roger Toothaker [one of the fence-viewers] who ran off and would not hear me notify him, and Abraham Locke, whom I missed by mistaking his place of residence, and Silas Goddard."

At a meeting held in August, the selectmen were authorized to hire money, "to meet the expense occasioned by the military movements."

It was voted to dismiss the article in the warrant "to see if the town will afford any assistance to the unfortunate sufferers by the freshet," which occurred that spring and did a great deal of damage.

[1815.] In 1815 the selectmen were directed to collect the resolves, maps, etc., belonging to the town, and to deposit them in their office.

[1816.] The town, at its annual meeting, in 1816, gave Russell Stoddard and others permission to place some hay-scales[1] between the road that went by Mrs. Robson's and that going by John Pollard's.

At a meeting held May 20, a majority of twenty-two votes was cast by the town against a separation of the District of Maine from the State of Massachusetts. At this meeting a committee was also appointed to provide a code of by-laws for the town.

At a meeting held September 2, the town again voted against the formation of a new State by a majority of fifty-one votes. The town also at this meeting chose Robert Dunning, Doctor Jonathan Page, and Joseph McKeen, delegates to a convention to be held in Brunswick on the last Monday in September following, to count the votes cast in the District upon this question, and if a majority of the votes cast were favorable, to form the draft of a constitution for a new State.

[1818.] The town, at its annual meeting in 1818, authorized the selectmen to purchase a hearse at a cost not exceeding one hundred dollars.

---

[1] *The scales were located in what is now the mall, opposite Green Street.*

At this meeting it was voted inexpedient to build a poorhouse. The one built in 1807 was sold by the town in 1812.

An article in the warrant of this meeting, in regard to a separation of the east and west parts of the town, was dismissed. Its insertion in the warrant was probably owing to some slight disaffection in one of these sections.

[1819.] At a meeting held May 3, the representative from the town was instructed to use all fair and honorable means towards effecting the separation of the District of Maine from the State. This act shows an evident change on the part of the citizens of Brunswick in regard to this question. The representative was also instructed to use all fair and honorable means to oppose the passage of a law allowing Wingate and others the exclusive right of navigating the Kennebec River with steamboats. Apart from all questions of propriety or of constitutional right, Brunswick and Topsham both had a special interest in opposing a law which would affect the navigation of their own river.

At a special meeting on July 26, the town voted, by a majority of one hundred and thirty-three votes, in favor of a new State, and at a subsequent meeting, held September 20, Robert D. Dunning, Doctor Jonathan Page, and Reverend Benjamin Titcomb were chosen delegates to the convention to be held in Portland on the second Monday in October, for the purpose of forming a Constitution for the new State.

At a meeting held December 6, the town voted its approval of the Constitution framed by that convention.

UNDER STATE OF MAINE.

[1820.] On March 15, 1820, the State of Maine was, by act of Congress, admitted into the Union.

At the annual town meeting this year, the selectmen were authorized to provide a place for the hearse, which they had been authorized to purchase two years before. Whether the hearse had been kept out of doors or in somebody's barn, or whether it was not purchased until this year, does not appear. At this meeting Doctor Jonathan Page bid off the care of the town's poor for six hundred dollars.

At the first election for governor of Maine, held this year, the vote of Brunswick stood: for Honorable William King, 195; for Stephen Longfellow, Esquire, 23; scattering, 9.

At a meeting in May, the selectmen were directed to petition the legislature to incorporate the town of Brunswick, together with a number of other towns in the counties of Cumberland and Lincoln, into a new county.

The selectmen were also, at a meeting held in November, directed to petition the legislature to make a deduction from the valuation of the town, as taken by the selectmen in August, in consequence of the loss of property occasioned by the great freshet of October previous.

[1821.] At the annual meeting in 1821 the town passed a resolve that the public good required the formation of a new county, to be composed of the towns of Brunswick, Bath, Phipsburg, Durham, Harpswell, Freeport, Pownal, Danville, Topsham, Bowdoinham, Bowdoin, Litchfield, Lisbon, Lewiston, and Wales; and the representative from Brunswick was instructed to endeavor to effect the object at that session of the legislature. This attempt was, however, unsuccessful.

The town this year, instead of building a poorhouse, instructed the overseers of the poor to hire suitable houses and land to accommodate the poor of the town and to appoint a person to take charge of them. This was for the purpose of making available, for the benefit of the town, the labor of the paupers.

[1822.] At a meeting of the town, held September 9, 1822, the representative to the legislature was directed to endeavor to obtain the passage of a law granting compensation from the State treasury to the soldiers of the militia.

[1823.] At a town meeting held January 20, 1823, it was voted to be inexpedient to make any offer to the legislature to induce that body to fix the seat of government in Brunswick. What effect a different vote might have had upon the prosperity of the town is a matter of some doubt, though had such an offer been accepted, there is no doubt but that it would greatly have benefited the community. The town, also, at this meeting, directed its representative to oppose in the legislature the erection of any new county which should include Brunswick within its limits.

The annual meeting in March was adjourned to the first Monday in April, "in consequence of the severity of the cold and the small number present."

[1824.] At a meeting held the fifth of April, 1824, the selectmen were authorized to receive all money or other property that may have been raised by subscription for the sufferers by the great fire in Brunswick, which occurred the previous year, and to divide the same among them according to their necessities. The selectmen were also authorized to pay twenty cents to each soldier of the militia, in lieu of rations, if the application for the same was made as the law prescribed.

At a meeting held September 6th, the town passed resolutions inviting General Lafayette to visit Brunswick while on his tour through New England, and a committee of eleven gentlemen, in addition to the selectmen, were appointed as a committee of arrangements for his reception, if he accepted. He was also invited by the authorities of the college, but was obliged to decline both invitations.

[1825.] At a meeting held January 1, 1825, the town voted an appropriation of one hundred and fifty dollars towards defraying the expense of exchanging the bell then hanging in the steeple of the new meeting-house for a larger one. A committee was appointed to purchase a fire-engine, and eight hundred dollars was appropriated for the purpose. $1,500 was appropriated this year for schools.

The selectmen were authorized to settle with Joseph Storer for damages suffered by him in crossing the bridge on Federal Street [1] with a horse and chaise.

A committee of fifteen was chosen to solicit aid for the relief of the sufferers at the late fire.

[1826.] The town, in 1826, voted to purchase the house, barn, out-buildings, and farm, near the lower landing, then owned by Roger Merrill,[2] and which contained about forty acres of land, at a price not exceeding $1,500. The town also voted to raise six hundred dollars per year, for three years, to meet the above expense.

The selectmen were authorized, this year, to furnish blank cartridges for the use of the militia of the town, when at reviews.

[1827.] At a meeting of the town, held January 4, 1827, the representative was instructed to use all fair and honorable means to prevent the passage of any legislative act which would deprive the town of Brunswick of any of its territory or in any way disturb the line established between the counties of Cumberland and Lincoln. This action was taken upon an article in the warrant to see if the town would consent that the islands below the falls should be set off, with their improvements, to Topsham, agreeably to a petition to the legislature of George F. Richardson and others.

The town voted, November 3, that the bills incurred in consequence of depredations on the Indians, the previous August, by Jere O'Brien and John McKeen, should be accepted to the amount of seven dollars and twenty cents. It seems that this year a party of Indians had encamped near "the landing," in Brunswick, and that a number of evil-disposed young men made a raid upon them, tore down their tents, and drove them off. O'Brien and McKeen entered a complaint

---

[1] *This was a small pole-bridge at the foot of the hill, across a brook leading from the swamp west of Maine Street.*

[2] *The present poor-farm.*

against the rioters, and the above vote was intended to compensate them for their legal expenses.

[1828.] In the year 1828, five gentlemen were chosen as agents of the town to oppose any division of the town that might be urged upon the legislature, which was then in session at Portland. One hundred dollars was appropriated for keeping in repair the two fire-engines, for ringing the bell, and for such other purposes as might tend to the security of the town against fire.

[1829.] The same amount was appropriated for the same purpose, in 1829, and the town voted to have the bell rung at nine o'clock on Sunday evenings.

The town voted to hold its future meetings in the village, provided a house could be obtained without expense to the town. Accordingly the next meeting, September 14, was held in the Baptist meeting-house on School Street.

At the September meeting of the town, a code of By-Laws was adopted. The provisions of these By-Laws were, in brief, as follows: —

Article 1. Provided against injury or loss of fire apparatus.

Article 2. Against the building of bonfires in the streets, and against the careless use of lights in houses, barns, and stables.

Article 3. Against coasting on or across the streets, and also against obtaining rides by taking hold of or getting upon vehicles, without the consent of persons riding therein.

Article 4. Against the wanton or unnecessary discharge of fire-arms near any dwelling-house, shop, or store.

Article 5. Against playing ball within ten rods of any dwelling, throwing snow-balls, playing with kites, or doing anything in public streets to annoy passengers.

Article 6. Against the assembling of noisy crowds in the night, and against rude or disorderly behavior, indecent or profane language, or the injuring of trees, fences, or buildings. The penalty for the violation of this article was five dollars.

Article 7. Against allowing geese to go at large. The penalty in this case was six cents per goose.

These By-Laws were approved by the Court of Appeals in the December following, and the town voted to have them printed, and one copy furnished to each family.

[1831.] In the year 1831, the town authorized the selectmen to appropriate a piece of land near the poorhouse for a paupers' cemetery. Also, that future town meetings should be held in the old west meeting-house.

[1832.] In 1832 the town appointed a committee to draw up some resolutions expressing the opinions of the inhabitants of Brunswick "in relation to the alarming modifications of the tariff now proposed to be made by the Congress of the United States." Another committee was also appointed to report suitable resolutions expressing the opinions of the citizens in regard to the sale of the disputed territory on the northeast boundary.

The reports of both committees were read and accepted, and the selectmen were instructed to furnish copies of them for publication to the Portland *Advertiser* and Kennebec *Journal.*

The selectmen were this year instructed to sell the "poor lot" on Federal Street, by auction or by private sale as they might deem best.

The dividing line between Brunswick and Freeport was this year defined. There seems to have been some doubt as to its location before this, for on October 15, 1828, the selectmen of the two towns met at the house of Samuel Chase, and proceeded to perambulate the line. Robert D. Dunning was the surveyor for Brunswick and Barstow Sylvester for Freeport. The line surveyed by them appears from the record to have been the same, or nearly the same, as that previously established.

For some reason, however, the line was not satisfactory to some of the citizens of the two towns. Depositions were taken in January, 1832, from various residents, testifying as to the location of the original line. Depositions were made by David Curtis, William Alexander, and Daniel Given.

On the seventh of February, 1832, the legislature appointed Joseph Sewall of Bath, William Bradbury of New Gloucester, and William Cummings of Cape Elizabeth, a committee to establish the dividing line between Brunswick and Freeport.

On the eleventh of June following, the committee met and viewed the premises on that day and succeeding days, closing their labors on the twenty-third of June.

Their report, which we give below, furnishes the result of their labors: —

"Pursuant to the foregoing Resolve for establishing the line between Brunswick and Freeport, we the subscribers, the Committee therein appointed, having been duly sworn, and having given due notice to the parties, and having met them by their committees and counsel at the house of Alexander Moorhead, in Brunswick, the eleventh day of June in the year of our Lord one thousand eight hundred and thirty-two, and by adjournment from day to day until this twenty third day of said June, and having heard all their pleas, proofs and arguments, and having viewed the premises, and maturely considered the same, have determined and established the dividing line between the towns of Brunswick and Freeport, in the County of Cumberland, agreeably to the Acts of Incorporation of said Towns, to be as follows to wit: Beginning on the Western shore of Maquoit Bay at the mouth of Bungamunganock so called at a ledge which we have marked B, thence North twenty eight and one eighth degrees West, passing by a hemlock tree in Vincent Mountfort's pasture, and through said Vincent Mountfort's house, and by a beach stump one rod and two links westerly of an ash tree in William Alexander's pasture by a stone in the wall on the western side of the county road on David Curtis' land marked + and over a ledge in said Curtis' pasture marked FB and by a spruce tree, a yellow birch tree, a ledge in Grouse's field marked +, a ledge in Skolfield's pasture marked +, a maple tree, a yellow birch tree, a stone set in the ground on the easterly side of the county road, twelve rods & sixteen links from the corner of Thomas Pennell's house, marked FB, a beach tree, a ledge in Samuel Sylvester's pasture marked FB, a stone in the wall on the westerly side of the Story road so called, a ledge in John Field's field marked FB, a beach tree, a hemlock tree, a spruce tree, a pine tree five miles & seventy rods to a stone marked FB at the middle of the Quaker road so called, and one rod and a half from William Jordan's wall, thence North East one hundred & ninety six rods to a stone marked DB at the corner of Durham and including within the town of Brunswick all Mair Point so called, and to include within said town of Brunswick all the estate of the late Benjamin Chase which was annexed to said Brunswick by virtue of an act of the Legislature of Massachusetts passed in 1790, entitled an Act setting off Benjamin Chase, his family and estate from the town of Freeport and annexing them to the town of Brunswick.

" JOSEPH SEWALL.
WM. BRADBURY.
WM. CUMMINGS."[1]

The same committee also established the Durham line.

According to McKeen the survey of the west part of the town was made by John Merrill while B. Ring lived in Brunswick, though the plan of the "Great Lots" was never laid down by any actual survey. According to the same authority, if Merrill's plan had been regarded

---

[1] *Pejepscot Records.*

and the boundaries preserved, the line would have gone farther south upon Freeport than was established by the committee in 1832, and would have taken sixteen rods on to what Durham now holds.[1]

[1833.] The town appropriated for schools in 1833, $2,000; for support of poor, $700; for highways, $2,500.

The town clerk was this year directed to procure all plans and papers, of every description, of the Pejepscot Company, which might be of use to the town hereafter, and which related in any way to the settlement of the town, at as moderate an expense as possible. The papers of the Pejepscot Company were, at this time, in the hands of Josiah Little, Jr., of Newburyport (or of Amesbury), Mass. By a sworn statement by John McKeen, the then town clerk, it appears that Mr. Little placed the Pejepscot Papers in his hands upon condition that they should be finally placed in the library of the Maine Historical Society, where they now are. This was certainly the best disposition that could have been made of them, particularly as many of the papers relate not only to Brunswick but to the whole region embraced in the Pejepscot purchase, and it would be difficult, if not impossible, to separate from them those relating exclusively to Brunswick.

The selectmen were this year authorized to grant licenses to retail ardent spirits, on condition that no spirits should be drank in or about the premises of the retailer.

John Coburn was appointed an agent to appear before a committee of the legislature, and to use his best endeavors to carry into effect the vote of the town in favor of the formation of a new county from parts of Cumberland and Lincoln Counties.

[1834.] At a meeting of the town, held July 4, 1834, a lengthy report of the Committee on Town Commons was read and accepted.[2] A committee was also chosen to consider the practicability and advisability of having the town farm upon the Commons, and to estimate the expense of removing the buildings thereto.

At a meeting held August 30, the Report of the Committee on Town Commons, Poorhouse, etc., was read, but its consideration was postponed to a further meeting. The selectmen were instructed to have the report printed and also to have the Commons surveyed.

The selectmen were also directed to petition the legislature for permission to use the Commons for agricultural purposes or to dispose of them at some future day, should the town ever so direct. They were,

---

[1] *McKeen, MSS. Lecture.* [2] *See Chapter XIX.*

moreover, directed to procure the same permission from the Pejepscot proprietors; and also to demand a rent from all parties occupying the Commons, and to remove all persons refusing or neglecting to pay the rent.

[1835.] At a town meeting, held April 27, 1835, it was voted to build a town-house without unnecessary delay.

The village school district this year applied for an Act of Incorporation, for certain municipal purposes, and an Act to this effect was passed by the legislature and received the approval of the governor, January 28, 1836.

At the annual meeting this year the town appropriated seven hundred dollars to pay for the town-house, and the Building Committee were authorized to borrow the needed balance of three hundred dollars. The town-house was completed this year.

[1837.] The town met at the town-house for the first time on January 16, 1837. The town, at this meeting, voted to receive its proportion of the money deposited with the State by the United States, in pursuance of "an Act to regulate the deposits of the public money," on the condition specified in the Act of this State entitled "An Act providing for the disposition and repayment of the public money apportioned to the State of Maine, on deposit, by the government of the United States." James F. Matthews was appointed the agent of the town to receive this money. The revenue of the United States had for some years been in excess of the demands of government, and this Act of Congress was to distribute the surplus to the States.

At a meeting of the town in April, the selectmen were authorized to loan the town's share of the surplus revenue to citizens of the town, on good personal security, in sums not exceeding two hundred dollars to any one individual.

At a meeting held in July, the selectmen were directed to collect what had been loaned, as it became due, and to deposit the amount, together with the remaining portion of the surplus revenue, with the citizens in the following manner: —

The sum total was to be divided into as many shares as there were inhabitants of the town at the last enumeration, and each male head of a family, and each female head of a family where there was no male head, should be entitled to receive, on deposit, one share for each member of his or her family actually resident at home in the family on the first day of the preceding March, including the heads of the family, the daughters, the sons, under the age of twenty-one years, and the regular apprentices. Each male above twenty-one years of age, without a family, was entitled to receive one share.

The receipts, which were to be taken in all cases, were to contain a promise of repayment, without interest, of the sum given, whenever the town should be required to repay it to the treasury of the State.

At a meeting held in September, the preceding vote was so amended as to entitle all who were residents of the town on the first of March previous to a share of the surplus money, and that persons since, but not then, residents should not be entitled to it.

[1838.] At the annual meeting in April, 1838, the town voted to relieve those who had received shares of the surplus revenue money from all obligation to return it, since the legislature had passed an Act releasing towns from a similar obligation.

The town voted to refer to the Building Committee the deeds of the gifts from Reverend William Allen and David Dunlap, Esquire. The above vote refers to the deeds of the land upon which the town-house was built.

[1841.] The overseers of the poor were authorized in 1841 to sell the poorhouse and farm whenever they could do so for a not less sum than $1,500.

In regard to several proposed amendments to the Constitution of the State, the town voted as follows: —

In favor of increasing the number of representatives, but against establishing the number at one hundred and fifty-one; in favor of electing the governor for two years instead of one, and in favor of having the legislative meeting but once in two years.

[1842.] In 1842 a petition from Isaac Lincoln and others, to have the town house sold or else to have it moved to the village, was dismissed.

[1844.] The town in 1844 voted in favor of an amendment to the Constitution of the State, changing the meeting of the legislature to May.

[1845.] A new hearse was purchased in 1845, by order of the town, and the old one was repaired and fitted with runners for use in the winter season.

[1847.] At the annual meeting in 1847 the selectmen were instructed to have the bell on the Universalist Church rung daily, for the ensuing year, at the expense of the town.

The town also at this meeting appropriated two hundred dollars towards the purchase of a clock to be located in the tower of the Universalist Church.

The town this year voted in favor of so amending the Constitution of the State as to prohibit the loaning of the credit of the State to any amount exceeding $300,000 in the aggregate; and also, against an amendment providing that the governor, senators, and representatives should be elected by a plurality instead of majority vote.

[1849.] In 1849 the town voted to dispose of Engine No. 1 and to purchase a new one, and for that purpose the sum of three hundred dollars was appropriated. The town this year refused, by a vote of one hundred and fourteen to sixteen, to adopt an Act of the legislature, which was passed July 16, 1846, and was entitled "An Act for the License and Regulation of Stationary Steam-Engines."

[1850.] The town voted in 1850 in favor of a constitutional amendment, which provided for a meeting of the legislature in January instead of May.

At a subsequent meeting this year the town voted to accept an Act of the legislature authorizing certain cities and towns to grant aid in the construction and completion of the Kennebeck and Portland Railroad, and also voted to loan its credit to that company for the sum of $75,000, according to the conditions and for the security provided in the Act. The vote was five hundred and eighty-eight in favor, and two hundred and fifty-two against the measure.

The inhabitants changed their minds in regard to stationary steam-engines, and the town accordingly voted this year to accept the Act in reference to the same, which was approved July 16, 1846.

[1851.] A protest, signed by one hundred and thirty-five of the inhabitants of Brunswick, was presented to the town in 1851. This protest was against the vote to loan money to the Kennebec and Portland Railroad, and was made on the ground that the Act of the legislature authorizing it was illegal, unconstitutional, and not binding upon the town.

[1856.] In 1856 the town authorized the selectmen to grant the use of the town-house to the Brunswick Light Infantry for an armory.

[1857.] The Act of the legislature, approved March 13, 1855, granting authority to cities and towns to adopt ordinances or by laws for sidewalks, was accepted in 1857, and a committee, consisting of the selectmen and Richard Greenleaf, Esquire, was appointed to lay out and determine the width of the different sidewalks in Brunswick, and to prepare some by-laws in reference to the same, which they were to report at a future meeting.

Another committee was also appointed this year, consisting of Messrs. Abner B. Thompson, John C. Humphreys, William G. Barrows, Samuel R. Jackson, Richard Greenleaf, and John McKeen, to investigate all matters relating to the town Commons; to ascertain what title the town had to them, and the boundaries thereof; to ascertain what encroachments had been made upon them, and all other facts relating to the subject, and to make a report at some future meeting.

Some time between March 16 and the first Monday in June, the town-house was destroyed by fire. The June meeting met — by adjournment — at the ruins of the town-house, and adjourned to McLellan's Hall.

The committee on sidewalks reported at this meeting the names of the streets upon which they had constructed sidewalks, the widths of the walks, and a code of by-laws in regard to the same.

The selectmen were authorized to dispose of the materials of the town-house which remained after the fire, and of the lot upon which it stood.

[1858.] At a meeting of the town, held January 18, 1858, to see what measures the town would adopt for the purpose of obtaining a charter for a city government, it was voted to appoint a committee of nine, — three from the village, three from the east, and three from the west part of the town, — to consider the matter and to report in one week. This committee reported, January 25, that the east and west portions of the town were opposed to a city form of government, but that the village was strongly in favor of it. A motion to petition the legislature for a charter as a city was lost by a vote of twenty-six majority. It was, however, voted that the village school-district should have leave to petition the legislature for a city charter for said district, under the name of the city of Brunswick, and the selectmen and town clerk were directed to petition the legislature to that effect. This they did, and upon February 10, a committee of the legislature reported a bill to incorporate the village district as the city of Brunswick. This bill was laid on the table and ordered to be printed. It was afterwards passed, and was approved by the governor, March 29. The bill provided for its acceptance by the whole town within thirty days, or to be null and void. At a meeting of the town, April 27, the charter was read, and rejected by a majority vote of one hundred and one.

At the annual meeting in March, the sum of seven hundred dollars was appropriated for a night watch. The committee on town Commons reported at this time. The report was accepted, and it was voted that the town agent be empowered and directed to communicate with the several parties whose lots abutted on the Commons, and in case any of them should decline to give the matter to referees, he was instructed to institute legal proceedings against them, that the rights of the town might be maintained and protected. The selectmen were also instructed to cause permanent stone monuments to be erected, in order to mark clearly the boundary lines of the Commons, whenever these lines should be authoritatively ascertained.

At a meeting held June 7, the town voted almost unanimously for the Prohibitory Liquor Law of 1858, there being but one vote for the License Law of 1856. This vote shows either an unparalleled sentiment in the town in favor of prohibition, or else that those in heart opposed to a temperance reform believed that its advocates had overshot the mark and that there would be a speedy reaction.

The town this year voted against granting State aid to a proposed Aroostook Railroad, and in favor of exempting future manufacturing establishments from taxation for a period of ten years.

[1860.] A committee was appointed in 1860 to consider the propriety of building a new town hall. They recommended the erection of a building on the corner of Maine and Pleasant Streets, at an estimated cost of $5,000. The town, however, refused to build.

[1862.] In 1862 the town lines between Brunswick and Freeport, Brunswick and Durham, Brunswick and Harpswell, and Brunswick and Bath, were perambulated by the selectmen of Brunswick and the authorities of the other places named, and monuments were erected to mark the line.

[1866.] An article in the warrant for a special meeting in November, 1866, in relation to petitioning the legislature to set Brunswick off from Cumberland County, was dismissed.

A new hearse was this year procured.

[1869, 1870.] In 1869, and again in 1870, propositions were made looking to the erection of a town hall, but they were defeated, and none has yet [1877] been erected.

[1872.] In 1872 a proposition was made for the erection of a monument in memory of the fallen heroes of the Rebellion. A committee was appointed to consider the subject, and at a subsequent meeting reported in favor of such a monument, but the town decided adversely to its erection.

All important acts of the town not embraced in this chapter will be found in other connections.

CHAPTER III.

MUNICIPAL HISTORY OF HARPSWELL.

UNDER COMMONWEALTH OF MASSACHUSETTS.

THE place formerly known as Wescustego was, on September 22, 1680, incorporated as a plantation by the name of North Yarmouth.

In 1731 the limits of North Yarmouth were determined by order of the General Court as follows: —

"To begin at a white Rock by the side of the Bay dividing between Falmouth & North Yarmouth & to extend from thence into the woods North west by Falmouth line eight miles, and from y^e s^d white Rock to extend by the Bay to the mouth of Bungamunganock River, from thence to extend eight miles into the woods on a line parallel to Falmouth line & from thence to Falmouth line aforesaid, & from the $afores^d$ white Rock & mouth of Bungamunganock River S^d Township to extend south east, the width of s^d Township to the Main Sea so as to include the Islands within s^d courses."

On April 6, 1733, the township was incorporated as a town.[1]

In 1735 a committee appointed by the General Court ran the line of the town as follows: —

"Beginning at the mouth of Bungamunganock River on the westerly side thence south east over Maquoit Bay to Mare Point and said line runs over Minot's Barn which stands on s^d Point, thence over Middle Bay to Merriconeag neck, thence across s^d neck and Merriconeag river to a point on Sebascodegan Island to an Inlet of water called the Basin, thence crossing another part of s^d Island to a small Island called Egg Island in Quahaug River, thence crossing another part of s^d Island running a S. E. course across the bay to small Point, thence to Hunnewell's Cove, thence crossing s^d cove and so on in a S. E. line to the Main sea at mouth of Kennebec River."

The present town of Harpswell, or the greater portion of it, was, it will be observed, at this time embraced within the limits of the town of North Yarmouth, of which town it constituted a parish.[2]

---

[1] *Maine Historical Society Collection*, 2, *pp.* 172, 176. *Russell's History of North Yarmouth.*

[2] *Maine Historical Collection*, 2, *p.* 180.

[1740.] In the year 1740 Merriconeag Neck was annexed to Brunswick, as will be seen by the following petitions to and order of the General Court: —

"TO HIS EXCELENCY JONATHAN BELCHER ESQ. CAPTAIN GENERAL AND GOVERNOUR IN CHIEF, THE HONOURABLE THE COUNCIL AND HONOURABLE HOUSE OF REPRESENTATIVES OF HIS MAJESTY'S PROVINCE OF THE MASSACHUSETTS BAY IN NEW ENGLAND IN GENERAL COURT ASSEMBLED MAY 28TH, 1740.

"THE PETITION OF THE PROPRIETORS OF THE NECK OF LAND IN CASCO BAY IN THE COUNTY OF YORK, CALLED BY THE NAME OF MERECONEGE NECK:—

"HUMBLY SHEWETH

"That Whereas the said Neck of Land, is one half part of it within the line of the Township of North Yarmouth, and having Paid Rates and Taxes to said Township, both to Church and State, altho' the Inhabitants there live above Thirty miles distant by Land from the Meeting House, and twelve miles by Sea across two very Dangerous Bays, (Especially in the Winter time) being also many times Impassable in canous, with their Familys thereby depriving them of the Public Worship of God, for a great part of their time, which is a very great discouragement to the Setlers, and Whereas this Honourable Court have been pleased Two years since to Invest the Township of Brunswick with all priviledges as the other Towns in this Province Enjoy and that Brunswick Meeting House is but Three Miles distant from the upper end of said Neck, adjoyning to Brunswick Town, and no Water to pass over which makes it easy to repair thereto without the Danger and Dificulty of the Winter and Tempests by Water and the very great length of way by Land.

"May it please your Excellency and Honours, We Humbly pray, That you would be pleased for the prevention of the aforesaid Inconveniences to set off the Familys that may Inhabit said Neck of Land, from the Town of North Yarmouth, and annex them to the Town of Brunswick, especially since but a part of said neck of Land is couched within the line of North Yarmouth Township. And as in Duty Bound your Petitioners shall ever pray.

"JOSEPH WADSWORTH
ADAM WINTHROP
HENRY GIBBS
BELCHER NOYES
JOB LEWIS
for ourselves and Partners."

"We the Inhabitants of the said Neck of Land Most Humbly [Pray?] That your Excelency and Honours would be pleased to grant the Prayer of the above named Proprietors of said Neck of Land that we may be Released under our very Great hardships, and as in Duty Bound shall ever pray.

"JAMES BREWER
JOHN MATHEWS
WILLIAM MAGRAY
EDWARD QUINGHAM
WILLIAM GIBSON
MOSES GATCHELL
JOSHUA CROMWELL
SAMUEL WINCHELL
JOHN ORR
WILLIAM MACKNESS
THOMAS McGREGOR
JOHN SMART
JOHN LINDSEY
BENJAMIN DENSLOW
RICHARD JAQUES
JOHN STOVER
ELISHA ALLEN
ISAAC HALL
SAMUEL STANDWOOD
DAVID STANDWOOD
JOHN STEVENS
JOHN ROSS JUN[R].
SETH TOOTHAKER
JOB MOULTON
ABIEL SPRAGE
WAIT WEBBER
EBENEZER TOOTHAKER"

"IN THE HOUSE OF REPRESENTATIVES, June 3, 1740.

"Read and ordered, That the Petitioners serve the Town of North Yarmouth with a copy of this Petition that they Shew Cause if any they have on Tuesday the 24th Instant, if the Court be then sitting, if not, on the first Thursday of the next Sitting of this Court, why the Prayer thereof should not be granted.

"Sent up for concurrence

"J. QUINCY, *Sp[ker].*

"IN COUNCIL June 4th 1740.

"Read and Concurred

"SIMON FROST *Dep[y]. Sec[ry]*

"Consented to

"J. BELCHER.

"A true Copy Exam[d].

"SIMON FROST *Dep[y]. Sec[ry]*"

"The following order passed on the petition of the Propriet[rs] of Merriconeag Neck, viz[t].

"IN COUNCIL June 27, 1740

"Read again and it appearing that the Town of North Yarmouth has been duly served with a copy of the Petition but no answer given in, Ordered that the prayer of the Petition be granted, and that that part of the Neck of Land within Mentioned which heretofore belonged to the Town of North Yarmouth together with the Inhabitants thereon, be and hereby are set off from the said Town of North Yarmouth, and annexed to & accounted as part of the Town of Brunswick there to do Duty and receive Priviledge accordingly.

"Sent down for Concurrence

"SIMON FROST *Dep^y Sec^ry*

"IN THE HOUSE OF REPRESENTATIVES June 28, 1740.

"Read & Concurred

"J. QUINCY *Sp^kr*

"Consented to

"J. BELCHER.

"A true copy Examined

"SIMON FROST *Dep^y Sec^ry*"[1]

[1741.] Merriconeag Neck remained, however, annexed to Brunswick for a short time only, as on August 1, 1741, the foregoing bill was again brought before the Council, together with the answer of Ammi Ruhamat Cutter, agent for the town of North Yarmouth, and the matter having been thoroughly considered, it was voted "that the order of this Court within written passed the twenty seventh of June *last* (A) be & is hereby superseded & set aside, and that such of the Inhabitants of the neck of land within mentioned, (B) as are consenting thereto and shall give in their names to the Town Clerk of Brunswick for that purpose be & hereby are set off to the Town of Brunswick so far as relates to the Ministry, to do duty and receive priviledge accordingly." This vote was sent to the House of Representatives August 5, where it was read and concurred in, with the addition of some amendments at the places marked A and B. The first amendment simply inserted the date, and the second one added the words, "with their estates."[2]

This legislation was not satisfactory to the people of Brunswick, nor to many of those upon Merriconeag Neck, and accordingly the following petitions were sent to the General Court this same year: —

[1] *Pejepscot Papers.* [2] *Ibid.*

"To His Excellency William Shirly Esq Governour & Comander in Chief in & over his Majestyes Province of the Massachusetts bay in New England,

The Honourable his Majestyes Councill, and the Honourable House of Representatives in Generall court assembled Anno Domini, 1741.

"THE PETITION OF THE SELECTMEN OF THE TOWN OF BRUNSWICK IN THE COUNTY OF YORK IN BEHALF OF SAID TOWN,

Humbly Sheweth

"That the Sd town being of but small Extent and the Inhabitants as yet but few in number & a considerable part of the Soil not so rich and fitt for tillage as in many other towns, and tho' the said Inhabitants from a Principle of Loyalty & dutifullness to the Government, are ready & desirous to do what they can towards the support of the publick charge, yet for the reasons above mentioned, they find it very difficult to maintain their families & support the ministry, & much more to pay the Province tax which the Honourable Court was pleased to lay upon them last year, and they find this Disability in some measure Increased by reason that a considerable part of Mericoneag Neck, which hapens to fall within the line of North yarmouth, by reason of the large extent of Sd township into the Sea Cuting of the whole front of Brunswick next the sea, which was the last year by order of the Generall Court annexed to Brunswick has been since Set back to North yarmouth; Now we beg leave Humbly to Represent to your Excellency & Honours that the town of North yarmouth is in extent of land more than three times as large as Brunswick, without reconing in the Necks & Islands Couched within the lines of Sd town, which much Increase the proportion, and the Sd town is much more numerous in Inhabitants, & their land by long Cultivation is become much more profitable, so that they cannot be reasonably suposed to stand in need of so small an addition as Mericoneag Neck. Now whereas the uper part of Sd neck, is Contiguous to Brunswick and the rest of it by land, is 18 miles nearer to the center of Brunswick & to Sd meeting house than to North yarmouth meeting house, & a much nearer & safer way to Brunswick in time of danger, where they can be relieved by land from Brunswick town, which they cannot readily, by North yarmouth, by land or water, and the addition of it to Brunswick, would something increase their number, & at present in Some measure Enable them to discharge the heavy tax laid upon them, which is very burthensom by reason of their Continuall fears and great poverty of the Inhabitants (excepting four or five familyes) Your Petitioners therefore Humbly pray that your Honours will so far Compassionate & Encourage them as to annex unto Brunswick the whole of S^{d} neck viz: that part of it that is couched within North yarmouth line & the uper part of it that lies between the lines of North yarmouth and Brunswick and which at present is within the bounds of no town and your Petitioners as in Duty bound Shall ever pray &c.

"BENJ^{A} LARRABEE,
WYMOND BRADBURY,
SAML HINKLEY, } *Selectmen of Brunswick.*

"We the Subscribers Inhabitants of Merriconeag Neck in Casco bay, such of us as fall within the line of North-yarmouth finding ourselves under a great burthen & disadvantage in being subjected to that town from whence we are so very remote & from whence we can expect no manner of benefit on account of the Ministry, School, or otherwise, & others of us who are not within the bounds of any town but lying between the lines of North yarmouth & Brunswick, but lying contiguous to Brunswick & Judging it to be very much for our Comfort & benefit to belong to s^{d} town, do Humbly Joyn with the Inhabitants of Brunswick in the within Petition, and earnestly Supplicate your Excllency & Honours that for the reasons therein set forth you will be pleased to annex the whole of Mericoneag Neck to the town of Brunswick & your petitioners as in duty bound shall ever pray.

"RICHARD JAQUES
WAIT WEBBER
JOHN STOVER
JOHN M^{c}ATHEWS
THOMAS MCGREGOR
NATH^{L} L. BARNES"[1]

These petitions were not favorably received by the General Court, but on June 14, 1749, that body, in response to a petition of the inhabitants of that portion of Merriconeag Neck and the adjoining islands, which was within the limits of North Yarmouth, passed an order to the effect that the Neck, the land and islands mentioned in the petition, and the northeast part of Sebascodegan Island, should be a distinct and separate precinct.[2]

---

[1] *Pejepscot Papers. Original Petition.* [2] *Massachusetts Records*, 1749.

In 1758 the following Act of Incorporation was passed: —

"ANNO REGNI REGIS GEORGII

SECUNDI TRICESIMO PRIMO.

"AN ACT

For incorporating a neck of land called Mericoneag Neck, and certain Islands adjacent, in the County of York into a Separate District by the name of ———

"*Whereas* the Inhabitants of Mericoneag Neck and the Islands adjacent have humbly represented to this Court the difficulties and great inconveniences they labour under in their present situation and have earnestly requested that they may be invested with powers privileges and immunities of a District.

"*Therefore be it enacted* by the Governor, Council, and House of Representatives, That the said Neck of Land beginning where Brunswick line intersects the upper end of said Neck which is four rods above the Narrows of said Neck commonly called the Carrying Place, from thence including the whole of said Neck down to the Sea, together with the Islands adjacent hereafter mentioned, viz: Great Sebascodegan Island alias Shapleighs Island, Little Sebascodegan Island,[1] and Wills[2] Island lying to the South east side of said Neck; Birch Island, Whites Island and the two Goose Islands lying on the Northwest side of said neck and Damariscove Islands[3] lying at the lower end of said Neck, be and hereby are incorporated into a separate District by the name of *Harpswell.*

"And the Inhabitants of said Neck of land and Islands shall be and hereby are invested with all the powers, privileges and immunities that the several towns in this Province by law do or may enjoy, that of sending a Representative only excepted.

"And be it further enacted That John Minot Esq. be and hereby is empowered to issue his warrant to some principal Inhabitant of the said District requiring him in his Majestys name to warn and notify the said Inhabitants qualified to vote in town affairs to meet together at such time and place in said District as by said Warrant shall be appointed to choose such officers as the law directs and may be necessary to manage the affairs of said District:

"And the said Inhabitants being so met shall be and hereby are empowered to choose officers accordingly.

---

1 *Now Orr's Island.*

2 *Now Bailey's Island.*

3 *One of which is now called Haskell's Island.*

"JANUARY 20th 1758,

"This bill having been read three several times in the House of Representatives passed to be enacted

"F. HUBBARD, *Speaker.*

"JANUARY 20th 1758,

"This bill having been read three several times in Council passed to be enacted

"A. OLIVER, *Sec'y.*

"JANUARY 25th 1758,

"By the Governor I consent to the enacting of this bill

"T. POWNAL.

"Copy examined

"A. BRADFORD
"*Sec'y of Commonwealth of Massachusetts*"

It will be observed that no reference is made in the foregoing Act to the town of North Yarmouth. This would convey the impression that when Harpswell was made a precinct, it became legally separated from that town, which was probably the case.

The present name of the town is not known to have been used prior to the incorporation. By whom it was first suggested is not known. One authority [1] states that it was so named by the General Court, but according to traditionary accounts the name was given by the Dunnings. There is a Harpswell in Lincolnshire, England, and the name was probably first suggested by some emigrant from that vicinity and was favored by the Dunnings, who were English people, though from another county.

Harpswell, though similar to an incorporated town in most respects, had not the privilege of being represented at the General Court, and was therefore only a district.

The first recorded meeting of the district was held March 30, 1758. At this meeting Captain John Stover was chosen moderator; Andrew Dunning, clerk; David Curtis, Isaac Hall, and Andrew Dunning, selectmen and assessors; Lieutenant Lemuel Turner, district treasurer; Elijah Douglas and Taylor Small, constables; James Babbage, Seth Toothaker, and John Coombs, tithing-men; Waitstill Webber, William Alexander, and Joseph Thompson, surveyors of highways;

---

[1] *Kellogg, MSS. Lecture.*

Edward Easters, Thomas McGregor, and Joseph Linscott, fence-viewers; Nathan Adams, James Gardner, and John Snow, hog-reeves; and Elisha Allen, sealer of leather. It was voted at this meeting that hogs and horses should be allowed to run at large, according to the existing law. The meeting adjourned to the last Wednesday in May.

At the adjourned meeting on May 25, the following votes were passed: —

That Alexander Wilson and Andrew Dunning should be a committee to settle with North Yarmouth, and to receive whatever money was due the town.

To have no schoolmaster this year.

That the selectmen should lay out the highways as they might deem advisable.

That the selectmen should settle "with Mr. Jaques, the former treasurer" probably of the former precinct or parish, "and should remove the Treasury into Lemuel Turner's hands."

That Thomas McGregor should be collector for that year, on the Neck, and should be allowed thirteen shillings and four pence for his services.

That Mr. William Harsey should be paid fifteen shillings for his trouble in making out the rates for the parish in 1755.

That Mr. William Blake and Mrs. Mary Young should be paid twelve shillings each, for making out the rates at the same time.

That Captain Timothy Bailey should be paid one pound for a note that he gave in the year 1751 "for the Place being presented."

That Mr. Curtis be paid £33 1*s.* 1*d.* "for taking up Mr. Pattishalls execution against the Parish."

That he have eighteen shillings for his time and expense in taking up the execution.

That Benjamin Jaques be paid thirteen shillings four pence "for going with Mr. Curtis to take up Patishal's execution."

That Benjamin Jaques and Alexander Wilson be paid three shillings each "for getting a power [of attorney?] to give Mr. Ralph Farnan."

That fourteen shillings be allowed Richard Starbird on his assessment for 1754.

That Samuel Eaton be paid three pounds for serving as clerk for four years; and that Lieutenant Lemuel Turner be paid eighteen shillings, David Curtis twenty-four shillings, and Captain Timothy Bailey three shillings, for going to North Yarmouth. It will be seen that most of the foregoing relates to past transactions of the precinct, or parish, which have not been preserved as matters of record.

[1759.] On May 9, 1759, a committee was chosen to settle the district and parish affairs, and another committee was also chosen to settle with the town of North Yarmouth, and to receive what money was due to Harpswell. At this meeting it was also voted to build a pound near the meeting-house, and also one on Mr. Joseph Thompson's land on the island called Great Sebascodegan.

On May 30, of this year, the town voted to purchase scales, weights, and measures for use as a standard. Jonathan Flint was allowed £1 9*s*. for laying out the main road from the Brunswick line to the lower end of the Neck; James Gardner was also paid 3*s*. for carrying a pole to lay out the road, and Thomas Jones, Jr., and Captain John Stover, 3*s*. each, for assistance in laying out this road. £13 6*s*. 8*d*. was appropriated for the poor.

[1760.] In 1760 the town appropriated 35*s*. 4*d*. to pay David Curtis for his expense in obtaining books, scales, and weights.

[1762.] At the May meeting in 1762, it was voted that 2*d*. per head should be paid for all crows killed on the Neck before the October following.

[1763.] In May, 1763, the town voted to pay Benjamin Jaques, Alexander Wilson, and John Alexander the sums assessed against them for the sloop built the previous year.

[1765.] In 1765 the town voted to allow Nicholas Pinkham the sum assessed upon his father "for the fine laid on the Quakers as appears by State and Rate Bills, 1760." [1]

[1768.] At a meeting held March 25, 1768, the town voted — twenty-six to twelve — not to set off Great Sebascodegan Island as a parish. At a meeting held September 28th, it was voted not to send a delegate to the convention to be held at Boston, but the selectmen, with Andrew Dunning and Benjamin Jaques, were chosen as a committee to prepare and forward a letter to that convention.

[1770.] The records of the meeting on May 22, 1770, contain the following entry: —

"The majority of votes for Mr. Samuel Stanwood as Representative were 20." This is the first mention to be found of the town's being represented at the General Court.

[1772.] In 1772 the town voted to pay David Curtis and Elijah

---

[1] *This is the first and only record in either of the three towns where Quakers are spoken of as having been fined.*

Douglas one dollar each "for haling Boards from Brunswick." What the boards were for is not stated, but probably for the school-houses.

[1773.] On January 28, 1773, a communication from the town of Boston, setting forth the rights of the colonies and a statement of the infringement of their rights, was laid before the town for their consideration.

A committee, consisting of William Sylvester, Deacon Andrew Dunning, and Captain Benjamin Jaques, was chosen to write a reply and to submit it to the town at a special meeting to be held on the eighth day of March, at which time the committee reported as follows: —

"That generous Ardor for Civil and Religious Liberty which in the Face of every Danger and even Death itself induced our fore Fathers to forsake the Bosom of their Native Country their Pleasant Seats and Fertile Fields and begin a Settlement in this then a howling Wilderness is not extinct in us their Posterity.

"they Dearly purchased (with many Tears Prayers Mortifications & Self Denials) those happy Gospel Priviledges and Religious Liberties which we enjoy in Conjunction with the Royal Charter these we esteem dear and Sacred — we are greatly alarmed at the Innovations made upon our Charter Rights and think them a Real Grievance — We fear not Poverty but disdain Slavery.

'whatever Day,
Makes Man a Slave takes half his worth away.'

"We shall not particularly enumerate our Grievances but only Say we Concur with the Sentiments of the Committy of Correspondence at Boston as they have stated the rights of the Colonists and of this Province in Particular, and of the Infringements on those Rights. We openly and Frankly declare that we hold Fast our Loyalty to our Sovereign (Independency we have not in View — we abhor the Thought) and hold our Selves in Readiness at all times with our lives and Fortunes to assist his Majesty in his Defence as we have heretofore done (when for the Enlargement of the Brittish Empire, upon the Ruins of their Perfidious French Neighbors we have Cheerfully Emptied our Purses and furnished out our Quota of Men to join the Countless Numbers of loyal Americans who have Sacrificed their lives in the high Places of the Field & Desert — Many of whose Bones are to this Day whitning in the sun) yet we groan under our Burdens we sensibly feel them, but do not despair of Redress If the Importunity of a Poor widow May Moove an unjust Judge to avenge her How much More

May we hope for Redress by Frequent application to our Gracious and good King which application we humbly conceive Should be Dutiful and loyal — Vewing our Selves to be the children and our Gracious Sovereign the Parent. And Could his Excelency Our Governour (whom we highly esteem & think to be endow[d] with Singular abilities) be prevailed upon to join the other Branches of the Legislature Supplicating the Throne for Redress it appears to us the Most probable way of obtaining his Majestys Royal Attention and Relief.

"WILLIAM SYLVESTER
AND[W] DUNING
BENJ[N] JAQUES } *Committy.*"

The records continue as follows: —

"The question being put whether the foregoing Report be accepted it Passed in the Affirmative *Nemine contradicente* and thereupon voted William Sylvester Esqr., Deacon Andrew Duning & Capt. Benj. Jaques a Committy to Transmit an attested Coppy from the Clerk to the Comitty of Correspondence at Boston with the Thanks of this District to that Respectable Patriotic Town."

[1774.] At the annual meeting in 1774, the town passed the following votes: "to allow Andrew Duning 6 shillings a year since 1759 for services as Clerk," and "to fence the burying place with stone or boards, as the Committee think proper."

At a special meeting, held August 11, William Sylvester, Esquire, Andrew Dunning, and Deacon Isaac Snow were chosen a committee to reply to sundry letters from the town of Boston, relative to entering into a covenant for the non-consumption of British goods.

The committee reported as follows: —

"That the Town of Boston is Now Suffering in the Common Cause, a Cause which we Esteem to be Our Own that it is our Fixed Resolution not to be Awed into Acquiesence by a Mad Exertion of Mere Power on the Part of Our Enemies but to hold and Defend Our Charter Rights to the Last. that a general Agreement between the Colonies of non importation & non exportation faithfully observed would (under God) be a Means of the Salvation of our falling Country that as the Honourable House of Representatives Did on June 17th 1774 Resolve that a Committy Should be appointed to Meet as Soon as May be the Committies that are or shall be appointed by the Several Colonies on this Continant to Consult together upon the Present State of the Colonies and to Deliberate & Determine upon Wise and Propper Measures to be by them Recomended to All the

Colonies for the Recovery & Establishment of their Just Rights — & it is our Opinion that our now Coming into the non-Consumption agreement Previous to the Result of the Congress would be Premature and that We should Anticipate the Verry End of that Respectable Body we therefore think it More Regular and Advisable first to hear the Measures advised to by the Congress and we hold our Selves in Readiness to Comply with the Same."

This report was accepted.

On September 14th, Joseph Ewing, Captain John Stover, and Andrew Dunning were chosen a committee "to go to Falmouth to meet the Falmouth and other Town Committees at Falmouth, y[e] 21st of Sept. Inst."

[1775.] On March 20, 1775, the town passed the following vote: "to Give the Men that Shall Engage as Minute Men too Shillings & Eight Pence p[r] Week allowing they Meet three Days each week & spend three Hours Each Day in exercising or Learning the Art Military for One Month from Date Agreeable to the Advice of the Congress — and if Legually called by the Chief Officers to March Out of Town Shall be entitled to forty eight Shillings as A Bounty or Incouragement and the like Incouragement to Any Others that shall be Legally Called as above & comply with the call."

The selectmen were this year instructed to have the town's proportion of the Province rate paid to Henry Gardner, Esquire, "as soon as may be."

William Sylvester, Joseph Orr, Nathaniel Purinton, John Snow, Samuel Bartlett, James Ridley, Joseph Ewing, Andrew Dunning, Benjamin Jaques, Paul Curtis, John Stover, Ebenezer Toothaker, John Roduck, John Farnham, Mark Rogers, William Morgridge, Simeon Hopkins, Ezekiel Curtis, and Anthony Coombs, Jr., were chosen a Committee of Inspection and of Correspondence.

The town also voted to provide a stock of ammunition, double in quantity the amount required by law. On May 1st, William Sylvester, Nathaniel Purinton, John Snow, Benjamin Jaques, and Andrew Dunning were chosen a Committee of Supply.

At a meeting held on the 5th of June, it was voted that "the Remainder of the half barrel of Powder Purchased by the Committy of Supply be a Town Stock." It was also, at this time, "Voted to keep four Watches — One at the intervale By the Harbour or there Abouts One at the High Land Near Benj. Webbers One at the Lookout and One at Jaqueses Hill And Every Person Deficient being Duly Notified to Pay Six Shillings as a fine." It was also voted,

"Not to fire a gun between Sun Set & Sun Rise except at the enemy or an Alarm on Penalty of Setting in the Stocks One Hour."

The town also voted that the powder should be furnished to those needing it, in the quantity of half a pound for each man, who applied and who should pay or give his note for it.

Captain John Snow, Paul Randall, and William Sylvester were chosen a Committee of Supply and Safety.

At a meeting held July 6th, Captain Nehemiah Curtis was selected to join with the committees of other towns in the county, for the purpose of distributing in the most important places the men who were stationed for a guard upon the sea-coast.

[1776.] At a meeting of the town held January 16, 1776, the selectmen were chosen a committee to embody in a petition to the General Court the necessity there was for an armed guard and a supply of ammunition in the town.

On March 4, William Sylvester, Nathaniel Purinton, Captain Nehemiah Curtis, Captain John Snow, and Lieutenant Benjamin Dunning were chosen a Committee of Correspondence, Inspection, and Safety. At a meeting held May 6, the vote of the District in 1775, giving minute-men 2*s.* 8*d.* per week for meeting for military practice on three days in each week, for three hours each day, was rescinded. On July 30 it was voted that the selectmen should take charge of the ammunition and arms, receipt for the same, and then distribute them among the officers of the militia, who should be accountable for them. It was also voted to pay Nathaniel Purinton and the seven men who assisted him in bringing guns down the Kennebec River, 4*s.* each, for two days' labor. It was also voted to pay Deacon Isaac Snow 12*s.* for his expenses and charge in bringing twenty-five fire-arms from Falmouth. Andrew Dunning was, at this meeting, chosen to take recognizances in Harpswell. At a meeting held on December 20, the following resolutions were passed: —

"Voted the great & General Court or Assembly of this State Do Take up a Form of Government as Soon as they think Propper & that form that Shall tend most to Piety, Peace, Safety and Good Order in this State and agreeable to the Honourable Continental Congress — the vote unanimus at a full Meeting.

"Voted the Selectmen Send to the General Court or Treasurer for Axes, Kittles, Canteens and Money to hire Waggons & Pay the Men that are Draughted their Milage to the Place of Destination."

[1777.] At the March meeting in 1777, Nathaniel Purinton, Captain John Snow, Captain Nehemiah Curtis, Ezekiel Curtis, and

Andrew Dunning were chosen a Committee of Correspondence and Safety. It was also voted, "Not to Have a Hospetal Built in the County for an Enocolating Hospetal." It was also voted this year to pay Andrew Dunning 12*s*. for superintending the delivery of powder and flints, and for recording the Declaration of Independence. On November 25, a committee was chosen to supply the families of soldiers with necessary articles.

[1778.] The entry of the May meeting in 1778 commences, "At a meeting of the Town of Harpswell." It is the first time that the records were thus commenced, heretofore the words "parish," "district," or "inhabitants" being used. Yet Harpswell must have been in all respects a town prior to this, having in 1770 elected a representative. At this meeting, Captain John Snow, Joseph Ewing, Benjamin Dunning, Ezekiel Curtis, Captain Thomas Merryman, Paul Randall, and Alexander Ewing were chosen a Committee of Inspection, Safety, and Supply. It was voted to raise £420 "for the reinforcement of nine men now to be raised, and proportioned as hereafter mentioned, viz. to four men for the militia one hundred *dollars* per man. To five men for the Continental Army two hundred *dollars* per man." The selectmen were instructed to hire the money to pay the above bounties, and also the mileage of the soldiers.

At a meeting, held June 24, the town voted to purchase some clothing which had been provided for the soldiers and also to raise the sum of £56 for the four men who had that day enlisted. At another meeting, held on the third of August, it was voted that the selectmen should provide the town's proportion of clothing for the army, in accordance with the order of the General Court, passed the previous June, and that each article of clothing should be of the same price as previously, if of as good quality, and that it should be valued by the same committees.

[1779.] At the March meeting in 1779, Thomas Merryman, James Ridley, and Alexander Ewing were chosen a Committee of Correspondence, Inspection, Safety, and Supply. At a meeting, held July 2, it was voted that all the male inhabitants of Harpswell above the age of sixteen years should take the oath of allegiance to the United States. It was also voted to supply powder and balls from the town stock to such as might need them; that the price of the powder should be £3, and of balls 15*s*. per pound. — each one being allowed half a pound of powder, and balls in proportion. It was also voted that Michael Curtis, Thomas Farr, Paul Randall, and John Blake should be a committee "to wait on the Justice to tender the oath of allegiance to the United States," and that all males over the age of sixteen years who refused to take that oath should be disarmed. At a meeting held in August, it was voted to sell eight fire-arms, that had been recently purchased, at forty two and one half dollars each.

[1780.] At the March meeting in 1780, William Sylvester, Esquire, Captain Nehemiah Curtis, Paul Curtis, Thomas Farr, Captain Isaac Snow, Lieutenant Anthony Coombs, and Simeon Hopkins were chosen a Committee of Correspondence, Inspection, and Safety. At the May meeting the town voted to raise £2,000 for expenses and £300 for support of the poor.

The proposed new constitution for the State of Massachusetts was read and considered article by article. It was amended "in Page 27th, last line, for the word Christian to have the word Protestant and in Page 33d — the House of Representatives to have a voice in the appointment of officers for the Continental army." Thus amended, thirty voted in favor of, and one against it. At a meeting held in September, the town voted for governor, lieutenant-governor, and senator. John Hancock received fourteen votes as governor; Samuel Adams eight, and James Bowdoin seven, as lieutenant-governor; and John Lewis, fifteen as senator. This is the first record of a vote of this town for State officers.

At a meeting held October 23, a committee was chosen to procure beef for the army.

[1781.] On January 11, 1781, a committee was chosen to procure soldiers for the Continental army, and on the thirtieth of the month the town voted "to give Sixty Pounds L. M. Paid in the Old Way in hard money, Stock, Produce or Equal in other things as shall be agreed on by the Town and Persons Engageing."

At a subsequent meeting, held the third of February, the town voted that the above-named sum should be given as a bounty to each man that should enlist for three years as a soldier, and that it should be paid "by the tenth Day of May next, or as Many Midling Cows & Calfs as shall amount to the Sum at five Pounds for each Cow & Calf or Intrest for the same till Paid."

At a meeting held in March, the town voted that "the Pools [polls] & estates in the Town be Divided into ten classes as Near as may be to Pay the Bounty Given the ten Continental soldiers, the Assessors to assess the Inhabitants & Each Class to collect their Part & Pay to the Agents for the Soldiers according to Agreement." And that "the whole sum contained in the Notes Given the Soldiers be assessed except the Cows that were Promised at the three years end, the Town to be assessed for the money."

At a meeting held in April, a Committee of Correspondence, Inspection, and Safety was chosen as usual.

At a June meeting it was voted to raise thirty-five pounds for current expenses and fifteen pounds for the support of the poor, the money to be reckoned in silver dollars at six shillings each, or in other currency equivalent to silver.

In July the town voted to raise £50 in silver, or its equivalent, for the purchase of the beef called for by the General Court in its requisition of June 22.

On December 5, the town voted to pay twenty-two shillings per hundred-weight for the beef needed to fill the second and third requisitions, and to raise £16 for that purpose.

[1782.] In May, 1782, the town voted to relieve the tax collector of all responsibility for the counterfeit money he had received prior to July, 1781, upon his making oath to the facts. The usual Committee of Correspondence, etc., was chosen this year.

[1783.] In March, of this year, the town voted to build two pounds, one to be erected on the neck and the other on the island.

In May, Nathaniel Purinton, Esquire, Lieutenant Anthony Coombs, Deacon Andrew Dunning, Benjamin Dunning, and Lieutenant Michael Curtis were chosen a Committee of Inspection, "on account of the Return of the Absentees."

[1785.] In March, 1785, the town voted to rent a workhouse, also to pay for labor on the highways the following rates: 4*s.* per day per man, 2*s.* for oxen, 8*d.* for a cart, and 1*s.* for a plough.

[1787.] On January 8, 1787, the town voted in favor of the three eastern counties being made a separate State, and Captain Isaac Snow was elected to represent the town at the convention to be held at Portland on the last Wednesday in January.

On December 10, Captain Isaac Snow was elected a delegate to attend the convention to be held at Boston on the second Wednesday of the succeeding January, and a committee was chosen to give him instructions. On the twenty-eighth of the month the town met to hear the instructions which the committee had prepared, and it was at this meeting voted to "except [accept] the federal Constitution with Amendments." This vote explains the object of the convention for which the town had chosen a delegate.

[1792.] The town appears to have been very undecided as to the utility of a separation of the eastern counties from Massachusetts. In January it voted in favor of it and in May against it.

[1794] On August 11, 1794, it was voted "to give the men that

shall go on *this* detachment five dollars as a bounty if they are called for into service. Voted to make up to the men that shall List with the Continental Pay, twelve dollars per month for three months if they should be called into actual service." The object for which a detachment was made from the Harpswell company of militia has not been ascertained. It is evident, however, from the above vote, that it was of a national character.

In November of this year, Stephen Purinton, Johnson Stover, and Benjamin Dunning were chosen to make a survey and plan of the town, in accordance with the provisions of an Act of the General Court passed the preceding eighteenth of June.

[1795.] This year the town voted — thirty-eight to twelve — against a revision of the Constitution.

[1796.] In May of this year the town voted "That if any let his Ram go at Large between the first day of September and the Tenth Day of November he shall forfeit the Ram."

[1797.] On May 10, 1797, the town again voted against a separation of the District of Maine from the State of Massachusetts.

[1798.] At a meeting held October 15, 1798, the town voted against "the formation of a new county to be composed of the towns of Brunswick, Harpswell, Durham, Georgetown, Bath, Topsham, Bowdoin, Bowdoinham, Little River, Litchfield, Green, Lewiston, Wales, and Littleborough."

[1803.] In 1803 the town offered a bounty of four cents for each crow killed during that year.

[1805.] In 1805 it was voted that "if the Treasurer shall receive any bank bills that will not pass that the town will receipt for the same." This was a singular way to discountenance the counterfeiting of money.

[1810.] This town seems to have been remarkably lenient towards those who had been imposed upon by counterfeit, or bad money, for this year it was voted "to receive a three dollar bill of the Widow Sarah Haskell, on Vermont State Bank, said not to be good, and give her good money in lieu of the same, and voted that Paul Raymond have the bill and *make sale of it to the best advantage*."

[1812.] At the annual meeting in 1812, the town voted "that Peter Birthright [and his family] live on the premises where they are and the Selectmen supply them with necessarys."

A present of ten dollars was also voted to Samuel Clark. At a special meeting, held August 24th, Stephen Purinton and John Curtis were elected delegates to a County Convention to be held at Gray "to take measures to alleviate the miseries of war, and bring about a speedy and lasting peace." The selectmen, with Stephen Purinton and Marlborough Sylvester, were chosen a Committee of Safety and Correspondence.

[1814.] At a meeting held July 25th, the town chose Stephen Purinton as an agent to go to Boston to receive Harpswell's quota of the State stock of arms and ammunition, provided that he could get them at the expense of the State and without cost to the town.

At a town meeting held the seventh of November, the selectmen were chosen a committee to receive into their care the arms and equipments for the town, and were authorized to dispose of the arms, one to a person, on sufficient security that those who received them would deliver them up when called for.

[1816.] In May, 1816, the town again voted against a separation from Massachusetts, and in September also, by a still stronger vote. At this latter meeting Reverend Samuel Eaton was chosen as delegate to the convention to be held at Brunswick on the last Monday in September.

[1817.] In 1817 the collectorship of taxes on the Great Island was struck off at auction to John Reed at five and a quarter cents, and that on the Neck to David Orr at four and a half cents on the dollar.

[1819.] In July, 1819, the town again voted against the separation of Maine, but at a meeting held in September, Stephen Purinton was elected delegate to the Portland convention, and on the sixth of December the town voted in favor of accepting the Constitution prepared by that convention.

UNDER STATE OF MAINE.

[1821.] At a meeting held February 25, 1821, the town voted to send a representative to the legislature for their proportionate part of the time, but objected to being classed for representation with any other town. At this meeting the town also voted against being set off from the county of Cumberland, and also against the formation of a new county. At a meeting held in May, it was voted "that Joseph Eaton shall purchase locks and hinges for the town chest, at the expense of the town."

[1822.] In 1822 the town's poor were, according to custom, set at vendue, but a vote was passed that those who bid them off should furnish them with suitable food and with tobacco, but should provide no clothing without the consent of the overseers of the poor. At a meeting of the town, held on December 21, a committee was chosen to present to the legislature a remonstrance against the proposed division of Cumberland County. At this meeting the selectmen were instructed to remonstrate to the legislature "against the now extended limits of the jail yard in this county."[1] The town also voted that the selectmen and town clerk should "instruct the representative in future events."

[1823.] In 1823 the town voted in favor of allowing the inhabitants of Great Island to be set off as a separate town.

[1825.] At the annual fall meeting this year, "it was motioned and seconded to take the minds of the people whether to send a representative or not, and the vote was not to send. The presiding selectman then told the people if there were any who wished to bring in their votes he should receive them." The result was that John Curtis had twenty-two votes, Paul Randall thirteen, and Peleg Curtis one vote.

[1826.] At the September meeting, in 1826, the town voted that the militia should be furnished with one quarter of a pound of powder for each man — made into blank cartridges — and that the commanders of companies should cause it to be expended in teaching the men precision in firing. Luther Dana was, in November of this year, licensed "as a retailer of strong liquors to be spent out of his shop." This is the first license of the kind recorded in the town records.

[1827.] In 1827 the town voted to let the powder remain in the magazine, and to pay the militia money instead of rations; also, to deliver to each non-commissioned officer and private — at the review inspection — one quarter of a pound of powder to be made into blank cartridges.

[1829.] In 1829 the town voted that the selectmen should grant licenses to sell intoxicating liquors to all suitable persons, who were victuallers or retailers, that should apply for a license agreeably to the provisions of an Act passed in March of that year.

[1831.] On January 3, 1831, the town voted *unanimously* against the formation of a new county, if Harpswell was to be included in it.

On January 25, it was voted to petition the legislature not to class Harpswell with any other town for representation, but for it to authorize the town to elect a representative for such a portion of time and at such period as should be equal to their portion of representation. The request was not granted.

---

[1] *Was this an exquisite bit of satire, implying that the jail was so insecure that the prisoners roamed all over the county?*

[1832.] On July 7, 1832, a law of March, 1832, relating to vaccination was read, and the town then voted to make no provision for vaccinating the inhabitants, and to raise no money for such a purpose. Peleg Curtis, Joseph Eaton, Levi L. Totman, Stephen Snow, and David Johnson, 2d, were chosen a Health Committee, and were instructed to use all reasonable means to prevent the introduction and spread of the cholera in that town.

[1834.] On February 15, 1834, the town voted, for a fourth time, against the formation of a new county, and still again at a meeting in September. It was also voted this year that no licenses should be granted to retailers, permitting them to sell liquor to be drank in their stores. The selectmen were authorized to grant permits for the taking of lobsters, and the next year (1835), they were instructed to grant a license to Captain John Smith, of Waterford, Connecticut, and company, to take lobsters, — he not to employ more than six smacks, — and to none others, for the sum of one hundred dollars per year until the town ordered otherwise.

[1836.] An article in the warrant for the annual meeting of the town in 1836, for purchasing one or more hearses, was "passed over," and until the year 1877 there was no hearse in town.

[1837.] In March of this year the representative was instructed to favor the passage of an Act so that the town might receive its proportion of the surplus revenue. At a meeting, held the next April, Benjamin Randall was chosen an agent to receive the town's proportion of the surplus revenue, and it was voted to have this money loaned to the citizens, and a committee was chosen to superintend the loan. It was also, at this meeting, voted that the overseers of the poor should try to remove all negroes from the town. This action may have been due to antipathy against the race, but it was more probably because the negroes were all paupers. The town, also, this year, voted almost unanimously against an amendment to the State Constitution relative to bail.

[1838.] This year the town voted that the surplus revenue money should be divided among the citizens, *per capita*, as soon as it could be collected. Paul Randall was chosen an agent to collect and distribute it, and he was authorized to collect it "in Union Bank bills and small change."

[1839.] The town this year voted against a proposed amendment to the State Constitution, relating to the tenure of judicial officers.

[1840.] At the regular meeting this year a committee was appointed to consider and report concerning the annual value of the lobster privilege. They reported that it was worth one hundred and ten dollars per year, and the town voted to lease it at that price.

[1841.] The town, this year, voted in favor of a resolve of the legislature, passed in April, which reduced the number of representatives to one hundred and fifty-one. Also, in favor of diminishing the number of representatives when they reached two hundred. The town, this year, again petitioned the legislature not to class Harpswell with any other town, but to assign its proportion of representation.

[1843.] A committee was chosen, this year, to ascertain where land could be purchased for an almshouse.

[1844.] The town, in 1844, voted very strongly against a resolve of the legislature for amending the Constitution, which was passed March 19, and it also voted unanimously against an Act to establish town courts, which was passed by the legislature, March 22.

[1845.] In February, 1845, a committee was chosen to petition the legislature for a separate representation. Several meetings were held in the winter and spring of this year, to fill the vacancy caused by the resignation of Samuel Mayall, the representative to the legislature. There was no choice, as this town voted each time for a Harpswell man instead of one from Gray, the town with which it was classed in representation. The town this year purchased land and built a house — which it still owns — on Lamboe's Point, for Thomas J. Pennell and family, who had lately removed from Gray. Pennell was a poor man, but able-bodied, and the town furnished this assistance as a precautionary measure to keep him from becoming a pauper.

[1846.] This year the town had the same trouble as the year before in regard to electing a representative.

[1847.] The town in 1847 voted against a resolve of the legislature which provided for the election of representatives to the legislature by a plurality vote; also, against an Act pledging the credit of the State and creating a State debt.

[1851.] In 1851 the town again petitioned for a separate representation in the State legislature.

[1852.] In 1852 the selectmen were instructed to appoint an agent to sell liquors.

[1853.] At a special meeting, held on February 26, 1853, the town was found to be unanimously opposed to Harpswell being set off from Cumberland and annexed to another county, and it was voted to remonstrate against all petitions for new counties that included Harpswell.

[1855.] In March of this year the town voted not to dispense with a liquor agency, but that if the selectmen should appoint an agent they should buy the liquor and pay him a reasonable compensation for selling it, the town receiving the profits thereof. In September the town voted against certain proposed amendments to the State Constitution, by which judges of probate, registers of probate, sheriffs, municipal and police judges, land-agent, attorney-general, and adjutant-general should be elected by the people.

[1856.] In March, 1856, the selectmen were instructed to see if the old meeting-house could be obtained of the proprietors, and in September the town voted to buy it for a town-house, for one hundred dollars, the price being that fixed by the proprietors.

[1857.] The selectmen were instructed in 1857 to remove the body pews in the town-house, build a chimney, provide wood, etc.

[1858.] At a special meeting, held in May of this year, the town voted unanimously in favor of the prohibitory law; fifty-nine votes being cast.

[1859.] The town in 1859 voted against State aid to the "Aroostook Railroad Company." It was also voted that the selectmen should take counsel in reference to some disputed islands adjacent to Harpswell, and should report as to the probability of the town's being able to deny them. The representative to the legislature was instructed to use all means in his power to reduce the expenses of the State government.

[1861.] In 1861 the town voted to petition the legislature for a separate representation for the term of ten years. The request was not granted.

The town records, subsequently to the last date, contain nothing of general interest, except what relates to the enlistment of volunteers and the support of their families, which will be mentioned in another connection, until 1865.

[1865.] At a meeting, held April 8, of this year, it was voted to raise $2,500 to purchase a town farm. Charles Stover, Paul C. Alexander, and Paul A. Durgan were chosen to hire the money and were instructed to hire it on town bonds, running fifteen years. This vote, however, was evidently never carried into effect.

[1866.] At the annual meeting in 1866 the town voted to leave the poor in the care of the overseers. It was also voted to raise $1,500 for the support of the poor.

[1867.] In 1867 the selectmen were authorized and instructed to have a room finished in the gallery of the town-house for an office, and also to build a chimney and procure a stove, and to have the building shingled. At a meeting held June 3d, the town voted unanimously in favor of an Act of the legislature for the suppression of drinking-houses and tippling-shops.

[1869.] At the annual meeting this year it was voted to buy a town farm, and L. H. Stover, William C. Eaton, and S. S. Toothaker were chosen a committee to get proposals, and were instructed to report at a meeting to be called for the purpose. The committee reported on the twenty-fourth of April, and the town voted to raise $3,000 by loan to purchase a farm, and the selectmen were instructed (if in their judgment the interests of the town required the purchase of a town farm) to purchase such a farm as they should think proper, and make the necessary repairs on the same.

[1870.] At the annual meeting in 1870, the town voted to leave the care of the poor with the overseers, and also to raise $1,500 for their support. The town also voted "that the treasurer be instructed to keep the State bonds arising from equalization in his own house."

[1871.] On January 14, 1871, the town voted that the selectmen and overseers of the poor "be and are hereby instructed to build a new barn for James Alexander in place of the one destroyed by fire, and that they furnish him with hay and sufficient farming tools, using their discretion in the matter."

The town also passed the following resolve: —

"That in our candid judgment the burning of the barn of James Alexander, 2d, and the maiming of his cattle in the night-time by some person or persons unknown, is an outrage upon a peaceable community which demands the most vigorous efforts to detect and convict the perpetrator, as no person is safe in his person or property in a community containing at large such a person.

"Therefore, *Resolved*, That the selectmen be authorized and instructed and are hereby required to make diligent search to apprehend and convict the offender, using their discretion as to the methods to be taken to produce that result."

The selectmen were also instructed to oppose the repeal of the Porgie Law, before the Committee on Fisheries at Augusta.

At a meeting held February 6th, the following preamble and resolution were passed by unanimous vote: —

"Whereas the location of our town of Harpswell is so isolated and is so far removed from any town not entitled to a representative, that it would be very inconvenient, and of no benefit to have it classed for representation.

"Therefore, *Resolved*, That we in our corporate capacity, agreeable to the requirements of the constitution of Maine, do hereby determine against a classification with any other town or plantation, and we do hereby instruct the town clerk to forward a copy of this resolution to the speaker of the House of Representatives, praying that the legislature may authorize the town of Harpswell to elect a representative for such portion of time and such periods as shall be equal to its portion of representation."

The prayer was not granted, however, and Harpswell still continues to be a classed town.

At the annual meeting this year, the town voted that the selectmen "be authorized to purchase a town farm the present year and to hire money for the purpose." This vote, however, was never carried into effect.

[1873.] At a meeting held in October, 1873, the town voted to exempt from taxation for six years the property located and the capital invested in Harpswell, of S. F. Perley and twenty-five others, who were associated for the manufacture of superphosphates, bone, plaster, fertilizers, and acids.

The important doings of the town not already mentioned will be found incorporated in other chapters.

CHAPTER IV.

MUNICIPAL HISTORY OF TOPSHAM.

THE town of Topsham first received its name, legally, in the year 1717, when a vote passed in the House of Representatives of the Commonwealth of Massachusetts, "That the other Town Plotted In a square of a Mile to y[e] eastward of Androscoggin River fronting to Merrimeeting Bay be allowed and accepted by the name of *Topsham* and be Plotted & Laid out the quantity of Six miles Square as the Land will allow." [1] This tract of land was mainly settled by English emigrants, the greater number of whom are supposed to have come from the town of Topsham, England, and to have named the place in memory of their former home. The situation of the place on the bank of a river may possibly have given it, to the minds of its founders, a fancied resemblance to its English namesake.

The settlement of the town under the Pejepscot proprietors has already been given in previous chapters. No records of any municipal doings of the inhabitants previous to the incorporation of the town have been preserved, if, indeed, there ever were such.

UNDER THE COMMONWEALTH OF MASSACHUSETTS.

[1764.] The municipal history of the town commences, therefore, with its incorporation in January, 1764. The petition for an Act of Incorporation was as follows: —

"*PROVINCE OF THE MASS[A] BAY.*

"TO HIS EXCELLENCY FRANCIS BARNARD ESQ GOV[R] & COMMANDER IN CHIEF OF SAID PROVINCE, THE HON[BLE] HIS MAJESTYS COUNCILL AND THE HON[BLE] HOUSE OF REPRESENTATIVES IN GENERAL COURT ASSEMBLED, DEC. 21, 1763.

"THE PETITION OF THE INHABITANTS OF THE SETTLEMENT OF TOPSHAM IN THE COUNTY OF LINCOLN.

MOST HUMBLY SHEWETH.

"That from the Year 1715 under the Sanction & approbation of this Honoured court the Settlement of said Place was projected at the

---

[1] *Massachusetts Records*, 1717.

Desire & Expense of the Pejepscot Proprietors under whose Right the said Inhabitants originally settled & so continue to this present time: That we always have been and still are an Exposed Frontier & have greatly suffered by the Indian Enemy Nevertheless by the Divine Favour have maintained said Settlement under the Protection of this Government and there are at this time to the number of thirty five families who are desirous of being incorporated that so they may be enabled to have the Gospell setled among them having already erected a Frame for the Meeting house in said Place; also that they may be qualified to transact their Affairs among themselves necessary to their better Settlement in Town Order the said Inhabitants having laboured under many Inconveniences on these Accounts and by their Situation have been Subjected to be taxed by the Town of Brunswick on which account they have had Just Cause to think themselves no so fairly treated by them.

"Therefore your Petitioners most humbly entreat this Honourd Court would be pleased to incorporate them into a Township or District that they may be entitled to the Advantages & Priviledges other Towns enjoy by virtue of the Royall Charter and that the said present Settlement may thrive & flourish under the encouragement & Protection of this Hon^{d} Court, And your Petitioners as in Duty bound shall ever pray.

"Adam Hunter
William Thorne
James Beveridge
Ezra Randall
William Reed Junr
Charles Robinson
John Reed
William Reed
David Reed
John Orr
John Patten
Sam^{ll} Winchell
Sam^{ll} Staples
John Winchell
Stephen Staples
Joseph Graves
Johnson Graves
Samuel Graves
Archibald Moffatt
Gowen Fulton
James Mustard
James Work
Eben^{r} Work
James Hunter
Wm Hunter
James Fulton
Robert Fulton
John Fulton
Wm Patten"[1]

[1] *Pejepscot Papers.*

In accordance with this petition, Topsham was duly incorporated in 1764. The following is a copy of the Act of Incorporation: —

"ANNO REGNI REGIS GEORGII III TERTIO QUARTO, 1764.

"TOPSHAM A TOWNSHIP.

"*AN ACT*

for erecting a Town in the County of *Lincoln* by the Name of *Topsham.*

"WHEREAS *the Inhabitants settled on a Tract of Land situate on the easterly Side of* Androscoggin River, *lying convenient for a Town, hitherto called and known by the name of* Topsham, *within the County of* Lincoln, *have humbly petitioned this Court, that for the Reasons therein mentioned, they may be Incorporated into a Town, and vested with the Powers and Authorities belonging to other Towns.*

Preamble.

Therefore for the Encouragement of said Settlement:

"BE IT ENACTED BY HIS EXCELLENCY THE GOVERNOR, COUNCIL AND HOUSE OF REPRESENTATIVES IN GENERAL COURT ASSEMBLED.

Bounds of Topsham.

"That the Said Tract of Land described as follows, *viz.* to begin upon the Southerly Line of the Town of *Bowdoinham*, where Said Line strikes the Water, and from thence to run a West Northwest Course upon said *Bowdoinham* Line, as far as it goes, and from thence on the same Streight Course to *Little River* so called, which is about eight Miles from the Water aforesaid, and from thence Southwardly down said *Little River* to *Androscoggin* River, and down said *Androscoggin* River to Merry-meeting Bay, and from thence to the Line of *Bowdoinham* aforesaid, including several small Islands or Islets lying in said *Androscoggin* River, between the Said *Little River* and the Falls at *Brunswick* Fort, be, and hereby is erected into a Town to be called *Topsham*, and the Inhabitants thereof shall have and enjoy all such Immunities and Priviledges as other Towns in this Province have and do by Law enjoy.

"AND BE IT FURTHER ENACTED, That *Aaron Hinkley*, Esq. be and hereby is empowered to issue his Warrant to some principal Inhabitant of the said Town of *Topsham*, requiring him in his Majesty's Name to warn and notify the said Inhabitants

First meeting how to be called.

qualified to vote in Town Affairs, to meet together at such Time and Place in Said Town as shall be appointed in said Warrant, to chuse such Officers as the Law directs and may be necessary to manage the Affairs of Said Town; and the Inhabitants being so met shall be and hereby are impowered to Chuse such Officers accordingly."[1]

The first town meeting was held May 9, 1764. In accordance with the Act of Incorporation, the warrant for this meeting was issued by Aaron Hinkley, of Brunswick, a justice of the peace, and was addressed to Adam Hunter. The following officers were elected at this meeting, viz.: —

Gowen Fulton, moderator; William Thorne, clerk; Adam Hunter, treasurer; John Fulton, John Read, and John Merrill, selectmen; Hugh Wilson, constable; David Reed, Paul Randall, and Samuel Wilson, surveyors of highways; James Work and Thomas Wilson, tithing-men; Ezra Randall and William Wilson, fence-viewers; Robert Gore, sealer of leather; James Beverage and William Alexander, hog constables; Stephen Staples and John Winchell, surveyors of boards, at Cathance; John Merrill and William Wilson, surveyors of boards; Samuel Staples, pound-keeper; James Mustard, field-driver; James Hendry (?), surveyor of staves, shingles, and hoop poles; Adam Hunter, sealer of weights and measures; James Hunter and Robert Gore, wardens.

At a meeting, held June 2, Thomas Wilson, Adam Hunter, John Reed, John Fulton, and John Merrill were chosen a committee to lay out the highways and roads through the town. The town at this meeting voted to raise £34 13*s.* 4*d.* as a contingent fund. There is no record to be found of any meetings of the town in 1765.

[1766.] At a meeting of the town, held May 8, 1766, Mr. William Patten was chosen to prefer a petition to the General Court "in order to get Kate Hance Point annexed to Topsham, and likewise all the islands in Brunswick River, below the falls."

[1767.] The above-mentioned petition was presented to the House of Representatives, and in 1767 the committee to which it was referred reported in favor of its dismissal, and it was dismissed.[2]

At a town meeting, held in July of this year, it was voted to allow men 3*s.* per day for work on the highways, and 2*s.* per day for each yoke of oxen.

[1769.] In 1769 Messrs. John Patten, William Patten, Robert

---

[1] *Topsham Town Records.* [2] *Massachusetts Records, Vol.* 26, 1767, *p.* 49.

Fulton, and Robert Patten, inhabitants of Cathance Point in the town of Bowdoinham, presented a petition to the General Court, asking to be set off from Bowdoinham and annexed to Topsham. The petition was considered by the General Court, and an order issued that the petitioners should notify the town of Bowdoinham that they might show cause at the next session of the Court why the prayer of the petitioners should not be granted.[1]

At the March meeting of the town, this year, James Potter, Jr., was chosen "to go to the General Court to get Cow Island, together with all the islands in the Narrows, annexed to Topsham."

[1771.] On the petition from Topsham it was ordered, in 1771, that the petitioners should notify the town of Brunswick that their petition was revived, in order that the agents of that town might be on hand at the next session of the Court.[2]

At the May meeting, this year, the town requested Mr. John Merrill to draw up a memorial to the General Court, asking to have the line determined between Brunswick and Topsham.

[1774.] At a meeting of the town, held November 19, 1774, it was unanimously voted that the town would stand by what the Continental and Provincial Congresses had done.

[1775.] At a town meeting, held April 30, 1775, Robert Gower and William Randall were chosen a committee to meet the committees of other towns at Pownalborough on the second of May, to represent the town of Topsham, as to the matter of provisions and ammunition, and to consider the method of furnishing the same.

The selectmen having petitioned the General Court for a supply of powder, that body passed a resolve to the effect that Topsham, being a seaport place in the eastern part of the colony, and much exposed to the attacks of the Indians, therefore it was recommended to the selectmen of Wrentham, Massachusetts, to furnish the town with one half barrel of gunpowder at the expense of the colony.[3]

[1776.] The town, at its March meeting this year, instructed the selectmen to petition the General Court to take off the provincial tax, "till the trade is opened." At this meeting James Potter, Junior, David Reed, James Fulton, John Merrill, and Robert Hunter were chosen a Committee of Inspection, Safety, and Correspondence.

At a meeting held June 12th, the selectmen were authorized to hire £30, lawful money, to furnish the town with a stock of powder. In

---

[1] *Massachusetts Records, Vol.* 28, 1769, *p.* 144.
[2] *Massachusetts Records, Vol.* 29, 1771, *p.* 257.
[3] *Massachusetts Records, Vol.* 31, 1775, *p.* 212.

December, the town voted to keep this powder at Captain James Mustard's and at Captain Actor Patten's.

[1777.] At the annual meeting of the town in March, 1777, a new Committee of Safety, etc., was chosen, consisting of Joseph Graves, David Robinson, Joseph Foster, James Purinton, and Pelatiah Haley. At another meeting, held the latter part of this same month, it was voted to petition the General Court for authority to collect the "Province Taxes" for 1776. Also, to send an agent to meet with other committees in other towns of the county, to regulate the prices of goods, etc.

[1778.] At the May meeting in 1778, the number voting against the constitution of the government, as it then was, was nineteen, and there were none in favor of it. The small number voting may possibly be due to a bad state of the weather and a consequently thin attendance, rather than to indifference. This vote was in reference to the ratification of the first Constitution of Massachusetts.[1]

A good deal of doubt was felt in town about this time in regard to the legality of a number of previous meetings, in consequence of there having been a neglect on the part of the constables to make a regular return on the warrants for holding these meetings. The matter was laid before the General Court in a petition. The General Court accordingly passed a resolve this year, "That none of the proceedings of said meetings or of any town meetings since March, 1776, shall be considered as invalid on account of the irregularity of the said returns, or neglect in recording the same."[2]

[1779.] In March, 1779, the town requested John Merrill, Esquire, to furnish a plan of the whole township. At a meeting held in July, the town voted to procure the number of shoes, stockings, and shirts which the General Court called for, for the use of the army.

[1780.] At the annual meeting in 1780, the town voted to give fifty dollars a pair for the shoes referred to above, sixty dollars a pair for the shirts, and forty dollars a pair for the stockings. The town at this meeting appropriated £1,600 for highways, and voted to pay twenty dollars per day for work on the same. £1,000 was also appropriated for current expenses.

At a meeting of the town held November 20, the selectmen were instructed to inform the General Court that the beef called for by them[3] could not be obtained without great difficulty.

---

[1] *Bancroft, History of United States*, 9, *p* 260.

[2] *Massachusetts Records Vol* 38, 1778, *p.* 674.

[3] *Each town was required to furnish its proportion of beef, etc , for the support of the Massachusetts army.*

[1781.] At a special meeting, held February 6, 1781, the town voted to postpone getting the beef referred to above, "until further orders." At this meeting a committee was chosen to procure the enlistment of seven men for the army, as required by the General Court. At the April meeting, Actor Patten, Lieutenant David Reed, and John Rogers were chosen a Committee of Correspondence and Safety. At a meeting held in May, the selectmen were directed to purchase the cows "promised to the Continental soldiers." The town also, at this meeting, voted that if the General Court had released or would release this county from sending its quota of men to the Continental Army, in that case the selectmen would "settle with the soldiers for this town as they think proper." The town also voted to raise £486, hard money, or cows with calf or with calves by their side, — cows to be reckoned equivalent to eight pounds each, — or £3,000 in paper-money.

At a meeting held the July following, it was voted to petition the General Court to release the town from providing the beef called for by them.

[1782.] At a meeting held January 14, 1782, the town voted to petition the General Court in regard to the difficulty they experienced in paying their taxes, and to employ William Lithgow, Esquire, of Boston, to speak in favor of the petition. In March, John Merrill and William Wilson were chosen a committee to petition the General Court in regard to the people at Little River settlement refusing to pay their taxes. Probably the settlement at Little River was an "adjacent" of Topsham.

At a meeting of the town, held on the last day of August, Captain George White was chosen delegate to a convention to be held at Wiscasset, to consider the question of a separation of the District of Maine from the Commonwealth of Massachusetts.

[1783.] At the March meeting in 1783 it was voted to rate the islands below the Falls to the town of Topsham. The wolves must have been committing depredations about this time, as at this meeting a bounty of 40*s*. per head was offered for all that were killed. At a meeting held in May, the town voted to comply with the resolve of the town of Boston, in regard to permitting absent refugees to return. Captain David Reed, John Winchell, and Robert Alexander were chosen a Committee of Correspondence and Safety, this year.

[1784.] William Reed, Ezekiel Thompson, and John Rogers were chosen a Committee of Correspondence and Safety for 1784.

[1785.] William Randall, Actor Patten, and Joseph Berry were the Committee of Correspondence, Inspection, and Safety for the year 1785. At a meeting held in November of this year, Samuel Thompson was chosen a delegate to a convention to be held at Falmouth, to consider as to the advisability of having the eastern counties made into a new State. The town at this time voted to petition the General Court to relieve them, wholly or in part, of their taxes, then due, or about to become due, on account of "the great loss the town had sustained by the late great freshet." It was, also, at this meeting, resolved, "that the former petition sent to the General Court, with regard to the islands in the Androscoggin River being annexed to Topsham," was agreeable to the present wishes of the town.

The General Court this year, on the petition of the inhabitants of Topsham with regard to the islands before mentioned, ordered that the petitioners serve the town of Brunswick with an attested copy of their petition, and of this order, twenty days before the second Wednesday of the next session of the Court.[1]

On the petition for an abatement of taxes, the General Court so far granted the request as to direct the treasurer of the Commonwealth to credit the town of Topsham with the sum of £126 6*s.* 2*d.* on the second tax set on the town in the year 1780.[2]

[1786.] At the annual town meeting in 1786, Samuel Thompson was chosen a delegate to the convention to be held at Falmouth on the first Wednesday of the following September. The question as to whether the District of Maine should be separated from Massachusetts was brought before the people in November, and this town voted in favor of a separation.

[1787.] At the annual meeting in 1787, the selectmen were directed to see that the town was provided with a stock of powder and ammunition, as provided by law. They were also directed to join in a petition of the people of Cathance in regard to having Cathance Neck annexed to Topsham. At this meeting a committee was chosen to take care of the fishery, agreeable to an act of the General Court in 1780, providing for its protection.[3] At a meeting held September 29, it was voted to petition the General Court "to consider us with regard to our deficiency in not [?] paying our taxes." At a meeting held the last day of the year, the town voted "against the constitution," and Samuel Thompson was chosen a delegate to a convention to be held at Boston.[4]

---

[1] *Massachusetts Records, Vol.* 46, 1785, *p.* 97.
[2] *Ibid., p.* 534.
[3] *Massachusetts Records, Vol.* 48, *p.* 472.
[4] *See p.* 132.

[1788.] On March 29, 1788, the General Court decided, on the petition of John Patten and others, of Bowdoinham, and of the town of Topsham, that Patten's Point, so called, be set off from the town of Bowdoinham, and annexed to the town of Topsham.[1]

At the May meeting, 1788, the selectmen were instructed to employ some person as agent to discharge the beef tax then standing against the town, and to authorize him to draw the money out of the town treasury. The town at this meeting voted that an application should be made to the General Court for an act to stop the catching of salmon by dip-nets and seines, and to prevent the building of weirs. Samuel Thompson was elected representative to the General Court, but was instructed not to attend its next session without orders from the selectmen. Another petition was also ordered to be sent to the General Court, in regard to the deficiency in taxes. At a meeting held in December the town gave its consent to the building of a boom from Mason's Rock to Ferry Point,[2] and fixed a scale of prices to be paid the owners of the boom, for stopping masts, bowsprits, logs, etc.

[1791.] In 1791 the representative was instructed not to attend the session of the General Court except so ordered by the authorities of the town, unless at his own expense. The town this year voted in favor of a separation of the District of Maine from Massachusetts. The town also voted against the proposed plan of cutting a canal from the Carrying-Place in Brunswick to Maquoit. But one person voted in favor of this project, while there were fifty voting in the negative. The town also voted to raise this year one half of the money allowed by the General Court for the damages caused by the great freshet of 1785. The excessive depreciation of the old paper currency at this time is shown by the instructions given to the selectmen, which were to the effect that they should take the paper-money belonging to the town and sell it as best they could, but not for a less price than seven dollars, current money, for $1,000 of the old.

[1792.] In 1792 the town voted to distribute, among the sufferers by the great freshet of 1785, one half of the money allowed by the General Court for this purpose. At the May meeting the town again voted in favor of a separation of the District from the Commonwealth. In November the town cast its vote in favor of Samuel Thompson as a Presidential elector. In the list of votes for Presidential electors,

---

[1] *Massachusetts Special Laws, Vol.* 1, *p.* 194.

[2] *Ferry Point, the point of land at the Topsham end of the iron bridge. Before the toll-bridge was built, there was a ferry from this point to the landing in Brunswick below Mason's Rock, hence its name.*

in the Massachusetts archives, the number of votes for him is recorded as seventy-seven.

[1793.] In 1793 Samuel Thompson was chosen a delegate to the convention, to be held at Portland in December, to consider the expediency of forming a new State.

[1794.] At the annual meeting in 1794, the town voted to purchase a stock of ammunition. At a meeting, held September 18, William King, afterwards governor, being moderator, the town voted "that those men who shall this day enlist, agreeably to the Act of Congress of the 10th of May last,[1] shall receive a bounty of four dollars per man, whether called for or not." The town, moreover, voted that those who should enlist should have their wages made equal, by the town, to ten dollars a month, from the time they should march to actual service until their discharge from the service, allowing them a reasonable time to return home; and that they should have one month's wages advanced on their march. Also, that one dollar of the aforesaid bounty should be paid on enlistment, and the remaining three dollars on producing a certificate of having passed muster. Colonel John Read, Jr., Captain Actor Patten, and Doctor Benjamin Jones Porter were chosen a committee to draw up the enlistment orders and to wait on the men and see that their names were enrolled. In November it was voted that a survey of the town be taken, agreeably to a resolve of the General Court. This year, for the first time, several persons were warned to leave the town, not having its consent to reside therein.

[1795.] At the meeting, this year, the selectmen were authorized to take measures to secure the lot of land called the school lot, which was said to belong to the town.

Samuel Thompson was chosen a delegate to a convention, held at Portland, for the same purpose as the previous conventions, and William King was chosen representative to the General Court.

[1797.] The question in regard to a separation of the District from the Commonwealth again came before the people in May, 1797, and the town voted forty-six in favor to one against a separation.

[1798.] This year William King was chosen delegate to a convention to be held at Hallowell, on the fourth Tuesday of the October following, to consider the expediency of dividing Lincoln County, and if judged expedient, to agree on the dividing line.

[1799.] At a meeting held May 6, 1799, the town voted to petition the General Court to have a Court of Common Pleas and General

---

[1] *For the improvement of the militia, Williamson, 2, p. 570.*

Sessions of the Peace held in Topsham thereafter. Reverend Jonathan Ellis, Doctor Benjamin Jones Porter, and James Purington were chosen a committee to draft and present the petition.

[1801.] In 1801 Captain Robert Patten was exempted from paying taxes for that year "by reason of his house being burnt."

[1802.] At its March meeting in 1802, the town voted to hold its meetings in future in the *Court House*, and the meeting in the May following was held there.[1] At this same meeting it was voted not to send any representative to the General Court that year. A motion was made to reconsider this vote, but it was not carried. "After the moderator (Reverend Jonathan Ellis) had declared the meeting dissolved, some person (not one of the selectmen) called for the people to bring in their votes for a representative. One of the selectmen protested against the disorderly manner of introducing the business, and declined having anything to do in receiving the votes. Two of the selectmen, however, with the town clerk, received and counted the votes, receiving, however, a number of unqualified votes and refusing some qualified votes which were offered while the votes were being assorted. The moderator then declared that the town had chosen Jonathan Ellis their representative." The town, at a meeting held on the last day of the same month, had a statement to the above effect prepared for presentation to the legislature, containing a remonstrance against Reverend Jonathan Ellis holding a seat as their representative. He was allowed, however, to take his seat.

[1804.] In 1804 a premium of twenty-five cents per head was offered for crows.

[1806.] A Mrs. Drybury became a town charge in 1806. She was the first pauper the town ever had. She lived in a little cot near the First Parish meeting-house. Her house was sold this year by the town for a small sum.

At the meeting for choice of governor this year, considerable feeling was manifested at what was considered the unfair management of the polls, and a protest was sent to the General Court.

The protest was signed by: —

ROGER MERRILL.	JONATHAN BLAISDELL.
GIDEON WALKER.	LUTHER KIMBALL.
DAVID PATTERSON.	JAMES PURINTON, JR.
SAMUEL EMERY.	JAMES COOK.

[1] *The town meetings had previously been held in the old meeting-house east of the village. Sometimes, in extreme cold weather, the meetings were adjourned to Mrs. Hunter's inn.*

PETER H. GREEN.	DAVID FOSTER.
GIDEON LARRABEE.	MOSES WAYMOUTH.
NATHANIEL GREEN.	WILLIAM FROST.
SAMUEL TOWNS.	JOHN ROGERS.
NATHANIEL WALKER.	JOHN HALEY, JR.

[1807.] In 1807 the town instructed its senator and representative to make application to the legislature for its consent to a separation of the District of Maine from the Commonwealth of Massachusetts.

[1808.] The EMBARGO which Congress had, December 22, 1807, declared, was a source of great vexation and suffering to all the New England towns, especially to those on or near the seaboard. Topsham suffered from this cause equally with Brunswick or Harpswell, and accordingly, at a meeting held August 20, 1808, the town resolved that it "unanimously approves of the doings of the town of Boston," respecting the petitioning for the repeal of the embargo laws, and the selectmen were directed to communicate this action to the selectmen of Boston. The town also voted to present to the President of the United States a memorial requesting him to suspend the embargo, in whole or in part, and Benjamin Orr, Esquire, William Wilson, and Henry Wilson were chosen a committee to draft the address. It was at once prepared and unanimously accepted by the town. The address, probably for the most part the production of Mr. Orr, was as follows: —

"TO THOS. JEFFERSON,
President of the United States: —

"The inhabitants of the town of Topsham in the State of Massachusetts, legally assembled in town meeting on the twentieth day of August, 1808, respectfully represent:

"That having always been influenced by a regard for the general interests and welfare of their country, sincerely attached to its Constitution and duly impressed with the necessity of conforming to the laws of their government, they have hitherto submitted to the privations and losses occasioned by the embargo laws, without opposition or complaint, at the same time indulging an anxious hope, that when experience should ascertain the extent and degree of their sufferings, in common with their fellow-citizens, and events in Europe should render it safe and expedient, a speedy relief would be afforded them, through the existing provisions of Congress for that purpose.

"And could your memorialists entertain a belief that the further suspension of all foreign commerce and the existing restrictions on domestics were necessary to the essential interests of their country, or consistent with the original views and policy of the government in passing the embargo laws, they would still wait the pleasure of government, without an expression of their wishes for relief.

"But concurring in opinion with numerous other sections of citizens assembled to express their sentiments on this subject, your memorialists are impressed with a conviction that the late attempt to subjugate the people of Spain to a foreign yoke, and their consequent declaration of independence, and of war against the power attempting to impose it, have materially altered the relations of the United States to some of the powers of Europe; and also believing that the avenues of a safe and lucrative commerce to the people of this country are by these events laid open, which the wisdom of the legislature has rendered available by placing the power to suspend the laws restricting it, in your hands:

"They therefore pray that the embargo laws may be suspended, in whole or in part, as your wisdom may direct, agreeably to the powers vested in you by Congress for that purpose."

A reply was received from President Jefferson to this memorial, which is entered in full on the records of the town. As it is identically the same answer that was given to similar memorials from the majority of the New England towns, and as it has often been published in documents of State and other works, it is not judged necessary to give it in this connection.

[1809.] At a meeting held February 4, 1809, the following resolutions and memorial were adopted, — the resolutions to be printed in the Portland *Gazette*, and the memorial signed by the selectmen and clerk, to be sent to the representative, to be by him presented to the General Court: —

"*Resolved*, That it becomes us not to despair of the safety of our Republic, while we enjoy the constitutional right and liberty of assembling peaceably to consult upon the common good and to petition the legislature to devise and promote the redress of the wrongs and grievances we suffer.

"That as it is our privilege 'in prosperity to rejoice,' it is our duty 'in adversity to consider,' to investigate, to ascertain the causes of the calamities we experience and the most effectual means to remove them.

"That we are convinced the people in many instances have not been sufficiently cautious in the exercise of their electoral rights, but have permitted themselves to be deceived by crafty and unprincipled men and have frequently conferred their suffrages on seekers of popular favor, without making the important inquiries, 'Are they capable?' 'Are they honest?' 'Are they attached to the Constitution?'

"Hence it has happened that many, destitute of requisite talents and integrity, have been promoted to offices of the highest trust and importance; and that we now feel the extensive mischief naturally arising from this want of caution and inquiry in the people; for power obtained by fraud will always resort to violence for support.

"That the principles and public conduct of our rulers are the fair objects of a manly and public-spirited scrutiny, for the purposes of merited censure or approbation, their continuance or removal from office, in the prescribed forms.

"That, when we take into view the great prosperity generally diffused through our once happy land, under the arduous administration of the revered Washington and his immediate successor, we are compelled to believe, that the numerous and heavy evils since fallen and daily accumulating upon us have been principally occasioned by the departure of our rulers from that wise, firm, liberal, and impartial policy which regulated the conduct of those distinguished patriots.

"That, with sorrow, we must confess that the present executive of the United States has appeared to us, in the course of his administration, more like the dependant and humble friend of a foreign despot than the brave and generous chief of a great spirited and free people, — more devoted to the nefarious schemes of the republic-destroying, King-making Napoleon, than to the security, peace, and happiness of his own country, or to the rights and privileges of those nations, who, having made a noble stand, are now contending from the pure spirit of patriotism against that rapacious tyrant of boundless ambition.

"That the people have a right to require of their lawgivers and magistrates, who are at all times accountable to them, an exact and constant observance of constitutional principles in the formation and execution of the laws.

"That our national legislature, apparently from the impulse of executive influence, have enacted a system of embargo laws, in our decided opinion, unconstitutional in principle and ruinous in operation, that must subject us abroad to contempt, at home to want and wretchedness.

"That we consider the act entitled 'An Act to enforce the several Embargo Laws of the United States,' a most flagrant violation of many articles in our federal and State Constitution and the measures prescribed to carry it into effect to be utterly subversive of our dearest rights and privileges; that it is a law which the people are not bound to obey and which we believe, from their strong attachment to the liberties of their country, they will not obey.

"That we most cordially approve the patriotic conduct of those officers of the revenue department who, disdaining to be the instruments of arbitrary power, and having a more tender concern for the rights of their fellow-citizen than for the emoluments of office, have lately retired to the post of honor, — a private station. That we sincerely hope these patriotic examples will excite a general emulation, and should deeply lament that any from a penurious, calculating spirit, from a mere regard to private property, should submit to or aid the execution of laws destructive of our civil liberties."

"MEMORIAL.

"TO THE HONORABLE SENATE AND HOUSE OF REPRESENTATIVES IN GENERAL COURT ASSEMBLED.

"The inhabitants of the town of Topsham in legal town meeting assembled on the fourth day of February, A. D. 1809, respectfully represent,

"That in the late recess of Congress, they petitioned the President of the United States to relieve them from the sufferings occasioned by the embargo, and, finding no hope of relief, they have made a similar application to Congress, by whom their petition has also been neglected.

"To your honorable body, therefore, your memorialists are induced to resort for relief, not only from the evils and sufferings of which they had reason to complain to the President and to Congress, but also from others of more serious moment emanating from those high authorities.

"At the time of the passing of the first embargo law, the respect due to the constituted authorities induced your memorialists to hope that it would not be continued in force beyond the ability of the people to endure it; but in the Act recently passed, not only to enforce that law and its supplementary appendages, but to extort additional sacrifices the most exorbitant, they recognize a policy equally ruinous and oppressive.

"Had this law been wholly original it would have been less dreadful in its aspects; but in the French decree of April, 1808, it has both an example and guarantee, by which all vessels of citizens of the United States found at sea after that time are declared forfeited to France for breach of the embargo.

"When such is the concurrence of laws, your memorialists can entertain no hope of relief or of safety from the constituted guardians of their national rights and privileges.

"To enumerate the losses, privations, and sufferings resulting from the embargo system would be but a recapitulation of circumstances familiar to every mind.

"The protection they afford to seamen brings with it want and misery; the benefits they confer on merchants are waste and bankruptcy, and to the hand of charity they consign the necessitous laborer and his dependants. As to their effects abroad, none are perceptible to your memorialists, except the approbation of the nation to whom alone they are beneficial and the disregard of that which they were manifestly intended to restrain and humble.

"The act to enforce the embargo, in its relation to the Constitution, cannot escape the notice of your honorable body. By this act the property of your memorialists, as well as their fellow-citizens, is rendered liable to seizure by military force, without evidence, without process or trial, and on the suspicion alone of an accuser, and neither their possessions nor buildings remain a secure depository against the combination of jealousy and force to assail them; these, with the exaction of exorbitant bonds for acts in themselves lawful at the time of doing them, appear to your memorialists calculated to deprive them of their most essential constitutional rights.

"In recurring to the transactions of the last session of your honorable body, your memorialists derive the highest satisfaction from the consideration that the opposing voice of a free people was distinctly expressed to an administration that had been offering up an essential part of their national rights a sacrifice to the boundless ambition of a foreign despot, rights that were obtained by the toils of the illustrious Washington and his companions and fellow-sufferers, and secured by a Constitution that will never be abandoned by free men, to the merciless hands that opposed it in its origin and still seek to destroy it. In the wisdom and firmness of your honorable body to restore to your memorialists and their fellow-citizens of the State the full enjoyment of those rights by rescuing them from the destructive grasp of the tyrant of Europe and his minions, they repose the most implicit confidence, and they pledge themselves by all the lawful means in their power to support the measures that your honors may adopt for the general safety and relief, against the various acts of violence and oppression with which they have been assailed by foreign and domestic usurpers. They therefore pray your honors to take the subject of their grievances into consideration and adopt such measures of redress as you, in your wisdom, shall deem proper and expedient."

[1810.] In the year 1810 a committee was chosen to superintend the inoculation with the kine-pox of all such persons as had not had the small-pox, and one hundred dollars was appropriated for the vaccination of those unable to bear the expense themselves.

[1811.] In 1811 a committee was chosen to discover what method should be taken to keep the highways from being encumbered with mill logs, timber, etc., especially on the island, and in the village near Granny's Hole. This committee reported at a subsequent meeting to the effect that increased diligence should be required on the part of surveyors, etc. The committee on vaccination reported that Doctor Isaac Lincoln had vaccinated four hundred and three persons, of which number three hundred and ninety-one cases had been successful and twelve were doubtful. The committee complimented Doctor Lincoln for the zeal and attention which he had shown in the matter.

[1812.] In 1812 Benjamin Hasey, Esquire, and Thomas G. Sandford were chosen delegates to a county convention, to be held at Wiscasset on August the third, "to take into consideration the alarming state of public affairs, to ascertain and express by memorial, or otherwise, the voice of the people relative to the WAR in which we are now involved, and to devise and recommend the most speedy means of relief from its awful calamities." On August the first, the following resolutions were adopted as the sentiments of the people of Topsham, and a copy of them was sent to the Portland *Gazette* for publication: —

"*Resolved*, That 'in the present season of calamity and war' it behooves the people to exercise their essential and unalienable right of consulting and seeking their safety and happiness; that, at all times, it is their duty to approve and support, with zeal and alacrity, laws for the vindication of their rights and the advancement of their welfare, and their right and privilege to expose and control, by the powers of reason and argument, all public measures endangering their security, their prosperity and peace.

"*Resolved*, That we cannot cease to cherish our fond attachment to the union of the States and the federal Constitution, endeared to us by the upright, wise, and liberal administration of Washington; that we cannot cease to hope that the innumerable evils already inflicted by the partial, degrading, and destructive 'exercise of restrictive energies,' commenced by the last administration and consummated by the present, will awaken in ourselves and our fellow-citizens a lively sense of our common dangers, and unite us, as the surest means of relief, in a firm resolution to intrust with power those only who are true to the example and faithful to the precepts of the departed Father of our Country.

"*Resolved*, 'That we cannot insult the free and gallant citizens of America with the suspicion that they are less able to defend their rights, than the debased subjects of arbitrary power to rescue theirs from the hands of their oppressors; that we will not insult them with the supposition that they can ever reduce themselves to the necessity of making the experiment "to regain their lost liberties" by a blind and tame submission to a long train of insidious measures which must precede and produce it.'[1]

"*Resolved*, 'That a state of war does not destroy or diminish the rights of citizens to examine the conduct of public men and the tendency of public measures';[2] that all attempts to impair the liberty of opinion and inquiry, the freedom of speech and of the press, are infringements upon our most invaluable constitutional rights and privileges, meriting the pointed disapprobation of all except Napoleon and his humble worshippers.

"*Resolved*, That we deeply lament the numerous facts which loudly proclaim that, in too many instances, the spirit of faction has misguided the deliberations of our State and national legislature. That by faction we understand a number of citizens, whether amounting to a majority or minority of the whole, who are united and actuated by some common impulse of passion or interest adverse to the rights of other citizens, or to the permanent and aggregate interests of the whole.

"*Resolved*, That to a factious spirit only can we attribute the *contrivance* of our senatorial districts by which nearly three fourths of the present Senate have been elected by a minority of votes of the whole State. That to intemperate party zeal in the Senate so chosen we must ascribe their obstinate refusal to adopt any one of the various propositions made to them by the House of Representatives, at their last session, for dividing the Commonwealth into electoral districts, and especially their refusing to concur in the resolve providing for the choice of electors by the people at large. That we consider these proceedings as disgraceful to the Commonwealth as grievances of the most alarming magnitude, demanding redress without delay; that we have full confidence that our representative in the General Court will

---

[1] *Madison.* [2] *De Witt Clinton.*

not be wanting in his endeavors to correct procedures so reproachful and oppressive.

"*Resolved*, That to a spirit adverse to the rights of the maritime States we must impute the long neglect and repeated refusals of our Congressional legislature to provide a navy in some degree competent to protect our commerce and guard our extensive and almost defenceless coasts; that our surprise at this neglect is greatly aggravated when we call to mind the solemn truths long since announced by the present chief magistrate of the Union, truths the more important and interesting now we are placed in 'an attitude' if not in 'an armor' of war. 'Naval batteries, the most capable of repelling foreign enterprises upon our safety, are happily such as can never be turned by a *perfidious* government against our liberties. The inhabitants of the Atlantic frontier are all of them deeply interested in this provision for naval protection: and if they have hitherto been suffered to sleep quietly in their beds; if their property has remained safe against the predatory spirit of licentious adventurers; if their maritime towns have not been compelled to ransom themselves from the terrors of a conflagration by yielding to the exaction of daring and sudden invaders, these instances of good fortune are not to be attributed to the *protection* of the existing government that claims *their allegiance*, but to causes that are fugitive and fallacious.'[1]

"*Resolved*, That the closest examination we have been able to make of the long train of our foreign negotiations compels us to believe that the unnecessary and ruinous war, into which we are now plunged, is to be attributed more to the impulse of faction, combined with the intriguing, flattering, menacing, confiscating, plundering, and burning policy of the modern Attila, operating upon our own government with magic influence, than to the 'injustice of a foreign power,' declared to be our enemy.

"That a war so forced upon us we can neither approve nor voluntarily support; that we cannot consent to forego the abundant and honorable returns of legitimate commerce for the scanty and disgraceful plunder of legalized piracy; we cannot freely exchange the cheering scenes of domestic peace for the chilling horrors of the 'bloody arena.' Indeed we are unwilling wantonly to put to hazard the noblest gifts of God to man, — our liberty and independence, — to assist even our *loving* friend Napoleon in his aim to destroy the remnant of liberty in Europe, that he may the more easily bring within his iron grasp the

---

[1] *Madison.*

'ships, colonies, and commerce of the world.' In short, this war we must reprobate and abhor chiefly because it tends to draw us into a close connection, into a fatal alliance with this tyrant of nations, the enemy of the human race, whose tender mercies are cruel, whose friendship is slavery and death.

"*Resolved*, That, undismayed at the gloomy and threatning aspect of our public affairs, we will not despair of the safety of our confederated Republic, trusting that the discerning, enlightened, and resolute spirit of a free people, not to be shaken by the ruffian assaults of faction, not to be seduced by the insidious arts of tyranny, will speedily arise in vindication of their honor and in defence of their rights, and make manifest to the world that their *confidence* cannot be *betrayed* nor their *interests sacrificed* with *impunity*."

[1814.] In 1814 it was voted to accept the offer of the Court House, for the purpose of holding town meetings, on the terms named by the Court of Sessions.

[1816.] At a meeting held May 20, 1816, the town voted strongly against a separation of the District of Maine from Massachusetts, and the representative from Topsham was instructed to use all means in his power to prevent such separation.

At a meeting held September 16, Benjamin Hasey was elected delegate to the convention to be held the latter part of the month in Brunswick.

At a meeting held November 4, the memorial strongly opposing separation, which was adopted by the convention at Brunswick on the last Monday in September, relative to the separation of the District of Maine from the Commonwealth of Massachusetts, was read, and it was then voted that the same should be signed by the selectmen and town clerk, and by them be presented in behalf of the inhabitants of the town of Topsham to the honorable General Court.

[1818.] At the annual meeting in 1818, Messrs. Abel Merrill, Thomas G. Sandford, and Captain Nathaniel Walker were chosen a committee to adopt measures for the maintenance of paupers. They reported at the May meeting in favor of the town poor being collected together and provided for by some one individual.

[1819.] At a meeting held July 6th, 1819, the town again, and for the last time, voted in favor of a separation of the District from the Commonwealth. This was the fourth time that the town had voted in favor of a separation, never having voted against it but once. September 20th, Mr. Nathaniel Greene was elected delegate to the convention to be held at Portland in October, for the purpose of framing a constitution for the new State. On December 6th, the town voted unanimously in favor of the Constitution framed at that convention.

UNDER STATE OF MAINE.

[1820.] The annual town meeting this year was held April 3d. This was the first meeting of the town after the admission to the Union of the State of Maine. At this meeting Mr. Pelatiah Haley declined any longer service as a selectman, and the thanks of the town were tendered him "for the ability and punctuality displayed in his service in that capacity for many years past."

At a meeting held in May following, the representative to the legislature was instructed to advocate a petition in favor of a new county.

[1821.] In 1821 the selectmen were instructed to provide a hearse for the use of the town.

[1822.] The vote for county officers was this year thrown out by the Court, on account of unlawful proceedings at the town meeting.

[1824.] In 1824 the selectmen were instructed to pay each soldier belonging to Topsham, who was entitled to receive rations, agreeably to a late law, twenty cents in cash. This was to enable the soldiers to buy their dinner on muster days. They were also instructed to employ a physician to vaccinate the town. The town this year voted to purchase the farm occupied by Aaron Thompson, "for the use of the town," paying for the same three hundred dollars in three annual payments. Probably the vote never went into effect.

The following by-laws were adopted by the town and approved by the Court of General Sessions this year: —

"1. Sliding down hill in winter on sleds or boards, in any of the public streets, prohibited under a penalty of twenty-five cents for each offence.

"2. Playing with, or knocking, a ball in the streets, within three fourths of a mile from the toll-bridge, prohibited, under a fine of twenty-five cents.

"3. Smoking a pipe or cigar on the streets prohibited under a fine of twenty-five cents for each offence.

"Carrying fire through the streets strictly prohibited, under a penalty of one dollar, unless it was properly secured in some metallic case or pan."

[1825.] At a meeting of the town, held in September, 1825, it voted to accept the land on Great Island, purchased by the selectmen for the use and benefit of the town, at the price of one hundred and twenty-five dollars. This land was for the erection of a building in which to confine an insane person.

At a meeting held in December following, the representative to the legislature was instructed "to oppose the petition of George Jewett and one other," unless the whole expense occasioned by its being granted should be imposed upon the county. It is probable that this petition was for a bridge across the Cathance River, at the eastern part of the town. Persons now living recollect that there was, about this time, considerable discussion in regard to this bridge, and no one has any knowledge of any other purpose for which a petition was likely to be presented at this time.

[1829.] This year the selectmen were instructed to petition the legislature for a new county.

[1832.] In 1832 the representative to the legislature was instructed to confer with the representatives of other towns on the subject of a modification of the militia law, so as to dispense with all trainings except the annual inspection in September, and such other meetings of companies as might be deemed necessary for the proper organization of the militia, and to request their co-operation.

[1833.] The selectmen were again instructed by the town, in 1833, to petition the legislature for a new county. They were also authorized to defend the town against any suit brought by the Maine Stage Company to recover damages for the upsetting of one of their carriages near James Purinton's tannery, in Topsham, on the evening of the 12th of January, 1833, or were authorized to settle the matter with the company, if judged expedient.

[1837.] The town, at its annual meeting in 1837, voted to receive its proportion of the surplus revenue deposited with the State of Maine by the United States government, and to deposit this money in Androscoggin Bank, provided the bank would allow interest at five per cent per annum, the interest to be paid annually to the town treasurer. Mr. John Coburn was appointed an agent to receive and receipt for the money in the name of the town. The September meeting was held in the Freewill Baptist vestry, near the brick schoolhouse. At this meeting the selectmen and treasurer were appointed a committee to consider the subject of building a town-house.

The town also voted that the surplus revenue money should be put at interest and the interest divided among the school districts. This vote was, however, reconsidered the next year [1838], and the town voted to divide it *per capita* amongst the inhabitants, and Gardner

Green was chosen agent to collect and distribute it. The money having already been loaned to individuals, the agent was authorized to borrow the same amount and distribute it *per capita*, as directed for the surplus revenue money. Messrs. Charles Thompson, Joshua Haskell, and William Frost protested against this action of the town as illegal, and gave notice that they would severally hold all persons, and particularly the agent, responsible, who should be instrumental in carrying the vote into effect.

[1841.] In 1841 the town voted in favor of the proposed constitutional amendments, in regard to the election of State officers, but voted against any increase of the number of representatives.

[1842.] In the year 1842 the town was classed, for election of representative, with the town of Bowdoin. Previous to this date it had elected its own representative.

[1843.] At a meeting, held February 6, in accordance with an Act of the legislature to see if the town would consent to the annexation of a part of Bowdoin, agreeably to a petition of sixty-three of the inhabitants of Bowdoin, the town chose Abel Merrill and Nathaniel Walker a committee to remonstrate against and oppose the proposed annexation. At the annual meeting in April, the selectmen were authorized to appoint one or more persons to sell ardent spirits for medicinal and mechanical purposes, and were instructed to prosecute all who were guilty of a violation of the law in regard to such sales. At a meeting held in September following, the selectmen were instructed to petition the legislature for a separate representation of the town.

[1846.] The following by-law was adopted by the town in 1846: "Any person sliding in the streets or highway in the town of Topsham, within three fourths of a mile from the Androscoggin toll-bridge, upon a sled, board, or any other vehicle or thing; or who shall skate in said streets or highways, as aforesaid; or shall knock, throw, or play at ball, in said streets or highways, as aforesaid; or be accessory thereto; shall be punished by a fine not exceeding five dollars for each and every offence so committed, together with costs, to be recovered on a complaint before a justice of the peace.

[1847.] In 1847 the town voted in favor of amendments to the Constitution providing that State officers should be elected by a plurality instead of a majority vote, and also in regard to the State loaning its credit.

[1850.] At a meeting held September 9, the town voted against an amendment to the Constitution providing for a change of the meeting of the legislature from May to January.

[1853.] At a special town meeting, held February 28, 1853, the representative was instructed to use his greatest exertions to prevent any change in the territory of the county of Lincoln, and the senator from the district was requested to co-operate with him. At the annual meeting the article in the warrant, to see if the town would choose an agent to sell liquors for medicinal and mechanical purposes, was dismissed. This was, of course, a total prohibition of the sale of intoxicating liquors for any purpose.

[1854.] In October, 1854, the town was called upon to express by vote its preference of a town to be the shire town of the new county of Sagadahoc, which was incorporated on the fourth day of April previous. The vote stood:

In favor of Topsham for shire town, one hundred and fifty-one. Of Bath, five.

[1855.] The town voted, in 1855, almost unanimously, against amendments to the Constitution of the State which provided that judges of probate, registers of probate, sheriffs, and municipal and police judges should be chosen by the people; and also providing that the land agent, attorney general, and adjutant general should be chosen by the legislature. The representative was chosen this year from the town of Lisbon, Topsham and Lisbon being classed together.

[1858.] In June, 1858, the town voted unanimously in favor of a Prohibitory Liquor Law.

[1859.] At the annual meeting in 1859, the selectmen were authorized to hire out to suitable persons such town paupers as might be able to perform labor, and also to bind out the children of such persons to suitable individuals, who should be required to give bonds for the faithful discharge of their trust. They were also authorized to provide a suitable building or buildings, in which to take care of the aged and of all others unable to do anything for their own support, and to employ some judicious person to take care of them under the general supervision of the overseers of the poor.

At a meeting held in June the town voted to exempt from taxation for ten years all capital which might be invested in manufactures in the town. The town also voted, at this meeting, against "an Act to aid the Aroostook Railroad Company, increase the value and promote the sale and settlement of the public lands."

[1860.] The town concluded in 1860 to make a different provision for its poor, and accordingly, at the annual meeting, it was voted that the selectmen and overseers of the poor be authorized to purchase a farm and to stock the same by hiring or purchasing stock, as they deemed most expedient. The town's poor were to be kept upon the farm and a superintendent was to be chosen who should be under the direction and control of the overseers. The selectmen were also authorized to hire money for the purchase of the farm, and to give notes payable in ten years in equal annual instalments.

The sum of $2,200 was raised this year for the support of the poor, and $1,250 for schools.

[1861.] At the annual meeting in 1861, the town expressed its choice of the candidates for the office of POSTMASTER, and Robert P. Whitney received a majority of the votes. This was an unusual, but at the same time eminently fitting way of securing the appointment of an efficient and honest officer. This year, Topsham and West Bath were classed together for representation.

[1863.] The town-house being in need of repairs, it was voted this year that the selectmen should ascertain what terms could be made with the Sagadahoc Agricultural Society, for the use of their hall for future town meetings. The next year, 1864, the town obtained the privilege of using the Agricultural Hall and authorized the sale of the town-house.

[1865.] This year the town voted to dispense with a liquor agency.

[1867.] At the September election in 1867, the town voted in favor of authorizing the county commissioners to effect a loan of $25,000 to complete the county court house at Bath.

[1868.] In 1868 an appropriation of six hundred dollars was voted for the purchase of a new hearse.

The municipal acts of this town, in reference to the enlistment of volunteers and the support of their families, as well as to all other matters not already given, will be found in their appropriate connection in other chapters.

CHAPTER V.

GENERAL AND SOCIAL.

At the time of the earliest occupation of these towns, the settlers lived far apart, and days, perhaps even weeks, must often have elapsed without a family seeing any of its neighbors. They had few, if any, roads, except the Indian trails, and almost invariably, therefore, settled upon or near some stream which might serve to them as a highway. This accounts for the fact that the houses of the early settlers fronted the water.

EARLY CONDITION AND CIRCUMSTANCES.

The early settlers of Topsham were nearly all English and partook of the national characteristics. Those in the vicinity of the New Meadows River were principally from Cape Cod. Those between New Meadows and Maquoit, who constituted a majority of the inhabitants of Brunswick, were Irish. They were usually called "wild Irish" by the native New-Englanders.[1] It is said of these early settlers that "they used to peek out through a crack or partly opened door, to see whether their callers were friends or foes, and that the same habit of peeking out through a half-open door to see whom their callers may be, is noticed to this day in their descendants." These settlers were nearly all poor, and often suffered for the necessaries of life. They had to work hard for their living, and dress in the plainest manner. Those, however, who came into this vicinity later, somewhere about 1750, were in better circumstances, and the appearance of their rich and fashionable apparel, especially the hoop in the dresses of the ladies, whenever they went to church or showed themselves abroad, drew forth the gaze and wonder of the earlier and more rustic settlers.[2]

The later settlers, and a few of the earlier ones, were sufficiently well off to be able to own slaves. The act of holding fellow-creatures, white or black, in involuntary bondage, was not, at that time, consid-

---

[1] *Pejepscot Papers.*

[2] *McKeen, MSS. Lecture.*

ered to be wrong. Andrew Dunning, who came to Brunswick in 1717 and who died in 1735, kept slaves during his life, and his family continued to own them for some time after his decease. Captain Benjamin Stone, who kept a tavern in Fort George in 1767, and subsequently, had a slave named Sarah Mingo as his house-servant. After she obtained her freedom she kept house for Timothy Weymouth, near where the Congregational Church now stands. Judge Minot also owned slaves. Brigadier Thompson had a negro servant named Hallup. It is uncertain, however, that she was a slave. As late as 1765 there are said to have been four slaves in Brunswick and no less than fourteen in Harpswell. Captain Nehemiah Curtis owned two or three, one of whom was a female.

MANNERS AND CUSTOMS.

Nothing is known concerning the social relations of the very early settlers. During the period embraced by the Indian wars, the character of the people differed materially from what it afterwards was. Instead of gayety and dissipation, a melancholy spirit prevailed. Almost the only topic of conversation with the people was in regard to their troubles with the Indians and the individual difficulties of their situation. Their chief relaxation consisted in singing psalms and doggerel rhymes. The only news that reached them was of cruel murders, by the savages, of their friends and acquaintance, or else of the wonderful escapes and marvellous exploits of the latter. Some of these accounts of personal adventure with the Indians have come down to us and will be noticed. Even when there was no open war with the Indians, the latter would mingle with the inhabitants and were apt to take offence, and revenge themselves by committing indiscriminate depredations. It cannot be denied that oftentimes the settlers were to blame, and that there were many among them who had the same deadly hostility against the savage that they had against a venomous reptile. The only time they could attend to their business without fear of molestation was in the winter, when the Indians usually retired to the interior. At these times they employed themselves in getting lumber to the landings, ready to be sent to Boston and other markets as soon as the spring opened. In summer they cultivated their fields, but always with their guns within easy reach.

In times of peace the Indians were in the habit of trading with the settlers. It is narrated that on one occasion one of the Indians, feeling in a merry mood and ready for sport, challenged old Lieutenant Woodside to run a race with him, and laid down upon the door-stone of the fort six beaver-skins as a wager. The Indian evidently expected, from Mr. Woodside's corpulency, that he would decline the challenge. The Lieutenant, however, contrary to the Indian's expectation, accepted it. The race was to commence at the brook under the hill, and the one who could get the skins first was to have them. At the commencement of the race the old man feigned himself rather more clumsy than he really was. The Indian found he could keep up with him at his leisure, and was quite amused at the clumsy running of so fat a man, and continued indulging in violent fits of laughing until at last the old gentleman began to wax warmer, to become more earnest, and to extend his steps. He thus obtained the advance and took the beavers, while the Indian was exhausted with laughing and running. This Mr. Woodside was a remarkably stout, athletic man, who could face danger, endure fatigue, and accomplish much.[1]

During this period old Mr. Joseph Foster, of Topsham, had a large dog that he had trained to attack an Indian whenever he met one. One day, during the French and Indian War, the women and children were sent for safety to the block-house, near where the late Lithgow Hunter afterwards lived. One afternoon while they were there, some of the children wanted to go to the river-side berrying. As no Indians were known to be about at that time, permission was given them to go, but the dog was sent with them for safety. While the children, laughing and chatting, were picking berries, the big dog suddenly became excited, and getting between a pile of brush and the children, bristled up and began to growl and display his teeth as if there were mischief lurking in the brush-heap. Mrs. Foster was nearest to the brush-pile, and having her attention called to it by the unwonted fierceness of the dog, saw an Indian there. She screamed, and the alarm being given all the children ran up the hill toward the block-house, the dog protecting the rear all the way. Several years after the war this same Indian was in the vicinity, and referred to the incident by saying that had it not been for the big dog he would have "made a great haul of pappoose."[2]

"The late David Alexander's father was remarkable when a youth for his agility and uncommon strength. In muscular vigor he far exceeded any of the lads in town who were anywhere near his own age. One day he and another boy by the name of Thorn were on the hill near the river and opposite where Mr. David Work now (1875) lives. Suddenly a couple of stout Indians pounced upon them,

---

[1] *Pejepscot Papers.* [2] *Dr. James McKeen's Notes.*

each Indian singling out one of the boys. Their object was to run the lads off into the woods, where they would be comparatively safe from pursuit. The stout resistance, however, made by young Alexander, although a mere boy, made the Indian feel as if he had more than his hands full. At every step he encountered a resolute resistance, and although a powerful Indian he was making slow progress. The boys' outcries at length attracted the attention of the settlers up and down the river, and his father being first to comprehend the true state of things outstripped all others in going to the relief of his son, guided partly by the voice of the lad and partly by the zigzag trail of the furrowed earth which was a conspicuous mark and was made by the boy's stubborn obstinacy and resistance. The father at length came in full sight of his son and was hastening to his rescue when the Indian, letting go the lad, fired, killing Mr. Alexander, who fell instantly dead. The son, the moment he saw his father fall, ran, and the Indian, fearing pursuit, desisted from attempting his recapture. The inhabitants of the neighborhood having provided themselves with guns, and guided by the Alexander boy, started off in pursuit. They found Mr. Alexander dead. Pursuing farther they came to the apparently lifeless body of the lad Thorn. His comparatively feeble resistance had enabled the Indian to carry him off to a greater distance, but hearing the gun and apprised by the Indian who had just shot Mr. Alexander that they were in danger of being captured themselves, they knocked the boy in the head and scalped him. The boy was found still alive and eventually recovered. It is said that he afterwards died at Farmington from a curious accident. Coming in one day to dinner and the meal not being ready, he sat down in a chair near the wooden ceiling (there were no lathed and plastered rooms then) and tipping his chair back leaned against the partition just under where a hog's head (what was called a 'minister's face') was suspended by a nail in the ceiling. The jar broke the string, and the hog's head fell, the nose, it is said, hitting the unfortunate man on the very spot where he had been scalped in his boyhood. The concussion caused his instant death.'[1]

"Not far from this time (time of Moffitt's death, — 1747) four men were killed, all at one time, a few rods from the old Flagg house, just beyond Joseph Foster's. One of these was a friendly Indian, the other three were white settlers. They were going to look at a field of corn to see if it had been molested. The bodies were all found near together.

---

[1] *Dr. James McKeen's Notes.*

Upon the day of the funeral of these men it was reported that the Indians intended lying in wait for the funeral procession, and killing and scalping or making prisoners of them all. In consequence, the bodies were not buried in the ground northwest of Joseph Foster's, in the old graveyard in the woods, but were carried up by water to Ferry Point, and buried there. The bodies were none of them mutilated, except that of the friendly Indian, which was hacked all to pieces."[1]

During this period of anxious care and oft-renewed strife, the tradesmen and their families used to live a good portion of the time in the fort or garrisons. Invalids, especially, often made their residence there.

The early settlers were men accustomed to track the pathless forests and often to spend their nights with nothing over them save the glittering canopy of the heavens. They were fond of hunting, and often ranged over large tracts of land in pursuit of game. In this way they became acquainted with localities quite a distance off. Mr. Thomas Wilson was a famous hunter. On one occasion he led a party, consisting of Stephen Titcomb, Robert Gower, James Henry, Robert Alexander, and James McDonnell, all of Topsham, through the wilderness to the place now called Farmington, the territory of which they thoroughly explored. Some of them afterwards settled there.[2] John Dunlap, son of Reverend Robert Dunlap, was a noted hunter. The following narrative, written by him, illustrates the dangers and sufferings to which these early settlers were exposed: —

"When a young man at the age of 18 years my father lost his only cow. He lived near the old meeting-house, and I found her dead in Mair Brook. So dependent was the family on this useful domestic that the loss seemed almost irreparable. So great was the distress of the family that I resolved with myself, that if industry and perseverance would effect anything, I would never be poor. This resolution remained by me and was continually urging me on to exertion. I left my father and served some time as a soldier in Fort George, but I soon found that this compensation but ill comported with my resolution, — but little was left after contributing to the absolute necessities of my father's family. I immediately concluded upon some other business. This town was then in its infancy, and nothing that could satisfy my ambition and desire of wealth presented itself, and I concluded to try my chance in hunting in the wild wilderness. I accordingly took my gun and made several excursions in pursuit of beaver.

---

[1] *Dr. McKeen's Notes.* [2] *History of Farmington, p.* 9.

I was successful, and found that if the business was well followed that there would be a good prospect of making money. I accordingly extended my range further into the wilderness, and the further I went the more was I encouraged. It was a very hazardous undertaking. I was exposed every night to the wolves which were continually prowling around me, and nothing but my fire, which they feared, deterred them from encountering me. While I kept a brisk fire I feared no harm. I have been several times to the heads of the Kennebeck and Penobscot. I used to go in the month of March, sometimes the last of February, and would be gone about forty days. My return home was always the most fatiguing, from carrying an immense pack of about two hundred pounds. The beaver-skins I took in one of these excursions usually turned me about two hundred dollars. Sometimes when I returned home, I was so altered that the family did not know me. I once lost my hat immediately after I left home, and the effect of the wind and weather, and having a long beard, not having shaved while gone, gave me really a frightful appearance.

"The most eventful tour I ever took was with one Robert Spear. We left this town together, determined on a cruise to the Penobscot, and to its rise. It was in the month of March, and the ground was covered with deep snow. We took with us each a gun, ammunition, four ounces of salt, and of bread what was equal to a dozen biscuit, and each a pair of snow-shoes. We commenced travel, and made the best of our way to the Kennebeck and Penobscot. We passed some rivers and many small streams which were frozen over. On our arrival at the Penobscot, we divided. Mr. Spear took the north side of the river, and I took the south. We were to proceed up the river to its source, and there wait seven days for each other. I traversed the woods, and frequently met with small streams which had been flowed by the beaver, and generally met with good success. After ten or fifteen days I arrived at the source of the river, and there I spent seven long anxious days, listening continually to hear the footsteps of my companion. My nights were long and dreary in the extreme. The day I spent in wandering about, killing what I could find that was profitable. At the expiration of the seven long days, seeing nothing of Spear, I resolved to return home, and had travelled one or two days, when the thought occurred to me about what account I should give Mr. Spear's family on my return. As I was a single man, I concluded to return, and if possible, find him. I travelled along down on the north side of the river, looking for some vestiges of human beings. What had become of Spear I could not imagine.

Whether he had fallen into the hands of the Indians, or had been devoured by wild beasts, I had no means of ascertaining. My mind was the whole time vacillating between hope and fear. After I had been travelling a number of days, and had been looking and listening, a pole stuck up in the middle of the river in the snow arrested my attention. I at once concluded it must be placed there by some human being, and thought I would go and see if there were any tracks. I repaired immediately to it, and on it found a piece of birch bark with writing upon it, to inform me that Spear was sick close by on the bank of the river. It is impossible to describe my feelings, — how long it had been there, whether he was dead or alive, — a thousand conjectures passed over my mind. I concluded to search, and immediately fired my gun, which was in about a minute answered. I followed the direction of the report, and in a few minutes found poor Spear lying under a log with some bark laid upon it, which afforded him but a scanty shelter. He was suffering from an acute rheumatic fever. He seemed overjoyed at my appearance. What to do for him I was at a stand. For this complaint, and indeed for any, I had nothing to administer; I built a camp, built him a good fire, and stayed by him, doing everything for him I could. Necessity, the mother of invention, suggested one application after another. His pains were extreme, and his spirits almost exhausted. I at length concluded to dig away some snow, get some good turf, green as I could find it, heated by the fire, and apply it to the part of the body most affected with pain. This proved a lucky expedient, he grew better, and after a while he was able to start for Fort Halifax, where, after a tedious travel, we arrived. I left him and came home. Spear followed in about a month." [1]

These early settlers were not only accustomed to the chase as a means of obtaining a livelihood, but were also obliged to draw a part of their subsistence from the water. Fishing was with them a necessity as well as a means of amusement. The catching of sturgeon, shad, and salmon was the constant occupation of many, while it served as a means of relaxation from their ordinary avocations to a few. Captain David Dunning probably belonged to this latter class. Salmon were formerly caught in dip-nets at the foot of Fishing Rock Island, or Shad Island, as it is now called, and also in set nets at Middle Rock, or the rock upon which the pier of the bridge rests. These set nets had corks attached to them, so that the attendant

---

[1] *Pejepscot Papers.*

could tell by the sinking of the corks when a salmon was caught. One day a man was sitting on Middle Rock watching his net, while Captain Dunning was catching salmon at the falls above with a dip-net. The man on the rock observing the corks on his net to sink in the water, drew in the net, and with it drew in Dunning, still alive. It appears that the latter, in reaching over to dip up a salmon, had slipped, and falling into the river had floated down until he caught in the net. Two other versions of this story are given. In one account he is represented as having fallen into the water from a ladder and being caught in his own net. In another, the accident is given as first narrated, but Captain Dunning is represented as drawing himself out of the water by the aid of the net.[1]

Going to meeting was, in the last century, an event of considerable interest. Meeting-houses were well filled and in some cases it was thought necessary to shore them up. All went to the same meeting. Ministers appeared with their large white wigs and commanded more awe than just respect. Nearly every one walked to meeting, and in some instances women would walk four or five miles and carry a child. Some of those who lived at a distance from the meeting-house owned a horse, a saddle, and a pillion, which would accommodate a man, his wife, and one child, and often two children. In the summer boys and girls both went barefooted. When within sight of the meeting-house, the girls would step into the bushes at the side of the road and put on their stockings and shoes, which they carried with them. The boys, however, usually went barefooted into the meeting-house. All the people carried their dinners with them, and in summer ate them in the woods near by. In the winter the meeting-house was their dining-room. The men usually resorted to the neighboring inn for their luncheon and grog. In the winter season many carried foot-stoves with them. There were separate seats in the meeting-house provided for colored people, and they were never allowed to sit in the same pew with white people. It is said that Deacon Dunning had a negro lad for a servant of whom he was very fond, and whom he always took to meeting with him. As the boy at first was too young to sit in the seats provided for persons of his race, and as it would not do to allow him to sit in the deacon's pew, he had to take his seat on the floor of the aisle beside the pew.

Sermons were lengthy in those days, which often made it necessary for the parson, after a pause, to exclaim, "Wake up, my hearers!"

---

[1] *Field Book of the survey of Bakerstown, in Pejepscot Papers.*

Parson Miller was, however, relieved from this task at length by old Mr. G. Coombs, who, with repeated raps with his rattan on the side of his pew, would make the meeting-house ring. At the east meeting-house, Deacon Snow, who wore a white wig, sat under or in front of the pulpit, and "lined out" the hymn, so that every man present might have an opportunity to sing. This was the common practice.[1]

One of the established institutions of those times was the board of tithing-men. It was their duty to preserve order during religious services, and to enforce the observance of the Sabbath. The most remarkable of all the men who ever filled this office was Mr. Crispus Graves. He was born and attained his majority in Topsham. He possessed a strong, muscular frame, and was quite tall. He had a large, strongly marked face. As far as his knowledge extended, his reasoning powers were good, and he could express his thoughts with conciseness and energy. He was a tithing-man for many years. In the old first meeting-house in Topsham, his pew was near the outside door. It was a wall pew with a large window. From his seat he could look the minister in the face, or turning around, could inspect the passers-by on the different roads in sight. He always had with him a remarkably long whipstock and lash. If he chanced to spy, during religious services, any "descendant of Belial, strolling about, or sitting on the fences, or in any way desecrating the Lord's day," he felt it incumbent upon him to leave the church and administer the necessary reproof. He hesitated not, also, if need were, to threaten the culprits with both the administration of the law and of his whip. He was an object of dread to all Sabbath-breakers. He did not consider, moreover, that his care was restricted to the oversight of human beings only. During his twenty-five years in office, he taught all owners of dogs to be sure and see them locked up before they themselves went to meeting. Occasionally, however, some unlucky cur would escape from his confinement and would follow his master to meeting. As surely as such an event happened, Mr. Graves would be on the watch, and if the dog came within his reach, it would receive as smart a stroke from him as his arm and whip could inflict. It made no difference whether it was in prayer-time or in sermon-time, the whip was sure to descend if the dog came within reach. Even during the singing the yelling of the dog might be heard exceeding even "the voice of the chorister or the double altos of his choir." Mr. Graves was so perfectly serious and solemn in his manner and so firm in his

---

[1] *James Curtis's Journal, in Library of Maine Historical Society.*

belief that it was his bounden duty thus to disturb the services, that the ministers were greatly at a loss to determine in what manner to interfere. Remonstrance would not only give offence, but would be useless; while without some interference, the evil was sure to continue if it did not become increased. It was a hard matter for Mr. Graves to give up his place in the old meeting-house and go to the new one. He got bravely over the struggle, however, and bought a pew in the new building. This time it was noticed by every one that he chose a pew the very farthest from the door, at the northern extremity of the house. The window at his pew faced the hearse-house only. There were now no tithing-men, and no culprits to watch, but Mr. Graves never forgot or forgave the canine desecrators of the solemnity of the Sabbath. It was remarked at the time that he had taken the back-most pew of all, because he thought his services would no longer be needed. This, however, was not so.

The dogs took much greater liberty in the new house than they had taken in the old, though they seldom got so far up the aisle as Mr. Graves's pew. On two occasions, however, when he was nearly eighty years of age, his old enemies "traversed the whole length of the aisle, as if to defy the old lion in his lair and try his mettle. But he was up to them and in service-time too. The ruling passion was too strong, even with the hearse-house his only perspective. He gave the dogs a good sound thrashing, and their loud yells and yelpings instantly, of course, arrested all devotional feelings, although Mr. Goss kept straight on with his prayer." The narrator[1] of the above concludes his account as follows: "I was present at the time, and no doubt many others now living were witnesses."

During the early days of the society of the First Parish of Topsham, when it used the old meeting-house at the east end of the town, the choir was large, and for a time was led by a Mr. Nichols, a shoemaker in Brunswick, who was a very fine singer. It was afterwards led by a Mr. Ripley, and still later by a Mr. Blanchard. No instrumental music was made use of in those days. At one time, probably about 1821, an attempt was made to introduce a bass-viol, but the project was thwarted by Mr. William Randall, an influential member of the society, who declared that he would n't "hear a fiddle in God's house."

In those old times people were better church-goers than now, even if the standard of morality was no higher. In those times almost every one attended religious services on Sunday, some walking sev-

---

[1] *The late James McKeen, M. D.*

eral miles, while others, riding from a greater distance, would, in the winter time, drive to the house of Mr. Alexander Rogers, who lived near by. This was absolutely necessary if they needed to get warmed, as the old church was never heated, even in the most severe weather, save by the fervor of the parson's theme and the little foot-stoves carried by the ladies. It was never considered time to start for church from Mr. Randall's until Mr. John Graves, who, from his exact regularity in attendance, was called "the clock," was seen to pass.

After the close of the Indian wars Brunswick and Topsham progressed rapidly in wealth and importance. Agriculture became the chief employment of the people, though a few were engaged in coasting, — carrying wood and lumber to other markets. As the prospects of the town grew better and better, the proprietors became more encouraged and assisted the purchasers of their lands by taking their pay in lumber or such products of their labor as could be spared.

As previously mentioned, the earlier inhabitants travelled mostly on foot, though a few owned horses and did their visiting on horseback. Indeed, nearly everything that a man could not transport himself was carried in that manner, and the saddle-bags were made capacious enough to hold veal, mutton, and produce of all kinds. At the meeting-house and at every retail store there was a horse-block with three steps, for the convenience of persons when mounting their steeds.

It is uncertain to whom belongs the honor of owning the first two-wheeled chaise. Judge Minot of Brunswick, and Robert Patten of Topsham, who were contemporaries, each owned one prior to the Revolution. Robert Patten, very likely, bought his soon after his marriage in 1768, although a ride in his "shay" may have been one of the inducements to his fair lady-love to wed him. Mr. James Curtis in 1830 wrote in his journal that fifty years previously (1780), when he was twelve years of age, "there was not a wheel carriage nor even a sleigh in Brunswick."

There is, however, no question that Judge Minot owned one previous to that time, but as Curtis lived at New Meadows, and the judge at Mair Point, the former may never have seen it. About the year 1790, Captain William Stanwood, Captain John Dunlap, and Benjamin Stone each owned a chaise. These chaises are described as clumsy, lumbersome vehicles, without springs and very heavy.

The first *balanced* two-wheel chaise in Brunswick is said to have been owned by William Alexander. Professor Cleaveland once hired this chaise to journey in to Boston, having first measured it and tested its strength in order to be assured that it was a safe vehicle.

Wagons were not introduced until about the year 1816 or 1817, and there had been but two or three carts, in Brunswick at least, previous to that date. The late Captain Peter Jordan, who lived at New Meadows, stated that he had the first wagon at the eastern part of Brunswick. He said that at the time of his purchase it was considered a great luxury, but that it was in reality little better than a cart. It was very heavy and was clumsily built, and as the body rested directly upon the axles, without the intervention of springs of any kind, the rider was apt to be jolted about not a little.

During the early part of the Revolutionary War, nails were so high that many used wooden pegs for shingling, boarding, and flooring their houses.[1] At this time such luxuries as carpets were unheard of here. The first one ever made in Topsham (for they were all home-made at first) was made in 1799, by Miss Margaret Rogers (the late Mrs. Nathaniel Green). This carpet was made of small squares of cloth about ten inches in diameter. These squares were alternately light and dark colored, and each one had some figure upon it, either an oak-leaf, a heart, or two hearts joined. A light-colored figure was always put on a dark square and *vice versa*. In 1800, at the time when the death of Washington was commemorated at the old meeting-house in Topsham, this carpet was borrowed to cover the rough platform which was built up in front of the pulpit, and upon which were seated the poet of the occasion and the dignitaries of the day. There was one other carpet in town at this time, belonging to the wife of Doctor Porter, but as it was fastened to the floor she objected to having it taken up.[2]

Weddings in those days were so similar to each other and differed so little from the present fashion, except in the amount of display attending and the sports following them, that it seems unnecessary to go into details concerning them. Three occurrences of this kind, however, were so peculiar as to demand special mention here. The first occurred in 1783 or 1785, and the facts have been deposed to under oath. Mr. William Walker, of Falmouth, and Miss Sybil Staples, of Topsham, had long been affianced and were anxious to be married. The day was fixed upon, and Reverend John Miller, of Brunswick, was requested to officiate. The wedding was to take

---

[1] *McKeen, MSS. Lectures; also James Curtis's Journal.*
[2] *Diary of the late Dr. James McKeen.*

place in Topsham, either at the residence of the bride's parents or at the meeting-house. "The course of true love ne'er runs smooth." There was no bridge across the river at this time and a sudden and unusual freshet prevented all crossing at the ferry, so that Mr. Miller was unable to keep his appointment. The bride and groom, determined not to delay, were equal to the emergency. By some means communication was established with Mr. Miller. The bridal party took their place on the Topsham side at the ferry-landing. After the bridegroom and bride had joined hands, Mr. Miller, on the opposite shore, lifted up his voice, and in a speech heard distinctly across the river, pronounced the twain to be one flesh.[1]

The following marriage certificate was copied verbatim from the original, now in the possession of Mr. J. L. Douglas, of Bath, and shows the ancient form of marriage of the Friends, which has been slightly modified, and is in use by this society at the present time: —

"Whereas, Cornalas Duglas of Harpswell, in the County of Cumberland, son of Elijah Duglas and Phebe his wife, and Ann Estis, Daughter of Edward Estes and Patience his wife, both of the afore sd town And County and Provence of the Massachusetts baye, in newengland, having declared their intentions of taking Eich other in marige, before two publick meeting of the people Called quakers, in Harpswell and falmouth, acording to Good order used amongst them, and Procedeing thirein after Delibarate Consideration, they allso appearing Clear of all others, And haveing Concent of parents and Relatives Concerned, ware approved by sd meeting. Now these are to certify all whome it may concern, that for accompleshing their sd Intentions, this 10th day of the 11th month called november, annodomi seventeen hundred and sixty seven, they the sd Cornalas Duglas and Ann Estes, appeared in a publick assembly of the aforesaid people, And others met together att their publick meeting house att Harpswell, aforesaid. And he, the said Cornalas Duglas, in a solom maner, takeing the said Ann Estes by the Hand, Did openly Declared as follows: friends, I Desire you to be my witnesses, that I take this friend, Ann Estis, to be my wife, promising through the Lord's assistance, to be unto Her a true and Loveing Husband untel it Shall pleas the Lord by Death to sepperate us. And then and their in the said assembley, the said ann Estis did in like manner Declare as followeth: friends, I Desire you to be my witnesses, that I take this friend, Cornelas Duglas, to be my Husband, promasing through the

[1] *Pejepscot Papers.*

Lord's assistance, to be unto him A true and Loveing wife, until it Shall pleas the Lord by Death to sepperate us. And as a further conformation theirof, the said Cornelas Duglas and ann Estis did then and their, by these Presents, set their hands, she according to Custom, assuming the name of her Husband,

"CORNELAS DUGLAS.
ANN DUGLAS.

"And we, whose names are hearunto Subscribed, being present at the Solomnizing of Said marrige and Subcribtion in manner aforesaid, as witnesses, have allso to these Presents Subscribed our names, the Daye and year above writen.

"JOSHUA BABB,
NATHANIEL PINKHAM,
ROGER TOOTHAKER,
GIDEON TOOTHAKER,
THANKFUL JONES,
SARAH PINKHAM,
ELEANOR HAIS,
MARY HAIS,
BETY WEBER,
ABAGAIL RODEX,
CATHRINE PINKHAM,
ELIJAH DUGLAS,
PATIENCE ESTES,
LEMUEL JONES,
JOHN BARKER,
JOHN BARKER, JR.,
ELIZABETH DUGLAS,
WAIT JONES,
SARAH ESTES,
ELENOR ESTES,
MARCY JONES,
RACHEL JONES,
SARAH PINKHAM."

The other wedding to which reference was made is remarkable only for the coincidence of the relationship. On September 28, 1825, in the Friends' Meeting-House, in Durham, Elijah and Reuben Cole, of China, *twin brothers*, were married to Elizabeth and Mary Jones, daughters of Edward Jones, of Brunswick, and *twin sisters*.

In the last century all, both men and women, except the few more wealthy ones, wore home-made garments. The men wore cloth of a light blue color, not fulled. Some few of the older men wore knee-breeches. Shoe-buckles were generally worn, and many of the men and even boys wore their hair long and done up in a queue behind. Mr. Dean Swift, when a boy of ten, had a queue six or eight inches long. James Curtis writes in his journal that in 1780 "not one man in ten had a pair of boots. Parson Miller attended meeting at the east meeting-house with a good pair of blue buskins hauled up over his breeches knees."

The dress of the ladies was as changeable, if not as complicated, as at the present day. The skirt of a lady's dress was composed of but two breadths, one in front, and one behind, with a small gore on each side. Skirts were very short, except for party dresses, which had the hind breadth made into a long train for the house. This train a lady, when preparing for the street, would pin up to her waist. The waists were made very short and full, such as we now call *baby waists*. The sleeves were short, and there was a broad band went over the shoulders. The neck was covered with a white muslin neckerchief, which was fitted to the neck and shoulders, and came down under the band of the waist. The arms were covered with long white kid mits which came nearly to the elbow. The hair was arranged in various modes, but the favorite way was to comb it all on top of the head and confine it with a large high-top comb; some would puff and roll their hair, but in every case powder was considered indispensable. It is said that one Patience Wallace, a young girl living on Small Point, was going to a party one night, and having no powder, flour, or chalk to dust her hair with, she took some unslacked lime. During the evening she danced, and as she got heated the perspiration slacked the lime, which entirely destroyed the hair. She never thereafter had any hair, but had to wear a man's cap on her head, both in doors and out.[1]

Mr. Curtis also wrote in the journal referred to that "in those days, women would collect in groups for the purpose of braiding wool, it being a hard, laborious work. When at length a carding-mill or machine was heard of, it was hailed with an enthusiastic welcome, and must have been as great a relief to the women as when, at an earlier date, water-power was applied to grain-mills, before which time it would take two women to grind or turn a corn-mill. Cotton was about three shillings per pound, and such was the labor of carding, spinning, weaving, etc., that cotton and linen cloth was worth fifty cents a yard, and a man must work half a month in the best of the season on a pair of shirts made of this coarse cloth." About 1780 "the nearest fulling-mill was in North Yarmouth, and the cloth was ordinary, as no one knew or thought that the quality of wool could be improved.

"Houses were built for convenience and not for show, and ceilings were just high enough to clear a tall man's hat. Chimneys were generally topped out above the ridge-pole. Fireplaces were from seven to nine feet between the jambs, and more than a proportionable depth, which would receive a log which it took two men to handle. Every family was provided, however, with a good strong hand-sled, on which to remove the logs to the fireside, which was done with convenience,

---

[1] *This description was given by a Mrs. Price, aged ninety-two years.*

as the sills of houses were laid close to the surface of the earth. In 1780 not one house in ten in Brunswick had a crane in the chimney, being supplied with long trammels and what was called a lug-pole, a stick across the chimney about four feet up, and there were more than six wooden mantel-trees to an iron one.

"In 1780 there were not more than two or three painted houses in Brunswick.

"Bears were frequently seen. The hideous cry of the wolf was commonly heard from our forests, and their ravages were not infrequent. Every family kept a large dog, some two, but commonly a large and a small one, which did not fail to annoy every traveller that passed with their yelping. This practice of keeping dogs was probably the result of the great utility of that animal in the French and Indian war.

"Every sorry old woman was deputed a witch, and spirits were frequently seen, and much feared, children having been brought up to hear such stories as an evening amusement, terrifying as they were, which had a lasting and pernicious effect." A great many superstitious beliefs were rife at this time, among which was one that toothache could be cured by cutting off one's finger and toe nails, and a lock of one's hair, and placing them in a hole bored in a tree with an auger. About the year 1850 a tree was cut on Oak Hill in Topsham, and was sawed at one of the mills. Near the centre of the log was found a lock of hair, and as Artemus Ward would have said, "a large and well-selected assortment" of the corneous extremities of the fingers and toes, doubtless placed there many years previously by a believer in this remedy for the toothache.

It is also stated in Curtis's Journal that "farming was done in a style very different from the present. A tolerable crop of corn was obtained by a shovelful of manure in the hill, but it must be hilled or banked up to a great height. The following crop was generally rye, flax, or barley. The land was then, not stocked down, but left to produce hay, and to be seeded by Providence or chance.

"Calves were snatched from the cows at eight or ten weeks old, without any previous care to introduce a substitute for milk, and turned out to hay or grass, to rend the air with their cries till starvation should teach them the use of such coarse food, and which they would not fail to learn before flesh and strength were quite exhausted. Probably, however, not more than three out of four got up 'May Hill,' as it was then called.

"Potatoes were raised at a great expense. The ground being

broken up, but not harrowed, a large hole was made by cutting out a piece of the sod the whole depth of the ploughing. Into the bottom of this hole was thrown a shovelful of dung, if so much could be spared, then a scanty portion of seed, which lay far below the surface of the ground, over which was made an enormous hill which must receive considerable addition at hoeing. In this way, with double the necessary labor, something like half a crop was obtained. A sufficiency was, however, generally raised. As it was not known that potatoes would save the lives of calves in the spring, or be of any use to pigs after wintering, any surplus was frequently lost.

"Hogs were generally kept over two winters, and at two and a half years old would commonly weigh over two hundred, but would seldom go as high as three hundred.

"Scarce a bushel of wheat was raised and bolting-mills were not known."[1]

Oil lamps and even tallow candles were for many years unknown. It is related that when Reverend Jonathan Ellis came to Topsham (as late as 1788), he spent his first night at Esquire Merrill's. Upon retiring for the night, Mrs. Merrill lighted a pitch-pine knot for him, and showed him to his room up stairs. Finding no other place to put his light, Mr. Ellis stood it up in the fireplace and in a few minutes the chimney was all ablaze.

The manner of cooking at that time was not very different from that of to-day, though it differed in some respects. One of the principal dishes was rather peculiar. It consisted of a piece of fresh beef boiled, with hulled corn and beans added. Every family had baked beans and brown bread on Sunday morning and noon. The rye and Indian corn bread was generally made in great troughs and then baked in iron kettles in a brick oven. From a half-dozen to a dozen loaves were usually made at one time. Doughnuts, instead of being made with molasses, were sweetened with maple sugar, which was very abundant in those days.

All kinds of liquors were freely drank, though West India rum was the most generally used. Various kinds of fancy drinks were also made, prominent among which was a winter beverage called *flip*. It was made of spruce beer, rum, sugar, and water. At all taverns it was customary to keep two iron rods, called pokers, heated in the coals. When flip was called for, the beer would be drawn, into which would be plunged a red-hot poker. The rum,

---

[1] *This Journal is in the Library of the Maine Historical Society.*

sugar, and water would then be added. Half a pint of rum to a quart of beer was considered to be the right proportion. This beverage was deemed delicious by all who indulged in it. Punch was the summer beverage. It was made in about the same manner as it is at present in those places where its use is indulged in, — of rum, sugar, and water, flavored with the juice of a lemon. Some of the citizens were too fond of these beverages for their own welfare. There was one such man named Andrews, who was very fond of making rhymes and equally fond of his punch or flip. One day a load of goods was brought from Maquoit to Brunswick village, and Andrews volunteered to assist in unloading. While doing so, a barrel of rum fell out of the cart, and striking his leg, fractured it. He was taken into a store and a surgeon sent for. His ruling passions displayed themselves even in his agony, for while waiting for the doctor he composed the following rhyme : —

> "By a sudden stroke my leg is broke,
> My heart is sore offended;
> The doctor 's come — let 's have some rum,
> And then we 'll have it mended."

Some of the customs of these times were so discreditable to the towns that it is with reluctance that any mention is made of them. Of this character were the quarrels between the students of the college and the rowdies of Brunswick, who were designated "Yaggers." The latter were almost invariably the aggressors. At times it was necessary for students, if alone, to go armed. There was an equal disaffection between the "Yaggers" and the rowdies of Topsham, and this fact was often a matter for rejoicing to the student. It is pleasant to know that a better feeling now prevails, and that such quarrels are events of the past. They would never have occurred had a proper police force been sustained, and the laws been enforced.

AMUSEMENTS.

In the earliest period of the settlement of these towns, but little real amusement was known to the citizens. Near the close of the last century, however, balls and parties, huskings and apple-bees, came in vogue, and served to enliven the otherwise monotonous life of the people. From the number of dancing-schools which have been kept in Brunswick and Topsham, it is reasonable to suppose that the citizens of these towns were fond of this method of relaxation from care, and that their dancing parties were well attended. The earliest dancing-school kept in either town is believed to have been the one taught by a Mr. Allen, in 1799, in the Godfrey House, in Topsham.

The amusements of the college students at a somewhat later date were generally confined to themselves, and were apt to give occasion to other feelings than those of merriment on the part of the citizens. Students' pranks have been altogether too numerous to admit even of their enumeration in this connection; nevertheless, the following is introduced, not only as being one of the earliest occurrences of the kind, but as affording a fair sample of all. Such tricks, if they did not afford amusement to those of the inhabitants immediately affected by them, yet served as good topics for general conversation for quite a while. The following anecdote is given in the words of another, himself a student and very likely an eye-witness, we dare not say a participant.

"A countryman bound to Portland with a two-horse team, laden with butter in firkins, beans in bags, and three dead hogs (for it was cold weather, being the first of the spring term), drove up to the tavern that stood near the college, and put up for the night. In the morning when he got up, his cart and load were gone. Search was made in all directions. They followed the wheel-tracks to the college, and there lost them. About the middle of the forenoon some one espied the vehicle on the roof of North College, the wheels astride the ridge-pole, laden ready to hitch on to. Who put it there and how they effected it was a mystery; but it was a deal of work for a good many hands to get it down by taking the cart to pieces." [1]

Of public amusements, such as caravans and circuses, theatrical performances, concerts, lectures, etc., the number is so great as to admit of but limited notice.

Mr. Dean Swift says that the first public exhibition in Brunswick or vicinity was given in the year 1798. One McGinness, an Englishman, gave a Punch and Judy show in the northeast chamber of the dwelling-house on Maine Street, now owned and occupied by Mrs. Rodney Forsaith. The exhibition was well attended, everybody was satisfied, and Mr. Swift says it was really quite a good show.

According to the same authority, the first caravan was exhibited here about the year 1818 on the lot now owned by the town, back of the Post-Office. This was followed, in the year 1825, by one which exhibited on the same lot. In 1829 a caravan, owned by Macomber & Co., exhibited near the Tontine Hotel. In 1836 there was a combined

---

[1] *Kellogg, Sophomores of Radcliffe.*

menagerie and circus. In 1843 Raymond & Co. gave their zoölogical exhibition, and in 1845 Rockwell & Stone's New York Circus was exhibited near the Universalist Church, on Federal Street. Since that time entertainments of this kind have been of more frequent occurrence.

In 1824 a Mr. Taylor gave an exhibition of ventriloquism at Stoddard's Hall. The first theatrical performance was that given in 1828, for one week, at Nichols Hall, by a company of comedians from the Tremont Theatre, Boston. The entertainment the first evening consisted of Tobias's comedy of "The Honeymoon" and the farce of "The Young Widow." The price of admission was fifty cents. Children under twelve years of age were admitted for half price.

The first public concert of vocal music of which we find any record was given at Richards Hotel, July 28, 1836, by Mr. and Mrs. G. Andrews and Miss A. Woodward of Boston. It is quite probable, however, that concerts were given at an earlier date by the Hayden Society, a musical organization in existence as early as 1825. Of late years concerts have been of too frequent occurrence to call for further notice.

The first instrumental concert was probably that given by the Brunswick Brass Band, March 1, 1844.

The first regatta ever given on the Androscoggin River took place October 12, 1870. There were four races for the championship of Maine and for silver goblets. The first race was for six-oared boats, three miles; the second, for wherries pulled by the students, one mile; the third for single shell wherries, two miles; the fourth for double shell boats, two miles.

The *burlesque* May trainings of the students of Bowdoin College may properly be classed under the head of amusements. The first occurred in 1836, the company appearing dressed in the most grotesque costumes, and with arms and equipments of not the most approved patterns. The following year the company again made its appearance. The cannon of the Brunswick Artillery Company, to which about forty of them belonged, having been concealed, the company marched over to Topsham and took the pieces belonging to the Topsham Artillery Company. Similar annual trainings by the students were kept up for many years, the last one occurring in 1855 or 1856. In these fantastic processions, the students generally personified public men or characters of fiction. Sometimes, though not often, they adopted costumes in ridicule of some worthy citizen of the town. More frequently they illustrated in a laughable manner some event of a local character. The causes which led to the appearance of these fantastic trainings in the first place will be given in the chapter upon the military history of the town.

In Topsham, public entertainments have not been of frequent occurrence. The reason for this is obvious: Brunswick, being the larger town and in such close proximity to Topsham, offers the better field for securing a full attendance upon such occasions. Of fairs, levees, school exhibitions, private dramatic entertainments, concerts by local singers, etc., Topsham has doubtless had her full share. Few travelling shows have, however. exhibited there.

About 1832 a caravan exhibited on the high land above the present Free-Will Baptist Meeting-House. Much curiosity was excited as to the elephants passing over the bridges from Brunswick, fears being entertained that they would break through or else refuse to walk over them.

About the year 1850 a company of Indians from the State of New York gave an exhibition at the Court House, illustrative of the Indian mode of life, and of warfare. It was the first exhibition of the kind in the vicinity, and it attracted a large audience.

Harpswell has always been obliged to content herself with amusements of a purely local character. The location of the town, and the scattered situation of its inhabitants, offer little inducement to proprietors of travelling exhibitions to exhibit there. But what the citizens lose in this way is probably made up by a greater degree of sociability and by more varied home amusements.

LECTURES.

Public lectures, either gratuitous or otherwise, have been of quite frequent occurrence in these towns, and especially in Brunswick. Mention of orations and lectures delivered upon public occasions will be made under the head of Public Celebrations.

The earliest known course of lectures was given by a Miss Prescott, in 1825. The subject was "English Grammar," and the tickets were three dollars for a course of forty lectures. In 1826 John Cleaves Symmes, a believer in an interior world, access to which was open to voyagers in the southern hemisphere, gave a course of three lectures, which was well attended, and commanded respect and interest, as Mr. Symmes was not considered a charlatan, however erroneous might be his theory.

In the summer of 1832, or about that time, through the influence of the distinguished Doctor Reuben Dimond Mussey, a professor in the Medical School, Doctor Sylvester Graham, noted for his theory of vegetable diet to the exclusion of animal, gave a course of lectures on his specialty. They were given in the Congregational Church, and were fully attended. The doctor was an attractive lecturer, and his theory gained many adherents. The meat-market ran low, and butchers feared for their calling. Some really feared that their occupation was gone.

About this time also. Professor Espy, of Philadelphia, an admirable lecturer, and eminent in his specialty, gave a very interesting course upon the theory of "Storms and Meteorology." He was called the "Storm King." Professor Smyth gave a course on "Electricity." Professor De la Mater, of the Medical School, gave his regular course on "Hygiene," as a lyceum course, at which the medical class attended. Doctor Benjamin Lincoln, of the class of 1823, and then professor in the Vermont Medical School, gave a course on "Vegetable Life." Single lectures were also given by Professor Packard, Ebenezer Everett, Esquire, Reverend Mr. Adams, and Professor Cleaveland. The most of these were free lectures, delivered under the auspices of the Brunswick and Topsham Athenæum. They were given in the Tontine Hall.

In March, 1833, a Mr. Wilbur, of Newburyport, Massachusetts, delivered a course of lectures on "Astronomy"; and in the following August, Reverend Mr. Farley gave a lecture before the Brunswick and Topsham Athenæum, at Reverend Mr. Titcomb's meeting-house, on the subject of "True Enterprise" In 1834 Mr. John McKeen gave a course of lectures before the above-mentioned society, upon the History of Brunswick and Topsham, and soon afterwards Mr. C. Hamlin gave a lecture at Pike's Hall, on "Steam Enginery." In the winter and spring of 1836 Professor Packard delivered a lecture on the subject of "Primary Schools," and Doctor Adams gave a course of lectures on "Physiology." The above lectures were given before the Athenæum.

In 1843 a lyceum was organized, and lectures were given by the following gentlemen: Reverend D. C. Haines, on "Education"; Professor Packard, on "Nationality"; R. H. Dunlap, Poem, "A Defence of Poetry."

The course was continued in 1844, by Professor Goodwin, on "Machiavelli"; Professor Smyth, on "Explosions of Steam Boilers"; Reverend Mr. Bailey, on "Reading"; Wm. G. Barrows, Esquire, on "The Saracens"; John W. Davis, on "American History"; Reverend Asahel Moore, on "Popular Education"; Colonel T. L. McKenny, on "Origin, History, and Character of the Indians."

In 1857 a lyceum was organized by members of the Unitarian Society, and lectures were delivered by Reverend Doctors Sheldon, of Waterville, and Peabody, of Boston, Mass., and by Professor C. C. Everett, of Brunswick, Reverend Mr. Stebbins, of Portland, Thomas H. Talbot, Esquire, of Portland, and by Reverend A. D. Wheeler, D. D.

In 1859 a course of lectures was given at the Congregational Vestry, by Professor Paul A. Chadbourne, on "Natural History as related to Intellect"; by Augustus C. Robbins, on "Rags and Paper"; by Reverend Cyril Pearl, of Baldwin, on the "Past, Present, and Future of Maine"; and by Professor Egbert C. Smyth, on "Walking."

In 1860 a course of six lectures was given by Professor Chadbourne on "Iceland and the Icelanders"; "Natural History as related to the Fine Arts, on General Principles of Classification, etc."; "General Description of Invertebrates"; "The Relations of Natural History and Religion."

In 1862 there was a course of free lectures. A record of two only has been preserved: the first by Reverend Doctor Ballard, on "Common-Sense"; and the second by Professor Packard, on the "Acadians, or French Neutrals."

Topsham, not being the seat of a literary institution, does not show so large a list of lectures, though its citizens have usually constituted a fair proportion of Brunswick audiences. A lyceum was inaugurated in Topsham in 1842, but no record of any lectures has been kept, except of one in December by Reverend Paul S. Adams, and one in January, 1843, by John W. Davis, Esquire. In 1850 Reverend Amos D. Wheeler gave a lecture at the Court House on the different methods of reckoning time.

In 1859 lectures were delivered before the Topsham Farmers and Mechanics' Club by Warren Johnson, A. M., Topsham; Reverend Wm. A. Drew, Augusta; Reverend H. C. Leonard, Waterville; and by Reverend S. F. Dike, of Bath; Doctor N. S. True, Bethel; Professor Paul A. Chadbourne, of Bowdoin College; A. G. Tenney, Esquire, Brunswick; Reverend H Q. Butterfield, Hallowell.

CELEBRATIONS.

The first observance of any public event in either of these towns, of which any account has been preserved to us, was that of Washington's death, the observance of which, in accordance with a resolution of the national Congress, took place on February 22, 1800. But little is preserved of the proceedings of that day in Brunswick. The only spectator now known to be living was at that time but eight years of age. A procession of citizens was formed in front of what was afterwards the residence of the late Doctor Lincoln; they were escorted by boys under the leadership of Mr. David Dunlap, and proceeded to the old west meeting-house, where a eulogy was delivered by Doctor Page. The eulogy has not been preserved, but the closing words are said to have been, "If Washington is dead, we can thank our God that we have an Adams in the chair."

In Topsham, a procession was formed at the house of Captain Alexander Rogers, and moved to the old east meeting-house in the following order: —

Marshal.
Military Officers
(in uniform, with side arms draped in mourning).
Soldiers of the Revolution.
The Orator.
Civil Officers of the United States.
Selectmen.
Citizens.

The exercises at the meeting-house consisted of music, a prayer, music, an elegy, and the singing of an anthem. "The whole attended to with decency, order, and decorum." The elegy was delivered by the Reverend Jonathan Ellis. The following introductory lines are given as a specimen of his muse: —

"Ye who have often heard his praises sung
In strains sublime by many an abler tongue,
Now hear my grief-taught muse her grief impart,
A grief deep felt by every patriot heart, —
Our Washington 's no more."

There was no observance of the occasion in Harpswell, the citizens of that town attending the exercises in Brunswick.

The first observance in this vicinity, of the anniversary of the Declaration of National Independence, took place in Topsham, in 1805. Samuel Willard, then a tutor in Bowdoin College, delivered an oration "at the request of the Federal Republicans of Brunswick and Topsham."

The following year, 1806, the Reverend Jonathan Ellis delivered an oration at the Court House, before the members of the same political organization.

No account has been found of any other celebration of this day prior to 1825, although it is known with tolerable certainty that such celebrations were had almost every year during the first quarter of the century. In the year 1825 the citizens assembled on July 4, at one o'clock, P. M., at the "Falstaff Inn," Brunswick. Here Charles Packard, Esquire, delivered "an appropriate and very interesting address," and concluded by reading the Declaration of Independence. A public dinner, enlivened with a variety of toasts, was then partaken of.

March 4, 1829, the inauguration at Washington of General Jackson as President of the United States, was duly celebrated in Brunswick. "Father" Stetson writes in his diary, on this day, "Great parading in our wide street, guns fired, bells rung, boys mustered."

July 4, 1830, was celebrated by a procession of young men, escorted by the Light Infantry Company. An oration was delivered at the meeting-house on the hill, by Mr. Webster Kelly, of Topsham. It was followed by a dinner at the Tontine Hotel, furnished by Mr. Elijah P. Pike. The festivities of the day were marred by a fatal accident. The boys in their patriotic zeal had obtained a swivel about eight inches in length. This they had filled with paper wadding, but without any bullet. The force of its discharge was sufficient, however, to cause the death of Mr. Theophilus Miller, who was accidentally hit by the wadding.

On July 4, 1836, the members of the Young Men's Temperance Society, of Brunswick, together with other friends of temperance, assembled at Stone's Hall, and formed a procession under the escort of the Mechanic Volunteers. The procession embraced a large number of the temperance people from different parts of the town, including a portion of the Temperance Society of Bowdoin College. A company of youth, named the "Juvenile Guards," formed the rear rank. At half past ten A. M., the procession moved up Maine Street to the Congregational Church, where the following exercises were held: —

"National Hymn, by the choir. Prayer, by Reverend Asahel Moore.[1] 117th Psalm; tune, *Old Hundred*. A Declaration of Independence, written for the occasion by Mr. Alonzo Garcelon,[2] member of the Senior Class of Bowdoin College. Address, by Mr. Andrew Dunning. Temperance hymn. Benediction. 'The services were interesting and the audience was large and attentive.'"

The Fourth of July, 1842, was celebrated in Brunswick with unusual eclat. At ten o'clock, A. M., a procession formed near Washington Hall, under the direction of Colonel Estabrook, marshal of the

---

[1] *Methodist. — Bowdoin, Class of* 1835.

[2] *Now a physician in Lewiston.*

day, marched through the various streets, and entered the Congregational Church at eleven o'clock. The escort was formed by the Mechanic Volunteers. The order of exercises at the church was as follows: —

A voluntary on the organ; singing by the choir; reading of Scripture by Reverend Doctor Adams; reading of the 136th Psalm, with responses by the audience; prayer; reading of the Declaration of Independence, by George C. Swallow; singing by choir and congregation; oration by Washington Gilbert; benediction. After the benediction, the audience separated, and, the procession being re-formed, they proceeded to the grove near the town-house, where a collation had been provided under the superintendence of Mr. William R. Field, Senior. The band enlivened the scene with appropriate music, and all seemed to enjoy the festival.

In the course of the afternoon, the young ladies of Brunswick received their friends in the Tontine Hall. The younger misses assembled at the house of Ebenezer Everett, Esquire, and passed the afternoon in a pleasant manner. In the evening there was a display of fire-works.

In 1843 the Young Men's Temperance Society of Brunswick celebrated the return of the anniversary of National Independence by a procession, of which Captain John A. Cleaveland was the chief marshal. Public exercises were had at the church on the hill. There was music by the band, a prayer, an original ode sung by the choir, and an oration delivered by Reverend George Knox, of Topsham, which was followed by more music, a poem by Mr. Albert W. Knight, and an original ode was sung by the choir.

In 1845 the day was celebrated in Topsham by the Temperance Society. The procession marched to the Unitarian Meeting-House, where an address was delivered by M. B. Goodwin, of the Senior Class of Bowdoin College. After the exercises, there was a dinner at the Washingtonian House.

Probably the celebration of the Fourth of July which was attended with the most eclat of any that ever occurred in either of these towns was that in 1854.

At ten A. M. a procession was formed in the following order: —

Marshal.

Bowdoinham Artillery,
Fire Companies of Brunswick,
Fire Company of Topsham, } as escort.

Band.

Aid — Chief Marshal — Aid.

Marshal — Fire Companies from Abroad.
Marshal — Committee of Arrangements.
President of the Day and Chaplain.
Vice-Presidents.
Orator, Poet, and Reader.
Marshal — Selectmen of Brunswick and Topsham.
Marshal — Fire Wards.
Marshal — Superintending School Committee of Brunswick and Topsham.
Marshal — United States Officers.
State Officers.
Marshal — Clergy.
Members of the Bar.
Town Officers (present and past) of Brunswick and Topsham.
Marshal — Officers of Bowdoin College.
Students of same.
Marshal — Agent and Overseers of the Cabot Manufacturing Company.
Operatives of the same.
Marshal — Schools of Brunswick and Topsham, with their respective Teachers.
Marshal — Preceptor and Pupils of Topsham Academy.
Marshal — Strangers.
Marshal — Citizens of Brunswick and Topsham.
Marshal — FLORAL PROCESSION of the Young Ladies of Brunswick and Topsham, in carriages.
Marshal — Juvenile Temperance Watchmen Club.

The procession, after passing through the principal streets, entered the church upon the hill. Here Professor R. D. Hitchcock offered a prayer, and the Declaration of Independence was read by Professor H. H. Boody, after which Ex-Governor Robert P. Dunlap, the president of the day, introduced to the audience Mr. William P. Drew, the orator of the day. The oration was followed by a poem by Reverend Elijah Kellogg. In the afternoon a trial of fire-engines for the prize, a silver trumpet, took place at the upper mills. The prize was awarded to Androscoggin No. 2, of Topsham, which played a stream of one hundred and seventy-four feet and some inches. Atlantic Company No. 2, of Portland, was so unfortunate as to burst their hose at each trial. An exhibition of fire-works, which would have been a fine one, was marred by a shower which hurried it to a close. The festivities of the day closed with a ball at the Tontine Hall, under the direction of Protector Engine Company No. 4, of Brunswick.

In 1860 the day was observed in a similar way. William P. Tucker, tutor of Bowdoin College, read the Declaration of Independence; and Augustus C. Robbins, Esquire, of Brunswick, delivered an oration.

Doubtless the day has been occasionally observed in Harpswell, but no account of any special celebration has been obtained. The day is often chosen for Sabbath-school picnics.

On Monday, August 16, 1858, a public meeting was held at the depot in Brunswick, to celebrate the successful laying of the Atlantic cable. General Abner B. Thompson called the meeting to order. Albert G. Tenney, Esquire, was elected chairman, and Daniel Elliot, secretary. The messages between the Directors of the Atlantic Telegraph Company, and between the Queen of England and the President of the United States, were then read. A volunteer choir sang an ode, speeches were made by A. G. Tenney, Reverend John S. C. Abbot, Reverend Amos D. Wheeler, D.D., of Topsham, Honorable Charles J. Gilman, Reverend Aaron C. Adams, of Manchester, New Hampshire, Honorable Ebenezer Everett, Reverend Doctor Ballard, and Reverend George E. Adams, D. D., and the exercises were concluded by another ode from the choir. The depot and telegraph office were illuminated, as were also the houses of many of the citizens of Brunswick and Topsham.

February 22, 1862, the anniversary of Washington's birthday was celebrated in the Congregational Church in Brunswick. Reverend Doctor Wheeler, of Topsham, read the hymn, "My country, 't is of thee"; Professor Whittlesey read selections from the Scriptures; Reverend Doctor Ballard read the prayers for the occasion, from the Episcopal Collection. Washington's Farewell Address was then read by Reverend Doctor Adams, a hymn to the tune of "St. Martin's" was then sung by the choir, and the benediction pronounced.

On Saturday, April 15, 1865, upon the reception of the news of the assassination of President Lincoln, a public meeting was held at the church of the First Parish in Brunswick. Honorable Marshall Cram presided. Reverend Doctor Wheeler, of Topsham, made a prayer, which was followed by addresses from Reverend Doctor Ballard, Honorable Charles J. Gilman, Reverend T. J. B. House, Reverend Doctor Adams, A. G. Tenney, President Leonard Woods, Reverend Mr. Baldwin, Professor C. F. Brackett, and Warren Johnson. A resolution was passed expressive of great grief at the calamity which had fallen upon the nation, and of faith in the stability of the government. The pulpit and choir gallery were appropriately draped in mourning, as were also many stores and private residences. All the flags were at half mast.

On Wednesday, April 19, 1865, a union meeting of the different religious societies of Brunswick was held in the Mason Street Church, at 12 M., in commemoration of the death of the late President of the

United States, Abraham Lincoln, whose funeral services were then being held at Washington, D. C. The exercises were as follows: —

A portion of Scripture was read by Reverend A. D. Wheeler, D. D., a hymn by Reverend J. T. B. House, a prayer by Reverend Doctor Adams; a second hymn was then read by Reverend Doctor Wheeler, who delivered an appropriate discourse. Prayer was then offered by Reverend Mr. House, a national hymn sung by the choir, and the benediction pronounced by Doctor Adams. The church was appropriately draped with mourning.

April 19, 1875, the anniversary of the battles of Concord and Lexington was celebrated in Brunswick, by the display of flags, ringing of bells, and a national salute fired by a detachment of the Artillery Company, of Bowdoin College.

Memorial Day has also been observed annually in Brunswick and Topsham by the decoration of the graves of the fallen heroes of the Rebellion, and frequently by a public address.

PUBLIC MEETINGS.

A meeting of the surviving soldiers of the Revolution was held October 5, 1825. Philip Owen was chosen chairman, and John Given secretary. A vote of thanks was passed to Honorable Peleg Sprague of Hallowell, Honorable John Anderson of Portland, and Honorable Edward Everett of Massachusetts, "for their generous and able pleas before the Congress of the United States, in behalf of themselves and companions in the perilous services of the Revolution."

On April 23, 1827, a citizens' meeting was held, "for the relief of the Greeks." Speeches were made by Honorable Robert P. Dunlap and Professor Thomas C. Upham. The amount of one hundred and sixteen dollars was contributed.

In 1833 a meeting of the citizens of Brunswick was held on the third of July, for the purposes of taking measures to extend an invitation to President Jackson to visit the town while on his proposed tour through New England.

The antislavery agitation commenced in this vicinity by the appointment at a public meeting in January, 1838, of Professor William Smyth and David Dunlap, Esquire, of Brunswick, and Reverend Thomas N. Lord and Reverend Edwin R. Warren, of Topsham, as delegates to the Maine Antislavery Society, to be held in Augusta. At the meeting of this society Professor Smyth was chosen its secretary.

In November, 1838, Mr. Codding, the general agent of the above-named society, delivered several lectures in Brunswick upon the subject of slavery and its abolition. The antislavery cause met with much opposition in Brunswick.

A meeting was held October 27, 1838, "to take into consideration the measures at present pursued by the Abolitionists," at which both the friends and foes of the measures were present.

An attempt was made to introduce some resolutions which had been prepared prior to the meeting by opponents of the cause. This action was warmly opposed by Professor William Smyth, who said they "had not come together to pass resolutions prepared to our hand without deliberation on our part," and that the call for the meeting implied that they were to "deliberate, examine, discuss." Hisses and "Down with him!" were heard in different parts of the house, but he concluded his remarks without any regard to them. He was followed and warmly sustained by General John C. Humphreys, and the meeting adjourned without transacting any business, to meet again on the following Tuesday evening.

At the adjourned meeting General A. B. Thompson offered resolutions to the following effect: —

Against any interference with slavery by the people of non-slaveholding States. Admitting the *right* of free discussion, but against the exercise of it and against any unlawful opposition to it. That the opinions expressed in these resolutions were in accordance with the sentiments of the vast majority of the citizens of that community. Mr. Adams spoke in opposition to the resolutions, though his remarks met with frequent interruption. The resolutions were adopted by a vote of one hundred and sixty-three to one hundred and seventeen.

On Wednesday, October 31, the citizens of Brunswick and Topsham met at the Congregational Church in Topsham to consider the action of the meeting held the previous evening in Brunswick.

The meeting was opened by a strain of pithy, pungent remarks from Doctor James McKeen, in reference to the late meeting in Brunswick. Addresses were also made by John M. O'Brien, Esquire, Mr. Codding, and others. The meeting was highly interesting in its character, and cheering to the friends of free discussion and of equal and impartial liberty. It was agreed to call another meeting of the citizens of the two villages, to assemble in Brunswick on the Friday evening following, and a committee was raised for that purpose.

In accordance with this arrangement, a call was issued on Friday morning, inviting "the friends of free discussion and the right of the people freely to assemble for the purpose of discussing any subject in morals, politics, or religion, in which they feel an interest," to meet at the Second Baptist Meeting-House, in Brunswick, on that evening, to give such expression of their sentiments in relation to this right as in existing circumstances might appear suitable and necessary. The house was well filled. Professor William Smyth addressed the meeting at some length, reviewing the action of the former meeting, and taking strong ground in favor of free speech. Professor William Smyth, Doctor James McKeen, and Major Nahum Perkins were appointed a committee to prepare business for the meeting. They reported the following resolution: —

"*Resolved*, That freedom of thought and of speech is the natural right of every human being; and that our Federal Constitution sacredly guarantees its protection to every citizen of this Republic."

Brief remarks were made by John M. O'Brien, Esquire, in favor of the resolution. He was followed by Mr. Codding, who addressed the meeting at some length. A vote was then taken upon the resolution, which was almost unanimous in its favor. Resolutions were then passed, that while the meeting would express no opinion either for or against the principles and measures of the Abolitionists, that they have a perfect right to hold and utter and defend their sentiments, and "that as good citizens they should patiently bear with each others' supposed mistakes and errors, not doubting but, in the end, from the collision of mind with mind in open, fair, and manly discussion, the truth on every important subject will shine forth clear as the noonday, commanding the united assent of all."

A public meeting was held October 20, 1853, at the Congregational Vestry, to consider the importance of ornamenting the village with shade trees. Doctor Isaac Lincoln, Charles J. Gilman, John L. Swift, Hugh McClellan, George W. Carlton, Joseph McKeen, Jr., Valentine G. Colby, Francis Owen, William M. Hall, and Augustus C. Robbins were chosen a committee to obtain the necessary funds and to superintend the transplanting of trees throughout the village. One hundred and thirty-two dollars and sixty-one cents was raised and paid out for transplanting trees, etc. Thirty cents was the average price paid for the trees.

On Saturday, June 14, 1856, a public meeting of the citizens of Brunswick and Topsham was held, to give expression to the feelings of these communities in regard to the wanton attack on Senator Sumner by Representative Preston C. Brooks in the Senate Chamber in Congress. The meeting was called to order by Doctor Isaac Lincoln. Reverend Leonard Woods, D. D., was chosen to preside. Speeches were made by President Leonard Woods, Honorable Charles J. Gilman, Ebenezer Everett, Esquire, and Reverend Mr. Jaquis, and an address given by Reverend John S. C. Abbott. Spirited resolutions were offered by Professor William Smyth, which were unanimously passed. The meeting was a large and earnest one.

The question of petitioning for a city charter began to be agitated by the citizens of Brunswick in the latter part of the year 1857. On January 7, 1858, a meeting of citizens was held at McLellan's Hall to consider the matter. The meeting voted that the citizens of the village ought to apply for a charter, and Daniel Elliott, A. G. Tenney, and A. C. Robbins were elected a Committee of Correspondence in regard to the matter. Ebenezer Everett, Joseph McKeen, Richard Greenleaf, Benjamin Furbish, and Charles J. Noyes were chosen a committee to draft a charter to be presented to the legislature.

A second meeting was held January 26. A. G. Tenney, Daniel Elliott, Benjamin Furbish, A. B. Thompson, and Thomas Skolfield were elected a committee to obtain signers to a petition. The meeting agreed to accept the whole town in the petition for a charter instead of the village, if it was generally desired.

A third meeting was held February 13th, at which it was voted to embrace the whole town in a petition for a charter if the town would so vote.

A charter was granted by the legislature, to take effect if accepted by the whole town at its first meeting. It was not accepted by the town.

From 1861 to 1865 inclusive, nearly all the public meetings held hereabouts had reference to the civil war then going on. The first one of which any record has been preserved was held at White's Hall, in Topsham, on April 23, 1861. It was to encourage the raising of a company of volunteers. Francis Adams, Esquire, was chosen chairman, and Sandford A. Perkins, clerk. Speeches were made by Reverend Amos D. Wheeler, D. D., Reverend George Knox, and others. Captain Edward W. Thompson marched over with his company of Brunswick Volunteers, and addressed the meeting. William Whitten, George A. Rogers, and Francis T. Littlefield were chosen a committee to solicit subscriptions, and two hundred dollars was subscribed on the spot. Some patriotic resolutions were also adopted.

On May 2, a meeting was held in Brunswick, at which a beautiful silk flag was presented to the Brunswick Volunteers by Mrs. Arabella Greenleaf, in behalf of the ladies of the town. Captain Thompson responded for the company.

A meeting was held in the depot, in Brunswick, on the afternoon of

October 17, and another on the evening of the same day, at which speeches were made by Colonel L. D. M. Sweat. and C. C. Woodman, Esquire, of Portland, Honorable Charles J. Gilman, of Brunswick, and J. T. Gilman, of Bath.

On the nineteenth of July, 1862, a meeting was held at the depot in Brunswick, which was opened with a prayer by Reverend George E. Adams. Speeches were made by Professors Whittlesey and Chamberlain, of Bowdoin College, and by General Oliver O. Howard, U. S. A.

July 25 a meeting was held at McLellan's Hall, and speeches were made by Honorable Charles J. Gilman, Professors Chamberlain and Whittlesey, Reverend Doctor Ballard, John M. O'Brien, Esquire, and J. T. Magrath, of Bowdoin College.

On the 29th a meeting was also held, at which speeches were made by Reverend Doctor Ballard, J. M. O'Brien, Esquire, Reverend Doctor Tenney, of Ellsworth, Reverend Doctor Adams, A. G. Tenney, and by a Mr. Temple, of Bowdoin College.

Another meeting of the same kind was held August 30, at which speeches were made by John M. O'Brien, Esquire, and A. G. Tenney.

September 1, a meeting was held in the meeting-house at Growstown, where speeches were made by Honorable Charles J. Gilman and A. G. Tenney.

On the next day two meetings were held, — one in the afternoon, in the Baptist Meeting-House at New Meadows, at which speeches were made by Charlton C. Lewis, of New York, and by Honorable Charles J. Gilman; the other was held in the evening at McLellan's Hall, and was addressed by Honorable Josiah H. Drummond, and J. T. Gilman, Esquire, of Portland, and by Reverend Mr. Rugg, of Bath.

On September 8, 1863, there was a public meeting at the Brunswick depot, which was addressed by Honorable F. O. J. Smith, of Portland, on the unconstitutionality of the Conscription Act. This could with more propriety be termed an *anti-war* meeting.

In January, 1864, a meeting of citizens was held at the Congregational Vestry in Brunswick, in favor of giving aid to the freedmen. Several speeches were made, and a committee was appointed to solicit aid. They issued circulars in regard to this object, and reported subsequently that they had received and forwarded to the Freedman's Bureau eleven boxes of clothing, the estimated value of which was $1,000.

Several meetings were held in the summer of 1865, in Topsham, for the purpose of taking action in relation to offering inducements to the trustees of the State Agricultural College to locate that institution in Topsham. Sufficient funds were obtained, but the trustees deemed it expedient to locate the college at Orono.

In 1866, some time in July, a meeting of the citizens of Brunswick was held to take measures for furnishing aid to the sufferers by the Portland fire. A relief committee was chosen, and supplies and money were sent by it to the city authorities.

Doubtless many other meetings of the citizens of these towns have been held besides those which are here mentioned. Some others are mentioned in other connections, and there are some, doubtless, of which no record has been found.

That our citizens have always been eminent for their cultivation of the moral and social virtues, no less than for their zeal for improvement in knowledge, is evident from the attention they gave to the formation of

ASSOCIATIONS,

The number of which, of various kinds and for various purposes, in Brunswick and vicinity, formed from time to time during the present century, is so large as to admit of but brief mention in these pages.

AGRICULTURAL AND MECHANICAL ASSOCIATIONS. — The earliest association of this kind was the MECHANICS' ASSOCIATION, of Brunswick, which was formed August 8, 1842. The first officers were, James Derby, president; Benjamin Furbish, vice-president; Theodore S. McLellan, secretary; Ezra Drew, treasurer. The object of the society was "the promotion of business and the improvement of intellect."

On April 14, 1854, the SAGADAHOC AGRICULTURAL AND HORTICULTURAL SOCIETY was incorporated. Though not a town society, it is mentioned here because all its buildings and grounds are situated in Topsham, and most of its meetings have been held there. The first meeting of this society was held in Bath, at the City Hall, July 1, 1854. At this meeting a code of by-laws was adopted and permanent officers elected, and the meeting then adjourned to the tenth of August following. At this latter meeting it was voted to hold a fair that autumn, at such time and place as the executive officers of the society might determine. Some of the principal officers, however, declined serving, and no fair was held that season. The society held its meetings annually at Bath for several years, but had, at first, a hard struggle for existence. In 1855 Mr. Francis T. Purinton, of Topsham, was elected its president. Though not nominally, yet in reality, he was the first person to serve in that capacity. In the autumn of 1855 the society held its first fair in the old town-house in Topsham, and Reverend Amos D. Wheeler, of that town, delivered an address. The exhibition was a marked success. Since then annual exhibitions have been held, and the condition of the society has steadily improved. It now ranks among the very best of the agricultural societies in the State. It owns upwards of nineteen acres of land, a large two-story building, in which the exhibitions are held, a dining-hall, stable, and other buildings. The society is free from debt, and has a large membership.

September 19, 1774, a grange of THE PATRONS OF HUSBANDRY was organized at Topsham, and about the same time one was organized in Brunswick. Both are in a flourishing condition.

CHARITABLE ASSOCIATIONS.

The oldest association for charitable and social purposes is UNITED LODGE, NO. 8, OF FREE AND ACCEPTED MASONS. The charter for this lodge was granted by the Grand Lodge of Massachusetts, December 14, 1801. The charter members were Jacob Brown, William Fairfield, James Rogers, Daniel Holden, Ziba Eaton, Samuel Snow, Jonathan Snow, David Patterson, James McLellan, and Joshua Emery. The first master was Jacob Brown.

The lodge was established in Topsham, holding its first meeting under the charter, February 20, 1802, at the house of Mr. Gideon Walker. The record furnishes no clew as to the exact place of meeting after that above mentioned, it simply reading "Mason's Hall"; and although a committee was raised at the first meeting "for the purpose of hiring a hall and furnishing furniture, clothing, etc.," no record of the report of that committee is found. In 1804 a committee was chosen to "draw a draft" (for a new hall), and on February 12, 1805, it was "voted that there be a committee chosen for the purpose of making all the necessary arrangements for building a Masonic Hall and to carry the same into effect."

On May 27, 1806, a committee was chosen to complete a Masonic Hall, and September 23, 1806, it was "voted that the secretary be empowered to subscribe five shares for United Lodge for the purpose of building a hall"; and the new hall was dedicated January 1, 1807. The lodge was evidently not at that time full owner of the hall, as a vote passed March 17, 1807, provides "that the lodge take all individual shares and pay for them, when the lodge is in capacity to do the same." This hall was in the building now known as the Franklin Family School. Several public displays are recorded while the lodge was located in Topsham. On June 24, 1806, the Festival of St. John the Baptist, a "procession formed (under direction of David Patterson, as marshal), and moved to Mr. Daniel Owen's hall, at Brunswick, where thirty-one Masons, together with five musicians, dined and then returned."

On June 24, 1808, the Festival of St. John the Baptist was celebrated by United Lodge and Solar Lodge of Bath. Jacob Herrick delivered an address at the new meeting-house in Brunswick.

In 1810 the question of moving the lodge to Brunswick was considered, and in 1814 it was voted to petition the Grand Lodge for permission to remove it. The answer to this petition was as follows; —

GRAND LODGE OF MASSACHUSETTS,
JUNE 10, A. L. 5816.

"On the petition of the officers and members of the United Lodge, situated at Topsham, voted that United Lodge have leave to remove from the town of Topsham to the town of Brunswick, of which the officers and members will take due notice and govern themselves accordingly.

"JOHN FOLEY, *Grand Secretary.*"

"BOSTON, June 29, A. L. 5816."

The above is a correct copy of the indorsement on the charter.

On June 24, 1816, a procession being formed, the lodge was joined by the officers and members of Freeport and Solar Lodges, and by the District Deputy Grand Master Oliver Bray, Esquire. The procession, preceded by a band of music, marched to the meeting-house in Brunswick, where an oration was delivered by Robert Pinckney Dunlap. The procession was again formed, moved to Washington Hall, and partook of a bountiful dinner provided by Robert Eastman. The lodge did not return to Topsham, but met in Washington Hall. from this date until January 16, 1817, when a new hall, on Mason Street, was dedicated. Only Masonic visitors were present at this ceremony. Robert P. Dunlap delivered an oration, and the fraternity afterwards "partook of a sumptuous dinner" at the house of the master, Doctor Jonathan Page. In January, 1822, this lodge was incorporated into a body politic, "with all the privileges usually granted to other societies, instituted for purposes of charity and beneficence." In the year 1844 the Masonic Hall was enlarged and refurnished at considerable expense. This hall was over the Mason Street School-house, and the whole building (and land) was in 1872 sold to the town for an engine-house. The lodge moved from the hall on Mason Street, October 3, 1872, into spacious rooms in the third story of the new building, known as "Lemont Block," on the corner of Maine and Pleasant Streets.[1]

The following anecdote comes in naturally in this connection. Early in the century a man came to Brunswick, who claimed that he was a Free Mason when he was not one. The deception was at once detected, but a few of the members of that fraternity determined to have some sport with the man, and at the same time give him a lesson that would be likely in future to deter him from attempting to gain a clandestine admission into other lodges. He was told that it was the custom of the Masons there to initiate all strangers before admitting them to the lodge, and that no exception could be made in his case. He consented to submit to the ordeal, and a room over Schwartkins's shop was at once prepared for the ceremony. The details of the initiation have not been preserved, but it is known that he was anointed with *water* in such quantity that it ran down through the floor on to the table at which Schwartkins and his family were at dinner. After the ceremony was finished the candidate was asked whether it was similar to what he had previously experienced when he was admitted to the fraternity. He replied, "It resembles it some, but you use a great deal more water here."

THE BRUNSWICK HUMANE SOCIETY was organized May 2, 1820. This was, as its name would indicate, a benevolent society, its object being to make gratuitous provision for the sick and destitute, of bedding and clothing, as far as it was able; and to assist such destitute children as manifested a desire to attend the Sabbath school, with suitable clothing. The meetings of the society were held at the residences of members. During the first year there were weekly meetings at which the time was occupied in making or repairing such garments as they were able to procure for the above purposes. After the first year the meetings were less frequent.

In March, 1822, the society contributed clothing, bedding, etc., "to students who had suffered in consequence of the fire on March 4," and it was at this time voted "that the sum of thirty dollars be delivered to Reverend William Allen to be expended in such articles as he shall judge proper for indigent students."

The last meeting recorded was held October 30, 1834.

During its existence this society did a good work in relieving the wants of the poor and adding to the comfort of the sick.

---

[1] *For the foregoing account we are indebted to Ira P. Booker and to L. H. Stover, Secretary of United Lodge.*

The Pejepscot Lodge, No. 13, Independent Order of Odd Fellows, was chartered May 2, 1844, and was instituted June 13, of the same year. The charter members were Giles Bailey, John S. Cushing, John D. Coburn, Leonard P. Merrill, William H. Morse, and Horatio Hall.

The first officers were, John S. Cushing, N. G.; Wm. H. Morse, V. G.; Jos. Lunt, 2d, T.; L. P. Merrill, Sec.

A hall was leased for five years of John S. Cushing, over his store on the corner of Maine and Pleasant Streets. It was neatly and elegantly furnished. The carpets, drapery, curtains, etc., were of the best material, and the regalia compared favorably with any in the State. There were forty-two members the first year, and in 1849 the number had increased to eighty-six. In December of that year the hall, which the lodge had occupied for five years and six months, was destroyed by fire together with its contents, including nearly all of the books and papers belonging to the lodge.

After the fire, the lodge held its meetings in a room over the store on the corner of Maine and Lincoln Streets, now A. T. Campbell's store.

The lodge did not flourish after the fire as it had done previously, and the number of its members grew less each year, and finally, in 1858, the charter was surrendered. From that year until 1875, there was no lodge of Odd Fellows in Brunswick.

In the fall of 1875 the old lodge was revived, and on the evening of October 6 there was a public installation of officers. Grand Master Stone was the installing officer, and the following were installed officers of the lodge, Frank Johnson, Noble Grand; Ed. Beaumont, Vice-Grand; R. B. Melcher, R. S.; W. F. Tyler, P. S.; E. T. Gatchell, Treasurer.

The Ladies' Soldiers Aid Society was organized September 16, 1862. It lasted during the civil war. In 1863 a series of public tableaux was given by it for the purpose of raising funds.

LITERARY AND SCIENTIFIC SOCIETIES.

Of the numerous associations of a literary and scientific character, which have existed in either of the three towns, the Nucleus Club, of Brunswick and Topsham, deservedly takes the highest rank. It was instituted April 7, 1820, and existed under the name of the Nucleus Club until about 1832, when its name was changed to that of the *Brunswick and Topsham Athenæum*, and under that name it flourished for some years longer, when it was disbanded.

In the year 1830 the constitution, by-laws, and rules of the club were printed, together with a list of its members at that time.

The exercises at the regular meetings of the club were a discussion of a subject which had been proposed, and accepted by the club, at a previous meeting, a lecture, dissertation, or such other performance as may have been provided for by the superintending committee or by the by-laws.

On the evening of each anniversary an address was delivered by the president, and a poem or dissertation by some member, previously appointed by the club for the purpose.

The by-laws provided for "a superintending committee," whose duty it was to select subjects and assign them to different members for discussion; to procure lecturers; purchase apparatus; and to have the general superintendence of all matters not otherwise provided for.

Standing committees were also chosen annually, for the consideration of the subjects mentioned in the list given below. The club possessed quite a large library, which was procured by purchase and by donations. When the club disbanded the books were distributed by lot among the members.

The following is a list of the officers and committees in 1830: —

John C. Humphreys, *President;* James Cary, *Vice-President;* Francis D. Cushing, *Secretary;* ———, *Librarian.*

Library Committee. — A. B. Thompson, John Coburn.

Superintending Committee. — Ebenezer Everett, John Coburn, Wm. Smyth, Charles Weld, John McKeen, Samuel P. Newman, Alpheus S. Packard, Elijah P. Pike, and Abner B. Thompson.

On Chemistry. — Parker Cleaveland, Geo. E. Adams, Geo. W. Holden, A. S. Packard, and Joseph McKeen.

Political Economy and Civil Polity. — Robert P. Dunlap, S. P. Newman, C. Packard, R. T. Dunlap, M. E. Woodman, S. Veazie, C. Thompson, and P. O. Alden.

Literature and Belles-Lettres. — S. P. Newman, E. Everett, and R. P. Dunlap.

Banking and a Circulating Medium. — E. Everett, Thos. G. Sandford, N. Hinkley, N. Perkins. and A. B. Thompson.

Electricity and Magnetism. — Wm. Smyth, I. Lincoln, James McKeen, and L. T. Jackson.

Navigation and Commerce. — A. B. Thompson, S. Veazie, W. Frost, John Dunlap, and N. Hinkley.

Astronomy. — C. Weld and James McKeen.

Agriculture. — David Dunlap, John McKeen, Nath. Dunning, and G. W. Holden.

Subjects connected with the Business and future Prospects of the Villages of Brunswick and Topsham. — John Coburn, J. C. Humphreys, F. D. Cushing, Dennis Gillett, J. S. Cushing, R. Forsaith, C. Waterhouse, John Owen, and Jos. Dunning,

Mathematics and Surveying. — E. P. Pike, Wm. Smyth, and R. D. Dunning.

Hydrostatics and Mechanics. — P. Cleaveland, J. Cary, Joseph Griffin, N. Houghton, L. T. Jackson, J. W. Moore, L. T. Cushing, J. R. Larrabee, H. M. Prescott, J. Stinchfield, and E. P. Pike.

Public Schools. — John McKeen, Geo. E. Adams, N. Perkins, Asa Dodge, and J. B. Cleaveland.

Roads and Canals. — Charles Packard, John Coburn, Joseph McKeen, M. E. Woodman, and C. Thompson.

History. — A. S. Packard and C. Weld.

The Pythonian Society was organized in January, 1825. Its object was debating, composition, and friendly and social intercourse. Only persons desirous of cultivating literary tastes by reading and discussions were invited to join. Dissertations were required from each member in turn.

Its anniversary was observed every year in January, at which time officers were chosen, and an address delivered by the president; sometimes there was also a poem, and always a supper.

The society had a small but select library, which was distributed among its members when it was disbanded, which was about 1853, having had an existence for upwards of twenty-five years.

The average membership was small, perhaps fifteen or sixteen. We are unable to give a list of its members, but it is worthy of remark that John S. Cushing was a member for upwards of twenty-five years, he having joined it the first year of its existence and continued an active member until he removed from town in 1852. The constitution, by-laws, and a list of members of this organization were once printed, but no copy has been obtained and it is doubtful whether one now exists.

In the winter of 1829–30 the Brunswick Lyceum was formed. It originated in the following manner. The Washington Fire Club had been accustomed to hold its annual meeting and to have an address delivered, in the winter season. This year the address was by Professor A. S. Packard, on the organization and importance of lyceums.

This address was favorably received, and the club voted to call a meeting of the citizens to hear the address and to consider the propriety of forming a lyceum. A meeting was held in the Universalist Church on Federal Street (now Dirigo Hall, on Gilman Avenue), and a lyceum was formed Committees were chosen to provide dissertations or essays on the particular subjects of which they had charge. Several lectures were given, but the society lasted only for a short time.

The BRUNSWICK AND TOPSHAM ATHENÆUM was the *Nucleus Club* under a different name. It received this name about 1832. This society was in existence in 1836, but no later reference to it has been found. At a meeting of this society in May, 1833, a committee was chosen to inquire into the practicability of building a railway from Brunswick to the tide waters in Casco Bay.

In November, 1842, the BRUNSWICK AND TOPSHAM LYCEUM SOCIETY was formed. It was in existence in 1845, perhaps later. The society not only provided lectures, but public discussions were held by it in the Maine Street Baptist Church in Brunswick.

The CASTALIAN SOCIETY OF BRUNSWICK was in existence in 1845. Nothing more is known concerning it. The name would indicate that its object was to encourage a taste for poetry.

The BRUNSWICK LINNÆAN SOCIETY, organized in May, 1845, was formed at the suggestion of Professor Cleaveland, the object being to "acquire a systematic knowledge of natural history." Meetings were held once a week at the residences of its members. At each meeting a dissertation was read by some member, and various subjects were analyzed. During the summer, botany was the subject of study. At other times, ornithology, conchology, entomology, ichthyology, meteorology, mammalogy, physiology, and geology.

In the summer, excursions were made. July 1, 1846, the society went to Harpswell Island to visit a grove of the mountain laurel. The next summer an excursion was made to Merrymeeting Bay, in the steamer "Rough and Ready." Other excursions were made at different times to localities of interest in the vicinity.

Each anniversary was observed in a fitting manner. The first by an excursion and picnic to Harpswell Island. The second by a social meeting, with invited friends, at Common's Hall, at which an oration was delivered by W. G. Barrows, a poem by G. F. Dunning, and an original ode by A. W. Knight. Upon the third anniversary a social gathering was held at the Brunswick Seminary, an oration was delivered by H. K. Craig, and a poem by A. W. Knight.

In 1848 a number of lectures were delivered before the society (not public) by Professor Cleaveland, G. C. Swallow, A. W. Knight, Oliver Stevens, S. J. Humphrey, L. P. Merrill, W. G. Barrows, and Doctor J. D. Lincoln.

The society flourished until the spring of 1849 (a period of four years), when it was " voted not to assign any regular parts during the summer, but to come together in a social way once a fortnight and occasionally for a walk." Meetings were thus held for a short time, when they ceased altogether.

The average membership of the society was from twenty-five to thirty.

A Town History and Natural History Society was organized in Brunswick, March 30, 1870, by the choice of A. G. Tenney, chairman, and John Furbish, secretary. Apart from creating an interest in its members for the objects for which it was formed, this society resulted in a failure.

Debating societies and lyceums of minor importance have also existed in various parts of each of these towns, but they do not call for particular mention here.

MUSICAL SOCIETIES.

The first musical society in this vicinity was the Hayden Society, formed about 1825.

This was followed in 1829 by the Mozart Society. This society was formed for the cultivation of musical tastes and for social intercourse. Its meetings were held at the Tontine Hotel, Maine Hotel, and at Robert Orr's office. It embraced members from Topsham as well as from Brunswick. Robert Orr, General Abner B. Thompson, James McKeen, M. D., John H. Thompson, and Benjamin Dennison are known to have been members.

About 1844 the Brunswick Brass Band was formed. It was probably the earliest band formed in this vicinity. It consisted of fifteen members and was in existence five or six years. William R. Field, Jr., was the leader during the last year of its existence.

The musical organizations of a later date have been too numerous to admit of mention here.

MORAL ASSOCIATIONS.

In 1826 the Peace Society of Brunswick was organized. It continued in existence for seven years, perhaps longer. Nothing has been ascertained in regard to its membership or its meetings.

March 20, 1838, the Topsham Antislavery Society was organized. James McKeen, M. D., was elected president; David Scribner, vice-president; and Joseph Barron, secretary. The whole number of members was fifty-eight. Their constitution required them to meet quarterly for the purpose of discussing the subject of slavery.

About 1845 the Liberty Association of Brunswick was formed. Nothing has been ascertained in regard to this society, but judging from its name, it was probably a political society.

PROTECTIVE ASSOCIATIONS.

The earliest society of this kind, not including insurance companies, etc., which appear in another connection, was the Brunswick Watch Association. This was an organization of citizens voluntarily associated together to secure the village against fire during the winter season, when it was difficult to obtain water. At that time, there being no suction hose, the engines had to be filled by buckets.

The association was formed January 14, 1826, a meeting of citizens being called for this purpose. At this meeting Joseph McKeen, Parker Cleaveland, Caleb Cushing, Richard T. Dunlap, Abner B. Thompson, and Benj. Weld were chosen a committee to prepare a system of rules for regulating the watch. They reported, and the association adopted, the following

BY-LAWS FOR THE WATCH.

1. "The watch for each night shall consist of four citizens, two of whom shall remain at the place of rendezvous, while the other two are out upon duty.

2. "The watch shall so divide themselves every night, that each half shall perform duty in that part of the village in which they reside, so far as this may be practicable.

3. "The watch shall make *five* rounds of the village during the night, the rounds commencing at *ten* o'clock, *half past eleven*, *one* o'clock, *half past two*, and *four* o'clock.

4. "Each round shall be divided into two parts, viz., *one part*, commencing at the place of rendezvous, shall proceed up Main Street to the Academy, thence returning by the meeting-house to the store of Joseph McKeen, Esquire, pass through Cross Street to Federal Street, thence down the same to School Street, through that to Pleasant Street, proceeding up that street to the house of Captain John A. Dunning, and thence return to the place of rendezvous.

"The *other part*, commencing at the same place of rendezvous, shall proceed down Main Street to the bridge, thence through Bow Street to Mill Street, and up that street to the house of Mr. B. Wells, thence back through Mill Street to Main Street, thence through Mason Street to Federal Street, up that street to the house of Mr. C. Waterhouse, thence back through Centre Street to Main Street, and thence to the place of rendezvous.

5. "The watch will proceed on their rounds without causing any unnecessary noise or disturbance to the inhabitants. In case of *fire* they will give the most prompt and effectual alarm.

6. "One member of the committee, in the afore-mentioned order of their names, will superintend the watch, as expressed in the subjoined list of the watch.

7. "Every member of the association who may be necessarily prevented from watching in his turn, shall furnish a suitable substitute, who, if not a member of the association, shall be approved by the committee for the week, or instead thereof, he shall pay the sum of one dollar; and the name of the substitute shall be presented, or the money paid to the committee for the week, as early as twelve o'clock of the day preceding his turn to watch.

8. "Each watchman, when out on duty, shall carry a watch-pole; and the poles during the day shall be deposited at the place of rendezvous, together with lanterns, to be used when necessary.

9. "The names of those who may be delinquent, or fail to comply with the by-laws established, shall be communicated by the committee to the association at the close of the season."

The by-laws were printed in sheet form, together with the "Order of the Watch," which gave the names of the members and the dates upon which they were expected to watch. The place of rendezvous was, at first, the counting-room of Farrin & Dunning. In 1827 it was at Barker and Rogers's Inn.

The Executive Committee in 1826 were: —

Joseph McKeen, Parker Cleaveland, Caleb Cushing, Richard T. Dunlap, Abner B. Thompson, Benjamin Weld. The association contained at that time one hundred and thirty-one members, some of whom were professors in college, and nearly all of whom were amongst the most esteemed citizens of the town.

The expense of the watch was paid by voluntary subscription the first year, but afterwards it was assessed by the committee upon the citizens, according to the amount of property they had exposed to fire. Hot coffee, bread, butter, cheese, and cold meats were furnished the watch at midnight. The watch-poles which were carried by the watchmen were about three feet long, with a hook at one end. The poles were used to walk with, and the hooks were used to catch into the clothing of any culprit who sought to escape from the watch by running.

A "Watch Book" was kept at the rendezvous, in which the watch each morning recorded any interesting event which occurred during the night. A book containing the records from January 1st to March 31st, 1827, is the only one we have been able to find. It contains no record of historical value, but has much of a humorous character, as the following extracts will show: —

"January 6th. Nothing material happened during the night. Found one light in a dangerous position (viz. at the head of a bed in a chair); two fires badly taken care of, and some courting on hand, people up late."

"January 30th. On the fifth watch saw a young man returning home from particular business. Detained him awhile, demanded his business for being out so late; he gave us good satisfaction; we let him go by paying one bottle of wine."

"February 15th. First round, half past twelve o'clock, met Hannah S. and Geo. W., all was well."

"March 4th. One thing is deserving of particular notice, viz., not a hundred rods distant a fine lady was observed to be sitting in the lap of a fine gentleman, and as our respected major and squire would say, 'all as fine as silk.'"

The watch was continued for several winters and then given up.

In 1849 a similar watch was established upon a modified plan. John M. Hall was appointed superintendent of the watch. The watch for each night consisted of six citizens, who were divided into three parties of two each, and it was so arranged that four persons were on the watch at all times through the night until daylight.

The watch was discontinued at the end of the season and was not afterwards revived.

In 1852 and 1853 a watch, consisting of six citizens appointed each night by the justices of the peace and selectmen, was kept in Brunswick. The chamber of the engine-house on Pleasant Street was used as the watch-room, where the watch met at nine o'clock each evening and organized themselves for the night.

TEMPERANCE SOCIETIES AND TEMPERANCE REFORM.

The first movement toward the suppression of intemperance in this vicinity, and possibly as early a movement as any of the kind in the State (then District) of Maine, was in the year 1813.

On the second day of April of that year a society was formed under the title of THE BRUNSWICK, TOPSHAM, AND HARPSWELL SOCIETY FOR THE SUPPRESSION OF INTEMPERANCE. The constitution of this society at first limited its exertions to the single object of restraining intemperance, but by an amendment adopted at its first anniversary in 1814, it was provided that the efforts of the society should also be directed against other immoralities.

The following extracts from the constitution, as published in 1814, will show the character of the organization and the nature of its work: —

"Article 2. The object of this society is the suppression of vice and immorality, and the encouragement of reformation and virtue. The accomplishment of this design is to be sought by admonition and persuasion, and by promoting a faithful execution of the laws."

Article 7 provided for a "Board of Council." Among the duties of this board were the following: "To make communications to other similar societies; to receive communications from them; to collect, combine, and digest facts and general information relating to the general purposes of the society; to devise ways and means for the furtherance of these purposes, and at each annual meeting to report to the society their doings; a digest of the facts and general information which they may have collected, and such measures as they may judge suitable for the society to adopt and pursue."

The eighth article provided that each member of the society should make it an object to discountenance and prevent as far as may be, by his own example and influence, every kind of vice and immorality.

April 27, 1814, Professor Cleaveland delivered an address before the society. A copy of the constitution and a copy of Prof. Cleaveland's address may be found in the library of the Maine Historical Society.

That there was need enough of a movement in favor of temperance at this period is evident from a statement made by a competent person, of the amount of spirits of various kinds that were sold in Brunswick between November 1, 1826, and November 5, 1830. From this statement it appears that in 1826 more than 12,000 gallons of liquor were sold. In 1830, owing to the temperance reform, the amount had been lessened one half.

The second temperance movement commenced in Brunswick about the year 1826. The subject was brought before the people by a lecture on temperance by some gentleman from Massachusetts. Some of the citizens of the place became interested in the subject, foremost amongst whom was Professor Packard, then a young man. The first movement made after the lecture mentioned above was the meeting together of the traders of the village to consult on measures for promoting temperance in Brunswick. This meeting was held at the old stage-house kept by Russell Stoddard, and consisted of all the grocers, tavern-keepers, and victuallers in the village. Various plans were discussed, but, about the close of the meeting, one of the oldest traders arose and submitted a plan and resolution. The resolution was as follows: —

"*Resolved*, That hereafter the retailers of spirits in this village charge four cents per glass and six cents per gill for all New England rum drank in their places of business, instead of three cents per glass and five cents per gill, as heretofore; and be it further resolved, that we add one cent per glass and one cent per gill to the price of all other liquors sold at our places of business."

This resolution was probably not adopted, as it is said that the patrons of this trader found much fault with him, complaining that he had always made more profit by his sales than the other traders, because when he drew his liquors for them "he placed his large thumb in the measure so that they did not get more than three fourths as much for a glassful as they did at other stores." A good way, surely, of compelling men to drink moderately!

The lecture and meeting referred to did good by attracting attention to the subject, though no real measures were taken to prevent the spread of intemperance. In 1828 the surveyors of highways were instructed by the town of Brunswick to use no ardent spirits at the expense of the town. It is extremely doubtful, though, whether this vote was due so much to the growth of a temperance sentiment in town as it was to a desire for retrenchment of expenses.

The second organization for the purpose of promoting a temperance reform was known as THE TEMPERANCE SOCIETY OF BRUNSWICK. It was organized on the twenty-third of November, 1830. The fundamental article of its constitution, or "the pledge," was as follows: —

"We agree that we will not drink ardent spirits, nor furnish them for others to drink, except when they are prescribed by a temperate physician as an indispensable medicine."

The society was at first quite small, there being in January, 1831, only twenty-seven members. The number soon after increased to eighty, and in the year 1835 there was a total membership of four hundred and sixty. Many of the members were so liberal in their interpretation of the pledge as to suppose they might drink wine or strong beer without violating it, and as a natural consequence, after a while, they disregarded the pledge altogether. Others, however, adhered firmly to their pledge, and remained ever after strictly temperate men. The society continued in existence until about 1842. Those, however, who adhered strictly to the spirit of the pledge had previously left the ranks and joined other organizations. It is said of those who remained that it was customary with them to drink wine at their meetings. However that may be, it is a matter of record that the Washington Temperance Society, in 1841, requested the clergymen of Brunswick not to take up any contribution in their meetings for the old temperance society, on account of the bad influence of its example.

We have been unable to find any records of the society, and cannot, therefore, give a list of its officers or any of its transactions. A copy of the pledge, containing one hundred and thirty-five names, is in our possession. Among the signers are the names of professors, clergymen, lawyers, physicians, and other prominent men as well as those of humbler citizens. The names contained in this list were obtained as early as 1833, possibly earlier.

In 1834 the BRUNSWICK TOTAL ABSTINENCE AND CHARITABLE SOCIETY was in existence and was probably organized that year.

In 1835 the YOUNG MEN'S TEMPERANCE SOCIETY, of Brunswick, and the TEMPERANCE SOCIETY OF BOWDOIN COLLEGE, were formed. There was also one other in addition to those already mentioned as formed in 1830 and 1834, making five temperance societies in existence in Brunswick at this time. From the "Annual Report of the Directors of the Cumberland County Temperance Society" we obtain the names of all the officers of these five societies, but no clew is given as to which society a given set of officers belongs.

Of one society Doctor S. P. Cushman was the president, and Professor A. S. Packard the secretary. Of another, Reverend George Lamb was president, and James Elliot, secretary. Elder John Bailey was the president, and Jonathan Snow the secretary, of a third. Of another, Ezekiel Thompson was the president. Of the last, John S. Grows was the president, and Samuel Holbrook the secretary. The total membership of the five societies numbered nine hundred and thirty-four.

About this time, as early at least as 1836, the TOPSHAM TEMPERANCE SOCIETY was formed. This was the first society of the kind amongst the people of that town. with the exception of the one formed in 1813, which included citizens of several towns.

THE WASHINGTON TOTAL ABSTINENCE SOCIETY OF TOPSHAM was

formed on the seventh of June, 1841. In November of the following year, there were one hundred and thirty-three members. Meetings were held weekly, and a good degree of interest was manifested. The officers, in 1842, were Samuel W. Swett, president; Nathaniel Quint, vice-president; Charles J. Harris, secretary; Cyrus M. Purington, treasurer and collector; E. Sawyer, Charles Barron, and Henry C. Haynes, prudential committee. We have been unable to obtain any further information regarding this society.

The Washington Total Abstinence Society of Brunswick was formed on Wednesday, June 16, 1841, fourteen persons affixing their names to the pledge. From this small beginning the society gradually increased in numbers, and in May, 1842, there were five hundred and eighty members. The officers chosen at the time of the organization of the society were General John C. Humphreys, president; Moses Towns, vice-president; George W. Carleton, secretary; Colonel A. J. Stone, treasurer.

Weekly meetings were held, at first, in the "Red School-House" on School Street, afterwards in Humphreys Hall, and still later (in 1842) in Washington Hall, in the old tavern which stood on the site of the present post-office and engine-house.

During the first year the society held occasional public meetings, at which addresses upon temperance were made and the pledge offered for signatures. One of these meetings was held in the Congregational Church, and was addressed by William H. Hawkins, of Baltimore. After the address *one hundred and one* persons came forward and signed the pledge of total abstinence. Meetings were also held at New Meadows and Growstown, and in Harpswell, Freeport, and other towns in the vicinity, under the direction of delegations from the Brunswick society.

The society decided by a *unanimous* vote that moral suasion and not coercion should be the method by which its members should seek to reform the intemperate and to prevent the sale of ardent spirits.

On the twenty-second of February, 1842, Washington's birthday was celebrated by a public meeting which was addrsssed by Reverend George E. Adams and Reverend Mr. Hillman, after which the society partook of a supper at Washington Hall. Dean Swift furnished an appropriate banner.

On the fourth of March, 1842, Reverend Mr. Thompson delivered an address before the society at the Congregational Church, the members marching in procession to the church, escorted by Captain Newman's company of militia.

The society existed for several years, precisely how many we are unable to state.

In 1841 the selectmen of Brunswick voted not to license any innholders, "unless they pledge themselves in writing, in the most solemn and positive manner, that they will not keep liquors in or about their premises to sell or to give away." They were also, at the annual meeting of the town, directed to prosecute all persons selling liquors without a license. They were led to the adoption of these measures in consequence of the growth of the sentiment in favor of temperance reform which was promoted by the temperance organizations.

The Martha Washington Society of Brunswick was organized on the seventeenth of March, 1842. A number of ladies, feeling the importance of aiding the cause of temperance, met at that time and formed a society. Meetings were held once a fortnight. In July following the society numbered two hundred and seventy-five members. The society not only labored for the reformation of the intemperate, but rendered substantial relief to worthy destitute families.

The Young Men's Washingtonian Society of Brunswick was, as its name would imply, an association of young men for the promotion of the cause of temperance. It was formed in April, 1843. The officers at that time were M. B. Bartlett, president; C. P. Stetson, vice-president; A. W. Knight, secretary; and E. A. Dunlap, treasurer.

In 1845 the True Washingtonian Temperance Society of Topsham was formed. Nothing more than this fact has been ascertained in regard to it. It was probably formed by those who, though temperate, could not conscientiously join a strictly total-abstinence society.

In 1846 the popular feeling in regard to temperance had become sufficiently powerful to enable the town of Brunswick at its annual meeting to pass the following resolve: —

"*Resolved*, That the traffic in intoxicating liquors as a beverage is injurious and unnecessary, and that, therefore, said traffic ought to cease; that the selectmen be directed to take all legal measures for its suppression in this town, and that in so doing the town will sustain them."

On the seventeenth of February of this year a public temperance meeting was held in Brunswick, at which a committee, consisting of sixty-three prominent citizens of the town, with John F. Hall as chairman, was chosen to devise means for suppressing the sale of intoxicating liquors. This committee issued a circular letter to each retail dealer in liquor in the town, requesting him to relinquish the traffic.

These letters had the effect of inducing some to abandon the sale of liquor, though many still persisted in it.

In the fall of 1849 the SAWACOOK DIVISION OF THE SONS OF TEMPERANCE was instituted in Topsham. It lasted for several years, and accomplished much good.

The BRUNSWICK DIVISION, NO. 142, OF SONS OF TEMPERANCE was instituted on the fifth day of February, 1850, by the Sawacook Division of Topsham. The charter was surrendered on the twenty-third of November, 1852.

BRUNSWICK DIVISION, NO. 20 (Sons of Temperance), was instituted March 22, 1858, by the Grand Worthy Patriarch.

In August, 1859, it was voted to admit "lady visitors." On the thirtieth of September, 1860, there were seventy-eight members, and one hundred and nineteen lady visitors. During the three months previous, sixteen members had been expelled, eight had withdrawn, five had violated the pledge, four had been admitted, three suspended, and three resigned. The division broke up in the fall of 1862.

TEMPERANCE WATCHMEN. — A temperance society with the above appellation was organized in the year 1850 or 1851. Its members were required to watch for, and report to the society, all violations of the law of the State, prohibiting the sale of intoxicating liquors. The ceremonies of the society were simpler than those of most other orders, and the expenses were less.

PEJEPSCOT DIVISION, NO. 13, OF JUVENILE TEMPERANCE WATCHMEN, of Brunswick, was organized in the fall of 1851, and in the course of two or three months there was a membership of about fifty. Weekly meetings were held, at which were debates, declamations, and other exercises of a like character. In the autumn of 1852 a fine banner was presented to the society by lady friends. It is now in the possession of Mr. Fessenden I. Day, of Lewiston, who was the treasurer of the club. The founder and first president of the club was Mr. George W. M. Hall. The club gave a public exhibition on the fifth of January, 1854.

A TEMPERANCE SOCIETY was organized in Topsham, on the nineteenth of January, 1857. It had no other title than "The Temperance Society." Sixty-two persons signed the pledge. David Scribner was chosen president; Joshua Haskell, vice-president; William Whitten, secretary; Sandford A. Perkins, treasurer; Humphrey P. Mallett, William Barron, Eben Colby, committee.

THE CADETS OF TEMPERANCE, a society of young men under eighteen years of age, was formed in the spring of 1859 or 1860.

There were two divisions of the cadets, one in Brunswick and the other in Topsham.

THE BOWDOIN TEMPLE OF HONOR AND TEMPERANCE, No. 5, a subordinate society of the Good Templars, was instituted in Brunswick, August 29, 1866. The society was located in Brunswick, but contained some members from Topsham.

The JOSHUA NYE LODGE, No. 126, OF GOOD TEMPLARS was organized on the eleventh of April, 1870, and is still in existence.

The REFORM CLUB was organized in 1871. It has held a number of public meetings which have been addressed by prominent temperance men from abroad, and which were productive of much good. The organization is still in existence and in a flourishing condition.

No account has been obtained of any associations in Harpswell except temperance societies, though without doubt there have been some others. Besides the Brunswick, Topsham, and Harpswell Temperance Society already mentioned, there was in 1842 a Washingtonian Society, with a membership of over two hundred, upon Sebascodegan Island, and there is now a reform club of about forty members on that island.

Other associations not given in this chapter, such as religious societies, military companies, etc., will be mentioned in their appropriate places in other connections.

CHAPTER VI.

FIRES AND FIRE COMPANIES.

CONFLAGRATIONS have been of rather frequent occurrence in Brunswick, Topsham, and Harpswell, considering the population of the towns. The first-named town has suffered by far the most and the latter the least from this cause. The following account of the different fires that have occurred in these towns is obtained mainly from the accounts given at the time in different newspapers, from the records of the fire companies, and from private journals. It is believed to be as full and accurate as is possible from the data to be obtained.

LIST OF FIRES IN BRUNSWICK.

[1671.] The beech woods, where the pine plains now are, were destroyed by fire.[1]

[1676.] A house and other buildings, near where Pennell's Wharf now is, were fired by the Indians. It had been occupied by a Mr. Wakely, who was killed and his body cast into the flames.[1]

[1690.] This year the whole settlement was destroyed by the Indians.

[1722.] The Indians destroyed nearly all the settlement. Among the houses burnt were those of Thomas Tregoweth and James Thornton. The latter was the father of Matthew Thornton, one of the signers of the Declaration of Independence.

[1735.] A block house, probably the one at Maquoit, was accidentally burned.

[1737.] The house of Andrew Dunning was accidentally destroyed by fire, and his widow lost her life.

[1770.] Deacon Samuel Stanwood's house, which occupied the ground where Mrs. Joseph McKeen's house now stands, was burnt.

[1777.] There was a fire in some house, not known, which was caused by hot ashes in a barrel.

---

[1] *Traditional.*

[1798.] The store of Stone & Veazie was burnt. It was a two-story building.

[1805.] A two-story dwelling-house, by whom occupied or owned is unknown, was destroyed by fire.

[1809.] On April 30, an extensive fire on the plains near the colleges. On June 29, at 11 A. M., the Gun House, on Center Street, was burnt. A new one was at once built on the same spot.

[1810.] In January, day unknown, 9.15 P. M., Captain Richard Tappan's house, store, and barn, and the house of Colonel William Stanwood. Deacon John Perry's house was torn down to prevent the spread of the fire. At midnight Secomb Jordan's house, near Pollard & Green's tannery, was burnt. The thermometer at the time indicated —10°.

[1814.] Samuel Page's house and James Jones's blacksmith shop were burnt.

For the next eight years there has no record been found of any fire. It is hardly to be presumed, however, that so long a time could have elapsed without some such occurrence. Newspapers at that time gave but little attention to such items, and they may easily have failed to be recorded in private journals.

[1822.] On March 4, the principal college building was burned about three o'clock in the afternoon; the whole of the woodwork was consumed by seven o'clock in the evening. The fire was undoubtedly accidental. $1,000 was contributed by the citizens to aid the sufferers, and the town of Dorchester, Massachusetts, also gave voluntary assistance.

[1823.] On February 12, the house of Mr. Benjamin Orr, occupied by the Misses Tappan, was destroyed. In March, James Nelson's house, near the landing, was burnt. September 4, a fire arose in the woods of Washington Bowker, near Rocky Hill, and made such alarming progress that it soon came within a mile of the village, where, however, its progress was fortunately stayed. It destroyed nearly every building for four miles in length and one in breadth. Twenty[1] buildings were burnt in all, amongst which were the houses of Andrew Toothaker, Lemuel Morse, and the Widow Douglass. There was also a great loss in woods, fences, sheep, and cattle. Among the sufferers were two widows. One of them, possibly Mrs. Douglass, "passed through a scene of peculiar anguish. After nearly exhausting her strength in fruitless efforts to save her house, she was

---

[1] *Cleaveland's Journal.*

compelled to bear away her sick son, with only the assistance of small children, to a place of safety." It is handed down as a tradition, that this fire was caused by a boy setting fire to a hornets' nest, in revenge for the hornets having stung him.

[1825.] On Tuesday morning, March 28, the store of Jotham Stone, occupied by Ammi R. West, was destroyed by fire, together with all his goods, valued at $2,000, his account books, and six hundred dollars in bank-notes, partly insured. This is the first instance met with in this town where any damages were covered by insurance.

December 1, the post-office caught fire, but was only slightly damaged.

On December 13, occurred what is known as the "Great Fire." Thirty-three[1] buildings were burnt, among which were the two factory buildings, five dwelling-houses (occupied by eleven families), two stores, two saw-mills, one grist-mill, and a number of mechanic shops. The thermometer showed the temperature at the time to be —13°. Many persons were badly frozen. The fire broke out in the then new factory building. The total loss was estimated at $90,000. There was an insurance on the factory of $1,800.

At a town meeting in Brunswick, held on the twenty-second of December of this year, it was voted that a committee of fifteen persons be appointed to solicit aid for the relief of the sufferers by the late fire, and to distribute what might be collected. This committee appointed a subcommittee of three, to ascertain the actual loss sustained by the citizens, exclusive of that of the factory company and of property which was insured. In their report it is stated that fifty-seven heads of families had lost $13,918, sixty-eight persons had been deprived of a shelter, and more than fifty persons had been thrown out of employment. $1,044 was contributed by the citizens for the relief of the sufferers.

In consequence of the frequency and severity of fires at this time a citizens' watch was established soon after the last-mentioned fire, and all citizens were requested to have holes made in the shutters of their houses and stores, in order that fires might be more easily discovered.

[1826.] On November 3, of this year, the following advertisement appeared in the columns of the *Baptist Herald:* —

"WANTED, A SMART, ACTIVE BOY to set fires and burn brush on Brunswick plains. A college-learnt lad would be preferred; one who has little else to do, and can afford to work very cheap. Apply to Doctor Shame, next door to the House of Correction."

---

[1] *A. C. Raymond's Diary.*

No record of any fires has been found for this year, but it would seem from the foregoing advertisement as though some parties had been kindling fires in the woods for purposes of mischief, and that the college students were the ones suspected.

[1827.] In the night of November 7, the stage tavern, kept by Charles M. Rogers, was burnt. Several travellers who were passing the night there had barely time to leave their beds and get out, unclad, into the deep, newly fallen snow.

On December 27, the house of Theodore S. McLellan was burnt.

At some time this year, the exact date not known, the store of Colonel Jesse Pierce was partially destroyed by fire. After the flames were subdued a *keg of powder* was taken out of the building, the outside of which had been *scorched* by the fire.

[1829.] On July 26, the house of Stephen Sawyer was destroyed by fire, together with most of its contents. Loss about eight hundred dollars; no insurance.

[1830.] On March 9, J. Nelson's cabinet shop was burnt.

[1833.] At midday on January 11, the store of John McKeen was burnt. The contents were mostly saved. The building was estimated to be worth between six and seven hundred dollars, on which there was an insurance of four hundred dollars.

[1834.] August 7, of this year, the lightning struck Captain Given's barn and burned it, together with three other barns and ten cattle.

On October 26, the old west meeting-house was burned by an incendiary. In consequence, the town, at a meeting held November 15, appointed a committee to legally investigate the matter, in order that the incendiary might be punished, and voted a reward of one hundred dollars for the detection of the offender.

[1835.] The Dunning house, on the west side of Maine Street, on the hill, nearly opposite the meeting-house, was burned either this year or (possibly) in 1834. The building was two stories high.

[1836.] On February 17, at half past two o'clock, A. M., the college building known as Maine Hall was totally destroyed by fire.

On September 26, the drying-house, near and belonging to the factory, was burned.

On November 7, the new two-story building of Messrs. Stone & Morse, near the corner of Maine and Bow Streets, was burned. It was occupied by John L. Swift, tailor.

[1837.] This year Messrs. Stone & Morse were again sufferers from fire, their store being burned on May 11.

[1838.] On May 3, a "factory and picking machine was burnt." The newspaper account does not state what factory it was.

[1841.] August 14, a portion of the McKeen woods was destroyed by fire. December 17, the toll-bridge burned. At some time this year, date unknown, the grist-mill at the Lower Falls was burned.

[1843.] The house of Thomas Crowell, two miles from Brunswick Village, was burned on July 23 or 24.

[1845.] On March 27, a destructive fire occurred, at which property to the value of $7,000 was destroyed. No other particulars in regard to it have been ascertained.

On September 24, there was a slight fire at Humphrey's Dye House.

On October 3, at four P. M., the "Growse" house was burned. Loss, two hundred dollars. Fully insured.

On October 13, a two-story house at Mair Brook, owned by Mrs. Garcelon, William R. Field, and George Woodside, was destroyed. It was unoccupied. Loss, six hundred dollars. Fully insured.

On October 19 (Sunday), between twelve and one o'clock at night, the houses of Stephen Harris and Joseph Badger were burnt. They were insured for $2,450.

On December 26, a school-house on the Portland road was destroyed by fire.

[1846.] On February 12, Humphrey's Dye House was burnt. On February 18, Major Willett's house, near the factory, was partially destroyed. Partly insured. The fire was extinguished by the Force-Pump Water Works. The fire was the work of an incendiary.

In September, Nichols's store, No. 7 Hinkley Block, was slightly damaged by fire and the goods injured by water. Insured.

[1847.] On April 14, the woollen-mill of Whitten & Meder was partially destroyed. Loss, three hundred dollars. Insured.

On November 13, a saw-mill was burned.

[1849.] On May 3, the woollen factory of Whitten & Meder (owned at the time wholly by William Whitten) was again attacked by fire. The total loss was between $6,000 and $7,000. Insured for $4,200.

On December 2, three buildings on Maine Street, beginning at the northern corner of Pleasant Street, where Lemont Block is now, were destroyed by fire. John S. Cushing occupied the corner store, and lost everything. The second story of this building was occupied by the Odd Fellows, who saved nothing. In the second building was a tailor's shop; and in the third, a shoe store. The second story of these buildings was occupied by different individuals for offices.

[1851.] On March 12, the bookstore of Nathaniel Davis was burned at half past twelve o'clock in the night. July 30, a Mr. Cobbett's house was destroyed by fire.

[1852.] On June 15, Mr. Larrabee's barn at New Meadows was burnt; and at four o'clock in the morning of the twenty-sixth of the same month, a tannery was burnt.

[1853.] The building on the corner of Maine and Mason Streets was destroyed by fire in February. Lorenzo Day and James Cary built one on the same spot that fall.

[1854.] On Saturday afternoon, January 14, one of the mills on Shad Island took fire. The fire had made considerable progress before it was discovered, but by the untiring exertions of the fire companies, assisted by the company from Topsham, the flames were soon subdued. The mill was owned by the Granite Bank Company of Exeter, New Hampshire, whose loss was estimated at $300. It was used by Mr. B. E. Parkhurst as a match-box manufactory. His loss was about three hundred dollars, but was partially covered by insurance. The machinery in the mill was the property of Messrs. Byam & Pearsons, of Boston, was only partially injured, and was probably insured. July 6, the house of Christopher Mitchell, on the Portland road, was burned. No insurance.

[1855.] On March 7, a loaded freight car was burned near the depot. The loss was estimated at $3,000. April 19, there was a fire at Carleton's gum factory. Amount of damage not stated.

On June 25, the freight and engine houses of the Kennebec and Portland Railroad Company were destroyed by fire about nine o'clock P. M. The contents of the buildings were saved.

On July 1, an old stable on School Street, the house and stable belonging to the Misses McLellan, and the Stoddard house, corner of Federal and School Streets, were destroyed by fire. The buildings on the "Stoddard lot" were owned by General R. T. Dunlap, and were not insured. The loss on them was about six hundred dollars. The McLellan house was partially insured.

[1856.] On May 17, Miss Narcissa Stone's steam-mill on Pleasant Street was burned. It was uninsured, and the loss amounted to $1,600. This fire is supposed to have been the work of an incendiary. In November the house of Isaac Varney, near the depot, was burned to the ground.

On December 10, the Washington Hall building and Parshley's store were destroyed by fire. The former was occupied by the barber shop of E. Eaton, by Johnson & Goddard's confectionery shop, and by four families; and the hall was used by the Brunswick Light Infantry as their armory. The building was owned by General R. T. Dunlap and S. Thompson. Dunlap's share was uninsured. Thompson was insured for five hundred dollars. Eaton's loss was some over fifty dollars. Johnson & Goddard were fully insured. The loss to the Infantry Company was about eight hundred dollars.

Parshley's store was occupied in the basement by Mr. H. A. Thompson, and in the second story by two families. Parshley's loss was about five hundred dollars in excess of his insurance. The whole loss due to the fire was estimated at $3,000.

[1857.] In the spring of 1857 the town-house was burnt. It was the work of an incendiary. On September 29, the Kennebec and Portland Railroad depot burned down. A great many papers and considerable baggage were destroyed. though some of the baggage and freight was saved. John A. Cleaveland lost one hundred and twenty-five, William R. Field four hundred, and Doctor Haley twenty-five dollars. The loss to the company was about $7,000. They were uninsured. One trunk that was burned was said to contain jewelry to the value of three hundred dollars. This fire was thought to be the work of an incendiary.

On October 20, Darius Newman's shop, and on October 23, James Spollett's shop on Pleasant Street, were burned. October 30, Leonard Merrill's house, at the Landing, was partially destroyed. November 22, Jotham Varney's building, occupied by W. J. Harmon & Co. as a billiard and refreshment saloon, was burnt. December 15, about four o'clock A. M., the Bourne mill, in the cove, was burnt. It belonged to R. T. Dunlap, C. J. Gilman, A. B. Thompson, and Ward Coburn.

[1858.] February 25, there was a fire in the picking-room of the factory.

[1859.] At one o'clock A. M., on July 15, the barn, shed, and back part of the house of the Misses T. and J. Hinkley, on Maine Street, which was formerly owned and occupied by Reverend John S. C. Abbot, were burned. The buildings were insured. The fire was supposed to be the work of an incendiary.

On July 20, four or five acres of swampy land, near Rocky Hill, were burned over.

In August there was a fire in the woods south of the McKeen Road, and also on the Plains.

[1860.] On September 16, the house, barn, shed, etc., of Mr. Hiram Campbell, on the Bath road, burned down.

[1862.] June 27, the McKeen Store, occupied by D. B. Libby, and by Joseph McKeen, treasurer of Bowdoin College, was destroyed by fire. The more valuable books of the college were saved, though many papers were lost. Henry Bowker's house and H. A. Thompson's store were slightly damaged by this fire.

On August 5, Gideon Kincaid's house, barn, and shed were burnt.

[1863.] At eight o'clock P. M., on December 2, the stable attached to the dwelling of James Hall was destroyed by fire. Insured.

[1864.] July 27, the house and barn of Calvin Cooper, one mile from the village, on the Bath road, was burned, together with its contents.

About midnight of August 12, the house of Washington Stanwood, near Mair Brook, was consumed by fire, together with the out-buildings and contents. It was occupied by Emery Hersey. Buildings insured for five hundred dollars.

At ten o'clock P. M., on October 14, one of Humphrey's steam-mills (the most southerly one) was consumed by fire. The loss was estimated at $5,000. Partially insured. Lumber valued at $1,000 and not insured was also destroyed by this fire.

October 20, Captain Nathaniel Badger's barn was burned, together with his horse and carriages.

[1865.] On the tenth of April the barn of the poorhouse was fired by an insane person. The loss was about seven hundred dollars. Insured for two hundred dollars.

At eleven o'clock P. M., on May 3, the grocery store of R. Crockett & Co. was entirely burned. Partially insured.

On September 26, the picking-room in the cotton factory took fire, but the flames were soon subdued and but little damage was done.

[1866.] At half past eleven P. M., on March 7, a loaded freight car was burned on the track near the depot.

In the night of June 23, a car loaded with hay took fire near the depot.

At three o'clock A. M., on December 22, Forsaith & Dunning's house and out-buildings, and the house and stable occupied by G. B. Tenney, were burned. The loss of Messrs. Dunning & Forsaith was estimated to be $2,000 over and above the insurance to each. Tenney's loss was estimated at about five hundred dollars more than the insurance, and the house occupied by him was valued at seven hundred dollars more than its insurance. This fire was supposed to be the work of an incendiary.

[1867.] On April 16, the stable of W. A. Campbell, including four horses, three top-buggies, and one open buggy, one Concord wagon, four single sleighs, one double sleigh, six single harnesses, one double and one team harness, fifteen robes, an express wagon, and a hearse; also the barn of J. Lufkin and that of the double house belonging to Albert C. Otis and Mrs. M. G. Merryman, were all destroyed by fire. Campbell's property, exclusive of building, was estimated at $3,250. He was insured for $2,000. The stable was worth five hundred dollars, and was insured for two hundred. The other parties were all fully insured.

At half past five o'clock A. M., on November 2, Jotham Varney's building, containing Haley's apothecary store and York's barber shop, was burned. No insurance.

[1868.] On February 15, the woodshed of the poorhouse was consumed by fire. Estimated value, one hundred and fifty dollars. Uninsured.

At half past nine o'clock P. M., on June 29, an engine-house of the Androscoggin Railroad Company was burnt.

About midnight of September 2, the barn and a portion of the house of Waitstill Merryman was burned. It was occupied by D. S. Perkins. Merryman was insured, but Perkins was not.

On November 26, the house of Harvey Stetson was partially consumed by fire. The loss was estimated at eight hundred dollars. No insurance.

On December 4, a house below Mair Brook was slightly injured by fire.

December 5, the house, barn, shed, and several cords of wood, belonging to Captain Jesse Coolidge, on the river road to Rocky Hill, about one and a half miles from the village, were burnt. The loss amounted to $2,200. Insured for $1,000.

[1869.] At four o'clock A. M., January 21, Mr. Robert Bowker's house was partially burned. Fully insured.

At seven o'clock P. M., on January 29, Charles Cobb's tool shop, on Cushing Street, was destroyed by fire. The loss was about four hundred dollars. No insurance.

At ten P. M., on May 9, Moses Freeman's house and shed, on the Bath road, were burnt. Everything was lost, even to the clothing of the inmates. House insured. At twelve o'clock P. M., John Snow's house, a mile and a half from the village, was burned.

[1870.] On the evening of July 19th, a farm-house on the estate of Captain Larrabee at New Meadows was burned.

[1871.] At six and a half o'clock A. M., on February 17th, there was an extensive conflagration at the cove, with the following loss:—

Colby & Co.'s sash and blind, saw, shingle, and clapboard mill, two planers, etc., estimated at	$10,000
Wing's grist-mill, estimated at	2,000
Coburn's saw-mill, estimated at	5,000
Blethen, Booker & Given, tools, machinery, etc.	1,000
David Dennison, plug-borers, etc.	400
Edward Stone's sash and blind mill,	4,000
William Whitten's mill, carding-machines, etc.	4,000
Sundry others	2,000
Total loss	$35,400

The shore-string of the toll-bridge was burnt, and one span and one abutment spoiled.

On the morning of May 20th, Samuel Gummer's house at Maquoit was injured by fire; loss estimated at two hundred dollars.

[1872.] At two o'clock A. M., on April 3d, the Portland and Kennebec Railroad bridge across the Androscoggin took fire and was entirely destroyed.

[1873.] On March 16th the farm-house of Horace Philbrook, with its contents, was entirely consumed by fire.

July 14th, two miles of woods at New Meadows were burned. The fire caught from a locomotive.

At fifteen minutes past eight o'clock A. M., of August 8th, fire was discovered in the stable of the Weld house on Federal Street. The fire was chiefly confined to the stable and woodshed, which were a total loss. The L attached to the main house was slightly damaged by fire and water. A portion of the library of Reverend Doctor Woods was burned and many valuable historical documents were destroyed. The loss on the buildings was about $2,200, on which there was an insurance of $1,300. The loss to the library was estimated at $1,000, but this was a *low* estimate. There was no insurance on the library.

At nine o'clock A. M., on October 31st, fire broke out in a house on Bow Street, occupied by a French family. It was speedily extinguished and but slight damage was done.

[1874.] At half past five P. M., on May 15th, Benjamin Dunning's house was partially burnt. It was insured.

At three o'clock A. M., on July 19th, the High School-House was damaged by fire to the amount of $1,500. It was supposed to be the work of an incendiary.

In the night of November 28th the soap factory of Levi F.

Andrews, in East Brunswick, was destroyed by fire. The loss was eight hundred dollars; no insurance.

In the forenoon of November 30, the house and barn, with their contents, of Martin Eaton was consumed by fire. There was no insurance, and the family was left destitute.

[1875.] In the night of March 3d the old Hunt house on the Maquoit road was burned, together with the adjoining barn.

In the morning of August 6, the house of Charles J. Noyes, occupied by Miss Estabrook and Mrs. Cutler, was somewhat injured by fire, but not consumed; insured.

[1876.] On April 27, a large fire occurred on the Commons, near the Harpswell road.

September 15, at one o'clock A. M., the Bradford Cobb house on Pleasant Street was totally destroyed. Loss, $2,000; insurance, $1.500.

November 6, at one o'clock A. M., the barn and L of the Melcher house on Noble Street were burned. Two horses were burned to death.

On December 5, Stephen Walker's house on the River road was destroyed. Loss, six hundred and twenty-five dollars; insured.

The following is a *résumé* of the list given above: —

There have been, during the time from 1671 to 1877, at least one hundred and twenty occurrences of fire in town. This would make an average of a little over one fire every two years. Probably a correct average would be about one fire a year.

Of the one hundred and nine fires in which the season is stated, twenty-six occurred in the winter time, twenty-seven occurred in the spring, twenty-five occurred in the summer, and thirty-one occurred in the autumn.

Of the forty-three fires in which the time of day is stated, thirteen occurred between 6 A. M. and 6 P. M., and thirty between 6 P. M. and 6 A. M. The largest number of fires occurred in the month of December (12), and the least in January (6).

LIST OF FIRES IN TOPSHAM.

Though the town of Topsham has suffered from no very extensive conflagration, it has had the usual experience in fires of other manufacturing and ship-building towns of its size. The only accounts of such occurrences before the present century are of the burning by the Indians of the houses of Gyles, Thomas, and York, and the traditional account of the house of Robert Patten having been twice destroyed by fire. The dates of all the above fires are unknown.

[1801.] In March or April of this year Captain Robert Patten's house was destroyed by fire.

[1810.] On Saturday, July 21, a large building, occupied by Messrs. Coombs and Hodgdon, the office of Benjamin Orr, Esquire, and three stables (probably misprint for stores in the newspaper account), belonging to H. Purinton, N. Green, and Messrs. T. & N. Sandford, were consumed by fire.

[1826.] Saturday, January 14, "Sager's house in Topsham was burnt about three o'clock."

On Sunday, January 15, between three and six o'clock A. M., the large three-story building owned by George F. Richardson, and a shop owned by Daniel Dennett, were burned. The upper stories of the house were occupied by the families of Messrs. Richardson, Oliver Conant, and Eliphalet Bryant. The inmates escaped, but saved nothing. The lower story was occupied by Major Nahum Perkins and Samuel R. Jackson as a grocery store. Richardson's loss was estimated at $4,000, Perkins & Jackson's about $4,000, and S. & N. Perkins, in notes and accounts, about $7,000, together with all their account-books. Mr. Gillet lost his shop and stock, about $1,000. There was no insurance. It rained hard and there was snow on the roofs, or the greater part of the village would have been destroyed.

Saturday, July 8, P. Dinsmore's tavern, owned by Captain Samuel Perkins, with the barns and out-houses, was destroyed by fire. The Brunswick people had to lay planks across the stringers of the bridge (which was being repaired), to get their engine across.

December 24, about 12.30 at night, the store owned by General Samuel Veazie, and occupied by Abel Merrill, Junior, was burned. The goods, valued at $1,900, were all consumed, together with three hundred and fifty dollars in cash. The building was not insured, but the goods were insured for $1,500.

[1828.] On January 27, General Veazie's house, situated where Mr. Woodbury B. Purinton now lives, was partially burned.

[1842.] July 25, a fine new ship of about four hundred tons, on the stocks, and nearly completed, was destroyed by fire at the yard of John Godfrey. The heat was so intense that the house of Mr. F. T. Purinton, a few rods distant (near the junction of Main and Green Streets), took fire several times, but was saved by the exertions of the firemen. A stable and chaise-house near, belonging to Mr. Purinton, were consumed, and a dwelling-house, occupied by Mr. Small, was much damaged by fire and water.

The vessel was valued, as she stood, at $15,000. She was owned by Mr. Godfrey, and Messrs. Frost, Haskell, Perkins, and Mallet, the greater part of the loss falling, however, upon Mr. Godfrey. No insurance. The whole loss, including buildings, etc., was estimated at not less than $20,000.

[1843.] The woods in the eastern part of the town were burned. Probably what was known as the "undivided."

[1844.] March 25, the house of Mr. Leiden Cook was destroyed by fire.

[1845.] May 12, woods burned.

[1850.] December 23, Mr. Rufus Rogers's mill, at the upper dam, was destroyed by fire.

December 29, Mr. Charles Thompson's store, occupied by F. T. Littlefield, tailor, and C. A. Berry, harness-maker, was totally consumed. The contents were saved.

[1851.] January 20, Ephraim Griffin's stable was partially burned.

[1854.] Railroad bridge was partially burned this year.

[1857.] December 3, at a quarter before two o'clock in the morning, Mr. Alfred White's store was destroyed by fire.

On the 9th, about eleven and a half o'clock in the forenoon, the old Court House (Academy) was burned. It was owned at the time by Charles Thompson, Joshua Haskell, W. B. Purinton, William Dennett, and Warren Johnson.

On the 17th, John Flagg's house was totally consumed.

[1858.] January 11, the Walker house suffered slightly from fire. It was supposed to have been set on fire by an incendiary.

[1859.] In August some woods were burned.

[1860.] February 18, the old store of F. T. & W. B. Purinton, on Main Street, was burnt. Dunlap's paint-shop, also, at the same time. It was thought to be the work of an incendiary.

April 23, at one o'clock in the night, the house, barn, and sheds, with their contents, of Mr. F. W. Dearborn caught fire, and were consumed. The house was unoccupied at the time. Loss $1,800. Partially insured.

May 30, John F. Blondell's house, four miles from the village, with barn, sheds, etc., and from forty to fifty cords of wood belonging to Messrs. William and Charles T. Patten, was destroyed by fire.

[1862.] April 2, John Preston's house, barn, and sheds on the mill road, together with eight cords of wood, one half ton of hay, and two fowl, were consumed by fire. Insured partially.

[1863.] August 25, at one o'clock at night, Maxwell & Jameson's blacksmith shop was burnt. Supposed to be the work of an incendiary. Loss, four hundred dollars. No insurance.

[1864.] April 23, the house owned by Miss Hannah Thompson and her sister, and occupied by Miss Thompson and Mrs. Merris, was burned. No insurance. July 17, the woods north of the fair grounds were burned. Considerable damage done.

[1865.] October 7, an old dwelling, belonging to Mr. Rufus Rogers, was totally consumed by fire. October 12, Wildes P. Walker's barn was set on fire, but was extinguished with but slight damage.

[1868.] April 21, at three o'clock in the morning, the barn and shed of W. D. Haskell and the barn and shed of H. P. Mallett were consumed by fire. Both were insured.

July 3, at ten o'clock in the evening, Perkins's saw-mill on the west side of the Topsham end of the toll-bridge was burned. It was the work of an incendiary. Loss $1,500. No insurance.

[1871.] May 24, in the night, a blacksmith's shop near Mr. Rufus Rogers's mill was burned.

[1873.] April 14 (to 19), Cornelius Gleason's house on the old Bowdoinham road was destroyed by fire. No insurance.

April 19, the old "Fuller" Haley house was burned. It had been unoccupied for a long time, and the fire was undoubtedly incendiary.

[1874.] June 11, the barn and hay of Charles E. White, and lumber worth $1,000, were destroyed by fire. No insurance.

August 8, at two o'clock in the morning on the Mallet road, some three or four miles from the village, Mr. Charles Purinton's house, stable, and barn were burned. Loss about $4,000. Insured for $2,000.

The following is the *résumé* of the foregoing list.

The number of fires known to have occurred in this town is thirty-eight, an average of one in two and a half years. Of the thirty fires in which the month is given, twelve occurred in the winter, eleven in the spring, nine in the summer, and two in the autumn. The largest number occurred in December, and none in September or November. Five fires are recorded as occurring in the daytime and eight at night.

LIST OF FIRES IN HARPSWELL.

Tradition says that the lower end of Harpswell Neck was at one time burned over and the cinders, flying across to Bailey's Island, set fire to the woods on that island, and they were all destroyed. No date is given of this occurrence, but it was probably very early in the history of the town, quite likely before its incorporation. Very few buildings have ever been destroyed by fire in this town. It is said that the only building ever burnt on Bailey's Island was an old, dilapidated school-house.

On the 23d of January, 1822, James Barstow's house on Orr's Island was burned to the ground. Mrs. Barstow, who was then seventy-four years of age and who was very fleshy, was taken out in her night-clothes and carried some distance to the house of a friend. A portion of the way she had to walk. She died three days after in consequence of the exposure. Mr. Barstow never recovered from the shock and exposure, and was at times insane. He died in 1826. The origin of the fire was a candle which was placed under and in too close proximity to a shelf.

Phineas Webber's house on Great Island caught fire, date unknown, from some boiling tar upon a stove. The house and contents were entirely destroyed. The loss was about $1,000. Insured for two hundred dollars. It was the first house in Harpswell that was ever insured.

On July 4, 1868, the Mansion House on Harpswell Neck was burned. The cause of the fire is unknown. The loss was $3,000.

There have doubtless been other fires than those enumerated, but these are all of which we have been able to learn.

Owing to the few cases recorded, no *résumé* of the fires in this town is needed.

The first fire-engine in Brunswick was purchased in 1810, by individuals. It was a small " tub " and had to be filled by buckets. An effort was made in 1810 to induce the town to appropriate some amount towards the purchase of this engine, but the article in the warrant for this object was dismissed. In 1814 an attempt was made to induce the town " to accept of the engine," but it declined so to do. This engine was used as late as 1847, at which time Whitten & Meder's factory was burned. This engine had no name at first, but was after some years named the " Mechanic."

The first fire company in Brunswick was called the Washington Fire Club. It was certainly formed as early as 1821, and very likely at the time of purchase of the engine, in 1810. No records of this company have been found, but it is known that the membership was voluntary, and that each member agreed to have in readiness for use, one canvas bag, one bed-key, and two leathern fire-buckets. In 1825 this company had charge of the engine, as is shown by a bill against the company for repairs to the pumps of the engine. In 1826 there were about fifty members to this club, among whom were Doctor Isaac Lincoln, Professor Parker Cleaveland, General Richard T. Dunlap, General Abner B. Thompson, General John C. Humphreys, and Mr. John Coburn.

After the "Great Fire" in 1825, the town appointed Professor Parker Cleaveland, Robert Eastman, Doctor Isaac Lincoln, Doctor Jonathan Page, and John Coburn a committee to purchase a new engine, and eight hundred dollars was appropriated for the purpose, with the proviso that any unexpended balance should be used for building an engine-house. The selectmen were also this year directed to increase the number of engine-men to twenty-five. This second engine was the "Hydraulian." It was made in Philadelphia. It had a suction attachment, not flexible like those of the present day, but of straight copper tubing, with curved joints. There were platforms over each wheel, upon which three or four men stood to aid those who stood on the ground in working the breaks. This engine was sold in 1852, in exchange for the "Protector No. 4."

No records of the Hydraulian Engine Company have been found previous to its reorganization in 1843, but it is known that Professor Cleaveland was especially instrumental in its organization. He was its first commander, and held the position for twenty years. He was always one of the first on the ground at a fire, always managed the hose pipe, and always stood, when duty required, in the place of the greatest exposure and danger.

In the summer of 1828 or 1830, a force pump was erected at the upper dam. It was operated by water power, and it forced water from the river through pipes, into a large tank which was situated on the high ground west of Union Street, about where the corn-house of the Honorable C. J. Gilman now stands. From thence the water was carried, by its own gravity, through pipes to Maine Street, just north of Lincoln Street, where it flowed continuously through a standing pipe, and thence along the gutter at the side of the street to the cove, where it entered the river. This arrangement worked well in summer, but when winter came the water froze in the gutter, the street and sidewalks were overflowed and covered with ice for a long distance, and the experiment was abandoned. It was probably a private enterprise to secure the property of individuals from loss by fire, as there is nothing in the town records to indicate that the town had anything to do with it.

The third engine in Brunswick was the "Niagara, No. 3." It was purchased by the town in 1848. This engine was exchanged in 1870 for a larger and better one, called the "Niagara, No. 3," also, but which was really the fourth engine.

The early records of Niagara Engine Company have not been found. The only thing known about it prior to its reorganization is that on the evening of June 11, 1855, the company paraded the streets with torch-lights.

The records which we have seen commence in 1858. The officers of the company at that time consisted of three directors, a standing committee of four, exclusive of the first director, one steward, one assistant steward, three pipemen, one foreman of hose, five leading hosemen, three suction hosemen, two axemen, and one clerk. The latter was paid between five and ten dollars per year. During the year there were sixty-seven members in the company.

The only events worthy of mention, to be gleaned from the records, are the following: —

October 17, 1858, the company attended the funeral of Professor Cleaveland. August 7, 1860, the company was presented with a flag by Edward W. Thompson, Esquire. On December 4, of the same year, a flag was also presented by Colonel Alfred J. Stone. Probably one of these was an ensign. On July 4, 1865, the company went to Lewiston to celebrate the day. August 7, 1866, the company was disbanded, but was reorganized on the thirteenth of that month, and the old constitution and by-laws were adopted.

No entry appears in the records later than the year 1871. The fifth engine in Brunswick was called the "Protector No. 4." It was purchased in 1852. The town that year authorized the selectmen to dispose of the two *old* engines and to purchase a new one. Two hundred dollars was appropriated, to be added to the proceeds of the sale of the old engines. The first book of records of the Protector Company has not been found. From the second book it appears that at the first meeting, held April 3, 1854, the following officers were chosen: H. M. Bowker, first director; J. H. Toothaker, second director; R. L. McManus, third director; Hiram Talbot, clerk; John Andrews, steward; John Andrews, Joseph McKeen, Charles Hinkley, A. S. Aubins, suction hosemen; Charles E. Owen, first pipeman; Jordan Snow, second pipeman; John D. Stanwood, third pipeman. C. R. Lunt, William Reed, B. Boutelle, John Hinkley, G. W. Swett, I. Taylor, A. Colby, hosemen; Curtis Harmon, A. Underhill, axemen; David Bonney, James French, torch-boys.

The sixth engine in Brunswick was the "Kennebec No. 1." It was bought in 1875.

In 1836 the village of Brunswick was created a corporation, by an act of the legislature, and invested with power "to raise money for the purchase, repair and preservation of one or more fire-engines, hose, or other apparatus for the extinguishment of fire, for the construction of reservoirs and aqueducts for procuring of water, and for organizing and maintaining within the limits of said territory an efficient fire department. The officers were a supervisor, clerk, treasurer, prudential committee of three, and from five to nine fire-wardens.

At a meeting of this corporation, held in November, 1836, a committee was appointed "to devise ways and means for protecting the village against fire."

This committee reported in favor of building eighteen brick cisterns, circular, and about twelve feet in diameter and fourteen feet deep. They also recommended the purchase of a double-chambered engine for raising the water from the cisterns and conveying it to different parts of the village. How far these recommendations were carried out is not known.

In 1875 the town purchased the two and a half inch iron pipe which had been laid by the Compressed Air Company, from the bridge to the railroad station. It was connected with the force pump of the Pulp Company, and was found to throw a powerful stream of water for a long distance, through two hundred feet of hose.

The following was the condition of the fire department of Brunswick, in March, 1876.

The number of engines was three, viz., the "Niagara, No. 3," "Protector, No. 4," and "Kennebec, No. 1."

The "Niagara" was built by Hunneman & Co., of Boston, in 1870. The diameter of its cylinder is five and three fourths inches. It is a first-class machine and is provided with folding brakes. The "Protector" was built by Hunneman & Co. in 1852. The diameter of its cylinder is five inches. The "Kennebec" was made by Button & Son of Waterford, New York, in 1867. The diameter of its cylinder is ten inches. There were at this time twenty-three reservoirs in good condition.

The first engine in Topsham was purchased about 1810 by private individuals. In 1813 an effort was made to induce the town to take charge of it, but the town voted "not to accept" the gift. The next year, however, it was generously voted to accept it, "*provided the town should never be at any expense either for the purchase or repairs.*" The town did, however, in 1826, vote, without any reservation, to accept and take care of this engine. Like the first engine in Brunswick, this one was a small affair, and had to be filled by buckets.

The earliest fire company established in Topsham, of which there is any record, was the Lincoln Fire Club. The exact date of its organization is not known, but the regulations of the club were printed in 1829. It may, however, have been in existence for some years previously. According to their regulations, the club met four times a year, on the first Tuesdays of January, April, July, and October. Whoever was absent the whole evening was fined twenty-five cents, and if any member left the meeting without the express consent of the club he was fined twenty-five cents also. The officers were a chairman, secretary, and treasurer. In order to be eligible for membership, one must be proposed at a previous meeting and receive three fourths of the ballots of those present on the night of his election. He must also pay in the sum of one dollar as an admission fee. Honorary members were elected in the same way, but were exempt from all assessments and fines.

Each member was required, within three months after his admission to the club, to furnish himself with two good leathern fire-buckets, holding at least ten quarts each. The fire hooks and ladders were under the control of and were probably owned by this club. From there being no other officers than those mentioned, it would appear as though this club had nothing to do with Engine No. 1.

At the annual meeting in 1850 the town appropriated $1,250 to purchase a fire-engine and other apparatus, and Nahum Perkins, Sparrow Chase, and Sandford A. Perkins were chosen a committee to make the purchase.

The engine bought at this time was the "Androscoggin, No. 2." It is one of the Hunneman make, and is the only one ever bought by the town. It ranks No. 2 in size. It is one of the best engines of its class ever made, and the citizens of Topsham justly feel some pride in the good work it has done.

The company having control of this engine was formed in 1850. The first meeting was held over the store of George S. Holt on April 5. The first meeting for the election of officers was held April 15, at which time Sandford A. Perkins was chosen first foreman; Varius Stearns, second foreman; John R. Hebbard, third foreman; David Farrar, treasurer; A. G. Poland, clerk; and James Maxwell, R. P. Whitney, and Eben Colby were chosen as a standing committee.

At this meeting it was voted to have a uniform, consisting of a blue frock with red collar, red webbing belts, a glazed cap, and dark pants.

The constitution and by-laws of the company were adopted at the annual meeting on the first Monday in May. The company at this time numbered seventy-one. June 28, 1850, the company voted to purchase an ensign. December 2, of this same year, a flag-staff was raised in front of the engine-house. July 25, 1851, the company voted to attend the firemen's jubilee to be held in Hallowell on August 6. At this celebration the company took the prize — a silver trumpet — as being the best engine of its class present. It also has taken several prizes since that time, at different celebrations of firemen.

On March 3, 1852, the company was reorganized by the choice of the following officers: F. T. Littlefield, first director; E. E. Maxwell, second director; D. A. Hall, third director; C. G. Jaques, secretary; D. A. Hall, steward. The number of members was fifty-five.

The new organization appears to have been for some reason unsatisfactory, as in August, 1853, the company was again reorganized.

In 1857, at a special town meeting held December 28, it was voted, "To authorize the selectmen to pay each man (not to exceed sixty in number) who shall faithfully perform his duty, twelve and a half cents per hour for his services while at fires, so long as there may be a well-organized fire company in Topsham village." The selectmen were also authorized to offer a reward of fifty dollars for the detection of incendiaries.

In 1860 the town forbade the company to take the engine out of town, except for fires and upon July the Fourth.

In 1869 the town voted to buy two hundred feet of hose, and to pay the members of the engine company twenty-five cents per hour when in active service.

There was never a fire-engine or a fire company in Harpswell. Fire-wardens are chosen by the town annually, and the citizens generally are provided with buckets, etc., to protect their own property. The population of Harpswell is so scattered that an engine would be of no service to a large majority of the people.

CHAPTER VII.

COURTS AND TRIALS, CRIMES AND CRIMINALS, LAWYERS.

THE earliest court ever held in this *vicinity* was the one held, in 1654, at the house of Thomas Ashley, which has already been mentioned. The meeting held at his house was for the purpose of organization merely, and there is no evidence that Thomas Purchase, who was appointed at that time an assistant to the commissioner, ever tried any cases. The laws and regulations adopted at this meeting, however, are sufficiently interesting to warrant their insertion here in a condensed form. They were as follows: —

1. All capital crimes, such as treason, murder, witchcraft, arson, rape, and adultery, were to be tried by the General Court at New Plymouth.

2. All other crimes were within the jurisdiction of the commissioner or the assistant. Theft was punishable by the restitution by the offender of three or four times the value stolen. Drunkards were fined five shillings on conviction for the first offence, ten shillings for the second, and for the third were put in the stocks. The punishment for Sabbath-breaking was left at the discretion of the assistant. For selling liquor to the Indians, the punishment for the first offence was the forfeiture of double, and for the second offence, of four times the value sold, or if the transgressor was a stranger, a fine of either £10 or £20.

3. All fishing and fowling were expressly continued free to every inhabitant. All actions between party and party were to be tried before a jury of twelve men; but no civil cause above £20 sterling was triable in the local courts without the consent of both parties.

From this time until the province of Lygonia came under the jurisdiction of Masssachusetts, there is reason to suppose that all minor offences were tried — if tried at all — by Thomas Purchase, a magistrate under the authority of the New Plymouth Colony (1652). In 1660 all legal cases in this vicinity were tried at York.

No cases of trial of persons from this vicinity, prior to 1722, have been discovered. This year the case of John Giles, of Brunswick, gentleman, *vs.* John Goddard, of Roxbury, gentleman and cordwainer, is recorded. The plaintiff let the defendant a horse, with bridle and saddle, at the beginning of June, 1722, and by order of the plaintiff, one Robert Dunning, soon after, in the same month, delivered the said horse, at Falmouth, to the defendant, which the defendant promised to deliver to the plaintiff at Roxbury, or to his order, with bridle and saddle, of value of £12; yet the defendant, though often requested, never delivered to the said plaintiff, horse, bridle, or saddle. The jury brought in a verdict for plaintiff of £8 damage, and cost of court, against the said John Goddard.[1]

The next case met with occurred in 1726, when Captain William Woodside was tried by a committee appointed by Governor Dummer for cheating the Indians in trade, and otherwise defrauding them. Some of the charges were proved against him, and he was required to make ample remuneration, acknowledge his fault, and give assurance that he would defraud them no more.[2]

Mr. John Minot was appointed a magistrate and chief justice of the Court of Common Sessions under George II about the year 1730 or 1732. An old account-book of his has been preserved, which contains on its blank leaves an account of some cases tried by him in 1732, which are here presented to the reader: —

"Y ss. TO THE SHERRIF OF Y^E COUNTY OF YORK HIS UNDER SHERRIF OR DEPUTY GREETING.
◇

"Whereas Complaint upon Oath hath bin made before me by Saml Boone of Northyarmouth in ye County of York that some time past he had Stole and Carried away from Merryconeag neck a black Cow with a white face and also Stole and carried away from Chebeag Island three Calves one being a Bull Calf the other a Stear and the other a heffer Calfe, which were mark'd with a Cross in the left ear and a slit in it and a flower Dlue in ye right ear — These are therefore in his Maj^ies name to require you to make Diligent Search after said Cattle if they may be found in your precinct and them safely to keep in your Custody maiking a returne of these your proceedings to me or some other of his Maj^ies Justice of ye peace in said County that the Affair may be Examined into, and the partyes with whom said Cattle may be found may be dealt with according to law — you are also hereby required to Summons Moses Gatchell, Hannah Smith,

[1] *York County Records, C. C. P., Vol.* 7, *p.* 88.
[2] *McKeen, MSS. Lecture.*

Wm Woodside Jas. Malcum and Eliz^a^ Malcum to give Evidence relating to this Affair hereof you are not to fail given under my hand and Seal the 16th day of Aug^st^ 1732.

"[Coppy.] "JN^n^ MINOT.

"THE RETURNE.

"BRUNSWICK, Aug^st^ 20th 1732.

"Having made search after the within mentioned Cattle this may certifye that I have found and taiken up three young Cattle uppon Suspision which were in the hands of Capt Willm Woodside which I have taken into Custody.

"EBENEZER STANWOOD, *D. Sherriff.*

"THE JUDGMENT

"Y ss "BRUNSWICK, Aug 21st 1732

"SAM^L^ BOON *Plant.* AND WILL^M^ WOODSIDE *Defend.*

"Having issued out a warrant to search for severall Cattle that Saml Boone uppon Oath Swore he lost at Chebeag Isl. & Merryconeage neck and having Summons'd Sundry witnesses as by said warrant will appear, I have Examined said witnesses uppon Oath (they all having veiw'd the Cattle) whether they knew them Cattle to be Mr. Boons which they all deny to have any knowledge of saving Mrs Malcum who says she remembers something of one of them but not perfecktly so as to give her Oath to it. I find therefore Cost for said Boon to pay and have ordered the Cattle to be Delivered to the said Wil^m^ Woodside again.

"[Coppy] "JNO. MINOT J. P."

Notice of complaint of James Smith against Anthony Vincent for calling his wife Hannah Smith improper names.

"The Complaint of Hannah Smith against Willm Mackness in behalfe of our Soveraign Lord the King that shee goes in Dainger of her Life."

"The Complaint of Willm Mackness against James Smith and his wife Hannah that he lives in dainger of his Cattle and Substance that they will be destroyed by them they using threatening words to kill their piggs &c. and that they will burn his house.

"[Signed] "JOHN MINOTT."

No other records of Judge Minot's cases have been met with.

At the October term of the Court of General Sessions in 1743 the selectmen of the town of Brunswick made a complaint against Isaac

Snow, "in manner following, viz., that Isaac Snow of Brunswick aforesaid, husbandman, the thirtieth day of August, 1743, at a legal town meeting held at Brunswick aforesaid, was chosen one of the constables for said town for the year 1743, who was legally notified thereof, but refused either to take the oath of a constable or to pay the fine for not serving as a constable." After a full hearing by the court the case was decided in favor of the defendant, and the complainants were charged with the costs.

At the April term of the same court, in 1744, committees were appointed by the court "to inform against and prosecute the violators of an act made in the seventeenth year of his Majesty's reign, entitled 'an act to prevent the great injury and injustice arising to the inhabitants of this province by the frequent and very large emissions of bills of public credit in the neighboring governments.' . . . And Messrs. William Woodside, Peter Cooms, David Dunning, Samuel Hinkley and James Thompson, Inhabitants of the Town of Brunswick in said County, were appointed by said Court to the office aforesaid."

At the April term of the Court of General Sessions for Cumberland County, in 1765, William Hasty, of Harpswell, was fined ten shillings "for sailing his coasting schooner in Quohog Bay to the open sea, the space of three miles, on the Lord's day." At the same term of court, William Blake, of Harpswell, was fined ten shillings, and costs, £1 5*s.* 4*d.*, for neglecting to attend public worship for the space of two months.

About this time, probably the next year, John Orr, of Mair Point, accused Captain William Woodside of cheating the Indians "by selling them *brass* rings for *gold* rings," and the case was *informally* tried by the judges of the Court of Sessions in a dining-room at Falmouth. Woodside was acquitted, made friends with Orr, and having just obtained his commission as a justice of the peace for Cumberland County, he "stood treat" for the court.

In those old times physical punishment was often made use of towards offenders. The whipping-post and the stocks were found in every settlement and generally in close proximity to the meeting-house. These implements of the law were, doubtless, at the time they were in vogue, of great service in restraining the evil-intentioned from committing many misdemeanors and minor crimes, and although the objections to their use are many and serious, yet one is tempted to believe that their occasional use might be fraught with good even in these days. The punishments by means of these implements were inflicted by the constables, in accordance with the sentence of the selectmen, when there was no justice of the peace, or other magistrate, to give sentence. Petty crimes, in which the damage did not exceed forty shillings, came under their cognizance. No account has been preserved of any stocks or whipping-post in Topsham. The only reference in regard to Harpswell is the indictment of that town, in the April term of the Court of Sessions for 1769, "for not being supplied with stocks against the Peace of the Lord, the King and the law of the Province." The selectmen appeared, and after a full hearing, the attorney for the king decided he would not further prosecute. Possibly the selectmen promised to provide these necessary instruments of correction thereafter.

Frequent allusion is, however, made to the stocks in the Brunswick records. In the latter town they are said to have stood a short distance back of the old west meeting-house.

The whipping-post was about a foot square, sharpened at the top like a picket, and the sharpened part was painted red.

At the time stocks and whipping-posts were used, many towns had also a ducking-stool, and at one time all towns in Massachusetts were, by law, required to have one. No account, however, has been found of any in this vicinity. This implement of punishment consisted of an upright post, with a cross-piece, from which was suspended a seat. The arm could be swung out over the water, and the occupant of the seat could thus be easily ducked. It was used more especially for the punishment of *scolding wives*.

The following description of the stocks actually used in Brunswick is from the pen of a former minister of Harpswell: "They consisted of two upright posts of oak, set in foot-pieces of the same material, and strongly braced. Between them was secured a thick plank, set on one edge, rising up a short distance from the ground. The posts above this were grooved, and in these another plank was inserted, which could be raised or lowered. In the lower edge of this were arched holes, just large enough to fit a person's legs above the ankle. In the top edge of this plank were hollows to receive the wrists, while another came down upon it to secure them. The criminal was made to sit on the ground and place his legs in the hollows of the lower plank, when the upper one was let down by the constable, and locked with a key, as a door. Sometimes this was the only punishment; at other times both hands and feet were put in,

when the officer, putting the key in his pocket, left the prisoner exposed to sun, wind, and rain."[1]

The only person in this place known to have been punished by being put in the stocks was one Jenny Eaton. When Deacon Stanwood's house was torn down, Mr. James Dunning found an old document purporting to be a decision upon the trial of this individual. She had permitted the embrace of a man named Rogers, on the promise of some sugar, tea, and coffee. The man failed to keep his word, she averred, and she therefore entered a complaint against him, and the case was tried before Esquire Woodside. The plaintiff could not prove the charge, and the magistrate gave the following verdict: "That Jenny Eaton be stretched upon the public stocks and rotten eggs thrown at her by the passing spectators for abfaming the character of an innocent man."[2]

Some time, probably between 1752 and 1770, one Ann Conner committed suicide by hanging herself from a pine-tree. The magistrates ordered (old Roman law) that she be buried where four roads met, and a stake be driven through her body. It was done on the Harpswell road a little way south of the college. It is said that, although it was in force at that time, this was probably the only instance when the law was put into execution in this country.[3]

Cumberland County was set off from York County in 1760, and, as a matter of course, a new county court was soon established. The first grand jurors drawn for this county from Brunswick were Isaac Snow and John Orr; from Harpswell, Thomas McGregor and John Hall.

At the June term of the Court of General Sessions of the Peace, held at Pownalborough in 1777, Mr. John Merrill, of Topsham, took his place on the bench as one of the justices. He officiated in that capacity as late as 1783, but no records of any cases tried before him have come to hand.

In 1783 James Hunter, Esquire, George White, John Reed, William Malcom, all of Topsham, and John Lemont, Esquire, Samuel Lemont, Esquire, William Swanton, George Andrews, and Stephen Sampson, the two latter blacksmiths, all of Bath, were bound over to the court to answer to the charge of breaking open the jail at Pownalborough, and for rescuing two prisoners who were lawfully committed. They were tried, and each sentenced to pay a fine of six shillings and costs.

---

[1] *The Sophomores of Radcliffe. Kellogg.* [2] *Pejepscot Papers.*
[3] *Pejepscot Papers. McKeen, MSS. Lecture.*

At the May term of the court for Cumberland County, the next year, Isaac Rolf, of Brunswick, was sentenced to pay a fine of £7 10*s*., and to receive *five stripes on his naked back*, for stealing five sheep. If he returned any of the sheep, "the owner was to restore him back one fold, the fine being treble value of the property stolen."

In 1796 a Commissioner's Court was held in an old red schoolhouse, which stood near the lower end of the Mall, in Brunswick. It was held to consider the respective claims of the Plymouth and Pejepscot proprietors. Governor Sullivan and other distinguished persons were present. This building was afterwards moved away and placed on the bank of the cove, near the building where General A. B. Thompson afterwards had an office, and which is now a factory boarding-house.

In 1800 terms of the Court of Common Pleas for Lincoln County were appointed to be holden in Topsham, and on the ninth of September of that year the court opened there for the first time.[1] It is said that this first court was held in an unfinished house belonging to a Mr. Sprague, the Court House not being finished until some time the next year. Mr. James Wilson, father of the James Wilson now living, gave the land for it, for a term of years. Few cases of importance, affecting the citizens of the three towns, were ever tried in it, but such as have been found will be given in the proper order.

December 24, 1822, a military court was held at Brunswick for the trial of Lieutenant-Colonel David Stanwood. It will be referred to hereafter, in another connection.

At the May term of the court, held in Portland in 1823, one Patrick Cole, of Brunswick, was convicted of manslaughter, and was sentenced to undergo six months of solitary imprisonment and four years at hard labor.

In 1824 the selectmen of Brunswick were authorized by the town to erect forthwith a House of Correction on the town lot in the village, and one hundred and fifty dollars was appropriated. This building, which to judge from its cost could have been nothing more than a lock-up, stood where the poorhouse used to be, back of the present residence of Mr. Robert Bowker.

At the August term of the Court of Common Pleas, at Topsham, in 1825, Honorable John Dole, a justice of the Court of Sessions for Lincoln County, was tried on a charge of slander against Samuel H. Clark, of Jefferson, the former having charged the latter with having com-

---

[1] *Jonathan Ellis's Diary.*

mitted adultery and other such crimes. Verdict for plaintiff. Damages, $1,058.

In 1826 five persons were brought before Charles R. Porter, a justice of the peace, of Topsham, on suspicion of having set fire to the barn of a Mr. Millet, of Bowdoin. Four of them were discharged, but the fifth, Reuben Jones, was bound over for trial before the Supreme Judicial Court, to be held at Wiscasset.

This year a case was tried in the Court of Common Pleas, of Cumberland County, of considerable interest. It was the First Parish of Brunswick *vs.* Joseph McKeen, on a plea of trespass. The First Parish had erected a fence from the meeting-house to the corner of what is now Cleaveland Street, claiming the land enclosed as belonging to the parish. Mr. McKeen caused the fence to be torn down, and the parish thereupon prosecuted him for trespass. His defence was that the Harpswell road was laid out in the rear of the church, and had always been used as such until fenced by the parish. On the other side, the parish claimed that the Harpswell road came out south of the church. The case was carried to the Supreme Judicial Court, and was there decided in favor of the defendant. Packard and Longfellow were the counsel for the plaintiffs, and Orr and Greenleaf for the defendants.

In 1827 a case was tried at Topsham which excited considerable local attention at the time, on account of the character and standing of the parties, and the questions involved. The case was that of General Samuel Veazie *vs.* Henry Jewell, both of Topsham. It was an action for damages on account of assault and battery, brought, in reality, to test the ownership of property.

The facts in the case seem to be as follows: Messrs. Henry Jewell, Stephen Jewell, Gardner Green, Samuel Perkins, and Nahum Perkins owned the "Great Mills" and the ground under the same. Four undivided fourteenth parts of the land (a bed of rocks) was within twenty-four feet of this mill, on the south side below the dam, which was owned by Gardner Green, Ezekiel Thompson, James Thompson, and Mary Thompson, the three last being heirs of Brigadier Thompson. General Veazie, without permission from Green or the Thompsons, and against their wish, attempted to lay the foundation of a saw-mill, and collected several sticks of timber and placed them under the floor of a mill-shed on the premises claimed by Green and others. Thereupon Jewell, by direction of Green and the Thompsons, in order to compel him to desist and to leave the premises, threw slabs, and afterwards emptied buckets of water upon Veazie and his workmen. Veazie defended himself with an axe-haft and a pitchfork, and for a while a serious quarrel was threatened. Veazie at length desisted from his attempt, and this suit was ultimately brought to test the respective rights of the two parties to the bed of rocks. Veazie had purchased the right to it from some of the heirs of Brigadier Thompson, but not from those mentioned. The case was decided against Veazie. This decision, though undoubtedly a just one, in all probability was a cause of depriving the towns of Brunswick and Topsham of the services of one who afterwards did so much for the manufacturing interests of Bangor and the neighboring towns upon the Penobscot. The above-mentioned affray occurred February 5, 1827.

In November, 1829, one Patrick Kincaid, of Brunswick, was fined by the Supreme Judicial Court $1,100 and costs, for breach of promise to a young lady whom he had engaged to wed, — a warning, it doubtless proved, to all bachelors, hereabouts, of inconstant minds.

In 1843 occurred the trial, at Portland, of Thomas Thorn and Mrs. Lois Wilson, for the murder of Mr. Elisha Wilson, of Harpswell. The facts of this case were as follows: —

In 1840, Thomas Thorn came to Great Island, Harpswell, from New York, to visit his sister, the Widow Dyer. He remained in Harpswell during the summer, and while there he made the acquaintance of a young lady named Lois Alexander, with whom he became quite intimate. He, however, left town and did not return until early in the winter of 1842–43. In the mean time, Miss Alexander had married Elisha Wilson, and Mrs. Dyer had married Elisha's brother Benjamin. On his return, Thorn went to Elisha Wilson's, where he remained. On the morning of the fifth of February, 1843, between the hours of three and four, Mr. Samuel Toothaker was aroused by Thorn, who told him that Elisha had fallen out of his bed in the night, in a fit, and was dead. Toothaker immediately repaired to the house, and found Wilson dead, and to all appearances as if he had been so for some hours. Some bedclothes, which had been washed and carried up stairs wet, at once aroused suspicion of foul play. An inquest was held, and Thorn and Mrs. Wilson were apprehended, and bound over to the April term of the Supreme Court, at Portland, at which time they were indicted for the murder by the grand jury, and were tried. Mrs. Wilson was acquitted, but Thorn was convicted and sentenced to be hung. His sentence was afterwards commuted to imprisonment for life. He was taken to the State prison, where he remained for over thirty years. A few years ago, on account of his good behavior while in prison and his failing health, he was pardoned, and returned to New York, where he was recently living. The following letter, which had been passed to Thorn wrapped up in a piece of tobacco, was produced at the trial: —

"poor lois i pity you and my hart akes for you and you must mind when you Come to Cort and clear me if you dont tha will hang me and you must mind how you talk i will wright to you once in fore days i whant to see you once more and then if you dont clear me i shall be willing to dy fore you i want you to write back."

This letter, with the piece of tobacco, are, it is said, on file in the clerk of court's office in Portland.

In 1847, Topsham ceased to be a half-shire town, and Mr. Jonah Morrow was appointed by the court a committee to sell the Topsham Court House. He did so, and reported the amount received for the building to be nine hundred and ten dollars; and for the furniture, eleven dollars and forty-seven cents. The bell was reserved to be afterwards disposed of as might be directed by the county commissioners.

The state of morals among the young in Brunswick must have been rather low about this time, as the town in 1849 passed the following resolution: —

"Whereas it is currently reported that boys and other persons are in the habit of visiting the mills and other places near the water on the Sabbath, for the purpose of gambling, voted, that the selectmen employ a suitable person to see that the Sabbath and the laws of the State are not violated; also, to stop the playing at ball or flying of kites in the streets."

In 1850 the legislature passed an Act, approved August 28, entitled "An Act to establish a Municipal Court in the town of Brunswick, in the county of Cumberland." At a meeting of the town subsequent to the passage of this Act, it was voted to accept its provisions and to establish such a court.

In April, 1855, Charles Crips, of Topsham, was indicted before the grand jury at Bath for the murder of his wife in the fall of the previous year. He caused her death by beating her with a club. He was tried before the Supreme Judicial Court at Bath, in the September following, and was convicted of manslaughter, and was sentenced to the State prison for life. He was pardoned by the governor before the expiration of his sentence.

This year there were numerous burglaries committed in Topsham, but the perpetrators of them were not discovered.

On Monday night, November 9, of this year, Eliphalet Berry, of Topsham, was murdered near Perkins's lumber-shed on "the island."

He and several others had been to Brunswick and were returning home, intoxicated, with a jug of rum. A difficulty arose between Berry and David Y. Dudley in regard to the possession of the jug. They both disappeared for a few minutes, and Dudley returned alone. Berry was soon found a short distance off in a dying condition, having been stabbed to the heart. Dudley was tried before the Supreme Judicial Court at Bath in 1858, and on September 4, the jury in the case brought in a verdict of manslaughter, and he was sentenced to five years of hard labor in the State prison. He was pardoned for good behavior before the expiration of his term of service.

In 1875, John Miller, of Birch Island, opposite Mair Point, was convicted of manslaughter and sentenced to the State prison for life. Miller was abusing his wife. His son interfered and his father shot him. Miller is a descendant of Reverend John Miller, a former minister of the First Parish in Brunswick.

It will be seen from the foregoing accounts that Topsham suffers from rather an unenviable reputation, for so small a town, on account of the number of persons it has had of marked homicidal proclivities. Besides those already mentioned, two other persons from this town, a Mr. Clough and Henry Richards, have suffered the penalty of the law for murders committed by them elsewhere. Notwithstanding this unpleasant fact, it is believed that the integrity of its business men and the general character of its citizens for morality, justness, and temperance will compare favorably with that of other similar communities of even a larger population.

Of late years but few trials, except of minor importance, of any of the citizens of either of the three towns, have been had, and but few crimes of importance have occurred here.

MEMBERS OF THE BAR.

The earliest lawyer in Brunswick is said to have been a man by the name of Hobbs, who is described as a shrewd, smart man, but not very well educated. Next to him came Peter O. Alden, who was admitted to the Cumberland bar in 1797. He was the only lawyer in town for the remainder of that century and for several years in the present one. He continued to practise his profession until his death in 1843, but his business was very small for many years previous to his death.[1]

After Alden came Henry Putnam, who practised law in Brunswick

---

[1] *See Biography.*

from 1806 to 1823, or thereabouts. His practice was not extensive. From 1807, ISAAC GATES, for a few years only, practised law in this town.

DAVID STANWOOD, of the class of 1808, Bowdoin College, studied law for one year with Peter O. Alden, then with Benjamin Hasey for one year, and afterwards one year with Samuel Thatcher. He was admitted to the bar in 1811, and removed from Brunswick in 1833.

EBENEZER EVERETT commenced the practice of his profession in Brunswick in 1817, from which time to 1828 he was also cashier of the Union Bank. He afterwards devoted his whole time to his profession until 1858, when the infirmities of age compelled him to retire from its active duties. He had a large practice and was deemed a very excellent counsellor.[1]

ROBERT P. DUNLAP[1] was in practice from 1818 until about 1830, when he entered into politics and gave up his law business.

BENJAMIN ORR[1] moved to Brunswick from Topsham about 1822, and continued in practice until his death, in 1828. He was one of the most eminent lawyers in the State.

CHARLES PACKARD[1] had a remunerative practice in town between the years 1825 and 1834, at which latter date he entered upon a course of study for the ministry.

PHINEAS BARNES practised law in town between 1839 and 1841. He was likewise a cashier of one of the banks at the time.

LEONARD P. MERRILL[1] was in the practice of the law, for a few years, about 1845.

WILLIAM G. BARROWS, now judge of the Supreme Judicial Court of Maine, practised law in Brunswick from 1842 to 1863.

HENRY ORR commenced the practice of his profession in town in 1850, and has pursued it up to the present time. In 1853 he was appointed by Governor Crosby a judge of the Municipal Court.

J. D. SIMMONS also practised here from 1850 to 1870.

From 1859 until 1861, George Barron and Edward Thompson, the latter of the class of 1856, Bowdoin College, followed the practice of law in partnership. Mr. Thompson entered the army in 1861, and since then Mr. Barron has practised alone. Since 1871, Mr. Weston Thompson has been a practising lawyer in town.

The first lawyer to settle in the town of Topsham was BENJAMIN HASEY,[1] Esquire. He commenced practice in June, 1794, and continued it for many years, but abandoned its active duties for some

---

[1] *See Biography.*

time before his death. His office was at first in a small building which stood just south of the Bank building. It was afterwards removed to the northeast corner of Summer and Main Streets, where he continued to occupy it for many years. Still later his office was over the bank.

In 1801, BENJAMIN ORR commenced practice here. His office was over T. G. & N. Sandford's store, in the building where Mountford's shop is now. He removed to Brunswick about 1822, and was succeeded by his brother, ROBERT ORR, who practised there until his death, in 1829.

During the latter year MOSES E. WOODMAN opened an office in the building formerly occupied by Nathaniel Green as a post-office and Registry of Deeds. He remained for a few years only.

In 1843, JOHN W. DAVIS was practising law in Topsham. When he first came, or how long he remained, has not been ascertained.

The town of Harpswell can boast of never having a professional lawyer settled within its limits. There were, of course, trial justices, but never any lawyers. The first justice of the peace in this town, that is now remembered, was Benjamin Dunning.

CHAPTER VIII.

TAVERNS AND PUBLIC HALLS, NEWSPAPERS, ETC.

TAVERNS IN BRUNSWICK.

WITHOUT doubt, the first public house in this vicinity was established in the year 1740. On the twenty-ninth of October of that year, at a meeting of the Pejepscot proprietors, application having been previously made for encouragement on the part of the proprietors to some suitable person to erect a house for the entertainment of travellers on Brunswick Plain, at the place where the North Yarmouth and several other roads met, it was voted, "That a tract of Land be granted to such person as shall be approved of by the Committee of the proprietors, he giving security for the faithfull and seasonable performance thereof."[1]

This offer was undoubtedly accepted by some one, and there is reason to believe it was by Robert Spear, who kept a tavern a little west of the old meeting-house, between the years 1744 and 1760, perhaps later. This inn was also a garrison house, protected by a timber fortification, and soldiers were kept in it by the government, for the safety of travellers, as well as for the protection of the citizens. It was used as a public house after the Spanish or Fifth Indian War had terminated, in 1748. Town meetings were frequently held in this inn in cold weather, and here, on Sunday, the people were wont to congregate for lunch and grog.[2]

The next inn, in point of time, was the one kept, about 1750, by James Thompson.[3] This was on the farm at New Meadows, where Bartlett Adams now lives. It was afterwards, it is said,[4] kept by his son, Brigadier Thompson, until he removed to Topsham, about 1784. It was certainly kept either by the Brigadier or some one of that family as late as 1780.[5] About 1762, Samuel Coombs was licensed as an innholder.[6]

---

[1] *Pejepscot Records.* [2] *McKeen, MSS. Lecture, and elsewhere.*
[3] *McKeen, MSS. Lecture. He was licensed in* 1761 *by the Court of General Sessions for Lincoln County.*
[4] *Peter Jordan.* [5] *Low's Almanac,* 1780. [6] *Court Records, Portland.*

In 1764[1] a man by the name of Ross kept a tavern, which tradition places near the site of the present dwelling of Mr. Rufus Jordan, on the Maquoit road, a short distance north of the Morse road. This inn was certainly kept as late as 1777.[2]

As early as 1767, Benjamin Stone kept a tavern in or near the fort, as is plainly shown by the following extract from the field-book of the company who made the survey of Bakerstown, now Minot, November, 1767. A part of the company, wishing to visit Brunswick, hired a boat, and on Wednesday, November 25, 1767, about "ten of the clock, started, and after rowing about three hours over a calm bay, covered with abundance of wild fowl (we) arrived at the head of Maquoit Bay at the house of Squire Woodside. . . . From Maquoit, we travelled three and a half miles to Brunswick Fort, which is founded on a rock, and built in an exact and regular manner, of stone and lime, in a four-square form, with two bastions on two of the corners, defended by two wooden towers or watch-boxes. This day fair weather. Here we lodged this night, and a pretty good house of entertainment is kept by Benjamin Stone."

From the foregoing, it would appear that Mr. Stone was at this time keeping a public house inside the fort, where tradition says there was a comfortable, two-story house, but it is possible, though not probable, that this tavern was outside, but near the fort, and that the allusion in the foregoing extract to "Brunswick Fort" referred to the settlement around it as much as to the fortification itself. Stone is known to have kept tavern near the Brunswick Falls as late as 1799.[3]

About 1776, later rather than earlier, a Mr. Curtis is said to have kept a tavern where Thomas Grouse now lives, near where the railroad crosses the New Meadows River.[4] This house was kept as an inn as late as 1791.

The house owned and occupied by the late Doctor John D. Lincoln, which was built in 1772, was kept by Captain John Dunlap as a public house a portion of the time between then and 1800.[5]

In 1796 or 1797, Talleyrand, the distinguished French priest and political character, visited this country. He landed at Castine, and on his way to Boston he passed through Brunswick, and spent the greater part of the day at this house.[6]

Where the post-office and engine-house now stand on Maine Street,

---

[1] *Nathaniel Ames's Almanac*, 1764.
[2] *Farmers' Almanac*, 1777.
[3] *Nathaniel Low's Almanac*, 1799.
[4] *Peter Jordan. Low's Almanac*, 1791.
[5] *McKeen, in Brunswick Telegraph.*
[6] *Ibid.*

there was formerly a building which was for many years a tavern, and was known, a part of the time, as WASHINGTON HALL. It was built by David Dunning about 1772, and was occupied by him for some years as a private residence. It was afterwards occupied by his son John, who kept a tavern there until 1807, when David Owen bought it and put on a large addition in front, using the old building as an L. Here Owen kept a tavern until about 1812, when Isaac O. Robertson took it and occupied it as an inn until 1815. The latter was succeeded by Russell Stoddard, who remained about two years.

Ebenezer Nichols, who had been keeping tavern directly opposite, then took it, and Stoddard moved to a building where the Tontine now stands. Nichols continued as landlord until his death, in 1824, and his widow carried on the business until 1827, when she moved back across the street to the building her husband had previously occupied. While she kept this inn it was called "Mrs. Nichols's Inn." William Hodgkins moved from the corner of Maine and Pleasant Streets into this Washington Hall building when Mrs. Nichols left it. Here he remained for a few years. After it was vacated by him it was occupied as a tenement house and for business purposes, till it was burned, in 1856.[1]

In 1799[2] a Mr. Chase kept a tavern which tradition places on the Captain William Woodside place, at Bunganock Landing.

The old tavern which stood in the northwest corner of the college yard, best known as MOORHEAD'S TAVERN, was built in 1802 by Ebenezer Nichols, but was not finished or occupied until early in 1803. Nichols was landlord of it until 1809. During this time it was the principal public and stage house in the town. Mr. Nichols was succeeded, in 1810, by Colonel T. S. Estabrook, who continued in it for some years. After Estabrook left it, a man by the name of Coffin took it, and kept it until 1818, when he sold out to Isaac Dow. The latter kept it until 1820, when he committed suicide. In September of this year it was offered for sale. It was occupied at that time by William Hodgkins. The advertisement stated that it had "six rooms on the lower floor, some large and well furnished; a spacious and convenient hall, a good cellar and never-failing well. The appurtenances are a large, well-finished stable, with other out-buildings; a good garden of more than an acre."[3]

Whether the house was sold at this time is not known, but in 1825 Alexander Moorhead was the proprietor. About the year 1831,

---

[1] *Dean Swift, Samuel Dunning, and other old residents.*

[2] *Low's Almanac*, 1799.

[3] *Maine Intelligencer*, 1820.

Moorhead retired from business, removed from town, and engaged in farming. He was succeeded by John L. Seavey, who kept the house for two or three years. The latter was succeeded by James Elliot, who was proprietor until 1839, at which time Mr. Moorhead returned to Brunswick and again assumed the management of this public house. Moorhead continued to keep it until 1842, when the building was purchased by the trustees of Bowdoin College. It was taken down in 1847 and rebuilt on Noble Street, and is now the residence of Mr. Joyce.[1]

A short distance west of Cook's Corner there stood for many years what was known as the PUMPKIN TAVERN, so called on account of its sign, which was a large ball about the size of a pumpkin, which it greatly resembled. It was a two-story house built by one Wadsworth previous to the war of 1812–14. Here he kept a public house until about 1836 or 1837. It was seldom patronized by travellers, and was in fact more a groggery than a tavern.

In the early part of this century "pumpkin taverns" were quite common, there being one in nearly every town, and they were all of about the same character, — the resort of the intemperate and depraved.

Soon after the war of 1812–14, Ebenezer Nichols, who had formerly kept the tavern on the hill, bought a one-story house, situated between what is now the residence of Doctor N. T. Palmer and that of the late L. T. Jackson, put a second story upon it, and fitted it up for a public house. Here he kept tavern for a few years, and then moved into the Washington Hall building.

About the year 1817, Russell Stoddard opened a public house, called STODDARD'S INN, in a large building which stood on the site of the present Tontine Hotel. It was built in 1803 for a store, and was occupied as such until Mr. Stoddard took it for a tavern. It was occupied by him until 1825, when it passed into the hands of John Barker and Charles M. Rogers. Barker soon sold out his interest, and Rogers assumed the sole management. The building was destroyed by fire in 1827. This house during its existence was the stage office and principal public house in Brunswick. It had a hall in which entertainments of various kinds were occasionally held. Stoddard had kept in the Washington Hall building for a year or two previous to opening this house.

---

[1] *McKeen, in Brunswick Telegraph; also Dean Swift, Samuel Dunning, Mrs. Lamb, and other old citizens.*

The dwelling-house on the corner of Maine and Pleasant Streets, now owned and occupied by Captain Alfred H. Merryman, was built by the Honorable Jacob Abbott for his residence, in 1807. At his death, in 1820, it passed into the hands of his son Jacob, who occupied it until 1823, when he removed to a house opposite the colleges, and this house passed into the hands of William Hodgkins, who fitted it up for a tavern, and occupied it as such from January, 1824, until some time in 1827. The house was known as HODGKINS'S INN, and a hall which was situated in the L of the building was known as HODGKINS'S HALL. In 1827, Hodgkins sold out to Charles M. Rogers, and moved into the Washington Hall building, which had just been vacated by Mrs. Nichols. Mr. Rogers had been burned out on the opposite side of the street, where he had been proprietor of the Stoddard House. He remained in his new quarters for about a year, when he moved to Topsham and opened the Lincoln House in November, 1828. He was succeeded in the charge of Hodgkins's Inn by John L. Seavey, who occupied it as the MAINE HOTEL until 1830. At this time it was repaired and refitted, and Major John Stinchfield took it and kept it until 1837, at which time he bought the house now occupied by Captain Isaac L. Skolfield, and fitted it up for a public house. Mr. James Mustard then became proprietor of the Maine Hotel. In 1840, Mr. Mustard died. The house was then kept for two years by Erastus Niles, and then for a single year by Joseph W. Sargent, when Mr. Niles again assumed the management and kept it until 1845.

James Mustard, son of the former landlord, took it in 1845 and continued until 1849, when Aaron Adams became the proprietor. While under the management of the latter, the house was known as the PEJEPSCOT HOUSE. In 1853 a Mr. Marston became proprietor, but he died within a year, and the house passed into the hands of J. R. W. Hoitt, and was known as the AMERICAN HOUSE. In 1856 it was kept as a boarding-house, called the BRUNSWICK HOUSE, by Benjamin Libby. In 1860, John R. Daly occupied it as a boarding-house. He was succeeded, in 1861 by Timothy Bradley, and in 1862 by E. F. Anderson, who kept a public house for a short time.

In 1863, Captain Merryman purchased the house and fitted it up for his residence. The house and grounds were greatly improved and are now an ornament to the village.

The TONTINE HOTEL was built in the year 1828 by a corporation known as "The Brunswick Tontine Hotel Company." The incorporators were Roger Merrill, David Dunlap, Benjamin Weld, Richard

T. Dunlap, and John Owen, 2d. The Act of Incorporation limited the capital stock to "not less than $6,000 nor more than $15,000, in shares of one hundred dollars each. Among the original stockholders were Ebenezer Everett, Esquire, Doctor Isaac Lincoln, General A. B. Thompson, Colonel A. J. Stone, General J. C. Humphreys, L. T. Jackson, Caleb Cushing, R. P. Dunlap, David Shaw, George Skolfield,

THE TONTINE HOTEL.

James Otis, and others. The hotel was built during the summer and fall of 1828, by Anthony C. Raymond, and was opened to the public on New Year's day, 1829. The establishment cost nearly $7,000. On the evening of January 2, the landlord, Colonel Elijah P. Pike, gave a supper to about fifty citizens of Brunswick and Topsham.

The *Androscoggin Free Press* of January 14, 1829, in a paragraph describing the building, says: —

"It contains thirty apartments besides closets, store-rooms, etc., and a hall which, for elegance and spaciousness, is not surpassed in the State."!

Colonel Pike continued landlord of the hotel until 1836, when Erastus Richards leased it for two or three years. He was succeeded, in 1839, by ——— Holland and Jacob M. Berry. The next year Mr. Berry assumed the sole management of the hotel, and continued its landlord until 1850, when he went to California, leaving the management of the hotel in the hands of Mr. Leonard Townsend. Mr. Berry had been in California only a few months when he died. The contract with Mr. Townsend having been made for a year, he continued the management of the hotel until 1851, when the control of the property passed into the hands of Mr. James Berry, a brother of Jacob. Mr. Berry at once assumed the management of the hotel, and continued landlord until 1867, when he sold out to Mr. H. B. Pinkham, who conducted the hotel until 1875. He was succeeded by Mr. S. B. Harmon, and the latter was in 1877 succeeded by Mr. Brewster, the present landlord. From the building of the hotel till the completion of the railroad, this hotel was the stage office and the principal public house in town.

STINCHFIELD HOUSE.— The house now owned and occupied as a residence by Captain Isaac L. Skolfield, on the corner of Maine and School Streets, was in 1837 purchased of the heirs of Honorable Benjamin Orr, by Major John Stinchfield, and fitted up for a public house. Major Stinchfield kept a tavern there until his death, in September, 1844. His family continued the business for a short time longer, after which the building was occupied by Mr. G. C. Swallow, who kept school in it. From the opening of this public house, in 1837, until the Moorhead tavern was sold, in 1842, there were four public houses in the village, viz., the TONTINE, the MAINE HOTEL, STINCHFIELD'S, and MOORHEAD'S.

An inn called GATCHELL'S TAVERN was kept near Gatchell's Mills, in the southeastern part of the town, from 1837 to 1850, or thereabouts. It was kept at first by Joseph and Francis Gatchell, and after 1840 by Francis Gatchell alone. It was a famous place for "sprees," and was the resort of students and others bent upon having "a good time."

William P. Storer kept a public house for three or four years from 1837, in the western part of the town, near the Durham line, at what was then known as Storer's Corner.

In 1838, Paul R. Cleaves opened a public house west of "Powder-House Hill," just beyond the corner of Mill and Pleasant Streets. He remained only a year or two, not receiving sufficient patronage to warrant his continuing the business in that location.

About the year 1825, Benjamin Peterson kept a tavern on the Bath road, about a mile beyond Cook's Corner, which was known as the HALF-WAY HOUSE. In 1835 he bought a farm in the town of Jefferson, sold this tavern, and moved away. Probably Thomas Wheeler bought it at this time, as he kept a tavern at this place for some years prior to 1845, which always went, with the college students, by the name of OLD WHEELER'S. It was a large one-story building. Like most of the public houses out of the village, it was a noted resort for carousals.

In 1870, John T. Smith purchased the residence of the late General Richard T. Dunlap, and converted it into a public house, called the BOWDOIN HOTEL.

In 1868 the building owned by Mr. Jotham Varney on Maine Street, opposite the mall, was converted into a public house, and has been occupied as such by different parties until the present time. It is now called the BRUNSWICK HOUSE.

The foregoing comprise all the public houses known to have been kept, at any period, in Brunswick.

The earliest public hall to which we have found any reference was the one in the tavern which stood where the post-office and engine-house are now. At first the hall was known by the name of its proprietor, as OWEN'S HALL in 1807, ROBERTSON'S HALL in 1812. It received the name of WASHINGTON HALL about the year 1815. It was for many years the only hall in which public entertainments were given. In this hall, also, private schools were taught at different times.

STONE'S HALL, on the corner of Maine and Mill Streets, was, in 1812 and subsequently, used for religious meetings and for other purposes not requiring a larger hall.

MASONIC HALL, on Mason Street, now the engine-house and hall of "Niagara, No. 3," was built in the year 1817, and besides being used for masonic purposes, the building has been used at different times for private schools, and, if we mistake not, for public lectures.

STODDARD'S HALL was in the tavern kept by Russell Stoddard in a building which occupied the site of the present Tontine Hotel, and which was destroyed by fire in 1827. Frequent allusions have been found to this hall, and it was probably large and comfortable, and adapted to the requirements of the town at that time.

While Hodgkins kept an inn in the house, now the residence of Captain Alfred Merryman, there was a hall in the L which was known as HODGKINS HALL. In this hall religious and political meetings were sometimes held, and it was also used as a school-room, and for public entertainments.

The TONTINE HALL was, for many years subsequent to its erection in 1828, the principal hall in Brunswick for all sorts of public gatherings, and it has always been a favorite place for balls and assemblies.

HUMPHREY'S HALL was over the store now occupied by Mr. Balcom as a hardware store, and in 1841, and thereabouts, was used for dances and for public meetings, not requiring a large hall.

ODD FELLOWS HALL was, from 1844 to 1849, over the store of John S. Cushing, where Lemont Block is now. The building was burned in 1849, and the Odd Fellows then went into a room over the store of A. T. Campbell, on the corner of Maine and Lincoln Streets.

McLELLAN'S HALL was opened as a public hall about the year 1851, and from that time until the erection of Lemont Hall, in 1870, it was used almost exclusively for public meetings of all kinds and for public entertainments.

LEMONT HALL has been, since its erection, the best hall in town. It is a neat and comfortable room, with a seating capacity of about eight hundred. It is not adapted to all classes of entertainments, but for lectures, concerts, fairs, etc., it is far superior to any of its predecessors.

IN TOPSHAM.

There is some doubt in regard to who kept the first house of entertainment in Topsham. Adam Hunter, who came to town in 1718, and who died about the year 1770, is said to have kept the first, though not a licensed one. On the other hand, the statement is made by the very same authority [1] that Colonel Samuel Winchell, who settled on the Cathance in 1750, "kept the first public house, not a tavern, as is usual now, but his house was deemed the first in town, and for his house strangers used to inquire."

Next to this house, in order of time, was the one kept by David Reed, five miles below the Falls on the lower road to Bowdoinham, near the line. He was licensed May 26, 1761, as an innholder, in the six following years as a retailer, and again as an innholder in 1772, 1873, and 1874.[2]

In 1762, Samuel Wilson was licensed as an innholder, and for each successive year, down to September, 1766, when his last license was granted.[3] John Reed kept an inn, probably this one, in 1768. This last year, William Wilson is mentioned in the Pejepscot Papers as an innholder in Topsham. He was licensed in 1761, and an Isabella Wilson in 1767.[4] The precise locality of the two inns kept by the Wilsons is not known, but they were doubtless within the limits of what now constitutes the village of Topsham. The reason for this supposition is, that Samuel and William Wilson owned lots in 1768 opposite the fort,[5] and in 1773 there was a tavern kept at Topsham Ferry by a Mr. Wilson.[6]

About 1770, Mr. John Hunter kept a tavern about two miles from the village, on the road to Bowdoinham. Nothing definite is known as to the length of time Mr. Hunter kept an inn, but it was probably

---

1 *Woodman's Journal.* 2 *Pejepscot Papers.* 3 *Ibid.*
4 *Lincoln County Court Records.* 5 *Plan of Topsham in* 1768.
6 *Low's Almanac,* 1773.

for five or six years. He was town clerk from 1773 to 1775. He died when thirty-two years of age. In 1777 a town meeting was held at "Widow Hunter's." From these facts it is probable that Mr. Hunter died in 1775 or 1776, and he had probably kept tavern for some years previous to that time. Mrs. Hunter carried on the business for some years, until she married Mr. Alexander Rogers. It used to be the custom for parties of five or six to ride from the village to this inn, and for the last one who arrived to pay for the "treat." Town meetings were occasionally held at this house, when the severity of the cold made the meeting-house too uncomfortable. It was at this house that an old negro, who lived in the vicinity, known as "Bill Fortin," attacked the mistress with warm words of invective, because some one had told him, in sport, that she had said that they had never any *black sheep* in their flocks until he sheared them.

While Mrs. Hunter carried on this house, an old soldier named Pike (pronounced Peek), returning from the war in tattered clothes and with his faithful musket upon his shoulder, begged of her to allow him to remain and work upon her farm. She consented and gave him plenty to eat and a new suit of clothes; whereupon he remarked that he would stay as long as he lived. In after years he remarked in still stronger terms, that he would remain with her "as long as a single shingle remained on the roof." The old house still stands in its oaken strength, while Pike, a faithful servant, has long since mouldered in the dust. After Widow Hunter's marriage, the house ceased to be a tavern. Mr. Rogers, however, in 1803 and for some years after his marriage to Mrs. Hunter, kept an inn at his own house, and it was the resort for lunch and grog on Sunday noons of all who attended meeting in the old east meeting-house. Here, too, the militia collected on training days, and here the procession was formed when Washington's death was observed, in 1800. The house descended from Mr. Rogers to his son, Honorable George Rogers, and from him to the late George A. Rogers, Esquire, in whose family it now remains.

In 1773, John Merrill was licensed as an innholder. For how long a time he kept a public house is not known.

In 1774, James Purington, and in 1779, John Whitney, kept tavern somewhere in Topsham. Samuel Tilton was licensed in 1778, and John Blanchard in 1791.

In 1792, Brigadier Samuel Thompson kept a public house in the building afterwards occupied by Harvey Thompson, now destroyed, near the entrance to the depot grounds. Hezekiah Wyman was licensed the same year.

From about 1800 to 1829, Francis Tucker kept a public house in the building which is still standing on Main Street nearly opposite the Bank building. This was for many years the principal public house in town.

The old Gideon Walker house, which stood a few rods south of the present Walker homestead, was used as a tavern for some years in the latter part of the last century, as early as 1792 and as lately as 1803.

About 1812 the SAGER HOUSE was kept by a Mr. Sager. It was situated on the northwest corner of Main and Winter Streets, where the Perkins Building is now. It was afterwards destroyed by fire.

From 1822 until about 1855, John Jack kept a tavern in what is known as the Jack neighborhood, near the little river line. During the early part of the time there was a great deal of travel, and the house was generally full. Lewiston was then a small village, and Topsham, Brunswick, and Bath were the markets for all of the interior towns.

From 1814 to 1829, Nathaniel Green was a licensed innholder in Topsham. Between the years 1831 and 1836 he kept a public house for the accommodation of persons attending court, in the building now used by the Franklin Family School. The next year, 1837, he went to Augusta, where he kept the Palmer House.

Prior to 1826 a public house was kept by Sullivan Haynes, and in 1826 by Prince Dinsmore, in a building which stood on the site of the late residence of Mr. Edwin M. Stone on Winter Street. In 1826 the house was burned. It was owned at that time by Captain Samuel Perkins. It must have been rebuilt at once, as in 1828, Charles M. Rogers, of Brunswick, took it and advertised it as the LINCOLN HOTEL, "a new and commodious house." From 1830 to 1834 this tavern was kept by James Mustard. In 1836 it was kept by Suel and Alden Baker as the TEMPERANCE HOTEL. In 1837 it was kept by Jeremiah Clough. In 1838 and 1839 (and probably later), by Aaron Crowley. Afterwards, for a short time, by a Mr. Moulton. In 1844 by Joseph C. Snow, and in 1845 by A. W. Hewey, during which time it again went by the name of the Lincoln House. After this it was kept by Leeman Hebberd for a while.

In 1817, Thomas G. Sandford, Jonathan Baker, George F. Richardson, Daniel E. Tucker, and Samuel Veazie were all licensed as innholders.

In 1829, Daniel Dennett was a licensed innholder. His house was on the east side of Main Street, a little above the present post office. It was not much of an establishment.

About 1845, George Green had a tavern on the island, known as the WASHINGTONIAN HOUSE. It was afterwards called the ELM HOUSE.

Several of the above-named public houses had halls attached for dancing and other public purposes. Besides these there have been at different times in Topsham the following public halls: —

In a building which stood on the site of the Godfrey House, on Green Street, there was a hall in which a dancing-school was kept in 1799. This house was purchased about 1804 by Reverend Jonathan Ellis. The hall had a swinging partition in it, the hinges of which were at the top. When this partition was opened it was fastened up to the ceiling by hooks and staples.[1]

The Court House was occasionally used as a public hall during the whole period of its existence. It was used for a public oration as early as 1804. At a later period it was occupied on Sundays by different religious organizations, and by the town for many years for its annual meetings. It was also occasionally used for travelling shows and other exhibitions.

At a later day the town-house, situated opposite the village burying-ground, was the principal place for public entertainments.

Still later, the hall of the Sagadahoc Agricultural Society was, and now is, used for fairs, dances, etc., but it is too large for lectures or for any ordinary entertainments.

Perkins Hall and White's Hall, over stores on Main Street, have been used for meetings of one kind and another, not requiring larger accommodations. The engine hall has also been used for small gatherings. Topsham has never had a hall suitable, in all respects, for public entertainments, the halls referred to being either too large or too small, and not adapted for all occasions for which a hall is required.

IN HARPSWELL.

About 1762, Richard Starbird and Timothy Bailey were licensed as innholders, in Harpswell.

A Mr. Eastman kept a sailor boarding-house on the east side of Condy's Point, Great Island, before and during the Revolution. The only public house on this island since that time is believed to be the UNION HOUSE, which was built in 1862 by David W. Simpson, and was conducted by him for one year. It not proving a success, he

---

[1] *Statement by Dr. Asher Ellis.*

gave it up and went to sea. It was bought by Robert Watson, and in 1865 was changed to a church and parsonage, and part of the pews were sold. In 1866 or 1867, Watson bought back the pews, changed the church to a tavern again, and carried on the house for one year. In 1867, James Jewell, the present landlord, hired the house and opened it for company. In 1876, Moses Paul bought the house and had last summer considerable patronage.

On Orr's Island there has never been a tavern or public house of any kind.

In 1829, Elijah Walker was licensed as an innholder on Harpswell Neck.

The MANSION HOUSE was built by Alexander P. Wentworth, now of Brunswick, in 1835, and was occupied by him as a public house for a short time, and was then sold to John Colby, who was succeeded by others whose names have not been ascertained. Frederic W. Dearborn, of Topsham, was the last owner and landlord. The house was destroyed by fire in 1868. Mr. Charles Johnson was licensed as an innholder in 1837, but whether he had charge of this house does not appear.

MAILS AND POST-OFFICES.

At the time of the earlier settlements here, before the establishment of any post-office, letters were brought to the inhabitants by the coasters which plied between Maquoit and the larger towns, or by any chance traveller who might be journeying this way. For a time even after the establishment of a mail-route, letters were sent by coasters as a matter of convenience.

The first mail-route from Boston to the Kennebec was established a little while before the commencement of the Revolutionary war, when, for a short time, Luke Lambard carried the mail on horseback once a fortnight, leaving the letters for Brunswick and vicinity as he passed by.[1] The mail was first carried between Portland and Bath, once a fortnight, by Richard Kimball, who went on foot and often carried the letters in his pocket. It was not until about 1800 that the mail was carried oftener than once a week.[1] In 1803 there were three mails a week from Boston, which arrived in Brunswick on the third day. In 1804 it reached that place in the afternoon, and in 1805 in the morning of the second day from Boston.[2]

---

[1] *Maine Historical Collection*, 2, *p.* 219.

[2] *McKeen, in Brunswick Telegraph, July* 30, 1853.

Henry McIntyre drove the first four-horse stage from Portland to Brunswick about 1803. He was living, at the age of ninety-three, at New Sharon, Maine, on April 30, 1875.[1]

In 1802, T. S. Estabrook, of Brunswick (afterwards Colonel), began to carry the mail to Augusta, passing through Topsham and Litchfield. He carried it at first on horseback, leaving Brunswick every Monday. In 1806 he commenced running a passenger coach twice a week. It left Brunswick on Saturday and Tuesday at eleven o'clock A. M., and arrived in Augusta on Sunday and Wednesday at ten A. M. Returning, it left Augusta at noon on Sunday, and at eight A. M. on Thursday.[2]

The first daily mail is thought to have commenced in 1810.[3] In 1824 "no mail from Brunswick could reach the towns on the Androscoggin River, except by way of Portland and Hallowell, and not all of said towns were reached in that way; consequently the publisher of the *Baptist Herald* found it necessary to establish at his own expense a weekly mail-route as far as Jay, about forty-five miles; passing up the west side of the river and down the east. The United States government, two years later, assumed the route and continued it until other facilities of transportation made it unnecessary." [4]

In 1836 a new mail-route was established between Brunswick and Turner, passing through Durham, Danville, Lewiston, and Minot. It left Brunswick at eight o'clock on Tuesday, Thursday, and Saturday. Another route was established at the same time to Lewiston, through Topsham and Lisbon. A route was also established this year between Brunswick and Harpswell. After the cars commenced to run on the Kennebec and Portland Railroad, there was a daily mail from each end of the road, and in 1864 two mails daily were received and sent.

The first post-office established in Brunswick was in 1793, and Deacon Andrew Dunning was the first postmaster. The office was kept until shortly before the death of Deacon Dunning in his dwelling on Maine Street, just north of what is now Noble Street. The estate remains in the Dunning family, but the present house is not the one in which the post-office was kept. Mr. Dean Swift distinctly remembers being sent to Deacon Dunning's for letters, when a boy, and he says that the deacon kept them in a desk in a corner of the room, and that it was customary for the citizens to look over the letters themselves,

---

[1] *Brunswick Telegraph.*

[2] *North, History of Augusta, p.* 333.

[3] *Farmers' Almanac,* 1810.

[4] *Griffin, Press of Maine, p.* 74.

and to select therefrom such as bore their address. Robert Dunning, who succeeded his father in 1801, kept the office on the northern corner of Maine and Dunlap Streets.[1]

In 1824 the office was kept on Mill Street, near the present residence of Mrs. A. J. Stone. In 1826 it was removed to the corner of Maine and Mason Streets, where Lorenzo Day's store now stands. The next year, the office was removed to a building south of the stage house, on the lot now occupied by James Berry, near the foot of the mall, where it remained until 1842, when it was removed to its present location. It was subsequently moved back to the Berry building, and in 1871 it was moved to its present location.

The income of the postmaster at this office during the year 1826 was one hundred and sixty dollars, and in 1845 was eight hundred and sixteen dollars and eighty-one cents. From these sums the postmaster was required to pay for office rent, clerk hire, wood and lights. The mails in the latter year arrived at eleven P. M. and two A. M.

On July 14, 1803, Major Lemuel Swift was appointed postmaster, in place of Robert Dunning. The appointment was probably made without the knowledge, or at least consent, of Mr. Swift, as he declined to accept it then, as he did also at other times.

The following is a correct list of all the postmasters of Brunswick and the date of their appointment. It is derived from the official records of the Post Office Department at Washington: —

Andrew Dunning, appointed March 20, 1793; Robert Dunning, appointed January 1, 1801; Henry Quinby, appointed January 1, 1804; Jonathan Stone, appointed May 20, 1807; Joseph McLellan, appointed September 15, 1823; Theodore S. McLellan, appointed December 29, 1840; Elijah P. Pike, appointed February 9, 1842; Theodore S. McLellan, appointed September 11, 1843; Joseph F. Dunning, appointed May 2, 1849; John McKeen, appointed September 28, 1850; Robert P. Dunlap, appointed May 13, 1853; Alfred J. Stone, appointed March 24, 1858; Benjamin G. Dennison, appointed April 8, 1861; Albert G. Tenney, appointed August 24, 1866; George C. Crawford, appointed April 3, 1867.

The first post-office in Topsham was up stairs in a building which stood directly opposite the bank. Charles R. Porter, the postmaster, was a lawyer, and the mail was kept in his office. He had for an assistant, Oliver, son of Major Nathaniel Walker, who remained with

[1] *Pejepscot Papers.*

him for two or three years, and was then succeeded by his brother, Wildes P. Walker, then a lad of ten or eleven years of age. The following is the list of postmasters in Topsham, derived from the same source as the preceding: —

Charles R. Porter, appointed February 6, 1821; Nathaniel Green, appointed July 13, 1826; Nathaniel Walker, appointed April 19, 1831; John H. Thompson, appointed August 12, 1841; Nathaniel Walker, appointed November 26, 1844; William Ricker, appointed July 19, 1845; Charles E. White, appointed February 9, 1849; John Tebbets, appointed April 11, 1849; Octavius A. Merrill, appointed May 3, 1853; Lewis M. Work, appointed September 22, 1853; Amos D. Wheeler, appointed February 29, 1856; Alexander Ridley, appointed October 6, 1856; Robert P. Whitney, appointed May 6, 1861.

The first post-office in Harpswell was established at the lower end of Harpswell Neck in 1842, about three miles from the old meeting-house, the mail being received at that time every Tuesday. The first postmaster was Washington Garcelon. Residents of Great Island and the upper part of the Neck continued to go to Brunswick for their letters for many years afterwards. There are several separate offices in the town of Harpswell, and the following is the official list of the postmasters in each.

The office in West Harpswell was established October 14, 1847. The postmasters were, Washington Garcelon, appointed October 14, 1847; Ebenezer Pinkham, appointed July 14, 1849; Alcot S. Merriman, appointed April 10, 1850. The office was discontinued May 27, 1854, but was re-established in September, 1862. David Webber, appointed September 11, 1862; Miss Helen M. Webber, appointed December 22, 1865; Miss Lydia F. Webber, appointed June 16, 1868; Miss Margaret M. Thomas, appointed February 28, 1871; Miss Eleanor Thomas, appointed June 15, 1872.

The office at North Harpswell was established February 25, 1864, and Charles Johnson was appointed postmaster on that day.

The office on Orr's Island was established May 13, 1868, and Samuel E. Smullen was appointed postmaster at that time.

Postage on a letter to Boston in 1833 was twelve and a half cents, eighteen and three fourths cents to New York, and twenty-five cents for any distance over five hundred miles.

In 1820 the rates were as follows: —

Single letters, for any distance not exceeding thirty miles, six cents; over thirty and not over eighty miles, ten cents; over eighty and not over one hundred and fifty miles, twelve and a half cents; over one hundred and fifty and not over four hundred miles, eighteen and a half cents; over four hundred miles, twenty-five cents.

Double letters, or those composed of two pieces of paper, double the above rates.

Ship letters, not carried by mail, six cents.

NEWSPAPERS, ETC.

The following account of the newspapers and press in Brunswick, Topsham, and Harpswell is mainly derived from a recent work by the late Joseph Griffin, entitled "The Press of Maine," with a few additions, which the character of his work led him to omit.

The first press in Brunswick was set up early in December, 1819, by Joseph Griffin, who graduated at the printing-office of Messrs. Flagg & Gould, in Andover, Massachusetts. His office was, at first, on the east side of Maine Street, facing Pleasant Street. In 1821 he removed to the building opposite the north end of the mall, and which he occupied until his death, in 1875.

For twenty-nine years Mr. Griffin printed, annually, one edition of the Catalogue of Bowdoin College, and for twenty years he printed two editions each year. He also printed sixteen editions (1,600 copies each) of the College Triennial Catalogue.

The first work approximating to a newspaper, or rather to a periodical, which emanated from his press, was in pamphlet form. It was issued in June, 1820. The third number had the following title-page: —

"The Management of the Tongue and Moral Observer. No. III. Price per annum, $1.50. Published & Printed by Joseph Griffin. Issued on the second Tuesday of each Month.

"CONTENTS. — Part 1. The Boaster, consisting of Two Maxims and Reflections. Part 2. The Ill Tongue, consisting of Three Maxims and Reflections. Part 3. Moral Observer, No. III. Melissa; a tale. Observation upon the Passions, addressed to the ladies. Poetry: Mathon's Return. The Season. Communication, suggesting a Legal Act in favor of 'Sitters' or Loafers. An Anecdote."

On the last page was an advertisement of Griffin & Hazelton's bookstore. Only three numbers were printed.

It was followed by the first newspaper that was printed in Brunswick. This was the *Maine Intelligencer*, a demiquarto of eight pages, published by Joseph Griffin, and edited by John M. O'Brien, Esquire, who graduated at Bowdoin College in the class of 1806.

The publication of this paper was commenced in September, 1820, and was given up at the end of six months, not proving remunerative to the publisher.

The Maine Baptist Herald. — The first number of this paper was printed by Mr. Griffin, July 17, 1824. It was a demifolio. It was edited for about six months by Benjamin Titcomb, Jr., a graduate of Bowdoin College, 1806, and son of the first printer in Maine. After the time named the *Herald* was under the sole management of the publisher. At the commencement of the second volume it was enlarged to a royal folio size, and continued weekly for six years. During the last two years of its existence it was called the *Eastern Galaxy and Herald*, the name having been changed in consequence of a larger part of its columns being subsequently devoted to secular interests. In the latter years of this publication the subscribers numbered over eleven hundred, — a larger circulation than can be claimed for any other of the many papers subsequently commenced in Brunswick.

The *Herald* was the first paper coinciding fully with the faith and practices of the primitive Baptists ever published in the United States. It was also one of the earliest papers in New England to take a stand against the inroads of intemperance, by exposing the causes leading thereto. In 1826 appears in the *Herald* the first complaint and argument against indiscriminate licenses for the sale of alcoholic liquors.

Androscoggin Free Press. — This paper was a royal folio, twenty-six by twenty. It was edited and published by Moore & Wells, assisted by Charles Packard, Esquire. It was commenced in 1827 and continued about two years. In politics it was the exponent of the principles of the Whig party.

The Escritoir was a semi-monthly magazine of thirty-two pages, octavo, published in 1826–27 by a club of students, of which John Hodgdon was chairman. It was printed by Joseph Griffin.

The Northern Iris, a monthly of thirty-two pages, went forth from the Bowdoin press for six months, in 1829. The editor and publisher was Sumner Lincoln Fairfield, a gentleman from the South. It was edited with ability, but depending on unsolicited patronage it was not remunerative. Mr. Fairfield had considerable reputation as a poet. He died while young.

In 1830 the *Brunswick Journal* made its appearance. It was a royal folio sheet, published by William Noyes, now one of the editors and publishers of the *Saco Independent*. Associated with him a part of the time was Henry W. Fairfield, now the printer of the *New*

England Farmer, Boston. The *Journal* was a Whig paper, supporting J. G. Hunton for governor of Maine, and Henry Clay for President of the United States. Charles Packard, Esquire, then attorney at law, edited it for a short time, after which Francis D. and John S. Cushing were the principal writers. It was a well-conducted paper, but it was published for only a year and three months.

The *Juvenile Key*, commenced in 1831, was a children's paper, nine by seven, in neatly printed newspaper form, published weekly for two years. A considerable portion of the type-work of this paper was done by two children of Joseph Griffin who, at the commencement, were only nine and seven years of age, respectively. Their names appeared as publishers. The first, a daughter, is now the wife of a clergyman in New Hampshire; the second, a son, Joseph Warren Griffin, was lost at sea in February, 1849, on his passage to California.

After the suspension of the *Brunswick Journal*, the *Key* was enlarged to a twelve by nine size, four pages, to make it more completely a family paper and give room for advertising. From this time it was called the *Family Pioneer and Juvenile Key*, and was published with good success for four years. It was the endeavor of the editor of the *Family Pioneer and Juvenile Key* to operate upon the public mind, especially that of the young, by the publication of interesting narratives, setting forth in a clear light, not only the evils of an intemperate use of intoxicating drinks, but the dangers of temperate drinking. The abolition of negro slavery, and of the death penalty for crime, were strongly advocated in the columns of the *Pioneer and Key*.

The Eastern Baptist was commenced in November, 1837, by Thomas W. Newman, and was continued about a year and a half, when it was discontinued, and the list of subscribers transferred to the *Zion's Advocate*, in Portland. The paper was started and edited by an association of Baptist ministers. These were, in 1838, David Nutter, Edwin R. Warren, A. J. W. Stevens, and Luther C. Stevens.[1]

Mr. Newman also published at this time, at No. 2 Forsaith's Block, the *Advocate of Freedom*. This was a semi-monthly sheet, published under the direction of the Executive Committee of the Maine Anti-slavery Society, and issued at fifty cents per annum. The prospectus stated, "It will explain and defend the principles held by the society and the measures approved by it. It will be a vehicle of the anti-slavery intelligence of the day, and a repository of facts and argu-

---

[1] *This account is not given in the Press of Maine. It was furnished us by Mr. Newman.*

ments on the subject of slavery and the measures for its speedy and peaceful removal." The editorial work was done principally by Professor William Smyth. The paper was devoted exclusively to the antislavery cause. There were no local items or advertisements in it. Number 1, Volume I, was printed March 8, 1838. Number 25, the last printed here, was printed February 21, 1839. The size of the paper was twenty by twenty-five. The publication of this paper was continued at Augusta as a weekly paper.

The *Regulator*, a royal folio, Democratic paper, was published for two years, 1837 and 1838, by Theodore S. McLellan. I. A. Beard was the editor.

The Brunswicker, a neutral paper, was printed and published for one year, 1842, by T. S. McLellan. John Dunlap, B. A., was the editor. It was succeeded by a paper called *The Yagerhamer*, of which, however, but two or three numbers were issued.

The Forester was printed in 1845 by Noyes & Stanwood. Its editor was H. A. Stanwood. Only one volume of this paper was published.

The *Pejepscot Journal*, a weekly sheet, was published at Brunswick in 1846, one year; edited by G. C. Swallow, now Professor of Geology and Agriculture in Missouri.

The *Juvenile Watchman* was edited and published in 1854 by Howard Owen, who is now one of the enterprising publishers of the *Kennebec Journal*. It was a small sheet, eleven by sixteen. It was issued on the first and third Monday of each month at the office of the *Brunswick Telegraph*. It was devoted principally to the cause of temperance, especially among the young. It was discontinued at the expiration of six months.

The *Musical Journal* was published monthly in 1855 by George W. Chase, editor and proprietor. It had but a short existence.

The *Brunswick Telegraph* was commenced in 1853 by Waldron & Moore, as publishers, and Wm. G. Barrows, Esquire, as editor. It was afterwards issued by Waldron & Fowler, then by Fowler & Chase.

The publishers in 1856 transferred their interest to Geo. W. Chase, who published it as editor and proprietor about one year, when Howard Owen, now of the *Kennebec Journal*, was admitted as a partner, and took charge of the agricultural department. After being connected with the establishment about five months, Mr. Owen became dissatisfied with his unremunerated labors and sold his interest to Mr. Chase. Early in 1857 Mr. Chase abandoned the *Telegraph* and went to Bath, where he published the *Masonic Journal* and taught music.

Mr. A. G. Tenney, a graduate of Bowdoin College, class of 1835, purchased the *Telegraph* establishment in 1857, reissued the paper, and has since continued to edit and publish it weekly. Of Mr. Tenney's fitness for the position of editor, the *Press of Maine* [1] well says, "To a liberal education and a mind capable of close reasoning and of arriving at logical conclusions, he adds unwearied industry and constant application." Under Mr. Tenney's management, the paper has been particularly valuable for the energy and fidelity which the editor has displayed in his efforts to make it a good *local* paper, and in this respect it has no superior in the State.

The only paper ever published in Topsham was a Second Adventist paper, which was printed about the year 1844, in a chamber over John Larrabee's workshop on Elm Street. No copy of the paper has been found, and its name is forgotten. The enterprise was abandoned at the expiration of a few months.

In Harpswell there has been but one paper published. It was the *Harpswell Banner*. The first number was issued in May, 1832. It was published weekly, for six months, by Josiah S. Swift and Jonathan R. Snow. Jesse Snow, 2d, was the agent. It was printed on a sheet six by ten, and the price was four cents for six numbers. In August, J. S. Swift became the sole proprietor and editor. In September, the paper was enlarged to a sheet seven by thirteen, and the next week eight and one half to thirteen and one half, and the title was changed to that of the *Literary Banner*, terms thirty-two cents per annum; semi-monthly. The last number, however, was issued October 24 of this year. One number contained an advertisement by the editor that he would draw "with accuracy, for one shilling, views of country seats, buildings, etc.; also land and marine views." This paper was printed at the editor's home on Sebascodigan Island. Swift, then a lad, now a clergyman, residing in Farmington, "procured a small font of worn-out type, which had been thrown into *pi* in the office of the *Bath Maine Inquirer*. This he sorted out, laid in a case of his own construction, and having made a wooden chase, some tin rules, and cut a head on a block of wood, he printed a seven by nine weekly paper on an old cheese-press. He received the patronage and encouragement of many of the *literati* of Bath and Brunswick. The late John McKeen became a regular correspondent" [2] The boy finally abandoned the enterprise to enter the office of the *Bath Inquirer*, where he remained for some years, and finally became the proprietor of that paper.

---

[1] *Page* 171. [2] *Griffin, Press of Maine, p.* 197.

CHAPTER IX.

DISEASES[1] AND ACCIDENTS, FRESHETS.

We are unable to give an extended comparison, as to the relative healthfulness of the towns of Topsham, Brunswick, and Harpswell, or of their average rate of mortality. It may be said briefly, however, that as regards both endemics and epidemics, Harpswell is the most healthy of the three towns, and Brunswick the least so. Topsham probably occupies an intermediate position between the two. The cause of the difference is in the configuration of the land, the nature of the soil, the proximity to the sea, and the density of the population. Topsham and Harpswell possess by far the best drainage, though that of Brunswick is amply sufficient, if properly cared for. No data exist from which to calculate accurately the death-rate of either town, but in each there have been a few individuals who have lived to an advanced age. Harpswell probably bears off the palm in this respect, for in one house four persons are said to have died, whose average age was ninety-nine and a half years. They were Taylor Small, who died in 1812, aged ninety-six; Peter Birthright, who died in 1822, at the age, it is said, of one hundred and fifteen; Tabitha Small, who died in 1846, at the age of ninety-nine; and Mark Small, who died in 1852, at the age of eighty-eight.

In this connection a brief mention of the different *physicians*, who have from time to time settled here, will not be inappropriate.

The first physician who settled in either of these towns was undoubtedly Samuel Gyles, who died in Brunswick in 1738, and who had practised there for a short time previously. He came from Salisbury, Mass.

Next in Brunswick was William Spear, son of Robert Spear, one of the early settlers. Dr. Spear was in practice about the year 1740,

[1] *The late Dr. John D. Lincoln commenced to prepare for the authors a chapter on the sanitary condition and mortality of the three towns. His sickness and death prevented its completion or revision, and we are consequently obliged to give a more meagre sketch than we otherwise should.*

but for how long a time is not known, and nothing is known as to his professional qualifications.

Doctor Phineas Nevers was in Brunswick from 1755 to 1765, and perhaps longer. Nothing is known of him as a physician.

Doctor Samuel Duncan came to Brunswick from Topsham in 1770, and was in practice until his death, in 1784. He was a young man, but was called a skilful physician, and he had an extensive practice. He lived at New Meadows.

Doctor Ebenezer H. Goss[1] came to Brunswick during the Revolution. He lived at Maquoit until 1804, when he moved to the village, and soon after moved to Paris, Maine. He had an extensive practice and was accounted a good physician.

Doctor Balthazar Stilkey was a Hessian surgeon, who came over with Burgoyne's forces, and after the war (about 1790) settled in Brunswick near the present residence of Mr. Martin Storer, north of Cook's Corner. He practised there for several years. But little is known of him. He is said to have been something of a quack.

Doctor Jonathan Richardson Parker was in Brunswick for one or two years only, about 1799.

Doctor Jonathan Page[1] came to Brunswick in 1795, and commenced the practice of medicine in 1800. His practice soon became extensive, and continued increasingly so until his death, in 1842. He held a highly respectable rank in his profession. His residence was for many years in the house just south of the Mason Street Church.

Doctor Isaac Lincoln[1] moved to Brunswick from Topsham in 1820. He enjoyed a very extensive practice until a short time before his death, in 1868. He held a high rank in his profession. He was a graduate of Harvard College, 1800, and is supposed to have been the first physician in Brunswick who had received a collegiate education.

John D. Lincoln,[1] son of Doctor Isaac Lincoln, was a graduate of Bowdoin College, class of 1843, and of the Medical School of Maine, class of 1846. He practised in Brunswick from 1846 till within a few weeks of his death, in 1877. He was a most excellent physician and his practice extended into many of the neighboring towns, and even to more remote portions of the State.

Other physicians in Brunswick, for a short time only, have been J. D. Wells, 1829; ——— Cushman, 1836; J. E. Shaw, 1857; T. S. Foster, 1864; J. B. Soto, 1871 to 1873.

Of those now residing in Brunswick, Asher Ellis commenced prac-

---

[1] *See Biography.*

tice in Brunswick in 1842, NATHANIEL T. PALMER in 1845, ALFRED MITCHELL in 1865, and DANIEL F. ELLIS in 1866.

The earliest physician in Topsham, the date of whose residence can be determined, was DOCTOR PHILIP HOYT, who died in June, 1790 (see epitaph). Tradition reports him as an excellent physician. In 1793 there was, if no mistake has been made in the recorded dates, a Doctor Hoyt in town who was a member of the church. Possibly he was a son of the one first named.

DOCTOR EBENEZER EMERSON came to Topsham prior to 1792. He came to Maine from Reading, Mass. At first he boarded with James Wilson, but he afterwards built and occupied the house now occupied by Swansey Wilson, just beyond Cyrus Purington's on the Bowdoinham road. He was settled here at least six years and probably longer.

While Doctor Emerson boarded at Mr. Wilson's there was also another physician named HAY who boarded with him. Doctor Hay did not, however, long remain.

A DOCTOR PARKER succeeded Doctor Emerson and lived in the same house that the latter had previously occupied. He remained in town several years.

A DOCTOR OSBORNE practised in Topsham prior to Doctor Phineas Never's residence in Brunswick, probably about 1754. He boarded at a Mr. Gray's, who lived near Ferry Point. His stay in town was short.

DOCTOR DUNCAN is supposed to have located himself in Topsham before he went to Brunswick. If so, his stay could not have been for more than a few weeks. Both of these last are said to have died at New Meadows, from consumption.

A young man named DOCTOR GUILD was here for a few years, about 1796.

In some old papers of Brigadier Thompson a DOCTOR WHITTAKER is alluded to in a manner to imply that he was a resident of Topsham. Nothing is positively known, however, in regard to it.

Prior to 1804, DOCTOR STOCKBRIDGE (the elder Dr. Stockbridge of Bath, deceased) settled in Topsham for a short time. He boarded with Jacob Abbott in what is known as the "Rachel Patten" house. Stockbridge Howland and John Stockbridge Patten are said to have been named for him.

About the same time a DOCTOR SAWYER settled in Topsham, kept an apothecary store, and practised his profession. DOCTOR SIMS and DOCTOR FAIRFIELD both practised here not far from this time, certainly before 1804. The latter also had an apothecary store.

In 1804, DOCTOR ISAAC LINCOLN [1] moved to Topsham and soon had an extensive practice. In 1820 he removed to Brunswick.

In 1820, DOCTOR JAMES MCKEEN[1] commenced to practise in Topsham. His office, at that time, was over Jonathan Baker's store, and he boarded at Humphrey Purinton's boarding-house. He continued in practice until a short time before his death, in 1873.

In 1813 a "botanic doctor," by the name of NORTON, came to town, but did not remain more than a year or two.

Between the last date and 1856, DOCTORS J. S. CUSHMAN, COOK, and SPRINGER were settled in Topsham for short periods.

In 1856, DOCTOR JOSEPH MCKEEN, JR., commenced practice, and is, at the present time, the only resident physician of this town.

Although the town of Harpswell has been unable to dispense entirely with the services of physicians, yet it has done so to a great extent. There have been but four physicians located in the town, and, with one exception, they remained but a few years. The practice in the town has been mainly carried on by Brunswick doctors. Prior to 1840 a DOCTOR NORTON resided in the town for several years. He was succeeded about 1843 by a DOCTOR BLISS. In 1850, or thereabouts, DOCTOR DAILEY settled in this town and has remained to the present time. In 1870, DOCTOR J. B. SOTO settled here, but remained but one year, when he removed to Brunswick, where he died.

DISEASES AND ACCIDENTS.

If Brunswick and Topsham cannot be considered as pre-eminently healthy places, yet it can with truth be asserted that they are as healthy as other towns of like character, situation, and population. Since the Great Plague among the Indians, about 1615 or 1616 (which extended all over New England), there has no devastating epidemic occurred here. Pulmonary consumption, pneumonia, acute rheumatism, typhoid fever, scarlet fever, measles, epidemic dysentery, and cholera infantum produce the same ravages here as elsewhere, but are none of them endemic. Cholera and yellow fever have never, it is believed, appeared here, and no quarantine has ever been established here.

Small-pox has prevailed a number of times, but never to an alarming extent. Its first appearance was in the early part of the fall of 1792.[2] How many cases there were in this epidemic is not known,

[1] *See Biography.* [2] *Pejepscot Papers.*

but the citizens were greatly alarmed, and the town of Brunswick very properly took all the precautions possible to prevent the spread of the disease. In October of that year, the town "voted not to allow any person in this town to inoculate for to take the small-pox, but to take all possible care to prevent the spreading of the disorder." Eighteen inspectors were chosen from the different parts of the town, whose duties were to erect "smoke-houses" wherever they thought best; to examine, smoke, and clean all goods brought into town for the space of two months, and to stop, examine, and cleanse any person whom they might suspect of being infected. The town also voted to build a hospital twenty-eight feet long by fourteen feet wide and one story high. The hospital was to be on the Commons, but the exact location was left to the decision of the selectmen. No physician was allowed to attend small-pox patients without the authority of the selectmen. After this epidemic had passed by, there were no cases of this disease for thirty-two years, unless, perchance, there were a few cases not known to the public.

In 1824, owing to fears of an epidemic of this disease, the town of Brunswick, at a meeting held May 10, appointed the selectmen as a committee to take prompt and efficient measures to have all in town vaccinated who had not previously been. The agents of the different school districts were directed to be present and see that all not previously vaccinated, attended at the time appointed by the physician. The names of all persons vaccinated were to be recorded on the town records, and the expense of the vaccination was to be paid by the town. Nothing further is known in regard to an epidemic at this time. In 1851 there were a few cases of small-pox in this vicinity, and at the May meeting in Brunswick, the town instructed the selectmen "to cause the inhabitants of the town to be vaccinated without delay." Doctors N. T. Palmer, Asher Ellis, and J. D. Lincoln were also chosen at this time as a Board of Health. There were a few cases of this disease in 1861, and a number in 1866, when there were three fatal cases. But few cases of this disease can have occurred in Topsham, since no record is to be found of any, except single cases.

In 1810 a committee was chosen to vaccinate all who had not had the small-pox, and this committee reported the next year that Doctor Isaac Lincoln had vaccinated four hundred and three persons, of which number three hundred and ninety-one cases were successful and twelve were doubtful.

In 1824 the people of Topsham were again vaccinated. Harpswell seems to have been quite free from this disease, so much so, apparently, as to have no dread of it, for in 1832 the town voted against having the people vaccinated.

It is thought that the ratio of cases of insanity was greater in the early part of the century, in this vicinity, than it is at present. At one time, about 1820, there were four insane persons in Brunswick and five in Topsham. In 1836 the town of Brunswick authorized the erection of a building for the accommodation of this class of patients, at an expense not exceeding three hundred dollars. The apparently greater number of cases of this kind in former years may be partially accounted for by the fact that there were not at that time so many of this unfortunate class under treatment in asylums abroad, and consequently each case was well known to the whole community.

Besides the ordinary cases of disease affecting the mortality of this vicinity, many cases of accident resulting in premature death have occurred from time to time. Foremost among these are the accidents from falling into the water. From the list of cases we have collected, only a few of the earliest or most remarkable ones are inserted here. The earliest case of the kind of which we have received any account, occurred in March, 1765, a Mrs. Babbage and son, who lived on the farm now owned by the heirs of the late John Pennell, and a young man by the name of Barnes, a son of Henry and brother of the late William Barnes, who lived on the farm now owned by James Alexander, in Harpswell, while crossing Merriconeag River to a grist-mill on the old Ewing place, had their float caught in the running ice and overset, and were all three drowned. Mrs. Barnes and William were watching them from the shore when the accident happened. Their bodies were recovered the following June. The only other similar deaths occurring prior to 1800 were of Daniel Winchell, before 1777, at some place unknown; Adam Hunter, at sea, in 1778; Samuel Potter, date and place both unknown, but some time in the last century; Robert Potter, at sea, before 1794; James and Robert Winchell, at the same time, at Cathance, date unknown; John Winchell, at Bath, between 1790 and 1800; Benjamin Randall and Thomas Wilson, both at sea and prior to 1800.

Some time previous to 1820, Major Burt Townsend and a Mr. Gross were on a raft of logs above the upper dam on the Androscoggin, at Brunswick. The raft broke loose and went over the dam. Just as they reached the falls, Major Townsend, with great presence of mind, leaped ahead into the river below and thus escaped both the undertow and the falling logs, and was thus able to swim ashore, while Mr. Gross, who either did not jump at all, or else not sufficiently far, was drowned.

From the list referred to, we are able to give the following summary: The number of cases of drowning in Brunswick and Topsham (exclusive of those drowned at sea, of which the list is, as a matter of course, very incomplete) is forty-five. Of these forty-five cases, there were drowned on the Cathance River, in Topsham, five; on the Androscoggin River (including Merrymeeting Bay), twenty-seven; on the New Meadows River, in Brunswick, one; at Maquoit, three; at other places mentioned, five; and where the place was unknown, four. Of the twenty-seven drowned in the Androscoggin, eight were drowned on the Topsham side, ten on the Brunswick side, five in Merrymeeting Bay, and four in the stream, away from the shore. Of the ten persons drowned on the Brunswick side, seven were drowned near the Factory or lower mills and two near the upper bridge. Of the eight on the Topsham side, four were drowned at the bathing-place above the upper bridge and two near the mills.

Next in the list of fatal accidents come those by fire. The first of these to which reference has been found was in 1737, when the house of the widow of Andrew Dunning was burned, and she was burned in it. No reference to any other death by fire in the last century has been found. In September, 1829, Hannah J. Brown, of Topsham, aged eight years, was badly burned by a brand which fell from the andirons on her cotton gown and set it on fire. She lingered for twenty-six days before she succumbed to her injuries. On January 15, 1857, Mrs. James Maxwell, of Topsham, was fatally burned, in consequence of the overflowing of a lighted lamp containing camphene. She lived but a short time. On January 25, 1859, a daughter of John Merritt, of Brunswick, was fatally burned in consequence of her clothes being caught in the blaze of the fire. On March 11th of this same year, Mr. Isaac Center was fatally burned by the explosion in his hand of a lighted lamp, containing burning fluid.

In this connection may be mentioned with propriety the cases (though not fatal) of accidents in consequence of lightning. The first occurrence of this kind was in 1828, when a house in Mill Street was struck by lightning, and a man injured. The next case occurred September 5, 1845, when one person was stunned and another prostrated by the lightning, which struck Common's Hall. At the time the "Henry Jordan" house, on Cleaveland Street was struck by lightning, June 23, 1874, two persons standing on the doorsill were struck, but not seriously injured. Other cases have probably occurred of which no account has been preserved.

Numerous accidents have occurred from time to time at the mills and factories, though fortunately but few have resulted fatally. The earliest occurrence of this kind was in the last century, though the precise date is unknown. Hugh Wilson, of Topsham, who was married in 1785, had his leg broken among the mill logs on the eastern branch of the Cathance River An amputation was performed by a physician from Casco (Portland), but he did not long survive the operation. The next occurrence of which we have seen any account, also in Topsham, was in August, 1825. At this time a little child, aged four years, fell through a saw-mill and fractured his skull. On October 7, of the same year, another child, aged ten years, while asleep in a saw-mill in Brunswick, where his father was working at the time, got up and fell out on to the rocks, a distance of twenty-five feet, and was instantly killed. Record has been found of only two accidents in the mills since this date, but there were doubtless many others which were unrecorded, save in the memory of afflicted friends.

At least eight fatal accidents are known to have happened upon the railroad in this vicinity, and it is possible there have been more. Only one of these cases happened in Topsham.

The following are a few of the cases of death that have occurred from other causes than those already specified: —

November 30, 1833, William B. Merriman, of Brunswick, mate of the brig "Veto," was murdered by the pilot, a Spaniard, while at Barbaras, in the lagoon of Maracaibo. In November, 1858, Richard L. McManus fell into the hold from the deck of the ship "Screamer," in the port of London, and died on December 7, in consequence of lockjaw induced by the injury he sustained.

On August 27, 1861, a young lad fell on to the rocks from the high bluff in front of the residence of Miss Narcissa Stone, in Brunswick, and was instantly killed. On the 27th of September, 1866, a young child was accidentally shot in Topsham.

The deaths caused by the personal violence of another have been mentioned in a different connection. The cases of suicide occurring in Brunswick and Topsham have been (including that of Ann Conner already referred to) only eight, so far as can be ascertained. These cases occurred in the years 1752 to 1770, 1820, 1823, 1833, 1852, 1855, 1858, and 1869. Two of these were destroyed by cutting their own throats, one by hanging, one by shooting, and two by drowning. The manner of death of the other two is not known. There have undoubtedly been other cases of this kind, but these are all in which the facts have been found recorded.

Among what might be classed under the head of accidents to property, but which might with even more propriety be classed under a meteorological heading, and which for convenience merely are introduced in this place, are

FRESHETS.

The earliest reference found to any freshet in the Androscoggin was to one that occurred in February, 1723. At that time the river was very full, "the lowland full of water and the river open not only below but even to the falls thirty miles above Pejepscot." This it will be noticed was in *midwinter*.[1]

The next great freshet occurred in 1780, in the winter season.[2] There was considerable ice in the river at the time, which dammed up the water so that it flowed across the lower part of Topsham village, and men went across Main Street below the bank in boats. Ice was carried by the water into the cellar of the Hodge house, which stood where the bank now stands, and it was also brought up the gully by the town landing, nearly as far as the present Congregational Church.

The next freshet was in 1784. It occurred some time in the fall. The barn of Andrew and John Dunning was brought down by the water from the intervale east of Rocky Hill. This barn continued entire until it reached the falls. The standing corn in the fields along the banks of the river remained fixed, but pumpkins came down in great abundance. The great mills on the island were carried off at this time.[3] In October of the next year[4] there was another freshet that carried off a saw-mill and nine saws, two grist-mills, a fulling mill, and three houses. On account of the amount of damage done by the sudden rise of water at this time, the town of Topsham preferred a petition to the General Court for an abatement in the tax for that year. The next unusual rise of water in the river occurred in 1811. At this time the toll-bridge was partially carried off. It was at this time, also, that two men, Johnson Wilson and "Noggin" Potter, went across the ice to Shad Island, where Wilson owned a mill, and went to work. There had been a rain, but Wilson and Potter did not anticipate a rise of water sufficient to break up the ice. At noon, however, when they left work and started for home, they found the ice had broken up and, as there was no bridge to the island at that time, they were unable to reach the shore. The ice was running rapidly, and it would be dangerous to attempt to reach them by boat; they were therefore obliged to remain on the island. As it

---

[1] *Pejepscot Papers.* [2] *Ibid.* [3] *Ibid.* [4] *Ibid.*

was uncertain how long they might have to remain there, their friends, who were on the Brunswick shore, threw crackers, pieces of fish, etc., to them, and thus their hunger was appeased. They were obliged to remain on the island nearly two days, when Major William Frost and some one else took a boat and brought them safely ashore.[1]

In the great freshet of 1814 twenty-one saw-mills were swept away, or rendered useless, and many other buildings and manufactories were destroyed. An expensive viaduct for conveying boards past the falls was also destroyed. Mills, barns, etc., came down to the falls erect, as though resting on their foundations, and were there dashed to pieces. The Patten mill, in Topsham, was carried down the river and across the island about where the paper-mill now stands; catching for a moment on the rocks at this place, the roof came off. Four saw-mills on the lower falls started at one time and carried off the greater portion of the bridge. The toll-man had just quitted his dwelling. There was a rise of water of twenty-eight feet in this freshet. In October, 1819, there was a heavy freshet which carried off the upper mills. The town of Brunswick petitioned the legislature to make a deduction from their valuation in consequence of the loss of property occasioned by it.

In the summer of 1820 the river was lower than it had been for sixty years previous, and all business in mills and factories was suspended for some time. This unusual drought was, however, only the precursor of a great freshet which occurred on the sixteenth and seventeenth of October following. At this time all the booms about the falls broke, containing logs, it was said, sufficient to supply twenty-three saws for two years, — the greatest number ever on hand at that season of the year. The lower dam on the Brunswick side started and carried with it about sixty feet of the Androscoggin bridge, and two mills for manufacturing clapboards, owned by Jaquith and Eastman. "A greater portion of the most expensive dam on the falls" then started, and it was supposed it could not be repaired under nine or ten months. Fifteen saws, two grist-mills, a carding-machine, two clapboard-mills, and a lath-mill were rendered useless until this dam was repaired. The estimated loss was over $125,000. There was also great loss of property at Lisbon.

On April 15, 1824, a "very great freshet" is recorded, but no particulars are given. On August 30, 1826, the most unexpected and rapid rise of water in the Androscoggin occurred that had ever been

---

[1] *James Wilson.*

known. In Livermore and Jay the water rose eight feet in one night. It swept away in its course every movable thing on the shores, such as timber, ferry-boats, etc. The swell of water reached Brunswick on Tuesday eve. Between one and two thousand logs that had been rafted below the booms at this place were swept over the dams, and some damage was done to a number of the mills. The loss at this point was, however, more than balanced by a fine run of logs from above. There had been no rains in this vicinity.

Another serious rise of water occurred on April 25 and April 26, 1827. The boom broke on the night of the twenty-fifth, and allowed about one hundred and fifty thousand logs to come down the river. In their course they carried off the new double saw-mill belonging to Doctor Jonathan Page, about two hundred feet of the toll-bridge, and the gulf dam. The Eagle Factory was also injured.

No freshet is recorded as occurring in 1829, but in November of that year the tide in the river is said to have risen five feet higher than ever before known, and to have done some slight damage.

Other considerable freshets occurred on January 2, 1831, May 22, 1832, and April 7, 1833. At the one in 1832, the Roger Merrill saw-mill and also the Patten mill and the bridge dam were carried away.

In February, 1839, there was a serious ice freshet, which carried away the upper dam and booms, and the Goat Island mill, and seriously injured the Great Mills. The ice became gorged at the Narrows, and was sixty feet high below the toll-bridge. It was piled so high between the bridge and the lower falls, that a man stepped off the bridge and walked on the ice to the roof of the mill on Shad Island.

A freshet occurred on May 22, 1843, at which the dam on the Topsham side gave way, and the lower boom above the falls also gave way, carrying off the Rogers mill in Topsham, and about thirty feet of the Shad Island bridge. The bank on the "Intervale" road in Brunswick was washed away, and a house undermined at this time.

The next noteworthy freshet was in May, 1854. It was said at the time to be the greatest of any since 1814, though but little damage was done. The old Hodge mill was carried off, but the new Hodge mill was uninjured.

In 1857, April 6, the water in the river was very high, and the old Purinton mill in Topsham was carried off.

On March 31, 1859, the ice carried away Maxwell & Jameson's blacksmith shop, on the island, and also an old grist-mill near by.

On April 19, 1862, an unoccupied house on the island in Topsham, next to the small bridge, was carried away by the water, and the draw and about two hundred feet of the Bay Bridge, on the Brunswick side, were also destroyed. Cow Island was entirely submerged.

On November 19, 1863, there was a high freshet. The northern abutment of the small bridge in Topsham was undermined, and carriage travel stopped. There were some logs lost, but no other damage is known to have been done at this time.

April 19, 1865, the water was quite high, but did no damage. There was, however, at this time, an extremely high wind, which blew down fences, signs, etc., and did considerable harm. A barn on the Island, in Topsham, was blown into the river with all its contents, even the hens.

On April 26, 1866, there was a heavy ice freshet. A small portion of the dam of Perkins's saw-mill, and the outer tier of posts of the Purinton flour-mill, both in Topsham, were carried away. Some damage was also done to the Coburn mill in Brunswick. There was also another, though lighter, freshet in November of this year.

In 1869 there were two freshets. At the first, on April 20, a boom broke, and a large number of logs belonging to Hiram Toothaker, and to Coburn & Thompson, went down river. The loss was estimated at about $40,000.

At the other freshet, October 5, several cows on Cow Island were drowned, and two hundred bushels of corn, belonging to John Merryman, at Rocky Hill, were washed away.

The last freshet of consequence was on April 16, 1873. The ice became gorged, and carried away the flume at the paper-mill in Topsham.

CHAPTER X.

STAGES, RAILROADS, NAVIGATION, TELEGRAPH, EXPRESSES, PUBLIC CARRIAGES.

STAGES, ETC.

THE first regular stage for the accommodation of passengers is thought to have commenced running about the year 1800. The first four-horse stage between Brunswick and Portland is known to have been driven in 1803 by Henry McIntyre. In 1806, Colonel Estabrook drove a biweekly stage between Brunswick and Augusta.

In 1807, or soon after, Nahum Perkins, of Topsham, drove a through stage between Portland and Augusta.

The first daily stage commenced, in connection with the mails, in 1810. It was between Portland and Brunswick.

A writer in 1820 remarks concerning the stages to and from Brunswick at that time, "From the great eastern, western, and northern routes the stages arrive at twelve o'clock at noon, and so well are they regulated that they often arrive at the same moment. There is no other place in Maine so well situated in this respect. From the east, west, and north, they arrive and depart every day in the week." These coaches were probably run by the Maine Stage Company, as that is the earliest company to which any reference has been found.

On January 1, 1821, William B. Peters commenced running a stage between Portland and Bath, leaving the former place on Monday. Wednesday, and Friday, and the latter on Tuesday, Thursday, and Saturday. The Brunswick office was at Hodgkins's tavern. The fare was the same as in the mail stage. This was an *opposition line* to the regular mail stage. How long it was maintained is not known.

On August 20, 1836, the Brunswick and Turner Stage Company began running a stage between those two towns, leaving Stinchfield's Hotel in Brunswick, Tuesdays, Thursdays, and Saturdays at eight o'clock A. M., passing through Durham, Danville, Lewiston, East Minot, East Turner, and arriving in Turner at three o'clock P. M. Returning, it left Turner on Mondays, Wednesdays, and Fridays at eight o'clock A. M , and arrived in Brunswick at four P. M. The fare to Lewiston was one dollar and twenty-five cents, and to Turner one dollar and seventy-five cents During the winter of this year, Jacob Harris drove a two-horse team twice a week to Portland, for freight and passengers.

On December 25, 1854, the Brunswick and Lewiston stage line was established, John Holland, Jr., being the agent. A passenger coach, capable of seating nine persons inside, left Lewiston for Brunswick every Monday, Wednesday, and Friday, and arrived at the latter place in season for the noon train for Bath and Augusta. It left Brunswick on its return at half past nine A. M. It passed through Topsham, Little River, and Lisbon. The fare between Brunswick and Lewiston was one dollar and twenty-five cents. This line was kept up for several years. In 1856 M. K. Marean was its agent. The last stage run to any point accessible by the cars was in 1858. In November of that year, C. M. Plummer commenced to run a daily stage to Bath *in opposition to the cars.* The fare by stage was forty cents, and by cars twenty-five cents.

There are at present three lines of stages leaving Brunswick. One is a daily stage to Potts's Point on Harpswell Neck; another, thrice weekly, to Condy's Harbor on Great Island; and another, thrice weekly, to Orr's Island. The first stage over the latter route was driven by Ephraim Johnson of Orr's Island, on June 1, 1868.

Among the different lines of stages which have been enumerated, the Maine Stage Company deservedly takes the first rank. The company at one time owned $60,000 worth of stock. Its coaches were large and comfortable, and its horses were of the best The line was well patronized and the profits were large. A quarterly dividend of thirty dollars on the hundred is known to have been distributed. The stages of this line continued running to Portland for some time after the railroad was completed. The fare to Portland by stage was one dollar, and by cars ninety cents, but the stage called for and delivered passengers at their residences, thus saving carriage hire. Among the drivers for the Maine Stage Company were Calvin Gossam, Charles Owen (son of Elder Shimuel Owen), Hiram Tibbetts (father of Mr. J. H. Tibbetts), Jabez Sawin, ——— Savage, Jacob Sands, ——— Stanwood, ——— Plummer, Job Sawyer, ——— Hobbs, and John Beals.

Gossam was a careful driver, prompt in business, attentive to the wants of his passengers, and scrupulously neat in his apparel; his hat, boots, and gloves were always stylish; when he announced, "Stage ready," no better dressed gentleman entered the coach. Gossam went to California, where he drove successfully several years before his death.

Mr. Sands drove a part of the time between Brunswick and Augusta, and a part between Brunswick and Portland. In 1849, when the steamer *Flushing* made her daily trips between New Wharf and Portland, he drove a stage connecting with the steamer. He was a careful driver and a pleasant, genial, whole-souled man. Those who desired to relieve the monotony of a stage journey by pleasant, facetious, and ofttimes instructive conversation, invariably chose a seat beside him upon the box.

Concerning the other drivers, nothing has been learned, except what would naturally be inferred, that they were all good "whips" and handled the "ribbons" skilfully.

Accidents were not infrequent in old stage times. In several instances the towns of Brunswick and Topsham were obliged to pay damages to the stage company, in consequence of injuries to their coaches caused by defects in the highways.

One incident is perhaps illustrative of the whole. On November 17, 1829, a stage containing eleven passengers, among whom were Governor Dunlap, and Mr. Charles J. Noyes, of Brunswick, was upset on McKeen Street, and tipped, top down, into a ditch full of water, so that the doors could not be opened. No one was seriously injured, but all were bedaubed with mud. A mother and her babe were among the inside passengers, and the child was found safely preserved on the shelf made by the inverted coach-seat.

RAILROADS.

The first local project for rail communication from Brunswick was broached some time in 1833. No serious attempt toward anything of the sort was inaugurated, however, until 1835. That year the legislature incorporated Elijah P. Pike, Nathaniel Davis, Alfred J. Stone, Charles Stetson, Roger Merrill, Jordan Woodward, Benjamin Pennell, John S. Cushing, and Solomon P. Cushman and their associates, successors, and assigns, "into a body politic and corporate" by the name of the Brunswick Railroad Company. This company was authorized "to locate and construct a railroad from the Androscoggin River, near Brunswick village, to some navigable waters of Casco Bay, with one or more branches," and were invested with all the necessary powers to carry their intention into effect. This corporation met June 4th of that year, and adopted a code of by-laws, and elected their officers. The road, however, was never laid out, and no other meeting of the company is known to have been held.

The first railroad to enter Brunswick was the Kennebec and Portland, which was incorporated in 1836, and was soon after surveyed. In 1845 the time of building was extended ten years, and of locating, five years. On May 1, 1845, the corporators met and chose a committee to confer with a committee of the Bath and Portland Railroad Company, which had been incorporated a short time previously. The result of the conference was a union of the two roads. On August 6th, of this year, a citizens' meeting was held at the Baptist Church, Maine Street, Brunswick, "to adopt measures in relation to the Portland, Bath, and Augusta Railroad." Honorable R. P. Dunlap was chosen chairman, and John D. Coburn, secretary. Speeches in favor of the road were made by the chairman, and by George Evans, of Gardiner, and P. Sheldon, and a committee was chosen to present subscription papers to the citizens. The town of Brunswick, in 1850, voted to loan its credit, to aid in the completion of this road, to the amount of $75,000. The same year Topsham voted to loan its credit for the same purpose to the amount of $30,000. The first work upon the railroad, near Brunswick, was commenced in 1847.

In March, 1849, Mr. John S. Cushing was called by the directors of the Kennebec and Portland Railroad to take charge of the grounds now occupied by the depot of the Maine Central Railroad Company, and prepare them for the use of the former company; to provide wood and materials for the construction of the road, which was then in process of building; and to pay the gravel-train men, and others in the employ of the company.

On the ninth of June, 1849, a locomotive steam-engine entered Brunswick for the first time. On the fourth of July, 1849, the track having been laid from Bath to Yarmouth, it was decided to put on a train of gravel cars, and with the first engine, the "Kennebec," and with such accommodations as could be prepared, to run the train back and forth between Bath and Yarmouth for the day, giving every one who desired it a "free ride." Though the train was composed chiefly of dump-cars, and the passengers probably paid for their ride in the discomfort attending it, yet it was to them a new and gratifying experience, and such was the delight of the public that many urged the directors to commence running a passenger train at once. To this request the directors acceded, and without any preparation of books, blanks, or tariffs, the train was put on the fifth of July, and continued to run regularly, carrying passengers to Yarmouth, and there transferring them to the cars of the Atlantic and St. Lawrence Railroad for Portland.

This sudden and unprepared-for event cast a good deal of labor and responsibility upon Mr. Cushing, who at once had tickets printed at the office of Mr. Griffin, for the four stations. In addition to this, freight began to flow on the road, and Mr. Cushing was instructed to fix such rates as he thought proper on all merchandise as it came in.

Mr. Joseph McKeen was the first treasurer of the road, and it was by his request that Mr. Cushing did whatever was necessary to meet the emergencies as they arose, and collect all moneys from ticket sales and conductors, and return to him. Thus Brunswick became suddenly a place of importance as the headquarters of the Kennebec and Portland Railroad Company, and as the place where the first impulse was given to the trains of this road.

The fares between the stations of the Kennebec and Portland Road and Portland were adjusted on the presumption that the Atlantic and St. Lawrence Company (now the Grand Trunk) would gladly receive so large a contribution of passengers at the same rate, twenty-five cents each, at which they transported stage passengers from Yarmouth to Portland. This amount the agent of the Kennebec and Portland Company added to the price of their tickets to Yarmouth, for all Portland passengers. Upon settlement with the Atlantic and St. Lawrence Company, at the close of the month of July, they claimed thirty-five cents, which was their local fare from Yarmouth to Portland, on all passengers coming over the Kennebec and Portland Road. They consented, however, to deduct *one half cent* from each ticket issued by the latter company, obliging them to pay thirty-four and a half cents on each passenger to Portland, although they had only received twenty-five cents each for that portion of the route. This action of the Atlantic and St. Lawrence Company was received with great indignation by the directors of the Kennebec and Portland Company. Two members each said that they would be one among ten to build a new road from Yarmouth to Portland, and it was in consequence of the unjust advantage thus taken of their necessities that the road was built about two years subsequently. This, however, was not the only disagreement between the two companies. The directors of the Kennebec and Portland Company solicited the other company to put down a third rail, and allow their trains (of a different gauge) to run on that road to Portland. This the Atlantic and St. Lawrence Company, speaking through their engineer, declared impracticable. After the new road was contracted for, however, they offered to give this accommodation, but were told, in reply, that it was then "impracticable." Thus the short-sighted policy of the Atlantic and St. Lawrence Company's directors was the cause of the building of the new road into Portland.[1]

Included in the purchase of the depot lot was a small, one-story, unfinished wooden building, which stood near Maine Street. This was hastily fitted up with ladies' and gentlemen's rooms, and a ticket-office between the two. The L was used for a baggage-room. The accommodations for passengers were small and poorly arranged. The building stood much nearer Maine Street than the present one. After the second depot was built, the first one was moved over to the north, next to the building once occupied by Isaac Center, and, at a later date by Mr. Poland, and was occupied by Ezekiel Thompson, the first baggage-master. It is still owned by the railroad company and leased by them as a dwelling. At the time the first depot was prepared, John S. Cushing acted as station agent, and George French as switchman. This was the force as organized at Brunswick, which was the *headquarters* of the road at that time.

The first engine went over the railroad bridge across the Androscoggin, below the falls, on the thirteenth of December, 1850, and cars ran to Augusta not long afterwards. The Topsham depot was erected in 1850–51.

The first large depot in Brunswick was finished in July, 1855. It was one hundred and sixty feet in length and about one hundred feet in width, including the two wings, the main body of the building being sixty feet in width, with a height of fifty-two feet to the ridge-pole. Three tracks ran through it. The north wing was divided into a ticket-office, with public waiting-rooms for gentlemen and ladies on either side, a refreshment-room, and a baggage-room. Space was also left for a stairway into the upper story of the building, where it was intended to have some of the office rooms of the company. The south wing was used for freight. This depot was burned in 1857. The present building was erected soon after. It is much larger now than it was originally, having received additions several times since its erection. Until 1870 there were but two tracks running through the depot, and the southern side of the building, where the third track is now, was used for the freight department. The freight-office

---

[1] *This matter, though rather beyond the scope of this History, is introduced here as a matter of interest to our citizens, and because it has never before appeared in print.*

and telegraph-office were in the southeastern corner. The waiting-rooms, refreshment-room, and ticket-office were small and inconvenient. In 1870 the present freight depot was built, and the passenger depot was enlarged and improved. Since then the refreshment-saloon and the ticket-office have been still further improved.

In the latter part of 1849, Mr. Cushing was taken into the office of Treasurer McKeen as book-keeper, in the place of Mr. George F. Dunning, who removed to Philadelphia.

In 1851, Mr. McKeen resigned his treasurership, and Mr. A. H. Gilman, of Portland, was elected; and in the following year the treasurer's office was removed to Augusta, where Mr. Cushing was continued as general ticket agent and freight accountant until 1857, when he was elected treasurer. In this capacity he has been continued through the different organizations of Portland and Kennebec and Maine Central Railroad Companies to the present time, — a period of twenty years. The length of the Kennebec and Portland Railroad was twenty-four miles in 1849, and that of the Maine Central in 1871 was three hundred and fifty-five miles.[1]

The LEWISTON AND TOPSHAM RAILROAD COMPANY was formed about 1853, with Francis T. Purinton, of Topsham, as its president. A road between these two places was surveyed but never laid out, and the company failed to do anything. This company was, however, the forerunner of the ANDROSCOGGIN RAILROAD, work on which was commenced in 1860, and the first trains on which ran regularly in October, 1861.

As illustrative of the difference in travel between the present and former times, it may be stated that in 1819, the time of travel between Brunswick and Boston was ordinarily three days, the very quickest being two and a half days, and the expense attending a trip was twelve dollars. Now, the time required is but six hours, and the expense three dollars and a quarter. Then there was one stage daily in each direction, passing through Brunswick. For a number of years after the railroad went into operation, there was but one passenger train a day each way, and the trains seldom had more than two passenger cars and a baggage car. At the same time a thrice-weekly freight train, each way, was all that was required.

Now, four passenger trains each way are run on the main line, with

---

[1] *For most of the facts given in the foregoing account we are indebted to Mr. Cushing, whose connection with this road from its first inception up to the present time renders his statements entitled to the fullest credence.*

from two to eight cars in each, and there are two regular freight trains each way daily, besides almost daily extra trains. In addition to these trains, there are on the Bath branch six trains daily, each way, including freight trains, and on the Lewiston branch there are four trains each way daily, including freight trains.

NAVIGATION.

In the very earliest times, before the era of stages or even of the introduction of horses to this region, before roads were even thought of, the travel was conducted exclusively by means of boats and vessels. The pioneer settlers always located themselves at or near the head of some navigable stream. It should be remembered that in those times the streams were all undammed and were all of them navigable for much larger craft than at present. Large vessels might then come to the foot of the falls of the Pejepscot without difficulty, and it was even possible to tow boats over the rapids.[1]

The earliest provision made for a boat of any size for use in this vicinity was in 1716. At a meeting of the proprietors, held February 21, of that year, it was voted, "That a proper boat be provided by Messrs. Minot & Watts with sails, oars, etc."[2] The intention of this vote may have been to furnish a boat for travel upon the river, but as the proprietors soon after purchased a sloop called the *Pejepscot*, for the purpose of establishing communication with Boston,[3] it is probable that the latter object was what was intended by their vote.

The next vessel to which reference is to be found was the sloop *Maquoit*, which was built by the proprietors and was used in carrying lumber and provisions between Maquoit and Boston.

There is some uncertainty as to whom belongs the credit of building the first vessel in this region, though it is probable that it was built on the New Meadows River. According to one authority, it was built by John Lemont, in 1745,[4] but by another it is said to have been constructed by George Harwood (with others).[5] Probably it was the same vessel, and more than one or two were interested in it.

The first vessel constructed at Middle Bay or Maquoit was built previous to the Revolution by Robert Dunning. The exact time is

---

[1] *Maine Historical Collection*, 3, *p*. 318.
[2] *Pejepscot Records*. [3] *McKeen, MS. Lecture.*
[4] *Lemont, Historical Dates of Bath, etc.*, *p*. 52.
[5] *McKeen, in Brunswick Telegraph*, "*Gleanings*," *No*. 4.

not known. In 1753 there were three sloops owned at Maquoit and New Meadows.[1]

In 1767 the schooner *Unity*, of Topsham, is mentioned in Brigadier Thompson's papers.

The first vessel launched above the Chops and the second above Bath was built by John Patten, William Patten, John Fulton, and Adam Hunter, of Topsham, about the year 1768. She was a sloop of about ninety tons, and was named the *Merry Meeting*. She was built for the purpose of coasting to Boston. When she was launched all the people in the neighboring towns came to see her, and were provided with a dinner. Captain William Patten was master of the *Merry Meeting*. He loaded her with wood and went to Boston and sold it for $1.50 per cord, two thirds of which went to the owners. At other times she was loaded with boards and timber.

Wages at that time were very low. Howard, the shipwright who built the *Merry Meeting*, received four shillings per day. He lived at New Meadows. Captains in the West India business received four pounds per month; mates, three pounds; seamen's wages were about six dollars. The sails and rigging for the *Merry Meeting* were purchased of Mr. Hooper ("King" Hooper he was called), of Salem.[2]

The *Defiance* was afterwards built and owned, principally, by John Patten. She was employed in coasting to Boston [3]

The schooner *Industry*, the first that ever went to the West Indies from the Kennebec, was owned by John Patten, his son Robert, his son-in-law Robert Fulton, Mr. Jameson, and Captain Harward. She was built about 1772. Captain James Maxwell was master. She was loaded the first time with boards, shingles, and four masts. A part of the boards were sawed at Cathance Mills and the rest at Topsham Falls. They were sold for four dollars per thousand. Captain Maxwell went twice to the West Indies in the *Industry*. She was sold during the Revolutionary war for paper money. Captain Robert Patten's eighth part enabled him to buy a horse and saddle for four hundred dollars.[4]

About 1790 the *Speedwell*, a coaster of ninety-seven tons' burden, under command of the Captain McLellan who married Molly Finney, ran between Brunswick and Boston. On one of her trips she landed at Bunganock, and took on board ninety cords of wood for Boston. The price here was three shillings and ninepence, and at Boston,

---

[1] *Memorandum on cover of Brunswick Records in Pejepscot Collections.*

[2] *Dr. Ellis. Notes of Robert Patten.* [3] *Ibid.* [4] *Ibid.*

twelve shillings per cord. The crew were four in number, and the average wages of each was seven dollars per month.

Several vessels were owned in Brunswick in 1790. On September 13, 1791, John Peterson made a request to the selectmen of Brunswick for an abatement of the tax on "one of my vessels, as she was cast ashore last Christmas day on Cape Cod, and by that accident I lost the value of one year's earnings of said schooner."[1]

The brig *Hope* was built in Brunswick by William Stanwood and John Dunlap, a short time previous to 1800. They sold a portion to Richard Tappan. In January, 1800, she sailed from Bath for Barbadoes, West Indies, loaded with about one hundred and thirty thousand feet of boards, and one hundred and five thousand shingles and other small lumber. The crew consisted of Richard Tappan, master; John Dunlap, Junior, mate; and Melzer House, John McDonald, Noah Moulton, Thomas Stanwood, and Philip Cornish, seamen. They reached Barbadoes safely, and from thence proceeded to the island of Tobago, where Captain Tappan met with a Mr. Kerr, of Grenada, to whom he sold his cargo of boards at the rate of forty dollars per thousand, and the shingles at four or five dollars per thousand, to be delivered at the island of Grenada. They sailed from Tobago on the third of March, and the same night, between Tobago and Grenada, they were boarded and taken possession of by a French privateer from Gaudaloupe. All the crew except the captain were taken out, and the brig was sent into Basseterre, Gaudaloupe, where she was condemned. The first officer and crew were imprisoned, but through the interference of a Danish merchant they were released and went on board of a vessel which he had purchased there and went with him to Santa Cruz. From thence they went to Saint Thomas, where they waited for an American convoy from St. Kitts, which arrived in a few days. With this convoy was the brig *Hannibal*, owned by the Dunlaps, commanded by Captain Nehemiah Peterson. This brig had also been taken by a French privateer, but had been retaken by the United States man-of-war *John Adams*. Captain Tappan and John Dunlap returned home in the *Hannibal*, the rest of the crew in the *Iris*, commanded by Captain Samuel Snow.

About the year 1800 the ship-yard at Brunswick called Skolfield's was constructed, and vessels began to be built there.

About the year 1802 a vessel of sixty-three tons was built at Lisbon by a Captain Woodward, launched into the Androscoggin during

---

[1] *Pejepscot Papers.*

a freshet and brought down as far as the booms above the upper dam. Here she was taken out of the water and hauled on rollers through the woods to what is now McKeen Street, thence down Maine Street to the cove, where she was again launched into the river and did good service for about twenty-five years. Dean Swift well remembers the circumstance, though but a boy at the time. He says one hundred yoke of oxen were employed in hauling the vessel on the land.

In 1808, Mr. Robert Given built a gunboat for the United States navy, in a yard a little north of the ship-yard of the Skolfields, on Harpswell Neck. The contract, still preserved, was for thirty dollars per ton, the iron to cost twelve dollars and fifty cents per one hundred pounds, the vessel to be heavily timbered, and the gun-deck to be of white oak and yellow pine.

In 1819, George F. Patten & Brothers built the brig *Statira*, of one hundred and eighty-three tons, at Muddy River, Topsham.

About 1820 there were in the neighborhood of 1,000 tons of shipping in Brunswick and Topsham, and about 2,000 tons in Harpswell, besides numerous small fishing-vessels. On September 20, of this year, the shipping list of the *Maine Intelligencer* contained the announcement of the arrival at Brunswick of the brig *America*, Otis, from Martinique, with one hundred and forty-six hogsheads of molasses consigned to the owners, Messrs. Dunlap; of the sloop *Eliza*, Douglas (regular packet), from Boston; of the brig *Maine*, Sylvester, with a cargo of molasses and sugar, and schooner *Susan*, Rodick, from the southward, both to D. Stone and others.

The brig *Maine* appears to have been a regular packet, as this same list, under date of September 29, mentions its arrival from Boston, together with the sloop *Ambition*, with freight and passengers. A brig also arrived the same day from Bath.

A wharf was built about this time on the New Meadows River, and one, seven hundred and fifty feet in length, at Maquoit.[1]

Pennell's ship-yard, at Middle Bay, was built about 1822. Wharves were also erected on the west side of Maquoit Bay about this time.

In 1823 a small schooner called the *Elizabeth*, which was built about 1793 on Sebascodegan Island, was cast away at the southern part of Condy's Point in the month of February. The crew, consisting of four men, were all badly frost-bitten. They were taken care of by the good people on the island until they were sufficiently recovered to go to their homes in Massachusetts. The schooner was loaded with fruit, groceries, and spirit.

---

[1] *Putnam, Description of Brunswick.*

About the same year a vessel was built at Durham and hauled over land to Maquoit. It was built by a person of doubtful gender, who at first wore woman's apparel and afterwards changed them for man's, and who was at first called Hannah, but afterwards Stover.

Not far from this time Mr. Robert Labish built a vessel of about four hundred tons in Topsham. He had his lumber all ready at Lisbon to be conveyed to Topsham, but the winter being mild and the roads bare, he was unable to have it carried where he wished. Being a man of energy and determination, he went with a party of men, and, guided by a compass, cut a road through the woods to Lisbon, and hauled his timber through it. This road (not a highway) is still in existence, and is called Labish's Road.

In the winter of 1824, Mr. Godfrey, of Topsham, built a vessel in Lisbon and had it conveyed on runners to Topsham, where it was launched. The experiment was a costly one, as the expense of getting her to Topsham more than offset the cheapness of the materials at Lisbon.

October 11, 1825, the sloop *Ambition*, owned by Samuel Lemont, of Brunswick, and commanded by a Captain Perkins, went ashore at Sandy Bay, on Cape Ann, Massachusetts, on her way to Brunswick, and went to pieces. She had a full cargo of dry goods, valued at $10,000, none of which was insured. A part was saved, however, in a damaged condition. The goods were for Messrs. Stone & Morse, E. Earle & Co., O. Nichols, and William Snowdon, of Brunswick, J. Dwinal, of Lisbon, and the Maine Cotton and Woollen Factory, of Brunswick.

March 27, 1830, during a severe northeast snow-storm, several sloops in Maquoit Bay were stranded and a portion of the wharf there was carried away.

What is known now as the New Wharf Ship-Yard was first used as such in 1830. The new wharf itself was built in 1837, by Captain Anthony Chase, Captain William Stanwood, Israel Simpson, Samuel Dunning, Captain Robert Simpson, Captain John Given, David Dunlap, Doctor Isaac Lincoln, and Stone & Morse.[1] Its cost was between $3,000 and $4,000.

The earliest reference to what is known as the Alfred White Ship-Yard, in Topsham, is in 1842. On October 8, of that year, the brig *Bernard*, of one hundred and sixty tons, owned by B. C. Bailey, of Bath, was launched there.

---

[1] *Samuel Dunning.*

The first regular packet vessel, excepting those under the control of the proprietors, is believed to have been the sloop *Friendship*. In May, 1814, she was advertised to ply between Portland, Harpswell, Bath, and Brunswick, coming up the New Meadows River to the Turnpike bridge, until she could have permission to go round Small Point, and then she was to run to Hallowell and Augusta, as usual.[1] She was, possibly, debarred from going up the Kennebec in consequence of the smuggling carried on at that time beween Augusta and Castine, the latter being then under British authority.

The next packet to which any reference has been found was the sloop *Caroline*, Skolfield, master, which was advertised on September 9, 1824, to sail from Brunswick for Norfolk and Baltimore. She had "superior accommodations for eight or ten passengers."

On April 1, 1829, the sloop *Hope*, Captain Connelly, having been completely repaired, was advertised to ply regularly between Bourne's Wharf, at New Meadows, and Boston. The *Hope* continued on this route for several years.

On March 24, 1830, the packet *Maquoit*, Captain Anthony Chase, was advertised to ply between Brunswick and Portland. At the same time the sloop *Orlando*, Captain Dunning, was advertised to go between Maquoit and Boston.

March 7, 1834, the sloop *Union*, Captain Jordan Woodward, was advertised to make regular trips between Maquoit and Boston. In 1836 the schooner *Boston* took her place on this route.

In 1842 the "new and splendid" schooner *Alice*, Captain Robert Chase, made regular trips between Brunswick and Boston, touching at Portland. Her first trip was on May fourth. She was built expressly for this route and contained "superior accommodations for passengers." On June fifteenth, of the same year, an opposition packet, the schooner *Accommodation*, Captain Anthony Morse, was put upon the same route.

Some uncertainty exists as to the first steamer which ever made its appearance on the Androscoggin. Mr. Dean Swift, who has an excellent memory, and whose statements relative to many other events have been proved by recorded facts to be remarkably correct, says that the first steamer was a small, flat-bottomed one that was built about 1819, in Wiscasset, by a lawyer of the name of Gordon; that he came up the Androscoggin in this little steamer, and then returned to Wiscasset with her. Mr. Swift says, furthermore, that a year or

---

[1] *North's History of Augusta*, p. 417.

two later Gordon built another small, flat-bottomed steamboat at Brunswick, and went with her to Hallowell and thence to Bath, where he sold her to Jere Hunt, who took her to New Meadows, cut her in two, and made two gondolas of her. This statement is undoubtedly *substantially* correct. Mr. Samuel Dunning, however, thinks Gordon built his steamer on the Androscoggin as early as 1816, and he is positive that it was sold to the owners of Maquoit Wharf, and not to Mr. Hunt.

Lemont[1] says that the first steamer which ever went up the *Kennebec* was the *Tom Thumb*. He says she was brought down from Boston in tow of a packet in 1818, and steamed up the river; that she was an open boat, about twenty-five or thirty feet long, with side wheels and with her machinery all in sight. He says, further, that the second steamer was fitted up on Governor King's Wharf, in Bath, in 1822, and that she was a flat-bottomed boat, and was called the *Kennebec*.

This statement conflicts with that of Mr. Swift only so far as relates to the Kennebec River. Very likely the *Tom Thumb* was the first steamer to ascend the Kennebec, and the fact of a steamer coming from Wiscasset to Brunswick and Topsham a year later may not have come to the knowledge of Mr. Lemont.

In 1823 the steamer *Patent*, Captain Porter, which had just been put on the route between Boston and Bath,[2] touched at Pennell's Wharf at Commencement time at Bowdoin College. In 1824[3] she ran between Boston and St. John, Nova Scotia. In 1825[4] she was advertised to run between New Wharf, in Brunswick, and Portland. It is thought she made but a few trips to New Wharf before her landing-place was changed to Bourne's Wharf, at New Meadows, where a stage for Bath connected with her.[5]

The first and only steamboat that ever made regular trips to Middle Bay was the *Flushing*, Captain Robert Chase, which plied regularly between Portland and New Wharf from 1846 to 1849. J. S. Cushing was the agent. No steamboat is known to have ever run regularly from Maquoit.

The steamboat *Rough and Ready* used to go up and down the Androscoggin, about 1847, on excursions.

On May 12, 1855, the steamboat *Victor*, built by Master Sampson, and owned by John R. Hebberd, F. T. Littlefield, and Mr. Woodside,

---

[1] *Historical Dates of Bath, etc.*, pp. 71, 72.
[2] *History of Camden*, p. 153.
[3] *Ibid.*
[4] *Advertisement.*
[5] *Traditional.*

was launched at Topsham. She was well modelled and thoroughly built, was eighty feet long and twenty-four feet beam. Her engine was rated at forty horse-power. John R. Hebberd commanded her. She was intended for pleasure excursions and for a tow-boat. She made her first pleasure trip about the first of June. She was the first steamboat ever built in Topsham, and the second built on the Androscoggin.

In 1856 the pleasure-boat *Elijah Kellogg*, twenty-two feet in keel and seven feet in beam, built by John Given, was advertised to take pleasure parties from Pennell's or Chase's Wharf. She was built expressly for this business, and is thought to be the first of the kind built here. There are numerous pleasure-yachts owned here at the present day.

TELEGRAPH.

The first movement for a telegraph office in Brunswick was in 1853. On August 6, of that year, a meeting was held at the Tontine Hotel to take some action relative to securing the establishment of a telegraph office in the town. Remarks were made by General A. B. Thompson, Honorable C. J. Gilman, and General J. C. Humphreys. Messrs. W. G. Barrows, C. J. Noyes, and T. S. McLellan were appointed a committee to procure the necessary information upon which to proceed, and the meeting adjourned to be called together again by the chairman, Colonel A. J. Stone, whenever the committee were ready to report. There is no report of another meeting, but the exertions of this committee undoubtedly led the way to the establishment of an office in town. The telegraph office was opened for the first time to the public in Brunswick, in January, 1854.

The line was owned by the Maine Telegraph Company, and its wires extended from Boston to Calais. This line was afterwards leased to the American Telegraph Company, and still later to the Western Union Telegraph Company.

The first operator in Brunswick was M. H. Prescott. The office was situated on the corner of Maine Street and the depot grounds. It was afterwards removed to the depot, where, with the exception of a single year, it has remained.

The only opposition line east of Portland, previous to 1877, was that of the International Telegraph Company, which established an office in Brunswick in 1867. In 1872 the line was sold to the Western Union Company, and the instruments were removed to their office.

In 1877 the Atlantic and Pacific Telegraph Company opened an office in Brunswick.

EXPRESSES AND HACKS.

Upon the completion of the railroad in 1849, Carpenter & Co. established an express route and opened an office in Brunswick on the first day of August of that year. Mr. A. L. Stanwood was appointed agent, and the office was in his store under the Mason Street Church. Subsequently the company consolidated with other companies under the name of the Eastern Express Company. In 1852 the office was moved to a building which stood on the lot opposite the foot of the mall, where Eaton's harness-shop is now. A few years later the building and office were removed to their present location adjoining the Tontine Hotel. Mr. Stanwood has continued the agent up to the present time, and it is worthy of record that during all this time he has not been absent from duty for any cause, excepting for one day about the year 1854.

The first public carriage other than stages was run to the depot by a Mr. Bean, upon the first opening of the road in 1849, and for a few years subsequently. Mr. Ephraim Griffin began during the same year, and has served the public faithfully as a hackman from that time to the present. Other persons have owned or driven public carriages for a longer or shorter time.

CHAPTER XI.

BURIAL-PLACES AND EPITAPHS.

"I WOULD *rather*," remarks Edmund Burke, "*sleep in the southern corner of a little country churchyard than in the tomb of the Capulets*"; and doubtless the same sentiment is felt, if not expressed, by many whose departed friends repose in rural graveyards.

The method of conducting funerals in olden times was substantially the same as at present, so far as relates to the performance or non-performance of religious rites. The mode of carrying the remains of the dead, however, from the house to their last resting-place, was slightly different.

Previous to the introduction of the first hearse, in 1818 in Brunswick, and still later in Topsham and Harpswell, bodies were carried to the grave on stretchers and the coffin covered with a pall. In Brunswick, the pall was kept, at one time, by Mrs. Benjamin Stone. Usually eight men accompanied the corpse, four carrying it until tired and then being relieved by the other four. The stretchers, or biers, were made of poles, young trees with the bark on, and were discarded after being once used. They were not made for permanent use, but were hastily made for each occasion.

Many of the burying-grounds in this vicinity are of old date. The earliest one in Brunswick of which there is any record or tradition was situated about midway between Bow and Mill Streets, fronting on Maine Street. It was just south of and adjoining the stone fort built by Governor Andross in 1689. This graveyard was used for the burial of the dead until about the time of the incorporation of the town. In this yard was the stone marking the burial-place of Benjamin Larrabee, agent of the Pejepscot proprietors, one of the commanders of Fort George, and the ancestor of the Larrabees now living in this vicinity. Here also were the gravestones of Robert and Andrew Dunning, who were killed by the Indians at Mason's rock. The site of this yard is now covered with buildings.

Another graveyard, probably of still earlier date, though nothing whatever is known in regard to it, was situated on what is now a portion of Woodlawn Street, on the estate of Miss Narcissa Stone.

On the thirty-first of May, 1856, two skeletons were exhumed by the workmen engaged in grading the street. It is not unreasonable to suppose that these were the remains of some of Purchase's fishermen, and if so, they were undoubtedly the first white people buried in this village, though perhaps not the first in the town.

The old graveyard of the First Parish, Brunswick, situated one mile south of the colleges, has been occupied as such since 1735. In this burying-ground are many stones the inscriptions upon which are illegible, and in some instances the stones themselves have crumbled to pieces, so that only a small portion of each one remains. Of those which can be deciphered the following are of interest on account of their age, the quaintness of the inscriptions, or the character of those they commemorate: —

HERE LYETH THE BO
DY OF MR ANDREW
DUNING
WHO DEPARTED THIS
LIFE JANUARY THE
18TH ANNODOM
1736
AGED 72 YRS.

1660 Charles 2d
1685 James 2d
1689 Wm & Mary
1702 Queen Ann
1714 George 1st
1727 George 2d

1664

1666 Lordon Burnt

HERE LYES BURIED THE BODY OF
SAMUEL MOODY, ESQ.
one of his Majesty's Justs of ye
Peace for the County of York
& Commander of his Majestys Fort
George at Brunswick who D'ceas'd
Sept. 22-1758.

Sacred
TO THE MEMORY OF
REV. ROBERT DUNLAP.
First settled minister of Brunswick,
Born in Ireland, Aug. 1715
Educated in Edinburgh;
Came to America, June 1736:
Settled at Brunswick, 1747;
Died June 26, 1775,
Æt. 60.
"Behold a Sower went forth to sow."

The two following epitaphs are from stones in the old Baptist Burying-Ground, at Maquoit. This graveyard was first used as such about 1794.

The first epitaph reads thus : —

> "To be much lov'd in life much mourn'd in death,
> A widow'd husband of a wife bereft,
> With tears inscribes this monumental stone,
> Which holds her ashes and expects his own."

The second is evidently that of a man accustomed to serious and deep thought. It runs thus : —

> "This languishing head is at rest,
> Its thinking and aching are o'er."

The old burying-ground at New Meadows was first used as such some time in the latter part of the last century. It contains the head-stones of many former residents of that part of the town, but there are none that require particular notice here.

The burying-ground at "Growstown" in Brunswick was first used about 1813. The following inscriptions are found in it : —

In memory of
ELD GEORGE LAMB
who departed this life
Dec 14 - 1836
Æt 48

Mr. Lamb was converted to God at the agė of 15 and engaged in the ministry at the age of 23. He laboured faithfully in his Masters service 25 years and died in full assurance of a blessed immortality beyond the grave.
Remember how he spake unto you when he was yet with you.

The following epitaph, which appears to us entitled to an insertion here, is to be found in this graveyard : —

> "Dear husband while you *spill* your tears
> In numbering o'er past happy years,
> But yet remember while you weep,
> With me you in the grave must sleep;
> But the last trumpet we shall hear,
> Before our God we must appear,
> And then with Jesus we shall reign
> And never part nor weep again."

Pine Grove Cemetery, in the village of Brunswick, a short distance east of the colleges, was laid out in the year 1825. The land originally was a part of the college grounds, but in 1821 it was deeded, by vote of the trustees, to Robert Eastman, Nahum Houghton, Abner Bourne, "and their associates, heirs, executors, administrators, or assigns," so long as it should be used for the interment of the dead, and if not so used, to revert to the college. The amount of land thus deeded was two acres, which was bounded as follows, "Beginning at the southwesterly side of the old County Road leading to Bath, at a stake and stone at or near the angle which it makes with the Bath turnpike, and running by said turnpike west 20°, north 12 rods, thence south 20°, west 26⅔ rods, thence east 20°, south 12 rods, and thence north 20°, east 26⅔ rods to the first boundary." The trustees also reserved the exclusive right at all times to hold as a place of interment for the dead "that part of the premises extending from said turnpike road on the westerly line of said lot, eighteen rods in length, and one and a half rods in breadth," subject only to such general regulations as should be binding upon other owners of lots.[1]

This cemetery is pleasantly situated, with handsome grounds and walks, which are kept in good order; it is enclosed with a neat and ornamental fence, and contains many handsome monuments and memorial tablets. Major Lemuel Swift was the first person buried here. Among the monuments and headstones to be seen there are those of Presidents McKeen and Appleton; Professors Cleaveland, Upham, and Smyth; and Governor Dunlap.

The tomb of President McKeen is in the extreme northwestern angle of the cemetery, the head toward Bath Street. In form, this tomb is an oblong rectangle, covering the grave, and about three feet in height. The pedestal is of Egyptian marble, and is surmounted by a heavy slab of white marble, which bears the following inscription:—

H. S. E.

QUOD MORTALE FUIT

VIRI ADMODUM REVERENDI,

DNI JOSEPHI McKEEN, S. T. D.

AC COLLEGII BOWDOINENSIS PRÆSIDIS PRIMI.

Natus est Octob^s^ die XV° Anno Dom. MDCCLVII,
in Republicâ Neo-Hautoniensi,
ubi primò in literis humanioribus institutus,
honores attigit Academicos.

---

[1] *From original deed.*

Postea VERBI DIVINI ministerio apud Beverleam,
in Republicâ Massachusettensi,
annos septendecim
strenuè juxta, ac benignè perfunctus est.
Novissimè autem, Nostratium omnium favore,
ac præcipuè doctorum piorumque,
Collegium hic loci auspicato fundatum,
quinque vix annos,
eâ, quâ par est, dignitate et sapentiâ,
fideliter, feliciter rexit;
donec, morbo Hydropico impeditus,
Julii die XV° Ann. MDCCCVII, in Domino abdormivit.
Ingenio fuit sagaci, judicio imprimis acerrimo,
priscorum temporum gravitate æmulus,
moribus autem facilis,
et benevolentiâ omninò Christianus.
Pietatem, doctrinam, artes optimas,
quoniam gnaviter excolebat ipse,
in aliis semper amavit, et quoad potuit, auxit.

M. S.

Monumentum hocce,
luctus, eheu! solamen leve,
at testimonium tamen,
SENATVS ACADEMICVS,
P. C.[1]

In the adjoining lot south is the monument of President Appleton. Its form is the same as that of President McKeen. The following is the inscription: —

---

[1] *Here is buried what was mortal of the reverend and most learned man, Joseph McKeen, S. T. D., the first president of Bowdoin College. He was born October* 15, *A D.* 1742, *in the State of New Hampshire, where, first of all, instructed in secular learning, he attained academic honors. Afterwards he discharged, actively as well as kindly, the duty of a minister of the Gospel, at Beverly, in the Commonwealth of Massachusetts, for seventeen years. But lately, a college having been auspiciously founded here in this town, not quite five years, with the approbation of all our countrymen, and especially of the educated and pious, he presided over it, as is meet, with dignity and wisdom, faithfully and fortunately, until, embarrassed by a dropsical disease, on the fifteenth day of July, in the year* 1807, *he fell asleep in the Lord. He was a Christian of sagacious mind, of especially acute discernment, in dignity emulous of former times, but courteous in manner and uniformly kind. He always loved in others, as he himself diligently cultivated, piety, education, the best occupations, and, so far as he could, he promoted them. Sacred to the memory, This monument of grief, alas! slight consolation, but yet a testimony, the Academic Council have caused to be placed.*

Huic tumulo mandantur reliquiæ
REV. JESSE APPLETON, S. T. D.
MARITI DESIDERATISSIMI. PATRIS OPTIMI.
ALMEQUE NOSTRÆ ACADEMIÆ
SECUNDI PRESIDIS.
Vir fuit ingenii acumine insignis, moribus
compositis, ac aspectu benigno,
majestatem quondam præ
se ferente;
sed morti inexorabili nihil est sanctum.
Eruditione magna,
inter literatorum principes justissime collocandus;
at theologicæ scientiæ lauream præcipue meritus:
hac enim, quo homines audeant,
cognovit et tentavit.
Integra fide, disciplinaque salutari,
duodecim annos,
res Academicas administravit.
Nimiis tandem vigiliis laboribusque consumptus,
sublimii ejus animo supernis intento,
ad quietem se contulit.
Ita vixit, ut omnes moribundi, sic se vixisse,
velint; ita mortuus est,
ut omnes, sic se morituros esse, optarent:
tamen voluit inscribi, se salutem sperasse in Jesu.
Natus est Novem.is die 17mo
Anno Domini MDCCLXXII.
Obiit Novem.is die 12mo Anno
Domini MDCCCXIX.[1]

On the south end of the tomb is inscribed: —

Senatus Academiæ Bowdoinensis,
summa reverentia,
hoc monumentum posuerunt.[2]

---

[1] *To this tomb are committed the remains of Reverend Jesse Appleton, S. T. D. The most regretted husband, the best father, and the revered second president of our college. He was a man distinguished by acuteness of mind, composed manners, and benign aspect, occasionally manifesting dignity: but nothing is sacred to inexorable death. Of great erudition, most justly placed amongst the first of teachers, but especially deserving the laurel in theological knowledge: for this, where men may presume, he examined and tested. He administered the affairs of the college with incorruptible fidelity and with salutary discipline for twelve years. At length, worn out by excessive vigils and labors, his exalted mind fixed upon celestial things, he betook himself to rest. He so lived as all who are at the point of death may wish themselves to have lived: thus he died, as all themselves about to die might desire. Yet he wished it to be inscribed that he hoped for salvation in Jesus. He was born November* 17, 1772. *He died November* 12, 1819.

[2] *The trustees and overseers of Bowdoin College, with the greatest reverence, have erected this monument.*

In the third lot south of President Appleton's is the monument of Professor Smyth. It is a heavy, rectangular pillar of granite, about ten feet in height. The pedestal bears the family name, while on the northern side of the shaft is the following inscription : —

WILLIAM SMYTH
born Feb. 2d 1797, died April 4th 1868.

Below this is the name of his wife, with the date of her birth and death, and on the eastern side is a record of the names and dates of birth and death of several children.

The second lot south of Professor Smyth's contains the monument of Professor Cleaveland, a plain yet elegant granite sarcophagus. On the eastern side it bears the words "Parker Cleaveland" ; on the south end is the date of his birth, 1780, while on the north is that of his death, 1852. Two headstones of white marble, one upon the east and one upon the west, mark the resting-places of wife and daughter.

The monument of Professor Upham stands in the next lot southward of Professor Cleaveland's. This also, like the two last, is of plain granite, and is in form an obelisk. The pedestal is proportionately large, and bears on the western side the initials T. C. U. ; while on the south side is the date of birth, 1799, and on the north are the figures 1872, the date of his death. The plinth bears the family name in distinct raised letters.

The Dunlap monument is situated near the principal entrance to the cemetery. It consists of a base, sub-base, plinth, die, — with three marble tablets inserted, — cap, and bust of Dunlap. It is, without the bust, ten feet, four inches high, and of granite, though the bust is of marble. It was made by Simmons. Upon the north tablet is the following inscription : —

To the Memory
of
ROBERT PINCKNEY DUNLAP,
who was three times
GRAND MASTER
of the
GRAND LODGE OF MAINE,
and
filled the highest places in the
Masonic Fraternity
of the State and the
UNITED STATES,

This monument is erected by the
FREE MASONS
of the
STATE OF MAINE.
They knew his virtues;
They honor his memory.

On the west side: —

ROBERT P. DUNLAP
was
GOVERNOR OF MAINE
from 1834 to 1838.
He had been
Representative, Senator, and
twice President of the Senate,
in the State Legislature;
and Executive Councillor; and was
afterwards representative in
Congress and Collector of the
Port of Portland.
He honored
every position he was called to fill
by an able and faithful discharge
of its duties.
THE STATE
gives to his memory the tribute
of its respect by inscribing
upon this tablet its grateful
recollection of his many virtues
and its high appreciation of
his public services.

On the east side is the following: —

DEAREST
TO THE NEAREST:
BEST
TO THEM WHO KNEW HIM BEST.
In Christ here:
With Christ forever.
Died
Oct. 20, 1859.
Æt. 65.
Inscribed
by wife and children
in loving and reverent
remembrance.

One of the oldest graveyards in town is that at New Meadows in the woods near Bartlett Adams's, where rest the remains of several members of the Thompson family. There are other burying grounds in Brunswick, some of which are of recent dates and require no particular mention in these pages.

The oldest burying-ground in Topsham of which there are now any traces was in the vicinity of James Mustard's residence, about two miles from the village on the road to Merrymeeting Bay. There are but three or four stones remaining. They are of slate, and are in a good state of preservation. They are in the woods about a third of a mile from the road. The earliest date given upon these stones is 1752, and the latest 1771.

The burying-ground near the old First Parish Meeting-House is the oldest in this town of which there is any *record*.

In 1769 the town purchased of James Hunter "the land on the south side of the county road where the graveyard is," paying therefor three pounds; and the same year the town appropriated £5 6*s*. 8*d*. "for fencing the graveyard, nine rods square, with white oak or cedar posts and good boards, with a good gate, with a lock and key, the fence to be five feet high." There are a few stones, the inscriptions upon which are illegible, whether from greater age or poorer slate cannot be determined. The earliest date to be found upon any stone is 1769. The following are a few of the more interesting inscriptions to be found in this burying ground: —

HIC JACENT SEPULTA
the Remains of
PHILIP G. HOYT PHYSICIAN
who died June 24th 1790
ÆTATIS 36.

I'm to this silent Grave retired,
Though once esteemed and desired;
All human ills had once a place,
And weighed justly in this breast,
All mortal griefs are now past o'er,
A broken heart can bleed no more.

PHILIP G. HOYT'S EPITAPH ON HIMSELF NOV ye 23d 1789.

Sacred to the memory of
JOHN REED ESQUIRE,
A Capt in the late American War where he served with reputation till
obliged to retire in consequence of a wound received in an action
a little preceding the capture of Genl Burgoine and
army. He so far recovered his health and
activity that he was elected to and
sustained the office of Lt.
Col. till his death.

He was an affectionate Husband and Parent and his hospitality endeared him to many who mourned his
departure which was suddenly, in a
paroxism of the cholic on the
20th day of Oct. A. D. 1797.
Aged 50 years.

LIEUT JAMES PURINTON
Dec 7th 1832
Aged 90 years.
One of the revolutionary officers and Staunch supporters of the
Republican Constitution.

Several stones bear the following inscription : —

Behold and see as you pass by,
As you are now so once was I,
As I am now so you must be,
Prepare for death and follow me.

The third burying-ground in Topsham, in point of age, is the one about a mile west of the village, where the first Baptist or "old yellow" meeting-house used to stand. In this ground are the remains of John Merrill, Esquire, Captain Peletiah Haley, and others of the early settlers who lived in that portion of the town.

There was formerly a private burying-ground on what was known as "Ferry Point" (the point of land at the Topsham end of the iron railroad bridge). Here were buried the remains of Brigadier-General Thompson and others of the family. When the railroad was laid out, the remains were removed to the village graveyard, those of Brigadier Thompson being placed in the grave with his son, Humphrey Thompson.

The village burying-ground in Topsham was laid out in 1825. It is owned by the proprietors of the lots. The unoccupied land is owned by Mrs. Susan T. Purinton. Among the inscriptions of particular interest in this ground are the following : —

ERECTED
by the Baptist
Church in Topsham
In Memory of
REV. CHARLES JOHNSON
their Pastor, who died
Feb. 29, 1836
in the 30th year
of his age.

Behold a Christian's grave — He walked with God
In the same path the dear Redeemer trod;
He loved the Church and prayed for its increase
Lived much belov'd & died in perfect peace.

Sacred
to
THE MEMORY OF
REV. OLIVER H. QUINBY
who, having zealously proclaimed a full and free Salvation
for all mankind through Christ, for nearly two
years, fell gently asleep in the arms of
Jesus, at his residence in Lisbon,
Jany. 23d 1842
Aged 23 years.

"Glory to God" he cried,
Then bowed his head and died,
His soul was borne on angels wings
To blissful rest, where seraphs sing.

There are four graveyards in Harpswell, one upon the Neck, one on Great Island, one upon Orr's, and one upon Bailey's Island, the oldest of which is the one adjoining the old First Parish Meeting-House. The oldest stone in this yard is undecipherable. It was probably placed there about 1758. There are several interesting gravestones in this yard, which the space at our disposal prevents us from giving. We insert here, however, the inscriptions upon the tombstones of the first pastor of that church, and of his wife, and also of William McNess, of the second pastor of the church, and of Deacon Andrew and Benjamin Dunning. The inscription upon Elisha Eaton's stone is as follows: —

HERE LYES INTERRED THE BODY OF THE
REVD MR. ELISHA EATON,
first Pastor of the Church in Harpswell who
triumphantly Departed this Life on
the 22d of April, A. D. 1764.
In the 62d Year of his Age.
Est Commune mori,
Mors nulli Parcit Honori,
Neque ulli Ætati
Ergo. MEMENTO MORI.[1]

---

[1] *To die is common, death spares no nobility nor any age. Therefore remember death.*

The inscription on his wife's tombstone is : —

To the Memory of
MRS KATHARINE EATON,
THE VIRTUOUS RELICT OF THE REV. MR
ELISHA EATON, WHO DEPARTED
THIS LIFE APRIL 12, 1767, Æ. 61.

Here, Passenger, confin'd reduc'd to Dust,
Lies what was once religious. wise & just,
Fixt, in deep Slumbers here the Dust is giv'n.
Til the last Trumpet shakes the Frame of Heav'n,
Then fresh to Life the Waking Saint shall rise,
And in new Triumphs glitter up the skies,
Like her be virtuous, you like her shall shine,
In Bliss above, immortal & divine.

The inscriptions upon the other stones are as follows : —

HERE LIES BURIED
the Body of
MR WILLIAM MACKNES,
who DeParted
this Life May
ye 12th 1782
Age 103
years Old.

THE REV. SAMUEL EATON,
2d MINISTER OF HARPSWELL,
born April 3 1737
graduated at Harvard College 1763
Ordained Oct 24, 1764,
& died Nov. 5, 1822.
in the 86 year of his age
& 59th of his Ministry.

Blessed are the dead who die in the Lord.

Sacred to the memory of
DEAC. ANDREW DUNNING,
who was chosen Deac. of the Church in this town, June 17, 1767;
which office he filled till his decease, March 27, 1808. Æ. 81.

His life was useful his death peaceful.

Sleep sweetly in the grave of rest,
Which Christ perfumed and also blest
Till he shall call thee to the skies,
Shall bid thy sacred dust arise!

Survivors walk Christ's path as straight
And enter in the heavenly gate.

To the memory of
BENJ'A DUNNING ESQ.
who with the utmost composure breathed his last Jan. 8, 1808
Æt 71. As a Husband, Parent, Christian, and civil Magistrate he was conspicuous. The Town, which for many years he represented, The Board of Overseers of Bowdoin College, and in fine, civil society, are deprived of a useful, wise and peaceful member.

But tho' his loss fills us with grief and pain
Our loss is his inestimable gain —— For
Thro' the ethereal blue, his soul immortal,
Borne on angelic wings, at the third Heaven
Arriv'd the spirits of just men made perfect,
Joined in lofty hallelujahs to the sacred
Time, eternity throughout.

In this connection it is proper to mention the discovery, in 1861, of an undoubted Indian burying-ground in Harpswell. It is on the farm of Henry Barnes, on the eastern side of Middle Bay, near the shore. Fourteen skeletons have been disinterred. Though of course there are no headstones, it is known to have been an Indian burying-place by the appearance of the skeletons, the ornaments found on or near them, its vicinity to the "carrying-place," a tradition to that effect, and lastly by the testimony of a party of seven Penobscot Indians who once stopped there on their way to Portland, and who pointed out the spot as an Indian burying-place and stated that there was once an Indian village near by.

CHAPTER XII.

ECCLESIASTICAL HISTORY OF BRUNSWICK.

EARLY PROVISIONS FOR PUBLIC WORSHIP.

The Commonwealth of Massachusetts, by its incorporation of the town of Lebanon in 1733, established the precedent, which it has generally followed since, of requiring towns, when incorporated, to set apart three lots, one for the ministry, one for schools, and one for the first settled minister.[1]

The Pejepscot proprietors did not, however, wait for any legal enactment of this kind, but very early set apart the required amount of land both in Brunswick and in Topsham, and also assisted in the erection of a meeting-house in each town.

In 1715 they voted that the meeting-house should be located midway between the fort and Maquoit, and that the lots for the ministry, the first minister, and the school be the centre lots.

In 1717 the General Court voted to pay seven hundred and fifty dollars annually for missions to the Indians, with board and lodging for the missionaries. The latter were accordingly sent to Brunswick as well as to other places.[2] It was probably in consequence of the above-mentioned vote that on October 3, 1717, several of the "praying" Indians sent a petition to the General Court, "That ye Great Governor and Councill would order a small Praying-house to be built near the ffort the English and VS to meet in on Sabbath days.

"Sabatis [Mark]
Warenowbe [Mark]
Heneque [Mark][3]

"Fort George at Brunswick
Oct ye 3 1717.
John Gyles, *Interpreter.*"

The missionary to Maine was Reverend Joseph Baxter, of Medfield, Massachusetts, and "he was particularly urged to use his best endeavors to bring over the Indians to the Christian Faith." [4]

---

[1] *Williamson, History of Maine,* 2, *p.* 180.
[2] *Varney's History of Maine, p.* 123.
[3] *Mass. Archives* 31, *p.* 94.
[4] *McKeen, MS. Lecture.*

The following extracts from Mr. Baxter's diary are of interest: —

"On Saturday, August 24th, [1717] I went up to Brunswick,[1] and the next day preached in ye fort, and 3 of ye Indians came to meeting in ye afternoon, when sermon was ended I repeated the heads of it, and Capt: Giles interpreted ym to ye Indians, & they seemed to be well pleased therewithal.

"On Monday I had some discourse with ye Indians to shew them ye necessity of sanctifying ye sabbath which was occasioned by their shooting a gun on ye Sabbath day.

"On Saturday, Aug. 31st, I discoursed with several Indians at Brunswick about Religion, and they seemed to be very well pleased with my discourse.

"September ye 1st I preached at Brunswick, and several Indians came to hear me. Capt Giles interpreted to them ye heads of ye sermons, and they seemed well pleased therewith.

"Octob; 6th I preached at Brunswick and staid there ye ensuing week & preached there on Octob. 13th."

"While I was at Brunswick I was informed by Captn Giles yt the Amberoscoggin Indians had sent a Petition to ye General Court to have a Praying-house built for them at Brunswick to meet with ye English."

[1718.] "January 19th I preached at Brunswick, and there came 3 Indians to meeting, the most of ye Indians being gone from thence before I came thither.

"January 26th I preached at Brunswick."

"April 20th I preached at Brunswick.

"April 23d. I discoursed with Three Indians, one of them was inquisitive about things in Religion, and I had a great deal of discourse with him."

"April ye 26th an Indian came to desire me to go to his squaw who was very sick & like to die, accordingly I went to her with Capn Giles, and discoursed with her about ye state of her soul, & directed her how to get prepared for death, and she seemed to be very well pleased with what was said to her.

"April ye 27th I preached at Brunswick."[2]

From the journal above referred to it would appear that Mr. Baxter did not remove to Brunswick with his family, but that he came here upon several occasions to preach, and that he was at Georgetown

---

[1] *From Georgetown.*

[2] *Baxter's Journal in MS. in Library of Maine Historical Society.*

during the greater portion of his stay in Maine. The proprietors, however, deeded him "the second Island in Pejepscot River, coming out of Merrymeeting bay," and he took up lots numbers 14 and 15 in Topsham, which were afterwards sold for non-fulfilment of conditions. It will also be seen a little farther on that there was a house on lot number 6 in Brunswick called "Mr. Baxter's house." In the absence of positive information, it is to be presumed that the proprietors built a house for him, in the hopes or expectation that he would settle there.

FIRST PARISH.

The first action in religious matters taken by the people was while Brunswick was a parish or plantation, under the Pejepscot proprietors. It appears by the records that: —

"Att a Leagual Town meeting in Brunswick Novm^ber^ 3^d^ 1718, It was Voted That whereas the Proprietors of S^d^ Township in their paternal Care for our Spiritual Good, have by there Joynt Letter Sought to ye Reverend Mr James Woodside to be our Minister & in order there to proposed Conditions for his Settlement on their part, Wee the Inhabitance of Brunswick will Give Fourty pounds pr annum toward ye support of ye S^d^ Mr. Woodside & a Sum in proportion there to from this time untill May next (if he Come to us) & God in his providence Should Then part us.

"It was also at this meeting Voted That Mr Baxters house on ye 6th Lott in Brunswick Be forthwith made habitable for ye s^d^ Mr. Woodside. That ye Charges there of ye Transporting him & his famoly from Falmouth to Brunswick be paid Equally by us ye inhabitance of s^d^ Brunswick & ye Capt Gyles is here by impowered to se ye Buisness effected.

"JOSEPH HEATH *Town C^lk^*"

The first meeting-house of the First Parish was probably commenced in 1719. It stood about a mile south of the colleges, where the old burying-ground is. It was not, however, finished for several years, and it is probable that Mr. Woodside preached in the fort.

On May 8, 1719, it was voted, that: —

"Whereas the Reverend Mr James Woodside for Some time past, has preached to us in order to his Settlement, some of us not being well Sattisfied with his Conversation,[1] And thinking It most reasonable ye Mr Woodside as well as our Selves should have further time

[1] *Used in the now obsolete sense of character.*

for consideration in so weighty an affair, Theirfore it is voted that if Mr Woodside please to Continue preaching to us Six Moneths Longer he Shall receive of ye town after ye rate of £40 per annum provided those of us who are Dissatisfied with his Conversation (as afore Said) Can by Treating with him as becomes Christians receive Such Sattisfaction from him as that they will heare him preach for ye Time afore s^d."

He did not give sufficient satisfaction, for "Att a Leagual Town Meeting in Brunswick Sept 10th 1719 it was voted that whereas the conversation of the Reverend Mr James woodside is Displeasing to ye most of us, which renders us unable to reverence him as our Minister, therefore wee will not heare him any Longer as such. And the Select men are Impowered & Desired to grant a rate & Commit it to ye Constable to Collect So y^t ye S^d Mr. Woodside may be paid according to our agreement with him viz. after ye rate of £40 pounds per annum his Time to begin ye 2^d Day of Novem^r & Continue to ye Date of this vote except ye several[1] weeks he was absent on his own buisness at Boston & elsewhere."

[1721.] At a meeting of the settlers held May 6, 1721, twelve pounds was assessed upon the inhabitants for the support of the Reverend Isaac Taylor, who agreed with the proprietors to preach alternately in Brunswick and Topsham for one year.

[1730.] In 1730 a chaplain was allowed at Fort George.

The first minister who preached here after the incorporation of the town was Reverend Robert Rutherford. In the petition for an Act of Incorporation it was stated that the people had obtained "a pious and orthodox minister" to settle with them, and he was doubtless the one to whom reference was made, as he commenced his labors here about 1735. He does not seem to have had a formal call, however, for several years, and was never actually settled.

[1739.] At the annual town meeting, held April 16, 1739, a committee was chosen to make an arrangement with Mr. Rutherford, or if he should decline his services, to agree with some other minister.

At a meeting held the following July it was voted, "That the minister should preach at the southeast end of the town [New Meadows] according to what rates and taxes the residents of that part of the town should pay towards the support of the Ministry." At another meeting held in September, it was voted "That the Reverend Mr. Rutherford should preach at the east part of the town *as often as*

---

[1] *Several or seven; the writing is illegible.*

he pleases." A vote was also passed "That James Hue should have the one half of the two hind seats to make a Pew of on the southeast end of the meeting-house."

[1740.] In the year 1740 the town appropriated £150 for Mr. Rutherford's salary, and also voted to raise £200 as a settlement, "if he lives and dies minister of Brunswick," and to raise £66 13*s.* 4*d.* that year.

[1741.] The town appropriated, in the year 1741, £150 for support of the minister and £66 towards his settlement. The proprietors also this year voted to lay out a "ministry lot" of one hundred acres, near the meeting-house, on the south side of the road. To judge from the record, the settlers must have been accompanied at church very frequently by their canine companions, as the town voted, "That each person that suffers his Dog to com to the meeten-hose one the Lords Day shall forfet the sum of twelve pence."

[1742.] Reverend Mr. Rutherford closed his labors here early in the year 1742, having preached in town for about seven years. In February of this year a committee was appointed by the town to obtain a minister to preach, on probation, with a view to settlement. This committee does not seem to have accomplished much, however, for in June following another committee was chosen "to agree with the Reverend Mr. Jonathan Pierpont, or some other minister, to preach to us for two or three months."

In September, the town voted "that ye Rev^d^ Mr. Sam^ll^ Orseborne and ye Rev^d^ Mr. James Morton be neither of them imployed in the publick woorke of the Ministrey in this town for the fughter." And a new committee was appointed to secure the services of some suitable "orthodox" minister to preach on probation during the winter, and to be permanently settled if an agreement could be had between him and the town. The committee were authorized to advance £3 a week to the minister who might be employed. This action was owing to the fact that there was a conflict between the eastern and western portions of the town arising from differences in religious views, and the town at this time having two ministers on its hands, in order to harmonize matters, voted that neither of them should be employed.

The people in the eastern part of the town were principally descendants of the first settlers of New England. Those who resided in the west part of the town were for the most part Scotch-Irish Presbyterians. The latter formed at this time the most numerous portion. The people of New Meadows wished to have the platform of the churches at York, Berwick, Kittery, etc., and "a Mr. Lumbers [or

Lombards], a busybody, was dispatched for a copy of Mr. Moody's platform."[1]

Besides the ministers already mentioned, Reverends Blowers, Crumbie, and McClanathan were employed for a longer or shorter time. The latter not only preached, but taught a school for some time.[2]

At a meeting of the Pejepscot proprietors at Boston, September 20, 1742, it was voted that: —

"Whereas the Town of Brunswick is at present destitute of a minister, and is in quest of another minister, That Lott Number Eight on the South easterly side of the Twelve Rod Road leading from Fort George to Maquoit containing one hundred acres and fifty acres more adjoining to it on the south westerly side of said Lott, making together one hundred and fifty acres, be and hereby is granted to the First Learned & Orthodox Minister who shall be Ordained and Settle there & shall continue in the Ministry there for the space of seven years, if he shall live so long, to be to him his heirs and assigns forever. And if he should continue in the Ministry there during his lifetime, though he should dye before the expiration of said term of seven years, to be to his Heirs and their assigns notwithstanding. Otherwise to revert to the Proprietors."

And it was also voted: —

"That Lott Number Seven[3] on the Southeasterly side of the Road be & hereby is granted to the Town of Brunswick for a ministry Lott, containing one hundred acres, to be & continue for said use forever. . . . Both the above granted Lotts lying near & commodious to the meeting house."

In November of this year the town made an agreement with the Reverend Mr. Hodges, of Falmouth, to preach for five or six months on a salary of £3 per week.

In May, Deacon Samuel Hinckley was authorized to secure a minister to preach on probation, with a view to settlement, and the town paid him £6 "for ten days going after a minister to supply the town." Some question, probably, arising about this time as to whom the control of the meeting-house was vested in, the proprietors, at a meeting held in Boston, June 1, 1743,

"*Voted*, Whereas the Proprietors out of an earnest desire to promote the preaching of the Gospell in the Town of Brunswick did some years since signify to the Setlers or Inhabitants of said Town,

---

[1] *Pejepscot Papers.* [2] *Ibid.*

[3] *This lot had been previously laid out for this purpose.*

That in case they would at their Charge provide & raise the Frame of a meeting house in said Town, the proprietors would at their Expence furnish Glass, Nails & other Materials & finish the said meeting house which they have accordingly done: It is therefore now agreed & Voted, That the said meeting house is to be & continue to the use of the Inhabitants of said Town, for carrying on the publick worship of God therein, and that no particular Inhabitant or Inhabitants, Proprietor or Proprietors, pretend to claim the same for their particular use or property contrary to the true Intent and design for which said house was erected, or to the Exclusion of any of the Inhabitants from enjoying the Benefitt of said House.

"Provided Notwithstanding that the Pew on the Right Side of the Front Door be & remain for the use of the Proprietors their Heirs & Assigns & wholly at our Disposal."

[1744.] There was no minister settled in the year 1744. A proposition was made in February, however, to extend a call to Reverend James Morton, but the town voted in the negative. In March a committee was chosen to procure a minister to supply the town "for some time," on as reasonable terms as possible.

[1745.] In May, 1745, Deacon Samuel Hinckley was selected as an agent to procure a minister, but he not meeting with success, in October, Mr. Ebenezer Stanwood was appointed agent for that purpose, and was promised forty shillings for his services.

[1746.] In December, 1746, the town voted to extend an invitation to Reverend Robert Dunlap, of Sheepscot Bridge, New Castle, Massachusetts, to preach with a view to settlement, and the selectmen were instructed to communicate with him by letter, and Messrs. Robert Given and Vincent Woodside were chosen a committee to go after him, and were to be allowed twelve shillings per day for their services. The town also voted to pay Mr. Dunlap £4 per Sabbath, and a committee was chosen to take up a contribution each Sabbath to help pay the minister's salary.

[1747.] In March of the following year the town voted to settle Mr. Robert Dunlap at a salary of £200 per year (old tenor), and with a settlement of £200 "when the war is over." The town also voted to hire a house for his use "during the present war,[1] and to pay the charge."

As Mr. Dunlap was a Presbyterian, and naturally desired to be ordained by a presbytery, and there being none nearer than London-

---

[1] *Spanish or fifth Indian.*

derry,[1] it was mutually agreed between him and the town that the ordination should take place at Boston, and Deacon Samuel Hinckley and Mr. Ebenezer Stanwood were appointed commissioners to appear at the ordination and receive Mr. Dunlap in behalf of the town. They were allowed £30 to defray the cost of the ordination dinner, but the expenses were afterwards found to amount to upwards of £60.

The ordination took place in Boston, in August or September, in the meeting-house of Reverend Andrew Le Mercier, minister of the Protestant French Church, by a presbytery composed of Reverend Mr. Le Mercier, Reverend Mr. Morton, of Colrain, Reverend Mr. Davidson, of Londonderry, Reverend Mr. Wilson, and Reverend Mr. M. Lothlius.[2]

[1750.] In March, 1750, the town voted a present to Mr. Dunlap, of £40 old tenor, and in May there was raised by the town for his salary £26 13*s.* 4*d.* lawful money, and £13 6*s.* 8*d.* to be given as a present, and the same amount for his "settlement."

At a meeting of the proprietors, held this year, July 9, it was voted by them to dispose of the vacant land at New Meadows, and to expend the money thus obtained in finishing the meeting-house.

A note at the bottom of the records says that this assistance was not accepted by the town.

[1751.] In 1751 the town voted to add £13 6*s.* 8*d.* lawful money, to Mr. Dunlap's salary, "providing he will take his pay in such specie as the town can pay him in, at the market price, otherwise Mr. Dunlap must adhere to his first agreement with the town." At its annual meeting the town also voted to raise for his salary £40 lawful money, "in such specie as it can produce in *lumber* at the market price," and £8 in cash.

[1752.] The next year the selectmen were directed to petition the General Court to have Topsham annexed to Brunswick in order to assist in maintaining the gospel, "unless the inhabitants of Topsham will bind themselves to the satisfaction of our selectmen, to pay the Reverend Mr. Dunlap eighty pounds, old tenour, this year." The Province laws at this time allowed the taxing of adjacents, which had no minister, and whose people attended preaching in the town which taxed them.[3]

The town also this year voted £40, lawful money, for his salary, "to be paid in lumber, landed in Boston at the market price, where

---

[1] *Pejepscot Papers.* [2] *Greenleaf's Ecclesiastical Sketches.*
[3] *McKeen, MS. Lecture.*

our minister shall order, two thirds to be delivered there by the first day of October next, and the other third by the first of May next." What effect the petition referred to above had, does not appear from the record, but in all probability it hastened the efforts made in Topsham to settle a minister. The cause of this petition was undoubtedly due to the fact that the people of Topsham, having no preaching in their own town, were accustomed to attend religious services in Brunswick, without contributing their due share towards the support of the same.

[1754.] This year the proprietors made a deed to Reverend Mr. Dunlap of the one hundred and fifty acres of land previously granted to the first settled minister.[1]

[1755.] About this time a meeting-house was built at the east end of the town, for the accommodation of the residents of that locality. Before the erection of this building, Mr. Dunlap used to preach in that part of the town in the barn of James Thompson,[2] which stood where Bartlett Adams now (1877) lives. During the war with the Indians he was escorted to the place by his neighbors, armed.[3]

[1756.] In the year 1756 the town, in addition to the usual appropriation of £40 for the minister's salary, voted to pay the rent of his house for that year.

[1759.] In 1759 the town voted that the inhabitants of the south-east part of the township should have preaching every second Sabbath.

[1760.] In October, 1760, a committee was chosen by the town to call a council of ministers "to decide our unhappy differences with the Reverend Mr. Dunlap." The council consisted of Reverend Messrs. Smith, of Falmouth, Morrill, of Biddeford, and of Reverend Mr. Lorrain. The council resulted in the speedy dismission of Mr. Dunlap. It will be noticed that although Mr. Dunlap was a Presbyterian, yet this was a Congregational council. The difficulties on account of which the council was held are said by Greenleaf[4] to have been in regard to the payment of his salary. McKeen,[5] however, implies that he was dismissed on account of "having become weak and imbecile in mind and body, owing to a paralytic shock." That Greenleaf was correct in his statement is evident from the following communication from Mr. Dunlap to the town, which is given verbatim: —

---

[1] *Brunswick Records in Pejepscot Collections.*

[2] *McKeen, MS. Lecture.*

[3] *Pejepscot Papers.*

[4] *Ecclesiastical Sketches of Maine.*

[5] *Brunswick Telegraph, July* 30, 1853.

"To the Town of Bruns^k June 30th 1760.

"Seeing It pleased Divine providence to obstruct my Being at Londonderrey at the Last Sitting of the Pres^by which will appear by my Journal & other evidence If Called: I By advice of some worthy men; offer to y^r Considderation these proposals —

"1st that no mans monney or Rates Shall Ever Come Into my pocket; or private use In aney Shape: as ministerial taxes In this town; that Do's not adhere to my min^ry

"2ly that Such as Be: or may be adherents To my min^ry Have Liberty to pay there ministerial taxes & other Ecclesiastical Dues when they Go to hear the word: or have or may Joine In Conection: with the old Church of Christ In Brunswick: & Such as pretend aney Scruple of Concience In Joineing with us: I Lord not over their Conciences they may use their Christian Liberty: their monney Shall be at their own Disposal: I have always tho't this was the Best way to pace: tho't I woud Rather quit my title to part of a town tax: or Rate then have a hand In Divisions: & uneasyness: I am no Longer able to Live under —

"2^d propos^l whether Deacon Hinkley & Capt. David Dunning: as we have a Rev^d & Good Presbr^y. to go to, will continue their adherence, as I think wee agreed & signifyd, and for which I am now preparing & still am Desirous of Such Government, & Do profess the west=minst^r. Confession of faith to be the Confession of my faith unless better light offer to my understandin

"3^ly that whereas you are or may Be aquainted: with my Going to the wes^rd Twice —

"1st to ask Counsel tending to the publig^e Benefit & Tranquility & that our unhappey Divisions might Be heald: 2^ly To waite on the Rev^d P BY which wind & weather Disapointed me In: my Journal will Demonstrate. I therefor Intreate you would let me have my Arears: of Last Sallary. I have no minnets of the exact time when I accepted ye Call But am pretty Certain It was In march or aprill after which I looked on my Self y^r min^r tho' not really ordained: and went to Boston: to prepare my self after which no pay was Rec^d By me from aney people for preaching the Gospel: as far as I can Remember: But Came to Bruns^k In the night of the eighth Day of July, which I am Readey to Depone.

"You may all See I am not wanting aney Charges: only my Just arears: which will Satisfy & may possibly make us Easey. Sure I think I aim at the Honest part.

"Altho I spent of my own monney about £30 Going to Boston: & hireing a horse, and riding to Derrey when I was ordained: —

"and these Last Expenses: which I am sure is more & not less: of which I say nothing at this time —

"pr

"Robt Dunlop"[1]

A meeting of the town was held not long after his dismissal, and a committee chosen to procure a minister to preach on probation.

[1761.] In March, 1761, the town chose a committee "to treat with Mr. Fairfield or Mr. Whitwell to preach to us for some time, on probation, and to offer neither of them over eight pounds, old tenour, per Sabbath, and, if they refuse, to get somebody else." Probably the inducement was not sufficient, as neither of these gentlemen was obtained, and in August following another committee was appointed to confer with Reverend John Miller, of Milton, Massachusetts, as to the terms upon which he would be willing to settle. At a meeting held in December the town voted "to concur with the church and give a call to Reverend John Miller to settle with us as a minister of the gospel." The town voted him a salary of £66 13*s*. 4*d*., lawful money, and to give him £100 to enable him to settle, this amount to be paid in three annual instalments, one third each year, and if he desired to settle on the "ministerial lot," it was voted to lay out £200 in a house and improvements. The arrangements for preaching were that Mr. Miller should be excused from preaching at New Meadows during the first three months of the year, and as a compensation to the residents of that portion of the town, he was to preach there every Sabbath for two of the summer months and every alternate Sunday for the rest of the year.

[1762.] In September, 1762, a committee was chosen to receive Mr. Miller's answer to the call given him by the church and town. His answer was as follows: —

"By virtue of your vote passed in your meeting the 14th day of September, 1762, as you then voted me a salary and settlement reference being had to said vote, I cheerfully accept of your unanimous and friendly offers and engage to settle with you as your minister dur-

---

[1] *Pejepscot Papers.*

ing life, unless something material happens, by being legally parted; and I engage to conform to your vote passed September 1st, 1762, in regard to preaching at New Meadows so long as my health will admit of, or till they are set off, or otherwise voted, and wishing that we may by our preaching and example edify and advance each other's eternal interest and live in love and peace as long as life lasts.

"JOHN MILLER JUNIOR."

The ordination took place on the third of November, the exercises being conducted by the Reverends Smith, Eaton, Lorain, Elvans, Weyburn, and Obens.

David Dunning provided an entertainment for the ministers and their attendants, by order of the town.

[1768.] In 1768 some difficulties began to arise in regard to the singing on the Sabbath, and a proposition was made to set off a part of the gallery in the west meeting-house for the use of the singers, but it was defeated by a vote of the town.

[1779.] The records contain nothing of special interest from this time until the year 1779, when the town voted to make Mr. Miller such a compensation for that year as might be agreed upon, in consideration of the scarcity and dearness of the necessaries of life, and Messrs. Aaron Hinkley, Thomas Skolfield, and Captain William Stanwood were chosen a committee to decide as to what sum was proper. Subsequently the town voted not to add anything to Mr. Miller's salary, but to leave it to the generosity of the people, and the usual salary of £66 13*s.* 4*d.* was accordingly voted.

[1780.] In 1780 the town voted to pay Mr. Miller's regular salary "in produce of the country, at the price such articles were in 1775, or so much of the present currency as will purchase so much of said articles."

[1786.] In the year 1786 the town voted to allow the people in the east end of the township to "regulate the way of singing in Divine Service in the east end as they shall think proper." In June of this year, owing to troubles now but imperfectly understood, but probably connected with matters of church government, the town voted to dismiss Mr. Miller from his pastoral office, and a committee was chosen to notify him of the action of the town. He must, however, have refused to accept his dismissal as [1787] on the eighth of May of the next year, agreeably to his own desire, a vote of the members of the *church* was taken, as to whether he should or should not be dismissed. The result of this vote was nine for dismission and five against it. As this did not seem satisfactory, the *congregation* was then called upon to vote on the subject. The result of this vote was twelve for dismission and eighteen against it. The town thereupon, without taking direct action,[1] voted to raise no money for his support.

[1788.] In 1788 the town again voted not to pay him any salary, and also voted to call a council of the neighboring churches to hear the grievances of those who were dissatisfied with him. As there is no evidence that a council was ever actually assembled, and as Mr. Miller died before the close of the year, it is probable that the calling of the council was deferred on account of his ill-health.

[1789.] The next year a committee was appointed to pay the executor of Mr. Miller's estate the amount of his salary due him at the time of his death. A committee was also chosen to secure another minister on trial.

[1790.] A committee was chosen in April, 1790, to invite Reverend Mr. Cornwell to preach on probation; but in August the town voted not to settle him, and a committee was chosen to secure some other minister.

[1791.] The following proposal was made to the town in December: —

"Six months I propose, at the desire of the Committee to supply the people of Brunswick as a Preacher, allowing me to be absent two months in the Winter, more or less as convenient, provided it is agreeable to the town.

"ABRA^M MOORE.

"DECEMB^R 2d 1791."[2]

[1792.] In January, 1792, the proposal of Mr. Moore was accepted, and he was engaged to preach for six months on probation. In August the town voted unanimously to give him a call to settle, at a salary of £100 and with a settlement of £100, to be paid him in one year after his settlement.

It was also voted that the Baptists in this town who can produce a certificate that they belong to a Baptist society shall have a right to draw the money that was last assessed as a ministerial tax, to be appropriated to pay their own preacher, and that they be no longer taxed in the ministerial tax.

It was also voted that the minister should preach every other Sunday at the east end of the town.

---

[1] *Which was needless, in view of the vote taken the preceding year.*

[2] *Pejepscot Papers.*

Mr. Moore declined the call to settle permanently and in September of the following year [1793], the town voted unanimously to extend a call to the Reverend Ebenezer Coffin, and to give him a salary of £100 and £200 for a settlement. He was ordained June 23, 1794.

[1801.] Mr. Coffin left in 1801. There is no account in either the town or church records of any formal dismissal, but there is probably no doubt that he was compelled to resign. From this time until 1806 there was occasional preaching in the old meeting-house.

[1806.] At that time the old house was abandoned by the First Parish, and a new one on the hill was occupied instead.

The participation of the town in the doings of the First Parish having now ceased, the remainder of its history will be included in that of the

CHURCH OF THE FIRST PARISH.

It does not appear anywhere, as a matter of record, that there was any church organization during the pastorate of Reverend Mr. Rutherford, or that he was regularly ordained. No mention is made of any church act at the time of the settlement of Reverend Mr. Dunlap, but it is said that, soon after that event, Reverend Mr. Murray formed a church in this place, in connection with the presbytery. Samuel Clark is said to have been the first deacon.[1]

It is narrated that on one occasion, while Mr. Murray, of Boothbay, was here for the purpose of organizing the church and was engaged in preaching, Aaron Hinkley, displeased with something that he had said, stepped out into the aisle, and addressing Mr. Murray, inquired of him if he knew in whose presence he was speaking; to which Mr. Murray replied that he was aware that he was in the presence of the Judge of the Inferior Court. Mr. Hinkley then said, "I say to you as the Lord said to Elijah, 'What dost thou here,' John Murray?" The question, with the verse following in this connection, "I have been very jealous for the Lord God of hosts; for the children of Israel have forsaken thy covenant, thrown down thine altars, and slain thy prophets with the sword" (1 Kings xix, 9, 10), gave a text to Mr. Murray upon which he continued to preach, making some very severe and sarcastic remarks, and putting an end to all further questions.[2]

There is no doubt but that this church was originally established on Presbyterian principles, and continued so during the ministry of Mr. Dunlap.

---

[1] *Woodman's notes.* [2] *McKeen, MS. Lecture.*

The male members of this church in 1761 were[1] John Minott, Samuel Clarke, Ebenezer Stanwood, William Simpson, David Dunning, John Orr, Samuel Whitney, Isaac Snow, James Thompson, Aaron Hinkley, Samuel Stanwood, James Elliott, William Ross, William Stanwood, Thomas Adams, Thomas Skolfield, and John Smart.

After the settlement of Mr. Miller, the church assumed a mixed character for about seven years. The number of church members was then about seventy, among whom were seven deacons.[2]

Mr. Miller was ordained November 3, 1762. The council consisted of Messrs. Smith, Loring, Elvin, Wibird, Robbins, and Eaton. At a church meeting held a few days subsequently, it was voted: "Whereas this church as to its government since it has been gathered and more especially while Mr Dunlap was their pastor, has not been duly kept up in the beauty and order of the Gospel, by reason of which they have greatly separated in the Ceremonials of Government, it was therefore voted: That all those who are not in full communion with the church and who never had any children baptized or were never baptized themselves, in order to receive the ordinances either for themselves or their children are required to be propounded to the church at least the Sabbath before Baptism, in order to own the Covenant of Baptism."

Reverend Mr. Miller was ordained as a Congregationalist, but after some years the church and parish returned to the Londonderry Presbytery, from which they had seceded.[3]

How much soever a portion of his congregation may have been edified by his preaching, some of them were not sufficiently so to give close attention to him, and it was not at all uncommon for numbers of people to be asleep. At such times, it is narrated, Mr. Miller was in the habit of stopping in the midst of his sermon, and saying, "Wake up, hearers!" After a while it was made the duty of old Mr. George Coombs to wake the sleepers by rapping on their pew-doors with his staff.[4]

At the council for the ordination of Mr. Miller, Reverend Thomas Smith was the moderator, and Mr. Loring, scribe. At the ordination, prayer was made by the Reverend Mr. Loring, the charge by Mr. Smith, the right hand of fellowship by Mr. Eaton, and the sermon by Mr. Miller himself.

The following, in regard to church government, was found on an old paper, undated, and very much worn: —

---

[1] *Pejepscot Papers.* [2] *Greenleaf, Ecclesiastical Sketches.* [3] *McKeen, MS. Lecture.*
[4] *James Curtis's Journal, in Library of Maine Historical Society.*

"These concerning the Church of Christ in Brunswick as to the order and Constitution of this Church. It was at first set up in the Presbyterian order to be governed by a Session and since we have left off that order and government we have got into Disorder and have no government at all, therefore we the subscribers hereof advise the members of the Church to look to God for a blessing and direction herein, in setting up their old Constitution and choose ten or twelve elders and have them ordained to their charge and duty, herein to act for the glory of God and the good of this church, and in all Ecclesiastical affairs belonging to this church that may come before them to decide them impartially without favor or affection. This is our deliberate judgement and advice and that we cannot come into peace and good government without taking these steps.

"JUDAH CHASE.
ROBERT DUNNING.
WILLIAM STANWOOD.
SAMUEL STANWOOD, JR.
SAMUEL STANWOOD, 3D.
LEWIS SIMPSON.
STEPHEN SKOLFIELD.
WILLIAM WOODSIDE.
DANIEL WOODSIDE, JR.
ANTHONY WOODSIDE.
DAVID DUNNING, JR.
DAVID DUNNING.
ANDREW DUNNING.
SAMUEL STANWOOD.
JOHN DUNLAP.
WILLIAM STANWOOD, 2D.
WILLIAM SPEAR.
SAMUEL DUNLAP.
JOHN SWETT.
JAMES CARY.
JAMES ELLIOTT.
WILLIAM STANWOOD, 3D."

[1762.] At a meeting of the church, held Monday, November 15, it was —

Voted, "That all such as desire admittance into full Communion with the Church, shall privately signify their desire to the minister, and [make a statement of their religious] views, after which the minister shall propound them to the Church at least a week before the Sacrament, that if any of the Communicants have anything to object, they may have time so to do before the Sacrament, which objection is to be made to the Deacons, who shall before Sacrament day acquaint the minister of it, that the minister may have time to inform the person, but if no objections appear, the minister shall proceed to admit the person." Also, "That the sacrament of the Lord's Supper be administered once in two months in the winter, beginning the first Sabbath of December, and once in six weeks in the summer months."

[1763.] On May 12, the church voted, "That the contribution be continued at both ends of the town in order to purchase utensils for this church.

"To purchase four flagons, eight tankards, twelve cups, four dishes, two tablecloths, and two napkins for the use of this church.

"That Aaron Hinkley and Deacon Dunning take charge of the contribution, and see the articles purchased as soon as may be.

"That Deacon Clark and Deacon Samuel Stanwood take an account of the money collected at the west meeting-house, and Deacon Snow and Deacon Whitney take account of the money collected at the east meeting-house, before delivered into the hands of Deacon Dunning and Mr. Hinkley."

It is difficult to understand the necessity for this vote to purchase flagons, etc., because (if there is no mistake in the date inscribed upon them) two flagons, three plates, and four cups were presented to the church in 1737 by Benjamin Larrabee and John Minot. They are now in the possession of Professor A. S. Packard.

At this same meeting of the church, it was "voted to sing Tate and Brady's version with the hymns annexed thereto, composed by Isaac Watts, D. D." Mr. Aaron Hinkley declined serving as deacon, and was excused.

[1764.] This year an individual who desired baptism for his two children was obliged to make a public confession of his criminal intimacy with Ann Conner, who subsequently committed suicide.

[1765.] September 8, the church met and voted to have a covenant drawn up and signed by each member.

The following is found on the cover of one of the old records: —

"October 1765 The people in Brunswick began to quarrel with their minister, John Miller, headed by William Woodside Senior."

[1766.] On May 9, a church meeting was held to consider this "quarrel"; and at an adjourned meeting, held May 22, the church voted that Mr. Woodside should apologize to the pastor. He refused to do so, and the church then voted that "Mr. Miller's Character stood fair in the eye of the church."

[1767.] May 13, William Woodside was suspended until he confessed his fault to the church and pastor.

[1768.] July 29. At a meeting of the church on this day objection was offered to the baptism of a child of Thomas Thompson, "on account of said Thomas standing up and reading the Psalm in the public worship of God." The child was, however, baptized. At a meeting on September 6, William Woodside, Senior, openly asked the forgiveness of the church and the pastor, as to his past misconduct, and was received again into the church. A number of the members were also reconciled to each other at this meeting, an uncommon spirit of forgiveness prevailing, and the members appearing to be "of one heart and of one mind." At this meeting Mr. Miller openly declared himself to be the pastor of a church on the Congregational plan.

[1770.] In May, 1770, the church records show that the members had been led to consider the decline of religion; and accordingly a day of fasting and prayer was appointed "to implore pardon of God, and his aid and help." The day was seriously observed. After public services the church met, confessions were made, alienations and differences composed, and tokens appeared of a reviving spiritual influence among the Christian portion of the community.

[1771.] The question whether the church should be Congregational or Presbyterian in form came up this year. A meeting was held at the west meeting-house, which the members of the east end did not attend. Subsequently a meeting was held at the east end which was attended by both parties. The next day some of the members at the east end met at Captain Thompson's, without notifying the other members. To reconcile the difficulties a meeting was held on [1772] June 16, and the following agreement was drawn up and signed: —

"In the first place we propose that this Church and the Discipline thereof be governed agreeable to the Congregational Constitution and platform of the churches in New England — excepting the administration of the ordinance of Baptism and the Lord's supper to be administered agreeable to the custom of the Presbyterian Churches, and to have only one preparation day before each sacrament.

"Consented to by me, "JOHN MILLER.

"DAVID DUNNING
AARON HINKLEY
SAMUEL CLARK
JAMES THOMPSON
SAMUEL STANWOOD
ISAAC SNOW
THOMAS SKOLFIELD
} *Church Committee.*

"Voted and accepted in Church.

"N.B. It is to be understood by the Pastor and the Church that the above writing was drawn up and executed in consequence of all differences and uneasiness that did subsist between the Pastor and Church, and the same were adjusted and settled in an amicable manner."

[1774.] At a meeting of the church, on May 16, at the west meeting-house, the above vote having caused some uneasiness, and some of the members at the east end of the town not being disposed to comply with it, it was voted that the sacrament might be administered at the west meeting-house from the long table, the communicants sitting around it or in the body-pews as they might see fit; and that it might be administered at the east meeting-house in the Congregational form. The ordinance of baptism to be administered in either form as persons might choose.

[1785.] At a meeting held on September 13, the church considered the matter of lay exhorters, who were becoming quite common in town. No action was taken, however, as some of the church evidently favored such persons.

[1786.] At a meeting held April 17, the subject of chosing ruling elders was brought forward, and it was voted not to choose any. The church then considered in regard to the new mode of singing adopted at the east end of the town, and it was voted that the psalms and hymns should be read by the deacons, *i. e.*, line by line, until all had had time to furnish themselves with books. Charles Thomas was chosen chorister at the east end, and John Dunning at the west end of the town, with liberty to appoint their own assistants.

At a meeting held July 5, there was a pretty warm discussion in regard to the mode of singing. After a while the discussion turned upon the question whether the church was Congregational or Presbyterian. The meeting closed without settling the point.

[1790.] At a meeting held in March, there being no minister, Stanwood Dunning was chosen permanent moderator. Several persons being asked why they had absented themselves from church meetings, etc., one replied, "because there was no order in the church"; another, that he could not sit down to the Lord's table with a certain member; and others answered that "they had joined the Baptists."

[1793.] December 18 the church voted a call to Reverend Mr. Coffin, and that the twenty-third of January be set for his ordination.

[1794.] January 22, the council for the ordination met. It consisted of Daniel Little, Kennebunk; Paul Coffin, Buxton; Thomas Brown, Stroudwater; Alfred Johnston, Freeport; Samuel Eaton, Harpswell; Jonathan Ellis, Topsham; and the usual lay delegates. The ordaining services were performed the next day in the west meeting-house.

The minutes of only two church meetings are recorded during the whole of Mr. Coffin's pastorate. May 10 of this year it was voted that there should be four communions a year. June 26 it was voted "that candidates for the baptism of their first child should be propounded as such one fortnight, that if there should be any objections made, they may be made in season to the minister that he may act accordingly."

On July 21, 1808, the new meeting-house, which had been built by subscription, was given to and accepted by the parish, the north gallery being reserved for the use of the students of Bowdoin College, that institution having contributed funds towards its erection. Afterward, in the present building, the south gallery was substituted in lieu of the north.

On February 8, 1810, the parish extended an invitation to Reverend John Bartlett to settle over them. The call was not, however, accepted. On the twenty-first of April, of this year, the parish voted to petition the Court of Common Pleas for a remission of the fine that had been imposed upon them "for not being supplied with preaching."

Since 1802 there had been no settled minister over them and a portion of the time no preaching, though during this time Presidents McKeen and Appleton often officiated.

On April 2, 1811, the parish voted "to appoint a suitable person to care for the meeting-house, sweep the same, and *ring the bell*." This is the first allusion to any bell in town and this bell was undoubtedly the one on the college chapel. In October, 1824, however, the parish authorized a bell to be put in the tower of the meeting-house, and it was done shortly after. This, the first *parish* bell, was bought by subscription, and cost about five hundred dollars.[1] The college paid fifty dollars towards its purchase, on condition that the parish would give them the right to use both it and the meeting-house, for literary exercises on Commencement week and at other times for special purposes, upon ten days' notice being given.

In 1817 the question of heating the meeting-house came up, and on the eighteenth of January the parish voted to grant permission to have stoves put in. This was probably not done, though, at this time, for in 1824 the matter again came up and was referred to a committee, who reported it inexpedient to use stoves. In November, 1838, the parish authorized the assessors "to adopt the plan used in Reverend Mr. Ellingwood's church, in Bath."

In 1819, John Schwartkin, of Holland, was allowed to partake of the communion without a letter of recommendation, because he was a stranger in a foreign country.

---

[1] *At all events, the subscriptions amounted to a trifle over this sum.*

In Reverend Mr. Mead's reply to a call of the church, in 18 2, he made it a condition of his acceptance that he should have the right to dissolve the connection with the church whenever the compensation he received failed to amount to seven hundred dollars a year.

His ordination services were held this year and were as follows: introductory prayer, by Reverend Mr. Mittimore, of Falmouth; sermon, by Reverend Doctor Payson, of Portland; consecrating prayer, by Reverend Mr. Gillet, of Hallowell; charge, by Reverend Doctor Packard, of Wiscasset; right hand of fellowship, by Reverend Mr. Smith, of Portland; address to the people, by Reverend Mr. Ellingwood, of Bath; closing prayer, by Reverend Mr. Pomeroy, of Gorham.

Mr. Mead was dismissed, at his own request, in July, 1829. On the fifth of that month he preached his farewell discourse, which was printed by request, and a copy of which is preserved in the library of the Maine Historical Society. During his ministry a creed and covenant were adopted by the church and a church library started, to which the books of the Brunswick Female Humane Society were added.

About this time the attention of the parish was directed to the question of the ownership and boundaries of the meeting-house lot. The fencing of this lot and the legal contest connected therewith is mentioned in another connection.

In November, 1829, Reverend George E. Adams was invited to become the pastor of this parish. Having already been ordained, although without a charge, he was installed Tuesday, December 29. The installation services were as follows: —

Introductory prayer, by Reverend Seneca White, of Bath; sermon, by Dr. Tyler, of Portland; installing prayer, by Dr. H. Packard, of Wiscasset; charge, by Reverend Asa Mead, of Gorham; right hand of fellowship, by Reverend Jacob C. Goss, of Topsham; address to the church and to the people, by Reverend Benjamin Tappan, of Augusta; concluding prayer, by Reverend William Mittimore, of Falmouth.

On November 27, 1834, Thanksgiving day, the meeting-house, having been repaired and somewhat altered, was dedicated anew.

In 1835 the parish voted to receive an organ, in trust, for the church. Two years later the debt due upon this organ was assumed by the parish. On May 16, 1840, a motion was made in parish meeting to pay the organist fifty dollars. This motion produced an animated discussion. One individual remarked, "I don't wish to wound the feelings of any one. I have felt very unpleasant ever since the organ came into the meeting-house. It is not acceptable to God. It is very offensive. It begins to make a noise after the hymn is read, — before they begin to sing. It has a very *immoral tendency.* It keeps our minds from other things." No objection to the motion was made by any one else, and the amount was therefore voted.

In 1842 a new bell was put in the tower in place of the old one, which had been cracked in consequence of ringing a fire alarm on the seventeenth of December of the previous year. The cost of this new bell was about one hundred and fifty dollars, and the sum was raised by subscription.

On February 15, 1845, the parish voted to have a new meeting-house built, and to dispose of the old one. Work was at once commenced on it, and it was finished early the next year. Its cost was $13,101.68. It was dedicated on March 18, 1846. The public exercises were as follows: A voluntary on the organ; an anthem by the choir; reading of Scripture by Reverend Ray Palmer, of Bath; prayer, by Reverend Jonathan Clement, of Topsham; hymn, by Reverend John O. Fisk, of Bath; sermon, by the pastor, Reverend George E. Adams; prayer, by Reverend John W. Chickering, of Portland; hymn, by Reverend E. G. Parsons, of Freeport; benediction, by Reverend James Drummond, of Lewiston.

Doctor Adams closed his ministry in August, 1870. When he went to Brunswick he was called from the Professorship of Sacred Rhetoric, in the Bangor Theological Seminary, and by experience and culture seemed unusually well endowed for the work of the ministry, which, with uninterrupted unanimity, was continued forty-one years. "With perhaps as few trials as have fallen to the lot of any of his contemporaries, he was permitted to witness repeated special manifestations of the Divine favor, and a large increase of the church and of the society. Having come to it when it was comparatively weak, he closed his long service when it had become one of the strong societies of the State. When at last, after an unusually prolonged pastorate, at his own request, moved to it by an inviting call to Orange, New Jersey, he asked to be released from this ministry, he received a united and costly testimonial from his whole people of their affectionate and grateful esteem and affection."[1]

Notwithstanding Doctor Adams's resignation was accepted by the parish, his formal connection therewith was never severed by any act of council, and he died the legal pastor of the society.

---

[1] *Church Manual.*

In December, 1870, Reverend Ezra H. Byington (University of Vermont, 1852) was invited to supply the pulpit, and on January 10, 1871, he received a quite unanimous call to settle. He accepted and has remained to the present time, but no *formal* settlement has yet occurred.

To this history of the church and society we add a brief notice of their Sabbath school.

The following sketch of the origin and early history of the Sabbath school is obtained from the church manual. The particulars were obtained from a private journal of the late Deacon John Perry, for many years an active and efficient member and officer of the church: —

"In the winter of 1811–12 an account of a Sabbath school in England, in a newspaper, suggested to Mr. Perry the idea of attempting the same agency for good in this community. He consulted the minister, Reverend Mr. Bailey, and President Appleton, about the expediency of such a movement and the proper method of conducting it. They favored the project, but were not informed of the way in which such schools were managed. They, however, thought that nothing but reading of a religious character should be allowed. To the inquiry whether small children, abecedarians, should be admitted, after deliberation of some days, they decided in favor of it, on the ground that unless such children were taught to read, they could never read the Scriptures. Mr. Perry then, May, 1812, gathered some eighteen of his own and neighbors' children in the red schoolhouse, School Street, during the hour before morning service. After the hour was spent, most of his school accompanied him to the church. The school was opened by Scripture reading and prayer; lessons were recited in the Bible and primer. Those that could read, read in the Bible at least once, and the portion read he explained as he best could. That first season, closing in October, passed without an assistant or a visitor; and so his service of love continued until in 1816, Mr. David Starret, a student in college (1819), was secured as an assistant, and more interest was taken in this humble work. President Appleton exhibited decided interest in the movement. At his suggestion, several of the church and parish met in 1817 to consider its claims, and the first formal organization of a Sabbath school, as an element in the work of the church, was made. A superintendent was chosen, teachers were appointed, wider interest awakened, and the institution permanently established."

According to another account with which we have been favored, "the first school of this kind was opened early in 1816, in the cloth-room of the factory, by Mr. Jacob Abbott, Mr Bourne, and Mr. Edwards, the credit of suggesting it belonging to the former gentleman. Deacon John Perry and several other gentlemen were invited to act as teachers. As the cold weather came on, the school was moved to the school-house near Miss Narcissa Stone's, and David Starrett and a Mr. Vance were the teachers. After a while it was moved to the red school-house." The writer of the above was connected with this school from its formation until 1826, and says that if one was formed earlier it certainly died out, as there was none in town when this school was formed, in 1816.

The following is a list of the settled pastors of the church, and of the deacons and members prior to the present century: —

PASTORS.

Reverend Robert Dunlap, 1747–1760; Reverend John Miller, 1762–1788; Reverend Ebenezer Coffin, 1794–1802; Reverend Winthrop Bailey, 1811–1814; Reverend Asa Mead, 1822–1829; Reverend George Eliashib Adams, 1829–1870; Reverend Ezra Byington, 1871.

DEACONS.

Samuel Stanwood, David Dunning, Samuel Clark, Isaac Snow.

MEMBERS.

(This list of members is supposed to be quite imperfect, but it includes all the names which can be found in the records.)

LIST IN THE HANDWRITING OF REVEREND JOHN MILLER, WHO WAS ORDAINED NOVEMBER 3, 1762. — John Miller, pastor; John Orr, Mair Point; Samuel Stanwood, deacon; Ebenezer Stanwood, died July 18, 1772; Thomas Adams, recommended to the church in Scotland, July, 1765; William Ross; David Dunning, deacon; William Simpson; Samuel Clark, deacon; James Hewey; Robert Given; John Given; Thomas Skolfield; John Gatchell, Senior; Isaac Snow, deacon; Peter Coombs, died January, 1768; Peter Coombs, Junior; Aaron Hinkley; James Thompson, renounced the church; Alexander Thompson; James Curtis, received May, 1763; Samuel Whitney, deacon, dismissed to a church to be gathered at St. John's River, eastward; Reverend Robert Dunlap; Enoch Danforth, received May, 1763, from church in Arundel; Benjamin Stone; George Hayden, or Headon, or Haddean, received September, 1765; Joseph Snow, received September, 1765; William Wilson, received December, 1762;

Samuel Snow, son of Deacon S., received October, 1765; Robin Miller (colored man); Robert Dunning, received May, 1772; ——— Allen; Andrew Dunning, deacon, received July, 1772; William Cotton; Daniel Browne, received July, 1772; Thomas Pennell; Susannah Orr; Hannah Moody, removed to Falmouth; Hannah Minot, Catherine Smart, removed to Penobscot; Jane Rutherford, removed to Georges, eastward; Eliza Stanwood, wife of William; Jane Stanwood; John Smart;[1] John Minot;[2] Jane Dunlap, wife of Reverend Robert; Mary Spear, wife of Robert; Elizabeth Ross, wife of William; Mary Dunning; Hannah Harward; Agnes Simpson, wife of William; Martha Clark, wife of Samuel; Anna Given; Mary Skolfield, wife of Thomas; Mary Snow, daughter of Deacon S., received October, 1765; Mary Whitney, wife of Deacon S. W., dismissed to St. John's River, October, 1765; Sarah Gray, received September, 1765; Dorothy Gray, received September, 1765; Thompson; Thompson; Hinkley; Ham; Elizabeth Hayden, wife of G., received September, 1762; Dorcas Danforth, wife of E., received May, 1763; Sarah Gray; Mary Snow; Sarah Dunning, wife of Robert, received July, 1772; Mary Hunt; Margaret Miller, wife of Reverend John; Elizabeth Dunning, wife of Andrew, received July, 1772; Mrs. William Cotton, received July, 1772; Mrs. Daniel Browne, received July, 1772; Alice Pennell, wife of Thomas, died 1839; Sarah Cary. Total number of members, seventy-two.

The following names are found in a list of those admitted to the church during Mr. Miller's ministry, which are not found in the preceding one. This list is apparently also in Mr. Miller's handwriting.

Daniel Hunt, James Elliot, William Dunning, Ephraim Hunt, Samuel Dunlap, Joseph Morse, Joseph Haley, Janett Hunt, wife of Daniel, Ruth Elliot, wife of James: all received April 20, 1783.

A List of Members who signed a Church Document which is without Date, but is at least as late as 1783, as it includes three Names admitted in 1783.—Judah Chase; Robert Dunning; William Stanwood; Samuel Stanwood, Junior; Samuel Stanwood, 3d; Lewis Simpson; Stephen Skolfield; William Woodside; Daniel Woodside, Junior; Anthony Woodside; David Dunning; David Dunning, Junior; Andrew Dunning; Samuel Stanwood; John Dunlap; William Stanwood, 2d; William Spear; Samuel Dunlap; John Swett; James Cary; William Stanwood, 3d.

---

[1] *Pejepscot Papers*, 5, *p.* 311, *et seq.* [2] *Ibid.*

In a list of church members during the ministry of Reverend Ebenezer Coffin and subsequently, the following are not found in previous lists: —

William Owen; Patrick Kincaid, deacon, July, 1800; Tobias Still; James Curtis, deacon, removed to Lisbon; Mary Owen; Sarah Given; Martha Ross; Mrs. Eunice Harding; Mrs. Hannah Lunt, received August, 1795; Jeremiah Minot, received August, 1796; Jane Dunlap, received August, 1796; Mrs. Goss, received May, 1801.

On account of the former connection of the First Parish with the town, an account is here inserted of the

PARISH FUND.

The origin of the fund was this: The meeting-house, which was built in 1806, was built by individuals with the understanding that the pews should be sold at auction, and that all that was paid over the amount needed to reimburse the builders was to go to the parish as a ministerial fund, only the interest of which was to be available for parish purposes. This fund could be added to by donations and otherwise, but the principal was not to be used. In 1816 the *overplus* of the town Commons — one hundred and ninety-seven acres — was set off to the parish and was afterwards sold to Mr. John Given. The proceeds of the sale were added to this fund. This *overplus* of the Commons was the amount of land over the one thousand acres, which by the proprietor's deed of 1783 was to go to the First Parish. It was not the "ministerial lot" of one hundred acres laid out by the proprietors in 1741. What became of the proceeds of the sale of the latter, we do not know. It may have been expended in building the first two meeting-houses. It formed no part of the parish fund. This fund is said at one time to have amounted to $5,000 or more. At first it was loaned to individuals, and some of the loans were lost by the parties dying insolvent. Afterwards the trustees of the fund bought some thirty or more pews in the meeting-house, and loaned the balance of the funds to the parish. By bad management this fund has dwindled away, and nothing now remains but a small lot of land back of the church.

BAPTIST SOCIETIES.

The first services in Brunswick by any preacher of the Baptist denomination were held in the year 1783. About this time Elders Case, Potter, and Lord preached here in some private houses, and though it is not known that they made any converts, the attention of the people was thus drawn to their particular theological views. On October 21, 1783, Reverend Isaac Case arrived in town. The next afternoon he preached at the house of a Mr. Woodard, and on the afternoon of the following day, he preached at the house of Mr. Samuel Getchell.[1]

In 1789 [2] or 1790,[3] Samuel Woodard and others formed themselves into a Baptist Society and refused taxes to the First Parish. In May, 1790, Joseph Morse entered in the town records his protest against ever paying anything to any Congregational or Presbyterian preacher.

On June 20, 1794, Judah Chase, William Mariner, Aaron Snow, Samuel Mariner, John Getchell, John Mariner, Charles Cowan, Peter Jordan, Robert Jordan, Anthony Woodside, David Ferrin, John Ferrin, Robert Dunning, David Clark, Benjamin Getchell, Stephen Getchell, John Williams, George Williams, Philip Higgins, Reuben Higgins, Sylvanus Combs, Philip Higgins, Jr., Samuel Williams, William Thompson, Joseph O'Donehue, Joseph Morse, Richard Orr, William Stanwood, Samuel Dunlap, Daniel Brown, Philip Owens,[4] Samuel Huey, Joseph Ross, John Mariner, Jr., Josiah Simpson, Michael Grows, Nathan Combs, George Winslow, Joseph Saint Combs, William Dunning, Samuel Woodward, Peter Woodward, William Gatchell, Jr., Ezekiel Spaulding, Ezekiel Spaulding, Jr., John S. Gatchell, John Ridout, Samuel Gatchell, John Matthews, David Linscot, William Woodside, Jr., George Combs, and George Combs, Jr., were incorporated by the name of "THE BAPTIST RELIGIOUS SOCIETY IN BRUNSWICK, HARPSWELL, AND BATH."[5] Previous to this time the society had no legal existence.

In May, 1795, the town voted to pass by the fourth article in the warrant concerning allowing the Baptists to use the meeting-houses a part of the time.

The following is a list of the names of those who joined the Baptists in 1796: —

On March 4, David Whitney, Simeon Whitney, Samuel Bean, Joshua Purinton, Abraham Capelon, Lemuel Standish, Jonathan Osgood, Jr., Jonathan Osgood, Francis Winter, Benjamin Chefford, Charles Peterson, William Grace, John Grace, James Ward, Thomas Crawford, Thomas McKenny, Isaiah Crooker, Hannah Crooker, Elijah Williams, Thomas Williams, Jr.

---

[1] *Millett.* [2] *Greenleaf's Ecclesiastical Sketches* [3] *Pejepscot Papers.*
[4] *Said to have been the first person ever baptized by immersion in Brunswick.*
[5] *Massachusetts Special Laws*, 1, *p.* 529.

On March 10, William Swanton, Jr., John Lowell, Otis Little, Patrick Murray.

On March 12, Joseph West, James Wakefield.

On March 14, John Whitmore, James Mitchell, Eliphalet Lowell, William S. Crooker, Samuel Lumber, Joseph Lumber, Birduck Berry, Thomas Mitchell.

On March 16, John McFarlan, John Eneos, Patrick Williams, Thomas Williams, John Williams, Joshua Williams, John Campbell, John Lemont, Stephen Combes, Stephen Combes, Jr., Thomas Combes, John Holbrook, John Sprague, Simeon Higgins, Jacob Low, James Low, Zedoc Lincoln, William Marshall, William Marshall, Jr.

On March 17, William Jackson, Edward Oliver, Christopher Daley.

On March 18, Samuel Davis, James Davidson, Samuel Todd, Simeon Tumor, Charles Lincoln, Jonathan Ryon, Benjamin Brown, Jr., Eliphalet Brown, David Coultson, Patrick Grace, Nathaniel Springot, John Sinclair.[1]

In 1798 the town voted "to allow the Baptist Society their extraordinary expense in the lawsuit between them and the other society in this town," which was to be in full of all demands. The object of this suit is nowhere stated, but the record of the Court of Common Pleas shows that at the October term of Court in 1795, "Samuel Woodward of Brunswick in the County of Cumberland, Clerk and Teacher of Piety, Religion and Morality," brought a suit against the inhabitants of Brunswick, one of whom was Thomas Thompson, a deputy sheriff, in a plea of the case that the inhabitants were indebted to the said Woodward in the sum of £10 17*s.* 6*d.* The plaintiff failed to recover, and costs were awarded to the defendants for nineteen dollars and eighty-six cents. The plaintiff appealed to a higher court. This was probably the lawsuit referred to, though we cannot be certain about the matter, since the original papers cannot be found. It is probable that there was an assessment of taxes made by the town, which was also the First Parish, upon property of some kind, to sustain preaching, and the suit was instituted by this society to obtain its share of the amount collected.

In 1799, Philip Owen, William Dunning, Daniel Brown, Judah Chase, Samuel Dunlap, Josiah Simpson, Anthony Woodside, Michael Grows, and Joseph Ross withdrew from this society and formed one at Maquoit.

---

[1] *Pejepscot Papers.*

The meeting-house of the Brunswick, Harpswell, and Bath society was at New Meadows. The date of its erection, according to the inscription upon the present building, was about 1800. The records of this church are in existence, but we have not been able to procure the loan of them and are therefore unable to give any further account of it.

FIRST BAPTIST CHURCH OF BRUNSWICK.

[1799.] A small number of persons having been led to embrace "Believers' Baptism," thought it might conduce to the glory of God and their comfort to be embodied together in church order. They therefore applied to the church in North Yarmouth and the church in Harpswell, of the Baptist order, for their assistance. Agreeably with this request the elders and messengers from those churches, together with Elder Williams, met at the Baptist meeting-house at Maquoit, on the second week in September, 1799. Elder Woodward preached a sermon in the forenoon on the nature of church order.

The brethren and sisters who met to be embodied were examined with regard to their articles of faith and covenant, and it appearing that they had adopted the same which is embraced by the Bowdoinham Association, a summary of which is printed in their minutes, the council decided to give them the hand of fellowship as a distinct Baptist church. The names of those thus embodied were, Judah Chase, Samuel Dunlap, William Stanwood, Sarah Woodside, Philip Owen, Mrs. Ross, wife of William Ross, and J. Merrill.

Mr. Merrill was dismissed from the Bowdoin church and the others from the Harpswell church in order to form this new church in Brunswick.

William Woodside was baptized, and then the church made choice of Samuel Dunlap as deacon.

Elder Williams having for some time preached to the Baptist society in Brunswick and in Topsham, they mutually requested him to remove his residence among them and preach for the two societies alternately. The invitation was accepted, and he moved with his family to Brunswick, January 24, 1800, preaching half the time for the Baptist society in Brunswick, and half for the Baptist society in Topsham.

On the fifteenth of April, 1800, an arrangement was made by which Elder Williams should preach for the ensuing year for the societies of Brunswick and Topsham, each society paying one hundred dollars for his services.

In April, 1801, Elder Williams was engaged to preach for the Brunswick society alone at a salary of two hundred dollars, and in April, 1802, he was engaged to supply the pulpit for another year. In the spring of 1803 he removed to Beverly, Massachusetts, having preached his farewell discourse on the twenty-fourth of April. "After Elder Williams left us, a Brother Kendall providentially fell in here and preached for us."[1]

On the twenty-second of February, 1803, Philip Owen, William Dunning, Daniel Brown, Judah Chase, Samuel Dunlap, Josiah Simpson, Anthony Woodside, Michael Grows, Joseph Ross, Samuel Stanwood, William Woodside, Andrew Blake, Abraham Toothaker, William Starbird, David Curtis, James Stanwood, Adam Woodside, David Dunning, William Ross, Frederic French, Nathaniel Chase, James Chase, William Swett, Shimuel Owen, Abner Melcher, William Low, Charles Ryan, Ephraim Hunt, William Lunt, Andrew Dunning, William Hunt, Anthony Chase, Gideon Toothaker, John Given, David Given, and Uriah Elliot were incorporated as the BAPTIST SOCIETY IN BRUNSWICK.

The following is a list of the members of the church in 1803: Deacon Samuel Dunlap, Judah Chase, Philip Owen, John Merrill, Esquire, Wm. Woodside, Mrs. Sarah Woodside, Mrs. Ross, wife of Wm. Ross, Abraham Toothaker and his wife, Betsey Owen, Molly Toothaker, Jane Curtiss, Molly Merryman, Mr. Browning and Mrs. Browning, Elisha Snow, Jean Dunning, Betsey Alexander, Martha Hunt, Jane Martin, Mrs. Snow, wife of Elisha Snow, Mrs. Brown, wife of Daniel Brown, Sarah Alexander, Mrs. Sparks, Hitty Hasey, Abner Melcher, Nabby Atherton, Katharine Willson, Andrew Blake, Heziah Blake, Peggy Stanwood, Ann Chase, and Shimuel Owen.

On September 8, 1804, Elder Titcomb, of Portland, at the request of the church and society, agreed "to minister to them in holy things." This invitation was formally extended by the society on August 29, 1805, and was accepted by him on the first of the following September.

On June 2, 1821, Elder Titcomb was dismissed at his own request, and received a letter of recommendation to other churches. The church was destitute of a settled pastor for some time, but had occasional preaching from Elder Titcomb and others.

On January 23, 1822, Benjamin Titcomb, Jr., was ordained, the churches in Topsham, Portland, North Yarmouth, Bath, Harpswell, and Freeport assisting. On November 11 of the same year a com-

---

[1] *All of this account is from the church and parish records.*

mittee consisting of David Given, John O'Brien, and Ephraim Brown was chosen "to provide a suitable place in the village and also another at Maquoit,[1] to meet in the winter for worship, and to take into consideration our present difficult situation in regard to making a selection of a teacher for the present year."

On the eleventh of March, 1824, it was voted that Elder Benjamin Titcomb continue his labors in the church as usual.

On the ninth of August of that year Shimuel Owen, a member of this church, was ordained as an evangelist. In November, a committee was appointed to ascertain the minds of the individual church members as to whether they were satisfied with the labors of Elder Titcomb.

It appears from the records that the church had been somewhat divided, and on the sixth of April, 1825, it was voted that "this church views with abhorrence and detestation their present state as a church, and feeling desirous to walk together in the faith and fellowship of the gospel, we do hereby unitedly agree to bury forever in oblivion all hardness which we may have felt or do now feel in our minds against any of our brethren or sisters, and that we will, with the help of the Divine Spirit, freely and voluntarily forgive all that may have trespassed against us." Up to this time the whole membership of the church was about one hundred and fifty.[2]

On the tenth of April the following members requested to be dismissed to form themselves into a church, or to join some other church, and the request was granted:—

Aaron Dunning, Philip Owen, Catharine H. Putnam, Mary Humphreys, Sarah Owen, Margaret Donahue, Elizabeth Gould, Nancy Swift, Elizabeth Dunning, Mary Blake, Mary Chase, Betsey Petingill, and Sarah Stanwood.

At the same meeting the church refused to grant permission to two of its members to withdraw and join the church of the Second Society, and a committee was chosen to prepare a statement of facts relative to the conduct of the other church since its formation.

On the twenty-sixth of June, 1826, a petition was addressed to Peter O. Alden, Esquire, a justice of the peace, requesting him to issue his warrant to one of the subscribers, directing him to call a meeting of those persons who were desirous of being incorporated into a religious society, to be called the FIRST BAPTIST RELIGIOUS SOCIETY OF BRUNSWICK.

---

[1] *There was no chimney in the Maquoit meeting-house, and there was therefore no way of heating it.*

[2] *Millet.*

In accordance with this petition, Esquire Alden issued his warrant to Ephraim Brown, directing him to call a meeting of the petitioners on the eighth day of July, 1826. At this meeting the society was organized by the choice of the following officers: —

John Brown, moderator; Jonathan Snow, clerk; David Given, John Brown, and Captain John Given, Jr., assessors; David Given, collector and treasurer; John Brown, David Given, Ephraim Brown, and Samuel Given, standing committee; Ephraim Brown, William H. Morse, William James, wardens; Nathaniel Melcher, sexton.

This organization was virtually the same as that incorporated in 1803 as the "Baptist Society in Brunswick." Many of its members had withdrawn and had established themselves as a society in the village, called the "Second Baptist Society." It is quite probable that the officers of the old society were among those who seceded, and being thus left without an organization, the remaining members applied to a justice of the peace under the laws of Maine, for authority to reorganize under a slightly different name.

In July the society voted to raise two hundred dollars for the ensuing year.

On September, 1826, the churches of the First and Second Societies met to discuss their differences. The church of the First Society claimed that the other church had no right to admit as members those who were excluded from the former, until they had been restored to fellowship and regularly dismissed by it. The church of the Second Society claimed that they had a right to admit such members, so long as the other church had nothing against the Christian character of these individuals. No agreement was reached between the two. In November, Adam Wilson was invited to preach one half the time.

On January 8, 1827, it was voted to join in fellowship with the Second Church, which had acknowledged some irregularities in receiving members who were excluded from the First Church.

On February 23, Elder Benjamin Titcomb asked permission to preach to those of the society who resided in the village, or to hold meetings in that part of the town, and it was voted "that it is the opinion of this church that Elder Titcomb is at liberty to preach anywhere in this town where he views it to be his duty." In April some of the members of the old society complained that many members absented themselves and attended Mr. Titcomb's meeting in the village instead of their own.

It had been the practice for some years to hold the meetings of the society in the village in the winter, and at the old meeting-house at

Maquoit in the summer. This year, on June 1, the village members requested that the meetings might continue in the village through the summer, but it was voted not to do so. A few days later thirteen members petitioned for liberty to attend meeting in the village, as it would be more convenient for them, but their request was not granted. In October, Elder Titcomb asked a dismissal, which was granted him, and also to Mary, his wife, and to Elizabeth Titcomb, Ephraim Brown, and Rebecca, his wife, Thomas Stanwood and wife, Thomas Noyes, Joanna Moore, and Mary R. Dunlap: and on the third of November, Joshua Bishop, David Wilson, William Randall, Mary Perkins, Patience Bishop, James Wilson, Isabelle Merryman, and Ruth Skolfield, of Harpswell, were dismissed to form a church in that town.

On January 4, 1828, a resolution was passed that Elder Titcomb, Ephraim Brown, John O'Brien, and others, "having asked dismission for the purpose of uniting with some other church, and having joined the First Church at Bath, and under their patronage have established a meeting in the village while there is already one church of this faith there, causes us grief, and we feel in duty bound to express disfellowship with such a procedure."

During the summer of this year, thirty-eight were added to the church.

In consequence of the action of the First Baptist Church in Bath in sustaining the new movement in Brunswick village, a council was held February 29, 1829, to settle the difficulties between that church and the First Baptist Church in Brunswick, but the action of the council is not recorded. On May 31, however, the Bath church sent a confession of their wrong-doing in having set up a branch church in Brunswick without consultation with the churches already existing there. This action of the Bath church evidently reconciled this church to the formation of the new one in the village, for on October 11, Jonathan Snow and Thomas Ward were chosen delegates to assist in organizing the branch of the Bath church, known as the Federal Street Church, in Brunswick, into an independent church.

The pulpit of the Maquoit or First Baptist Church had been supplied during the past three years by Elders Samuel Mariner, Adam Wilson, Shimuel Owen, and Henry Randall.[1]

On May 22, 1830, it was agreed to try to raise money by subscription for the support of the gospel.

On the twentieth of August, 1831, it was voted that Elder John

---

[1] *Millett.*

Bailey, formerly of Wiscasset, take the pastoral care of the church. He resigned his pastorate in June, 1833.

Elder William Johnson became pastor of the church in 1836, and continued in that capacity until 1840. In July, 1836, Elder Noah Norton and wife were received by letter from the Baptist Church in Bowdoin. In 1838 the parish voted to raise by tax one hundred and fifty dollars for the ensuing year's expenses.

In April, 1840, it was voted to engage Elder Noah Norton, and to raise one hundred and fifty dollars by tax, and fifty dollars by subscription.

It was voted this year that all pew-owners should give up their pews, and that thereafter they should all be free.

On May 1, 1841, it was voted to build a new meeting-house, and that it should stand on the west side of the twelve-rod road, near the road leading to Harpswell; and Captain William Stanwood, Jonathan Snow, Jacob Skolfield, and William Stanwood, 2d, were chosen a building committee. Although there is nothing further upon the subject in the records, it is known that instead of building a new meeting-house, the one on Federal Street, belonging to the Universalists, was, about 1846, purchased and moved to a lot near the junction of the old Harpswell and Mair Point roads, and it was thereafter known as the "Forest Church."

From 1841 to 1845, Elder Norton was annually chosen preacher.

Elder Joseph Hutchinson was chosen pastor in 1848, and in 1852 was dismissed at his own request.

Meetings seem to have been held in the years 1853, 1858, and 1866, but there is no record of any settled pastor, or of any important transactions.

On May 19, 1867, Grenville M. Atkins was invited to become their pastor, and accepted the invitation. He was ordained June 13, 1867. He preached a few days over a year, resigning his charge on May 31, 1868. Since then there has been no settled pastor of this church.

The last entry in the records is dated April 29, 1867, and is to the effect that the parish met on that day and reorganized, and voted "to raise all we can for the support of the gospel."

Connected with the history of this church is the following anecdote which is told of William Woodside. He became "converted" under the preaching of Elder Potter, and at one of the meetings related his "experience," and, as was the custom in those days, he had much to say derogatory of himself. He was in reality a very good man, but in his remarks he called himself a bad man, one who was wholly evil, whose every act was wicked, and whose imaginations were all vain. When he sat down, a relative arose and with becoming gravity said that he could vouch for the truth of all William had said!

SECOND BAPTIST CHURCH AND SOCIETY.

On Tuesday, May 5, 1825, a church was regularly constituted in this place, agreeably to the Baptist platform, by a council assembled for the purpose, under the title of the "Second Baptist Church in Brunswick." The council consisted of delegates from eight churches, who were unanimously agreed in giving the right hand of fellowship. The records of this church have not been found, and it is not positively known who were its members. It is probable, however, that Aaron Dunning, Philip Owen, Catharine H. Putnam, Mary Humphreys, Sarah Owen, Margaret Donahue, Elizabeth Gould, Nancy Swift, Elizabeth Dunning, Mary Blake, Mary Chase, Betsey Pettingill, Sarah Stanwood, Heman Pettingill, and Stanwood Dunning were among the first members All of these persons were previously members of the First Baptist Church, and were dismissed from that church on the tenth of April of that year in order "to form themselves into a church, or to join some other church." The Second Baptist *Society* was not formed for a year later.

In 1826 a meeting-house was erected on School Street. Elder Shimuel Owen was pastor of this society from 1827 until it dissolved, in 1840.[1] The building was then sold to the Congregationalists, and has been used by them ever since as a vestry.

FEDERAL STREET BAPTIST SOCIETY.

In 1828, Elder Benjamin Titcomb, Ephraim Brown, John O'Brien, and a few other members of the First Baptist Society, asked and received dismission from that church and united with the First Baptist Church of Bath, under whose patronage they established meetings in the village of Brunswick. Notwithstanding there was at the same time another Baptist society in the village (the Second Baptist), and notwithstanding the opposition made toward this new movement by the First Baptist Society, it was successful, and in 1829 it was organized as a church. In April, work was begun upon a meeting-house. and the building was completed on the twelfth of the following September. It was situated on Federal Street, at the corner of what is now Franklin Street.[2] This church, it is said, was under the pastoral

[1] *Millet.*

[2] *It is now the Catholic Church.*

care of Elder Titcomb during the whole period of its existence. It was dropped from the association of Baptist churches in 1839. No records of the church having been found, we are unable to give a more complete and accurate sketch.

MAINE STREET BAPTIST CHURCH AND SOCIETY.

In the early part of 1840 a very extensive revival took place in Topsham and Brunswick. In October, twenty-four persons from the church in Topsham, who resided in Brunswick, were organized into a church. The *society* was formed in the same year, and a meeting-house, containing seventy-five pews, was erected on Maine Street, a few rods north of Lincoln Street.[1] The Reverend Paul S. Adams, from South Berwick, was the first pastor, from January 3, 1841, to 1843. He was succeeded by Reverend Dudley C. Haynes, whose pastorate lasted between two and three years.

Reverend John Hubbard, Jr., was chosen pastor January, 1846, at a salary of two hundred dollars per annum. His pastorate ended October 4, 1851. Reverend J. W. Coburn was pastor from March 15, 1852, until June 2, 1853; and in November of the latter year he was succeeded by the Reverend Charles Ayer, who remained until September 1, 1856. Reverend E. Andrews, an evangelist, then supplied the pulpit for a few months, and was succeeded by the Reverend James D. Reid, in October, 1857. In 1859, Reverend Charles Ayer again supplied the pulpit.

In June, 1860, the Reverend George Knox was installed as pastor of the society. In June, 1861, Mr. Knox was granted a leave of absence to act as chaplain of a Maine regiment, and Reverend S. W. Taylor was engaged to supply the pulpit during his absence. The former was discharged from his pastorate, at his own request, November 17, 1861. He was afterward killed by a fall from his horse.

In 1862, Reverend T. J. B. House was chosen pastor, and remained with the society three years. In 1865, Reverend C. M. Herring was chosen pastor. During his pastorate a vestry was built and the meeting-house was repaired and remodelled.

Mr. Herring resigned his pastorate July 26, 1868, and was succeeded, the next spring, by Reverend S. W. Emerson, who remained but one year.

Reverend B. F. Lawrence became pastor in June, 1870, and

---

[1] *The present Baptist Church.*

remained for four years. Reverend E. S. Small, the present pastor, began his pastorate February 20, 1876.

The foregoing sketch of this parish is made from notes furnished by the parish clerk. It is not so full as could be wished, but is as complete as possible from the notes furnished.

SOCIETY OF FRIENDS.

There has never been any organized society of Friends in Brunswick, but about 1772 several Quakers moved into town and settled not far from the line between Brunswick and Durham. Some of them had previously been living in Harpswell.[1] Others joined them, and there are now a number of excellent people in the west end of the town who belong to this denomination. Their meeting-house is in the town of Durham, and they belong to the society of that town.

FREE-WILL BAPTIST SOCIETIES.

About 1793, Elder Pelatiah Tingley, of Waterboro', formerly of Sanford, began, with others, to hold religious meetings in Brunswick. These meetings were usually held at the house of William Alexander.[2] About 1799 the First Free-Will Baptist Society, or as it was sometimes called, the "Christian Church in Brunswick and Freeport," was formed. The first church meeting was held at James Elliot's on October 23. The members were Obadiah Curtis, Adam Elliot, William Alexander, Anthony Morse, Joseph Ward, John Coombs, Susannah Morey, Hannah and Margaret Coombs.

In 1807 the records state that there was considerable contention in the church, but the cause thereof is not given. On August 27, of this year, the church numbered forty members. In 1809 there was a "considerable want of union and many backsliders."

In 1810 the church was more prosperous, and many converts were made. This year their meeting-house was built. It was a one-story building, and was situated near Noah Melcher's, on the old Freeport road. It was, it is said, the second meeting-house of this denomination in the State.

In 1813, on December 16th, Elder Adam Elliot, who had been settled about August, 1803, died, and the pulpit became vacant. In 1816, Elder George Lamb was settled. The whole number of members up to June 1, 1817, was one hundred and fifty.

On May 2, 1818, a division occurred in the church, on the question

---

[1] *Pejepscot Papers.* [2] *Stewart's Free-Will Baptists.*

of washing of feet after the manner of the early disciples, and a few members withdrew because the rite was not observed.

On February 22, 1823, owing to the small number of members and the low state of interest existing, the society was declared dissolved. On January 17, 1826, the church was reorganized by a committee from the Quarterly Meeting. The first meeting after the reorganization was held on the fourth of February. On November 14, 1827, the Union Meeting-House at "Growstown" was finished, and the future meetings of this society were held in it.

In 1831, June 25, the church voted to use a bass-viol with their singing. A resolve to use no ardent spirits, except as a medicine, was passed at this meeting. On February 22, 1834, it was voted to deal with all church members who had taken the pledge of temperance and had violated it. Elder Lamb resigned his pastorate on September 25, 1835. He died in Brunswick, December 14, 1836, having served as pastor nineteen years. August 12, 1837, Elder Andrew Rollins was received as pastor of the church. The whole number of members, between 1826 and 1839, was one hundred and ninety-three.

On May 16, 1840, it was voted to increase Elder Rollins's salary from three hundred to three hundred and fifty dollars. February 20, 1841, it was voted to recognize singing as a means of worship, and to make regulations in regard to the same. On July 22, 1842, Amos Lunt, Amos Lunt, Jr., Thomas Coombs, George Cobb, and Phineas Collins were dismissed, to organize the Freeport and Brunswick Church. On June 30, Elder Ezra Crowell was ordained.

June 8, 1844, Elder E. G. Eaton was elected as pastor. He was dismissed February 12, 1847. During the latter year Elder E. F. Page officiated. On February 12, 1848, Elder Almon Libby was settled. He was dismissed February 14, 1852, and in May of that year Elder Rollins was again settled. The whole number of members up to 1851 was three hundred and sixty-eight, of which two hundred and twenty-five were females.

February 12, 1853, the church repealed the old covenant and adopted the *New Testament as a covenant.* On September 20, 1856, Elder D. Waterman was settled. In 1859, Elder Chaney was settled over the church, but his pastorate was a short one, as he resigned in the October following. On February 16, 1860, Elder Hutchinson was settled.

THE FREE BAPTIST SOCIETY OF BRUNSWICK VILLAGE was originally composed of members of the church at Topsham who resided in Brunswick, and who, on account of the distance, resolved to form a church of their own.

The first sermon was delivered in McLellan Hall, by Reverend Doctor Graham. No step had at that time been taken to form a society, though the matter had been somewhat discussed. On the evening of October 25, 1865, five men met at the house of Mr. Ezekiel Thompson to form a society. Church officers were appointed to serve six months, and on the next Sabbath Reverend A. H. Heath, then of Bates College Theological School, was invited to preach at the Good Templars' Hall. The Sunday school was organized at the second meeting of the society, November 5, 1865. Mr. Heath continued to preach until the spring of 1876, when he returned to his studies at the Theological School, and Reverend E. C. B. Hallam, a returned missionary, was engaged to preach in his stead.

On the afternoon of April 12, 1866, a council of ministers met at McLellan Hall, — to which place the society had moved its meetings, — to formally organize the church. Forty persons, including five converts, composed the society at this time. The council approved the course that had been taken, accepted the letters of recommendation that were presented, and extended the right hand of fellowship to the new society. Mr. Hallam was then installed as pastor. On the third of June following, the first communion service was held. Mr. Hallam was requested by the Missionary Board to return to India, and in consequence of his acquiescence, he was obliged to preach his farewell sermon on Sunday eve, November 11.

In 1867, Reverend S. D. Church was called to the pulpit, and preached for two years. During his pastorate eleven persons were received into the church. Reverend W. F. Smith commenced to preach to this society on August 22, 1869. The church at that time had sixty-five members and a growing congregation. Upon the completion of Lemont Hall, in 1870, the majority of the society desired to occupy it, and it was accordingly engaged for the Sabbath services. This change of place met with earnest opposition, however, from a few members, who refused to enter the new hall and withdrew their support to the society. Consequently, upon the eighth of June, nine persons, including both deacons, were excluded from church membership. During Mr. Smith's pastorate forty-three persons were added to the church by baptism or by letter.

On November 30, 1872, the resignation of Reverend Mr. Smith was accepted. He was succeeded by Reverend H. P. Lamprey, who preached for one year, then by Doctor Heath, of Hallowell. The time of the latter was divided between two churches and the practice of medicine.

In the early part of 1875, Reverend B. M. Edwards, the present pastor, was settled. The society had for some time desired a house of worship, and in 1874 a lot of land upon O'Brien Street was purchased for the site of one. In the autumn of 1875 the building was commenced. The vestry on the lower floor was finished before the middle of the following summer, and on the ninth of July, 1876, the first sermon in the new house was preached by Mr. Edwards. It was owing largely to the efforts of the pastor that the building was erected.

This church in its first years was unfortunate in losing many of its leading members by death, among whom were Deacon Dresser, Mr. Ezekiel Thompson, and Mrs. Smiley. "Aunt Smiley," as she was called, had prayer-meetings at her house for more than thirty years, and when this society was formed, their weekly prayer-meetings were held there until after her death. Mr. Thompson was elected a deacon after Mr. Dresser died, and served faithfully up to the time of his own decease. Deacon Dresser was one of the most active members in forming the society and was always zealous in its support.

A good degree of religious interest has always been kept up in this society, and the church shared largely in the revival work of the past winter. There are now one hundred and twenty-nine members. The Sunday school has been well supported, and there are now connected with it nine teachers and one hundred and thirty scholars.[1]

UNIVERSALIST AND UNITARIAN SOCIETIES.

The records of the UNIVERSALIST SOCIETY, previous to its uniting with the Unitarians in 1850, having been lost or destroyed, a perfectly accurate history of the society is impossible. It is believed, however, that the following sketch is substantially correct, and it is as complete as could be made from the material at our disposal.

The first movement toward sustaining Universalist preaching here was made in the year 1812. The nature of that movement is best shown by the following agreement, the original of which is now in the possession of Mr. Harvey Stetson, son of the Harvey Stetson who is named in the agreement: —

"BRUNSWICK, January 20th, 1812.

"We, whose names are here under written, Do Profess to believe in the Doctrine of Universal Salvation by our Lord and Saviour Jesus Christ: And feeling it our Duty as well as our privilege and

---

[1] *For the particulars of the foregoing sketch, we are indebted to the pastor and to the parish clerk.*

highest happiness to worship the one living and true God in Christ Jesus: Do hereby agree and enter into Solemn Covenant to assemble together as a Religious Society on the Sabbath as often as we can conveniently to worship the most high God: And that we will pay our proportion towards the expense of procuring a convenient place for convening together for publick and social Worship: and for the support of Publick Teachers of Piety, Religion and Christian Morality in our Society:

"Lemuel Swift
Jonathan Eastman
James Merrill
James Cary
James Jones
Robert Eastman
E. H. Goss
James Cary Jr.
Roger Merrill
Elijah Hall
John Marston
Abner Pratt
Benj. Stephens
John Gray
Abner A. Kelley
Stephen Lennox
Dean Swift
Nathl. Badger
Harvey Stetson
Edward Raymond
James Maxwell
Edward Welch
Phineas Taylor
Ira Fuller
Joseph Kimball
John Lee
Edmund Prady
Solomon Gray
Reed Welch
Burt Townsend
Allen Wing.
31"

They were incorporated in October of that year as the First Universal Christian Society in Brunswick. Mr. Dean Swift is probably the only one of the signers of the foregoing paper who is now living.

Soon after this agreement was made, arrangements were made with the Reverend Thomas Barnes, of Norway, to preach here once a month. The meetings were held in Washington Hall. Mr. Barnes came here on Saturday, on horseback, and returned on Monday. After the cotton-mill was built, in 1812–13, he received a good part of his pay in cotton yarn, which he carried home in his saddle-bags. He preached here for, probably, a year and a half. Mr. Barnes was called the "Father of Universalism in Maine." He came to Maine from Massachusetts in 1799 as an itinerant preacher. He was ordained over the united societies of Norway, New Gloucester, Falmouth, and Gray, January 6, 1802. He died in Poland in 1814.

Reverend Jacob Wood, of Saco, succeeded Mr. Barnes, preaching here occasionally, but for how long a time is uncertain. Probably other itinerants visited the place from time to time. In 1826, Reverend Sylvanus Cobb[1] preached here several Sabbaths.

On the twenty-seventh of January, 1827, Major Burt Townsend,[2] Captain Roger Merrill,[2] Captain Joseph McLellan,[2] Thomas Taylor,[2] Colonel Andrew Dennison,[2] Joshua Lufkin,[2] Harvey Stetson,[2] James Derby,[2] A. C. Raymond, Joseph Lunt, John L. Swift, and others whose names we cannot ascertain, formed a society under the name of THE UNIVERSALIST SOCIETY OF BRUNSWICK AND TOPSHAM.

Arrangements were at once made with Reverend Mr. Cobb to preach once in three or four weeks. The meetings were held in Washington Hall. This engagement continued until February, 1828 (about one year), when it terminated.

In April of that year Reverend Seth Stetson (Father Stetson, as he was called in later years) came East on a missionary tour, and preached here, for the first time, on Thursday evening, April 17, 1828. On the following Sunday, as he says in his diary, he "preached in a large hall to a good number of men." The next day he went to Topsham, where he was the guest of Major William Frost, and in the evening he preached in the court-house. From Topsham he went to Bowdoinham and other places in the vicinity, and soon after returned to Boston, where he then resided.

About the first of June following, he received an invitation to remove to Brunswick, and preach in the three towns of Brunswick, Bath, and Bowdoinham, alternately. He accepted the invitation, and on the twenty-second of June, 1828, he preached in Brunswick, and continued to preach there every third Sabbath until May 10, 1829, when his engagement closed.

A meeting-house for this parish was erected in 1829. It was situated on Federal Street, directly opposite the present high-school building. Reverend Mr. Stetson was invited to preach in the new meeting-house during the winter, for which he received eight dollars a Sabbath. After the twenty-first of February, 1830, he preached a few Sabbaths for what he could get, a collection being taken up each Sabbath. The amount collected being too small for his necessities, he gave up the field and went on a missionary tour, and in May following removed with his family to Buckfield.

---

[1] *He was afterwards settled at Malden, Massachusetts, where he died. He was a prominent clergyman in the denomination.*

[2] *Deceased.*

From this time until 1835 the Universalists were without preaching, and their meeting-house was occupied by the

UNITARIANS.

On the eleventh of December, 1829, a meeting of Unitarians was held, and it was decided to form a society for the establishment and maintenance of Unitarian preaching in Brunswick. The organization was effected on the third day of January, 1830, under the title of The Second Congregational Society of Brunswick,[1] and was composed of twenty-three members, all of whom were avowed Unitarians. No records having been kept, we are unable to give a complete list of the members. Among them, however, were the following: Benjamin Weld, Charles Weld, Governor Dunlap, Professor Henry W. Longfellow, Ebenezer Everett, John Coburn, John S. Cushing, Humphrey Purinton, and Major William Frost.

A subscription paper was soon after circulated to raise funds to support preaching. This list numbered fifty-five, and included some Universalists who sympathized with the Unitarians, and were willing to aid in support of Unitarian preaching.

The Universalists gave the use of their meeting-house, and in June, 1830, the first Unitarian sermon was preached in Brunswick. Reverend Andrew Bigelow was the preacher.

From June, 1830, to June, 1835, there was regular Unitarian preaching, but there was not any of this time a settled minister. Of those who supplied the pulpit, Mr. Wiswell remained the longest.[2] He preached here from 1832 to 1834,—a little more than two years.

The other ministers supplied for a longer or shorter time, varying from two to ten or twelve Sundays each. The meetings were well attended, the building being generally well filled, but seldom or never crowded. Professor Longfellow conducted a Bible class for several years, which was largely attended, and which is spoken of by members of the class as having been exceedingly interesting and instructive.

---

[1] *This society had, however no legal existence.*

[2] *The ministers supplying the pulpit after Mr. Bigelow, were: H. Edes, Allen Putnam, Caleb Stetson, William Newell, John H. Williams, Alonzo Hill, Sidney Willard, A. B. Muzzey, John Goldsbury, William D. Wiswell, William A. Whitwell, Jabez Whitman, R. A. Johnson, A. Davis, and Charles A. Farley.*

A part of the congregation was composed of Topsham people, and after a time the meetings alternated between Brunswick and Topsham to accommodate them. Finally it was agreed between the Universalists and Unitarians that the former should maintain preaching in Brunswick and the latter in Topsham. (See sketch of Unitarian society of Topsham.) In 1835 the

UNIVERSALISTS

Made a third engagement with Reverend Seth Stetson to supply their pulpits. Accordingly he again removed to Brunswick with his family, and ever after resided here. His engagement began on the twenty-eighth of June, 1835, and ended on the twenty-eighth of February, 1836.

Early in June, 1836, Reverend Stephen A. Sneathen came here from Massachusetts, and preached occasionally during the months of June, July, and August. Reverend G. M. Quinby, then settled at Yarmouth, also preached here occasionally during the same period. On the tenth of August, in this year, Mr. Sneathen entered into an engagement to preach every other Sabbath, a part of the time in Topsham. This arrangement was continued during the remainder of the year. On the twenty-fifth of January, 1837, Mr. Sneathen was ordained, and became the first settled minister of the society. He was a young man, physically a cripple, but said to be a speaker of more than ordinary ability. His pastorate ended in the spring of 1838.

Mr. Sneathen was succeeded by Reverend Sidney Turner, whose pastorate commenced in June or July, 1838, and lasted until about the first of September, 1840. Father Stetson says of him in his diary, "He was a young Congregational minister who turned Universalist, but after a year or two he turned back again. He married a minister's widow in Bingham, where he was settled in 1849"

In October, 1840, "Father" Stetson began his fourth and last engagement, preaching every other Sunday until April, 1842.

He was succeeded by Reverend Giles Bailey,[1] who began a supply of the pulpit in April, 1842. In July he removed here from Winthrop, the place of his first pastorate, and where he

---

[1] *Now pastor of the Universalist Church in Reading, Pennsylvania, and to whom we are indebted for many of the facts contained in this sketch.*

was ordained. He preached regularly during the year, but was not formally installed until January 7, 1843. The installation sermon was preached by Reverend Mr. Gardiner, of Waterville. The pastorate of Mr. Bailey continued until September, 1848, when he resigned to enter upon the duties of the missionary agency of the Maine Universalist Convention. The society was, during the pastorate of Mr. Bailey, in its most flourishing condition. The officers of the society at that time were Colonel Andrew Dennison, and Anthony Raymond (or "Father" Raymond, as he was called), deacons; Isaac Center, clerk; Nathaniel Badger, collector and treasurer. During this pastorate the Mason Street Church was built. It was dedicated in December, 1846.

After the resignation of Mr. Bailey the church was without a pastor for several months. Early in the year 1849, Reverend W. C. George was called to the charge. He remained only a year, when the society was again without a pastor.

The Universalist Society of Brunswick and the Unitarian Society of Topsham were both at this time in a feeble condition, the result chiefly of deaths and removals. It was therefore proposed to unite the two societies in one organization, to be known as

THE MASON STREET RELIGIOUS SOCIETY.

The necessary arrangements were made, and went into effect on the first Sunday in November, 1850. Reverend Amos D. Wheeler, of Topsham, Unitarian, was the pastor.

There was a debt of one thousand dollars upon the house, six hundred dollars of which was procured by the pastor from prominent Unitarians in Boston, and the balance was paid by individual subscriptions in the society.

The engagement of Reverend Doctor Wheeler was for five years only, and the salary was to be raised in equal proportions by the members of the society from the two towns. Doctor Wheeler's engagement was renewed from time to time, so that his services were not discontinued until October 1, 1865, at which time he delivered his farewell discourse, having been appointed by the American Unitarian Association to act in a missionary capacity in the State of Maine.

During Doctor Wheeler's pastorate the ladies of this society formed an association, the object of which was: —

"*First*, the promotion of kind, social, Christian intercourse and feeling among its members and generally throughout the society with which it is connected; and *secondly*, to aid in the accomplishment of any religious or benevolent purpose from its funds or otherwise as a majority of its members may determine."

Doctor Wheeler was succeeded by Reverend William Ellery Copeland, who was ordained on Thursday, July 26, 1866. The services were as follows: —

Introductory prayer, by Reverend Casneau Palfrey, D. D., of Belfast; reading of Scripture, by Reverend John Nichols, of Saco; anthem, by choir: sermon, by Reverend George Putnam, D. D., of Roxbury, Massachusetts; hymn; ordaining prayer, by Reverend A. D. Wheeler, D. D.; charge, by Reverend Edward E. Hale, of Boston; right hand of fellowship, by Reverend Charles C Salter, of West Cambridge, Massachusetts; address to the people, by Reverend Charles C. Everett, of Bangor; hymn; benediction, by the pastor.

Mr. Copeland, like his predecessor, was a Unitarian in his views. The society, however, owing to the various causes which usually combine to weaken any religious association, became gradually feeble, and as it became so, the Universalist element preponderated. Mr. Copeland gave good satisfaction while pastor, though he laid himself open to the objection that was made, that he cared more for the temperance cause than he did for the success of this church. He resigned his charge in 1869, and in 1870 Reverend William R. French, a Universalist, was chosen to fill his place, and continued as pastor of the society until 1875, when he resigned. During his pastorate Mr. French labored faithfully and well for the interests of the society. Since his resignation no regular services have been held by either the Universalists or Unitarians.

THE UNITARIAN SOCIETY OF BRUNSWICK.

This society was legally organized on the fifth day of August, 1874. The incorporators numbered fifty-three. Stephen J. Young, W. B. Purinton, A. G. Poland, Emeline Weld, and Harriet Tebbets were elected a standing committee; Henry W. Wheeler, clerk; A. V. Metcalf, treasurer; Humphrey Purinton, collector; H. P. Thompson and Alonzo Day, assessors.

A code of by-laws was adopted and a committee chosen to present, at some future time, plans for a chapel suitable for the accommodation of the society, and to take measures to secure a suitable lot.

In March, 1875, a lot was purchased on the corner of Federal and Pearl Streets for $1,500, the amount having been subscribed by members of the society. The society has not yet erected a church edifice, but the organization is maintained.

METHODIST EPISCOPAL SOCIETY OF BRUNSWICK.

The first Methodist preaching in Brunswick, of which we have any account, was in the year 1821. At that time Melville B. Cox, while laboring on a circuit approaching within eight miles of this place, came here and, securing the use of the school-house near the colleges, commenced a course of Sunday-evening lectures. His devout appearance and the pathos of his words interested his hearers and soon drew a considerable congregation, among whom were many students. One family in the place kindly opened their doors for his entertainment. After he had continued his appointment for some time, he came one Sabbath evening, wearied with the labors of the day and a long ride, from his place of preaching during the day, and called at the house of his host. He saw no signs of any one in the house, and knocked at the door several times, when at length the man came to the door and said that he was very sorry to inform him that he must turn him away from his house or be turned away himself. The preacher repaired to the place of meeting without a supper, preached his last sermon in Brunswick, and then rode eight miles to find a lodging; such was the opposition at that time against the Methodists.

In the latter part of 1828, or early in 1829, Reverend William H. Norris, then stationed at Bath, preached a few times in this place, after which meetings were held occasionally by local preachers from Bath. At the Maine Annual Conference, held in July, 1829, Reverend Benjamin Bryant was appointed to the Bath circuit, including the upper part of Bath, New Meadows, and Brunswick. He spent a few Sabbaths in this village and formed a "class" of five members, namely, Mrs. Snowden, Miss Jane Blake, Miss Eunice McLellan, Miss Margaret Todd, and Miss Maria Walker. The last two are still living.

The encouragement was so small that the place was abandoned, and at the succeeding Conference the circuit was merged in the Bath station.

Soon after the above-mentioned class was formed, two Methodist students entered Bowdoin College (in 1828 and 1829). One of these, John Johnston (afterwards Professor of Natural Science in Wesleyan University), manifested a firm attachment to Methodism and cordially identified himself with the humble society at Brunswick. The other, Charles Adams, was a licensed preacher, and preached in the neighborhood of Brunswick as occasion offered during his college course. Under his direction the small class increased in numbers, strengthened by occasional recruits from the college students.

In the fall of 1833 the class consisted of about fourteen persons, of whom five were students in college.

In the winter of 1834 an arrangement was made with a number of preachers in neighboring towns to supply preaching one half the time on the Sabbath, until the session of the Conference in the following July. The preaching was gratuitous, the society paying the travelling expenses of the minister.

At this Conference (1834) an application was made for a preacher to be supported in part by funds of the Missionary Society. But the condition of the funds would not allow such an appropriation. The services of Reverend James Warren, a very acceptable local preacher, were obtained one half of the time. The request for a preacher was renewed the next year, 1835, and Mr. Warren was appointed to Bowdoinham and Brunswick circuit. In consequence of ill-health, Mr. Warren retired from the circuit in two or three months, and Asahel Moore, who had just graduated at Bowdoin College, and who had always been warmly interested in the society, was engaged to take charge of it and visit it once in two or three weeks, being then engaged in teaching school at Gardiner. Early in the spring of 1836 he closed his school and devoted his whole time to the society in Brunswick. At this time there were about forty members in the society, including seven college students.

These meetings were held on the Sabbath in the Congregational conference-room, or in the Universalist meeting-house, which was hired for this purpose.

On the sixteenth of April, 1836, Eliphalet S. Bryant, Daniel Smith, Charles Evans, Rufus Rich, Ebenezer Stockbridge, and Albert Merrill requested Moses E. Woodman, Esquire, a justice of the peace, to issue a warrant to one of the applicants, directing him to call a meeting of the applicants for the purpose of organizing a religious society or parish, by the name of the Methodist Episcopal Society, in Brunswick. The warrrant was issued, and on the twenty-fifth of April the applicants referred to met at the Baptist Meeting-House on Federal Street, and after appointing Asahel Moore,

Sandford K. Ballard, Stephen M. Vail, and Samuel G. Lane to be their associates, organized by the choice of Sanford K. Ballard, chairman, and Stephen M. Vail, clerk. A constitution was then adopted, and a board of trustees was elected, consisting of Honorable Allen F. Cobb, of Durham, John Wilkinson, of Bath, Ebenezer Moore, of Gardiner, John Moore, of Gardiner, Eliphalet Bryant, of Brunswick, Ephraim Sturdivant, of Cumberland, and Samuel G. Lane, of Brunswick.

In September following, the meeting-house on the east side of Federal Street, called the "Baptist Branch Meeting-House," previously occupied by the society of which Reverend Mr. Titcomb was pastor, was bought by the trustees of the Methodist Episcopal Society for the sum of $1,900, and the lot upon which the building stood was purchased for fifty dollars additional. In payment the trustees gave notes payable at the expiration of one year. Something more than one half the amount was paid during the year, and new notes were given for the balance.

On the tenth of January, 1838, the house was paid for, and on the seventeenth of April following the society was entirely free from debt. The whole pecuniary responsibility in the purchase of the meeting-house was assumed by Mr. Sturdivant. Some help was received from abroad, but in order to relieve Mr. Sturdivant from his heavy burden the parsonage (which had been built mostly by the generosity of Thomas Knowlton) was deeded to him, and the debt due to him mostly paid.

At the annual Conference, held in August, 1836, the Reverend Mark Trafton was appointed to Brunswick. He remained with the society about three months, and left in the apprehension that he could not receive a support. The society was thus thrown into great discouragement. In this emergency the pulpit was supplied by Isaiah McMahon, a student in college.

In 1837, Reverend C. P. Bragdon took charge of the society. His labors were quite successful, and a considerable number were added to the church. From 1838 to 1840, Reverend C. C. Cone was the preacher in charge. His labors were quite successful, and the society was increased from seventy-five to one hundred and twenty-seven. He was succeeded by Reverend A. P. Hillman. During the two years' appointment of this preacher the society was reduced to ninety-three members. No cause for this diminution of membership is given in the society's records.

In the year 1842, Reverend Asahel Moore was appointed to Brunswick. The society was laboring under great embarrassment from its feebleness, but was considerably improved under the labors of Mr. Moore, there being one hundred and fifteen members at the close of his two years' labor.

Reverend Cornelius Stone was the preacher in charge in 1844. A few conversions occurred during the year, but the number of deaths and removals was more than sufficient to offset the gain.

In 1845, Reverend Daniel Fuller was appointed to Brunswick. During the second year of his labors his health broke down and he did not long survive. His last sermon was preached in January, 1857, his subject being the *Eternal World.* He was a good preacher and a faithful pastor.

His successor, Reverend John W. True, was appointed at the Conference held in Saco the same year. The church at this time was much enfeebled by removals and in consequence of being deprived of their pastor most of the year. The pastor was considerably interrupted in his work by sickness and other embarrassments, and the society hardly held its own during these two years.

During the year 1849 the society was without a preacher.

In the spring of 1850 the society raised the sum of two hundred dollars and repaired the meeting-house. Reverend Ezekiel Robinson was the preacher in charge.

Reverend Charles Munger was pastor in 1851–2, and Reverend Joseph Hawkes in 1853.

Reverend J. C. Perry was appointed to Brunswick in 1854, and a considerable revival occurred during the year.

In 1855, Reverend Parker Jaques was the preacher.

In 1856–59, Reverend Charles W. Morse spent three years and ten months at Brunswick with varied success.

From 1845 till 1854 Brunswick was a missionary station. There was no appropriation subsequent to that time. Mr. Morse was retired from active duties, but, on account of the protracted sickness of his wife, he had charge for the fourth year at Brunswick.

In 1860 and 1861 no material change occurred in the condition of the society. Reverend John Cobb was pastor.

In 1862–3, Reverend Josiah H. Newhall was preacher in charge. During the second year there was considerable religious excitement in the village, caused by the labors of the revivalist, Reverend Mr. Hammond, and a considerable revival occurred in the Methodist Society. Mr. Newhall was a fine scholar, a native of Lynn, and a graduate of Wesleyan University. He died suddenly of paralysis in 1866.

In 1864, Reverend W. W. Baldwin, an energetic young man, was preacher in charge and had considerable success. The following year he went to Montana as a missionary.

Reverend John B. Lapham was appointed to Brunswick in 1865 and 1867. Under his labors there was considerable revival and accession to the strength of the society. In 1866 the old meeting-house was sold and the present one erected. In 1868 furniture for a parsonage was purchased, and a new communion service was bought.

Reverend Stephen Allen was preacher in charge for two years, 1867 to 1869. Under his pastorate there was a gratifying gain in membership, and he left his charge with good prospects for the future. Mr. Allen was a graduate of Bowdoin College, class of 1835. He is a fine scholar, an interesting preacher, and is one of the leading men in the denomination. He was succeeded by Reverend James McMillan, who had charge of the parish for three years, 1869 to 1872. There was an extensive revival during his second year, resulting in large additions to the church.

Reverend H. C. Sheldon, a graduate of Yale College and a ripe scholar, succeeded Mr. McMillan, remaining here two years, 1872 to 1874. He is now a professor in the Boston University. He was succeeded, in 1874, by Reverend C. W. Morse, who was also pastor here from 1856 to 1859, and who has won the sincere respect, not only of the members of his parish, but of the citizens of the town generally.

Reverend W. S. Jones is the present pastor.

ST. PAUL'S PARISH.

The first Episcopalian service ever held in Brunswick was held in the college chapel in 1842. The Reverend J. Cook Richmond, on his way from Gardiner to Portland, was obliged to stop over night at Brunswick. Wishing to improve the opportunity to present the services of the church to the people of the town and the students of the college, he asked the consent of the Congregational minister to such a service, which he failed to receive. He then appealed to the president of the college (Doctor Woods), who said to him, "There is one place in this town over which I have control, and you can hold a service in the college chapel." Timely notice was given, and at half past seven in the evening a large congregation was gathered to hear (many of them for the first time) the evening service of the Prayer-Book. Mr. Richmond then preached and held the attention of his hearers for nearly two hours.

This was the first step towards introducing the services of the church here, and doubtless suggested and encouraged the idea of the permanent establishment of a parish. The next service of the church was held in the Congregational vestry on School Street, by the Right Reverend J. E. K. Henshaw, Bishop of Rhode Island and Provisional Bishop of Maine, on his first visitation to this State, in October, 1843. He was accompanied by the Reverend Messrs. James Pratt of Portland, and Thomas F. Fales of Rhode Island, and after evening prayer "preached to a respectable and attentive audience." Mr. Fales afterwards returned as a missionary, and on the fifth of November, 1843, being Sunday, he began regular services in what was then known as the Pleasant Street Seminary, nearly opposite the present Methodist Church, but which has since been removed to Maine Street, and is now used for business purposes.

Mr. Fales thus became the first rector of this parish. He was educated for the ministry at the General Theological Seminary in New York City; was ordained deacon by Bishop Griswold in Rhode Island, July 22, 1840, and priest by the same bishop in 1841; and on the same day of the same month, July 21, he received the degree of B. A. from Bristol College, Pennsylvania, and M. A. from the University of New York.

Mr. Fales continued to hold meetings in the school-house from November, 1840, until the completion of the church in July, 1845. There was at first considerable opposition to the establishment of this church, but it soon passed away. This parish has from the first been a mission, supported mainly by the "General Board" and by the "Diocesan Board of Missions." Up to 1848 no contribution had been made by the parish towards the support of the rector, and then it only amounted to a small sum. At the time Mr. Fales's labors began, the number of Episcopalians was very small. There were only three communicants, Daniel R. Goodwin, Mary R. Goodwin, and Isabella McDougal.

The families of Professor Goodwin, of the college, and of Mr. Samuel Harris, of Topsham, were the only entire households which identified themselves with the church. Five or six of the students were Churchmen. The attendance on the services, however, increased, and on the eighth of January, 1844, a parish was duly organized according to the laws of the State. There were seven original members, namely, Professor D. R. Goodwin, Joseph Badger, Samuel Harris, George Earle, John O B. Dunning, Ebenezer M. Johnson, and Samuel Dunning.

The first officers elected were, for wardens, D. R. Goodwin and

Joseph W. Sargent; for vestrymen, Abner B. Thompson, Joseph Badger, George Earle, Samuel Dunning, John O. B. Dunning, Ebenezer M. Johnson, and Samuel Harris.

It was then voted that the parish assume the name of *St. Paul's*, and that the Reverend T. F. Fales be invited to settle as rector of the church. The invitation was accepted on the twelfth day of February, 1844.

From the very organization of the parish, the Ladies' Society has been most faithful and most efficient in raising and supplying all that was needed. Nothing except the improvements made by Mr. Taylor has been done without them. In fact, if it had not been for the self-sacrificing labors of the ladies of the parish, it might never have lived for thirty years. In 1845 they furnished the church with the reading-desk and pulpit, altar and chairs. In 1848, chiefly through their exertions, an organ was procured and placed in the gallery. Previously stringed instruments were used.

The communion set used from the first till now was presented by Mrs. Griswold of the "Eastern Diocese," as it was called. The stone font was given in 1861 by a number of persons, chiefly graduates of Bowdoin College. The organ was removed from the gallery to the east transept in 1867, and was replaced by a new one in September, 1873.

There have been six rectors. The Reverend Thomas F. Fales, the first, remained here just six years. He has since been rector of Christ Church, Waltham, Mass.

The Reverend Andrew Croswell was here three years and five months. He now resides in Cambridge, Mass.

The Reverend Professor D. R. Goodwin supplied services for six months, when there was a vacancy for ten months with only occasional lay-reading.

The Reverend William Stone Chadwell was the third rector, and remained here three years and eight months. He is now rector of Grace Church, Brooklyn, Long Island, New York.

The Reverend Edward Ballard immediately succeeded him, and was rector of the parish for twelve years and seven months. (See Biographical Sketch.)

After a vacancy of six months, during which time there were occasional services, Reverend Joseph Pemberton Taylor entered on the charge of the parish, and remained here two years and four months. He was immediately succeeded by Reverend Frederick S. Sill, M. A., and is now residing in Camden, New Jersey.

Reverend Mr. Sill was succeeded by Reverend H. P. Nichols, who was ordained to the priesthood, May 27, 1877.

In this parish, since its formation, one hundred and thirty individuals have been baptized, eighty-three confirmed, sixty-three buried, and thirty married. The present number of communicants is about twenty-nine; of individuals, about seventy-five.

ROMAN CATHOLICS.

The formation of a society of believers in the doctrines of the Church of Rome was begun in this town about 1860, or a short time previously. Services were at first performed by the priest stationed at Bath. The society, however, gradually increased in numbers, and in 1866 purchased their present church building on Federal Street, of the Methodist Society, and Father Powers was soon after sent to them. This society is now, numerically, by far the largest in town. About five sixths of the congregation are French Canadians. They number about eight hundred. The present priest, Father Noiseux, is a French Canadian.

STATISTICS OF CHURCH-GOERS, ETC, IN 1873.

In 1873, Mr. Charles Hill, agent of the Brunswick Bible Society, canvassed the town and collected statistics relative to the number of church-goers, etc. The following is a summary of his report, and shows the religious views of the citizens as well as such a canvass can, but it is not, probably, absolutely correct.

Number attending church (nominally)	3,056
" not attending church	1,001
" children attending Sabbath schools	794
" children not attending Sabbath schools	122
" Catholics (French, 477; Irish, 131; colored, 59)	667
" Protestants	2,389
" Congregationalists (Orthodox)	598
" Free Baptists	574
" Methodists	361
" Baptists	306
" Friends	159
" Universalists	151
" Adventists	82
" Unitarians	61
" Episcopalians	56
" For Union of Churches	39
" Spiritualists	2

CHAPTER XIII.

ECCLESIASTICAL HISTORY OF TOPSHAM.

But little is known concerning the condition of religious matters in Topsham prior to the incorporation of the town. In the year 1721 the Reverend Isaac Taylor was employed by the proprietors to preach there one half the time. In 1730 there was a chaplain at the Fort in Brunswick, supported by the proprietors, who attended to the religious needs of the several neighboring communities, but who, most likely, preached only in Brunswick. There is little doubt that previous to the erection of the first meeting-house in Topsham, the inhabitants of that place were accustomed to attend religious services at Brunswick. In 1739 the inhabitants of Topsham contributed to the support of preaching in Brunswick, and it is probable that such had been the custom for some years previous.[1] The town was incorporated in 1764, and at this date, therefore, properly begins the history of the

FIRST PARISH.

[1764.] At the second meeting of the town, held June 2, 1764, John Fulton, John Reed, and John Merrill (the selectmen) were chosen a committee "to get an orthodox minister to preach for the space of three months." They evidently employed Reverend Mr. Buzzell, for at a subsequent meeting he was employed for "four Sabbaths longer."

Whether he was unwilling to remain still longer, or whether he failed to give satisfaction, is not known. He could not have remained over the parish more than the four months for which he had been employed, or the town would not have chosen a committee "to get a minister by next spring to preach to us."

[1766.] On March 18, £60 was raised "for a minister and schoolmaster" for this year. As the same individual was sometimes employed for both purposes, it is probable that such was the intent of that vote.

---

[1] *Pejepscot Papers.*

At a subsequent meeting the town decided very strongly in favor of the Presbyterian form of worship, and voted to extend a call to Reverend Stephen Scales. Goin Fulton, Adam Hunter, and Thomas Wilson were chosen a committee to make an agreement with him.

[1767.] In July, Reverend Mr. Thompson was engaged for two months after the expiration of his first contract.

In consideration of the agreement made at the time of the confirmation of their title by the government of Massachusetts, as well as in conformity to the laws, the proprietors about this time set apart a lot of land in Topsham "for the use of the Ministry" and one for "the first settled Minister." The ministerial or parsonage lot was "Number Twenty-six lying in the Range of Lotts fronting on Pejepscott River containing one hundred acres." The lot for the minister was "Number sixty four, containing One hundred acres, lying on the Rear of Lotts belonging to Alexander Potter and James Potter, Jr., bounding Northeast on Land of Robert M^c^Farlands and Southwest on the School Lott."

[1768.] In 1768 the town voted to give James Hunter a lot of land called the School-house Lot, in exchange for which he was to give the town one hundred acres where the meeting-house stood. Mr. Southmaid was employed to preach in the winter "as a probationer."

[1770.] At the annual meeting this year a Mr. Stuart was engaged to preach until the first of the following November, and it was voted to assess one fourth part of the minister's salary on the holders of pews.

[1771.] The first church organization, as distinct from that of the parish, was organized in 1771. It was of the Presbyterian order, and was organized by Reverend Mr. Murray, a Presbyterian minister of Boothbay, and by Reverend Joseph Prince. It consisted of twenty-seven members.[1] Who these members were is not now known, but it is not improbable that two of the early members of the Congregational Church, Messrs. Alexander Patten and James Fulton, were among the number. This church was at no time very strong, and ceased to exist about the year 1789. No records of its meetings can be found.

Committees were appointed in the years 1771 and 1772 to obtain the services of a minister, so that it is probable that there was preaching a part of this time.

[1773.] Reverend Samuel Wheeler probably officiated for a while this year, as the town voted, November 29, "to send a man west-

---

[1] *Greenleaf's Ecclesiastical Sketches.*

ward to bring Mr. Samuel Wheeler's character, provided Mr. Samuel Wheeler will pay the charges"; and John Merrill, consenting to go upon these terms, was duly chosen for that purpose.

[1774.] Mr. Merrill's report as to Mr. Wheeler's character must have been satisfactory, as he this year received a call at a salary of £66 13*s*. 4*d*., lawful money, and with £100 as a "settlement." The town this year reversed its former action, and decided to adhere to the Congregational form of worship. This action of the town gave serious offence to the minority. Messrs. Adam Hunter, Goin Fulton, James Henry, John Orr, John Fulton, James Fulton, and Alexander Potter entered their protest against the meeting as being illegal and *destructive to the church*. These persons were evidently strong in the Presbyterian faith, and probably some, if not all of them were members of the First Church. There is no evidence that Mr. Wheeler was ever formally installed over the church and society of the First Parish, and his pastorate could not have been a very satisfactory one, as the next year [1775] a committee was appointed to obtain a minister, and also one "to converse with Mr. Samuel Wheeler concerning the abatement of his wages and to make return."

[1776.] In December of the next year the town also voted not to pay his board nor his horse keeping. From this time to 1783, there is no record of any settled minister in the town, although there is no doubt but that there were religious services held for a few Sundays in each year, since the town in some at least of these years chose a committee to obtain a minister. In 1778, however, the committee were instructed not to agree with one for more than a service of two months without the consent of the town.

[1783.] At a meeting of the town held May 27, 1783, the committee to obtain a minister were instructed to employ the Reverend Mr. Urquhart to preach eight Sabbaths after the Sabbath next ensuing, and to use their own discretion as to the terms. At a later meeting of this year, held September 10, it was voted to employ Mr. Urquhart "one Sabbath when he returns from the westward." At this meeting there was also a committee appointed to see why the porch to the meeting-house, which the town voted in 1770 to have built, was not finished. The citizens of the town can easily be excused for getting a little impatient, after having waited thirteen years for the construction of this porch. At a meeting held two months later, Mr. Urquhart was employed for one year at a salary of £80, he to have the privilege of leaving if he had a call to settle elsewhere.

[1784.] At a meeting held in October, 1784, the town voted to hire Reverend Mr. Urquhart for one year more after the expiration of his first year. To this action of the town, Messrs. John Merrill, Jonathan Whitney, Actor Patten, Peletiah Haley, Alexander Gray, and William Reed declared their disapproval "for several reasons, but more particularly because we have reason to believe that the said Urquhart has two wives now living, and we think that disqualifies him to administer any of the Gospel ordinances."

This charge was sustained by the facts,[1] and it is not probable that Urquhart preached in Topsham after the expiration of his second year, if indeed he was allowed to complete his engagement.

In regard to Urquhart as a preacher, it has been said that "his mode of preaching was marked for its humor and quaintness, and he would arouse his drowsy listeners on a summer afternoon by some stirring anecdote or exclamation. On one occasion he stopped suddenly in his sermon and then exclaimed, 'I'm your shepurd o'er all o' ye, and Wully Wilson is me graut bull-dog.' The deacon, either not relishing this publicity, or to signalize that he *was not asleep*, sturdily called out yet louder still, 'I'm *not* your bull-dog! What did you say that for?'"[2]

[1786.] In 1786 the town voted to give Mr. Kellogg an invitation "to return and preach with us after he has been to study divinity six months, provided he will settle with us if desired."

[1788.] This year Reverend Jonathan Ellis was invited to settle in town at a salary of £85 and a "settlement" of £150. The "settlement to be paid in boards, shingles and other Lumber, or any produce of the country." Mr. Ellis did not accept this call, but [1789] the next year, at a meeting held June 9, the town agreed to settle him on condition that he would take his dismission if two thirds of the legal voters of the town should, at any future time, prefer not to remain under his ministry and should so declare at a legal town meeting, and that, in case such a thing should occur, he should be allowed to continue six months thereafter and no longer. Mr. Ellis was present at the meeting and agreed to these conditions.

On August 31 of this year there were two legal meetings of the town. The first was called by warrant of John Merrill, a justice of the peace, upon the application of more than ten voters, the principal object being to see if the town would consent that those not willing to settle under the ministry of Mr. Ellis should be allowed to withdraw from his support and maintain a minister for themselves. The second

---

[1] *See Annals of Warren, p.* 172 *et seq.*

[2] *Dr. James McKeen's Notes.*

meeting was on the usual warrant issued by the selectmen, and was for the purpose of taking action in regard to Mr. Ellis's ordination. At the first meeting thirty-five persons voted to withdraw from being under Mr. Ellis's ministry, and sixty-seven voted to be under his ministry. At this meeting the town also voted that one-fourth part of the expense of repairing the meeting-house should be assessed on the pew-holders, and the remainder paid by the town. At the second meeting the town voted that the council which was to be at the ordination of Mr. Ellis should meet and sit at Mr. Joseph Foster's house, and that they and their attendants should be entertained at Captain David Reed's and James Fulton's houses. It also voted that Doctor Philip Hoyt, James Wilson, and Joseph Haley, *clothier*, should be a committee to attend upon the council on the day of ordination.

The ordination of Mr. Ellis occurred September 16, 1789. The sermon on the occasion was preached by Reverend Andrew Lee, of Lisbon, Connecticut. The charge was by the Reverend John Ellis, of Rehoboth, Massachusetts. The right hand of fellowship by the Reverend Josiah Winship, of Woolwich, Maine. The sermon was printed, but no copy of it can now be found. The following is the title-page, which has been preserved: —

" The Duty of Gospel Ministers | Illustrated in a Discourse preached | at the ordination of the Rev. Jonathan Ellis | to the pastoral office in the church | at Topsham, Massachusetts, Sept. | 16th 1789. By Andrew Lee A. M., | Pastor of a church at Lisbon, | Conn, | Keep thyself pure — St. Paul. | Portland — Printed by Thomas | Baker Wait. MDCCXC."

The Congregationalist Church held its first meeting in June, 1789, at which a day of fasting was appointed, and it was voted to send for a council. This council met June 26, 1789, for the ordination of Reverend Jonathan Ellis, and voted " that the members of the church at Topsham be considered as a regular church of Christ, on the Congregational form of worship and discipline."

On October 23 of the same year the church adopted a covenant.

On June 27, 1790, the first sacrament since the organization was administered. It was administered in the Presbyterian manner, the communicants sitting around the table. Eleven members were present, beside five from the church in Brunswick.

[1791.] The only thing noticeable in any of the records this year is the fact that the town appointed a committee of three " to keep the dogs out of the meeting-house."

[1793.] This year the following names of members appear upon the church records: —

Captain John Patten (deacon),	Mrs. Mary Fulton,
Captain James Mustard,	Mrs. Esther Haley,
Alexander Patten,	Mrs. Hannah Henry,
James Fulton,	Mrs. Anna Winchell,
John Small,	Mrs. Mary Ellis,
Joseph Haley,	Mrs. Nancy Stockman,
——— Whitum,	Mrs. ——— Perry,
William Randall,	Mrs. Jane Randall,
Doctor Philip Hoyt,	Mrs. Rachel Reed,
Reverend Jonathan Ellis,	Widow Jameson,
Mrs. Mary Patten,	Widow Sarah Cobb.

[1794.] At a meeting of the town, held May 20, 1794, it was voted not to oppose the petition of John Merrill, Esquire, and others, praying the General Court for an Act of Incorporation as a Baptist society, *provided* they would withdraw their suit at law, of Job Macomber *vs.* The Town of Topsham, in which case the town agreed that the execution against Abraham Cummings[1] should not be put in force, and that all future taxes for the minister's salary, of members of the Baptist society, might be drawn by them from the treasurer or the constable, they producing a certificate that they had paid an equal sum for the Baptist society, *provided* they obtained an Act of Incorporation within one year. An attempt was made this year to obtain a two-thirds vote to dismiss Reverend Mr. Ellis, but faiied. After this date the First Parish held meetings distinct from those of the town, and the latter, therefore, has only occasionally since then taken any action in regard to religious matters.

[1795.] The incorporation of the Baptist Society which had just occurred had the unfortunate and rather singular effect of depriving the First Parish of all its officers. It is certainly rather remarkable that all these officers should have affiliated with the Baptists. That such was the actual fact, however, is shown by a petition to John Merrill, Esquire, justice of the peace, requesting him to call a meeting of the freeholders of the First Parish. This petition expressly sets forth the fact that the First Parish had no officers and "were consequently incapable of conducting and managing its affairs." This petition was dated April 20th, and on April 30th the first meeting of the parish, after the separation, was held at the meeting-house.

---

[1] *Probably for non-payment of minister's tax.*

A new board of parish officers was chosen, money raised for support of the minister, and Richard Knowles elected sexton, "with allowance of twelve shillings." At a subsequent meeting this year a committee was chosen to wait upon Mr. Ellis and to concert measures for rendering the ministerial lot of some benefit to the minister and parish.

[1797.] In 1796 and 1797 considerable repairs were made to the meeting-house. In May of the latter year a committee was chosen "to wait on the Reverend Jonathan Ellis for the purpose of obtaining information how his proposals may in the best way be answered, and report to the Parish." What proposals the pastor had made is not known, but on the twenty-sixth of June following, the parish decided not to increase his salary "at the present time, on account of the depreciation of money."

[1799.] At a meeting of the parish, held September 9, Captain Alexander Rogers, James Fulton, and Arthur Hunter were chosen to settle with Mr. Ellis and to pay him the arrearages due to him. They were also authorized to grant him a discharge from the parish if he desired, and to supply the pulpit for a while.

[1800.] At the annual meeting of the parish this year, the sum of three hundred dollars was raised for current expenses. This sum was between thirty and forty dollars less than had usually been raised for the minister's salary alone. At the annual meeting of the town, Messrs. John Merrill, William Wilson, James Purinton, Doctor Porter, and Alexander Thompson were chosen a committee to consider the practicability of uniting the two societies. The desire for such union probably arose in consequence of the difficulty experienced, at that time, in furnishing adequate support to two ministers.

[1801.] The committee for supplying the pulpit were instructed by the parish "to write to the Professor of Divinity at Harvard College requesting him to recommend a candidate to them of ability and good moral character," and were also instructed to employ no transient preacher until it was positively ascertained that no suitable candidate could be sent. The parish also voted "not to employ Mr. Thompson any longer to supply the Desk." It would appear from this action that Mr. Ellis had received his discharge from the committee appointed in 1799 to settle with him.

[1802.] The Reverend Mr. Western was employed as a preacher until October, 1802. At a meeting of the parish in June, Benjamin Hasey, Esquire, Doctor Porter, and Ezra Smith were chosen a committee to petition the legislature "for permission to sell the Parsonage

Lot, or take measures to render the same profitable to the Parish, agreeable to the original intentions of the Grantors "

[1803.] On April 23 of this year, the parish passed a vote inviting Mr. Ellis to preach for one year at a salary of two hundred and eighty-three dollars and thirty-three cents, he to have " the privilege of keeping school such part of said year as he shall choose."

[1805.] An effort was this year made to unite with the Second Parish in obtaining a minister to preach alternately in the two parishes.

[1806.] At a town-meeting, held November 3, 1806, it was voted "that the town having heard and duly considered the proposal of the Honorable Benjamin J. Porter. and others, to build a meeting-house near the Court House, do unitedly approve of the same and do earnestly recommend it to the members of both parishes of the town to become united as soon as may be into one corporate body for the purpose of supporting public worship in said town when [it shall be] erected.

" And it is further voted that the town, with a view to promote an union of the parishes, for the support of public worship, agreeably to the proposal of said Porter and others, will appoint a committee of seven persons with full power to pursue any measures necessary and proper on the part of the town to promote the building of said house and to support public worship therein."

In December the parish voted to hold their business meetings and religious services in the Court House until a new meeting-house should be built, but the vote was subsequently changed so as to have the meetings for public worship held one half the time at the Court House and the remainder of the time either at the old meeting house or at the school-house near it.

[1810.] At the annual meeting this year the parish voted " that the treasurer be directed to renew or exchange the securities or collect, if necessary, the money that is now at interest, belonging to the parish, and also to receive the interest annually or take notes for the same." It is evident from this that the parish had something of a fund at this time, but from what source it was derived is not so easy to understand. The amount of money raised each year was seldom more than enough to pay current expenses and often not sufficient for that purpose, and the ministerial lot was not sold, notwithstanding the vote in 1802, until 1819.

At this same meeting Benjamin Orr, Esquire, was appointed to obtain from the committee chosen in 1799 a certificate of the discharge of Reverend Mr. Ellis, and to deposit the same with the parish clerk. This document, which was the only legal annulment of the contract between the pastor and parish, was dated May 7, 1810.

Owing to the separation which had occurred in the parish, and to other causes, the church had gradually dwindled away, and after the dismissal of their pastor it became nearly extinct. During the period of Mr. Ellis's ministry it was Congregational in name, but not what would now be called strictly Orthodox, since it paid more attention to the form of church polity than it did to uniformity of belief. Reverend Ezra S. Goodwin had been preaching this year, and on October 12, the parish expressed to him their approbation of his past services and requested him to continue with them awhile longer.

[1811.] An attempt was made this year, unsuccessfully, to have the minister over the First Parish supply the pulpit of the Second Parish also. The thanks of the parish were again given to Mr. Goodwin for his services, and the regret expressed that the financial situation did not admit of their employing him longer.

[1814.] Nothing further of special importance occurs in the parish records until the year 1814, when an attempt was again made to unite the two parishes. The committee on the part of the First Parish chosen to confer with the other parish were instructed that "if an union of said parishes could not be obtained on any other principle, that the meetings for public worship be holden two thirds of the time at the Court House and the other third at the upper meeting-house."

[1815.] In 1815, Messrs. Benjamin Orr, Alexander Rogers, and Jehiel Abell were appointed a committee to petition the legislature, in behalf of the parish, "for leave to sell the parsonage lot in Topsham, under such restrictions and limitations as they shall think proper."

[1818.] The meeting-house, about this time, must have been getting sadly in need of repair, since, in April, 1818, the parish committee were instructed to repair it, "by building doors, glazing the windows, and underpinning the house so as to secure it from falling."

[1819.] On May 10, 1819, the committee appointed in 1815 to sell the ministerial lands, reported that "they have sold the whole of said lands at auction to the highest bidders on the 22d day of April 1819, as follows, to wit. To Samuel Hunter twelve acres and 80 rods for the sum of one hundred and twenty-five dollars: To Arthur Hunter thirty-eight acres and seventy rods for the sum of two hundred and thirty dollars and 62½ cents; To Thomas Patten twenty-four acres and ten rods for two hundred and sixteen dollars and fifty-six cents; To George Rogers twentyfive acres for two hundred dollars.

All and singular of which sums to be paid, with interest, in four years from the time of sale, one quarter part of the principal of each sum to be paid annually, and interest semi-annually on the whole amount of sales Amounting in the whole to the sum of $772.18

"(Signed) "ACTOR PATTEN,
HUMPHREY PURINTON,
THOS. G. SANDFORD."

[1821.] In the year 1821, a committee was chosen to ascertain and report, at an adjourned meeting, who were members of the First Parish. The parish this year, moreover, agreed to accept the *new* meeting-house on the terms offered by the proprietors of the same, which were as follows: "That the proprietors of the meeting-house present the same to the First Parish, reserving the right to the proprietors of selling all their right thereto and receiving the proceeds; and whether the same is sold or unsold, it shall not be liable in any manner whatever to be taxed by the First Parish; and it is understood by the foregoing reservation that the parish shall never assess any moneys that it may hereafter raise either wholly or in part upon the pews or seats of any individual proprietors therein; and the proprietors further present the parish with one of the front pews on the lower floor, numbered thirty-one, and the two pews in the gallery behind the singing seats, and the overplus of moneys arising from the sale of pews in said house, after paying the bills of said house, shall be annexed to the funds of the First Parish.

"That in future the meetings for publick worship be holden one third of the time at the old meeting-house, and two thirds of the time at the new meeting-house, for six months in the year, commencing the first Sabbath in May; the remainder of the year at the new meeting-house."

At a subsequent meeting, a number of persons who had previously joined the Second Parish were accepted as members of the First Parish. At the same meeting an agent was chosen to obtain a deed of the meeting-house from the proprietors, and to give deeds of pews to the owners thereof.

On August 26, 1821, the church was reorganized. The following persons constituted its membership at this time: —

William Randall, John Harmon, Deacon Samuel Winslow, Mrs. Jane Randall, Mrs. Margaret Patten, Mrs. Mary Ellis, Mrs. Hannah Patten, Mrs. Martha Rogers, Mrs. Betsey Perkins, Miss Hannah Patten, Widow Mary Foy, Widow Mary Patten, and Widow Rachel Reed.

[1823.] This year an attempt was made to settle Reverend Mr. Danforth, at first for five years and then for one year. There was a good deal of difficulty in raising the necessary amount of money by subscription, and it is evident that he was not engaged, as at a meeting held on the twenty-second of November, the parish committee were instructed to employ a preacher, and to pay him out of the money already raised.

[1824.] The parish this year invited Reverend Jacob C. Goss to settle as their pastor, "until six months' notice on either side shall be given for a discontinuance of his services." The salary offered was five hundred dollars. To this invitation Mr. Goss made an answer containing the following proposals, which were accepted by the parish: —

"*First.* Provided that I may have liberty to be absent four weeks each year, and during this time shall not be under obligation to supply the desk.

"*Second.* Provided either party may have liberty to dissolve this connection, giving to the other one year previous to such dissolution.

"*Third.* Should the salary which you offer me be found on trial insufficient to meet my expenses, I shall expect it will be increased."

Thomas G. Sandford, Actor Patten, Colonel Samuel Veazie, Charles R. Porter, Doctor James McKeen, and Major Nahum Perkins were chosen on behalf of the parish, and Samuel Winslow on behalf of the church, to make the arrangements for the ordination.

On December 7 the council for ordination met at the house of Nathaniel Green. There were present, Reverend Hezekiah Packard and David Owen, Wiscasset; Reverend Eliphalet Gillett and Samuel P. Ingraham, Hallowell; Reverend William Mittimore and Jonathan Moody, Falmouth; Reverend John W. Ellingwood, David Stinson, and Gillett Trufant, Bath; Reverend Enos Merrill and Nathan Scales, Freeport; Reverend Asa Cummings and Cushing Prince, Brunswick; Reverend Seneca White, Levi Houghton, and Daniel Marston, 2d, Bath; Reverend Caleb Hobart and Jacob Hayes, North Yarmouth; Reverend Benjamin Tappan and John Eveleth, Augusta, and William Allen, D. D., president of Bowdoin College.

Reverend Doctor Allen was chosen moderator, and Benjamin Tappan, scribe.

The ordination took place December 8, 1824. The introductory prayer was made by Reverend Mr. Mittimore; the sermon was by President Allen, from Isaiah lii, 7, "*How beautiful upon the mountains are the feet of him that bringeth good tidings*"; the consecrating prayer was by Reverend Doctor Gillett; the charge to the pastor, by Reverend Doctor Packard, of Wiscasset; the right hand of fellowship, by Reverend Mr. Mead; address to the church and society, by Reverend Mr. Tappan; and the concluding prayer, by Reverend Mr. Ellingwood.

[1825.] At a church meeting held January 20, it was decided "that the ordinance of the sacrament should be administered the first Sabbath in every other month, and that a regular church meeting should be held every Thursday previous to communion."

[1826.] This year the parish voted that the notice of its meetings "be in future posted on the meeting-house door and in the publishment-box [1] to said meeting-house."

On May 11 of this year Samuel Winslow was chosen as deacon, — the first one since the reorganization of the church. On August 10, one of the members was charged with a "too frequent use of spirituous liquors," and was suspended from fellowship and afterwards was excommunicated.

[1829.] In April, 1829, Mr. Goss sent in his request for a dismissal, on the ground of dissatisfaction with his present condition and prospects. A committee was appointed by the parish to confer with him and to make to him a full disclosure of the condition of the parish, and to inform him, if they found it expedient, that the parish felt unable to support him after the expiration of the year. At a subsequent meeting the assessors were instructed to devise measures for paying the arrearages due him. Notwithstanding his resignation, Mr. Goss seems to have remained for some time longer, for at a meeting held early the next year [1830] another committee was appointed to inform him "of the embarrassed situation of the parish on the subject of dissolving his connection with said parish"; and on July 16, a committee was chosen "to invite him to dissolve the connection between him and the parish and discontinue his services as early as may be convenient to him and prior to the first of December next, and that the connection be now accordingly dissolved." A week later Mr. Goss sent a letter to the parish in which he consented to the annulment of their contract, provided all arrearages were paid and his salary paid up to the date of the termination of his services, otherwise his resignation was to be null and void. Upon the receipt of this communication, the parish voted to use so much of the interest of

---

[1] *A box with a glass door, in which the town clerk posted the names of those intending marriage.*

the parish fund as might be found necessary to pay what was due. This terminated the civil contract between the parish and pastor, but the pastoral connection of the church with Mr. Goss was not severed by act of council until June 10, 1835. Mr. Goss commenced his labors under very favorable auspices, and so far as can be determined from the records there was no dissatisfaction with him, and his dismissal was owing solely to the feeble condition of the parish at this time.

[1836.] At the annual meeting of the parish in 1836, a committee was appointed to examine the records of the parish, and ascertain who were members of it and report a list of the same. This report, on account of the information it contains in regard to parishes in general, is herewith given in full: —

"The committee appointed at a meeting of the First Parish in Topsham, held on the twelfth instant, to ascertain who are the legal members thereof, respectfully report that they have examined the statutes and reported cases in point, and have unanimously come to the conclusion that all inhabitants of twenty-one years of age and upwards, within the bounds of said parish, and who have not withdrawn therefrom by leaving a written notice thereof with the parish clerk, are members of said parish, with the exception of such persons only as are legal members of some poll parish. That all inhabitants coming to reside within the limits of the said First Parish and who are not members of a poll parish, with all such as reside therein and withdrawn from the poll parish to which they were connected by leaving a written note thereof with the clerk of said parish, do on their claiming and exercising their rights of membership thereby become members of said First Parish.

"To visit each individual within the limits of said First Parish, and to ascertain from them personally whether they belong to the parish or not, would require more time than your committee could conveniently bestow on the subject. They therefore have examined the records of the poll parish, within the bounds of the First Parish, and from which it appears the following named persons[1] are members of the *Second* Parish of this town. . . . Your committee further report that they are divided in opinion, in regard to the point whether the members of a poll-parishioner's family, at arriving at twenty-one years of age, do thereby, without first withdrawing from the poll parish,

---

[1] *These names appear in the account of the Baptist Society, and are therefore omitted here.*

become members of the territorial parish within the bounds of which the poll is situated. A majority of your committee, Messrs. Perkins, Tibbets, and Ellis, are of opinion that they do. The other members of your committee are of a different opinion. The case has been submitted to two of our most able counsellors, who differ in opinion on the subject. Your committee, therefore, to avoid all uncertainty, recommend to persons so situated to withdraw from the poll parish, in case they are desirous of connecting themselves with the territorial, or from the territorial if they prefer continuing with the poll. They would further recommend, in case the parish should resort to taxes, that such persons so situated, and arriving at the age of twenty-one, should not be taxed or considered as members of said parish until they claim and exercise their rights of membership.

"NAHUM PERKINS,
per order of Committee."

The ministerial fund of the First Parish amounted at this time to seven hundred and thirty-sixty dollars and sixty-one cents. No parish meetings were held later than this, and the majority of the pew-holders became members of the Unitarian Society. The continuation of the history of the First Parish Church organization will be given further on, under the title of the "Congregational Church." The latter is the direct lineal descendant of the old First Parish Church, though, for reasons given elsewhere, the members of it no longer belonged to the First Parish, but formed a new poll parish.

THE FIRST BAPTIST CHURCH AND SOCIETY, OR SECOND AND THIRD PARISHES.

The first Baptist preaching in Topsham was by Elder Simon Locke, it is believed, in 1779. On the fifth of June of that year he baptized Miss R. Purington, who was the first one in town to receive the ordinance by immersion.

After 1782, Reverend Mr. Potter preached occasionally for several years, but without making many converts. During the years 1783 and 1784, Elders Case and Macomber preached occasionally.[1]

Reverend Job Macomber also preached here in 1789, 1790, and 1791. These ministers were paid for their services by the voluntary contribution of individuals, as appears from a receipt given by Macomber to Actor Patten, Joseph and Pelatiah Haley, and John Merrill.

The General Court of Massachusetts, by an Act passed in June,

---

[1] *From Millet.*

1794, incorporated John Merrill, Esquire, Stephen Douty, Actor Patten, Hugh Wilson, Robert Cleaves, Jr., James Purington, Jr., Ebenezer Farrin, William Bragdon, John Starboard, Jr., John Hewey, John Duggan, Joseph Jack, Elnathan Hinkley, Alexander Thompson, Elijah White, Benjamin Woodard, Moses Hodgkins, John Sandford, John Ware, William Hunter, Samuel Wilson, Calvin Wade, Thomas Smith, John Starboard, Luther Hall, Thomas Rideout, John Reed, William Malcom, Robert Cleaves, John Wilson, Joseph Haley, Humphrey Thompson, Willard Sears, Moses Owen, William Collamore, Nathan Wyman, Hezekiah Wyman, William Wyman, and James Purington into a society by the name of the "Baptist Religious Society in Topsham."[1]

The first meeting of this society was held at the house of Actor Patten on February 9, 1795. This society constituted the Second Parish of the town. At this meeting James Purington was chosen moderator, and John Merrill parish clerk. It was voted to build a meeting-house "forty feet long and thirty feet wide, this season, and that it be set between Joseph Haley's house and Benjamin Eaton's." It was to be owned by each proprietor in proportion to the amount subscribed.

This meeting-house, subsequently known as the "old yellow meeting-house," was built principally by Joseph Haley, Captain Actor Patten, 1st, John Merrill, Esquire, Captain Pelatiah Haley, and James Purington, the tanner.

April 17, 1797, the parish voted to give Elder Elihu Purington, of Bowdoinham, an invitation to preach for them one half the time. This invitation was accepted.

In the year 1800, Reverend Mr. Williams preached in the meeting-house of the Second Parish.[2]

The following is the list of members subsequent to the incorporation of the parish, down to April 7, 1808: 1796, James Sampson, Obed Burnham; 1797, Andrew Whitehouse, Joshua Whitten, Joseph Whitten, John Whitten, Stephen Pennell, William Wilson, Jr.; 1798, Nathaniel Melcher, Benjamin Eaton, Charles Gowell, Joseph Graves, Joshua Graves, Samuel Graves, Moses Plummer, Gideon Walker; 1799, Francis Douglass, Benjamin Metcalf; 1800, James Potter; 1803, John Rogers, John Hern, David Work, Jeremiah Staples, Winslow Staples, Moses Graves, Joseph Berry, James Staples, Thomas

---

[1] *Massachusetts Special Laws, Vol.* 1, *p.* 537.

[2] *Diary of Reverend Jonathan Ellis.*

Hunter, Arthur Hunter, Robert Alexander, William Malcom, Jr., John Given, William Reed, Thomas Reed, Robert Reed, David Reed, William Reed Hunter, Timothy Hern, Joseph Quint, Josiah Staples, John Graves, Jr., Jacob Graves, Samuel Staples, Ebenezer Work, William Given, Jacob Stockman, Daniel Gray, Caleb Curtis, Lemuel Thompson; 1808, Daniel Holden, Nathaniel Green, Jotham Chick, Stephen Harris, James Cook, Samuel Towns, Jonathan Blaisdell, Moses Weymouth, David Foster, Timothy Foster, Gideon Larrabee, Aaron Thompson, John Rogers, Jr., Joshua Haines, Isaac Johnson, Samuel Perkins, Joseph M. Perry, Robert Sager, Nathaniel Quint, James Thompson, John Jameson, Francis Card, James G. Goold, William Frost, Nahum Houghton, Joseph Haley, Jr., David Flagg, Jesse T. Haley, and Peter H. Green.

[1808.] On April 28, 1808, the parish voted to raise four hundred dollars for the support of the ministry, but the vote was reconsidered in June, and two hundred and fifty dollars was then voted. From this time until about 1833, the amount annually raised for the supply of the pulpit and all other expenses was, ordinarily, only one hundred dollars.

[1815.] In September of this year three males and five females belonging to this society were organized into a church at Oak Hill, under the title of "The Predestinarian Baptist Church of Topsham." It is probable that Mr. Elihu Purington was then ordained as an elder,[1] since the records of the church state that at this time Elder Kendall preached the introductory sermon, Elder Titcomb gave the *right hand of fellowship*, and Elder Temple made the concluding prayer.

[1818.] On June 4, 1818, Mr. Winslow Staples was ordained by council; Elder Stearns preached the sermon, Elder Persons offered a prayer, Elder Temple gave the right hand of fellowship, Elder Stinson gave the charge. and Elder Frost made the concluding prayer. The church at this time numbered over fifty members.[2]

At a meeting held April 18, of this year, the parish voted that a committee which had been chosen to settle the accounts of the parish should be authorized "to move the meeting" to any part of the town if they judged it expedient. Accordingly, the meetings were held this year in two places, — in the "old yellow meeting-house" and in a school-house.[3]

[1819.] In April, 1819, the frame of a new meeting-house was

---

1 *Adam Wilson's Historical Discourse*, p. 10. 2 *Millett.*
3 *Autobiography of Elder Kendall.*

raised, and in November the building was completed. It was small, containing only thirty pews.[1] This building was the one, opposite the village graveyard, which was afterward used as a town-house.

This year "one half of the male and several female members of the church were expelled for intemperance, until only eight were left."[2]

[1820.] Elder Staples's pastorate could not have been a very successful one, as in February 26, 1820, the church and parish, in joint session, passed a vote of censure against him. At a parish meeting, held April 15 of this year, a committee was appointed to confer with Elder Henry Kendall as to the terms on which he would consent to become their settled minister.

At a meeting held April 29, 1820, it was voted to accept Elder Henry Kendall's proposals, and to consider him as their settled minister, agreeably to the conditions specified by him. These conditions were as follows: —

"1. It will not be expected by me that the society bind itself to pay me any specified sum for my services as their minister, nor would it be pleasing to me on my settlement that any obligatory grant should be made to me, but that the whole subject should be left with the society to give me annually much or little as they may consider duty or proper.

"2. That a committee, to be composed of members of the church and society, be annually raised, whose duty it shall be to confer with me on the subject of my situation and the number of Sabbaths I ought to serve the society for the sum they may by grant or subscription annually raise, and report as soon as may be the result of this conference to me and the assessors of the society.

"3. That whenever I shall think it duty to request a dissolution of my ministerial connection with this society, and shall officially make known my desire, the society shall, without any unnecessary delay, attend to the subject, and if they are not disposed to grant my request they shall join me in choosing a council of the elders and churches of our order, to hear and determine the subject of the request, whose decision shall be binding on the parties.

"4. That whenever a majority in parish meeting, legally called for that purpose, shall by vote declare that my ministerial labours is no longer useful, and vote my dismission, then my ministerial connection shall be considered dissolved."

Up to this time the Second Parish contained both Calvinist and

---

[1] *Autobiography of Elder Kendall.* [2] *Ibid.*

Free-Will Baptists, but a separation now occurred, and in 1821 Joshua and John Whitten were dismissed to the Free-Will Baptist Society.

[1824.] At a meeting held April 17, 1824, the parish voted "to dismiss Elder Henry Kendall from being any longer their settled minister, — agreeable to his request." The church records contain a statement to the effect that the dismission of Elder Kendall gave rise to some dissatisfaction.

Nothing of importance occurs in the records of the Second Parish subsequent to this date, though the records do not close until the year 1832. As the Baptists withdrew that year, and formed a new society, it would seem as though the Second Parish must thereafter have been composed exclusively of Free-Will Baptists or else that there were two religious societies in one poll parish.

THE BAPTIST CHURCH SOCIETY.

On January 19, 1824, Henry Kendall, Jabez Perkins, James Cook, Richard Orr, Samuel Wilson, James Wilson, Elijah White, George Howland, and Daniel Welch petitioned the legislature for incorporation as a religious society. The petition was granted, and on February 2, 1824, the society met and elected Henry Kendall, moderator, and James Cook, clerk. Jabez Perkins was chosen collector, and Deacon Elijah White and Mr. James Cook as parish committee. The members of this society constituted the third parish of the town.

Joseph Foster, Jr., Daniel Welch, Leonard Blondell, Jabez Perkins, David Scribner, James Cole, John Owen, Charles White, Joshua Haskell, Aaron Hinkley, Charles Hunter, Edward Welch, David Dunlap, William Randall, Jr., Jonathan Baker, James Rogers, Benjamin Hasey, John Hunter, 2d, Benjamin Thompson, Francis Tucker, George Rogers, William Work, and John Mustard joined the society about this time, though a number of them afterwards went back to the First Parish. The members at their first meeting voted to call themselves by the name of "The Baptist Church Society." They built this year a small meeting-house in the village, at a cost of about six hundred dollars.

[1825.] This year there was a powerful revival in the church, though but little mention is made of it in the records.

[1826.] At a meeting held on April 3, the society voted that as less money than was needed had heretofore been raised, "if the society should not be able to raise by voluntary subscription at least one hundred dollars for Elder Kendall the present year, that they will not require his ministerial labors beyond a proportion of the time for the sum they shall raise and pay over to him."

[1834.] At a church meeting, held February 22, the subject of building a new meeting-house was discussed, and it was thereupon voted "that Jabez Perkins, David Scribner, Samuel Perkins, Josiah Sanford, and L. Hibbard be a committee to solicit means to carry the same into effect." On October 4, of this year, Samuel Perkins and David Scribner were chosen deacons.

At a meeting of the society, held April 7, it was decided to accept a lot of land for a meeting-house, that had been purchased of Pelatiah and Nancy Haley. Jabez Perkins and David Scribner were chosen a committee to raise subscriptions for and to build a new meeting-house.

[1835.] On April 6, 1835, this committee reported that they had contracted with S. & R. D. Melcher for the erection of a meeting-house. That the whole expense would be $2,250, and that the building would probably be completed in about six weeks. At this meeting Jabez Perkins, Samuel Perkins, and James Cook were appointed a committee to sell the pews, but were instructed to reserve one pew next the desk, on each side, and two floor pews near the stove, for *free* pews. The society also authorized their agent to sell the old meeting-house if the consent of the pew-owners could be had. It was bought by Deacon Joshua Haskell for the Free-Will Baptist Society. At a meeting of the church, held March 21, Elder Charles Johnson was invited to settle on a salary of three hundred dollars per annum. The next meeting of the society was held May 27 in the new or present Baptist meeting house. At this meeting, Elder Johnson was ordained and the new church building was dedicated. The year was remarkable for a revival in this and the other societies.

[1837.] On February 25, 1837, the church extended a call to Reverend Edwin R. Warren, and the amount of salary to be offered him was left to the discretion of the church officers.

[1838.] During the year 1838 a controversy commenced between the committee of management of the "*Eastern Baptist*" and Mr. E. Brown. It continued several years and caused considerable trouble in this church.

[1840.] At a meeting of the church held October 25, forty-four members were dismissed from this church, in order to be organized into a Baptist church in Brunswick village. There was a great revival this year. Meetings were held for more than one hundred successive evenings, and one hundred and fifty-two persons were added to the church by baptism.

[1841.] On July 25, Elder Warren resigned the pastorate, and Reverend George Knox was invited, November 1, to succeed him on a salary of four hundred dollars. On December 14, forty-nine delegates, representing eighteen churches, met in council for the purpose of his ordination. The services were as follows: —

An anthem; reading of Scriptures, by Elder P. S. Adams; a hymn; a prayer, by Elder F. Merriam; a sermon, by Elder Z. Bradford; an anthem; an ordaining prayer, by Elder Z. Adlam; the charge, by Elder Adam Wilson; a hymn; the right hand of fellowship, by Elder E. H. Gray; an address to the church, by Elder H. G. Gott; an anthem; a closing prayer, by Elder E. R. Warren; and the benediction, by the pastor.

[1846.] On May 25, 1845, Elder Knox resigned, and on February 1, of the following year, Reverend James Gilpatrick was invited to settle as pastor, on a salary of four hundred dollars. He accepted the call February 5, and was installed April 22, 1846. The services were as follows: —

Reading of Scripture, by Elder J. Hubbard; prayer, by Elder N. Norton; sermon, by Elder N. W. Williams; prayer, by Elder H. Hawes; charge, by Elder W. C. Grant; right hand of fellowship, by Elder M. Hanscom; address to church, etc. by Elder William Bailey; prayer, by Elder J. Ricker; benediction, by the pastor.

[1853.] Elder Gilpatrick, having determined to move with his family to Kansas, — then beginning to be settled, — sent in his resignation April 2, 1853, and it was accepted by the church to take place in June following. On July 17, Elder A. Robbins was invited to settle as pastor, on the same salary as his predecessor. On the twenty-fourth of the following September, however, his salary was increased to four hundred and fifty dollars.

[1859.] On June 5, 1859, Elder Robbins resigned under circumstances that led many to have doubts as to his fitness for his position. When his resignation was accepted, however, some commendatory resolutions were passed by the church. These resolutions were displeasing to some of the members, and for a time the matter seriously disturbed the church.

[1860.] March 25, 1860, Reverend L. P. Gurney received a call from the church to settle as their pastor, and accepted the invitation the following May.

[1862.] At a meeting held on April 6, 1862, the church was presented by Deacon William Barron with a complete silver communion service.

[1865.] At a meeting of the church, held July 1, 1865, Reverend L. P. Gurney, Deacons David Scribner and William Barron, William Skolfield, George A. Rogers, and W. E. Haley were chosen a Committee of Arrangements for a semi-centennial anniversary of the formation of the church. On September 2 the anniversary was celebrated in an appropriate manner, Reverend Adam Wilson, D. D., delivered an historical discourse, which, in accordance with a vote of the church, was printed in 1866.

[1866–1868.] March 1, 1866, Elder Gurney resigned his charge, and the church was for a time without any settled minister. On February 2, 1867, however, Reverend A. Bryant united with the church and supplied the pulpit until February 11, 1868.

In 1869, Reverend Ira P. Leland, the present pastor, was installed.

THE FREE-WILL BAPTIST CHURCH AND SOCIETY.[1]

[1783.] The first minister of this denomination who preached in Topsham was Elder Benjamin Randall, who preached once or twice in John Merrill's barn about the year 1783.

[1815.] The Second Parish, as already stated, was made up of both Calvinist and Free-Will Baptists. Their first pastor was Elder Purington. He sympathized in his views with the Free-Will Baptists. In 1815 he baptized six persons, who subsequently joined the Free-Will Baptist Church. The next preacher of this denomination was Elder Benjamin Thorn, who preached one season or more in the "old yellow meeting-house." The precise time that he was engaged with this church is not stated, but it must have been between the fall of 1815 and the fall of 1816.

[1816–17.] In 1816, Elder George Lamb preached a few times and was succeeded by Elder Farwell, who preached to the society in 1817.

[1822.] There was occasional but not regular preaching after this up to about 1822, when Elder Briggs settled for about one year. He preached a portion of the time in the Topsham Court House, and the remainder of the time in a hall in Brunswick village. Why services were not held in the yellow meeting-house is not known. It was not occupied by the Baptists, and the presumption is that the Court House was used because the meeting-house was so far out of the village. About this time the Free-Will Baptists began to leave the Calvinist

---

[1] *From a sketch of the same by the late Mr. William Whitten.*

Baptist Church. As the latter had given up the Second Parish Meeting-House, and had been incorporated into a new society, it is by no means unreasonable to suppose that the former constituted then, and are now, the Second Parish.

[1825–6.] In the autumn of 1825, Elders Clement Phinney, Allen Files, and Abizer Bridges came to Topsham and preached occasionally. On December 15, 1825, the church was organized by Elder Bridges, who baptized the eight individuals of which it was composed.

Additions continued to be made to the church, and on Saturday, February 4, 1826, a meeting was held at John Haley's, near the yellow meeting-house. At this meeting Elder Bridges, having been chosen moderator, the church elected Elder Allen Files, pastor; Andrew Jack and Joshua Haskell, deacons; and Uriah Jack, clerk.

[1830.] After five years' service, Elder Files resigned, and was succeeded by Elder Dexter Waterman, in 1830. He remained but one year, and after he left the church was without a pastor and had preaching only occasionally, for about five years. During this time the church became very low and feeble. Some of its members had died, others had left town, and but a few remained who were able to be of much assistance in sustaining a preacher.

[1836.] March 22, 1836, Elders George Lamb and Clement Phinney were sent by the Bowdoin Quarterly Meeting to visit the church, and try to revivify it. Accordingly, on that day, the church met at the old red school-house and chose Elder Lamb, moderator. At the commencement of the meeting the members were very much discouraged, and were inclined to give up their organization and join other churches. Elder Lamb, however, said to them, "You ought to be ashamed to let your own fire go out, and then crawl in and warm yourselves by another man's." This and similar remarks served to inspire them with new zeal, and they determined to make strenuous efforts to support a church and society. They at once voted to engage Elder Lamb to preach one half the time. As the society owned no meeting-house, the yellow one being owned by members of both Baptist societies, a committee was chosen to purchase one. This committee was, however, saved from all trouble in the matter by Deacon Joshua Haskell, who purchased the former Baptist meeting-house or vestry (the one afterwards used as a town-house) at an expense of about three hundred and fifty dollars. Elder Lamb commenced his pastoral labors in May, 1836, and remained over the church until his death, which occurred on the fourteenth of the following

December. At the same time that Elder Lamb was preaching in the village, Elder Charles Bean was preaching in the "Mallett" neighborhood. He made many converts, who all joined the church in the village.

In 1836 it was decided to build a new meeting-house. This enterprise received the hearty encouragement of all the members. and the present building was accordingly completed in August, 1837, at an expense of $3,000. A. C. Raymond, of Brunswick, was the builder.

Previously to the erection of this building a Sabbath school was organized, in which A. R. Bradbury and J. J. Butler, students in Bowdoin College, took an active part.

After the death of their pastor, Mr. J. J. Butler supplied the pulpit for a while. Elder Phinney also preached for a few months, but there was no one settled until May, 1837. On May 20, 1837, Elder Daniel Jackson moved to town with his family, and was settled as the pastor of this church. He remained over them until some time in 1840.

[1842.] He was succeeded in the autumn of that year by Elder Andrew Rollins, who remained until the spring of 1842.

[1843.] Elder Rollins was succeeded by Elder Peter Folsom, who continued until February, 1843, when he was obliged to leave on account of illness.

[1843–1846.] In the summer of 1843, Elder Daniel Jackson was again engaged to take the pastoral care of this church. He remained until some time in the early part of 1846. During his last pastorate, in 1843 and 1844, the "Miller" excitement prevailed in the town. The members of the church, not wishing "to stand against anything that looked like truth," permitted their church to be used for the promulgation of the new views. The result was a loss of some ten or more members, and some disaffection amongst those who remained. The trouble was not, however, of long duration.

Elder Peter Folsom succeeded Elder Jackson, and preached for one year, when he was himself succeeded by Elder Charles Bean, who remained about two years.

[1849.] In September, 1849, E. B. Fernald, a student from the Biblical School at Whitestown, received a call and commenced preaching to this church. He was ordained at the meeting-house in Topsham in October following. He remained pastor of this church about two years and a half.[1]

---

[1] *Mr. Whitten's sketch ends at this point. He intended bringing it down to a more recent date, but his sickness and death prevented, and we are now unable to give a more complete account.*

Since then the following preachers have been settled over this society: —

Reverend William T. Smith, from 1852 until 1857; Reverend M. W. Burlingame, from 1857 until 1863; Reverend S. D. Strout, from 1863 until 1864; Reverend A. A. Smith, from 1864 to 1870; Reverend E. Manson, from 1870 to 1874; J. A. Simpson, for about six months in 1874–5, after which there was no settled minister until June, 1877, when Reverend A. G. Hill, the present pastor, was settled over the society.

ORTHODOX CONGREGATIONAL CHURCH AND SOCIETY.

The Congregational Church was, as stated in the account of the First Parish, the *church* of that parish, though the *society* constituted only a portion of it. The following sketch is therefore, so far as it concerns the church, a continuation of that of the First Parish.

[1835.] On May 16, 1835, the church adopted their present confession of faith, and this date may be considered as probably the last meeting of the church prior to the dissolution of the First Parish.

[1836.] In May, 1836, Reverend J. T. Hawes, who had been settled over the First Parish in 1831, resigned, and was succeeded by Reverend Mr. High, who supplied the pulpit for eight weeks, by Reverend Mr. Cleaveland for eleven weeks, and by Professor Smyth, of Bowdoin College, for eight months. A new house of worship[1] was erected this year by voluntary subscriptions.

[1837.] In July, 1837, Reverend Thomas N. Lord commenced preaching to this society and was ordained in August. He was invited at a joint meeting of the church and society held in the Court House in January, 1837. His salary was five hundred dollars per annum. The council for his ordination met August 7.

The services were held on the next day and were as follows: —

Singing by the choir; prayer, by Reverend Ray Palmer, 2d church, Bath; singing by the choir; sermon, by Reverend David Thurston, Winthrop; consecrating prayer, by Reverend Josiah T. Hawes, Edgecomb; charge to pastor, by Reverend Jacob C. Goss, Woolwich; singing by choir; right hand of fellowship, by Reverend George E. Adams, Brunswick; address to church and people, by Reverend Timothy Davis, Litchfield; concluding prayer, by Professor Smyth, Bowdoin College; benediction, by the pastor.

[1841.] At a meeting held September 21, 1841, the church passed the following resolutions: —

---

[1] *The present edifice.*

"Resolved, that we have entire confidence in the ability and piety of our pastor, and that the welfare of this church and the interests of religion in this place demand that the connection be continued.

"Resolved, that in the opinion of this church, Reverend Mr. Lord has faithfully preached the gospel, and the church is willing to sustain him." The foregoing resolutions evidently indicate the existence of some dissatisfaction in the society, though not in the church.

At a joint meeting of the church and society, held July 2, 1842, Mr. Lord in a verbal communication requested to have the connection severed between himself and the society, on account chiefly of the state of his health, but partly on account of some disaffection which he thought existed. The meeting voted that Major Nahum Perkins and Matthew Patten be a committee to settle up the affairs of the society; "that John Barron, Alfred Perkins, and Samuel Douglass be a committee to take charge of the meeting-house, ring the bell, settle with the minister, etc.

"That Deacon Sprague, Nahum Perkins, Given Jameson, and Alfred S. Perkins be a committee to consult with Reverend Mr. Lord concerning his request."

[1842.] On July 5, 1842, this committee reported that Mr. Lord still wished to dissolve his connection with them, and the church and society accordingly gave their assent and voted to call an ecclesiastical council. On July 12 the council met, and after long deliberation agreed by a very small majority to sever the connection.

At a church meeting, held September 18 of this year, the standing committee of the church was instructed to make an agreement with Reverend Daniel Sewall to supply the pulpit for that year, commencing July 1, 1842, and ending July 1, 1843. He had already preached five Sabbaths.

[1843.] Between October 2, 1842, and August 5, 1843, the slavery question began to be discussed in the church, and caused some disaffection. One member was refused a letter of recommendation to a church of which the members were slave-owners, and several resolutions against slavery were passed, which so offended a number of the members that they absented themselves from church meetings for some time.

[1844.] At a meeting held May 16, 1844, complaint was made against several persons that they had withdrawn from the communion and had embraced "unscriptural and erroneous doctrines," having accepted the views of the Second Adventists. A committee was appointed to visit and argue the matter with them, but their arguments had no effect, and these individuals were excommunicated about a month later.

On July 14 of this year a letter was received from the *acting* pastor, Reverend David Sewall, urging the church to settle a permanent minister. Isaac L. Cook, Deacon Willis Sprague, and Samuel Jameson were chosen a committee "to ascertain if a sufficient sum could be raised to secure a minister."

[1845–6.] In August, 1845, the church extended an invitation to Reverend Jonathan Clement, of Chester, New Hampshire, to preach to them as a candidate for settlement, and on September 5, 1846, the church voted, "To concur with the parish in extending a call to the Reverend Jonathan Clement to become pastor over the church." He accepted, and was installed February 1, 1847.

[1852.] May 13, 1852, Reverend Mr. Clement and his wife were dismissed from this church, and recommended to the Congregational Church in Woodstock, Vermont, where he had received a call to settle. During Mr. Clement's pastorate the church was prosperous, and nothing appears on the records save a few cases of discipline not necessary to be mentioned.

From the time of the dismission of Mr. Clement until his successor was installed, the pulpit was supplied by Professor Alpheus S. Packard, of Bowdoin College.

In December, 1852, a call was extended to Reverend John Wilde, of Falmouth, and a council was called for his installation.

[1853.] This council met January 4, 1853, and the following services were held: —

Prayer, by Reverend P. F. Barnard; sermon, by Reverend William Warren; installing prayer, by Reverend J. W. Turner; charge to pastor, by Reverend J. W. Ellingwood; right hand of fellowship, by Reverend George E. Adams, D. D.; address to people, by Reverend J. O. Fisk; concluding prayer, by Reverend E. Whittlesey; benediction, by the pastor.

[1854.] On August 19, 1854, a letter was received from Mr. Wilde asking to have a council called to act upon his request for a dissolution of the pastoral relation, the reason of his request being the inadequacy of his salary. In compliance with this request the church, August 21, voted to call a council. This council met shortly afterwards, and dissolved the relation between the pastor and church.

[1856.] After Mr. Wilde left, Reverend James M. Palmer supplied the pulpit for one year. He was followed by Reverend J. Q. Peabody, of Ipswich, Mass., who supplied till October, 1856, when he accepted a call to settle at Fryeburg.

In December, 1856, Reverend Daniel F. Potter, of Union, was invited to preach for a few Sabbaths. He was then invited to settle, but declined, agreeing, however, to preach to the society during their mutual pleasure.

[1865–6.] June 3, 1865, Mr. Potter notified the church that on account of ill-health he should be unable to preach any more. Between this date and June, 1866, the desk was supplied by Professors Packard and Sewall, of Bowdoin College, and by Reverend Elijah Kellogg, of Boston.

[1868.] During the year 1868 a new and handsome spire was erected on the meeting-house, and the whole building was remodelled.

[1869–1875.] On February 4, 1869, the building was rededicated. The services of the occasion were as follows: —

Invocation, by Reverend Mr. Bryant, of the Baptist Church; reading of Scriptures, by Reverend Mr. Potter; sermon, by Professor Jotham S. Sewall, of Bowdoin College; dedicatory prayer, by Reverend Doctor Adams, of Brunswick; hymn, prayer, and benediction, by Reverend Mr. Smith, of the Free Baptist Church, Topsham.

From the records of this church the following facts have been gleaned: —

The number admitted to the church up to 1821 was	22
" " up to 1874 was	263
Whole number admitted on confession	238
" " " by letter	25
" " dismissed	49
" " suspended	5
" " excommunicated	6
" " who died up to 1874	92

The number of infants baptized between October, 1833, and July, 1871, was thirty-four, — twenty-two boys and twelve girls.

The number of members in 1874 was one hundred and twelve, of which the males numbered seventy-eight and the females one hundred and eighty-five. Reverend Nahum W. Grover has preached for this society since the fall of 1875.

THE UNITARIAN SOCIETY.

Previous to the formation of the Orthodox Congregational Society, in 1836, the First Parish had ceased to hold meetings as such. A majority of the owners of pews in the second meeting-house of the First Parish being Unitarians, meetings were held in the meeting-house for many years, which were conducted by Unitarian preachers.

The first preacher of this denomination who ever conducted religious services here is thought to have been a Reverend Mr. Greeley, who preached on one occasion in the old east meeting-house. He was afterwards a deacon of Doctor Channing's church, in Boston.

[1836–1838.] Reverend H. Edes preached in town on December 11, 1836, whether for more than one Sunday is not known. He was followed by Reverend Mr. Russell, Reverend J. O. Day, Reverend Mr. Crafts, and Reverend G. M. Rice. The engagement of the latter commenced in August, 1837, and ended August 25, 1839.

[1839.] On the date last mentioned Reverend Amos D. Wheeler, then of Standish, preached on an exchange with Mr. Rice. The same evening a committee of the "subscribers for the support of Unitarian preaching" invited him to take charge of the pulpit for the term of three years, that being the unexpired portion of the time for which their subscriptions had been made. The committee consisted of the following persons: —

Humphrey Purinton, William Frost, Benjamin Hasey, Gardner Green, Charles Thompson, John Coburn, and John S. Cushing.

The invitation was accepted, and he removed to Topsham with his family on the twenty-sixth day of October of that year, having in the mean time preached there two or three times.

From fear of losing their rights as members of the First Parish, this society refrained from asking for an Act of Incorporation, neither was any church formally constituted by council, according to Congregational usage.

The pastor, however, did collect together into a church such as were willing to sign the following covenant: —

"'One is your Master even Christ, and all ye are brethren.' — *Matthew* xxiii, 8.

"'One shall say, I am the Lord's, and another shall call himself by the name of Jacob, and another shall subscribe with his own hand unto the Lord.' — *Isaiah* xliv, 5.

"We whose names are hereunto annexed, receiving the Bible as the rule of our faith and practice, do hereby associate for our mutual improvement in truth and holiness, as the disciples of Christ. And we declare it to be our sincere desire and purpose, as far as lieth in us, to walk in all the commandments and ordinances of the Lord blameless, and to cherish and maintain towards all Christians 'the unity of the Spirit in the bond of peace.'"

From the pastor's records the following names of the communicants are obtained. The date at which they joined the church is not given: —

John Coburn, Nathaniel Dunning, John S. Cushing, Joseph N. Dunning, Amos D. Wheeler, Charles H. Wheeler, Javan H. Hall, Mr. Bicknell, Joshua Young, John M. Goodwin, George N. Richardson, Mr. Talbot, Mr. Fitch, Mr. Moreton, John D. Coburn, Sarah E. Purinton, Sarah C. Cushing, Isabella M. Dunning, Delia A. Dunning, Mary W. Green, Mary A. Green, Mary Thompson, Harriet N. Houghton, Louisa A. Wheeler, Mary B. H. Wheeler, Annie E. Thompson, Sarah A. Thompson, Hannah Rogers, Mrs. Coburn, Mrs. Dunning, Mrs. N. Walker, Mrs. H. Purinton, Mrs. Sarah Thompson, Miss Palmer, Miss Webb, Mrs. Shaw, Elizabeth W. Purinton, Penthea S. Hall. Many of these members belonged in Brunswick, and some of the males were students in college.

During the pastorate of Reverend Doctor Wheeler in this town the average attendance at meeting was about one hundred. The building, having been erected for the accommodation of the whole town, was of course too large for any one of the four societies which then existed in the town, and consequently the attendance at the Unitarian services always appeared smaller than it really was. Although small in numbers, it had, however, its full share of the intelligence and pecuniary ability of the community.

[1850.] At the expiration of a little more than ten years from the settlement of their last pastor, arrangements were made to unite the two "liberal" societies of Brunswick and Topsham. The arrangements were completed and went into effect in November, 1850.

[1853.] In 1853 the "proprietors of the Unitarian Meeting-House in Topsham" obtained authority from the legislature to sell it. It was accordingly sold, and in December of that year taken down and removed to a ship-yard at Middle Bays, owned by Robert Pennell, Jr., and others, where it was erected into a boarding-house.

The ministerial fund of the First Parish came into the hands of the pew-holders of the Unitarian Society. It amounted in 1836 to seven hundred and thirty-six dollars and sixty-one cents. This sum was in the hands of various individuals, who gave their notes for the several amounts in their possession. After the transference of the preaching to Brunswick, these notes were unintentionally allowed to become outlawed, and the fund has thus become lost beyond recovery, some of the parties owing the money having died.

Nothing, therefore, now remains in Topsham to remind one of the old First Parish Society except the graveyard attached to the old first meeting-house.

CHURCH AND SOCIETY OF THE SECOND ADVENTISTS.

About the year 1843 an individual by the name of Starkweather came to town, and preached the peculiar views of this society in the Free-Will Baptist Meeting-House. He was succeeded by several others of the followers of "Joe Miller," and quite a number of converts were made, some coming from nearly all the churches. A society was formed and regular meetings were held on Saturday. The society owned no place of worship, but were accustomed to meet at the houses of members. About the year 1844 a paper was issued for a short time by this society. It was devoted exclusively to the dissemination of their religious views. Several predictions were made as to the second coming of the Messiah, and on at least one occasion preparations were made for the event. The society gradually dwindled away, though meetings of its members were held each Saturday until about 1852.

OTHER DENOMINATIONS.

No other religious society was ever formed in this town, but other denominations have occasionally had preaching here for a short time, — the Universalists in the Court House in 1841,[1] and the Methodists and Episcopalians, and perhaps others, at other times.

---

[1] *A. D. Wheeler's Diary.*

CHAPTER XIV.

ECCLESIASTICAL HISTORY OF HARPSWELL.

The early settlers of Harpswell belonged, for the most part, either to the Congregational or to the Church of England denomination.[1] There were, however, amongst them a few Quakers, who set up a monthly meeting about the year 1751. The inhabitants at first contributed to the support of preaching in the First Parish of North Yarmouth, as it appears from the records of that town that on April 16, 1744, the town excused the inhabitants of Merriconeag from paying the minister's rate for that year. In 1751 Merriconeag became a parish, styled the Second Parish in North Yarmouth, and from this time, if not before, voluntarily employed a minister of their own. The first was Reverend Richard Pateshall, a graduate of Harvard College. He preached for two or three years, but was not permanently settled. He was succeeded by Reverend Mr. Packard, who preached only for a short time.

[1753.] In 1753 a church was formed and Reverend Elisha Eaton was settled. The council that met to ordain him assembled at the house of Lieutenant Eaton, it being the only house in town, at that date, that had plastered rooms.[2]

[1758–9.] In 1758 and 1759 the meeting-house on Merriconeag Neck was built, though it was not entirely completed for many years. This building will be more particularly described in another chapter.

In 1758 the town voted that "the Selectmen should proportion the preaching on the Island according to the Rates they pay, and to loose an equal proportion of the time that is deficient." Also to pay four shillings for each Sabbath to the persons who conveyed Mr. Eaton to the Island.

On May 19, 1759, the town voted that Mr. Eaton should preach "in the meeting-house for the future, except foul weather prevents." The selectmen were authorized to hire persons to convey him to the

---

[1] *Kellogg, MS. Lecture.* [2] *Ibid.*

Island. In 1760 the town voted that the people on the Island should be taxed in proportion to the amount of preaching they had. These votes show clearly that Mr. Eaton, thus early, was accustomed to preach on Sebascodigan Island, as well as on the Neck. But little is known concerning the affairs of this church during the ten or eleven years' pastorate of Mr. Eaton; no records have been found, and even our knowledge of its existence at that time, as an organized church, is traditional. What Mr. Eaton's salary was is not known with certainty. In 1758 the town raised for that purpose sixty-five pounds, in 1760 seventy pounds, and in 1762 seventy-five pounds.

[1764.] Reverend Elisha Eaton died on Sunday morning, April 22, 1764, aged sixty-two years. On May 22 a committee was chosen to supply the pulpit with a minister. The town also at this meeting voted £37 7*s.* to defray Mr. Eaton's funeral expenses, and "to give the widow of the Deceased Rev'd Mr. Eaton a Decent sute of mourning."

On July 3d of this year the town voted to pay William Modgridge eight shillings, for making Mr. Eaton's coffin, and to pay a Mr. Babb five shillings for assisting in making the coffin and digging the grave.

On July 17th the town voted to give Reverend Samuel Eaton, the son of their former pastor, an invitation to settle with them, the vote having been unanimous on the part of the church and congregation. It was also voted to give him £120 as a settlement and to pay £40 a year until the settlement was paid. £66 13*s.* 4*d.* was also voted as his yearly salary. Benjamin Jaques and Nathaniel Purinton were chosen to represent the town in the committee chosen by the church to deliver the invitation.

At a meeting of the town, held August 27, it was voted that the "minister should go to the Island called Great Island, fifteen Sabbaths a year, yearly, allowing each day that is appointed by s[d] Minister to be one of s[d] fifteen days, and the Minister to go when he pleases till the fifteen days each year are completed."

The town, at this meeting, also voted to fix upon a place for a meeting-house on the Great Island.

For some reason the invitation voted to Mr. Eaton seems to have been unsatisfactory, and accordingly it was renewed by both the town and the church, at a meeting held on the nineteenth of September.

At this latter meeting a committee was chosen to make the arrangements for his ordination. He was ordained the following October.

[1765.] In May, 1765, the town voted an appropriation of £206

6*s*. 11*d*., old tenor, to defray the charges attendant upon this ordination.

No further action appears to have been taken by the town in regard to ecclesiastical matters for some years, and no parish or church records have been found of an earlier date than the year 1770.

The first church records of Harpswell that are to be found begin with a church meeting, held August 2, 1770, on Sebascodigan Island, at which Isaac Snow was chosen deacon.

At a subsequent church meeting, October 24, 1770, the following preamble and votes were passed: —

"We that thro' God's Goodness, have been combin'd, & are still continued a Chh. of his, having heretofore consented unto the Covenant of Grace, according to the gracious Terms whereof, we have made Choice of the Lord Jehovah, Father, Son & Spirit as our God, and of the Lord Jesus Christ as the glorious Mediator, upon whose Fullness of Merit & Power we rely, as well to be strengthened for the Duties, as to be invested with ye Blessings of that well ordered Covenant; being withall sensible y^{t} our Justification by Faith in the Righteousness of him who is a Saviour and Surety for us, does very strongly oblidge us to close with all the Commands of God, as holy, just & good, and as those Rules, in Conformity to which alone, our Peace can be lengthened out: y^{t} its our Duty to walk circumspectly, not as Fools but as wise, redeeming the Time, because the Days are evil, and calling to Mind ye sinfull Miscarriages of some Professors, who are Spots in our Feasts of Charity, and our Duty to Watch over y^{m} for their good; and considering further that the Doors of the Chh. do not by God's Appointment stand so wide open, y^{t} all sorts of Persons good & bad may freely enter in at their pleasure; y^{t} the Eunuch of Ethiopia was examin'd by Philip; y^{t} the Angle of the Chh. of Ephesus is commended for trying such as said they were Apostles, and were not; and y^{t} twelve Angles were set at ye Gates of ye Temple, lest such as were ceremonially unclean should enter thereinto, (2 Chron. 23, 19. Mat. 13, 25, & 22, 12. Acts 8, 37. Rev. 2, 2, & 21, 12,) Have accordingly conveined at a Chh. Meeting, at the Meeting House duly notified by the Pastor, this 24 Oct^{o}. 1770, and made the following Resolves: —

"The Rev. Samuel Eaton Moderator.

"1. *Voted*, that it is the Intention of this Chh. according to the best of their knowledge, to adhere closely to ye sacred Scripture for their Guide, and to the Rules therein contained for their mode of Discipline, and to come into no Resolves, for which they have not a divine Warrant.

"2. *Voted*, y^t it would be a great evil in us, if we should not accord^g to ye best of our Capacity, attend & support ye Institutions of God in the Midst of us, & that Chh. Discipline wch he has commanded in his Word, that there may be Nothing wanting thereunto.

"3. *Voted*, y^t it is the Opinion of this Chh. y^t the receiving into Chh. Communion, or w^t is called owning the Covenant, those persons who live prayerless in their Families, is a scandal to our holy Religion. Therefore,

"4. *Voted*, y^t this Chh. will not for ye future receive into Chh. Communion, or what is called owning the Covenant, those persons who live prayerless in their Families.

"5. *Voted*, y^t it is the Opinion of this Chh. y^t maliciously to make, or injuriously to spread abroad any false Report, or Reports to ye Injury of the Innocent, is detestable in the sight of God, & ought to be so to us. Therefore,

"6. *Voted*, y^t if any chh. Member or p^{r}sons in Covenant, shall maliciously make, or injuriously spread abroad any false Report, or Reports, to the Injury of the Innocent, he or she, upon Conviction by the Mouth of two or three witnesses, shall be lyable to ye censure of this Church, as those who sin, are to be rebuked before all.

"7. *Voted*, y^t if any Chh. Member, absent him or herself from the Ordinance of the Lord's Supper, in its stated administration, he or she, shall be accounted in the eye of the Chh. as a disorderly Walker, & guilty of the Breach of his or her Covenant Obligations.

"8. *Voted*, y^t it is the Opinion of this chh. that the Custom of young People, of both sexes, getting together in the Night, in those Companies for Mirth & Jollity, Fiddling and Dancing y^t they call Frolicks, so spending the Time together till late in the Night, in their Jollity, to the neglect of family Prayer, and violating all Order, is a sin detestable in the sight of God, & ought to be so to us. Therefore,

"9. *Voted*, y^t if any chh. Member, or Members, or p^{r}sons in Covenant, shall assemble at those places, where such things are, or allow of the same in their Houses sh^{ll} come under the censure of this Chh. so far as to be debarr'd Chh. priviledges, til they give Scripture Satisfaction.

"10. *Voted*, y^t it is the Opinion of this Chh. y^t Churches ought to preserve Communion one wth another, because yy are all united unto Christ, not only as a mistical, but as a political Head: Therefore

"11. *Voted*, y^{t} this Chh. will not hold Communion wth the Member of another regular Chh. who is und^{r} the Censure or Suspension of y^{t} Chh. til he or she gives that Satisfaction agree^{ble} to Scripture, & as practiced by the Chh^{s} in N. England.

"12. *Voted*, y^{t} Messrs Edwd Cuningham, Benj^{a} Jaques, and Jacob Blake, be a Committee for the Neck, and John Snow & Nathl Purington for the Island called great Sebascodigin, to inspect ye walk of Professors, and enquire into Reports if any there may be, and accordingly make Report to the Pastor.

"13. *Voted*, y^{t} it is the Opinion of this Chh. y^{t} for Professors unnecessarily to frequent a Tavern on the Lords Day there to spend some part of it needlessly drinking spirituous Liquor, is a sin detestable in the sight of God, and ought to be so to us, Therefore,

"14. Voted, y^{t} if any Professor shall unnecessarily frequent any Tavern on the Lord's Day, or there repair with a view needlessly to drink spirituous Liquor, or shall at any Time be guilty of Drunkeness, or drinking to excess, he or she shall come und^{r} the Censure of this Church.

"15. Voted, y^{t} it is ye Opinion of this Chh. that some provision be made by them, for the Relief of such Chh. Members, (being well reported of) as are by the providence of God cast into indigent Circumstances. Therefore,

"16. Voted, y^{t} Messrs. Edward Cuningham, Ben^{a} Jaques, and Jacob Blake, be a Committee for the Neck, and John Snow & Nathaniel Purington for the Island, y^{t} if any Chh. Members, who conduct according to the Gosple, and are well reported of but by the providence of God are cast into those circumstances wch necessarily call for Releif, may apply to, and the Committee to make it known to the Pastor, and the Pastor to call the Brethren together that they may judge of their Case, and accord^{g} to their Liberality releive them.

"17. Voted, y^{t} this Chh. will receive No Report unless proved by the Mouth of Two or Three Witnesses.

"18. Voted, y^{t} these Resolves be entered upon the Chh. Records, and publicly read upon the Lords Day.

"A true Copy from the Minutes examined and attested,

"By SAML. EATON, *Moderator*.

"Consented to

"SAML EATON, *Pastor*."

[1777.] At a meeting held May 29, 1777, Joseph Ewing was chosen a deacon.

[1784.] At a church meeting held at the meeting-house, May 31, 1784, it was voted that those who desired church privileges should be examined before the church, and that those living holy lives might have their children baptized though they themselves were not church members. That the deacons should be a committee to inspect the walk of church members, and that the pastor had liberty, "provided he sees his way clear, to baptize by Immersion those who conscientiously desire it, provided they give Satisfaction to the Church of their Faith in Christ & live holy Lives."

At a meeting held August 31, 1786, the church unanimously voted to rescind the seventeenth vote, in regard to receiving reports against members, that was passed October 24, 1770.

[1787.] The previous unanimity in regard to religious affairs in this town began to be disturbed about this time. At a meeting of the town, held in March, 1787, it was voted that those persons who did not intend to pay the minister's tax should give in their names to the committee chosen for the purpose, and should give their reasons to this committee in writing. The committee were to report at a subsequent meeting, but no such report is in the records.

[1803.] At a church meeting, held on April 28, 1803, James Wilson was unanimously chosen a deacon.

[1806.] This year the town voted that Mr. Eaton need preach only in the west meeting-house, on account of the difficulty of a person of his age going to and from the Island.

[1813.] At the annual meeting of the town in 1813 it was agreed that Mr. Eaton should preach only in the west part of the town that year, and that the inhabitants of Great Island should be exempt from paying a tax for his support, "excepting the Ewings." The reason for thus excepting one family was undoubtedly because they lived so near, — just across the Narrows, — and could easily and were accustomed to attend the meetings on the Neck; and also because they were strong supporters of Mr. Eaton and were well-to-do people.

A special town meeting was held in September of this year, at which John Blake, Isaiah Snow, and Paul Raymond were chosen a committee "to go and converse with the Rev'd Samuel Eaton." The nature of the conversation is not recorded, but it may have been in regard to the taxing for his support of residents upon Sebascodigan Island, as following the record of the meeting is this entry: —

"HARPSWELL, Sept. 3d, 1813.

"I hereby Certify that I do from this Date for Ever Relinquish the Civil Contract between great Sebascodegin Island and my Self.

"SAMUEL EATON

"ANTHONY COOMBS, JR.
MARLBORO SYLVESTER

"MARLBORO SYLVESTER *T. Clerk*"

[1818.] At a special meeting of the town, held July 13, Marlboro Sylvester, Sylvester Stover, and Peleg Curtis were chosen to effect a settlement of accounts with Mr. Eaton. Their report was as follows: —

"We the subscribers chosen a Committee by the Town of Harpswell to settle with the Rev'd Sam'l Eaton in behalf of said Town, have attended the service of our appointment the 13th day of July 1818 and we find that since the last settlement, which was up to July 13th 1813, there is due to him from the Town, for five years past services, the sum of $1115. to this date, of which one third part was relinquished to Great Sebascodegin Island, which was $371.66, leaving a balance due to him from the westerly part of said town of $743.34.

"MARLBRO' SYLVESTER
SYLVESTER STOVER
PELEG CURTIS } *Committee*"

Following this report in the town records is this entry: —

"I do relinquish to the Town of Harpswell the whole of the above balance and acknowledge all accounts settled and balanced up to the above date of July 13th 1818.

"SAMUEL EATON."

The reason why Mr. Eaton chose to relinquish so large a sum which was justly his due requires some explanation. The attendance upon his services was at this time small. The Baptists had withdrawn, many citizens objected to being taxed for the support of a minister, and some had absolutely refused to pay their taxes. The parish officers did not like to urge payment, for fear of creating still further opposition, which would result in the further injury of the parish, and thus the unpaid taxes were allowed to accumulate. Mr. Eaton could have compelled the town to pay the amount, but he relinquished it for the sake of harmony.

Probably about this time, though the exact date is nowhere given, Reverend Mr. Samuel Eaton resigned his pastorate. From an examination of the church records, it appears that while Mr. Eaton had charge of this church, he baptized five hundred and eighty-four male children, five hundred and thirty-five female children, nine adult males, seventeen adult females, and two children of whom the sex was not designated, making in all one thousand one hundred and forty-seven persons baptized by him.

In this connection, the following document, obtained from an account-book of Reverend Elisha Eaton, will prove entertaining. It is certainly in the handwriting of Reverend Samuel Eaton, and is probably a portion of some report of his to the Missionary Association. From the number of baptisms recorded, it must have been written — judging from the list of baptisms in the church records — about the year 1767.

"If I am not mistaken in my Calculat^{n} I have preached 40 Serm^{ns} exclusive of Sabbath, & the N^{o} of Baptisms stands thus, —

Child^{n}	157
Adults	11
Total	168

"I now beg leave to make a few gen^{l} Remarks. The pple who were ye Objects of my mission, are, in ye main in a broken State as to Religion. So far as I am able to judge, I impute it to ye multiplicity of lay preachers, and ye paucity of those who are regular and learned. Y^{y} are an open Prey to every Imposter. Missionaries (as many well inclined & who even tremble for ye Ark of G. observed to me) were never more needed y^{n} at this Day. I have found some, I believe, who know genuine religion, who are clear & distinguishing in their notions, & are not carried about by every Wind of Doctrine. Others who app^{r} to me to boil over wth Enthusiasm, others who are thotless of y^{t} wch ought to be their chief Concern, and others who were enquiring w^{t} yy should do to be saved. I feel for ye pple; yy need Guides, yy need Instruction, yy need ye right sort of preach^{rs}. May G. of his infinite Mercy prevent their perishing for lack of vision. In my Public Discourses, as well as private Conv^{r}sation, I endeavoured to distinguish between Truth & Error, an imaginary & true religion, & ye Operat^{n} of both — to reclaim ye Erroneous — To detect ye Hypocrite, to encourage & help ye inquiring, to warn ye hardened Sinn^{r}, to comfort those who mourn in Zion, & to establish ye true Xtian. Neither have I omitted ye Inculcation of morality, & ye necessity of encouraging human Literature &c.

"So far as I am acquainted ye pple are hospitable, have treated me wth great respect & kindness, & all Denominations have industriously attended my preach^{g} on the Sabb^{h} and Lectures.

"I pray G. to water ye seed w^ch^, &c, & to have y^m^ und^r^ his keeping and Guidance, to bless y^m^ wth spiritu^l^ & tem[poral] Favours, & y^t^ each memb^r^ of ye Society may be reward^d^ wth an hund^d^ fold here, & hereafter wth an unfading Crown of Glory. I conclude only wth adding y^t^ I have endeavoured to execute my Mission in a mann^r^ most agreeable to ye Intentions of ye Society."

[1823.] The earliest records of the First *Parish* that have come to our hands commence August 23, 1823. At this meeting Jonathan Johnson was chosen moderator; Joseph Eaton, clerk; Samuel Skolfield, treasurer; Benjamin Dunning, collector; George Skolfield and Jonathan Johnson, assessors; Benjamin Dunning, Joseph Eaton, and Deacon James Wilson, a standing committee. This committee was to supply the pulpit until the middle of November, from the money that had already been subscribed.

The church this year, at a meeting held December 30, voted "to assent to the Cumberland Church Constitution."

[1826.] At a parish meeting held April 15, it was voted that the committee for supplying the pulpit be also a committee "to admit or reject the application of Strangers and others who may wish to hold meetings in the Meeting House."

[1828.] The parish at a meeting held July 14, 1828, voted, though not with unanimity, to give Reverend Ebenezer Halping an invitation to settle as their pastor. They also voted that the money for his support should be raised by subscription, and that James Orr, Sylvester Stover, and Joseph Eaton be a committee to wait upon Mr. Halping and see for what sum he would agree to settle with them. The parish also choose a committee of three to confer with a like committee of the Baptist Society, "to see if they concitute [conciliate?] Matters."

At a meeting held August 4, it was voted that "Captain James Orr be a committee to go and see Mr. Halping and state to him the means that we have to settle him and know if he would accept." It was also voted that Mr. Halping should have what he could obtain from the Cumberland Conference in addition to what the parish gave.

[1829.] On January 21 the church voted to have a copy of the covenant and articles of faith distributed to each family connected with the church.

[1830.] At a meeting of the parish on April 12, 1830, it was voted to supply the pulpit for that year by subscription, and it is therefore most likely that Mr. Halping did not accept the call, though he may have supplied the pulpit for a while. At a meeting held December 20, the parish voted to hire Reverend Moses Welch for one year at a salary of four hundred dollars.

[1831.] On October 3 the parish and church united in extending an invitation to Reverend William Harlow, who had been preaching to them through the summer, to settle as their pastor, provided they could obtain the sum of two hundred dollars, and that he should obtain what sum he could from the Maine Missionary Society and the Cumberland County Conference. At a meeting held December 7, it was decided to have a stove in the meeting-house. Reverend Mr. Harlow accepted the invitation to settle, and at this meeting it was determined that the council for his installation should be entertained by individuals without expense to the parish.

[1832.] Mr. Harlow was ordained and installed January 25, 1832. The services were as follows: —

Prayer, by Reverend Mr. Adams; sermon, by Reverend Mr. Mittimore; installing prayer and charge, by Reverend Mr. Ellingwood; right hand of fellowship, by Reverend Mr. Adams; address to the people, by Reverend Mr. Hawes.

Following the above in the church records appears the following entry: —

"The Reverend Mr. Harlow took the liberty (without asking the consent of his people) to absent himself from them from the ninth of July to the thirteenth or fourteenth of August, 1832, therefore it may be considered that the civil contract expired the day he went away."

This was signed, not by the real, but by an acting clerk. This mistake of taking a vacation without the consent of his parishioners was, however, afterwards rectified.

[1833.] At a parish meeting held November 9, 1833, it was voted to allow him four Sabbaths a year in which to visit his friends. A vote was also passed at this meeting that the Maine Missionary Society should be asked to give Mr. Harlow fifty dollars that year. The same request was made for several years in succession.

[1834.] At a meeting of the church in April of this year at the house of Stephen Sinnett, it was voted "that the record relative to the Reverend William Harlow, on the foregoing page, was made without the knowledge or approbation of the said church."

[1837.] At a meeting of the church held in May, 1837, in compliance with the vote of a council that was held in September of the previous year, the acting clerk, who had been excommunicated on account of his entry in the records and his subsequent conduct, was restored to the fellowship of the church. At this meeting also, Deacon Simeon

Orr and Benjamin Dunning were chosen a committee "to request Mr. Harlow to ask a dismission, if he declined to invite a council."

[1838–1840.] Mr. Harlow probably resigned in the winter of 1838, perhaps earlier. From March, 1839, to March, 1840, the pulpit was supplied in turn by Reverends Clark, Cornish, Gillett, Kenderick, Purington, Merrill, Parsons, and Peasley.

The dismission of Mr. Harlow, or some other cause, seems to have produced considerable disaffection in the church, and during the year 1838 several members of the church were suspended or excommunicated.

Reverend Jotham Sewall, of Freeport, filled the pulpit for a while after Mr. Harlow left, and at a church meeting, held February 29, 1840, it was voted, "That the thanks of this church be presented to the church in Freeport for the faithful and interesting labors of their pastor with us of late."

[1843.] About this time a new meeting-house was built and a new society formed. Though the church and society of the First Parish probably continued to exist for some time after this event, yet no records were kept after the year 1844, and the preaching was probably only occasional in the old meeting-house. The church organization may have connected itself with the new society.

FIRST BAPTIST CHURCH AND SOCIETY.

The first Baptist preaching in Harpswell was in the year 1783, by Reverend Isaac Case and Mr. Potter. The former preached twenty-five sermons to the people on Great Island in the course of a few months. There was some opposition, and Mr. Case said that he was treated "rather coolly" by Reverend Samuel Eaton. On the nineteenth of January, 1785, a church was organized on this island by Reverend Messrs. Case and J. Macomber. It consisted of thirty-one members, of whom only a portion belonged in Harpswell.

A short time after the organization of this church Mr. Potter was baptized and united with it, and on October 5, 1785, he was ordained as an evangelist by Messrs. Case and Macomber, Mr. Case preaching the sermon for the occasion. Elder Potter soon received an invitation and took the pastoral charge of this church. During his ministry about twenty were added to it. He resigned in 1788. In 1790, Elder Elisha Snow, of Thomaston, was ordained as his successor, and preached about two years. He was succeeded by Reverend Samuel Woodard, of Brunswick, who was ordained at his own house, October 11, 1792. Elder Woodard resigned his charge in the latter part of 1801, and was succeeded by Reverend Samuel Mariner, who was ordained in January, 1802. Elder Mariner remained as pastor until his death in 1832. After the death of Elder Mariner, up to the year 1845, this church had no settled minister, though its pulpit was supplied the greater part of the time by Elders S. Owen, Henry Kendall, D. Pierce, William Johnson, J. Butler, and N. Hooper.

This church has had at different times several distinct names. At first it was called the Harpswell Church, then Harpswell and Brunswick, and later it went by the name of the East Brunswick Church. The whole number of members up to the year 1843 was about two hundred and fifty.[1] Reference has been made to this church in the preceding chapter.

SECOND BAPTIST CHURCH AND SOCIETY OF HARPSWELL.

[1827.] This church was organized November 13, 1827. The records commence with the following: —

"We whose Names are hereunto affixed — Having a hope that God has Renewed our Hearts by his rich Grace, and has made it our duty to Glorify him on the Earth — We feel a desire to be embodied into a visible Predestinarian Baptist Church that we may More perfectly Glorify him and enjoy the ministration of his word and ordinances."

The above was signed by: —

John L. Lambert, Elizabeth Lambert, Hannah Thomas, Lozana Alexander, Jane Wilson, Robert B. Gardner, Lucy Ann Farr, James S. Wyer, Mary Alexander, Norton Stover, Joshua Bishop, Patience Bishop, Isabella Merryman, Perry Alexander, Rosanna Alexander, Margaret Wyer, David Wilson, 2d, James Wilson, Jr.

At a meeting held November 3, 1827, the following was sent to the Baptist churches in Topsham and Brunswick, and to the "*Harpswell* Church in *Brunswick*."

"Beloved Brethren: we wish you to send us your Elders and such brethren as you may think proper, to sit with us in Council for the purpose of organizing us into a Predestinarian Baptist Church, to meet with us at the Lower School House on the Neck, on Tuesday the 13th inst. at 10 o'clock A. M."

In reply to this request the Topsham church sent Elder Henry Kendall, Ebenezer Whittemore, and James Cook; the Brunswick church sent Elder Benjamin Titcomb, David Given, Jr., and Samuel Given; the Harpswell church in Brunswick sent Elder Samuel Mariner, Robert

---

[1] *The foregoing account is taken from a " History of the Baptists in Maine," by Reverend J. Millet,* 1845.

Jordan, and Henry Jordan. This council met November 13, and after choice of officers. they examined into the faith and order of the candidates, and voted to give them the right hand of fellowship.

The services were as follows: —

Prayer, by Mr. Hall; sermon, by Reverend Henry Kendall; after which the members arose and received the right hand of fellowship as a sister church; prayer, by Elder Mariner.

[1828.] At a meeting held January 5, 1828, William Randall and John L. Lambert were confirmed as deacons.

[1831.] The first elder to preach to them seems to have been Elder Kendall in 1831.

[1846–1850.] Elder Pinkham preached to them in 1846, and at a church meeting held August 15. 1847, he was formally invited to settle as their pastor. He was dismissed at his own request on October 4, 1850.

[1853–54.] Elder L. Barrows began to preach to this church about May, 1853, and on November 5 formally united with them. In July, 1854, he was dismissed in order to unite with the Baptist Church in Kennebunk.

[1856.] Elder J. Hutchinson of the Maquoit church in Brunswick preached occasionally after the dismissal of Elder Barrows, and on August 25, 1856, having been dismissed by the Maquoit church, was received into the fellowship of this church.

[1860.] In 1859, Elder Nelson was preaching to them; and on August 5, 1860, Elder Evans was sent as a delegate to a meeting of the Baptist Association, so it is safe to infer that he was preaching to this church.

[1862.] April 5, 1862, Reverend H. Perkins was received as a member of this church. On December 3 he received a certificate to enable him to join the church at Mechanic Falls, where he was already settled.

[1865.] On February 4, 1865, Elder N. P. Everett was admitted to fellowship.

[1866.] On August 4, 1866, Elder Sargent was chosen a delegate to the association.

[1869.] On August, 1869, Elder R. Goud was settled as pastor; and on the following twenty-fifth of December, Elder Everett was dismissed.

[1874.] On July 4, 1874, Reverend William R. Millett and wife were received into the church by letter from the church in South Auburn. He died in August, 1875.

The last entry in the church records is dated December 5, 1874. At this meeting it was voted to discontinue the Sunday school, and to hold Sabbath prayer-meetings immediately after the morning service instead of the evening.

THE FIRST FREE-WILL BAPTIST CHURCH AND SOCIETY.

This society was organized on Great Island, April 17, 1817. The following are the names of the original members: —

Daniel Curtis, Stephen Purinton, Anthony Coombs, Arthur Hall, John Snow, Swanzey Wilson, Jane Dingley, Ruth Snow, Mary Purinton, Mary Rich, Desire Dingley, Sally Kemp, Mary Totman, Mary Raymond, Polly Purington, Fanny Merritt,[1] Martha Hall, Deborah Rich, Mary Linscott, Betsey Rich, Almira Purinton, Mary Purinton, Hannah Totman, Ruth Page, Joanna Curtis, Hannah Curtis, Sally Dingley, Priscilla Purinton, Eunice H. Purinton, and Hannah Dingley.

Reverend George Lamb, of Brunswick, was the settled minister from the organization of the society until his death, in 1835 or 1836. From that time until 1839 the pulpit was supplied by transient preachers. In 1839, Reverend O. W. Smith was settled over the church until 1842, and during this time sixty members were added to it. From 1843 to 1854, Reverend Levi Hersey was the pastor. From 1857 to 1860, Reverend David Libby Hind was settled, and during his pastorate thirty-five new members were added to the church. In 1866, Reverend L. C. Burr was settled for three years. Since then Reverend Messrs. D. Libby, A. Libby, Heath, and Prescott have supplied the pulpit.

The meeting-house of this society is the Free Union Baptist Meeting-House on Great Island. It was built by subscription in 1843.

This society is now feeble and the number of its members is small. They are also quite scattered through the town. Its present membership is but thirty-two.

THE SECOND, OR ORR'S ISLAND FREE-WILL BAPTIST CHURCH AND SOCIETY.

This society was organized, in 1858, by Reverend J. Fuller. Its original members were: —

George W. Card, Reuben Dyer, John Black, Cummings Alexander, Sarah Dyer, Mary Green, Martha Sinnett, Adaline Orr, Henrietta Sinnett, Patience Orr, and Jane Alexander.

This society uses the Orr's Island Union Meeting-House, which was

---

[1] *The only one now living.*

built about 1855, alternately with the other societies owning the building. The society is quite small, its present membership being but thirty. No facts have been obtained as to the ministers who have had charge of it.

FIRST UNIVERSALIST SOCIETY IN HARPSWELL.

[1838.] The first preaching of Universalist doctrines in Harpswell was in April, 1838. Reverend Seth Stetson visited Harpswell at this time, and preached two sermons to about thirty hearers in the Number Two School-House on the Neck.

[1839.] The next summer Reverend Mr. Stoddard preached there on two Sundays. In 1839 the Universalists raised about thirty dollars, and employed Reverend Mr. Stetson for six or seven Sabbaths.

[1840.] In 1840 a similar amount was raised, and preaching was had for about the same length of time.

[1841.] In 1841 the Universalists, together with some of a different faith, built a Union Meeting-House, which was dedicated by the Universalists on September 21. The sermon was by Reverend John T. Gilman, of Bath. There was a sermon in the afternoon by Reverend E. Wellington, and another in the evening by Reverend G. Bates.

[1842.] In 1842 they raised about fifty dollars, and employed Reverend L. P. Rand to preach one fourth of the time during that year.

[1844.] On April 20, 1844, a Universalist society was legally organized by the choice of Isaac Stover, moderator; Thomas Alexander, clerk; Samuel Dunning, treasurer; and Samuel Dunning, Joshua Stover, and Thomas Alexander, parish committee. The following constitution was adopted: —

"We the subscribers being desirous of forming ourselves into a society, for the purpose of supporting and enjoying the preached Gospel of our Lord and Saviour Jesus Christ, do hereby unite and agree to walk together in harmony and love. And to guide ourselves understandingly we adopt the following rules: —

"1st. We take the name of the First Universalist Society of Harpswell.

"2d. We take the Bible, containing the Old and New Testaments, as the rule of our faith and practice.

"3d. We agree to meet together as often as convenient for the worship of the one living and true God, the Father of the spirits and the Father of our Lord Jesus Christ.

"4th. We agree to subscribe, so far as we are able, for the support of the preached Gospel and the maintenance of Christian worship.

"5th. We agree to strive to live in a moral and virtuous manner that we may give no occasion to the adversary to speak reproachfully, and that we may honor our God and Saviour by a well-ordered life and Christian conversation.

"6th. Any person of a sober, moral character may become a member of this society by subscribing his or her name to the foregoing rules.

"7th. Any member may withdraw from this society when they shall have paid their subscription and signified their desire so to do, to the clerk of this society."

The following names were affixed to this constitution: —

Isaac Stover, Thomas Alexander, Samuel Dunning, David Curtis, Joshua Stover, Paul R. Thomas, James Meryman, 2d, Alcot S. Pennell, Robert Pennell, Sylvester Stover, 2d, Jacob Blake, Alcot Stover, Harmon Pennell, Thomas Pennell, and Robert Dunning. In 1845 this society was received into the Kennebec Association of Universalists.

The entries in the records of this society are very brief, and contain little else than the lists of officers chosen annually.

At a meeting held April 14, 1849, it was voted to support a preacher that year by subscription, and not by taxation.

At a meeting held July 21, 1860, the treasurer in his report declared the society to be free from debt. The society, notwithstanding this fact, had only occasional preaching for nearly ten years.

[1870.] On January 29, 1870, the society was reorganized by the choice of Thomas Alexander as moderator; David Pennell, clerk; Alcot S. Pennell, Benjamin F. Randall, and Joshua Stover, standing committee; B. F. Randall and A. S. Pennell, collectors; and A. S. Pennell, treasurer. The last entry in the records is dated May 8, 1875. Between 1870 and 1875, Reverend William R. French, of Brunswick, preached a portion of the time in summer, in addition to his services at Brunswick. There is at present no settled minister, but the society is still in existence.

CENTRE CONGREGATIONAL PARISH.

[1843.] This society or parish originated in 1843 by certain individuals combining for the purpose of building a new meeting-house. It was formed, and the first meeting was held agreeably to the warrant for the same, on September 27. Daniel Randall was chosen moderator, and William C. Eaton, clerk. The following constitution was adopted at this meeting: —

"We the undersigned having organized ourselves into a parish under the name of the Centre Congregational Parish, in Harpswell, for the promotion of good morals, for religious teaching and instruction, and for sustaining and propagating the truths of the Gospel as held by the Orthodox Congregational denomination in this State, do adopt the following constitution: —

"Article 1st. This parish shall consist of those whose names are affixed to the application for a warrant for organization, together with such other persons as they may from time to time elect, and who shall sign this constitution.

"Art. 2d. The officers of this parish shall be a clerk, two or more assessors, a treasurer, a collector, and a standing committee of three, who shall be elected at the annual meetings.

"Art. 3d. The annual meeting of this parish shall be held in the month of April in each year, on some day to be specified by the assessors.

"Art. 4th. In case the annual meeting shall not be held at the time specified, the officers of the preceding year shall retain their offices until others are chosen and qualified in their stead.

"Art. 5th. This parish agree in the settlement of a minister, and in the support of the ordinances of the Gospel, to proceed upon the established principles of the Orthodox Congregational denomination in this State and to act in concert with the church in Harpswell of like order and faith.

"Art. 6th. A majority of two thirds of all the legal voters in this parish shall be necessary to alter or amend this constitution."

The original subscribers to the above constitution were: —

Silvester Stover, Joseph Eaton, James Stover, Simeon Orr, Jacob Meryman, Benjamin Dunning, George S. Dunning, Arthur Orr, Thomas U. Eaton, Lemuel H. Stover, Shubal Merryman, William C. Eaton, Daniel Randall, Henry Barnes, Joseph Stover, James Meryman, James Dunning, Jeremiah Meryman, Angier H. Curtis, Albert Stover, Paul C. Randall, Dominicus Jordan, William Barnes, James Curtis, Joseph Curtis, John Durgin, H. C. Martin, Ralph Johnson, Joseph A. Stover, Elisha S. Stover, and Isaac Merryman.

It was also at this meeting voted to accept the meeting-house offered by the proprietors, and to assume all the liabilities and duties of the latter.

The next day the new meeting-house was dedicated with the following services: —

Reading of Scriptures, by Reverend Elijah Kellogg, then on a missionary tour; prayer, by Reverend Daniel Sewall; sermon, by Reverend J. W. Chickering; address to the church, by Reverend George E. Adams; prayer, by Reverend Mr Parsons.

At a meeting of the church on November 12, it was voted: —

"That the *Centre Congregational Church* in Harpswell would tender their united thanks to the individuals in Bath, Freeport, Brunswick, and High Street Church, Portland, for their liberal donations to assist them in the erection of a house of worship; also to the Widow D. Dunlap, for the liberal present of a sofa; to the president and professors of Bowdoin College, for their services in supplying the pulpit; and to Professor Upham, for his unwearied exertions in our behalf."

[1844.] On April 25, 1844, the church voted, in concurrence with the parish, to extend an invitation to Reverend Elijah Kellogg to settle as their pastor for three hundred dollars per year, for four years. This invitation was accepted, and was subsequently renewed for an indefinite period.

[1847.] At a parish meeting, held November 1, this year, it was decided that Mr. Kellogg might go "to Orr's Island the coming winter, and preach three Sabbaths, if he see fit."

The church records are wanting entirely between the years 1844 and 1855, and from the latter date down to 1870 they contain only the admissions to church fellowship and lists of those baptized.

[1854.] In 1854, Mr. Kellogg gave up the immediate charge of the parish, in order to devote more time to literary pursuits, but his pastoral connection with the church has never been dissolved.

[1866.] At a meeting of the parish, held April 28 of this year, three hundred dollars was raised for repairing and painting the meeting-house.

[1870.] At a church meeting held on the twenty-eighth of August, it was voted that the thanks of the church "be hereby given to Honorable A. D. Lockwood, of Lewiston, for a highly valued, beautiful communion service, generously presented by him for our use. And our prayer is that the Great Head of the church will accept the act as done to himself, and bountifully reward the giver." On September 24 a church meeting was held on Orr's Island, the first one mentioned in the records as being held on that island.

[1874.] At a meeting of the parish, held April 23, 1874, it was voted to allow the sewing circle "to enlarge the stove-rooms by taking in the pews in front of each." The latest entry in these records is dated the sixth of the following September, at which time Paul C. Randall was chosen a deacon.

There has been no settled minister over this parish since Mr. Kellogg left, but the pulpit is supplied a good part of the time, and nearly every summer, by Mr. Kellogg himself, who makes Harpswell the place of his summer residence.

THE METHODIST CHURCH AND SOCIETY.

The introduction of Methodism into Harpswell dates back only to 1854, although as early as 1814 Fathers Lombard and Bennett, and perhaps others, had preached in town.

[1854.] In May, 1854, Reverend George C. Crawford, of Brunswick, was, at the solicitation of a number of people of West Harpswell, appointed to that field of labor. At that time there was not a member of the Methodist church on Harpswell Neck, with the exception of Sidney Bailey and wife. Mr. Crawford commenced his labors about the first of June, holding the meetings in the school-house near Mr. Simeon Webber's. On the third Sabbath of his ministry here, he read in public the "Doctrines, Discipline, and General Rules" of the Methodist Episcopal Church. A small "class" was then formed, consisting of Captain Norton Stover, Nathaniel Pinkham and wife, and Sidney Bailey and wife. A few weeks later Mr. William Gillam and wife, then of Orr's Island, joined. After two or three meetings it was decided to build a church at once. A suitable lot was secured in a central location. Captain Stover was chosen an agent to purchase lumber and other material; and W. W. Douglass, of Brunswick, was chosen to superintend the erection of the building.

[1855.] The work was hastened, and in less than one year from the time of the first meeting in the school-house, a beautiful and graceful chapel was dedicated. On the day of dedication people flocked to town from all directions, and Reverend William F. Farringdon, then of Portland, delivered the dedicatory address from the words, "Searching what, or what manner of time, the spirit of Christ which was in them did signify, when it testified beforehand the sufferings of Christ and the glory that should follow." The sale of pews took place in the afternoon of the same day. The society is largely indebted to Captain Norton Stover and Nathaniel Pinkham, who assumed the entire financial responsibility in the erection of the church.

At the Conference of 1855 Reverend Heman Nickerson was appointed to succeed Mr. Crawford. He was succeeded by Reverend Mr. Russell. Then followed, in succession, Reverends N. Andrews, John Collins, H. B. Mitchell, Alpha Turner, George C. Crawford (a second time), J. C. Perry, H. Briggs, Thomas Hillman, N. C. Clifford, D. Dudley, N. Andrews (a second time), and M. C. Baldwin. Under these preachers there were several revivals and a large number were added to the church. The society is now in a flourishing condition, and is composed in a large part of the wealth, intelligence, and refinement of that section of the town.

CHAPTER XV.

EDUCATIONAL HISTORY OF BRUNSWICK.

BRUNSWICK, the seat of Maine's oldest and most favored college, has generally shown herself fully mindful of the claims of education. So far, however, as the early introduction of schools is concerned, no especial credit attaches itself to the early settlers, who simply acted in accordance with the laws of the Commonwealth, and had, indeed, before the incorporation of the town, no volition in the matter. In all probability it has been well for the town that the establishment of schools was not left to the discretion of the earlier settlers, for they were, with a few notable exceptions, extremely ignorant as to all knowledge usually acquired from books. As an illustration of the average attainments of the time, it is related of Thomas Atkins, one of the earliest settlers in this vicinity, that he had ten daughters, of whom not one could sign her name to a deed.[1] Even so late as Judge Minot's time it was considered a rare accomplishment for one to be able to read, and it is given as a tradition among his descendants that on one occasion, when he had received a newspaper at the village, he stopped on his way home and read from it to some workmen on the road, who were greatly astonished that the judge should be able to read. The judge was not, however, the only man hereabouts at that time who could read, for there were then a number of educated people in town, one of whom (Thomas Skolfield) was a graduate of Dublin University.

Ample excuse is to be found for the neglect of the earlier settlers to provide means for education in the fact that they were few in numbers, constantly exposed to the incursions of a savage foe, and were obliged to till other fields than those of an intellectual kind, — to break up the rough soil of the wilderness, and raise the scanty crops absolutely required for their physical existence. It is simply another example of the fact that, in the order of time, physical must precede mental activity.

The first action looking to the establishment of a school in Bruns-

---

[1] *Reverend Dr. Ballard's Notes.*

wick was in the year 1715, at which time the Pejepscot proprietors voted that the ministerial, minister's, and school lots should be the centre lots of the town.[1]

In 1717 provision was made by the General Court of Massachusetts for a school-master to reside at Brunswick, and fifty dollars was voted for books and rewards for the young *Indians* who might become his pulpils.[2] This school was a part of the mission to the Indians. Who was sent as teacher has not been ascertained.

At the November session of the Court of General Sessions this year, Benjamin Larrabee, Esquire, appeared in behalf of the town of Brunswick, to answer to the "presentment of the town for not having and maintaining a school-master in said town to teach children and youth to read and write as the law directs and requires." Larrabee's excuse for the delinquency was accepted, but the town was required to pay sixteen shillings, the fees of court.

At a meeting held February 23, 1743, the proprietors voted:—

"That Lott number six on the southeasterly side of the Road adjoyning to the Ministry Lott be and hereby is granted to the Town of Brunswick for a school Lott containing one hundred acres, to be and Continue for said use."[3]

At a town meeting in 1739, a proposition to employ a school-master was "voted for and past in the negative," but the town afterwards reconsidered its action, and at a meeting in September chose a committee to secure the service of a school-master.

PUBLIC SCHOOLS.

The first school-teacher employed by the town was James McCashlen, who was employed in the year 1740, and was paid £40[4] for his services. In 1741 it appears from a statement in the Pejepscot Papers that Reverend Mr McClanethan taught a school here.

In 1742 a committee was appointed by the town to secure the services of a school-master, and they were authorized "to appoint him the time and places for keeping the Schoole in the Sevarel partes of the Town as they shall Think proper." Samuel Maffitt was selected as a teacher, and received £17 10*s.* as his pay, but the length of time he taught is not stated.[5]

About the year 1752, Mr. George Harwood was employed to teach by the year.[6] In order to give equal privileges of schooling to all, he

[1] *Pejepscot Records.* [2] *Varney, History of Maine, p.* 123. [3] *Pejepscot Records.*
[4] *Town Records* 1, *pp.* 23, 49, 50, 51. [5] *Ibid.* [6] *Pejepscot Papers.*

taught in three different parts of the town, — at the upper part of New Meadows, at the old west meeting house, and at lower New Meadows.

In 1753 a committee was chosen to secure a school-master at the rate of £220 old tenor. In 1754 another committee was raised for the same purpose, and £13 6*s.* 8*d.* voted for the salary. The committee were instructed to station the teacher in the several parts of the town, according to the amount paid by each part.

In 1755 the same amount was paid as salary, with the board additional. This year John Blake was employed as a school-master for six months from November 5. His engagement was probably not renewed, as the town in May, 1756, authorized the selectmen "to provide a school-master when they see the times to be convenient."

In 1759, John Farrin was employed as a teacher, the town paying him at the rate of £26 13*s.* 4*d.* per annum. He was re-engaged the next year at the same salary, and continued to teach until October 1, 1761, when his time expired. He is known to have taught again in 1776, because he that year gave the town £15 6*s.* 8*d.* of his salary, in consequence of the public distresses and the burdensome taxes. Whether he taught between 1761 and 1776 is not known, but it is to be presumed that he did.

In 1762 the town was virtually divided into two districts, by the employment of separate teachers for the eastern and western parts. Probably Mr. Farrin was one of the teachers employed.

In 1763, George Harwood was chosen as school-master, by vote of the town, "if he accepts of the same." He did accept, for in 1767 he was paid for four years' teaching.

In 1790 the town was, for the first time, legally divided into school districts, a committee being chosen at a regular meeting to divide the town into two districts.

In 1797 a vote was passed by the town, "that the school money be divided in future according to the number of scholars in each class,[1] the scholars to be numbered, all between four and twenty-one years of age, but if any others in any class are disposed to go, he or she shall have a right to do so, whether they are over or under the above age."

In 1798 the town voted, for the first time, to choose a school committee, and the selectmen were chosen to act in that capacity. The town also voted that no person should be allowed to teach in any district without the approbation of the committee.

---

[1] *Districts were then called classes.*

Previously to this time the red school-house at the foot of the mall was built.[1] It was afterwards moved to the Cove. Who the other teachers may have been, besides those already named, prior to 1800, is unknown. Mr. Richard Flaherty is mentioned as having taught here some time in the last century, but neither the date of his teaching is known, nor whether his school was a public or private one.

In 1810 the town was divided into nine school districts. About this time Mr. Dorman Perkins taught in the district schools of the town. He kept a school one term in Benjamin Larrabee's house, at New Meadows, near where Mrs. Thomas now lives. He kept school another term in the upper New Meadows district, and another term at Maquoit.

In 1820, if not before, the number of districts must have been increased, as there were this year twenty-three public or district schools.[2]

In 1820 the school committee were directed to report at the annual town meeting the names of two scholars "from each class, one boy and one girl, that shall have made best improvement and sustained good moral characters."

On November 29, 1824, the greater portion of the "school lot" was sold at auction. This was the origin of the school fund. A. Bourne, the auctioneer, was the chairman of the trustees of the school fund. The remainder of the school lot was sold in 1833.

At a town meeting, held in March, 1826, a petition of Benjamin Peterson and others, "that this town set off the colored people of School District Number 14, into a district by themselves," was referred to the selectmen. This district was at New Meadows, where there were quite a number of negroes, and the white citizens of that district had then the same feeling in regard to commingling with those of a darker race that is even now prevalent in some quarters. At another meeting, held on the eleventh of September following, the town voted that the money for District Number 14 should be divided, the white people to have a school summer and winter, and the colored population to have a school at the other seasons. The division of money was to be made according to the proportion of scholars in the separate schools.

Of the different districts of the town we have succeeded in obtaining the records of but two, viz., of District Number 5 (Growstown) and of the Village District.

---

[1] *The red school-house on School Street was of a later date.*

[2] *Putnam, "Letters to a Gentleman in South Carolina."*

The records of District Number 5 commence February 11, 1817. At this meeting a district school committee were chosen to superintend the school, and it was voted to have the school-mistress "board round."

In 1839 the district committee were instructed to visit the school every four weeks, and were to have three dollars each for their services if they attended to their duty.

On January 29, 1848, the district decided to build a new school-house, to be located "at the corner of the road on land owned by James Otis and occupied by E. T. Parsons, on the north side of the road leading by said Parsons's house; with the understanding that it be given gratis." Stephen Snow, George Woodside, and Harvey S. Otis were chosen a building committee, and at a meeting held the next month, it was voted to give them discretionary power to build a suitable school-house and to dispose of the old one.

On January 25, 1849, a new committee was chosen, and the building of a school-house was set up at auction to the lowest bidder, the old house to be given to the successful bidder, "except the stove and funnel." James Otis agreed to build it for two hundred and fifty dollars, and the district voted to raise two hundred. The school-house was built this year.

On April 11, 1857, the district voted to admit pupils from other districts, at the discretion of the agent, "at twenty-five cents per week and board of teacher a proportionate part of the time." This permission appears not to have worked well, or to have given dissatisfaction, for two years later the district voted not to admit pupils from other districts on any consideration.

The following are the early teachers in this district so far as known: Mary Noyes, Mary Merryman, and James McKeen, in 1814; Priscilla Melcher and John Winslow, in 1815; Margaret Ransom and John Winslow, in 1816; Deborah Small and Benjamin Thompson, in 1817; Mary Snow, in 1818; Mary Stanwood and Benjamin Thompson, in 1819.

THE VILLAGE SCHOOL DISTRICT.[1]

Brunswick village was formerly divided into three school districts, known as Numbers "1, 2, and 20." In the winter of 1848 several informal meetings of the inhabitants of the village were held, to take into consideration the condition of the village schools.

---

[1] *For this account we are largely indebted to MSS. of the late A. C. Robbins, Esquire, from which we have copied freely.*

A committee was appointed to collect information upon the subject of schools in other places, and to see what could be done for the improvement of the public schools in the village.

This committee proposed the plan of uniting Districts Numbers 1, 2, and 20 into one district, to be called the Village District, for the purpose of grading and classifying the schools, and of adopting the "high-school system."

On March 24, 1848, Benjamin H. Meder and fifteen others petitioned the selectmen to insert in their next annual warrant for a town meeting an article to so alter the school districts that Districts Numbers 1, 2, and 20 should constitute one district.

About the same time John C. Humphreys and Leonard C. Merrill presented to the selectmen a similar petition, except that it contained in addition the words "provided such shall be the wish of said districts respectively."

In the warrant for the annual town meeting, April 3, 1848, an article was inserted in accordance with the latter petition, and the town at that meeting voted: "That School Districts Numbers 1, 2, and 20 be discontinued and to be constituted one district, to be called the Village District, *provided* such shall be the wish of the several districts respectively."

At a meeting of the legal voters of *District Number* 1, on April 24, 1848, a committee of five were chosen to take measures for building a new school-house. This committee were Allen Colby, Ward Coburn, John Rogers, William H. Hall, and Benjamin H. Meder. It was also at this meeting voted: "To join District Number 1 and District Number 20, to form a High School." The meeting adjourned to May 6, at which time the district proceeded to act on sundry matters as though no vote to join the other district had been passed. The following votes were passed: 1. To accept the report of the committee, which was in favor of building a school-house on Bow Street, to be two stories high. 2. To choose a prudential committee of three. 3. To raise three hundred dollars by tax towards building a school-house. 4. To pay the agent and clerk each five dollars. 5, 6. To compel the children of the district, who were between the ages of four and fourteen years, to go to the summer school, and to forbid those between the ages of four and ten years to attend the winter school. 7. To require pupils between the ages of ten and twenty-one years to go to the school kept by a male teacher. This was the last meeting ever held by *District Number* 1.

The legal voters of *District Number* 2 held a meeting at the red school-house, on School Street, previously referred to, on April 22, 1848. This meeting was adjourned to May 6, at which time a committee, consisting of G. C. Swallow, A. C. Robbins, William Mountford, Thomas Knowlton, and E. S. Parshley, were chosen to obtain information in regard to the high-school system, and to report at a subsequent meeting. The next meeting of this district was held June 24. The committee reported in favor of the adoption of the high-school system, and it was voted "that the district concur with Districts Numbers 1 and 20 in adopting the system and in the formation of a Village District, agreeable to the petition of Benjamin Furbish and others and a vote of the town." G. C. Swallow, George F. Dunning, A. C. Robbins, John F. Titcomb, and John S. Cushing were chosen a committee to confer with Districts Numbers 1 and 20.

At a special meeting of *District Number* 20, held June 24, 1848, it was voted "to unite with School Districts Numbers 1 and 2 for the formation of the Village District." The district also chose Professor H. H. Boody, Charles J. Noyes, and Robert Melcher a committee to confer with the committees chosen by Districts Numbers 1 and 2, and they were authorized and empowered to adopt such measures as might be necessary on the part of the district, "to bring the object of said preceding vote into full and complete effect."

On June 20, 1848, a petition was sent to the legislature, stating that the three above-mentioned districts had united and formed one district, with the consent of the town, and requesting the passage of an Act confirming the action of the town "and giving to said district power to raise annually such sum of money as may be needed for the support of the public schools therein." This petition was signed by Abner B. Thompson and nineteen others in District Number 1, by Robert P. Dunlap and thirty-five others in District Number 2, and by Parker Cleaveland and twenty-three others in District Number 20.

In accordance with this petition the legislature, the same year, passed an Act confirming the vote of the town, and granting to the Village District all the powers and privileges of other districts in the State; authorizing the district to raise such sum of money as might be deemed necessary for support of the public schools within the district, the amount so raised not to exceed "three fifths of the amount apportioned to said district from the school money raised by the town for the same year"; requiring this money to be assessed and collected as other school-district taxes were; and authorizing the district to choose school agents and adopt proper by-laws.

Immediately after the passage of the preceding Act, measures were taken for the organization of the Village District. A meeting of the inhabitants of the three districts in the village was called by the selectmen, to be held on August 18, 1848. At this meeting a committee of seven were appointed to draft a plan of organization. To this committee were added the superintending school committee of the town, making a committee of ten. This committee reported, at a meeting held August 30, as follows: In favor of the annual election of a board of nine agents, three of whom might be from each of the former sections of the district, and this board were also authorized to act as an executive committee, and to prescribe a course of study and determine the text-books to be used; to examine teachers; to visit the schools; to conduct examinations; to promote deserving scholars; to admit pupils from without the district; and to establish by-laws. The committee also recommended that there should be three grades of schools, — primary, grammar, and high; determined which should be taught by male and which by female teachers; fixed the commencement and close of the several terms and vacations; prescribed the classification and course of studies for each school, and the requirements at examinations and for admission to school.

This report was accepted at this meeting and its recommendations approved and authorized to be put into execution, though they were afterwards (April 17 and May 8, 1849) somewhat modified.

The Board of Agents made a report, September 27, 1848, in which they recommended the purchase of a lot on Union Street, between O'Brien and Lincoln Streets, for the erection of a grammar and high school building, the renting and furnishing of rooms for these schools until such a building should be erected, and the enlargement and repair of the primary school-houses.

In their next report, this board state that all the schools had been organized according to the plan agreed upon. During the winter of 1848–9, four primary and two grammar schools had been taught, the average length of each being fifteen weeks. The number of teachers employed was eleven; eight in the primary schools, two in the principal grammar school, and one in the select grammar school. This was five more teachers than had been usually employed in previous years. The number of pupils at this time in the primary schools was four hundred and forty-six; the number in the principal grammar school was one hundred and twenty-five, and in the select grammar school, forty-six. The total number of pupils in the village schools was six hundred and seventeen.

As the number of scholars very much exceeded what had been anticipated, the committee had been under the necessity of establishing a fourth primary school on Union Street. The select grammar school was a temporary expedient made use of at this time, on account of the number of pupils really fitted to enter a high school being too small to justify the immediate establishment of such a school.

Some fault having been found with the result of the examinations, the board in this report explained their method of conducting them, and defended their action in the matter.

The total receipts for the village schools this year were $1,204,49. Of this sum, $1,137.09 was expended for rent and repair of school-houses, payment of teachers, and incidental expenses, leaving a balance unexpended of sixty-seven dollars and forty cents. If from these expenditures the unusual expense of rent, repairs, etc., be deducted, there remains a sum less by twenty dollars than that expended for the three winter schools of the previous year, which demonstrated the advantage of the system in a financial aspect.

The agents urged strongly the necessity of providing suitable accommodations for the high and for the principal grammar school. They say, "By next September, at least one hundred and forty scholars will be entitled to a place in the grammar school, — a number which it is totally impossible to accommodate in any room in the village of which the committee have knowledge."

In concluding this report the board congratulated the district "on the *successful* introduction of a new and better system of schools."

In their report for the year ending April 2, 1849, the superintending school committee also speak of the very decided improvement in the schools, in consequence of the adoption of the grading system and of a uniformity of school-books.

The Board of Agents, in their report for the year 1849–50, make the following statements: —

In the summer there were two grammar and four primary schools kept; in the fall and winter, two grammar, three primary, and one miscellaneous school. The number of teachers during the year was, in the summer, ten, — one male and nine females. The school year was thirty weeks, divided into three terms of ten weeks each. In the summer term there were five hundred and sixty-seven, and in the fall and winter terms five hundred and seventy-three pupils.

At the beginning of the year there were not enough children sufficiently advanced in their studies to enable the agents to constitute the high school with all its appropriate classes. No high school was established, therefore, but the pupils were taught in the grammar school. The time had then arrived, however, in their opinion, for establishing the school.

They affirm, "without fear of contradiction, that never has there been in this village schools, public or private, of so high an order as the schools of this district the last year."

The committee also stated that they had contracted with teachers, and conducted the schools on the assumption that the additional tax levied by the district would be paid promptly. A part only of this tax had thus far been collected, and the most of this had been paid to cancel a note of the district, and that in consequence the teachers had not been paid for their last term's service. They stated that most of the citizens had favored, or at least acquiesced in, the change in the school system, but all had not. "On the part of some, there is an avowed hostility to this system, which will not be satisfied with anything short of its entire overthrow."

The committee stated that this hostility was exhibited the previous summer in an effort to procure from the legislature a repeal of the Act of Incorporation of the Village District. Failing in this, they refused to pay the tax levied by the district, on the pretext that the district had not been legally constituted, and that the power granted to it in its Act of Incorporation was in violation of the Constitution. The committee added that this objection came with bad grace from those who signed the petition for incorporation. They considered the matter practically settled by the action of the legislature, but were ready to meet the matter at once before the Supreme Court. In accordance with a vote of the district they had taken legal advice, which was that the collector should be asked to proceed at once in the collection of these taxes and that he should be supported therein by the whole strength of the district.

The petition to the legislature, to which reference was made above, was signed by John Crawford and one hundred and four others, and declared that the plan of uniting the schools into one district had proved a failure, and therefore a repeal of the Act was prayed for. This petition was first referred to the Committee on the Judiciary, and was subsequently laid before the Committee on Education. Seventeen of the signers were petitioners for the Act of Incorporation of the Village District.

As soon as it was known that the above petition was in circulation, a remonstrance against a repeal was at once started. It was signed by Robert P. Dunlap, Adam Lemont, and two hundred and twenty-one others.

One of the positions taken by the opponents to the Village District was that District Number 1 never intended to unite and form with Districts Number 2 and 20 a *Village District*, and that they did not acquiesce in the matter. In refutation of this argument, Messrs. Isaac Lincoln, William H. Hall, and Alfred J. Stone deposed, June 8, 1850, "that since the organization of the Village District in Brunswick, in the summer of 1848, District Number 1 has claimed to have no legal existence, nor has the said District Number 1, since that time, performed any acts as a district, but has united with Districts Numbers 2 and 20 in the formation of the Village District.

"No public schools have been taught in what was District Number 1 since the summer of 1848 up to this date, excepting the schools which were under the control and supervision of the agents of the Village District, to which schools the people in the part of the Village District which was formerly District Number 1 have cheerfully sent their children for instruction, and have received their full share of benefit therefrom."

The truth in regard to the feeling in this district is shown by the following facts, which were certified to by John F. Hall, the last clerk of the district: Of the voters in District Number 1, *twenty* petitioned for the Act of Incorporation of the Village District, *thirty-five* petitioned for the repeal of the Act, and *sixty-seven* remonstrated against a repeal.

To show that the selectmen recognized the Village District as having an existence in November, 1848, the following certificate was written: —

"SELECTMEN'S OFFICE, BRUNSWICK, June 7, 1850.

"On the seventeenth of November, 1848, I was called upon by A. C. Robbins, one of the Board of Agents for the Village District, for that year. At his request I balanced the accounts with School Districts Numbers 1, 2, and 20, and carried the balances forward to the credit of the Village District. At that time there was due to District Number 1, $381.03; to District Number 2, $319.08; to District Number 20, $179.40. All which balances were credited to the Village District in Brunswick, since which time we have had no accounts with Districts Numbers 1, 2, and 20: the money formerly due to them being credited to the Village District in Brunswick.

"(Signed) "RICHARD GREENLEAF,
Chairman of Selectmen."

In July, 1849, the president and directors of the Warumbo Manufacturing Company petitioned the legislature "that the said company may be exempted from the payment of the taxes by special legislation imposed upon them, or that if they must be specially taxed for such objects *beyond the general provisions of law*, that the avails may go to the benefit of the whole town in which their property is situated."

Among the reasons given for asking for this exemption was that, in the passage of the Act, the corporation had no agency nor *notice*. It was true that they had no notice, as a corporation, but the company were represented in the petition for incorporation by their treasurer and one of their directors.

The petition for the repeal of the Act of Incorporation, the petition of the Warumbo Manufacturing Company, and the remonstrance, were all laid before the Committee on Education. On an appointed day the petitioners appeared, and were heard by their counsel, General A. B. Thompson and Honorable James W. Bradbury. The remonstrants were heard by their representatives, Professor William Smyth and Phineas Barnes, Esquire, of Portland. Richard Greenleaf, Esquire, appeared as a witness for the petitioners.

After the somewhat protracted hearing, the committee of nine, all of whom were present, voted eight to one to give the petitioners leave to withdraw. On July 20, 1849, this report of the committee passed both houses of the legislature without a dissenting vote.

At the annual town meetings in 1848, 1849, and 1850, it was voted: "That the several school districts be authorized to choose their several school agents."

The foregoing account relates to the *organization* of the Village District. What follows will relate to the doings of this district.

At a meeting of the Village District, held on the twenty-seventh of September, 1848, the Board of Agents were authorized to borrow such sums of money as might be needed from time to time for the expenditures already authorized, not to exceed $5,000. At the annual meeting of the district in 1849, it was voted "to raise three fifths of the amount of money raised by the town, apportioned to this district by a tax on the same." This vote was passed under the law of August 3, 1848.

Under the first vote, and by the authority therein given, the Board of Agents hired the sum of three hundred and twenty-five dollars for the purpose of altering and repairing the primary school-houses, and gave their note for the district.

This loan of three hundred and twenty-five dollars, together with the amount raised by vote of the district, April 17, 1849, was certified to the selectmen and assessors, and at the annual assessment in 1849 the assessors made one tax for both items.

The Board of Agents for the year 1849 were William Smyth, John C. Humphreys, Allen Colby, Benjamin Furbish, and Richard Greenleaf. They put the schools in operation, basing their expenditures and calculations upon the supposition that the extra tax of three fifths, voted in April, 1849, would be paid.

Early in the spring of 1850 it was ascertained that very many of the large tax-payers had declined and absolutely refused to pay the extra school-tax. The consequence was that the district was largely indebted to school-teachers, and had no means of paying their claims so long as the extra tax was withheld. A meeting of the district was held March 7, 1850, at which the following resolution was passed: —

"Whereas certain individuals in the district have declined the payment of their taxes upon the ground that the law under which the tax is levied is unconstitutional. Therefore, Resolved that the Board of Agents be instructed by this meeting to procure such legal advice as they may deem expedient and take such measures as may in the speediest manner test the constitutionality of said law and secure the collection of the taxes."

At the annual meeting in April, 1850, the following vote was passed: —

"*Voted*, that the town collector be requested at once to collect the taxes remaining unpaid, by distraint or otherwise, and that the district will indemnify him in the same."

This vote of the district was formally certified to the collector, yet he declined doing anything towards the collection of the extra tax.

The Board of Agents for the year 1850 found themselves very unpleasantly situated. The district was largely indebted to teachers. The larger part of the extra tax was uncollected, and the collector refused to perform his duty. At a meeting of the board, May 7, 1850, the following vote was passed, all being present: —

"Whereas Stephen Snow, the collector of the town of Brunswick to whom was committed a certain tax, assessed upon the inhabitants of the Village District in said town, by the proper authorities of said town, raising money for the support of schools in said Village District, has collected and paid over a part of said tax and neglects and refuses to collect and pay over the balance of said tax, the time mentioned in his warrant of commitment having expired some time ago, therefore: Voted, that John C. Humphreys be a committee to call upon the treasurer of the town of Brunswick and inform him of the neglect and refusal of Stephen Snow, the collector, to proceed in the collection of the taxes, and request the treasurer to issue his warrant against the said Stephen Snow, collector, agreeably to the provisions of the Revised Statutes, Chapter 14, Section 111, as the contingency has occurred which makes it the duty of the treasurer to issue his warrant against the collector for neglect of duty."

Mr. Humphreys reported that he called upon the treasurer May 11, 1850, and handed him a copy of the vote, after reading which he returned an answer that he would see the collector the first of the week and see what could be done about it.

At a meeting of the Board of Agents, May 7, 1850, the following vote was passed: —

"*Voted*, that A. C. Robbins be a committee to obtain legal advice as to certain points affecting the welfare of this district, and which are now in dispute between the friends and opposers of the schools."

Under this vote Mr. Robbins made a statement of all the facts in the case and laid it before Phineas Barnes, Esquire, and Honorable William Pitt Fessenden, of Portland, and received a written opinion from them in reply. Amongst other things they say, "No particular form of *assent* is specified in the vote, and the law regards *substance* rather than form. . . . If therefore the several proceedings in voting, certifying, and assessing the taxes, and their commitment to the collector, were correct and legal (all which we have taken for granted), we have no doubt that it is the collector's duty, and still remaining so, to collect these taxes, according to his warrant. The warrant constitutes both his authority and his protection." If he neglects, they say the treasurer should be requested to issue his warrant against him; and if the treasurer neglects or refuses to do so, the proper remedy is to apply to the Supreme Judicial Court for a writ of *mandamus*.

May 23, 1850, the treasurer of the town gave to the Board of Agents a written refusal to issue his warrant against the collector, as requested by them.

On the same date, the Board of Agents gave an order to Augustus I. Owen, one of the teachers, upon the treasurer of Brunswick.

The latter indorsed upon this order the following: —

"The subscriber declines paying the within, there being no funds in his hands subject to the order of the treasurer of the Village District."

On account of this action of the treasurer, the Board of Agents gave Mr. Owen an order on the selectmen, on which the latter indorsed the following: —

"The selectmen of Brunswick decline paying or accepting the above order for the reason that the district has already received its full proportion of school money raised by the town, and that the amount raised by extra taxation in the district has not been collected and is not therefore subject to their order."

May 25, 1850, William Smyth, Robert P. Dunlap, John C. Humphreys, Augustus C. Robbins, and Leonard Townsend, the Board of Agents, petitioned the Supreme Court at the session to be held at Paris, Maine, on the last Tuesday of the month, for a writ of mandamus against the treasurer. They showed in their petition all the facts given in the preceding pages.

Upon the foregoing petition, the affidavits in support thereof, by the petitioners, having been heard and considered by the court, it was, on the May term, 1850,

"Ordered, That a rule be issued to the said John F. Titcomb, treasurer of the town of Brunswick, requiring him to show cause, if any he have, why he has neglected and refused to issue his warrant of distress against the said Stephen Snow, named in said petition, and why a writ of mandamus should not be granted by the court, commanding him to issue such warrant of distress according to law; at the term of this court to be holden at Norridgewock, within and for our county of Somerset, on the second Tuesday of June, 1850, on the third day of the term, and that the petitioners give notice thereof to the said John F. Titcomb by causing an attested copy of this petition and of this order thereon, to be served upon him fourteen days at least before the said third day of the term of the court to be holden at Norridgewock aforesaid."

At the court held in Norridgewock, the petitioners appeared by their counsel, Phineas Barnes, Esquire, and the respondents appeared by John S. Abbot, Esquire. The respondents asked for a continuance, which was opposed by the petitioners. It was finally agreed between the parties that the case should be continued to the term of the court to be held at Belfast on the fourth Tuesday of July, 1850. It was also agreed that a hearing then and there should be had, and that the respondent should furnish the petitioners with an attested copy of his answer, fourteen days before the sitting of said court.

At the court held in Belfast no witnesses were introduced by either party. The petitioners put into the case the documents already mentioned. General Samuel Fessenden, of Portland, appeared for the respondents, and Phineas Barnes, Esquire, for the petitioners.

In his answer to the petition of the Board of Agents for a writ of mandamus, the treasurer gave the following reasons for refusing to issue his warrant of distress against the collector: —

1. That the Act of Incorporation of the Village District was unconstitutional, on account of its allowing them to raise money additional to that raised by the town.

2. That the district was not legally constituted: (*a*) because the several districts had not voted to form a Village District, but only to unite for a "high-school system"; (*b*) because the old districts had never been discontinued; (*c*) because the meetings had not been legal; (*d*) because the vote of the town was illegal; (*e*) because the Act of legislature was subsequent to the action of the town, which was itself conditional on an act of the district which it had no right to delegate to them the power to do; (*f*) because the legislature has no right to create a school district by direct legislation.

3. That the assessment of the tax by the district was illegal: (*a*) because there is no constitutional authority for the legislature to create a corporation of any kind, *compelling* individuals to become members thereof, and *subject to taxation* against their will, except in the case of the formation of a town; (*b*) because the assessors had never had any official notice that the conditions of the town had been complied with, and the district legally formed; (*c*) because the money assessed by the assessors was never raised by a legal vote of the district; the vote not only authorized the purchase of land and the erecting of a school-house (which would be legal), but also authorized the enlargement and repair of the old school-houses, and the renting and furnishing of rooms for the use of schools, and the whole was embraced in one vote, contrary to the law providing the way in which "incidental expenses" should be paid; that the money was neither *borrowed* nor *expended* for purposes for which a school district is authorized by law to borrow money; (*d*) because the several certificates and copies provided by law, to be given by the officers of the school district to the assessors, treasurer, and clerk, of the town, were not duly certified, filed, and recorded, as required by law; that no certificate of the vote of the district, authorizing the borrowing of money, was ever certified by the clerk thereof to the above officers; (*e*) that if the legislature has power to authorize school districts to raise money, such power cannot be given to a single district, but should be granted by a general law operating throughout the State; (*f*) that a school district is not such an organized body, nor has such interest as to enforce the collection, by a *town* collector, of a tax by mandamus, — the treasurer being the officer of the town and not of any school district.

Allen Colby, William H. Hall, and Benjamin H. Meder, in behalf of the petitioners, made depositions, July 18, 1850, to the following effect: —

1. That they resided in the district.

2. That they had never known any persons claiming a separate organization as *District Number* 1 subsequent to the formation of the *Village District.*

3. That they had never known of any public school kept in *District Number* 1, except what was under the authority of the Board of Agents of the *Village District.*

4. That the vote passed at the annual meeting of *District Number* 1, April 24, 1848, *did contemplate* the throwing up of the old organization and the formation of a new district.

6. That they never heard the plan of a high school spoken of at that or any other meeting of the district, except in connection with the formation of a Village District.

8. That they would have known if there had been any schools kept out of the public funds in that territory, other than those kept under the authority of the agents of the *Vil age District.*

9. That after the organization of the *Village District*, the people in what was formerly *District Number* 1 sent their children to the schools of the Village District.

The committee on accounts, in their report for 1850, under the "Treasurer's Account," give the amount received from the agents of the *Village District*, thus recognizing its existence.

The school committee, in 1850, recognized the district in their report and spoke of the manifest improvement of the schools therein.

Judge Howard, in ordering the issue of a writ of mandamus, made an exhaustive review of all the questions raised upon either side and fully sustained the Board of Agents in every material point, though he pointed out some errors made by them. Thus ended one of the most important lawsuits to which the village of Brunswick has ever been a party, and both sides in the suit deserve credit for persisting in bringing to a legal settlement questions of such momentous importance to the welfare of the town and to the interest of education in general.[1]

This opinion was delivered by the judge, March 1, 1851, and was received in Brunswick the same day. A meeting of the Village District was called on the nineteenth of the month. At this meeting Professor William Smyth made a report in behalf of the Building Committee. In this report a recapitulation was given of the *needs* of

---

[1] *For the full account of this trial, see Smith* v. *Titcomb*, 31 *Me.* 272.

the district in regard to school-houses, and of the *votes*. He reported that the Building Committee and Board of Agents had selected the lot of Miss Narcissa Stone, on the corner of Federal and Green Streets, and that he had been empowered by a vote of each committee separately to purchase the lot. This he had done at a price of $1,000, payment to be made in five equal annual instalments, with interest at six per cent. Possession was obtained June 1, 1851.

The committee had then turned their attention to the erection of a building upon this lot, but in the mean time it had been found that a portion of the tax-payers had positively refused to pay the taxes still due from them. The Building Committee had no alternative but to stay proceedings, and await the decision of the Supreme Court. After that decision had been given they at once resumed their labors and contracted at once for the brick and stone necessary for the erection of the building, and they were being at that time deposited upon the lot.

The report stated that the Board of Agents had been very much embarrassed by the want of suitable accommodations for the schools. They had been obliged to break up classes, separate the boys from the girls, and virtually to return to the confusion and inefficiency of the old system.

On April 19, 1851, William Smyth, chairman of the Board of Agents, made a report of which the following is a synopsis: —

He stated that the committee had been greatly embarrassed by want of accommodations and by the lawsuit. He remarked, those opposed "regarded themselves as maintaining an important constitutional principle and their own just rights." But the question had now been settled, and all acquiesced in it. The committee recommended that the thanks of the district should be given to their counsel, Phineas Barnes, Esquire, and especially to their colleague, A. C. Robbins, Esquire, "for the untiring effort and distinguished ability with which their case was prepared by him for argument, — services gratuitously rendered indeed, but upon which the success of the district in the late suit, so far, at least, as its legal existence is concerned, is mainly to be attributed." The report goes on to state that after the termination of the suit, the town collector had collected enough to pay off all the debts of the district, except the fees of the counsel and the expenses connected with the suit.

The report spoke favorably of the schools as a whole, but considered the primary schools as of the chief importance. It recommended the permanent establishment of an apprentices' school, and stated that the material did not at that time exist for the perfect organization of the

High School. Several suggestions were also made as to the best mode of raising the necessary money for school purposes.

The superintending school committee, in their report for April, 1851, say, "as their deliberate judgment, that at no period has there been so much to commend in the management and success of the village schools or so little to censure.

"In the general interests of education in the village, they think that a manifest advance has been made during the year." They were also of the opinion that the condition of the schools throughout the town would bear a favorable comparison with that of any former year.

The new brick school-house erected for the use of the schools of the Village District was dedicated on Tuesday, December 9, 1851. The services were opened by some remarks from Professor William Smyth. Then followed a somewhat detailed account of the schools for several years previously, by Professor D. R. Goodwin, which was followed by remarks by John S. C. Abbot. After a prayer by Reverend Doctor Adams, remarks were made by Messrs. Adams, Boody, and Smyth, a hymn was sung, and the benediction pronounced by Father Stetson. There was quite an audience present, and the occasion passed off very pleasantly.

In April, 1852, the superintending school committee reported that there were nine hundred school children in the village. They said that "the Village District has been greatly indebted to Mr. E. G. Parshley, who taught a separate school of older pupils of the primary schools, and who were not entitled to enter the grammar schools. About eighty attended this school, who were well taught and kept in admirable discipline. The only compensation Mr. Parshley had for this service was the thanks of the community."

Speaking of these village schools, Mr. John M. Adams, school commissioner for Cumberland County, in his report, published in the spring of 1853, says: —

"This system of graded schools comes as near perfection as any I have ever seen, not excepting even that of Portland, which under the fostering care of a few efficient and devoted friends, chief amongst whom stands Mr. Barnes, has acquired a high and well-merited reputation."

The cost of the brick school-house, as given in the financial report of the Board of Agents in 1853, was $5,885.44. The cost of the lot, which was $1,000, is not included. A portion ($5,000) of this amount was raised by loan, the balance by a direct tax.

In 1852 there were, including the Village District, twenty-six school districts in town. The whole amount received from all sources for the schools this year was $3,329.04.

On November 12, 1857, the High School pupils commenced a series of tableaux at their school-room, for the purpose of procuring funds for the purchase of apparatus. They met with good success.

In 1862 the apprentice school, which had been in operation in the winter season since 1851, was kept in the engine-hall on Pleasant Street.

In 1867 the brick school-house on Bath Street was built. The amount of money for schools received from all sources was $6,782.27.

In September, 1872, the school-house on the corner of Federal and Centre Streets was completed. It contains four rooms, with large halls in both stories.

The condition of the schools in 1876 was as follows: the whole number of schools in town was twenty-three; the number of teachers employed was thirty-one; the total amount of school money received from all sources was $10,403.08.

It has been found impossible to obtain a list of the number of pupils in Brunswick for each decade since the organization of the first town school, but the number at the different dates mentioned below will give some idea of the rate of increase.

In 1804 the number of pupils was 845; in 1805 it was 875; in 1806 it was 885; in 1825 it was 1,533; in 1826 it was 1,598; in 1829 it was 1,603; and in 1876 it was 1,782. The actual attendance this last year was, however, only 864.

ACADEMICAL INSTITUTIONS.

An account of Bowdoin College and the Medical School of Maine might with propriety be given in this connection, but on account of the length of the sketch, as well as for the reason that they are State and not town institutions, a separate chapter will be devoted to them.

The first academical institution which should be mentioned here was the BRUNSWICK ACADEMY.

This was a Gothic structure, which stood on Maine Street directly opposite the southwest corner of the college grounds. It was built by President Allen for a classical school. Mr. William Smyth (afterwards professor) taught it the first quarter, which *ended* on the eleventh of December, 1824. The second quarter began a week later, and was taught by William Hatch. The building was only used a few terms for a school and was then occupied by college students. Afterwards it was used as a dwelling by Mr. Charles J. Noyes, and still later it was torn down and rebuilt, and is now occupied as a dwelling.

THE BRUNSWICK ACADEMY.

PLEASANT STREET SEMINARY. — This seminary building was erected in the fall of 1842 or winter of 1843, on the south side of Pleasant Street, a few rods from Maine Street. It was dedicated on the twenty-seventh of March, 1843. An address was delivered by Professor A. S. Packard, and there was singing by a choir under the direction of Mr. Charles J. Noyes. The building was two stories, the upper story being leased for a club-room. The lower floor was the school-room. The first term began on the twentieth of March, 1843, under the instruction of M. B. Bartlett (Bowdoin, class of 1842). Mr. Bartlett is said to have been an excellent teacher, and the school was a good one. Mr. Bartlett conducted the school for about three years, and was succeeded by Mr. Alfred W. Pike, a graduate of Dartmouth College, who was already an experienced teacher. This building was afterwards, in 1843, used by the Episcopalian society as a chapel. It was subsequently removed to Maine Street, and is now occupied as a store by Mr. J. P. Weeman, a few doors north of the post-office.

THE BRUNSWICK SEMINARY was incorporated in 1845, with the design "of establishing an institution, in which the youth of both sexes might receive a *thorough* and *practical* knowledge of those branches of education which pertain especially to the *every-day* business of life; and, also, all those higher branches of a finished education, which are taught in boarding-schools and the higher seminaries."

In accordance with this design, a commodious building[1] was obtained, with apartments so arranged that the ladies and gentlemen, while they occupied different rooms, had all the advantages of being classed together, of meeting at recitations, lectures, and other general exercises of the school.

The trustees of the school were Honorable Robert P. Dunlap, president; John S. Cushing, Esquire, secretary; Parker Cleaveland, LL. D., treasurer; Leonard Woods, Jr., D. D., General Abner B. Thompson, Reverend George E. Adams, General John C. Humphreys.

The instructors in 1845–6 were G. Clinton Swallow, M. A., principal; Miss Tryphena B. Hinkley, preceptress; Miss Frances E. Stowe, teacher of music on the piano, etc.; Miss Olivia J. Record, teacher of drawing and painting; Albion K. Knight, M. A., teacher of vocal music; Miss Evelina Owen, assistant; Miss Mary B. Hill, Miss Ellen S. Shaw, Mr. John W. Watson, Mr. John S. Fuller, monitors.

During the first year there were one hundred and sixty-nine students, of whom eighty-one were young gentlemen and eighty-eight young ladies.

OTHER PRIVATE SCHOOLS.

In addition to the seminaries already mentioned there have been many other schools taught in town by private persons, some of which might, perhaps, from their size and the successful manner in which they have been conducted, be justly placed in the foregoing class. They have not been, for the reason that they did not assume any higher name than that simply of a private school.

All of these schools, concerning which we have been able to gain any exact information, will be mentioned under the name of their respective teachers.

MISS EUNICE BUSS came to Brunswick in 1802 as the friend and companion of Miss Lucy Abbott, daughter of Honorable Jacob Abbott. After Miss Abbott's marriage in 1805, Miss Buss taught a small school for young children. After Mr. Abbott's death in 1820, the family prepared a small house for her in a corner of the garden-lot, about where

---

[1] *This building was on the corner of Maine and School Streets, and is now the residence of Capt. Isaac L. Skolfield.*

Captain John Bishop's house now stands. Here she taught school for a number of years. She afterwards maintained herself as a seamstress. She was highly esteemed, and was the presiding officer in many of the charitable associations of the ladies. In 1835 her health became impaired, and she returned to her former home in Wilton, New Hampshire.

MRS. CAROLINE P. PUTNAM, wife of Henry Putnam, Esquire, and mother of George P. Putnam, the New York publisher (recently deceased), taught school in Brunswick for about eighteen years. From 1807[1] until about 1818 or 1819, she taught in what was then known as the old Dunlap house, now the residence of the family of the late Doctor John D. Lincoln. Miss Narcissa Stone was her assistant during a portion of that time.

MRS. PUTNAM next taught for a year or two in the Forsaith house, next south of Dr. Lincoln's,[2] occupying the southeast room for her school-room, and from there she moved into the old Stone Mansion, which was situated near the northerly corner of Maine and Mill Streets, but which stood a little back from both streets. She occupied one half of this house and Dean Swift the other half. In this house she taught until 1825, when it was destroyed by fire. Mrs. Putnam then moved to New York, where she ever after resided. She is spoken of by those who knew her as an excellent woman and a good teacher.

JOHN M. O'BRIEN, a member of the first class of Bowdoin College, kept a private school for two or three years. The exact date is not known with certainty, but the school was probably kept between the years 1806 and 1810.

MISS ELIZA CHAPMAN, a Boston lady, sister to Mrs. Governor Dunlap, kept a private school for young ladies from 1823 until 1829, in the conference room on Centre Street. She was a lady of fine education and was a very successful teacher.

MR. SMITH taught a private school in Hodgkins Hall, on the corner of Maine and Pleasant Streets, in 1824. This teacher is said to have been Mr. William Smyth, afterwards a professor in Bowdoin College.

ABRAHAM PREBLE kept a private school under Masonic Hall, in the winter of 1825, and announced another term to be kept in another place which would better accommodate his patrons. He kept school for several terms, but exactly how long is not known.

LOT JONES opened a school over the bank in September, 1828, where he taught the various branches usually taught in academies, and

---

[1] *Reminiscences of Mrs. Lamb.*

[2] *Reminiscences of Dean Swift.*

prepared students for college. He taught here for about one year and was a very successful teacher. He afterwards became an Episcopalian clergyman.

ASA DODGE, of the class of 1827, Bowdoin College, and afterwards a missionary physician in Syria, taught a school for young gentlemen and ladies, in 1829, and for two or three years after, in the conference room on Centre Street. His school was one of the best that was ever kept in Brunswick. He was a fine scholar and instructor, and is highly spoken of as a man by those who knew him. He died in Beirout, Syria.

DARIUS ADAMS taught a school in Washington Hall about the year 1830. He was succeeded by

SAMUEL ADAMS, who taught in the same place for a few terms.

HARRIET LEE kept a private school for misses in 1830, in the Rodney Forsaith house, on Maine Street.

The MISSES R. and S. OWEN kept a female boarding and day school in 1830, and for two or three years after, in the Owen house, which was situated on the corner of Maine and O'Brien Streets, on the lot now occupied by the residence of Mr. Benjamin Greene.

RICHARD WOODHULL, of the class of 1827, of Bowdoin College, taught a school for one or two terms about 1830, in the conference room on Centre Street. He succeeded Mr. Asa Dodge.

MR. THOMAS BAKER (Bowdoin, class of 1831) taught a school for young gentlemen in Washington Hall, from 1833 until 1838 or 1839. From here he went to Cape Ann, and from thence to Boston as a head master. He became quite celebrated as a teacher.

MISSES DEBORAH FOLSOM and MARY DUNNING kept a family school for girls for about three years, on Union Street, nearly opposite O'Brien Street. This was about the years 1836 to 1838 inclusive. They were both successful teachers.

MISS TRYPHENA B. HINKLEY came to Topsham in 1842 as an assistant in Mrs. Field's school. Two years later Mrs. Field resigned the school, and Miss Hinkley conducted it on her own account for about a year, when, at the solicitation of friends in Brunswick, she united her school with that of Professor Swallow, under the name of the Brunswick Seminary. At the end of about a year Miss Hinkley withdrew from this school and taught a day-school in the Pleasant Street Seminary. Here she taught for about a year. She then leased the house on the corner of Pleasant and Union Streets, recently owned and occupied by Mr. Samuel R. Jackson. She taught in this building for about five years, keeping a boarding-school for young ladies. From here she moved into the O'Brien house, which stood on Union Street, nearly opposite O'Brien Street. In this house she taught for about seven years. Here her school was large and prosperous. From the O'Brien house she moved into her present residence opposite the colleges, which she purchased of John S. C. Abbott, and to which she made additions and improvements.

In all of her schools Miss Hinkley has been assisted by her sister, Miss Josephine Hinkley, whose special department has been that of drawing. Among the other lady assistants she has had, at different times, Miss Fannie White, a teacher of music; Madam Zimmerman, a German lady and a fine music teacher; Miss Frances Adams (now Mrs. General Chamberlain), Miss Lizzie McKeen, Miss Fannie Stowe, Miss Sarah Newman, Miss Emily Poole, and Miss Sophia W. Wheeler.

For gentleman assistants Miss Hinkley has depended largely upon the college. Among those who have assisted her at different times have been C. C. Everett, William Packard, Egbert C. Smyth, William S. Tucker, Joshua Leighton, Henry Farrar, her brother Eugene B. Hinkley, and Professors Brackett, Russell, Taverner, and Briggs. The average number of boarding scholars has been about fifteen, the largest number about twenty-seven.

Alfred W. Pike advertised the eighth term of the "Brunswick High School" to begin April 10, 1843. It was kept in Washington Hall. In 1845 he advertised the "Brunswick High School and Teacher's Seminary." Vocal music to be taught by Jotham Sewall; mathematics and French, by Samuel J. Pike; drawing and painting, by Miss Frances Adams. In 1846, and for about three years after, he kept a school in the Pleasant Street Seminary, then in a building which stood on the spot cut through for the railroad on the east side of Maine Street, and lastly, in his own house, which was then a cottage on Potter Street, but which was afterwards removed to Maine Street, enlarged and improved, and is now the residence of General Chamberlain.

D. Kendrick, Junior, taught a private school for ladies in 1845, and for about a year, in Dunlap Block.

In addition to the foregoing private schools for general instruction, there have been from time to time others taught for instruction in special branches.

SPECIAL SCHOOLS.

The schools of this character will be given under the head of the branches taught in them.

DANCING ACADEMY. — In January, 1821, L. Champrosay began a school at Stoddard's Hall. The terms were six dollars for twelve lessons. He also advertised to give private lessons in French.

SCHOOL FOR EMBROIDERY. — In 1823 a school was established by a lady from Scotland, for working in embroidery.[1]

SCHOOL FOR INSTRUCTION IN FRENCH. — In 1836, J. G. Mivelle Dechene taught French at Mrs. Pollard's house.

SCHOOL FOR MUSICAL INSTRUCTION. — INSTRUMENTAL. — In 1826 a Miss Brown of Boston, gave instruction on the piano and harp.

SCHOOL FOR INSTRUCTION IN NAVIGATION. — In 1825 a school for instruction in the art of navigation was kept by B. F. Neally, and another one in 1843 by John F. Hall.

SCHOOL FOR INSTRUCTION IN FANCY PAINTING. — In 1827, A. B. Engstrom taught the art of fancy painting on paper, satin, or wood.

SINGING-SCHOOLS. — In 1825, Luke Hastings taught a school for instruction in vocal music. In 1836, Charles J. Noyes kept a similar school; and so did also L. W. Additon, in 1843. Since then schools of this character have been too numerous for specific mention to be made of them.

WRITING-SCHOOLS. — In 1824, I. Morgridge kept a school for instruction in penmanship, in Stone's Hall. He was succeeded the next winter by William Sawyer. In 1836 a Mr. Butler kept a school of this kind; in 1843, Mr. I. O. Richardson; and in 1845 a Mr. Fisk kept one in Dunlap Block. Further mention of such schools is unnecessary.

The above by no means completes the list of miscellaneous schools, but they are all which have come to our knowledge that are worthy of especial mention.

---

[1] *Putnam.*

CHAPTER XVI.

EDUCATIONAL HISTORY OF TOPSHAM.

THE earliest information to be obtained in regard to educational matters in Topsham is that contained in the town records. It appears from these that on March 18, 1766, the town voted to raise £60 for a "minister and school-master" for that year, and Thomas Wilson was chosen a committee to agree with him or them. At the annual meeting in 1768, John Reed and John Fulton were chosen a committee to obtain a minister and school-master for that year. At a meeting of the Pejepscot proprietors, held July 23 of this year, it was voted:—

"That Lott Number sixtyfive adjoyning to the aforesaid Lott granted to ye first settled Minister lying on the Rear of the Lotts conveyed to Benjam'in Thomas and bounding Northwest on Land belonging to Heirs of William Wilson as described and laid down in the Plan, be and hereby is granted to the Town of Topsham, for a Lott for the Benefitt and advantage of a Publick School, to continue for said use forever — said Lott contains one hundred Acres."[1]

On July 14, 1770, the town voted that the school-master should be hired for one year from the date of his first commencing school.

At the annual meeting in 1773, the selectmen were instructed to divide the town into several school districts and to proportion the taxes according to the number of children in each district. The amount raised this year for schools was £26 13*s*. 4*d*.

From 1786 to 1792 the employment of a teacher was left with the selectmen.

At the annual meeting of the town in 1795, the selectmen were instructed to take measures to secure the lot of land called the "School lot," "which was said to belong to the town." The article in the warrant to provide for the employment of a school-master was this year passed over.

At a town meeting held May 6, 1799, the selectmen were instructed

---

[1] *Pejepscot Records.*

to divide the town into such school districts as they should deem advisable. Three hundred dollars was appropriated for the support of schools this year.

The selectmen neglecting for some reason to divide the town into school districts, Reverend Jonathan Ellis, Alexander Thompson, Senior, James Wilson, Arthur Hunter, William Wilson, and Samuel Winchell were chosen a committee for this purpose in 1800. The town also voted to have six school districts and to build a school-house in each district within thirteen months, and $1,200 was appropriated for that purpose, upon the condition that each district should give the land needed for its school-house.

In 1801 the preceding action of the town was so far modified as to make seven instead of six districts. It was also voted this year that the school committee should consist of one person in each district.

In 1802, Benjamin Hasey, John Merrill, and Benjamin J. Porter were chosen a committee to petition the legislature for permission to sell the school lot and to place the proceeds of the sale as an accumulating fund until it should net an income of three hundred dollars per annum, or in any other way which the General Court might think proper.

In 1803 three of the school districts, Numbers 4, 5, and 6, were consolidated into one.

On March 6, 1804, the General Court authorized the sale of the school lot and the investment of the money accruing therefrom.[1]

Nothing of importance in relation to educational matters appears in the town records subsequently to this time, until the year 1825. In their report for that year, the school committee express doubts "whether knitting and sewing ought to be permitted in town schools," and express the hope "that parents in future will be convinced of the impropriety of imposing this service on the instructress."

In 1828 the town voted that the selectmen should make a sale of the school lot, in accordance with a former vote passed for that purpose.

In 1830 the trustees of the school fund reported that the school lot was sold on the twelfth day of December, 1829, to Captain Samuel Perkins, for three hundred and fifty dollars.

In 1833 the school fund arising from the sale of the school lot amounted to four hundred and twenty dollars and thirty-four cents.

In 1837 the town voted that the surplus revenue money, that was or was to be deposited with the town by the State, should be kept as a

---

[1] *Massachusetts Acts,* 1804.

fund, and that the town treasurer should be permitted to loan the money on interest, under the direction of the selectmen, who should see that good security was taken, and that the *interest* should be divided amongst the school districts. The next year, however, though a strong protest was made against it, this vote was reconsidered and the money was divided among the inhabitants.

Between 1851 and 1870 the superintending school committee kept a record of their doings. From this record it appears that the following persons were chosen for school committee in 1851: Reverend Jonathan Clement, James Gilpatrick, and A. D. Wheeler. At their first meeting they drew lots, as provided by law, to determine the time for which they were respectively to serve on the committee. Reverend Mr. Wheeler was selected to serve one year, Mr. Clement for two, and Mr. Gilpatrick for three years. There were at this time nine school districts in town, which were designated as follows: —

Number 1 was called the Jameson district.
" 3 " " " Oak Hill district.
" 4 " " " Middlesex district.
" 5 " " " Mallett district.
" 6 " " " Cathance district.
" 8 " " " Jack district.
" 9 " " " Bay Road district.
" 11 " " " Alexander district.
" 12 " " " Little River district.

Numbers 2, 7, and 10 were united into one district, which was called the Village District. Districts Number 1, 8, and 12 were up the river, Numbers 4, 6, and 9 were down the river, and Numbers 3, 5, and 11 were back from the river. The total amount of school money received this year, from all sources, was nine hundred and ninety dollars and thirty-two cents. The whole number of children in town, between the ages of four and twenty-one years, was six hundred and sixty.

In 1852 the total amount of school money was six dollars and thirteen cents more than the previous year. The school fund this year was six hundred and sixty-four dollars and fifty cents.

Nothing has been found to show the exact time when the grading system was applied to the village schools, but on November 18, 1854, the following entry occurs in the records of the committee: " Messrs. Adams and Cotton met in the selectmen's office and examined Mr. Gaslin for the Village High School. He was found well qualified." It would seem from this, since no previous reference to it has been found, that the High School must have been established this year.

On July 22, 1848, the school committee agreed upon the following as the requirements for admission to the High School, namely, that pupils should have gone in arithmetic as far as simple interest, in geography though Colton's book, and in grammar through etymology. For admission to the grammar schools, pupils were required to know the multiplication table and the simple rules of arithmetic and to have finished the primary geography.

In 1859 the town voted that "the trustees of the ministerial fund, derived from the sale of the ministerial land granted the town for the support of the ministry, transfer said fund, together with accrued interest, to the municipal officers, clerk, and treasurer of the town, as a fund for the support of the public schools, agreeably to the twelfth chapter of the Revised Statutes of Maine." This fund was not available, however, having been loaned to individuals, one of whom was dead, and the notes of all of whom had become outlawed.

In 1861 the town elected Mr. Warren Johnson as supervisor of schools. The following resolution was found in the town records on a slip of paper inserted between the leaves, and was apparently overlooked by the clerk in copying his minutes, as it does not appear on the records: —

"Whereas, in the judgment of the town, it is desirable that the management of schools be placed in the hands of one supervisor, and whereas the ill health of the Rev. Dr. Wheeler (the only member of the former board of school committee) would prevent him from discharging the laborious duties of a supervisor, and the election of another necessitates his retirement after a service of nearly thirty years.

"*Resolved*, That we sensibly recognize his long and effectual services as an able and earnest educator, to whom much is due for the former success of our school system."

In 1862 the trustees of the school fund reported at the annual meeting that this fund was invested in good notes to the amount of six hundred and sixty-four dollars and forty-eight cents, and that the interest, amounting to thirty-three dollars and eighty-seven cents, had been paid, and had been divided among the several school districts.

In 1863 the town returned to the practice of selecting a school committee instead of a supervisor. In December of this year the committee made the following changes in school-books: They voted to use the Progressive Series of Readers, in place of Town's Readers; Weld and Quackenbos, in the place of Bailey's grammar; and Greeneaf's new arithmetics, in place of his old ones.

In 1869 the Wilson Series of Readers was adopted for five years.

SCHOOL-TEACHERS.

The names of the school-teachers prior to 1800 are unknown. The earliest teacher in town of whom any record is found was Reverend Jonathan Ellis. Mr. Ellis taught school during a large portion of his residence in Topsham, between 1789 and 1811. At first he taught in a school-house at the eastern end of the town, near the old first meeting-house; afterwards in the school-house, which stood on the lot now owned by Captain William S. Skolfield, on the corner of Pleasant and Elm Streets. It was a small building directly opposite where the Orthodox Church now stands. Afterwards he kept a school for three or four years in the Court House. He was teaching there at the time of the great eclipse of the sun in 1806.

Mr. James Wilson distinctly remembers that the school closed at the time, and that the scholars came to his father's house to smoke pieces of glass in order to watch the eclipse. In his diary Mr. Ellis mentions the fact that he completed his school in District Number 4 on August 25, and in District Number 6 on October 7, 1800. On the first date there was a public exhibition by the school. Mr. Ellis was an excellent teacher.

In 1802, Mr. John Hern taught in a small school-house, which stood near the Benjamin Wilson house.

About 1825, Mr. Josiah Perham came to Topsham and taught the village school. He occupied the next room to the post-office, which then stood opposite the bank, where he cooked his own food, and lived by himself. He is said to have been a good teacher and a worthy, persevering young man. In later years he made himself famous by inaugurating a series of cheap excursions, known as "Perham's Excursions," and still later was proprietor of "Perham's Seven-Mile Mirror," a panorama which was exhibited in many of the principal cities and towns throughout the country. He is said to have been the first man to sign a petition for a charter for the Pacific Railroad.

Of other teachers prior to this date, sufficient is not known to enable us to make mention of them, and the subsequent teachers of the public schools of the town have been too numerous.

ACADEMICAL INSTITUTIONS.

The Topsham Academy was started in the year 1847 or 1848 by a few prominent citizens of the town. They purchased the old Court House and converted it into an excellent school-house, with recitation-rooms, library, etc. The teachers the first year were Messrs. Dexter A. Hawkins, class of 1848, and Charles H. Wheeler, class of 1847, Bowdoin College. They were succeeded by Messrs. Albert H. Ware and George O. Robinson, both of the class of 1849, of the same college. The latter was succeeded by Mr. Francis Adams, of the class of 1850. Mr. John Clement taught the school after Adams left. The school was given up about 1858, the last teacher being Mr. Joshua Laighton, of the class of 1857, Bowdoin.

The tuition at this academy was. for instruction in the lower department, four dollars; in the higher department, five dollars. There was a quite good library connected with this institution, and a literary society the name of which is not now remembered.

In 1856, Mr. Warren Johnson, of the class of 1854, Bowdoin College, purchased the residence of Major William Frost, deceased; enlarged it somewhat, and on May 20, 1857, opened it for a boarding-school, under the name of the FRANKLIN FAMILY SCHOOL. While under his management, as well as since, the school proved to be a very excellent one. It was afterwards kept by his brother, Samuel J. Johnson, then by H. A. Randall, then by R. O. Lindsey, and the latter was succeeded by a Mr. Billings. It is now under the management of Mr. D. L. Smith, an experienced and successful teacher.[1]

In 1865 an earnest but unsuccessful effort was made to secure the location of the State Agricultural College in Topsham. Mr. Daniel T. Coffin, of New York, formerly a resident of this town, sent a donation of two hundred and fifty dollars to aid in securing its location there. An account of the efforts made by the citizens is given in another chapter.

PRIVATE SCHOOLS.

Some time in the last century Mr. Samuel Thompson offered to keep a private school, if he could obtain twenty-five scholars, at a price ranging from sixteen to twenty-five cents a week. Whether or not he succeeded in getting up this school is not known, but it is certain that he taught a village school for a long time. He was subject to fits of derangement, and at times the town authorities had to confine him in a "cage." This was a one-story and one-room structure at the Topsham end of the toll-bridge, somewhere on the site of the present paper-mill. He was attended to here by Denem Winslow, the toll-gatherer.

---

[1] *Mr. Warren Johnson had begun to prepare for these pages an account of the school, but his sickness and death prevented its completion, and we are consequently unable to give a fuller sketch.*

Moses M. Marsh, a well-known school-master of Brunswick, once taught a school in Topsham. It may have been a public and not a private school. Enoch H. Hines also taught here prior to his death in 1828. He taught district schools, but may possibly have taught a private school also.

On May 8, 1826, the Topsham Female School was opened in Greene's Hall. It was taught by a lady.

On March 9, 1829, a Miss Eastman commenced a school for young ladies. The studies taught were reading, writing, grammar, geography, ancient and modern history, arithmetic, philosophy, geometry, French, and painting, according to the method of Engstrom.

Tuition was three to six dollars a term. How long a time this school was kept up is not known.

Mrs. Fields's School. — Mrs. Elizabeth Fields was the widow of Robert Fields, Esquire, barrister in England, a lawyer of no mean ability, who was induced to come to America, and resided for many years in Boston, in the practice of his profession. He died in 1812. In 1830, Mrs. Fields, while on a visit to General King's family of Bath, in an afternoon's drive, chanced to pass the Doctor Porter house,[1] in Topsham, which General King pointed out to her as "his property, once the residence of his sister, and now likely to remain unoccupied for years." At once the idea suggested itself to Mrs. Fields of taking possession of it as a boarding-school for young ladies, and after making the necessary arrangements with General King regarding repairs and rent, she immediately proceeded to place it in order for occupancy, and in 1831 opened her school with twelve boarding and as many day scholars. General King sent his only daughter, and used his influence, which was by no means small, in inducing many of his friends in Augusta and elsewhere to send their daughters. Miss Caroline Weld was the first assistant teacher. Subsequently Mrs. Fields secured the assistance of Miss Mary Thacher, daughter of Peter Thacher, Esquire, of Lubec, a young lady of unusually fine mind and intellectual acquirements, and a Mr. Purinton, who was previously in one of the principal Bath schools. Later, in 1838, when Miss Thacher left the school to be married, her place was filled by Miss Hester A. C. Hinkley, from Hallowell, equally competent, and who, in her turn, having left in 1842 to be married, was succeeded by an accomplished sister, Miss Tryphena Hinkley, who continued in that capacity until Mrs. Fields gave up the school in 1844, when Miss Hinkley took it,

---

[1] *Now the residence of Mrs. Susan T. Purinton.*

THE FRANKLIN FAMILY SCHOOL.

and continued it on her own account for some time.[1] After Mr. Purinton left, his place was always filled by competent male teachers, among whom were Doctors Williams, Parlin, and Hall, then students at the Medical School, and after them a Mr. Curtis, of Topsham. The average number of boarders was sixteen, and of day scholars about twelve. Mrs. Beers, the widowed daughter of Mrs. Fields, was music teacher all the time. This school was considered to be of a superior character, and Mrs. Fields was held in the highest esteem by the entire community.[2]

To this account we are enabled to add the following interesting reminiscence of a former pupil: —

"For four years I was a pupil of hers, with occasional vacations. As it was the first school I ever attended, I could not at the time compare it with others, but the more I know of other boarding-schools, the more clearly I see that she was unique, and in many respects superior. There were no written regulations. In fine weather we were encouraged to study out of doors. The grounds were ample, well provided with arbors, shade-trees, swings, and 'teeter-boards.' There was an old corn-house in view from the school-room windows, which sometimes was a summer resort for a difficult French lesson. Five or six of the Télémaque class, each with her book and one dictionary, would often have a fine social time while getting out the translation.

"Plenty of exercise, in the open air when the weather would allow, and in-doors in stormy weather, was enforced upon us. Whenever the evenings were cool enough to require a fire, a good dance, of at least an hour, was required before going to bed. The school-room was large, with an immense fireplace opposite the windows, and in one corner, farthest from the fireplace, stood a large box-stove. When the weather was very cold, both stove and fireplace were used.

"Mrs. Fields's seat was at the left hand of this fireplace by a large desk, and she used to play the guitar herself, and call off for the school-room dancing.

"The food was plain, wholesome, and abundant. She always presided at the table and fared exactly like her scholars.

"In the mornings we all met in the school-room, at half past six in summer and about eight in the shortest days of winter. Prayers were read, then came breakfast, and at eight in summer and nine in winter school began.

---

[1] *See "Miss Hinkley's School."*

[2] *The material for the foregoing is furnished by Mrs. Mary Beers McLellan, granddaughter of Mrs. Fields.*

"English studies came first, arithmetic, grammar, and spelling. No one was excused from spelling. Mrs. Fields would say, 'My dear, if you *can* spell, it takes but little of your time; if you *cannot*, you ought to learn.' One of her commonest criticisms upon a composition would be, 'Very well, my dear! Now take it and rewrite it, and see in how much less space you can get every idea' She used to say that diffuseness and obscurity were the great faults of modern literature. Writing from dictation was with her a favorite method of drill in spelling and punctuation.

"Some young lady was always assistant teacher for the beginners; but when the assistant least expected it, Mrs. Fields herself would step in and hear the recitations, sending the assistant to hear her own particular classes meanwhile.

"At about eleven A. M., Mrs. Beers, her daughter, who was a music teacher, came in and attended to penmanship, setting the copies herself. At noon we had an intermission of two hours in summer and one in winter, with dinner about one o'clock. We had the range of the extensive grounds, provided only that we did not go out of bounds without permission and were prompt in minding the bell.

"After dinner was playtime until two o'clock. Then came sewing of various kinds, embroidery and fancy, in all its branches; also lace mending and fine darning, plain and fancy knitting. When we were all fixed at our work, some one was called on to read aloud, not more than fifteen or twenty minutes at a time. At five, school was out. After supper we usually had an hour for study, and then the tables were cleared for a dance or some other frolic until bedtime.

"The standard of honor was very high with Mrs. Fields, and yet I can recall no instance of punishment for dishonorable conduct, except her withering sarcasm and a feeling that the offender was not trusted. There was no standard of rank and no public examination, though visitors were always welcome. There was one custom conducive to social training. The house was open for a weekly reception most of the time. Thursdays Mrs. Fields and her pupils were always 'at home' to all personal friends of herself and pupils. The latter were taught to behave as the daughters of the house in entertaining guests. I do not remember which was treated as the greatest fault, — a prudish avoidance of a gentleman guest, or an appearance of coquetry and flirtation. Music, dancing, and conversation were the amusements of these reunions."

For several years subsequent to 1840, private schools were kept in town by Miss Mary B. H. Wheeler, who had an excellent reputation as an instructress of young children. There are many middle-aged persons in town who received their earliest tuition from her, and many who remember her pleasant ways with children.

About the year 1840, MISS THEODOSIA WILSON commenced a private school. She taught schools, both public and private, in Topsham, for about thirty-four years. She was well known in the community as a successful and experienced teacher as well as an accomplished and estimable lady.

In the fall of 1842. Messrs. J. L. Nutting and J. F. Woodside both advertised that they would teach a private high school in Topsham. It is presumed that one, if not both, did keep such a school that year.

SPECIAL SCHOOLS.

Schools for special instruction, especially in writing and in singing, have been of quite frequent occurrence in Topsham. Sufficient material has not, however, been obtained to enable one to give any extended account of them. The earliest writing-school of which any account has been found was taught in the summer of 1824, at the school-house, near the Court House, by Mr. J. Morgridge. The earliest singing-schools known were those taught by Andrew Dennison, previous to 1820, and in 1844 by L. W. Additon.

CHAPTER XVII.

EDUCATIONAL HISTORY OF HARPSWELL.

THE earliest reference that has been found to any provision for a school in Harpswell is the appropriation of £20 for that purpose by the town on May 9, 1759. Where a school was kept this year and by whom is nowhere stated.

In May, 1760, the town voted that each part of the Neck, and also the Island, should draw their proportionate part of the school money that was collected and should hire mistresses.[1]

At the annual meeting in 1761, the town appropriated £20 for the support of a school and instructed the selectmen to provide one.

In 1762 the town voted to raise £20, as usual, for a school.

At the May meeting in 1763, the town voted not to build a school-house near the meeting-house. The town also voted to pay James Booker £1 and 13*s*. for going to Falmouth, "the Place being Presented for want of a school." By reference to the records of the Court of General Sessions for Cumberland County, October term, 1762, it appears that though the town had been presented, it was excused from a fine by reason of the selectmen testifying that they had employed a man as teacher who had been taken sick and had consequently been unable to attend to his duty.

In 1765 the town voted to pay William Sylvester, Esquire, £1 and 11*s*. "for the charges that he had paid on account of there being no school the last summer."

At the annual meeting in March, 1771, the town voted to build three school-houses. It is not known exactly where these buildings were located, but in all probability one of them was on Great Sebascodigan Island and the other two on the Neck.

In May, 1780, the town voted to raise £300 for the support of schools. The difference between this sum and £20 seems extreme. It is undoubtedly due to the depreciation of the currency.

---

[1] *No reference occurs in the records of Brunswick or Topsham to the employment of any mistresses in the last century.*

In June, 1781, £15 was voted by the town for school money, "to be reckoned in silver dollars as six shillings each, or in other currency equal to silver."

From this time until May, 1791, the town took no action in regard to school matters, except to pass the usual appropriation of money. On this latter date it was voted that "Orr's Island and Baylie's Island are to have five pounds of the school money for them to keep a school with them the present year, and for no other use." The appropriation for schools was this year £25.

In 1797 the town voted that "the selectmen should class the town into school classes, and appoint a day for each class to meet and choose a head for their respective classes."

In May, 1798, the town voted to accept the school classes or districts on the Island, as the selectmen had divided them. Marlborough Sylvester was chosen to be the head of the first district on the Neck; Captain William Tarr to be head of the second district on the Neck; Clement Orr, of the district on Orr's Island and Bailey's Island; Samuel Snow, of the first district on Sebascodigan; Stephen Purinton, of the second district on the latter island; and Josiah Totman, of the third district on this island. From this it appears that the town was divided into six districts, of which two were on the Neck; one included Orr's and Bailey's Islands; and the remainder were on Great Sebascodigan Island.

The records of the town contain nothing further in regard to schools until 1810. This year the town voted that school committees should be chosen in each district.

On November 7, 1814, the town passed a vote unlike any that we have ever met with in the doings of any other town. It voted "that the school money raised on the first Monday of May last shall be appropriated towards paying the expenses the selectmen were at for their attendance and expenses for the militia." *Inter arma leges silent!*

In September, 1821, the town voted to choose a superintending school committee of three, and Reverend Samuel Eaton, Alcot Stover, Jr., and Captain Stephen Snow were elected. Agents were also chosen this year for the different school districts.

In 1822 a school committee of seven members was chosen.

At a meeting of the town in September, 1828, it was voted that the school committee should not be paid for their services. As there is no evidence of any dissatisfaction with the committee, the above vote probably indicates the impression that existed in the town that the honor of holding such a weighty office ought to be considered a sufficient compensation.

In 1834 a new division of the town into school districts was made.

In 1857 the town voted to dispense with a superintending school committee and to choose a supervisor. Thomas U. Eaton was elected to this office. From this time until 1862, inclusive, a supervisor of schools was chosen each year.

In 1863 the town abandoned the idea of electing a supervisor, and went back to the old plan of choosing a school committee of three.

SCHOOL-HOUSES AND TEACHERS.

The town in 1771 voted to build three school-houses, but it is not known whether they were erected that year nor where they stood. If they were all built at that time, it is probable that two of them, at least, were built upon the Neck. If the other was built upon Sebascodigan Island, it was probably destroyed by fire, as according to very trustworthy traditional testimony the first school-house now known to have been built upon that island was not erected until about 1785. This school-house was first located a few rods south of the burying-ground, but about 1845 it was removed to its present location, about two hundred rods north of where it formerly stood. This house has been often repaired and is still quite sound, and is annually used for schools.

In 1786, or a year or two later, the second school-house on this island was built on the land of Nathaniel Purinton. It was destroyed by fire in 1826, and the present building was erected soon after on the site of the former.

No information has been obtained in regard to the erection of school-houses in other portions of the town, and but little can be said concerning the early teachers here.

An Irishman by the name of Patch is said to have taught the first public school on Great Island. He kept a school in the old school-house for seven or eight winters. Some of the later teachers in that district have been Wentworth Dresser, a Mr. Hill, T. Coten, and Mr. Edgecomb, of Topsham, who is the present teacher there.

The first teacher in the second school-house was John Sullivan, also an Irishman. He is said to have been a good teacher, but addicted to habits of intemperance and accustomed to close his school for a week or more in order to go upon drinking "sprees." Among his successors in that school have been Samuel Williams, Nathaniel Purinton, W. Dresser, Doctor Seward Garcelon, Jeremiah Hacker, S. Purinton, G. C. Smith, and the present teacher, Alvah A. Plummer.

There are upon Great Island six school districts, and the schools average from sixteen to twenty-eight weeks each in length. From twenty to forty dollars per month and board are the wages to male teachers, and from two to six dollars per week and board to female teachers. Board is from two to four and a half dollars per week. The average number of scholars in each school is about twenty.

ACADEMICAL INSTITUTIONS.

The only school of this character in town was the HARPSWELL ACADEMY. Some of the prominent citizens, desirous of having better advantages of education offered to the children of the town than were afforded by the common schools, formed a corporation for the promotion of that object in the year 1859.

The first meeting of the Harpswell Academy Corporation was held June 13, 1859, in Johnson's Hall. The Act of Incorporation was accepted, and a committee of three were chosen to prepare a code of by-laws. These by-laws, which were accepted at the next meeting, provided, amongst other things, that the annual meeting should be held on the second Monday in June, that the officers should consist of a president, secretary, treasurer, and a visiting committee of three, together forming a Board of Trustees; that the visiting committee should visit the school twice each term, and should have entire control of the school and building; that the Board of Trustees should employ the teachers, fix the terms of admission to the school, and make all purchases; and that "there shall never be a majority of the trustees elected from any one sect or denomination of Christians."

At this meeting, Paul Randall was chosen president, Harmon Pennell, vice-president; Robert Pennell, secretary; Henry Barnes, treasurer; and Clement Skolfield, Isaiah Snow, Stephen Purinton, Thomas Pennell, and Lemuel H. Stover, a visiting committee. A committee of three was also chosen to raise money and select a place for an academy building. On July 2d of this year, the trustees voted to accept a lot of one fourth of an acre of land offered by David S. Dunning at the sum of twenty-five dollars, and very shortly after this a neat and substantial building was erected on that part of the Neck which is designated North Harpswell. The corporators, however, went in debt for the building, and accordingly, at a meeting held March 1, 1860, the academy was mortgaged in order to raise money to pay the indebtedness. On April 18, 1865, the trustees voted to raise money by subscription to redeem this building.

How successful this attempt was, is not stated in the records.

The first term of school in this academy commenced Monday, September 5, 1859, under the instruction of H. C. White, M. D., with one or more assistants. The rates of tuition were as follows: —

In Primary Department,	per term . .	$2.00
" Common English,	" . .	3.00
" Higher Branches,	" . .	4.00
" Drawing and Painting,	" . .	1.50 to 2.00
" Music,	" . .	6.00

For use of instrument, one dollar extra.

The school was kept up a few years, but finally failed from want of adequate support and encouragement. The building is still standing.

PRIVATE SCHOOLS.

THE first school-teacher upon Great Island was a man named Hobby. He taught in private houses. Private schools were held in many families prior to the building of the first school-house, but there have been but few held in the part of the island where the second school-house is located. Stephen Purinton, however, is known to have had schools for his children. The only private teachers besides Hobby, who are remembered to have taught here in early times, were Messrs. Patch and Sullivan.

The first teacher on Orr's Island is said to have been a man by the name of Kinnecum, and the first one upon Merriconeag Neck is said to have been a Mr. Walker. Both of these teachers taught private schools.

The only teacher of a private school on the Neck beside Mr. Walker, of whom we have been able to learn, was Parson Eaton, who taught a few day-scholars in some of the higher branches. Although we have no positive information upon the subject, it is probable that Mr. Eaton's scholars were only those who desired to secure a higher education than could at that time be obtained at the common schools, and they very likely were the children of the more wealthy citizens.

CHAPTER XVIII.

BOWDOIN COLLEGE AND THE MEDICAL SCHOOL OF MAINE.

BOWDOIN COLLEGE IN 1821.

IN November, 1788, petitions were sent to the General Court of Massachusetts from the Cumberland Association of Ministers, as well as from the Cumberland County Court of General Sessions, for the incorporation of a college in that county. No decided action, however, was taken on these petitions until 1790, when a favorable report was made by a committee of the legislature, to which the matter had been referred. In March, 1791, in consequence principally of the exertions of Honorable Josiah Thatcher, a senator from Cumberland County, a bill for a college, to be called the Maine College, passed the Senate, but failed to pass the House.

At the next session, in the winter of 1791–2, upon the motion of H. Slocum, Esquire, a member from Bristol County, a committee was raised "to consider the expediency of establishing a college in the District of Maine." All mention of Cumberland County was avoided, and the motion was made by a member from another county in order that no prejudice might be excited against the measure. Governor Eustis was appointed chairman of the committee, and a bill was prepared, establishing a college which was first proposed to be called Winthrop College, but which was called in the Act of Incorporation Bowdoin College, " the name being selected as one of the most honored names that Massachusetts could boast." The bill passed the House at this session, but owing to a disagreement between the two houses in regard to the name and location of the college, the bill was not formally enacted until June 24, 1794, when it passed both houses and received the signature of the governor, Samuel Adams. The towns of Gorham, Portland, North Yarmouth, Brunswick, New Gloucester, Freeport, and Winthrop were pertinacious in urging their respective claims as being the most fitting seat of the college, and in some of them subscriptions were raised to secure the location. The town of Brunswick was at length selected as a compromise between the conflicting interests of the claimants, the citizens of the town having made what was considered at the time a valuable consideration for the preference.

The founders of this institution appear to have formed adequate conceptions of what such a college should be. Their evident design was, as expressed in their own words, to found a seminary which should " promote virtue and piety, and a knowledge of the languages and of the useful and liberal arts and sciences."

The government of the college was, by its Act of Incorporation, vested in a Board of Trustees and a Board of Overseers, the former consisting of thirteen, and the latter of forty-five members. The trustees are the legislative body, and the overseers possess a vetoing power. Five townships of land, each six miles square, of the unappropriated lands in the then District of Maine, were granted for the " use, benefit, and purpose of supporting " the college.

" Immediately after the charter was granted, establishing an institution which was to bear his family name, the Honorable James Bowdoin, of Boston, afterwards minister plenipotentiary at the Spanish court, generously bestowed both money and lands, the estimated value of which was $6,800. The first meeting of the Boards of the college was held at Portland, December, 1794. In consequence, however, of a deficiency of available funds (for the best lands of the State having been previously selected by other grantees, there was great difficulty in effecting a sale of the college townships, or any portion of them, without a sacrifice), eight years passed before the college went into operation. Indeed, notwithstanding the original grant of the legislature, and the patronage of the individual already named, nothing but great zeal and unwearied perseverance on the part of the most active friends of the project carried it through to its accomplishment. Besides two stated meetings of the Boards each year, special meetings were occasionally called: but it was no easy matter to sustain the interest of all the members in an institution which as yet existed but in name, and it was always difficult even to form a quorum for the transaction of business. Committees were repeatedly appointed by the Boards to solicit donations, but the public had not then learned to give, and when thousands were needed, the amount contributed was small, and mostly in books. Mutual recriminations of inefficiency and neglect passed between the two Boards, and some were almost ready to despair of success"

Although but few donations were made to the college at this time, it is gratifying to know that neither the citizens nor the Pejepscot proprietors were unmindful of the benefit the location of the college in Brunswick would be to this town. Thirty acres of land were given to the college for its location by Captain John Dunlap, William Stanwood, and Brigadier Thompson, though the college afterwards had to purchase a part of it from more rightful owners.[1]

The Pejepscot proprietors also, at a meeting held April 3, 1799, voted to give a deed of two hundred acres of land to the trustees, "for the use of the college forever."

The following were the original trustees and overseers of the college: —

TRUSTEES. — Reverend Thomas Brown, Falmouth; Samuel Dean, D. D., Portland; John Frothingham, Esquire, Portland; Reverend Daniel Little, Wells; Reverend Thomas Lancaster, Scarboro'; Honorable Josiah Thatcher, Gorham; David Mitchell, Esquire, North Yarmouth; Reverend Tristram Gilman, North Yarmouth; Reverend Alden Bradford, Wiscasset; Thomas Rice, Esquire, Pownalboro'; William Martin, North Yarmouth; and the president and treasurer of the college.

OVERSEERS. — Edward Cutts, Kittery; Thomas Cutts, Pepperelboro'; Simon Frye, Fryeburg; David Sewall, York; Nathaniel Wells, Wells; Reverend Moses Hemmenway, D. D., Wells; Reverend Silas Moody, Arundel; Reverend John Thompson, Berwick; Reverend Nathaniel Webster, Biddeford; Reverend Paul Coffin, Buxton; Rev-

[1] *John McKeen, Reminiscences of Brunswick in* 1802.

erend Benjamin Chadwick, Scarboro'; Reverend Samuel Eaton, Harpswell; Reverend Samuel Foxcroft, New Gloucester; Reverend Caleb Jewett; Reverend Alfred Johnson, Freeport; Reverend Elijah Kellogg, Portland; Reverend Ebenezer Williams, Falmouth; Reverend Charles Turner, Sandford; Daniel Davis, Portland; Samuel Freeman, Portland; Joshua Fabyan, Scarboro'; William Gorham, Gorham; Stephen Longfellow, Gorham; Joseph Noyes, Falmouth; Isaac Parsons, New Gloucester; Robert Southgate, Scarboro'; John Wait, Portland; Peleg Wadsworth, Thomaston; William Widgery, New Gloucester; Reverend Ezekiel Emerson, Georgetown; Reverend Jonathan Ellis, Topsham; Jonathan Bowman, Pownalboro'; Edmund Bridge, Augusta; Daniel Cony, Augusta; Henry Dearborn, Pittston; Dummer Sewall, Bath; Samuel Thompson, Topsham; John Dunlap, Brunswick; Francis Winter, Bath; Nathaniel Thwing, Woolwich; Alexander Campbell, No. 4 Washington County; Paul Dudley Sargeant, Sullivan; and the president and secretary of the college.

The site for the college was selected in 1796. It is situated on a plateau about three quarters of a mile south of the Androscoggin Bridge, near the pine plains. A beautiful grove of pines forms a part of the college grounds, and its proximity suggested the motto of one of the literary societies of the college.[1]

It was decided at this time to erect a building as soon as practicable, and in 1798 one was constructed of brick fifty feet long, forty feet wide, and three stories high. Owing to lack of means, however, it was not ready for use until the summer of 1802. In this latter year a wooden house was erected for the use of the president of the college.

About this time a part of the college lands was sold, and thus a new and more vigorous impulse was given to the growth of the college.

"In July, 1801, the Boards proceeded to elect a president. Among several candidates the choice fell upon Reverend Joseph McKeen, a clergyman of high standing, of Beverly, Mass. The selection was fortunate for the institution. Possessing sound judgment and great sagacity, President McKeen was enabled to give a wise direction to measures, and to establish precedents of great importance to the future stability and prosperity of the institution. Through his instrumentality the tenure of office, a point which elicited much discussion, was established on a proper basis. In the following November, John

---

[1] *The motto of the Peucinian Society is "Pinos loquentes semper habemus" (The murmuring pines we always have).*

Abbot, A. M., Harvard, was chosen Professor of Languages. The President and Professor of Languages were installed September, 1802. Great interest was felt by the friends of learning and education throughout the Commonwealth in this undertaking, and the ceremonies of the inauguration attracted to Brunswick a large assemblage, in which were men of the first distinction in the State. For want of a building suitable for the occasion, a platform with accommodations for spectators had been erected in the pine grove in the rear of the ground where the college grounds now stand. The scene in which they were participating could not but have deeply affected the principal actors. . . . On this occasion, the name of the college building, already erected, was proclaimed in due form, — Massachusetts Hall.

"On the day following this interesting occasion eight students were examined for admission into the college, two of whom came from the metropolis of the Commonwealth and its neighborhood, showing the interest and the confidence felt there in this new child of promise.

. . . . . .

"The duties to which President McKeen was called were arduous and highly responsible. For two years he was aided only by the faithful services of the Professor of Languages. The obstacles and the discouragements he was compelled to encounter in laying the foundation of an institution which was attracting notice and exciting much expectation in the community, without apparatus of any kind, and almost without funds, situated in a part of the country where superfluous wealth was not yet known, at a period when such an undertaking was a novel one, cannot now be duly appreciated. Before they were introduced to their labors, the president and professor visited the principal colleges of New England, that they might avail themselves of the best experience of the time for the successful management of the college. It should be mentioned as an honorable testimonial to the enlarged and independent views which governed the measures then adopted, that the requisitions for admission at once placed the new institution, in this respect, on a level with the oldest and best conducted institutions in the country, — a rank which it has ever maintained."

His house not having been completed in time, the president and his family, for a while, occupied rooms in Massachusetts Hall, the lower story of which had been fitted up, temporarily, as a chapel and recitation-room, and the upper portion for dormitories. There was no bell of any kind, and the pupils were summoned to prayers morning and evening by the thumping of the president's cane on the staircase.

In addition to these daily devotional exercises, President McKeen also preached on Sunday, either in the meeting-house of the First Parish or in the college chapel.

In 1804, Samuel Willard was appointed a tutor, and took up his residence within the college. One or two resident tutors were chosen annually after this until 1824.

Soon after its incorporation Mr. Bowdoin presented the college with £823 4*s*., with a "request that the interest thereof may be applied to the establishment and support of a professorship of Mathematics, and of Natural and Experimental Philosophy, and that this interest be added to the principal until a professor shall be appointed." To fill this professorship the boards, in May, 1805, elected Parker Cleaveland, A. M., Harvard, who was at that time a tutor at Cambridge. He was inducted into office in October. During this year the first chapel was erected. It was constructed of wood, with rooms for the library and philosophical apparatus in the second story. It was not designed for a permanent building, but was, however, enlarged and improved in 1817, and served the purposes for which it was built until 1845.

In 1805 the first literary society was instituted. This society, the Peucinian, was founded by Charles Stewart Daveis, Alfred Johnson, Nathan Lord, Robert Means, Enos Merrill, Benjamin Randall, Joseph Sprague, and Henry Wood, members of the three highest classes of the college. Robert Means was the first president. At first the society consisted solely of members of college, but in 1814 the members who had graduated held a meeting and, together with those belonging to the college society, formed a general society, of which Charles Stewart Daveis was elected the first president. With varying periods of prosperity and reverses, the society has continued to the present day. Its membership in 1858, the date of the last catalogue, was as follows: —

Whole number of members, 1,023; initiated members, 945; honorary members, 78; members of General Society, 882; members of College Society, 63.

The first Commencement of the college was celebrated in September, 1806, when the first class was graduated. The following-named individuals composed this class: —

Mr. Richard Cobb, who died in 1837, aged 49; Mr. Isaac Foster Coffin, who died in 1861, aged 74; John Davis, who died in 1841, aged 62; Mr. John Maurice O'Brien, who died in 1865, aged 79; Moses Quinby, S. H. S., who died in 1857, aged 71; Mr. George

Thorndike, who died in 1810, aged 21, and who also received his degree at Harvard, in 1807; Reverend Benjamin Titcomb, who died in 1829, aged 42.

At the same time the following fourteen persons, graduates of other colleges, received at their own solicitation honorary degrees: Ebenezer H. Beckford, of Harvard; Oliver Bray, of Yale; Jason Chamberlain, of the University of Brunswick; Thomas J. Eckley, of Harvard; Jacob H. Elliott, of Harvard; Abraham Eustis, of Harvard; Jacob C. Jewett, of Harvard; Thomas M. Jones, of Harvard; Isaac Lincoln, of Harvard; Samuel Orne, of Harvard and Yale; Albion K. Parris, of Dartmouth; Leverett Saltonstall, of Harvard and Yale; Ichabod Tucker, of Harvard; and Owen Warland, also of Harvard.

This being the first occasion of the kind in a portion of the Commonwealth then looked upon as almost a wilderness, excited much interest throughout Massachusetts. A large number of people attended from the District of Maine, and many from Boston and vicinity. There was, perhaps, a larger attendance than has been usual since that time. This Commencement is memorable not only on account of its being the first one, but also on account of a storm of uncommon severity, which began the day before the one appointed for the exercises of graduation, and for three days raged without abatement. The exercises were postponed one day, but were obliged to be held the next.

The successful working of the college at this time is shown by the fact that in 1807 forty-four students had been admitted to it, the library contained between fourteen and fifteen hundred volumes, and a philosophical and chemical apparatus had been obtained which was probably unsurpassed at that time by any in New England, except by that in Harvard University. A new building, subsequently named Maine Hall, was commenced this year. It was of brick, one hundred feet long, forty wide, and four stories high, and was intended for dormitories.

In consequence of the illness of the president at this time, his duties were distributed among the three remaining instructors. The tutor, Nathan Parker, A. M., Harvard, afterwards Reverend Doctor Parker, of Portsmouth, New Hampshire, "a most efficient and able officer, both of instruction and government," performed regularly the chapel duties of the president during the vacancy in that office.

In September, 1807, in consequence of the death of President McKeen, it became necessary to choose his successor. Some perplexity arose in consequence of the number of applicants for the position, but finally the Boards made selection of Reverend Jesse Appleton, A. M., Dartmouth, who was at the time settled in the ministry in Hampton, New Hampshire. His inauguration took place in December of the same year.

"President Appleton brought to the discharge of his duties a conscientiousness which forbade him to relax any effort, and a deep sense of responsibility both for the literary reputation and the moral and religious welfare of the institution. He possessed also rational views of collegiate discipline, great discretion, unshrinking integrity, an uncommon spirit of command, true love of learning, cultivated taste, habits of close application, and a delicacy and refinement of character which could not be surpassed. He had gained in a degree unusual for one of his age the respect of the clergy, both of Massachusetts and New Hampshire, as may be inferred from the fact that in 1803 he was one of the two most prominent candidates for the Theological Chair of Harvard University. The selection of such an individual for the presidency of the college was deemed highly auspicious. But he was called at the outset to encounter peculiar trials. Not to mention the relaxation of discipline likely to ensue on account of the protracted illness of the former president, and the interval between his decease and the coming of a successor, it was a time when there was throughout the community a tendency to looseness of sentiment and character. At no period in the history of our colleges has there been more recklessness on the part of youth. The habits of society, which then made the use of intoxicating liquors an essential even of common hospitality, exerted a most deleterious influence on all our colleges. . . . By the unwearied assiduity, however, of President Appleton, by a uniform system of discipline, great energy, and firmness tempered with parental solicitude for the welfare of his pupils, and the influence of high moral and religious principle, which pervaded in an uncommon degree all his intercourse with the students, the difficulties to which we have alluded were gradually overcome, and under his administration the college acquired high repute for good morals as well as sound scholarship."

In the month of June, 1808, a few students associated themselves together for literary purposes, under the name of the "Athenæan Society of Bowdoin College." Henry Wood was the first president. This society for a few years surpassed its rival the Peucinian, but soon languished, and in 1811 was temporarily discontinued. It was revived again in 1813, but was again disbanded in 1816 and its library divided. In 1818 it was again revived, and has continued till the present time. In 1820 the General Society was formed, and Levi Stowell was chosen as its first president. In 1822 its library was injured in the burning of Maine Hall, in which it was kept. In 1828 this society was incorporated by an Act of the legislature, and a new seal was adopted.[1] In 1836 its library was again almost totally destroyed by fire. In 1850 it received the cabinet of curiosities and other property of the "Caluvian Society." The membership of this society in 1856, the date of its last catalogue, was as follows: Whole number of members, 885; initiated members, 739; honorary members, 79; members of the General Society, 748; of the College Society, 67. Though these two literary societies still exist, yet neither of them, it is believed, are supported with the former vigor and enthusiasm.

In 1811, Mr. Bowdoin, the steadfast friend of the college, died. He bequeathed to this institution his valuable private library of more than two thousand volumes, besides a large number of pamphlets, charts, maps, and several articles of philosophical apparatus, a valuable collection of minerals, comprising nearly five hundred distinct specimens, arranged by Haüy, nearly four hundred models in crystallography, and a valuable collection of paintings and engravings which he had collected in Europe. The value of this legacy was certainly not less than $15,000.

At a meeting of the Board of Trustees of the college, on May 19, 1812, it was voted "that in consideration of the great munificence of the late Honorable James Bowdoin, Esquire, toward this institution, and the interest taken by it in his lamented decease, it is expedient and becoming that public notice be taken of the event; and therefore, voted, that the secretary of this Board be requested to deliver, at the ensuing Commencement, an eulogy on his memory." The Board of Overseers concurred in this request, and at the ensuing Commencement, September 2, the eulogy was delivered by Reverend Mr. Jenks, and was afterwards published in pamphlet form by a vote of the Boards.

This year Reverend William Jenks, A. M., Harvard, at that time settled in the ministry at Bath, the secretary of the Board of Trustees, was appointed Professor of Oriental and English Languages. He commenced his duties January 5, 1813. "The erudition of this gentleman, and his classical taste, rendered his services an important acquisition." His appointment was for three years only, and he kept up

[1] *On the seal was engraven a head of Minerva, with the inscription: "Athenæan Society, B. C., Cul Su. Sci. Cor." The abbreviations are for, "Bowdoin College, Cultores suos scientia coronat" (Science crowns her worshippers).*

his connection with his society in Bath. Efforts were made to retain him as a permanent instructor, but they were unsuccessful. At this time the finances of the college were in a low state, almost the only source of income being the sale from time to time of some of its wild lands, which were not then of much value.

In 1814 an Act was passed by the General Court, making an annual grant to the several colleges in the Commonwealth, for ten years. The portion allotted to this college was $3,000, one fourth of which was to be appropriated to the payment of the tuition of indigent students. This year the "Benevolent Society of Bowdoin College" was instituted. It was at first composed entirely of graduates and undergraduates of the college, but it afterwards admitted those not connected with the institution. It was incorporated and had, at one time, funds to the amount of seven hundred dollars. From the printed constitution of the society the following facts are obtained: —

The object of the society was to assist "indigent young men of promising talents and of good moral character in procuring an education at this college." No person could receive pecuniary assistance unless he had been a member of college, for at least one term. Any one of twenty-one years of age or over could become a member by paying one dollar on admission and one dollar annually, or a life member by paying ten dollars. The society received donations of books, furniture, clothing, or money, and the donor could designate the manner in which the gift should be appropriated, "provided it be for an object consistent with the design of the society." One half of the money received into the treasury and not appropriated by the donors was reserved as a permanent fund, of which only the annual income could be used.

The death of President Appleton occurred in November, 1819, and in consequence thereof a special meeting of the Boards was called in December, to elect his successor. Their choice fell upon Reverend William Allen, A. M., Harvard, of Hanover, New Hampshire, who had been president of Dartmouth College. In September previous, Samuel P. Newman, A. M., Harvard, was elected to the professorship of Latin and Greek, which had been rendered vacant by the resignation, in 1816, of Professor Abbot. The new professor and president were both inaugurated in May, 1820.

The formation of the new State of Maine in 1820 affected considerably the welfare of the college.

In the "Act of Separation," passed by the legislature of Massachusetts, June, 1819, it was provided that the grants already made to the college, which would not expire under four years, should continue in full force after the District of Maine became a State, and that all the chartered rights of the college should be enjoyed without change, "except by judicial process according to the principles of law. By the Constitution of Maine, on the other hand, the legislature were restrained from making any grant to any literary institution, unless they should have a certain right of control over such institution" The trustees and overseers of the college, therefore, deemed it wise to vest such right of control in the legislature of Maine, in order to be able to derive aid from the State. Accordingly an application was made by them to the legislatures of both States "for their assent to such modifications of the college charter as would remove any impediment in the way of the college receiving patronage from the legislature of Maine."

In response to this petition, the legislature of Massachusetts, on June 12 of this year, passed a resolve giving their consent to the alteration of the clause in the "Act of Separation" which referred to this college, provided the legislature of Maine consented thereto, and that the alteration did not affect the rights or interests of the Commonwealth. Four days later, the legislature of Maine passed an Act, so far modifying the "Act of Separation" as that the powers and privileges of the president, trustees, and overseers of the college should be subject to be "altered, limited, restrained, or extended by the legislature of the State of Maine, as shall by the said legislature be judged necessary to promote the best interests of said institution." The college having given its assent to this Act, the legislature of Maine granted a continuance of the sum which had been given by Massachusetts, and which had been appropriated for the purpose from a tax on the banks. By the power given them in this Act, the legislature also, in March, 1821, passed another Act increasing the number of trustees to twenty-five and of overseers to sixty, and the governor and council, by authority granted by the same Act, proceeded to fill by appointment the places which had been thus created. In this way thirty-three individuals were introduced into the two Boards.

The college buildings at this time were three in number, arranged to form the three sides of a square, but at suitable intervals from each other. The southern building was of wood and two stories high. The lower apartment contained the library, consisting at that time of about six thousand volumes. The building on the north was a large, square brick building, three stories high, divided into apartments for the philosophical apparatus, laboratory, mineralogical cabinet, etc. The eastern building was of brick, and was four stories high, and contained thirty-two rooms for students.

In 1822 an additional building, Winthrop Hall, was erected for dormitories. In March of this year, Maine Hall took fire and the entire interior was burnt, though the walls were not materially injured. The fire was discovered at three o'clock in the afternoon, and when first noticed was beyond control. It is supposed to have caught in the garret, but no satisfactory knowledge of its origin can be given. The loss by this fire was considerable. The building alone cost $16,000. The theological library, consisting of from three to four hundred volumes, was almost entirely consumed. Twelve of the students lost all their wearing apparel, except what they had on at the time, together with their furniture and bedding. The private property thus lost was estimated at the time at not far from $1,500.

This severe blow to the prosperity of the college was averted by the public liberality. Individual donations were extensively made, and contributions were received in a large number of the churches in Maine and Massachusetts, and thus the loss was fully repaired.

In 1824 two new professorships were created. Reverend Thomas C. Upham, A. M., Dartmouth, who was settled in the ministry in Rochester, New Hampshire, was chosen Professor of Metaphysics and Ethics; and Samuel P. Newman, Professor of Rhetoric and Oratory. They were inaugurated in February of the following year. Professor Newman also conducted the recitations in civil polity and political economy, and Hebrew was taught by Professor Upham.

This year Alpheus S. Packard, A. M., a graduate of the college in the class of 1816, who had been a tutor since 1819, was chosen Professor of Languages and Classical Literature.

Professor Packard was the son of Reverend Doctor Hezekiah Packard, and was born in Chelmsford, Massachusetts, on December 23, 1798. His connection with the college for a period of fifty-eight years is evidence not only of the high esteem in which he has always been held by the public, as well as by his colleagues and the alumni, but is also a proof of the wisdom originally displayed in his selection. Professor Packard, in addition to the professorship to which he was originally chosen, was appointed from 1842 to 1845 to fill the vacancy in the Chair of Rhetoric and Oratory, and in 1864 was made Professor of Natural and Revealed Religion. In addition to his college duties, he has, from time to time, supplied the pulpit in the churches of the neighboring towns. In 1860 he was honored with the title of S. T. D. from this college. In 1828 he was elected a member of the Maine Historical Society, in which he has for some years held and still holds the office of secretary. He has also for several years been one of its standing committee.

In 1825, William Smyth, A. M., a graduate of this college in the class of 1822, who had been a tutor for two years previously, was appointed Associate Professor of Mathematics and Natural Philosophy. In 1828 he was made a professor in full. This year, 1825, a branch of the literary society of graduates, known as the Phi Beta Kappa, of which there is a branch in nearly all of the older colleges of the country, was organized at this college.

In 1826 the first graduation[1] of a student belonging to the colored race occurred. John B. Russworm, afterwards governor of Liberia, was the name of this individual.

In 1829, Henry W. Longfellow, A. M., a graduate of the class of 1825, was chosen to the professorship of Modern Languages, towards the foundation of which $1,000 had been bequeathed by Mrs. Dearborn, formerly the widow of Honorable James Bowdoin. Professor Longfellow resigned his office in 1835, having been invited to a similar professorship in Harvard University. What is usually designated as "Commons Hall" was built this year. It was designed, and for many years was used, as a dining-room for the students. It is now used as a laboratory of analytical chemistry.

In March, 1831, an Act was passed by the legislature which provided that no person then holding the office of president in any college in the State should hold said office beyond the day of the next Commencement of the college, unless he should be re-elected; and that no person should be elected or *re-elected* to the office of president unless he should receive in each Board two thirds of all the votes given on the question of his election; and that any person elected to said office should be liable to be removed at the pleasure of the Board or Boards which should elect him. It was furthermore provided that the fees usually paid to the president for degrees should be paid into the treasury, for the use of the college, and be no longer a perquisite of office. "This unprecedented act of legislation excited the deep concern of all who felt an interest in the permanency and stability of our literary institutions. Though applicable alike to both colleges of the State, its immediate object and direct bearing no one has ever pretended to disguise."

---

[1] *In* 1858 *a colored gentleman named Jacob M. Moore was graduated from the Medical School.*

At their next meeting the trustees and overseers voted to acquiesce in this act of the legislature, and at once proceeded to choose a president, but failed in consequence of their inability to get a two-thirds majority in both Boards. A committee of the two Boards was chosen to petition the legislature for a repeal of the provision of the Act requiring a two-thirds majority in each Board. President Allen, however, did not wait the result of this petition, but at once proceeded to test the constitutionality of this legislative enactment by a suit in the Circuit Court of the United States. The case was argued before Honorable Joseph Story, associate justice of the Supreme Court, and Honorable Ashur Ware, district judge. The decision of the court had not only an important bearing upon the welfare of this college, but was also one which involved the chartered rights of all such institutions, and is deserving, therefore, of more particular mention in these pages.

The following abstract of this decision is taken from a published sketch of the college by Professor Packard, from which we have already freely quoted: —[1]

"1. A college established for the promotion of learning and piety is a private and not a public corporation. In the charter of Bowdoin College the visitatorial power is intrusted to the Boards of Trustees and Overseers; as soon as they accepted the charter, they acquired a permanent right and title in their offices, which could not be diverted except in the manner pointed out in the charter. The legislature was bound by the Act; they could not resume their grant, and they could not touch the vested rights, privileges, or franchises of the college, except so far as the power was reserved by the sixteenth section of the Act. The language of that section is certainly very broad, but it is not unlimited. It is there declared that the legislature 'may grant further powers to, or alter, limit, annul, or restrain any of the powers by this Act vested in the said corporation, *as shall be judged necessary to promote the best interest of the college*.' Whatever it may do, then, must be done to promote the best interest of the college. It is true that it is constituted the sole judge of what is the best interest of the college; but still it cannot do anything *pointedly destructive of that interest*. Its authority is confined to the enlarging, altering, annulling or restraining of the *powers* of the corporation. It cannot intermeddle with its *property;* it cannot extinguish its corporate existence; it cannot resume all its property, and annihilate all its powers and fran-

[1] *For the full text of this decision see Allen* v. *McKeen*, 1 *Sumner's Report*, 276.

chises. The legislature must leave its vitality and property, and enable it still to act as a college. It cannot remove the trustees or overseers, though it may abridge, as well as enlarge, their powers.

"2. Bowdoin College has never surrendered any of its rights. Whatever may have been the intentions of those concerned, at the outset, in regard to a surrender of the college to the State, there has been a miscarriage of the parties; it never has been *de jure* under the control of the legislature of Maine.

"3. But admitting that the college, as was contemplated, did come under the control of the legislature of Maine, when it is stated in the Act modifying the college charter, that the president and trustees and overseers of Bowdoin College shall enjoy their powers and privileges, subject to be altered, limited, restrained, or extended by the legislature, no authority is conferred upon the legislature to add new members to the Boards by its own nomination or by that of the governor and Council of the State. That would be an extension, not of the powers and privileges of the Boards, but of the legislative action over them. If the legislature could add one new member of its own choice or appointment, it could add any number whatsoever. It could annihilate the powers and privileges of the charter Boards under the pretence of alteration or extension. The legislature might authorize an enlargement of the Boards, but the places thus created must be filled by the Boards themselves.

"4. The Act of the legislature, removing the presidents of Bowdoin and Waterville Colleges out of office at a certain time, is a direct exercise of a power which was expressly and exclusively conferred on the College Boards by the original charter, and which has never been taken from them.

"5. President Allen was in office under a lawful contract made with the Boards, by which contract he was to hold that office during good behavior. The Act of the legislature directly impairs the obligations of that contract. It takes away from him his tenure of office, and removes him from it. Holding his office during good behavior, he could not be removed from it except for gross misbehavior; and then only by the Boards, in the manner pointed out in the original charter. Immediately upon the decision of the court being announced, President Allen resumed the discharge of the duties of his office."

In 1835, Daniel R. Goodwin, then a tutor in college, succeeded Longfellow as Professor of Modern Languages. He served in this capacity until 1853, when he resigned, for the purpose of accepting the presidency of Trinity College, Connecticut.

President Allen resigning in 1839, Reverend Leonard Woods, of Bangor Theological Seminary, son of Reverend Leonard Woods, a well-known divine, was elected as his successor. President Woods was at that time well known for his scholarly culture and attainments, and his reputation has steadily increased. In 1839 he received the honorary degree of D. D. from Waterville College, and in 1846 from Harvard College. In 1866 he received that of LL. D. from Bowdoin. He was not only an eminent scholar and a fine teacher, but he attracted students by his courteous demeanor and by his lenient disposition. He resigned in 1866, after a period of service extending over twenty-seven years, — a much longer service than that of any previous president.

In 1842 a professorship of Political Economy was founded, and Alpheus S. Packard was chosen as the first professor in that branch. He was succeeded in 1845 by Henry H. Boody, then a tutor.

On July 16 of this latter year, the corner-stone of King Chapel was laid with Masonic ceremonies. There were present the Grand Lodge of Maine, the Boston Encampment of Knight Templars, the Portland Encampment of Knight Templars, the Mount Vernon Chapter of Royal Arch Masons of Portland, the Montgomery Chapter of Bath, Ancient Landmark Lodge of Portland, Solar Lodge of Bath, Freeport Lodge of Freeport, and United Lodge of Brunswick. At the northwest angle of the ground there was a raised platform, upon which were the officers of the college, the Grand Lodge, and the Knight Templars. President Woods read the psalm "*Lætatus sum*," and made an address. Prayer was offered by Reverend William T. Dwight, and John T. Paine, Grand Master of the Grand Lodge of Maine, assisted by Honorable Robert P. Dunlap, ex-Grand Master, then laid the stone in due form. A silver plate provided by the college, and one provided by the Grand Lodge, were then deposited in the proper receptacle in the stone.

In 1855 the new chapel was completed. The entire cost was $45,000. On June 7 it was dedicated. The services of the occasion consisted of a selection from the Scriptures and a prayer by Reverend George E. Adams, a hymn, an address by President Woods, a second hymn, a sermon by Professor Hitchcock, and a concluding prayer by Reverend Doctor Dwight. The services were attended by the undergraduates, many graduates, the college boards and faculty, and many friends of the college, who assembled in the library, from whence they moved to the chapel in a procession conducted by Honorable Charles J. Gilman as marshal.

In 1848 a professorship of Rhetoric and Elocution was founded, that of Political Economy being merged in it, and Professor Henry H. Boody was appointed to this office. He was succeeded in 1856 by Egbert C. Smyth, son of Professor William Smyth, a graduate of the college in 1848, and a tutor in 1849.

A professorship of Natural and Revealed Religion was founded in 1850 by subscriptions among the Orthodox Congregationalists, and Calvin E. Stowe, D. D., of the class of 1829, an eminent scholar and theologian, was chosen to that office. He was succeeded in 1852 by Roswell D. Hitchcock, a graduate of Amherst in 1836, now of New York City. In 1856, Professor E. C. Smyth was transferred to this chair, and Joshua L. Chamberlain, of the class of 1852, was appointed to the Chair of Rhetoric and Oratory. In 1858, William Russell, a distinguished elocutionist, assisted in his branch.

Professor Goodwin resigned in 1855, and Charles Carroll Everett, now a professor in Harvard College, occupied the Chair of Modern Languages for two years, from 1855 to 1857. He was succeeded by Professor Chamberlain for two years, when William A. Packard, class of 1851, now professor at Princeton, gave the instruction for one year. In 1861, Professor Chamberlain was again placed in the Chair of Modern Languages, that of Rhetoric and Oratory being filled in 1862 by Reverend Eliphalet Whittlesey, a graduate of Yale.

In August of this year, 1862, Professor Chamberlain resigned his office to go into the army for the period of the war then raging. The boards, however, granted him leave of absence instead of accepting his resignation, and Stephen J. Young, class of 1859, was made Provisional Instructor in Modern Languages, to which, on Professor Chamberlain's resigning in 1865, he was elected as professor.

Professor Whittlesey also went into the army, and the duties of his chair were performed by members of the faculty. At the close of the war Professor Whittlesey resigned, and General Chamberlain was re-elected to the Chair of Rhetoric and Oratory, which, however, he again resigned in 1866, to accept the office of governor of Maine. He was followed by John S. Sewall, class of 1850, who held the chair until 1875, when Professor Henry L. Chapman, Bowdoin, class of 1866, was transferred to this from the Chair of Latin.

In 1859, Paul A. Chadbourne, a graduate of Williams, was chosen Professor of Chemistry and Natural History. He was succeeded in 1863 by Cyrus F. Brackett, a graduate in 1859, tutor in 1863. In 1864, Professor Brackett was appointed Adjunct Professor of Natural Science, and in 1865 to a full professorship in the Josiah Little Chair of

Natural Science, to which, however, in 1868, George L. Goodale, a graduate of Amherst in 1860, was elected.

In 1862, William P. Tucker, class of 1854, tutor since 1857, was instructor in mathematics for one year. He had, in the mean time, as librarian, prepared an elaborate and valuable catalogue of the college library. In 1865, Edward N. Packard, tutor since 1863, was instructor, and in 1866 Adjunct Professor of Mathematics. The death of Professor Smyth in 1868, while intensely engaged upon the building of Memorial Hall, left the Chair of Mathematics and Natural Philosophy vacant, and Charles E. Rockwood, a graduate of Yale, was chosen to the place.

In 1864, Professor E. C. Smyth resigned the Chair of Natural and Revealed Religion, and was succeeded by Professor Alpheus S. Packard, who was transferred from the Chair of Ancient Languages, to which, in 1865, Reverend Jotham B. Sewall, class of 1848, tutor in 1851, was chosen. In 1871, Henry L. Chapman was chosen Adjunct Professor of Latin, and in 1872 a full professor.

In 1865 the alumni of the college voted to erect a building to be called Memorial Hall, in honor of the graduates and students of the college who had died in the civil war. A subscription was at once started to carry the plan into execution, and a committee was raised for the purpose. A sufficient amount of funds was raised to warrant the prosecution of the work, and the corner-stone was accordingly laid in 1866. The outside of the building has since been completed, but enough funds have not yet been secured to enable it to be finished inside. When more prosperous times return, there is scarcely a doubt but that the original intention will be carried out.

President Woods resigning in 1866, Reverend Samuel Harris, S. T. D., a graduate of 1833, was elected to his place in 1867. He took upon himself, also, the duties of the Professor of Moral Philosophy and Metaphysics, Professor Upham being that year honored with the *Emeritus* title.

In 1871 the eminent scholar, civilian, and general, Ex-Governor Chamberlain, was chosen to succeed President Harris, and at this time quite a reorganization of the college occurred. A scientific department was established and several new chairs of instruction were founded. George L. Vose, C. E., was elected Professor of Civil Engineering; Edward S. Morse, Ph. D., of Salem, Professor of Comparative Anatomy and Zoölogy; Mr. James B. Taylor, Provisional Professor of Elocution and Oratory; the Chair of Latin was separated from that of Greek; and United States officers were brought here by orders of the government, — Brevet Major J. P. Sanger, Fourth United States Artillery, as Professor of Military Science, and John N. McClintock, class of 1867, of the United States Coast Survey, as instructor in Topographical Engineering.

In 1872, Professor Brackett was made Professor of Chemistry and Physics, and Robert L. Packard, class of 1868, Assistant Professor of Applied Chemistry, for one year. In 1873, however, Professors Brackett and Goodale resigned, and Henry Carmichael, a graduate of Amherst and of Göttingen, Germany, was elected Professor of Chemistry and Physics, and Doctor Charles A. White, of Iowa, Josiah Little Professor of Natural Science. In the winter of the same year, Professor Rockwood resigned, and Charles H. Smith, a graduate of Yale, was Professor of Mathematics. Doctor White resigned in 1875, and the instruction has since been given by different persons, Professor A. S. Packard, Jr., class of 1861, giving an annual course of lectures on entomology; Mr. George L. Chandler, class of 1868, giving instruction in natural history in 1875–6; and Mr. Leslie A. Lee, a graduate of St. Lawrence University (Canton, N. Y.), class of 1872, in 1876–7.

In connection with the new plan, arrangements were also made for other instruction in various branches, should such be needed. Professor Paul A. Chadbourne was engaged to give the instruction in mental philosophy. Exercise in the gymnasium was made regular and obligatory, and military science and tactics were required to a certain extent, of all not specially excused. Professor Chadbourne was succeeded in 1873 by Reverend E. C. Cummings, and by President Mark Hopkins in 1874. This year, however, the Edward Little Chair of Mental and Moral Philosophy was founded, and President Chamberlain was chosen as professor.

In 1875, Major Sanger's detail expired, and Brevet Captain Louis V. Caziarc, First United States Artillery, was appointed in his place as Professor of Military Science and Tactics. Mr. Charles H. Moore has been instructor in Latin since Professor Chapman's resignation, except one year, when Professor A. H. Davis held the chair provisionally.

Professor Young, having accepted the office of treasurer, relinquished the duties of his chair, and they were performed for one year by Instructor Moore, and since then by Charles E. Springer, class of 1874.

In 1873 the old Commons Hall was remodelled into a laboratory of analytical chemistry, and Mr. F. C. Robinson was chosen instructor in that department of chemistry. The same year the lower floor of Memorial Hall was fitted up as a gymnasium. Honorable Peleg W. Chandler, of Boston, also, this year, remodelled old Massachusetts Hall into a beautiful room, called the Cleaveland Cabinet, in memory of the late Professor Parker Cleaveland.

A picture gallery has also been finished in the chapel, over the library. Two fine pictures have been added to the panels of the chapel, one given by Mrs. William S. Perry, in memory of her husband, the subject being "The Transfiguration"; the other, "Moses giving the Law," which is the beautiful memento left by the class of 1877. The last makes the seventh of the pictures which have been, from time to time, added to the chapel panels.

Since 1872 over $25,000 have been given the college as scholarships to aid deserving students, and $100,000 towards a general endowment of the college.

Measures have been taken to endow a "Longfellow Professorship of Modern Languages," and a "Cleaveland Professorship of Chemistry and Mineralogy." Efforts are also being made to add the "Upham Professorship of Mental Philosophy."

Many valuable gifts have been made the college in the way of books and natural-history collections. Especially notable are the collection of Mrs. Frederick Allen, of Gardiner, comprising more than one thousand specimens, including many from Mount Ætna, presented by her daughter, Mrs. Elton, of Boston; the Cushman collection of birds of Maine; and the Blake herbarium.

The whole number of graduates from the college up to 1876 is one thousand eight hundred and eighty-seven. The number of students at present is about one hundred and thirty-seven, and of officers of instruction, fifteen.

The number of volumes in the college library is 17,500; in the medical library, 4,000; in the libraries of the Athenæan and Peucinian Societies, 13,100; and in the Historical Society's library, which is placed in a room of the college chapel, 3,000: making a total of books accessible to the student of 37,600 volumes. Large additions have also been made to the chemical and physical apparatus.

The public buildings of the college are at present: —

Massachusetts Hall, containing the Cleaveland Cabinet, lecture-room, and treasurer's office.

Winthrop Hall, containing, on the lower floor, the engineering-rooms and recitation-rooms, the upper floors being used as dormitories.

Maine Hall, having on the lower floors the Athenæan and Peucinian Societies' libraries and recitation-rooms; and on the upper floor, dormitories.

APPLETON HALL, containing dormitories.

KING CHAPEL, containing the picture gallery, library-rooms, and Historical Society's rooms.

ADAMS HALL, containing the lecture-rooms of chemistry and physics, and the rooms of the Medical School.

ANALYTICAL LABORATORY and MEMORIAL HALL, containing gymnasium. These buildings, with the exception of Adams Hall and the Analytical Laboratory, will, when the original plan is completed, form a quadrangle, the side towards the public road being open.

The present total estimated value of the college property, real estate and permanent material, is $375,000; the productive funds are $244,000; the total annual income is $30,000.

Besides the three literary societies of the college, already mentioned, it is proper to add that there have been, from time to time, several secret associations formed, which are presumably for literary purposes. The principal ones, if not all, are designated as the Alpha Delta Phi, Delta Kappa Epsilon, Chi Psi, Psi Upsilon, and Theta Delta Chi. The history of these societies is, of course, known only to the initiated.

THE MEDICAL SCHOOL OF MAINE.

In 1820 an Act was passed by the legislature, establishing a Medical School, to be connected with Bowdoin College, and also making an annual grant of $1,000, during the pleasure of the legislature, for the promotion of the objects designed in its establishment. Doctor Nathan Smith, a member of several societies, both in this country and in Europe, founder of the Medical School of New Hampshire, and an eminent physician and surgeon, was appointed Professor of the Theory and Practice of Medicine. He also assumed the duties of instructor in anatomy and surgery. He was assisted in the latter branches by Doctor John D. Wells, who had just taken his medical degree at Cambridge. At the close of the first course of lectures, Doctor Wells was chosen to fill the Chair of Anatomy, and immediately sailed for Europe, where he spent nearly two years, preparing himself for the discharge of the duties of his office. After a short but brilliant career as a lecturer at this college, at the Berkshire Medical Institution, and at Baltimore, he died, and was succeeded in 1831 by Doctor Reuben D. Mussey.

In 1825 the Chair of Obstetrics was founded, and Doctor James

McKeen was appointed professor. Doctor McKeen prepared himself for the duties of his office by a preliminary study in the lying-in hospitals of Europe, and served acceptably until 1839, when he resigned, and was succeeded by Ebenezer Wells, M. D., as lecturer.

In 1846 the Chair of Materia Medica and Therapeutics was founded, and Doctor Charles A. Lee was chosen as lecturer, and in 1854 as professor. He resigned in 1859, and was succeeded by Doctor Israel T. Dana as lecturer and afterwards as professor in full. Doctor Thorndike resigned in 1861, and was succeeded by Doctor William C. Robinson.

In 1849 the Chair of Medical Jurisprudence was founded, and Honorable John S. Tenney was chosen as lecturer.

In 1857 the Chair of Anatomy was separated from that of Surgery and joined to that of Physiology, and Doctor David S. Conant was elected, at first as lecturer, and afterwards as professor. He was succeeded in 1863 by Doctor Corydon L. Ford. Edmund R. Peaslee, M. D., who had been chosen as Lecturer on Anatomy and Surgery in 1843, and as a professor in these branches in 1845, was in 1857 appointed Professor of Surgery.

From 1820 until his death in 1858, Professor Parker Cleaveland gave an annual course of lectures on chemistry to the medical students.

Under the influence and by the exertions of these gentlemen and their successors, this Medical School has enjoyed a good degree of prosperity. At first, and for many years, the lectures were given in the upper room of Massachusetts Hall, but in 1861 the Adams Hall was built expressly for the accommodation of this school.

The present accommodations are ample, and the school has a valuable cabinet and an excellent library of choice works and expensive plates. Clinical instruction is given several times a week, and students can have the privilege of occasional visits to the hospitals of Portland at but slight expense.

This school, during the fifty-seven years of its existence, has graduated one thousand one hundred and seventy-four pupils, of whom seventy have been alumni of Bowdoin College. The last class numbered ninety members, and the present number of instructors is ten. The following is a list of the professors and lecturers not already mentioned: —

Of Chemistry, Professors Paul A. Chadbourne, Cyrus F. Brackett, and Henry Carmichael; of Theory and Practice, Henry H. Childs, Daniel Oliver, Professor John De La Mater, Professor William

Sweetzer, William Perry, James McKeen, Israel T. Dana, Professor Alonzo B. Palmer, and Alfred Mitchell, Adjunct Professor; of Anatomy and Surgery, Jedediah Cobb, and Joseph Roby; of Anatomy and Physiology, Professors Thomas T. Sabine and Thomas Dwight; of Anatomy, Professors Thomas Dwight and Stephen H. Weeks; of Physiology, Professors Robert Amory and Burt G. Wilder; of Surgery, Professors Timothy Childs, David S. Conant, and William W. Green; Lecturers, Alpheus B. Crosby and Thomas T. Sabine; of Obstetrics, Benjamin F. Barker, Professor Amos Nourse, Theodore H. Jewett, Professors William C. Robinson, Edward W. Jenks, and Alfred Mitchell; of Materia Medica and Therapeutics, Professors Dana, William C. Robinson, George L. Goodale, and Frederic H. Gerrish; of Medical Jurisprudence, Cyrus F. Brackett, John Appleton, and Professor Charles W. Goddard.

This school has exerted a very marked influence on the interests of medical science, and also upon the general interests of education in the State, and has annually sent forth a corps of physicians qualified not only to cope vigorously with the unseen, though certain foe of the human race, but who have also shown themselves, hitherto, alive to the material welfare and best interests of the State, and have thus far more than repaid the amount expended upon the school by the State.